THE OFFICIAL PRICE GUIDE TO

POTTERY

AND

PORCELAIN

Ninth Edition

Joe L. Rosson

House of Collectibles

New York Toronto London Sydney Auckland

House of Collectibles and colophon are registered trademarks of Random House, Inc.

RANDOM HOUSE is a registered trademark of Random House, Inc.

This book is available for special discounts for bulk purchases for sales promotions or premiums. Special editions, including personalized covers, excerpts of existing books, and corporate imprints, can be created in large quantities for special needs. For more information, write to Special Markets/Premium Sales, 1745 Broadway, MD 6-2, New York, NY, 10019 or e-mail specialmarkets@randomhouse.com.

Please address inquiries about electronic licensing of any products for use on a network, in software, or on CD-ROM to the Subsidiary Rights Department, Random House Information Group, fax 212-572-6003.

Visit the House of Collectibles Web site: www.houseofcollectibles.com

Library of Congress Cataloging-in-Publication Data is available.

Ninth Edition

Printed in the United States of America

10 9 8 7 6 5 4 3 2 1

ISBN 0-676-60091-3

ACKNOWLEDGMENTS

A person needs a great deal of help to assemble a price guide such as this one. This book could not have been finished without the help of Tony McCormack, Richard Hatch, Chris Paddleford, Wade and Brenda Ford, Elaine Tomber Tindell, and the people at Needful Things in Hendersonville, North Carolina. Their input and their permission to photograph items made all the difference in the world.

I also want to thank Rick Crane, who took the vast majority of the photographs featured in this book, and helped me keep this project going on a day-to-day basis. Without his hard work, information gathering, patience, computer talents, and general "do what needs to be done" attitude, I could not have completed this project.

All illustrations by Annie Parrott.

Photographs by Richard H. Crane and Tony McCormack.

TABLE OF CONTENTS

Introduction xi

The Potteries

Abingdon Potteries, Inc. 3

American Art China Works 13

American Bisque Company 14

Appleman Auto Works, Inc. 21

Arequipa Pottery 23

J. A. Bauer Pottery Company 25

Bennington Pottery 35

Brayton-Laguna Pottery 39

Brush-McCoy Pottery and Nelson McCoy Pottery 44

Buffalo Pottery 73

California Cleminsons 85

California Originals 87

Camark Pottery, Inc. 92

Canonsburg Pottery Company 96

Cardinal China Company 100

Castleton China 102

Catalina Island Pottery 113

Ceramic Arts Studio 116

Clewell Metal Art 129

Continental Kilns 131

Cowan Pottery 133

Coxon Belleek Pottery 137

Crooksville China Company 140

Cronin China Company 143

Dedham Pottery 145

Kay Finch 151

Florence Ceramics 154

Frankoma Pottery 162

Fulper Pottery/Stangl Pottery 173

W. S. George Pottery Company 206

Gilner Pottery 213

Gladding, McBean & Company 214

Glidden Pottery 239

Gonder Ceramic Art Company 241

Grueby Faience Company/Grueby Pottery 249

Haeger Potteries 253

Hagen-Renaker 264

Halderman Potteries 266

Hall China Company 268

Hampshire Pottery 311

Harker Pottery Company 315

Homer Laughlin China Company 325

A. E. Hull Pottery Company 363

Iroquois China Company 403

Jugtown Pottery 411

Kenton Hills 415

Edwin M. Knowles China Company 417

Knowles, Taylor and Knowles 421

Lenox Inc. and the Ceramic Art Company 424

Limoges China Company 455

Marblehead Pottery 457

Matt Morgan Pottery 459

Metlox Potteries 461

Morton Pottery Company 495

Mount Clemens Pottery Company 498

Muncie Clay Products and Muncie Potteries 501

Newcomb College Pottery 504

Niloak Pottery Company 507

North Dakota School of Mines 514

Ohr Pottery 517

Ott and Brewer 520

Overbeck Pottery 523

J. B. Owens Pottery Company 526

Paden City Pottery Company 533

Paul Revere Pottery 537

Pennsbury Pottery 540

Pewabic Pottery 543

Pfaltzgraff Pottery Company 546

Pickard China Company 553

Pisgah Forest Pottery 560

Pope-Gosser China Company 564

Pottery Guild 566

Purinton Pottery 567

Red Wing Potteries 572

Regal China Company 585

Robinson-Ransbottom Pottery Company 587

Rookwood Pottery 589

Roseville Pottery 604

Royal China Company 659

RumRill Pottery Company 670

Salem China Company 675

Scio Pottery 680

Sebring Pottery Company 683

Shawnee Pottery Company 690

Shenango China Company/Shenango Pottery Company 717

Southern Potteries 719

Stanford Pottery 732

Sterling China Company 733

Stetson China Company 736

Steubenville Pottery Company 740

Syracuse China Company 753

Tamac Pottery 764

Taylor, Smith and Taylor 766

Teco Gates 772

Tiffany Pottery 775

Treasure Craft 777

Twin Winton 781

Uhl Pottery 787

Universal Potteries, Inc. 795

Union Porcelain Works 803

Van Briggle Pottery 805

Vernon Potteries, Ltd./Vernon Kilns 809

Wahpeton Pottery (Rosemeade) 831

Watt Pottery Company 840

Weller Pottery 858

Willets Manufacturing Company 875

Glossary 879

Bibliography 893

INTRODUCTION

It has been said that the trouble with price guides is that they contain prices—and prices for antiques and collectibles can be extremely treacherous things. Prices have the disquieting tendency to vary from place to place and from time to time. They can also fluctuate greatly, depending on the context in which a person wants to know the monetary worth of a given item.

In the world of collecting, assigning a concrete value to an object can be a difficult task because there are many, many factors that can cause that value to change. Any reader of a price guide must understand these variables in order for the information offered by the guide to have meaning and validity. Two of the most significant factors affecting the prices of collectibles are regionality and venue, which are discussed below.

Regionality

The United States is a very large, very diverse country, and prices for antiques and collectibles obtained in one part of our nation might be quite different from those obtained in another.

As an example of this phenomenon, I remember a client who had a piece of American Brilliant Period cut glass appraised in Iowa before she sent it to her daughter, who lived in San Francisco, California. Upon receiving this piece of glass, the daughter decided to have it reappraised because she needed a formal document in order to have the piece added to her household insurance policy. Both mother and daughter were surprised when the price quoted was significantly lower than the price that had been quoted in Iowa.

Both of the appraisers used were highly reputable, and it was speculated that the reason for the discrepancy was that cut glass is somewhat more popular in Iowa than it is in San Francisco, where earthquakes may make the "shelf life" of this extremely fragile type of glass somewhat questionable.

Regionality—loosely defined as those aspects of a piece that relate to its place of origin—is an important concept because, as a general rule, antiques and collectibles tend to be most valuable near the places where they originate. For example, I once priced Pisgah Forest art pottery near Asheville, North Carolina, very near to where the pottery was actually made, and found that the pottery was more expensive near Asheville than it was in other parts of the country.

Another important aspect of regionality is that antiques indigenous to a particular region of the United States may not be recognized or appreciated in other parts of the country. A relatively simple redware pot signed "Cain," for instance, might bring relatively big dollars in Virginia and Tennessee, but be completely overlooked and undervalued in places where the potter's name is not immediately recognized or where his significance as an artist is not immediately understood. This phenomenon is perhaps most evident with respect to country pottery, which can differ widely in both style and form from one geographic area to another.

Venues from Which Prices Are Obtained

There are three basic sources for the prices reported in most price guides: auctions, retail sources such as antiques shows and shops, and specialist collectors.

Auctions are perhaps the main provider of prices for most guides, but there are inherent difficulties with values derived from these sources. Traditionally, auctions have been a wholesale market frequented by antiques dealers who then mark up the items they purchase (generally two to four times the price paid) before offering them for sale in a retail environment.

In the past few decades, however, more and more retail customers have started shopping at auctions, and the differential between wholesale and retail at this sort of venue has become somewhat blurred. It is now very difficult to tell whether a particular item was bought for resale, or simply purchased by an "end user" or collector who paid as much as a private consumer is willing to pay for that specific item. As a result, prices obtained at auctions are open to a great deal of interpretation.

There is yet another problem with auction prices and that is that prices obtained from a given event tend to be average prices. In other words, some objects sold at an auction brought less than they should, others sold for more than they were worth, and still others sold for exactly what they should have in terms of fair market value. I call this the "Goldilocks principle" of auction pricing: some prices at these events are "too hot," some prices are "too cold," and some prices are "just right."

On more occasions than I care to count, I have seen an item sell at auction for far more than it was worth, and have heard auction company personnel whisper wryly to one another about the price, "Well, there's a world record that'll never be broken." And in many cases they were absolutely right—the price paid was outrageous.

This can occur for a variety of reasons. Sometimes family members battle it out to own a precious family heirloom that has ended up being sold to settle an estate, or two rivals engage in bitter combat with a "hang the price, I *will* own this piece" attitude that sends prices into the stratosphere. There are, of course, other reasons (some that involve chicanery) why prices can be too high at auction, but these two are perhaps the most common.

Prices realized at auction can also be too low, for a variety of reasons. Generally, a low price is the result either of buyers' failure to recognize an item's worth, or of an auction gallery mistake. Individual auction prices that are either too high or too low are just the "nature of the beast," and it needs to be clearly understood that all prices taken from an auction are a record of what a specific item sold for at a specific time and place with a specific audience, and that this exact price might never be duplicated at another auction.

A similar problem exists with prices obtained from retail sources such as antiques shops and shows. These values are often unique to the dealer who did the pricing and reflect his or her understanding of the marketplace where the pieces are to be sold and his or her customer base. In addition, prices in this context are based to some degree on the amount of money the dealer paid for the item in question. As a result, because retail pricing is not based on a set formula, it can vary greatly depending on the business doing the pricing and its circumstances.

Prices can sometimes be obtained from specialists in a specific field of collecting who should have a clear understanding of what objects within their area of interest are worth. Sometimes, however, the bias of such specialists can cast doubt upon the prices they quote. It has been suggested by some observers, for example, that collectors who supply prices may exaggerate the value of items they own and wish to sell, and undervalue objects that they do not own and wish to buy at attractive prices. Though this is obviously not a common practice with all specialists, it may nonetheless skew the prices assigned to certain items from time to time.

The prices in this guide were obtained from all three of the basic sources listed above—auctions, retailers, and specialty collectors—with the last two being the major resources used by far. An attempt has been made to report only retail prices;

therefore, in the few instances in which data were obtained from auction sources, some interpretation and judgment was used to arrive at the retail prices that are listed.

The Cyclical Nature of Pricing

It is also important to note briefly the role played by fad and fashion in determining the prices of collectibles and antiques. In a market-driven economy such as ours, the price of any commodity is determined by the laws of supply and demand, and antiques and collectibles are no exception.

The pricing history of Homer Laughlin's "Fiesta" dinnerware provides a good example. Twenty-five years ago, few people were interested in these products other than as something on which to serve "beans and 'taters." Then, in the 1980s, "Fiesta" became fashionable with collectors, and Homer Laughlin reintroduced the ware in new colors and designs. Interest skyrocketed, the number of collectors increased dramatically, and as more collectors chased fewer and fewer goods, prices soared. "Fiesta" products became some of the strongest collectibles of the late-20th and early-21st centuries.

In spite of this success, however, the question remains: "How long will it last?" When will the bubble burst, and when will the fad cease to drive the marketplace? The answer is that no one knows for sure, but every experienced and serious collector knows that it will happen eventually, for two reasons. First, tastes will change and new items will come along to supplant the popularity of "Fiesta" products. And second, the prices of these products will become too high to sustain the market, the wider spectrum of buyers will no longer be willing to pay the inflated prices, and those prices will have to come down.

There is an inexplicable assumption among many collectors that the prices of antiques and collectibles never come down—they just keep going up and up and up. This is simply not true. Prices are cyclical: they go up when a group of objects is in fashion and buyers want to own them, but they go down when fashions change—and everybody knows in their hearts that fashions do change.

How and Why to Use This Guide

There are three main reasons why someone might want to know the value of an antique or vintage piece of pottery or porcelain. The first is to determine the price for which a similar item could be sold on the current collector market. The second is to know how much a piece is worth so that a judgment can be made as to how much to pay for a similar piece being offered for sale. The final reason is to know the amount for which a piece should be insured on a household insurance policy.

Since an attempt has been made to list only retail prices in this particular guide, a person using this guide to determine what an item might bring if it were offered for sale will have to use a little judgment and do a little interpreting. As a general rule, when private individuals try to sell their antiques, they can expect to receive between 30 and 60 percent of the retail value for each item, though that percentage may be significantly higher in the case of rare or eagerly sought-after items. Thus, if the value of an item for insurance replacement or retail purposes is $100, that item generally can be sold wholesale by a nonprofessional for somewhere between $30 and $60. Though this is not a hard-and-fast formula, it is a good "rule of thumb." An antiques dealer working in a retail environment should be able to get the full $100, though circumstance might force him or her to accept less, and good fortune might allow him or her to get a bit more.

Though the 30-to-60-percent rule generally applies, owners and collectors might find that the retail prices listed in any guide might be too low if, for example, the item being evaluated is an upper-end product from a well-regarded firm: an unusually large Newcomb College piece, or one with an early high-gloss glaze; a Rookwood Scenic Vellum piece; an example of Rookwood's Standard glaze with an exceptionally well-done portrait of a Native American chief; or a large, two-color Grueby vase, to name but a few examples. Pricing the upper-end products of such firms can be difficult, because the values of such items are highly volatile. Nonetheless, a guide such as this one can be very useful in helping to identify what such upper-end products actually are.

As for buying, prices listed in this guide are what one might expect to pay in a professionally run antiques shop or antiques mall. Savvy buyers will want to pay significantly less for the items they purchase than the prices listed in these pages—indeed, paying half these values (or less) is the goal that many experienced shoppers may wish to achieve.

As you peruse this guide, a few caveats are in order. First, always keep in mind that this is a price *guide*; the prices it lists are as accurate as they can be, but no one should assume that these values are "set in stone" or infallible. Second, it should be understood that, by the time this guide is published, the prices it lists will be at least six months old. For the vast majority of items, this lag time will have little or no adverse effect on pricing. For a very few items, however, the market will have changed significantly, and their values will have either increased or decreased (yes, prices for antiques and collectibles can decrease!) in the interim. This is simply the way the antiques marketplace works. Finally, though a great deal has been said about where the prices in this guide have come from, something should also be said about where they have *not* come from—namely, Internet auction sites. Though such sites can be wonderful places to buy and sell, they are simply too volatile to provide reliable prices for the purposes of this guide.

The manufacturers in the *Official Price Guide to Pottery and Porcelain* will be listed alphabetically, but they will fall into four main categories: makers of American Art Pottery, makers of American decorative pottery and commercial art wares, makers of American decorative porcelain, and makers of American dinnerware. In many instances, specific companies will make products that fall into more than one of these categories. The famous Lenox Company of Trenton, New Jersey, for example, is now primarily known for its dinnerware, though it originated as a maker of decorative porcelain and today actually produces both. Likewise, the firm of Fulper/Stangl made fine American art pottery while it was known as Fulper, and a huge array of everyday dinnerware when it was known as Stangl.

American Art Pottery

It can be argued with a great deal of validity that American Art Pottery is still being made to this day, but the classic period for this category of collectibles was from the 1870s through the 1920s. Unfortunately, since there is no clear definition of what constitutes American Art Pottery, the category usually ends up including whatever collectors of this genre say it should include.

The history of American Art Pottery is often said to have begun in earnest at the Philadelphia Centennial Exposition of 1876, when the American public was exposed to the arts and crafts of the world in a significant and concentrated way. Both the French and Japanese displays greatly influenced the Robertson family of potters (i.e., James Robertson and his sons, Hugh, Alexander, and George) and Mary Louise McLaughlin of Cincinnati, Ohio, who are usually credited with starting the art pottery movement in America.

American Art Pottery is made from earthenware, stoneware, and porcelain using a wide variety of decorative techniques, and it was produced by a large number of makers primarily for aesthetic purposes. In other words, these pieces were made primarily to be beautiful and not to be useful, although the vases could hold flowers and the large bowls could hold fruit.

American Decorative Pottery and Commercial Art Wares

One of the difficulties with defining American Art Pottery is that many of the companies that made this type of ware early in their histories may have turned to making other things later on. Both Weller and Roseville, for example, had all-too-brief periods when they produced true American Art Pottery, but they later turned to making more inexpensive decorative pottery. Such pottery is now more correctly known as "commercial art wares"—that is, pottery items that are molded with only a little hand finishing.

Other companies making decorative pottery items never made true art pottery, but always turned out commercial art wares. Examples of such firms include Hull, Gonder, Shawnee, and most of the California potteries that were operating from the 1920s to the late 1960s. These commercial art wares were largely mass produced, and many of today's collectors tend to lump them into the "art pottery" category when technically they do not belong there.

Decorative Porcelain

Porcelain was not widely made in the United States until the late 19th century. Until that time, fine-quality porcelain dinnerware or decorative objects were generally imported from Europe, China, or Japan. Much of the early decorative porcelain made in America was manufactured in Trenton, New Jersey, by such important companies as the Ceramic Art Company (CAC), which eventually evolved into Lenox, and Ott and Brewer, which made some of the finest and most valuable of the American decorative porcelains.

Much of the American decorative porcelain made during the late-19th and early-20th centuries was marked "Belleek," and in some cases these pieces were an attempt to imitate the lovely ware that had been made by the Belleek company in Ireland since the 1860s. In other cases, however, the marks were an attempt to make these beautiful hand-painted pieces more appealing to American customers who still preferred European porcelains. Besides Ott and Brewer and CAC, other makers of American Belleek included the Willets Manufacturing Company and the American Art China Works, both of Trenton.

Other cities in the United States where decorative porcelains were made during the 19th century included Philadelphia (Tucker & Hemphill and Tucker & Hulme), Greenpoint in Long Island, New York (The Union Porcelain Works), and Bennington, Vermont (United States Pottery Company). Each of the major companies in these cities was extremely important to the development of American decorative porcelain, and their products are hard to find (for the most part) and can thus be very valuable. Unfortunately, pricing for these manufacturers is not readily available, and the products of these firms will not be addressed to any significant degree in this book.

American Dinnerware

As was the case with American decorative porcelains, American consumers in the 19th century were interested in foreign dinnerware, mainly pieces from Europe—England, France, and Germany—and China. After the end of the Civil War, however, two significant pottery centers began to develop in the United States: one around Trenton, New Jersey, and the other around East Liverpool, Ohio, which extended into the part of West Virginia that was just on the other side of the Ohio River from East Liverpool. Later, the area around Los Angeles, California, would also develop into a region where large quantities of dinnerware and other pottery items were made.

Initially, American dinnerware was made mainly from some sort of earthenware. In the 20th century, however, companies such as Lenox and Syracuse began to produce dinnerware made from fine porcelain. Dinnerware was the "bread and butter" of many American pottery companies, which made vast quantities of this type of product in order to pay their bills and keep their doors open.

Country Pottery

The color insert featured in this guide is a special section on country pottery. Along with the color photographs you'll find descriptions and prices of a wide variety of country pottery pieces, ranging from blue decorated stoneware to earthenware mixing bowls made by a variety of Ohio and New Jersey companies. Country pottery is a very diverse category that encompasses all sorts of pottery made by individuals and small companies all across America. It is sometimes anonymous and the market can be very regional in nature, but it is one of the most popular areas with collectors.

The Potteries

ABINGDON POTTERIES, INC.

ABINGDON
USA

One of the marks found on
pottery made by *Abingdon
Potteries, Inc. of Abingdon,
Illinois.*

The Abingdon Sanitary Manufacturing Company of
Abington, Illinois, began manufacturing bathroom fixtures
in 1908, but by 1934 it had changed its name to Abingdon
Potteries, Inc. and had begun making a line of molded commercial art wares. These products were covered with a
number of glaze colors, including "Bronze Black" (later
called "Gunmetal Black"), "Copper Brown," "Fire Red," (brilliant red with crystalline specks), "Royal Red" (a purplish-
red shade), "Sudan Red" (matte reddish-tan), and "Riviera
Blue" (a dark blue). These hues are the most popular colors
with collectors and command a premium value; other colors such as white, ivory, yellow, light blue, and chartreuse
can be found, but are valued at about 25 percent less. The
company also made dinnerware and cookie jars, but it returned to making sanitary wares in 1950 and stopped producing its other lines.

Bookends
Prices below are for nonpremium colors unless otherwise
noted.

#370 Cactus, *6 inches, pair*	$ 175–225
#374 Cactus, *planter, 6¹/₂ inches*	$ 225–275
#444 Dolphin, *planter, 5¹/₂ inches*	$ 75–100

#428 Fern Leaf, *pair*	$ 275–325
#441 Horse Head, *7 inches, pair*	$ 125–175
#441 Horse Head, *black, 7 inches, pair*	$ 200–250
#595 Quill, *8¹/₄ inches, pair*	$ 325–375
#363 Reclining Colt, *6 inches, pair*	$ 700–750
#321 Russian Dancer, *8¹/₂ inches, pair*	$ 550–600
#650 Scotty, *7¹/₂ inches, pair*	$ 375–425
#305 Seagull, *6 inches, pair*	$ 275–325

Cookie Jars

It is important to note that when Abingdon stopped making commercial art wares in 1950 it sold its molds to other manufacturers. In many instances, these other companies continued making jars from the Abingdon molds, but they do not bear the "Abingdon" stamped mark (it has been estimated that 95 percent of all true Abingdon cookie jars are marked with the company's rubber stamp). These later non-Abingdon pieces were sometimes cold painted (i.e., unfired), though true pieces made by Abingdon were never cold painted.

#653 "Cookie Time" Clock	$ 225–275
#677 Daisy, *both color schemes*	$ 110–135
#549 Hippo, *solid color*	$ 375–425
#549 Hippo, *hand-painted, all designs*	$ 575–625
#602 Hobby Horse	$ 425–475
#663 Humpty-Dumpty	$ 275–325
#611 Jack-in-the-Box	$ 725–775
#674 Jack-O'-Lantern	$ 400–450
#622 Little Bo Peep	$ 475–525
#694 Little Bo Peep	$ 500–550
#471 Little Old Lady, *all color variations*	$ 575–625
#588 Money Bag	$ 110–135
#695 Mother Goose	$ 725–775
#664 Pineapple	$ 125–175
#665 Tepee	$ 925–975

#651 Train (Locomotive)	$ 300–350
#678 Windmill	$ 475–525
#692 Witch	$ 1,200–1,300

Dinnerware

#341 Bowl, *soup, coupe, 5¹/₂ inches*	$ 65–80
#338 Bowl, *soup, covered, square, 4³/₄ inches*	$ 50–65
#337 Dish, *square, 5 inches*	$ 50–65
#342 Plate, *round, 7¹/₂-inch diameter*	$ 50–65
#343 Plate, *round, 12-inch diameter*	$ 75–90
#339 Plate, *square, 7¹/₂ inches*	$ 50–65
#340 Plate, *square, 10¹/₂ inches*	$ 65–80

Figures

Animals

Prices are for nonpremium colors unless otherwise noted.

#571 Goose, *black, 5 inches*	$ 100–125
#571 Goose, *5 inches*	$ 65–75
#98 Goose, *leaning, 5 inches*	$ 75–90
#99 Goose, *upright, 2¹/₂ inches*	$ 75–90
#562 Gull, *5 inches*	$ 150–200
#574 Heron, *5¹/₂ inches*	$ 60–75
#605 Kangaroo, *decorated, 7 inches*	$ 350–400
#605 Kangaroo, *solid colors*	$ 175–200
#416 Peacock, *5 inches*	$ 90–110
#572 Pelican, *decorated, 5 inches*	$ 100–125
#572 Pelican, *solid colors, 5 inches*	$ 75–90
#573 Penguin, *5¹/₂ inches*	$ 80–100
#388 Pouter Pigeon, *4¹/₂ inches*	$ 80–100
#661 Swan, *3³/₄ inches*	$ 90–110
#657 Swordfish	$ 90–110

Chessmen

#03095B Bishop, *4¹/₂ inches*	$ 200–250
#03095C Castle, *4 inches*	$ 200–250
#03095K King, *5¹/₂ inches*	$ 200–250
#03095N Knight, *5 inches*	$ 200–250
#03095P Pawn, *3¹/₂ inches*	$ 150–200
#03095Q Queen, *5 inches*	$ 200–250

People

Most of these figures were produced in white, blonde, or black.

#497 Blackamoor, *black, 7¹/₂ inches*	$ 250–300
#497 Blackamoor, *chartreuse, 7¹/₂ inches*	$ 150–200
#3904 Fruit Girl, *10 inches*	$ 400–475
#3903 Kneeling Nude, *7 inches*	$ 450–525
#3902 Scarf Girl, *13 inches*	$ 500–600
#3906 Shepherdess and Fawn, *11¹/₂ inches*	$ 375–425

Kitchenware and Short Lines

"Daisy"

The bottom of "Daisy" pieces are ivory, and the lids are either blue daisies with yellow centers or yellow daisies with brown centers. The jam jars are an exception: they have yellow bodies and ivory tops with centers in the form of fruit—grape, plum, and strawberry. Some pieces, such as the wall pockets, have fronts that are all yellow.

#384 Candleholders	$ 50–65
#682 Creamer, *2¹/₂ inches*	$ 30–40
#679 Grease jar, *4¹/₂ inches*	$ 45–60
Jam jars, *all varieties*	$ 30–40
#690D Range set, *three pieces (salt, pepper, grease jar)*	$ 110–130
#680 Salt and pepper shakers, *4 inches, pair*	$ 35–45
#681 Sugar bowl, *3 inches*	$ 30–40
#683 Teapot, *6¹/₄ inches*	$ 85–100
#379 Wall pocket, *7³/₄ inches*	$ 90–110

"Asters"

#450 Bowl, flare, oval, $11^1/2$ by 8 inches	$ 55–65
#452 Bowl, *oval, 15 by 9 inches*	$ 75–90
#454 Bowl/Vase	$ 75–90
#451 Candleholder, *double, $4^1/2$ inches, pair*	$ 50–60
#453 Vase	$ 50–60
#455 Vase	$ 60–70

"Fern Leaf"

Described as a 20th-century interpretation of the feather motif associated with early 19th-century Empire design.

#423 Bowl, *$7^1/4$ inches*	$ 100–110
#424 Bowl, *$8^1/2$ inches*	$ 125–140
#425 Bowl, *$10^1/2$ inches*	$ 140–160
#427 Candleholder/Bud vase, *$5^1/2$ inches, pair*	$ 65–80
#429 Candleholder/Bud vase, *8 inches, pair*	$ 90–110
#426 Flower boat, *15 by $6^1/2$ inches*	$ 130–150
#432 Fruit boat, *13 by 4 inches*	$ 125–140
#430 Jug, *1-quart*	$ 150–175
#420 Vase, *$7^1/4$ inches*	$ 75–90
#421 Vase, *$8^3/4$ inches*	$ 100–110
#422 Vase, *$10^1/4$ inches*	$ 125–140
#433 Vase, *15 inches*	$ 175–200
#431 Wall pocket, *$7^1/2$ inches*	$ 130–150

"Morning Glory"

#393 Bowl, *7 inches*	$ 65–75
#390 Vase, *10 inches*	$ 65–75
#391 Vase, *$7^3/4$ inches*	$ 60–70
#392 Vase, *$5^1/2$ inches*	$ 50–60
#375 Wall pocket, *double, $7^3/4$ inches*	$ 50–65
#377 Wall pocket, *9 inches*	$ 40–50

"Shell"

#500 Bowl, *15 inches*	$ 45–55
#501 Bowl, *10¹/₂ inches*	$ 35–45
#502 Bowl, *7 inches*	$ 45–55
#506 Bowl, *6-inch diameter, 5¹/₂ inches high*	$ 35–45
#533 Bowl, *12 inches*	$ 35–45
#610 Bowl, *deep, 9 inches*	$ 60–75
#503 Candleholder/Ashtray, *single, 4 inches*	$ 15–25
#505 Candleholder, *double, 4 inches*	$ 35–45
#507 Vase, *oval, 7¹/₂ inches*	$ 35–45
#504 Vase, *planting, 7¹/₄ inches*	$ 60–70
#508 Wall pocket, *7 inches*	$ 120–140

"Star"

#713 Bowl, *console, 10 inches*	$ 75–85
#714 Candleholder, *pair, 4¹/₄ inches*	$ 60–75

"Tri-Fern"

#436 Candleholder, *8 inches, pair*	$ 110–125
#435 Wall pocket, *8 inches wide*	$ 150–175

Refrigerator Sets

Jugs in these sets were made in solid colors: Dusty Blue, April Green, Sudan Red, Eggshell, or Golden Yellow. Covered pieces come in either yellow with black covers or ivory with blue covers.

#RE4 Butter dish, *1-pound*	$ 100–120
#RE5 Casserole, *8 inches*	$ 100–120
#200 Jug, *ice lip, 2-quart*	$ 150–175
#201 Jug, *1-quart*	$ 120–135
#202 Jug, *1-pint*	$ 90–110
#RE1 Jug, *water, with lid, 2-quart*	$ 100–120
#RE2 Leftover, *oblong*	$ 80–100

#RE8 Leftover, *round, 4 inches*	$ 65–75
#RE7 Leftover, *round, 5-inch diameter*	$ 70–80
#RE6 Leftover, *round, 6 inches*	$ 80–100
#RE3 Leftover, *square*	$ 80–100

Planters

#673 Burro, *4¹/₂ inches*	$ 55–65
#668 Daffodil, *5¹/₂ inches*	$ 90–110
#669 Donkey, *7¹/₂ inches*	$ 90–110
#672 Fawn, *5 inches*	$ 55–65
#667 Gourd, *5¹/₂ inches*	$ 25–30
#670 Pooch, *5¹/₂ inches*	$ 65–75
#652 Puppy, *6³/₄ inches*	$ 65–75
#671 Ram, *4 inches*	$ 50–60

Vases

#485 Acanthus, *oval, 8 inches*	$ 60–70
#486 Acanthus, *oval, 11 inches*	$ 45–60
#468 Bird, *7¹/₂ inches*	$ 50–60
#584 Boot, *bud, 8 inches*	$ 60–75
#616D Cactus, *with sleeping man in sombrero, 6¹/₂ inches*	$ 80–90
#639 Calla Lily, *8¹/₂ inches*	$ 50–65
#469 Dutch Boy, *8 inches*	$ 95–115
#470 Dutch Girl, *8 inches*	$ 95–115
#487 Egret, *floor vase, relief, 14 inches*	$ 200–225
#524A Egret, *sand jar, 17¹/₂ inches*	$ 275–325
#389 Geranium, *7 inches*	$ 70–80
#659 Hackney, *8¹/₂ inches*	$ 60–75
#3801 Head, *large*	$ 350–400
#496D Hollyhock	$ 60–75
#594 Hourglass, *9 inches*	$ 45–55

#628D Iris, *8 inches*	$ 75–90
#708D Leaf, *square, embossed, 9 inches*	$ 100–120
#464 Medallion, *8 inches*	$ 55–65
#706D Oak Leaf, *9¹/₄ inches*	$ 90–110
#629 Poppy, *6¹/₂ inches*	$ 100–120
#472 Reeded, *8 inches*	$ 80–95
#625 Ribbed, *6¹/₂ inches*	$ 65–75
#566D Scallop	$ 60–75
#417 Scroll, *8 inches*	$ 100–120
#596D Sea Horse	$ 75–90
#494D Ship	$ 60–75
#703 Slant-top, *9¹/₂ inches*	$ 100–115
#463 Star, *7 inches*	$ 35–45
#626 Taper, *6 inches*	$ 65–75
#604D Tulip	$ 90–110
#654 Tulip, *6¹/₂ inches*	$ 90–110
#466 Wheel Handle, *8 inches*	$ 60–75
#467 Wreath, *8 inches*	$ 80–100

Wall Pockets

#589 Acanthus, *bracket, 7 inches*	$ 85–100
#649 Acanthus, *bracket, 8³/₄ inches*	$ 85–100
#648 Acanthus, *wall vase, 8³/₄ inches*	$ 85–100
#699 Apron, *6 inches*	$ 135–155
#676D Book, *6¹/₂ inches*	$ 125–145
#601D Butterfly, *8¹/₂ inches*	$ 125–145
#586D Calla Lily, *9 inches*	$ 65–80
#711 Carriage Lamp, *10 inches*	$ 100–125
#587 Cherub, *bracket, 7¹/₂ inches*	$ 90–110
#489 Dutch Boy, *10 inches*	$ 150–175
#490 Dutch Girl, *10 inches*	$ 150–175

Abingdon Potteries vase, 10¾ inches tall, $45–$55.
Item courtesy of Kingston Pike Antique Mall, Knoxville, Tennessee.

Abingdon Potteries vase, blue glaze with wreath decoration, 9 inches, $35–$45.
Item courtesy of Needful Things, Hendersonville, North Carolina.

#493 Horn shape, *double, 8¹/₂ inches*	$ 130–145
#457 Ionic, *9 inches*	$ 125–150
#590 Ivy, *hanging basket, 7 inches*	$ 80–95
#675D Matchbox, *5¹/₂ inches*	$ 110–125
#640 Triad, *5¹/₂ inches*	$ 65–80

Miscellany

#510 Ashtray, *Donkey, 5¹/₂ inches*	$ 180–225
#356 Ashtray, *duo, 6³/₄ inches*	$ 45–55
#509 Ashtray, *Elephant, 5¹/₂ inches*	$ 180–225
#326 Ashtray, *Greek, 4¹/₄ by 3 inches*	$ 75–85
#369 Ashtray, *guard, 5 inches*	$ 40–50
#316 Ashtray, *Trojan, 5 by 3¹/₂ inches*	$ 75–85
#317 Ashtray, *utility, round, 5¹/₂ inches*	$ 30–40
#700D Bowl, *Pineapple, 14³/₄ inches long*	$ 110–125

#580 Box, *Butterfly, 4³/₄ inches*	$ 100–120
#607 Box, *Candy Cane, 4¹/₂ inches*	$ 125–150
#612 Box, *Lily tray, 9¹/₂ inches long*	$ 160–175
#716D Candleholder, *bamboo, 3¹/₂ inches square, pair*	$ 60–75
#614 Candleholder, *reflector, 6¹/₂ inches, pair*	$ 125–145
#608 Cigarette Box, *Elephant, 6 inches*	$ 210–235
#715D Console plate, *bamboo, 10¹/₂-inch diameter*	$ 200–225
#606 Jar, *Elephant, 9³/₄ inches*	$ 250–300
#609D Jar, *Pelican*	$ 210–235
#378 Mask, *Female, 4 inches*	$ 200–250
#376F Mask, *Female, 7¹/₂ inches*	$ 250–300
#378 Mask, *Male, 4 inches*	$ 200–250
#376M Mask, *Male, 7¹/₂ inches*	$ 250–300
#702 String holder, *Chinese face, 5¹/₂ inches*	$ 200–225
#712D String holder, *Mouse, 8¹/₂ inches*	$ 200–225

AMERICAN ART CHINA WORKS

One of the marks used by the *American Art China Works of Trenton, New Jersey.*

Collectors often refer to this company as "Rittenhouse and Evans," after the names of its two founders. It opened in Trenton, New Jersey, in 1891 and an emphasis was placed on the fact that its fine-quality porcelain was American-made, which was something of a rarity for the day. The company made fine hand-painted decorative porcelains and some dinnerware items, but also sold white porcelain blanks that could be embellished by either professional decorators or amateur china painters.

Its products are marked with either a circular mark with "R E & Co. China Trenton, New Jersey" inside, or a monogram above the phrase "Belleek China."

The American Art China Works was very short-lived, and went out of business in 1895.

Cup and saucer,
chocolate, hand-painted floral $ 350–400

Pitcher,
gilt decoration, with gilt flowers, 4 inches tall $ 375–425

AMERICAN BISQUE COMPANY

B. E. Allen founded the American Bisque Company in Williamstown, West Virginia, in 1919 with the purpose of making bisque porcelain doll heads. One source reports that Allen did not become involved with the company until 1922, but whichever date is correct, the firm remained in the Allen family until the factory was closed in 1982.

Items sold by American Bisque to giftware stores were marked with a paper label bearing the image of a tree and the name "Sequoia Ware." Items sold to chain stores were marked with a label featuring a cloverleaf and the name "Berkeley." The company's cookie jars were marked with a label that featured three blocks—with "A" in one, "B" in another, and "C" in the third. Since these labels were generally removed after purchase, most cookie jars are found marked just "USA."

American Bisque made a variety of wares such as salad bowls, ashtrays, planters, banks, and serving dishes, but it is most famous for its cookie jars. Specifically, the company is known for unusual cookie jars featuring blackboards incorporated into the jar, lids that double as serving trays, and jars with elements called "flashers" that display movement (these jars were referred to in the American Bisque catalog as "Pan-Eye-Matic" cookie jars). The company is also known for its cartoon and other character jars.

Cookie Jars and Related Items

Acorn jar, *all color variations*	$ 225–275
After School Cookies	$ 65–85
Alice in Wonderland	$ 275–325
Baby Elephant, *no gold trim*	$ 225–275
Baby Elephant, *gold trim*	$ 325–375
Baby Huey	$ 3,400–3,600
Blackboard Boy	$ 375–425
Blackboard Clown	$ 375–425
Blackboard Girl, *"Mustn't Forget" above blackboard*	$ 375–425
Blackboard Girl, *"Don't Forget" above blackboard*	$ 575–625
Blackboard Hobo	$ 475–525
Blackboard Saddle	$ 325–375
Boy Pig, *all color variations, with or without patch on knee*	$ 175–225
Boy with Churn	$ 250–300
Casper, the Friendly Ghost bank, *8¹/₂ inches tall*	$ 525–575
Casper, the Friendly Ghost candy jar, *11³/₄ inches tall*	$ 625–675
Casper, the Friendly Ghost cookie jar, *13¹/₂ inches tall*	$ 725–775
Chef with cookie tray hat	$ 725–775
Chick, *all color variations*	$ 175–225
Chiffonier (chest of drawers)	$ 250–300
Churn, *with embossed flowers*	$ 50–65
Clown, *no paint*	$ 45–60
Clown, *painted*	$ 150–200
Coffeepot, *both styles*	$ 85–110
Collegiate Owl	$ 85–110
Cookie Basket, *tray as top*	$ 175–225
Cookies Out of This World, *spaceship and spaceman*	$ 950–1,100
Cowboy Boots	$ 175–225
Davy Crockett	$ 475–525
Davy (Crockett) in the Woods	$ 625–675

Cookie jar, American Bisque Company, Boy with Churn, 12 inches tall, $250–$300. *Item courtesy of Bill Brooker, Old School Antique Mall, Sylva, North Carolina.*

American Bisque Company cookie jar, churn with embossed flowers, $50–$65. *Item courtesy of Needful Things, Hendersonville, North Carolina.*

Dino with Golf Clubs (Flintstones)	$ 875–925
Dino with Golf Clubs (Flintstones), *bank*	$ 425–475
Elephant in Baseball Cap	$ 225–275
Feed Sack	$ 125–175
Fire Chief	$ 300–350
Flasher, *Bear and Beehive*	$ 325–375
Flasher, *Cheerleader*	$ 550–600
Flasher, *Clown on Stage, all variations*	$ 425–475
Flasher, *Cow Jumped Over the Moon*	$ 1,900–2,100
Flasher, *Sandman Cookies, dog on television screen*	$ 400–450
Flasher, *Sandman Cookies, clown on television screen*	$ 400–450
Flasher, *Tortoise and Hare*	$ 900–950
Fred and Dino (Flintstones)	$ 625–675
Grandma, *gold trim*	$ 225–275
Grandma, *yellow or green dress, no gold trim*	$ 175–225

Happy Clown	$ 150–200
Harvey & Katnip, *marked "Harvey Cartoons 1960" and "USA"*	$ 6,800–7,200
Ice Cream Freezer	$ 375–425
Jack-in-the-Box	$ 200–250
Jolly Pirate	$ 425–475
Kitten and Beehive	$ 150–200
Little Audrey *(from Casper, the Friendly Ghost)*	$ 1,800–2,200
Little Audrey, *bank*	$ 375–425
Little Lulu, *marked "Western Publishing," "Little Lulu," and "USA"*	$ 4,400–4,600
"Little Mo" or Mohawk Indian (made for Mohawk Carpet Company)	$ 4,400–4,600
Magic Bunny	$ 175–225
Majorette	$ 375–425
Milk Wagon	$ 150–200
Mr. Rabbit	$ 275–325
Mrs. Rabbit	$ 275–325
Oaken Bucket	$ 350–400
Olive Oyl	$ 2,800–3,200
Pennsylvania Dutch Boy	$ 675–725
Pennsylvania Dutch Girl	$ 625–675
Popeye	$ 775–825
Rubbles' House (Flintstones)	$ 525–575
Rudolph the Red-Nosed Reindeer	$ 825–875
Santa	$ 575–625
Sitting Horse	$ 950–1,100
Spool of Thread	$ 425–475
Strawberry, *marked "Sears Exclusively" and "USA"*	$ 150–200
Sweet Pea	$ 1,600–1,800
Sweet Pea, *bank*	$ 725–775
Toothache Dog	$ 375–425

Davy Crockett planter, American Bisque
Company, 5 inches, $145–$185.
*Item courtesy of Bill Brooker, Old School
Antique Mall, Sylva, North Carolina.*

Snow White planter, 6½ inches, American
Bisque Company, $175–$250.
*Item courtesy of Bill Brooker, Old School
Antique Mall, Sylva, North Carolina.*

Toy Soldier	$ 250–300
Treasure Chest, *closed*	$ 425–475
Treasure Chest, *open*	$ 250–300
Tugboat	$ 275–325
Umbrella Kids	$ 500–550
Wilma on the Telephone (Flintstones)	$ 875–925
Wooden Shoe	$ 975–1,100
Yarn Doll, *all variations*	$ 275–325
Yogi Bear, *all variations*	$ 350–400

† *Many of American Bisque's cookie jars are being reproduced. These include Dino with
Golf Clubs, Fred and Dino, Happy Clown, Little Lulu, "Little Mo," Olive Oyl, Popeye,
Rubbles' House, Sitting Horse, Sweet Pea, and Wilma on the Telephone.*

Donald Duck planter, 7 inches, American
Bisque Company, $200–$250.
*Item courtesy of Bill Brooker, Old School
Antique Mall, Sylva, North Carolina.*

Donald Duck planter, 5 inches, American
Bisque Company, $100–$145.
*Item courtesy of Bill Brooker, Old School
Antique Mall, Sylva, North Carolina.*

Roy Rogers and Trigger bank, 7½ inches,
American Bisque Company, $200–$250.
*Item courtesy of Bill Brooker, Old School
Antique Mall, Sylva, North Carolina.*

Dumbo bank, with gold trim, American
Bisque Company, $125–$150.
*Item courtesy of Bill Brooker, Old School
Antique Mall, Sylva, North Carolina.*

Bambi bank, marked, American Bisque
Company, $150–$200.
*Item courtesy of Bill Brooker, Old School
Antique Mall, Sylva, North Carolina.*

Dumbo, large salt and pepper shakers, set, American
Bisque Company, $85–$110.
*Item courtesy of Bill Brooker, Old School Antique Mall,
Sylva, North Carolina.*

APPLEMAN AUTO WORKS, INC.

Glenn Appleman was born in New York City in 1949, and earned a Fine Arts degree in 1971. He established his own studio, where he created sculptures of such diverse subjects as armadillos and Mao Tse-Tung. The cookie jars he created were manufactured from 1977 to 1987, with one reissue in 1992—first in New York City (until 1982), and thereafter in Union City, New Jersey. The jars were generally expensive, on account of the great deal of hand finishing required to produce them.

Cookie Jars

Buick Convertible, *black, red, white, green, and brown*	$10,000–10,100
Buick Convertible, *"Dewey Defeats Truman"*	$ 3,500–3,650
Buick Convertible, *red with ten cats*	$ 3,000–3,250
Buick Sedan, *black, brown, green, red, and white*	$ 1,000–1,100
Gotham Trucking	$ 1,750–1,850
Humperbump Police Car	$ 1,000–1,100
Humperbump Sedan, *all colors*	$ 900–1,000
Packard Police Car	$1,000–1,200

Phanta-Zoom, *black with red, gray with pink, turquoise with white*	$ 1,000–1,100
Phanta-Zoom, *with cat on fender*	$ 1,250–1,400
Rolls-Royce, *all color combinations*	$ 1,400–1,500
Sid's Taxi	$ 1,000–1,100
Skyway Cab	$ 1,250–1,400
Great American Trucks, *Vito's Veggies, with driver*	$ 2,000–2,200

AREQUIPA POTTERY

One of the marks used by the *Arequipa Pottery* of *Fairfax, California.*

In 1911, a pottery was established at the Arequipa Sanatorium in Fairfax, California, to provide occupational therapy and a little extra income to its female patients, who were suffering from tuberculosis. The patients did not have to perform heavy lifting, or any work that might have exposed them to clay dust in the air, but they did perform most of the decorating and finishing work in a well-lit and well-ventilated room.

The first ceramist at Arequipa was Frederick Hurten Rhead, who had served as art director at the famous Roseville Pottery in Zanesville, Ohio, from 1904 to 1908. Rhead and his wife, Agnes, taught the patients how to decorate pottery, but they had two significant problems. The first was that, while some of the women were very good at decorating pottery, others were not. As a result, the quality of Arequipa pottery can vary greatly. Rhead's second problem was that the patients working in his pottery only stayed in the sanatorium for an average of six months or less before returning to their former lives. This made it necessary to train new workers all the time, which gave the better decorators little time to develop and perfect their skills and techniques before leaving the facility.

The Rheads left Arequipa in 1913. The new ceramist was Albert L. Solon, who was the son of Louis L. Solon—a renowned ceramist who occupied important positions at both Sevres and Mintons. Solon expanded the pottery operation, and began using clay that was dug a little more than 50 yards from the pottery building. This clay was mixed with other clays, and then either thrown on a wheel or molded to make vessels on which designs created by Solon and other local artists could be sketched on the still-wet clay. The patients-cum-decorators then incised, carved, or painted decorations to finish the items and, if Solon liked the work, he allowed the patients to initial the bottom of their pieces.

Solon left Arequipa in 1916 and was replaced by Fred H. Wilde, who promoted the production of handmade tiles, which were quickly becoming a commercial success. Unfortunately, the war in Europe caused the pottery to close in 1918.

Vase, $4^1/2$ inches, globular form with a blue glaze on the exterior, cream glaze on the interior	$ 800–900
Vase, $4^1/2$ inches, bulbous, blue and brown matte glaze	$ 1,000–1,200
Vase, $4^1/2$ inches, globular form, incised floral decoration with brown and green glaze	$ 2,400–2,600
Vase, $5^1/2$ inches, broad base narrowing to top, matte mauve glaze, slight damage to rim	$ 500–600

J. A. BAUER POTTERY COMPANY

One of the marks used by the *J. A. Bauer Pottery Company* of Los Angeles, California.

BAUER
MADE IN
USA
LOS ANGELES

One of the marks typically found on pottery made by the *J. A. Bauer Pottery Company* of Los Angeles, California.

John Andrew Bauer established Paducah Pottery in Paducah, Kentucky, in 1885 and began supplying local distillers with whiskey jugs, and other businesses and homeowners with flowerpots and sanitary stoneware. The company also made beer containers, bean pots, mixing bowls, watercolors, mugs, and the like. This pottery was very successful and it allowed Bauer, who was an asthmatic, to spend his winters in Southern California finding relief from his chronic condition.

In 1909, Bauer decided to relocate his pottery to Los Angeles, and in 1910 the new facility became operational. Initially, his company specialized in making many of the same things the Paducah Pottery had made back in Kentucky. Flowerpots made from red clay were a big seller amongst local nurserymen, and the company made other garden wares in addition to pickle jars, chamber pots, and butter churns.

In either 1912 or 1913, Bauer hired Danish immigrant Louis Ipsen, who began designing fancier items made from redware. Ipsen was joined soon thereafter by Matterson Carlton, who was a talented turner, and it was Carlton who started producing a selection of hand-turned vases that were used both by local florists and homeowners. At about this time, Bauer developed a matte green glaze similar to the one being used on Grueby and Hampshire pottery, and this glaze became very popular for use on the hand-thrown vases.

In 1922, J. A. Bauer retired and the company passed into the hands of Watson E. Brockmon, who was in the Kentucky bourbon business and wanted the company for his two sons, Sam and Lynn. One-third of the pottery was also sold to Bauer's daughter, Eva, and her husband. The Brockmons did not do well with the business, and it was saved to some extent by Prohibition and the company's production of crocks that were useful for making and storing a wide variety of illicit alcoholic beverages.

In 1929, the company hired Victor F. Houser, a ceramics engineer who formulated some new, brightly colored glazes for some sturdy dishes that Ipsen had been ordered to design. Initially, Ipsen's dinnerware dishes had been glazed with an uninspired transparent glaze, and the finished products are said to have looked like the under plates used to keep plants from dripping on the floor. The addition of Houser's bright glazes, however, transformed these dishes from drab to glorious.

Actual dinnerware production did not start at Bauer until 1930, at which time the company began offering the consumer a new concept in dining. Before this time, dinnerware had been either too delicate or too expensive for casual outdoor use. But the California lifestyle called for sturdy dinnerware that was colorful and appropriate for use in either a patio or informal dining setting, and Bauer had invented the perfect product for both purposes. Initially this dinnerware was called "California Colored Pottery" or "Plain Ware," but it soon came to be known as "Ring Ware" because of the concentric rings on its surface.

In 1928, Bauer purchased an old, two-story winery in Atlanta, Georgia, and refitted it as a pottery. It was a somewhat makeshift effort and, in the beginning, Bauer Atlanta's only significant business came from a contract with the United States military to supply them with clunky hotel ware cereal bowls and tumblers for use by troops. The glory of Bauer's Atlanta operation, however, was the art pottery designed by Russel Wright that it produced from 1945 to 1946. Today, this pottery is very difficult to find.

Wright's wife, Mary, also wanted to get into the design business, and created a dinnerware set for Bauer Atlanta to manufacture. The pattern was called "Country Garden" and it never went into actual production, but pieces do turn up from time to time marked "Country Garden" and signed "Mary Wright." The Bauer Company went out of business in 1962.

"La Linda"

First introduced in 1939, this pattern was the result of a collaboration between Louis Ipsen and Ray Murray, who had come to Bauer from Frankoma Pottery in 1937. Murray, who was in his mid-twenties at the time, modeled the new California Art Pottery—or "Cal-Art" line—for Bauer, and later worked with Ipsen to spruce up his old "Plain" dinnerware line to make it more popular. The result was the "La Linda" pattern. "La Linda" pieces have no rings and the shapes are rather austere, with wide rims on the plates and modern shapes for the hollowware. The colors for this line are matte shades of green, blue, ivory, and dusty pink, and gloss colors of burgundy, chartreuse, dark brown, gray, green, ivory, light brown, olive green, pink, turquoise, and yellow. Gloss burgundy and dark brown are the colors most desired by collectors.

Bowl, *cereal, 6 inches, dark brown*	$ 30–34
Bowl, *individual fruit, 5 inches, light brown*	$ 20–24
Butter dish, *oblong, green*	$ 80–85
Cookie jar, *yellow*	$ 100–110
Creamer, *new style, Ray Murray, pink*	$ 15–18
Creamer, *old style, Louis Ipsen, burgundy*	$ 20–24
Cup and saucer, *coffee, matte blue*	$ 30–34
Cup and saucer, *jumbo, gray*	$ 75–80
Gravy boat, *olive green*	$ 45–50
Plate, *bread and butter, 6 inches, yellow*	$ 8–10
Plate, *chop, 13-inch diameter, green*	$ 38–42
Plate, *dinner, 9-inch diameter, matte ivory*	$ 18–22
Plate, *dinner, 9-inch diameter, dark brown*	$ 25–29
Plate, *salad, 7¹/₂-inch diameter, chartreuse*	$ 10–12
Plate, *salad, 7¹/₂-inch diameter, burgundy*	$ 13–15
Platter, *oblong, 10 inches, tab handles, dusty pink*	$ 25–30
Platter, *oblong, 12 inches, tab handles, blue*	$ 35–40

"Monterey Modern"

Designed in the late 1940s by Tracy Irwin, this pattern was first produced by Bauer in 1949 and was not discontinued until 1961. Unlike Bauer's other solid-colored ware, "Monterey Modern" pieces have a very sleek, modern look with coupe-shaped plates, gloss glaze, and, in the case of pieces produced toward the end of the 1950s, some decal-decorated items that are now rather rare and hard to find. There were two notable decal designs; the most spectacular features a spray of Epiphyllum in shades of pink, white, and green. On the dinner plates, this decoration covers most of the plates' centers, and depicts large opening blossoms with the suggestion of opening green leaves. The second notable decal design is known as "Barnyard," and features a red barn with a silo, a windmill, and a green field with a mailbox at the front edge. There was a lot of experimentation with "Monterey Modern" glazes, and Bauer thus produced a number of two-tone pieces—either with one color on top and another on the bottom, or with bands of color for borders or around rims. Colors used with the "Monterey Modern" pattern include yellow, pink, green, brown, chartreuse, burgundy, gray, and black. The most desired colors are burgundy and black, and the most desired items are two-tone pieces and pieces with decals.

Bowl, *vegetable, divided, 8¹/₂ inches, brown*	$ 55–60
Bowl, *salad, 13-inch diameter, gray*	$ 90–95
Bowl, *soup, 5¹/₂-inch diameter, black*	$ 45–50
Bowl, *soup, 5¹/₂-inch diameter, yellow*	$ 20–24
Butter dish, *round, covered, yellow*	$ 80–85
Canister, *rectangular, wooden top, "Barnyard" decal*	$ 50–55
Coffeepot, *6-cup, yellow*	$ 165–175
Cookie jar, *wood-and-metal top, "Barnyard" decal*	$ 145–150
Creamer, *pink*	$ 16–20
Cup and saucer, *tea or coffee, burgundy*	$ 45–50
Mug, *10-ounce, black*	$ 85–90
Mug, *10-ounce, green*	$ 45–50
Pitcher, *2¹/₂-quart, chartreuse*	$ 100–110
Plate, *dinner, 10¹/₂-inch diameter, Epiphyllum decal*	$ 50–55
Plate, *dinner, 10¹/₂-inch diameter, pink*	$ 35–40
Plate, *dinner, 9¹/₂-inch diameter, burgundy*	$ 25–30
Plate, *salad, 7¹/₂-inch diameter, chartreuse*	$ 12–15
Platter, *12 inches, rectangular, brown*	$ 30–35
Salt and pepper shakers, *chartreuse, pair*	$ 20–24
Sugar bowl, *pink*	$ 25–30
Teapot, *2-cup, black*	$ 100–110
Teapot, *2-cup, olive green*	$ 55–60
Teapot, *6-cup, green*	$ 80–85
Tray, *three-tier serving, chartreuse*	$ 75–80

"Ring"

Introduced in either 1931 or 1932, "Ring" was Bauer's most successful dinnerware line, and it is thought to be one of the main influences that led to the creation of "Fiesta" by the Homer Laughlin Company some four or five years later. As the name suggests, the "Ring" pattern is characterized by concentric rings that run around the edges of the flatware pieces and up and down the sides of bowls and tumblers. "Ring" evolved from the "California Colored Pottery" pattern, and it is thought that the rings derived from the markings that appear on a piece of pottery when it is hand-thrown on a potter's wheel.

The original colors for "Ring" (pre–World War II) are light brown, Chinese Yellow, orange red, jade green, cobalt blue, ivory, black, and white. Of these colors, the one least desirable to collectors is jade green because it is relatively common; the most desirable colors are cobalt blue, black, and white, with black being the rarest and most valuable. The "Ring" colors introduced after the end of World War II are red-brown, olive green, light blue, turquoise, chartreuse, gray, and burgundy. Of these colors, burgundy is the most desired by collectors, and gray is the least desirable. Pieces featuring the "Ring" pattern were last produced in the early 1960s.

Baker, *round, covered, individual, 5 inches, red orange*	$ 70–75
Bowl, *mixing, 5-inch diameter, Chinese Yellow*	$ 100–110
Bowl, *mixing, 7-inch diameter, cobalt blue*	$ 150–160
Bowl, *mixing, 9-inch diameter, Chinese Yellow*	$ 150–160
Bowl, *mixing, 9-inch diameter, jade green*	$ 150–160
Bowl, *soup, lug handle, 7$^{1}/_{2}$-inch diameter, jade green*	$ 100–110
Bowl, *vegetable, divided, oval, jade green*	$ 275–285
Cake stand, *metal pedestal, Chinese Yellow*	$ 120–130
Cake stand, *metal pedestal, red orange*	$ 120–130
Cake stand, *metal pedestal, cobalt blue*	$ 130–140
Casserole, *individual with lid, Chinese Yellow*	$ 275–285
Casserole, *individual with lid, red orange*	$ 275–285
Casserole, *individual with lid, jade green*	$ 245–255
Casserole, *individual with lid, cobalt blue*	$ 290–310
Cookie jar, *red orange*	$ 600–650
Creamer, *restyled, red orange*	$ 50–60
Cup and saucer, *coffee or tea, red orange*	$ 110–120

J. A. Bauer "Ring Ware," 17-inch diameter chop plate, jade green, $275–$325.
Item courtesy of Richard H. Crane, Knoxville, Tennessee.

Cup and saucer, *coffee or tea, Chinese Yellow*	$ 110–120
Cup and saucer, *coffee or tea, burgundy*	$ 145–155
Cup and saucer, *after-dinner, red orange*	$ 325–340
Cup and saucer, *after-dinner, burgundy*	$ 450–475
Jug, *beer, jade green*	$ 500–525
Mug, *jade green*	$ 130–140
Mug, *cobalt blue*	$ 120–130
Plate, *bread and butter, 6-inch diameter, red orange*	$ 50–60
Plate, *bread and butter, 6-inch diameter, cobalt blue*	$ 65–75
Plate, *bread and butter, 6-inch diameter, Delft Blue*	$ 50–60
Plate, *bread and butter, 6-inch diameter, jade green*	$ 50–60
Plate, *chop, 12-inch diameter, cobalt blue*	$ 270–280
Plate, *chop, 12-inch diameter, red orange*	$ 120–130
Plate, *chop, 14-inch diameter, Delft Blue*	$ 350–375
Plate, *chop, 17-inch diameter, jade green*	$ 275–325

Bauer vase, 5½ inches tall, orange-red glaze, $90–$110.
*Item courtesy of Bill Brooker, Old School Antique Mall,
Sylva, North Carolina.*

Plate, *dinner, 9¹/₂-inch diameter, black*	$ 225–240
Plate, *dinner, 9¹/₂-inch diameter, burgundy*	$ 145–155
Plate, *dinner, 9¹/₂-inch diameter, Chinese Yellow*	$ 100–110
Plate, *dinner, 9¹/₂-inch diameter, red orange*	$ 100–110
Plate, *dinner, 9¹/₂-inch diameter, olive green*	$ 120–130
Plate, *dinner, 9¹/₂-inch diameter, jade green*	$ 120–130
Plate, *dinner, 9¹/₂-inch diameter, Delft Blue*	$ 110–120
Plate, *dinner, 9¹/₂-inch diameter, cobalt blue*	$ 100–110
Plate, *dinner, 10¹/₂-inch diameter, cobalt blue*	$ 180–190
Plate, *salad, 7¹/₂-inch diameter, Chinese Yellow*	$ 60–70
Plate, *salad, 7¹/₂-inch diameter, red orange*	$ 65–75
Plate, *salad, 7¹/₂-inch diameter, jade green*	$ 60–70
Plate, *salad, 7¹/₂-inch diameter, Delft Blue*	$ 65–75
Plate, *salad, 7¹/₂-inch diameter, black*	$ 165–175
Serving plate with center handle, *Chinese Yellow*	$ 120–125

Serving plate with center handle, *red orange*	$ 130–140
Serving plate with center handle, *cobalt blue*	$ 130–140
Sugar bowl with lid, *red orange*	$ 100–110
Tumbler, *barrel-shaped, metal handle, ivory*	$ 225–240

Miscellany

Basket with twist handle, *Matt Carlton hand-thrown, royal blue*	$ 2,000–2,250
Bean pot, *4-quart, covered, brown glaze*	$ 75–85
Bean pot, *8-quart, covered, brown glaze*	$ 160–175
Dish, *"Cat" on front, high-gloss turquoise*	$ 250–275
Dish, *"Dog" on front, chartreuse*	$ 175–185
Figure, *Duck, head under wing, Cal-Art, red orange* (*unusual color and rarest form*)	$ 125–135
Figure, *Duck, head raised, Cal-Art, matte white* (*most common color*)	$ 45–55
Figure, *Duck, head down, matte white*	$ 40–50
Figure, *Hippo, 3¹/₄ by 4¹/₂ inches, Cal-Art, cream*	$ 375–385
Figure, *Madonna, 10 inches tall, Cal-Art, white*	$ 175–185
Figure, *Madonna, 8 inches tall, Cal-Art, green gloss*	$ 275–285
Figure, *Scottie Dog, 4 by 4¹/₂ inches, matte white*	$ 375–385
Jardinière, *"Lion" pot with raised lion's head masks and garlands, redware, 14-inch diameter*	$ 200–225
Jardinière, *in the shape of a stump, redware, 12-inch diameter*	$ 325–350
Jug, *5-gallon, brown glaze*	$ 200–225
Oil jar, *24 inches tall, jade green*	$ 2,000–2,200
Oil jar, *22 inches tall, red orange*	$ 1,200–1,400
Oil jar, *16 inches tall, royal blue*	$ 1,000–1,200
Oil jar, *12 inches tall, red orange*	$ 750–800
Vase, *ribbed with ruffled top, Matt Carlton, red orange*	$ 575–600
Vase, *18¹/₂ inches, Matt Carlton's hand-thrown "Signature" shape, twist handles, horizontal ribs, red orange*	$ 2,000–2,200
Vase, *14¹/₂ inches, Matt Carlton's hand-thrown "Signature" shape, twist handles, horizontal ribs, deep blue (rare color)*	$ 3,000–3,250

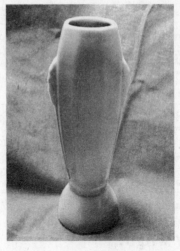

Bauer teapot, 10½ inches, Ray Murray gloss pastel glaze and gloss pastel design, 8-cup, $250–$300.
Item courtesy of Patty Tower, Old School Antique Mall, Sylva, North Carolina.

Bauer vase, "Cal-Art," 7 inches, light-green glaze, $80–$90.
Item courtesy of Richard Crane.

Vase, *fan shape, hand-thrown, Matt Carlton, 6 by 8 inches, uneven striations, white (rare color)*	$ 650–700
Vase, *fan shape, 6 inches, horizontal ribs, Matt Carlton, black (rare color)*	$ 650–700
Vase, *12 inches, Rebekah shape, baluster shape with two handles, Matt Carlton, hand-thrown, jade green*	$ 1,000–1,000

Russel and Mary Wright

Russel Wright began working with Bauer in 1945 to design an art pottery line. Wright was coming off of great success with his "American Modern" dinnerware, made by the Steubenville Pottery Company, which was the best-selling American dinnerware of the time. The art pottery line he designed for Bauer Atlanta was very avant-garde, and had flowing glazes that in some cases flowed so much that they damaged the kilns. Unfortunately, when the line was offered to buyers, Russel Wright enthusiasts bought his pieces but did not reorder, and the art pottery was a dismal failure that was discontinued by 1947.

#8A Ashtray, *pinch, 6¹/₂ inches, aqua and bronze*	$ 550–600
#7A Bowl, *centerpiece, 17 inches long by 9 inches wide, figured white and bronze*	$ 1,200–1,400
#11A Bowl, *"Manta Ray" or "Pancake," 3 inches, Jonquil Yellow and bronze*	$ 1,400–1,500
#15A Bowl, *centerpiece, candlestick ends, Atlanta Brick*	$ 900–1,000
#12A Pot, *flower, 4¹/₂ inches, Jonquil Yellow and Georgia Brown*	$ 600–650
#1A Vase, *pillow, figured white and aqua*	$ 800–850
#3A Vase, *corsage, 5 inches tall, gunmetal*	$ 600–650

Mary Wright

While her husband, Russel, was working on his art pottery line for Bauer Atlanta, Mary Wright was developing a dinnerware line that would come to be known as "Country Garden." Commercial production was to start in 1946 but, unfortunately, it never did. Prototypes and samples were made (the line was shown unsuccessfully at the Atlanta Housewares Show in 1946), but a disagreement over manufacturing costs caused Bauer to drop the line altogether. Experimental "Country Garden" pieces do turn up on rare occasions, and these can command rather high prices, but are not listed in this book.

"Country Garden" is basically a solid-color line, but some pieces do have raised flowers or leaves in a lighter color as decoration. The normal colors for "Country Garden" pieces are white, pink, green, beige, and brown. These pieces are easy to identify because they are signed by Mary Wright and have a "Bauer" backstamp.

Butter pat, *1¹/₂ inches, pink*	$ 110–120
Butter plateau, *6 inches, green*	$ 350–375
Casserole, *hinged, brown*	$ 400–425
Cup and saucer, *brown*	$ 150–165
Pitcher, *5-cup, pink*	$ 375–400
Plate, *8-inch diameter, green*	$ 150–165
Plate, *6-inch diameter, pink*	$ 90–100
Sauceboat, *deep, pink*	$ 225–250
Sauceboat, *shallow, pink*	$ 325–350
Skillet server, *green*	$ 325–350
Sugar bowl, *spoon cover, brown*	$ 250–275

BENNINGTON POTTERY

One of the marks used by the *United States Pottery Company of Bennington, Vermont.*

This listing is slightly different from the others in this book in that it covers the work of several potteries within a single geographical area: Bennington, Vermont. The Bennington potteries include Norton Pottery, Lyman Fenton and Company, United States Pottery Company, and Norton and Fenton, among others. The long and convoluted story of Bennington pottery begins with Captain John Norton, who established a pottery in Old Bennington, Vermont, in 1793, where he made common redware and, a little later, stoneware.

In 1831, Captain Norton's son, Judge Lyman Norton, moved to the town that today is called Bennington and built a kiln where he made yellowware and creamware, often covering it with a spattered brown glaze that goes by a number of names. It is often called "American Rockingham" (in reference to wares supposedly made on the estate of the Marquis of Rockingham in England), and pieces covered with the glaze are sometimes referred to as "tortoise-shell ware" (after the similar products made by Englishman Thomas Whieldon in the 18th century). Most American collectors, however, simply refer to this type of glaze as "Bennington."

Christopher Fenton, Judge Norton's son-in-law, joined the firm in 1839, and the company became Norton and Fenton. It should be noted that, over the course of its existence, this company changed names several other times to reflect its ownership at those times, but the pottery stayed within the Norton family until 1881, when the Norton interests were sold to C. W. Thatcher.

Christopher Fenton wanted to make parian wares (i.e., wares made from white porcelain that was left in the bisque state and was said to resemble Parian marble), and he began experimenting in the Norton and Fenton factory. In 1852, he went out on his own and established the United States Pottery, which was located across the street from the facility run by the Nortons. The United States Pottery made even finer wares than the Nortons' firm, using such materials as parian, white granite, and a glaze known as "flint enamel."

Flint enamel resembles the spotted and splotched "Rockingham" glaze that is widely associated with Bennington, but it features a variety of colors other than Manganese Brown on a yellow background. Flint enamel colors include black, yellow, several shades of green, and, rarely, red and blue. Unfortunately, the United States Pottery Company was short-lived, and reportedly closed its doors in 1858.

Baking dish, *octagonal, 12 inches, flint enamel*	$ 800–1,000
Bottle, *in the shape of a coachman, Rockingham, 11 inches tall*	$ 1,200–1,400
Bowl and pitcher set, *scroddled (marbleized with different-colored clay), molded diamond pattern, 13 inches*	$ 3,000–3,500
Candlesticks, *flint enamel, brown and green, 8 inches tall, waisted form with flared foot, pair*	$ 1,000–1,200
Chamberstick, *scroll handle, flint enamel, 3 inches*	$ 3,000–3,500
Coffee urn, *flint enamel, 20 inches tall, covered, marked*	$ 3,000–3,500
Coffeepot, *12 inches, baluster form, flint enamel*	$ 1,200–1,400
Cuspidor, *8 inches, Rockingham*	$ 225–275
Figure, *lion on plinth with foot on ball, coleslaw mane, flint enamel, mottled green, 11 inches*	$ 6,000–7,000
Figure, *poodle, with coleslaw fur, carrying basket of fruit in mouth, Rockingham*	$ 2,250–2,500
Figures, *poodles, with coleslaw fur, carrying baskets of fruit in their mouths, 8 inches, flint enamel, pair*	$ 5,000–6,000
Flask, *book form (also called a "hand warmer"), flint enamel, entitled* Bennington Battle	$ 1,100–1,250

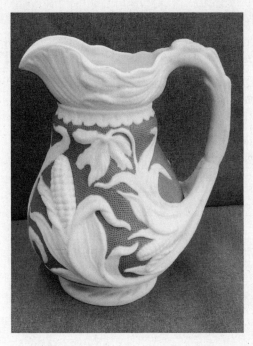

Bennington parian pitcher, marked with
the United States Pottery ribbon mark, 8¼
inches, $350–$450.
*Item courtesy of Kingston Pike Antique Mall,
Knoxville, Tennessee.*

Flask, *book form, (also called a "hand warmer"),* *flint enamel, entitled* Ladies Companion *(rare title)*	$ 4,000–5,000
Flask, *book form, (also called a "hand warmer"),* *flint enamel, entitled* Departed Spirits	$ 750–1,000
Flask, *book form, scroddled (marbleized with* *different-colored clay), star on spine, 6 inches*	$ 5,800–6,500
Footbath, *flint enamel, 21 inches*	$ 6,500–7,000
Frame, *oval, Rockingham, 9 inches*	$ 1,000–1,200
Jar, *slop, covered, paneled, flint enamel, 19 inches*	$ 3,000–3,500
Lamp, *astral, flint enamel base, original globe and prisms*	$ 10,000–11,000
Paperweight, *rectangular form with conical knob,* *flint enamel, green and amber, 5 inches*	$ 750–850
Pitcher, *parian, 10 inches tall, panel form,* *embossed "Wild Rose" design*	$ 450–650
Pitcher, *octagonal, flint enamel, 10 inches*	$ 450–550
Pitcher, *hound handle, 12 inches, Rockingham*	$ 2,250–2,750

Plate, *pie, serving, Rockingham, 9-inch diameter*	$ 700–800
Spill vase (a "spill" is a twist of paper used to light a fire), *form of recumbent male deer, with tree trunk, flint enamel, 10 inches*	$ 6,000–7,000
Spill vase (see above), *form of recumbent doe, flint enamel, 11 inches, marked*	$ 10,000–12,500
Sugar bowl, *9 inches, paneled baluster form, flint enamel, unusual coloration with bold olive-green splashes*	$ 2,500–3,000
Teapot, *Rockingham, 5 inches*	$ 800–900
Toby snuff jar, *flint enamel, mottled green, 4 inches*	$ 3,000–3,500
Toby snuff jar, *Rockingham, 4 inches*	$ 1,200–1,400
Vase, *tulip form, flint enamel, 10 inches, pair*	$ 1,800–2,200

BRAYTON-LAGUNA POTTERY

Brayton Laguna Pottery

One of the marks used by the *Brayton-Laguna Pottery of Laguna Beach, California.*

One of the marks of *Brayton-Laguna Pottery.*

Dulin E. Brayton was a graduate of the Chicago Art Institute who began making pottery in the garage at his home in South Laguna Beach, California, in 1927. His company flourished and, in 1938, he built larger facilities in Laguna Beach. Brayton-Laguna's first products were dinnerware, vases, flowerpots, and figures. After Brayton married artist Ellen Webster Grieve in 1936, the scope and artistic quality of the company's pottery expanded, and Brayton-Laguna began to make all sorts of items—from cookie jars and novelty items to pieces sanctioned by the Walt Disney Company. Ellen "Webb" Brayton died in 1948, and her husband followed in 1951. The company's employees kept the company going until 1968.

Early pieces are marked "Laguna Pottery," and later pieces are marked "Brayton Laguna Pottery" or just "Brayton's." Some pieces are unmarked, and some of the pieces produced for the Walt Disney movie *Pinocchio* are marked "Geppetto Pottery."

Blackamoor Items

Candleholders, *pair,* black/burgundy/green	$ 275–325
Candlesticks, *pair, pillow,* black/burgundy/green	$ 275–325

Brayton-Laguna Blackamoor planter,
8¼ inches, $325–$375.
*Item courtesy of Bill Brooker, Old School
Antique Mall, Sylva, North Carolina.*

Figure, *kneeling with cornucopia, 10 inches tall*	$ 275–325
Figure with bowl, *black/burgundy/green/white, 8 inches tall*	$ 325–375

Cookie Jars and Related Items

Black Maid, *black dress, white apron, holding pie*	$ 4,500–5,000
Black Maid, *blue dress, white apron, holding pie*	$ 8,000–8,500
Black Maid, *salt and pepper shakers, black pants and skirt*	$ 1,200–1,400
Circus Tent	$ 450–500
Gypsy Woman	$ 500–550
Lady with Concertina	$ 3,500–3,750
Lady with Goose, *all variations*	$ 2,250–2,500
Mammy, *green plaid dress, green kerchief, arms akimbo*	$ 1,900–2,100
Mammy, *green plaid dress, yellow kerchief, arms akimbo*	$ 1,800–2,000
Mammy, *red or yellow kerchief, zigzag pattern at hem of apron*	$ 1,500–1,650
Mammy and Black Chef, *salt and pepper shakers, green plaid*	$ 750–800

Matilda, *all variations*	$ 750–800
Plaid (or Gingham) Dog	$ 500–550
Ringmaster, *marked "Geppetto Pottery"*	$ 3,000–3,250
Wedding Ring Granny	$ 1,000–1,100

Figures

Animals

Carousel Horse, *rearing, 16 inches tall*	$ 175–200
Cat, *lying down, Siamese-type, 6^1/$_2$ inches long*	$ 85–95
Cat, *on oval base, hat with bluebird on head, 6^1/$_4$ inches long*	$ 145–160
Giraffes, *necks intertwined, 18 inches tall, pair*	$ 300–325
Monkeys, *male and female, 13 inches tall, white crackle glaze with brown faces and brown stain, pair*	$ 500–525
Pluto, *Walt Disney, 6 inches long*	$ 200–225
Purple Bull	$ 150–160
Purple Calf	$ 75–85
Purple Cow	$ 125–135
Quail, *on base, 10^3/$_4$ inches tall*	$ 165–175
Squirrel, *white crackle, 12^3/$_4$ inches long*	$ 150–160
Swan	$ 80–90

Calico/Gingham

The figures of calico cats are decorated with clusters of four dots in various colors (usually red, blue, and green, though green, yellow, and gold can also be found), while the figures of gingham dogs feature plaid decoration (usually in blue and red, though red and gold and brown, yellow, and green can also be found). Both types of figures have a representation of a stitched seam running down the middle of the face and body.

Cat, *Calico, 8 inches tall*	$ 125–135
Creamer, *calico cat*	$ 100–110
Dog, *Gingham, 8 inches tall*	$ 125–135
Fireside figure, *calico cat, 15 inches tall*	$ 200–225

Fireside figure, *gingham dog, 15 inches tall*	$ 200–225
Pencil holder, *gingham dog*	$ 100–110
Shakers, *gingham dog and calico cat, pair*	$ 100–110
Toothbrush holder, *gingham dog*	$ 165–175

Children: Boys

Arthur, *with elephant (1940)*	$ 125–135
Butch, *boxes under arms*	$ 125–135
John, *boy with horn*	$ 135–150
Jon, *with megaphone*	$ 125–135
Peanuts, *Asian boy*	$ 135–150
Pedro, *Mexican boy with serape*	$ 150–175
Sambo, *black boy, blue coveralls*	$ 175–200

Children: Girls

Ellen, *feet pointed in, pigtail sticking out*	$ 125–135
Emily, *with purse, knitting*	$ 125–135
Dorothy, *seated, legs sticking out*	$ 125–135
Francis, *flower holder, bluebird on right arm*	$ 85–95
Petunia, *black girl with basket and hair bows*	$ 175–200
Rosita, *Mexican girl with basket*	$ 150–175
Sally, *flower holder*	$ 85–95

Other Figures

African-American Boy and Girl, *on base, both holding baskets*	$ 525–550
Bedtime, *from Gay '90s Matrimony series, man and woman standing, dressed in nightclothes*	$ 200–225
Boy, *from Hillbilly Shotgun Wedding series, wearing bathing suit*	$ 225–250
Bride and Groom, *from Gay '90s Matrimony series, bride is standing, groom is seated*	$ 200–225
Hillbilly Shotgun Wedding, *6 figures*	$ 2,000–2,250

One Year Later, *from Gay '90s Matrimony series, bride is sitting holding infant, groom is standing*	$ 185–200
Seashore Honeymoon, *from Gay '90s Matrimony series, man and woman standing, wearing bathing costumes*	$ 200–225
Woman with Wolfhounds, *flower holder, 9¹/₂ inches tall*	$ 150–175

Miscellaneous pieces

Bookends, *Circus series, clown sitting with outstretched legs*	$ 350–375
Vase, *seahorse, 8¹/₂ inches high*	$ 300–325

BRUSH-McCOY POTTERY AND NELSON McCOY POTTERY

One of the marks used by the *Nelson McCoy Pottery of Roseville, Ohio.*

Examples of marks found on products made by the *Nelson McCoy Pottery of Roseville, Ohio.*

Nelson McCoy Pottery mark.

The history of the various McCoy pottery companies is very convoluted, but it begins in Putnam, Ohio, in 1848 when W. Nelson McCoy and W. F. McCoy began making stoneware crocks and jars. Putnam, Ohio, incidentally, is now part of Zanesville, Ohio, one of the most important centers for the making of American art and other kinds of pottery.

The McCoys' company was extremely successful, and began shipping its wares to destinations as far away as New Orleans, Louisiana. This was fairly unusual, because at that time the products of most crock makers stayed close to home where they could meet the storage needs of local residents and farmers.

How long this venture stayed in business is open to discussion, but the next important McCoy pottery was founded in Roseville, Ohio, in 1899, and was called the "J. W. McCoy Company." This concern made all sorts of products for household use, including jardinières, baking pans, and cuspidors, and by 1902 it also began making some fine art pottery. Perhaps its most distinctive line was a very rare line called "Mt. Pelee," which was made for only a short time—probably from 1902 to early 1903. In 1903, a fire destroyed most of the company's pottery-making facilities, including the entire stock of "Mt. Pelee" ware that had not yet been sold. After the fire, "Mt. Pelee" ware was never made again.

In a way, the destruction of the "Mt. Pelee" stock by fire was strangely appropriate, since the ware had been named after a volcano on the island of Martinique in the French West Indies, which had erupted in 1902 and killed 40,000 people. As their name suggests, pieces of "Mt. Pelee" ware were taken from molds and pushed and convoluted until they appeared to be made from volcanic rock. They were then glazed an iridescent black or, more rarely, a matte green. Many of the best pieces feature three-dimensional depictions of Art Nouveau-style women, who appear to be caught in the maelstrom of the volcanic cataclysm. When "Mt. Pelee" items have handles, the handles appear to be very distressed and, in some cases, they resemble crumpled ribbon.

In 1909, George Brush became General Manager of the J. W. McCoy Pottery Company and, in 1911, Brush and McCoy founded the Brush-McCoy Pottery Company in Roseville and Zanesville, Ohio. This company was a merger between the J. W. McCoy Pottery Company, with facilities in Roseville, Ohio, and Brush Pottery, which had been founded in the old J. B. Owens plant in Zanesville. Initially, the Roseville plant made utilitarian wares while the Zanesville operation made art ware, but when a fire in 1918 burned down the Zanesville plant, all manufacturing was moved to Roseville.

J. W. McCoy died in 1914 and, by that time, Brush-McCoy had become one of the largest makers of pottery in the United States. Nelson McCoy, J. W.'s son, took his father's place in the business and, in 1918, disaster struck again when the Zanesville plant burned to the ground and all manufacturing operations had to be moved to the Roseville facility. In 1925, the McCoys sold their interest in the company, and it continued to operate as the Brush Pottery Company. The McCoys' involvement in the pottery industry did not end, however, and the family instead concentrated its efforts on the Nelson McCoy Sanitary Stoneware Company, which had been founded in Roseville, Ohio, in 1910.

Originally, the Nelson McCoy Sanitary Stoneware Company made such utilitarian wares as stoneware churns, poultry fountains, and foot warmers. After 1925, however, it began branching out and making more decorative wares such as umbrella stands and jardinières with pedestals. Later it began making pieces covered with an onyx-style glaze in shades of brown, green, or blue, similar to the glaze that had been introduced at Brush-McCoy in 1923.

In 1933, the company was reorganized and became known as "The Nelson McCoy Pottery Company," and in the 1940s it began making a line of novelty cookie jars—very popular with today's collectors—and commercial art wares for use by homeowners and florists. The company produced prodigious amounts of these commercial art wares, and currently they are widely available and modestly priced, except for a few rare items. The Nelson McCoy Pottery Company went out of business in the late 1980s.

Most of the products made by The Nelson McCoy Pottery Company are easy to identify because they are plainly marked with the company name, "McCoy." However, general collectors sometimes have a problem identifying J. W. McCoy and Brush-McCoy art wares because the vast majority of them were not marked with the company's name. A list and description of some of the more important Brush-McCoy art lines follows.

- **"Florastone."** Pieces in this line have gray stoneware bodies and were decorated with high-gloss enamels using the squeeze-bag technique. In this process, a balloonlike bag was filled with stiff but liquid colored clay, and the end of the bag was fitted to an oil can spout. (This apparatus is called a "squeeze bag" because the colored clay is squeezed out through the tip and applied to the surface of a piece of pottery, in much the same way that a baker would decorate a fancy birthday or wedding cake.) "Florastone" pieces were decorated in shades of rose, green, blue, and white, and the decorations most often consisted of stylized flowers and leaves with white and blue dots and triangular accents. "Florastone" is one of Brush-McCoys' "Stoneart" lines, which also include "Jewel," "King Tut," "Jetwood," "Zuniart," and "Krackle-Kraft." No one is exactly sure when "Florastone" was produced, but it was probably made from the early 1920s until no later than 1928.

- **"Jetwood."** This very beautiful line was introduced in 1922 and was made for only a few years. "Jetwood" pieces are easily recognized because they depict twilight in the woods surrounding Roseville, Ohio. They feature distinctive bands of blue and orange on a cream ground, and generally depict low hills with black trees seen in silhouette against a sunset. Occasionally a rail fence is incorporated into the view, and on extremely rare pieces bunny rabbits are also included. The decoration on these pieces was achieved by applying small droplets of black enamel from a squeeze bag. (For details of this process, see "Florastone," above.)

- **"Jewel."** This line reportedly originated in 1923, and its pieces feature high-gloss decorations against matte backgrounds. Often these decorations, which were applied using the squeeze-bag technique, are composed of diamonds, triangles, dots, and ovals, arranged to suggest a fringed window shade with jewel-like pendants. These pieces have a real "1920s" feel to them. The colors of the raised squeeze-bag design elements are generally green, blue, rose, and white. Because these design elements were entirely hand-wrought, production of the "Jewel" line was extremely time-consuming. In fact, it is said that a decorator could spend more than one-third of his or her working day embellishing a single large "Jewel" piece.

- **"King Tut."** This line originated in 1923, after Howard Carter had opened the tomb of Egyptian pharaoh Tutankhamen in 1922. This line consists of banded ware, and its pieces feature green bands at the top and bottom (the shade of green may vary) and a band in the center decorated with either Egyptian kilted figures or scarab-themed artwork. (The decorations were created using the squeeze-bag technique.) In addition, the pieces featuring Egyptian figures may also feature crude renditions of hieroglyphics. As a general rule, pieces featuring figural decorations are more valuable than those featuring scarabs.

- **"Krackle-Kraft."** This is an Asian-inspired line. Its pieces feature a crackle glaze that is accented with a cobalt-blue overwash. The tops of these pieces often feature a single or double line of blue around the edge, though some pieces have a raised arabesque design applied using a squeeze bag, and some have an area of blue glaze around the rim that has been allowed to drip down the sides. Examples in this line are very hard to find, and should be considered fairly rare. Dates of manufacture are unclear, but the line was probably produced from the mid-1920s until no later than 1928.

- **"Loy-Nel-Art."** Named after J. W. McCoy's three sons—Loyd, Nelson, and Arthur—this line was McCoy's version of certain lines, known for their brown-glazed wares, that originated at Rookwood and were popular at Weller, Roseville, Owens, and other potteries. These pieces were slip-decorated with flowers and leaves—and, in some rare examples, grapes or berries—in shades of orange, yellow, and green. Made by both the J. W. McCoy Pottery Company and Brush-McCoy, this line was first produced as early as 1906, though most pieces are circa 1912.

- **"Navarre Faience"** (also called "Navarre" or "New Navarre"). Pieces in this line were made from molds originally used by the J. B. Owens factory to make its "Henri Deux" line. These pieces have deep, matte green backgrounds and white decoration featuring an Art Nouveau woman seen in profile. This woman is often depicted wearing what appears to be a ribbon, though foliage and flowers may sometimes appear, also done in white. This line reportedly originated in either 1912 or 1914.

- **"Olympia."** Pieces in this line feature a standard brown glaze with raised decorations of flowers, berries, leaves, or, occasionally, a coat of arms. In addition, some pieces may have diagonal orange stripes. Collectors should not confuse pieces in this line with similar raised-decoration pieces made by the Peters and Reed Company, also of Zanesville, Ohio. Both lines were unmarked. "Olympia" was made by J. W. McCoy Pottery during the first five years of the 20th century.

- **"Rosewood."** Another unmarked J. W. McCoy line with a standard brown glaze, but this line is distinguished by diagonal orange streaks that give the surface of its pieces the appearance of a mystic firestorm.

- **"Zuniart."** First made in 1923, the pieces in this line were supposed to resemble the pottery of the Zuni tribe of Native Americans, who call northwestern New Mexico home. Unfortunately, the resemblance was mainly in the minds of the Brush-McCoy designers. The background of these pieces is sand or beige, and the decoration is banded—with the central band containing a sun or peace symbol that many people associate with the infamous swastika. It should be noted, however, that the Nazi version of this symbol had arms placed in a clockwise rotation, while the Native American version has arms facing in a counterclockwise direction. The symbol appears on all "Zuniart" pieces, except the model of the moccasins (part of the Zuniart line), which features a star motif instead. The decoration on "Zuniart" pieces was achieved using several techniques, including "squeeze bag," which gives the design elements in the central band of each piece a raised profile. One rare piece from the "Zuniart" line is a round plaque featuring a molded portrait of an Indian chief in profile wearing a feather headdress.

Among the Brush-McCoy commercial art ware lines that are most often encountered by the collecting public is a line called "Onyx," which was made using either a brown, blue, or green gloss glaze, accented with a marbled effect in white and black. On pieces in this line, all the glaze colors were allowed to run together, producing a finished product that is supposed to resemble stone. Pieces from this line were produced in a wide variety of shapes that run the gamut from clock cases to vases encased in metal mounts. The "Onyx" line was produced for a very long time, and examples are relatively easy to find.

Brush-McCoy Cookie Jars

Cookie jars made by Brush-McCoy, which went out of business in 1982, can often be identified by style numbers that include the letter "W" as a prefix. The "W" is a reference to the Winton twins, Don and Ross, who designed many of Brush-Mc-Coys' cookie jars.

Angel, *with wings, "W17R"*	$ 900–1,000
Auto, *old-fashioned touring car, green and white*	$ 1,500–1,600

Basket, *with hen lid, also called "Hen on a Nest"*	$ 135–165
Boy with Balloons, *right hand in pocket*	$ 750–825
Chick and Nest, *"W38"*	$ 275–425
Cinderella Pumpkin Coach, *"W32," two mice as finial*	$ 250–300
Circus Horse, *"W9R," green mane, puppy finial*	$ 900–1,000
Clown Head, *with hat lid*	$ 300–350
Cookie Clock, *"W20," mantle clock with smiling face and poem on side: "It's cookie time the clock around...."*	$ 325–375
Cookie House, *"W31," chimney finial*	$ 110–135
Covered Wagon, *puppy finial, "W30R"*	$ 575–625
Cow, *cat finial, "W10," purple spots, blue bell*	$ 1,100–1,200
Cow, *cat finial, "W10," brown*	$ 125–175
Cow, *cat finial, "W10," blue spots*	$ 1,500–1,650
Cow, *cat finial, "W10," black spots*	$ 1,200–1,300
Davy Crocket, *standing figure, no gold trim*	$ 400–450
Davy Crockett, *standing figure, gold trim*	$ 750–800
Davy Crocket mug	$ 80–100
Dog with Basket, *dog's head with hat coming out of a basket*	$ 250–300
Donkey Cart, *"W33," ears up*	$ 875–925
Donkey Cart, *"W33," ears down*	$ 425–475
Elephant, *"W8," seated, in baby bonnet with ice cream cone in trunk*	$ 475–525
Elephant, *monkey finial on lid*	$ 5,000–5,200
Fish	$ 500–550
Formal Pig, *"W7," pig in top hat with cane, black coat, gold trim*	$ 475–525
Formal Pig, *"W7," pig in top hat with cane, black coat, no gold trim*	$ 275–325
Formal Pig, *"W7," pig in top hat with cane, green coat, gold trim*	$ 425–475
Formal Pig, *"W7," pig in top hat with cane, green coat, no gold trim*	$ 250–300

Formal Pig, *"W7," pig in top hat with cane, yellow coat, gold trim*	$ 575–625
Formal Pig, *"W7," pig in top hat with cane, yellow coat, no gold trim*	$ 325–375
Granny, *"W19," rolling pin at side, pink apron with blue dots on skirt*	$ 325–375
Granny, *"W19," rolling pin at side, plain green skirt*	$ 400–450
Hillbilly Frog, *"43D," green frog in brown peaked hat*	$ 4,500–4,750
Hobby Horse, *"W55," wooden barrel body, saddle lid*	$ 1,200–1,300
Humpty-Dumpty, *"W29," with peaked hat, black trim*	$ 225–275
Humpty-Dumpty, *"W29," with peaked hat, brown trim*	$ 175–225
Humpty-Dumpty, *"W18R," with beanie and bow tie*	$ 275–325
Laughing Hippo, *"W27," monkey finial on back*	$ 775–825
Little Boy Blue, *"K25," small*	$ 725–775
Little Boy Blue, *"K24," large*	$ 875–925
Little Boy Blue mug	$ 90–110
Little Girl, *patched skirt, eating a cookie*	$ 575–625
Little Red Riding Hood, *"K24," small*	$ 575–625
Little Red Riding Hood, *"K24," large*	$ 925–975
Little Red Riding Hood mug	$ 110–135
Owl, *"W40," "Nite Owl," gray and white*	$ 135–155
Owl, *"W40," yellow*	$ 200–250
Owl, *"W42," "Stylized Owl"*	$ 375–425
Panda Bear, *"W21," black and white*	$ 225–275
Panda Bear, *"W21," blue and white*	$ 350–400
Peter Pan, *small, no gold*	$ 575–625
Peter Pan, *small, with gold*	$ 725–775
Peter Pan, *"K23," large*	$ 725–775
Peter Pan, *"K23," with gold*	$ 825–875
Peter Pan mug	$ 150–200
Pumpkin, *"W24," elf finial, two children peaking out window*	$ 450–500
Puppy, *in basketweave container, "Cookies"*	$ 135–160

Puppy Police, *"W39"*	$ 600–650
Rabbit, *"W25," "Happy Rabbit," in chef's hat, white*	$ 225–275
Rabbit, *"W25," "Happy Bunny," in chef's hat, gray*	$ 275–325
Raggedy Ann, *"W16," arms out*	$ 475–525
Siamese Cat, *stylized, "W41"*	$ 475–525
Shoe, *"W23," shoe house*	$ 125–175
Sitting Hippo	$ 500–550
Sitting Pig, *"W37R"*	$ 400–450
Squirrel, *with top hat, "W15," black coat and hat*	$ 275–325
Squirrel, *with top hat, "W15," green coat*	$ 375–425
Standing Clown, *"W22," with pants in blue, yellow, pink, or brown (the brown pants are the earliest, but least desired)*	$ 175–225
Teddy Bear, *with blanket, feet apart, "O14 USA"*	$ 250–300
Teddy Bear, *feet together, no blanket, "W14 USA"*	$ 200–250
Treasure Chest, *"W28," shell finial*	$ 175–225

Nelson McCoy Cookie Jars

The Nelson McCoy Pottery Company made a variety of cookie jars between 1946 and the 1980s. Most of these jars are unmarked, except for "USA" or an impressed shape number.

Animal Cracker Box, *"Barnum Animals," clown head finial, #152*	$ 550–600
Apollo Spacecraft, *landing module, flag and paper label*	$ 1,400–1,600
Apple, *red, gold finial*	$ 100–125
Apple, *white, with green top (also known as "The Tooth")*	$ 75–100
Asparagus, *bunch*	$ 100–125
Astronaut, *spaceman finial, globular shape, light blue*	$ 1,400–1,600
Auto, *old-fashioned touring car, #139*	$ 125–150
Bag, *"Sack of Cookies" written on tag*	$ 200–225
Bananas, *bunch, stalk finial*	$ 275–325

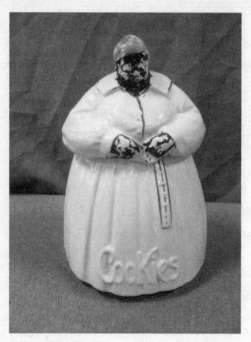

Nelson McCoy "Mammy" cookie jar, wear to cold-painted decoration, $200–$250. *Item courtesy of Needful Things, Hendersonville, North Carolina.*

Baseball Boy, *three-dimensional boy as finial, sitting on baseball*	$ 400–450
Basket with Hen on a Nest, *#139*	$ 85–100
Bear with Cookie in Vest, *cold painted white*	$ 125–150
Bear with Cookie in Vest, *brown bear, yellow coat*	$ 475–525
Bell Pepper, *green*	$ 90–110
Bell Pepper, *yellow*	$ 145–165
Caboose, *cold painted, #182*	$ 275–325
Cat, *black, painted face, "Coalby Cat," #207*	$ 425–475
Chairman of the Board, *burgundy pants, #162*	$ 850–900
Chairman of the Board, *brown pants, #162*	$ 1,000–1,100
Chef, *"Cookies" written on hat, mustache*	$ 225–250
Chipmunk with Acorn	$ 175–225
Christmas Tree, *#174*	$ 1,500–1,600
Circus Horse, *with monkey finial and plume, cold painted*	$ 225–275
Clown in Barrel, *cold painted*	$ 150–175

Clown in Barrel, *solid color, green*	$ 550–600
Clown, *sad, #255*	$ 175–200
Coal Scuttle, *white cat on top*	$ 425–475
Coffee Cup, *steam finial, #232*	$ 150–175
Cook Stove, *old-fashioned, black*	$ 30–40
Cookie Boy, *in kerchief, with hat, "Cookie Boy" written on chest, turquoise*	$ 400–450
Cookie Boy, *in kerchief, with hat, "Cookie Boy" written on chest, yellow or white*	$ 250–300
Cookie Cabin	$ 125–145
Cookie House, *lid is a bank, #192*	$ 125–145
Covered Wagon, *no finial, "Cookie Wagon" cold painted on end*	$ 100–125
Dalmatians in a Rocking Chair, *#189*	$ 650–700
Davy Crockett, *head and shoulders, #140*	$ 600–650
Drum, *small drum finial, #170*	$ 175–200
Ear of Corn, *#156*	$ 275–325
Eggs in a Basket, *#274*	$ 100–120
Elephant, *vest, cold painted, "split trunk" (part on lid, part on body)*	$ 350–400
Fireplace, *clock on mantle, pot on fire*	$ 225–250
Football Boy, *three-dimensional boy as finial, sitting on football, #222*	$ 450–500
Fox Squirrel	$ 3,500–4,000
Freddy the Gleep, *yellow, #189 (beware of reproductions)*	$ 700–750
Freddy the Gleep, *green, #189 (beware of reproductions)*	$ 750–800
Friendship 7, *space capsule, cold painted, #204*	$ 150–175
Globe, *on stand, cold-painted continents, #173*	$ 350–400
Granny, *gold trim, #159*	$ 275–325
Granny, *no gold trim, #159*	$ 175–200
Hat, *Uncle Sam's*	$ 1,000–1,100
Hot Air Balloon, *#353*	$ 100–125
Jack-O'-Lantern, *orange body with green or orange leaf and stem top*	$ 700–750

Jug, *"Cookie Jug," #145*	$ 50–65
Kangaroo, *with joey, #234*	$ 500–550
Kittens in a Basket, *two kittens*	$ 850–900
Leprechaun, *green or red costume, #169*	$ 2,000–2,200
Liberty Bell, *#264*	$ 100–120
Locomotive Engine, *black, #207*	$ 250–300
Locomotive Engine, *yellow, #207*	$ 325–375
Lunchbox, *#357*	$ 90–100
Mammy with Cauliflower, *cold paint badly worn (beware of reproductions)*	$ 650–750
Milk Can, *#7019*	$ 50–60
Nursery Rhyme, *cylinder with conical roof, "Mary, Mary, Quite Contrary"*	$ 200–225
Nursery Rhyme, *cylinder with conical roof, "Little Miss Muffet"*	$ 200–225
Nursery Rhyme, *cylinder with conical roof, "Humpty-Dumpty"*	$ 200–225
Nursery Rhyme, *cylinder with conical roof, "Baa, Baa Black Sheep"*	$ 200–225
Oak Leaves and Acorns	$ 275–325
Orange, *leaf-and-stem finial*	$ 125–140
Owls, *Mr. and Mrs., #38*	$ 125–150
Picnic Basket	$ 100–125
Puppy, *in basketweave container, "Cookies"*	$ 135–160
Raggedy Ann, *#741*	$ 200–225
Rocking Horse, *#36*	$ 425–475
School Bus, *#352*	$ 150–175
Smiley Face, *"Have a Happy Day"*	$ 80–100
Snoopy on Doghouse	$ 400–450
Soccer Ball, *whistle finial*	$ 1,750–1,900
Stagecoach, *driver, spirited horses*	$ 1,200–1,400
Tea Kettle, *gunmetal glaze, #188*	$ 60–75
Tepee, *#137*	$ 475–525

Cookie jar, Native American head, reproduction from the 1990s. The original McCoy Indian head cookie jars were 11½ inches; this one is 10½ inches (all reproductions are smaller than the originals), gray with gold highlights, $125–$150.
Item courtesy of Needful Things, Hendersonville, North Carolina.

Touring Car, *#139*	$ 125–150
Traffic Light, *vertical lights*	$ 100–120
Tugboat, *"Cookie Tug" cold painted on waves*	$ 9,500–11,000
Turkey, *#23*	$ 400–450
Turtle, *"Timmy Tortoise," butterfly finial*	$ 65–80
Winking Pig, *#150*	$ 500–550
Wishing Well	$ 70–90

McCoy Dinnerware

"Brown Drip"

Pieces in this line are very similar to wares made by other companies. Each piece has a dark-brown center with a foamy white drip around the rim or edges.

Baker, *oval, 9¹/₄ by 6¹/₄ inches*	$ 22–25
Baker, *oval, 10¹/₂ by 7¹/₄ inches*	$ 30–35
Baker, *oval, 12¹/₂ by 9¹/₂ inches*	$ 40–45

Baker, *oval, 14¹/₄ by 11¹/₄*	$ 45–50
Bean pot and lid, *3-quart*	$ 60–70
Bowl, *individual fruit, 5¹/₄-inch diameter*	$ 5–8
Bowl, *onion soup, open, two handles, 3³/₄ inches*	$ 3–5
Bowl, *soup, coupe shape, 7¹/₂-inch diameter*	$ 4–6
Bowl, *vegetable, oval, 9¹/₄ inches*	$ 22–26
Bowl, *vegetable, oval, divided, 12 inches*	$ 22–26
Butter, *¹/₄-pound, covered*	$ 10–14
Canister, *coffee*	$ 30–35
Canister, *flour*	$ 45–50
Canister, *sugar*	$ 30–35
Canister, *tea*	$ 20–35
Casserole, *round, covered, 5¹/₂ inches*	$ 55–65
Casserole, *round, covered, 7¹/₄ inches*	$ 60–70
Cookie jar	$ 45–50
Creamer	$ 14–16
Cup and saucer	$ 12–15
Dish, *au gratin, lug handles, 7-ounce*	$ 15–18
Dish, *au gratin. lug handles, 14-ounce*	$ 18–22
Gravy boat	$ 40–45
Jug, *32-ounce*	$ 25–30
Jug, *48-ounce*	$ 35–45
Jug, *80-ounce*	$ 40–50
Mug, *3³/₄ inches*	$ 2–4
Mug, *soup, 5¹/₂ inches*	$ 6–9
Pitcher and bowl set, *small*	$ 85–95
Pitcher and bowl set, *large*	$ 145–165
Plate, *salad, 7¹/₄-inch diameter*	$ 8–10
Plate, *dinner, 10-inch diameter*	$ 10–14
Plate, *grill, 11¹/₄ inches*	$ 11–14
Platter, *oval, 13¹/₄ inches*	$ 30–35

Soufflé, *7-inch diameter*	$ 25–30
Soufflé, *8-inch diameter*	$ 28–35
Sugar bowl, *covered*	$ 15–18
Teapot	$ 30–35
Tureen with lid	$ 110–125
Tureen ladle	$ 30–35

"Canyon"

Each piece in this line has a brown center with mottled, darker-brown trim.

Bean pot with lid	$ 65–75
Bowl, *cereal, 6¹/₂-inch diameter*	$ 10–14
Bowl, *onion soup, open*	$ 8–12
Bowl, *vegetable, oval, 10¹/₂ inches*	$ 30–35
Creamer	$ 10–14
Cup and saucer	$ 8–10
Jar, *jam or jelly, lidded*	$ 24–28
Plate, *chop, 12¹/₂-inch diameter*	$ 32–36
Plate, *dinner, 10¹/₂-inch diameter*	$ 12–17
Plate, *salad, 7¹/₂-inch diameter*	$ 6–9
Plate, *salad, square, 8¹/₂ inches*	$ 12–16
Salt and pepper shakers	$ 20–25
Sugar bowl, *lidded*	$ 18–22
Teapot	$ 45–55
Tureen with lid and ladle	$ 175–185

"El Rancho"

Coffee server	$ 165–185
Food warmer, *covered, chuck wagon shape, wire wheels*	$ 200–250
Iced tea server, *barrel-shaped, with spigot*	$ 225–275
Mug, *coffee*	$ 25–35
Tureen, *5-quart*	$ 375–425
Tureen lid, *"Serve-All"*	$ 165–185

"Pink and Blue Stripes"

As the name implies, this dinnerware is decorated with pink and blue stripes or, in the case of flatware pieces, pink and blue concentric circles. The blue stripes are narrow, and appear on either side of broader pink bands.

Bean pot, *lidded*	$ 115–125
Bowl, *cereal, 5¹/₄-inch diameter*	$ 22–26
Bowl, *dough, 14¹/₂ inches*	$ 190–210
Bowl, *mixing, 6-inch diameter*	$ 35–40
Bowl, *mixing, 10-inch diameter*	$ 55–65
Bowl, *soup, 6¹/₄-inch diameter*	$ 20–24
Bowl, *vegetable, round, 7-inch diameter*	$ 34–38
Canister, *coffee*	$ 32–38
Canister, *flour*	$ 50–60
Canister, *sugar*	$ 28–32
Canister, *tea*	$ 32–38
Casserole, *covered, 2-quart*	$ 95–105
Casserole, *covered, 3¹/₄-quart*	$ 100–110
Creamer	$ 25–30
Jug, *32-ounce*	$ 45–50
Mug, *3¹/₂ inches*	$ 12–16
Plate, *dinner, 10¹/₂-inch diameter*	$ 25–35
Salt and pepper shakers	$ 30–35
Sugar bowl, *open*	$ 28–32

"Strawberry Country"

This pattern features a white background decorated with vibrant red strawberries and green leaves.

Bean pot, *lidded*	$ 70–80
Bowl, *cereal, 6¹/₄-inch diameter*	$ 7–10
Butter, *¹/₄-pound, covered*	$ 20–25
Canister, *coffee*	$ 20–25
Canister, *flour*	$ 50–55

Canister, *sugar*	$ 35–40
Canister, *tea*	$ 20–25
Casserole, *2-quart, covered*	$ 70–80
Creamer	$ 15–20
Cup and saucer	$ 20–25
Jar, *jam or jelly, lidded*	$ 16–20
Mug, *3$^{1}/_{2}$ inches*	$ 7–10
Pitcher and bowl set, *small*	$ 65–75
Pitcher and bowl set, *large*	$ 130–145
Pitcher, *24-ounce*	$ 16–20
Plate, *dinner, 10$^{1}/_{4}$-inch diameter*	$ 12–15
Plate, *salad, 7$^{1}/_{2}$-inch diameter*	$ 6–9
Salt and pepper shakers	$ 20–25
Sugar bowl, *lidded*	$ 20–25
Teapot, *individual*	$ 25–30
Tureen with ladle and lid	$ 160–175

Teapots and Tea Sets

Cherries and leaves, *teapot, various colors*	$ 120–140
Cherries and leaves, *sugar bowl and creamer*	$ 120–140
Daisy, *sugar bowl and creamer*	$ 90–110
Grecian, *teapot, sugar bowl, creamer*	$ 165–185
Ivy, *teapot, sugar bowl, creamer*	$ 350–400
Pinecone, *teapot, sugar bowl, creamer*	$ 165–185
Pinecone, *sugar bowl and creamer, gold trim*	$ 90–110
Two-Tone, *teapot, sugar bowl, creamer*	$ 165–185

Nelson McCoy Kitchenware

Batter bowl, *spoon rest on rim, 7$^{1}/_{2}$ inches*	$ 275–325
Batter bowl, *spoon rest on rim, 9$^{1}/_{2}$ inches*	$ 400–450
Bowl, *mixing, ring pattern, 9 inches*	$ 225–275

Nelson McCoy three-piece child's tea set with bunny décor, 1970s blue glaze, $125–$135.
Item courtesy of Kingston Pike Antique Mall, Knoxville, Tennessee.

Nelson McCoy pitcher with embossed parading ducks, 7½ inches, late 1930s, aqua glaze, $200–$250.
Item courtesy of Bill Brooker, Old School Antique Mall, Sylva, North Carolina.

Bowl, *mixing, "Feather" pattern, 8-inch diameter*	$ 100–125
Bowl, *mixing, "Raspberries and Leaves" pattern, 9-inch diameter*	$ 275–325
Bowls, *mixing, "Wave" pattern, set of 6, nested, 5- to 11-inch diameters*	$ 1,500–1,750
Casserole, *concentric rings, covered, large*	$ 250–300
Crock, *covered, cheese, ring pattern*	$ 160–185
Juicer, *"Islander" line*	$ 70–80
Salt box, *covered, ring pattern, 6 inches*	$ 375–425
Spoon rest, *in form of penguin*	$ 225–275

Nelson McCoy Flowerpots

Basketweave (also called "Textured"), *with underliner, small*	$ 45–50
Basketweave (also called "Textured"), *with underliner, medium*	$ 50–60
Basketweave (also called "Textured"), *with underliner, large*	$ 60–75

Basketweave with Leaves, *with underliner, small*	$ 65–75
Basketweave with Leaves, *with underliner, medium*	$ 80–95
Basketweave with Leaves, *with underliner, large*	$ 100–120
Basketweave with Rings, *with underliner, small*	$ 70–85
Basketweave with Rings, *with underliner, medium*	$ 85–100
Basketweave with Rings, *with underliner, large*	$ 120–140
Butterfly, *with underliner, $3^1/_4$-inch diameter*	$ 85–100
Butterfly, *with underliner, $6^1/_2$-inch diameter*	$ 100–125
Daisy, *with underliner, small*	$ 70–80
Daisy, *with underliner, medium*	$ 85–100
Daisy, *with underliner, large*	$ 100–120
Diamond Quilted, *with underliner, 4 inches tall*	$ 50–60
Diamond Quilted, *with underliner, 5 inches tall*	$ 60–70
Dragonfly, *with underliner, $3^1/_2$-inch diameter*	$ 80–100
Dragonfly, *with underliner, 5-inch diameter*	$ 95–110
Dragonfly, *with underliner, 6-inch diameter*	$ 110–125
Flat-leaf, *with underliner, 3 inches tall*	$ 100–120
Flat-leaf, *with underliner, 4 inches tall*	$ 100–120
Flat-leaf, *with underliner, $5^1/_2$ inches tall*	$ 120–135
Flat-leaf, *with underliner, $6^1/_2$ inches tall*	$ 140–150
Hobnail and Leaves, *with underliner, small*	$ 75–85
Hobnail and Leaves, *with underliner, medium*	$ 85–100
Hobnail and Leaves, *with underliner, large*	$ 95–110
Icicles, *with underliner, small*	$ 40–45
Icicles, *with underliner, medium*	$ 45–50
Icicles, *with underliner, large*	$ 50–55
Lily Bud, *with underliner, small*	$ 65–75
Lily Bud, *with underliner, medium*	$ 75–85
Lily Bud, *with underliner, large*	$ 90–110
Lotus Leaf, *with underliner, small*	$ 65–75
Lotus Leaf, *with underliner, medium*	$ 80–90

Lotus Leaf, *with underliner, large*	$ 100–125
Lotus Leaf, *with underliner, extra-large, 10 inches tall*	$ 600–700
Quilted Rose, *with underliner, small*	$ 55–70
Quilted Rose, *with underliner, medium*	$ 60–75
Quilted Rose, *with underliner, large*	$ 65–80
Sand Dollar, *with underliner, medium*	$ 65–80
Sand Dollar, *with underliner, large*	$ 75–90
Stonewall, *or "Roses on a Wall," with underliner, small*	$ 45–50
Stonewall, *or "Roses on a Wall," with underliner, medium*	$ 50–60
Stonewall, *or "Roses on a Wall," with underliner, large*	$ 60–75
Swirl, *with underliner, 4 inches tall*	$ 65–75
Swirl, *with underliner, 7 inches tall*	$ 95–110

Nelson McCoy Jardinières

Basketweave and flower design, *with pedestal, ring handles, white with embossed design, 13 inches tall, 7$^1/_2$ inches in diameter*	$ 450–500
Butterfly pattern, *7$^1/_2$-inch diameter, matte yellow*	$ 200–225
Butterfly pattern, *square top, 3$^3/_4$ inches*	$ 85–100
Fish in a Net pattern, *7 inches*	$ 400–450
Flying Birds ("Swallows") pattern, *4-inch diameter, matte white*	$ 80–95
Flying Birds ("Swallows") pattern, *7$^1/_2$-inch diameter, matte white*	$ 150–175
Hobnail pattern, *3 inches*	$ 55–65
Hobnail pattern, *4 inches*	$ 65–75
Hobnail pattern, *6$^1/_2$ inches*	$ 95–120
Holly pattern, *4-inch diameter*	$ 60–70
Holly pattern, *5-inch diameter*	$ 70–80
Holly pattern, *7$^1/_2$-inch diameter*	$ 125–150
Holly pattern, *with pedestal, 13 inches tall, 7$^1/_2$-inch diameter*	$ 450–500
Ivy pattern, *brown and green, 8 inches tall*	$ 550–600

Leaves and Berries pattern, *with squat pedestal, 7^1/$_2$-inch diameter, brown and green glaze*	$ 375–425
Leaves and Berries pattern, *with pedestal, 8^1/$_2$-inch diameter, 12^1/$_2$ inches tall, matte green glaze*	$ 500–600

Nelson McCoy Planters

Basket, *low oval, crossed handles, basketweave body, 9 inches*	$ 110–135
Basket, *tulips, 8^3/$_4$ inches*	$ 225–275
Bookends, *flower pattern, 6 inches tall, pair*	$ 225–250
Bookends, *flying birds ("Swallows"), pair*	$ 400–450
Bowl, *with applied grapes, 12 inches*	$ 100–120
Bowl, *with pinecones, 8 inches, green and brown*	$ 750–800
Bowl, *with three-dimensional bird, 10 inches*	$ 45–60
Bowl, *leaf-shaped, one handle, 6^1/$_2$ inches*	$ 110–125
Bowl, *in the form of a rock, "Floraline," 8^1/$_2$ inches*	$ 70–85
Bowl, *rectangular, "W"-shaped top, applied butterfly*	$ 160–175
Bowl, *rectangular, embossed roses and leaves in pink and green, 8^1/$_4$ inches*	$ 90–110
Cornucopia, *8 inches*	$ 80–95
Dish, *rectangular, zigzag edges, 9^1/$_2$ inches*	$ 165–185
Figural, *Alligator, 10 inches*	$ 200–225
Figural, *Antelope, three-dimensional, leaping, four containers, 12 inches*	$ 525–575
Figural, *Asian man with basket, 5^1/$_2$ inches*	$ 55–70
Figural, *Automobile, 6 inches*	$ 70–85
Figural, *Baby's Bed, oval, 6^1/$_2$ inches*	$ 55–65
Figural, *Baby Buggy, gold trim, 6 inches*	$ 200–225
Figural, *Baby Buggy, no gold trim, 6 inches*	$ 100–125
Figural, *Banana Boat, with man playing guitar, 11 inches*	$ 250–300
Figural, *Bird Dog, bird in mouth, "No Hunting" sign, 8^1/$_2$ inches*	$ 275–325
Figural, *Bird of Paradise, long tail, 13 inches*	$ 80–100

Nelson McCoy planter, Asian man with basket, 5½ inches, $45–$60.
Item courtesy of Bill Brooker, Old School Antique Mall, Sylva, North Carolina.

Nelson McCoy planter, "Humpty-Dumpty," 4½ inches, $65–$80.
Item courtesy of Bill Brooker, Old School Antique Mall, Sylva, North Carolina.

Figural, *Buggy with Umbrella, 9 inches*	$ 250–300
Figural, *Butterfly*	$ 200–250
Figural, *Cat at Well, trees behind, 7 inches*	$ 200–225
Figural, *Caterpillar, 13½ inches long*	$ 65–75
Figural, *Duck with Egg, 3½ inches*	$ 60–70
Figural, *Ducks, pair flying, 10 inches*	$ 275–325
Figural, *Frog with Umbrella, 7½ inches*	$ 240–275
Figural, *Fruit, apple, leaf underliner, 6½ inches*	$ 85–100
Figural, *Fruit, grapes, leaf underliner, no gold trim, 6½ inches*	$ 225–250
Figural, *Fruit, grapes, leaf underliner, gold trim, 6½ inches*	$ 400–425
Figural, *Fruit, lemon, leaf underliner, 6½ inches*	$ 150–175
Figural, *Fruit, orange, leaf underliner, 6½ inches*	$ 125–150
Figural, *Goat*	$ 425–475
Figural, *"Humpty-Dumpty," 4½ inches*	$ 60–75
Figural, *Lamb, 6 inches*	$ 85–100

Nelson McCoy planter in the form of a
lamb, 6 inches, $85–$100.
*Item courtesy of Bill Brooker, Old School
Antique Mall, Sylva, North Carolina.*

Nelson McCoy Liberty Bell planter,
$425–$475.
*Item courtesy of Bill Brooker, Old School
Antique Mall, Sylva, North Carolina.*

Figural, *Liberty Bell, "4th of July," 8¹/₄ inches*	$ 425–475
Figural, *Lion, realistic representation, on rocks, 8¹/₄ inches*	$ 165–185
Figural, *Log, with wheel leaning up against it, gold trim, 12¹/₂ inches*	$ 160–175
Figural, *Log, with wheel leaning up against it, no gold trim, 12¹/₂ inches*	$ 110–125
Figural, *Mammy on Scoop, cold painted, 7¹/₂ inches*	$ 250–300
Figural, *Panda, with cradle, 5¹/₂ inches*	$ 165–185
Figural, *Parrot, with chain, leaves, feed cup, 7 inches*	$ 70–90
Figural, *Pelican, pulling cart, 4¹/₂ inches*	$ 80–95
Figural, *Piano, grand, black, no gold trim, 5 inches*	$ 225–275
Figural, *Piano, grand, color other than black, gold trim, 5 inches*	$ 425–475
Figural, *Poodle, nose in air, 7¹/₂ inches, green*	$ 125–150
Figural, *Rabbit, holding carrot, 7¹/₄ inches*	$ 200–225
Figural, *Shell, 7¹/₂ inches*	$ 80–95

Nelson McCoy planter, Poodle with its nose in the air, also called "Snooty Poodle," pink, 7½ inches, $125–$150. *Item courtesy of Bill Brooker, Old School Antique Mall, Sylva, North Carolina.*

Nelson McCoy Planter, urn-shaped, "Grecian" with embossed leaves, mottled gold, 6 inches, $75–$90. *Item courtesy of Kingston Pike Antique Mall; Knoxville, Tennessee.*

Figural, *Shoe, baby's*	$ 60–70
Figural, *"Stretch Goat," stylized, head and horns down, horns in and attack position, light blue*	$ 375–425
Figural, *"Stretch Lion," stylized, cobalt blue, 4 inches*	$ 375–425
Figural, *"Stretch Lion," stylized, light blue, 5½ inches*	$ 475–525
Figural, *Swan, rose on wing, 7 inches*	$ 75–90
Figural, *Turtle, lily pad on back, 8 inches long, green, brown, and rust red*	$ 250–300
Figural, *Turtle, lily pad on back, 8 inches long, yellow, cold painted*	$ 85–110
Figural, *Turtle, no lily pad, 12½ inches long*	$ 200–235
Figural, *Wishing Well, brown glaze, 6 inches*	$ 45–55
Figural, *Wishing Well, brown glaze, 7 inches*	$ 75–90
Strawberry jar, *6½ inches*	$ 110–125
Trough, *"Butterfly" line, 8¼ inches*	$ 100–120

Trough, *Hobnail, 8¹/₂ inches*	$ 75–85
Urn, *on pedestal, Grecian, with embossed leaves, 6 inches*	$ 75–90
Window box, *diamond shingle design, 10 inches*	$ 40–50

Nelson McCoy Vases

Arrowleaf, *embossed design, round flared mouth, 7¹/₂ inches*	$ 120–140
Arrowleaf handles, *heavily ribbed body, 8 inches*	$ 700–775
Basketweave, *ring handles, 5 inches*	$ 65–80
Bird of Paradise (tropical plant form), *cold painted, twig handles, 8¹/₄ inches*	$ 65–80
"Blossomtime," *flowers and leaves, two arched handles on either side, matte ivory with pink flowers and green leaves, 6³/₄ inches*	$ 100–125
Butterfly, *globular with ribs, 4¹/₄ inches*	$ 85–100
Butterfly, *"V"-shaped flared top, 9 inches*	$ 135–165
Cat-shaped, *black, 14 inches*	$ 300–350
Cherries, *embossed, leaves and stems, square, stoneware*	$ 165–185
Chrysanthemums, *three flowers on base with leaves and yellow flowers*	$ 240–260
Cornucopia, *tall, ribbed body, notched mouth, 10 inches*	$ 160–180
Cornucopia, *tall, ribbed body, notched mouth, 5 inches*	$ 125–150
Cornucopia with deer, *brown and green glaze*	$ 200–225
Ewer, *7¹/₂ inches*	$ 45–60
Grapes, *pitcher-shaped, embossed grapes with three-part handle, 9 inches*	$ 85–100
Hand, *opening in palm, 6¹/₂ inches*	$ 150–175
Hand holding bowl-like vase, *7¹/₂ inches*	$ 200–225
Hand holding flower bouquet, *3 inches, pink*	$ 150–200
Hand holding sacklike vase, *5 inches*	$ 80–95
Hobnail and Leaves, *flared cylinder, 7 inches*	$ 110–125
Hourglass-shaped, *embossed broad leaves and berries around top, 14 inches*	$ 325–375
Hourglass-shaped, *embossed broad leaves and berries around top, 12 inches*	$ 300–325

Nelson McCoy "Butterfly" line vase, 4¼ inches, $85–$100.
Item courtesy of Bill Brooker, Old School Antique Mall, Sylva, North Carolina.

Nelson McCoy vase, embossed wheat design, 8½ inches, $85–$100.
Item courtesy of Richard Hatch and Associates, Hendersonville, North Carolina.

Hourglass-shaped, *embossed broad leaves and berries around top, 6 inches*	$ 110–125
Hyacinth, *figural flowers with leaves, 8 inches tall, strong color*	$ 250–300
Leaves and berries, *brown and green matte glaze, two small handles between shoulder and neck, 7 inches*	$ 110–125
Lily Bud, *embossed leaves and bud at base with protruding stem, diamond shape, notched "V"-shaped top, 10 inches*	$ 185–220
Lily, *single, with leaf base, 8 inches*	$ 135–160
Lily, *triple, with leaf base, 8½ inches*	$ 150–175
Magnolia, *figural flowers with stems and leaves, 8½ inches*	$ 350–400
Pigeon, *wings stretched out behind to form vase, 3½ inches*	$ 150–175
Pitcher with rope handle, *7 inches*	$ 80–95
Poppy, *double, with leaves and log-type base, strong color*	$ 1,100–1,250
Ram's head, *chartreuse, 9½ inches*	$ 165–185
Ram's head, *white, 9½ inches*	$ 350–400

Rings, *two handles, 9¹/₄ inches*	$ 160–185
Sailboats, *embossed, round base, flared lip, two decorative handles*	$ 120–140
Square vase with open center, *three-dimensional bird in square center opening, 6³/₄ inches, green and yellow*	$ 75–90
Sunflower vase, *leaves in basketweave base, airbrushed decoration*	$ 650–700
Swan, *with tall aquatic plants behind, 9 inches*	$ 120–140
Tulips, *double, figural, leaves, tall, 8 inches*	$ 165–185
Tulips, *double, figural, leaves, low, 6¹/₂ inches*	$ 300–350
Uncle Sam, *bust with hat, 7¹/₂ inches tall (beware of reproductions)*	$ 85–100
Wheat, *embossed stalks of wheat, hexagonal, two handles, 8¹/₂ inches*	$ 85–100

Wall Pockets

Apple, *leaves behind, 7 inches*	$ 275–325
Bananas, *in a bunch with leaves behind, 7 inches*	$ 525–575
"Blossomtime," *panels with triangular tops, raised floral decoration, 7³/₄ inches*	$ 135–165
Butterfly, *with outstretched wings, 6 inches*	$ 625–675
Cuckoo Clock, *8 inches*	$ 275–325
Fan, *gold brocade, 8¹/₂ inches*	$ 125–150
Jester, *conical hat, ruffled collar, 8¹/₂ inches*	$ 140–165
Lovebirds, *pair on trivet base, 8 inches*	$ 110–135
Mailbox, *"Letters"*	$ 135–165
Violin, *10 inches, blue*	$ 375–425
Violin, *10 inches, black*	$ 475–525

"Loy-Nel-Art"

Pieces in this line look a great deal like the brown-glazed art wares produced by a number of potteries in Ohio, including Rookwood, Roseville, Owens, and Weller.

Nelson McCoy bank, "National Bank of Dayton," $100–$125.
Item courtesy of Bill Brooker, Old School Antique Mall, Sylva, North Carolina.

Nelson McCoy barrel-shaped bank, "Dollar Federal Bank," 8 inches, $85–$110.
Item courtesy of Bill Brooker, Old School Antique Mall, Sylva, North Carolina.

Nelson McCoy bank in the shape of a sailor, 6 inches, $135–$165.
Item courtesy of Bill Brooker, Old School Antique Mall, Sylva, North Carolina.

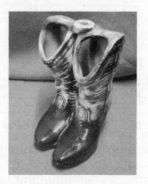

Nelson McCoy lamp base in the form of cowboy boots, 7 inches, $110–$130.
Item courtesy of Bill Brooker, Old School Antique Mall, Sylva, North Carolina.

Often unmarked, examples of "Loy-Nel-Art" can sometimes be distinguished by a splash of green on the front and orange on the back.

Bowl, *footed, 8¹/₂-inch diameter, marked, pansies*	$ 275–325
Cuspidor, *8 inches, unmarked, pansies*	$ 300–350
Jardinière, *10 inches tall, unmarked, leaves*	$ 375–425
Jardinière, *footed, globular, 5-inch diameter, marked, cherries*	$ 325–375

Brush-McCoy "Amaryllis" pattern planter,
8¼ inches, $325–$375.
*Item courtesy of Munday and Munday
Antiques, Benton, Illinois.*

Brush-McCoy "Amaryllis" pattern vase, 5¼
inches, $150–$175.
*Item courtesy of Munday and Munday
Antiques, Benton, Illinois.*

Brush-McCoy frog planter, 3½ inches,
$40–$50.
*Item courtesy of Richard Crane, Knoxville,
Tennessee.*

Brush-McCoy vase, #572, 10 inches tall,
$90–$110.
*Item courtesy of Bill Brooker, Old School
Antique Mall, Sylva, North Carolina.*

Jardinière and pedestal, *both marked, 16¹/₂ inches tall, jardinière has two handles between shoulder and rim, above-average painting of flowers*	$ 1,600–1,850
Pitcher, *cider, unmarked, 5¹/₂ inches, floral*	$ 300–350
Vase, *cylinder, 10 inches, marked, roses*	$ 375–425
Vase, *embossed Native American on back, flower painting on front, 12 inches, unmarked*	$ 650–725

Brush-McCoy Onyx bowl, 7 inches,
$55–$75.
*Item courtesy of Bill Brooker, Old School
Antique Mall, Sylva, North Carolina.*

J. W. McCoy carnelian vase, 9 inches, circa
1904, green, yellow, and orange glaze,
$325–$375.
*Item courtesy of Bill Brooker, Old School
Antique Mall, Sylva, North Carolina.*

Brush McCoy Miscellany

Bowl, *onyx, green, 6-inch diameter*	$ 45–65
Pitcher, *"Woodland Green," artist-signed: "Cusick"*	$ 350–425
Umbrella stand, *majolica-style, green, tan, and brown glaze, embossed floral border around top, griffin's heads, 20^1/$_2$ inches*	$ 450–500
Vase, *Onyx, ovoid, mottled green, 6 inches tall*	$ 45–65
Vase, *Onyx, brown drip, 8 inches*	$ 95–125
Vase, *Onyx, brown and cream, 10^1/$_2$ inches*	$ 175–225

BUFFALO POTTERY

One of the marks used by the *Buffalo Pottery Company.*

This is the signpost mark used on "Deldare Ware," which was made by the *Buffalo Pottery Company of Buffalo, New York.* Note the date on either side of the signboard.

The history of the Buffalo Pottery in Buffalo, New York, is inextricably linked to that of the Larkin Soap Company, also of Buffalo. The Larkin Soap Company was founded by John D. Larkin in 1875, and initially manufactured a product called "Sweet Home Soap." It was inexpensive, and was sold along the streets of Buffalo from handcarts. Elbert Hubbard, Larkin's brother-in-law and later the author of *A Message to Garcia* (1899), as well as the founder of the famous Roycroft Arts and Crafts community, was the company's first salesman—and, many say, the driving force behind the company's success.

In 1881, a new Larkin washing-powder product called Boraxine was introduced, and each box included a premium inside: a small chromolithographed picture. In 1885, Larkin began a program that allowed Boraxine labels to be redeemed for premiums, and Hubbard and Larkin later instituted a "factory-to-the-family" approach, which eliminated both the company's sales force and its wholesale and retail dealers in favor of selling directly to the public by mail order.

These changes so improved Larkin's cost structure that the company began offering a $10 premium to consumers for every $10 worth of soap and other Larkin products that they purchased. Ten dollars was a great deal of money to spend in the late 19th century, however, and so Larkin allowed buyers a full month to make payment, plus the added incentive of a desk, piano lamp, or even a stove as a premium with their purchases.

This system was very successful, and Larkin began mailing out catalogs to promote its soap and the other household items it produced, along with the premiums that were available with each purchase. Pottery products were often used as premiums, but delivery from the various pottery manufacturers was something of a problem. In 1901, to solve this problem, Louis Brown—then a salesman for Crescent Pottery—and John Larkin began discussing the feasibility of building a pottery factory in Buffalo that would fulfill the needs of the soap company.

The Buffalo Pottery was organized with John D. Larkin as president and Louis Brown as general manager, and the first firings occurred late in 1903. At this time, most pottery items offered by other companies as premiums were second-quality wares, but Larkin prided itself on offering its customers first-quality items made at the Buffalo Pottery. Previously, Larkin had offered Limoges, Dresden, and English china as premiums, and now it was competing head to head with these high-profile foreign manufacturers. English "Blue Willow" pattern dinnerware had previously been a popular premium item for Larkin, and Buffalo started producing its own version of this pattern, which some collectors believe to be of better quality than the original.

The first art wares produced by the Buffalo Pottery were called "Deldare Ware," and were first introduced in 1908. Each "Deldare" piece had an olive-green body decorated with a transfer print that was then hand-colored. "Deldare Ware" (the actual derivation of the name is unknown, and is a matter of some conjecture) was originally made only from 1908 to 1910 (only a calendar plate is known to have been made in 1910), but it was reissued from 1923 to 1925.

The scenes depicted on "Deldare" items tend to have English themes—for example, "The Fallowfield Hunt," "Ye Olden Days," and "Ye Lion Inn." The "Fallowfield Hunt" scenes are perhaps the best known of these decorations, and were derived from English fox-hunting prints created by Cecil Aldin and initially published around 1900. The scenes trace the progress of a traditional fox hunt—beginning with "Ye Breakfast at the Three Pigeons," and proceeding through "The Start," "The Dash," "Breaking Cover," "The Fallowfield Hunt," "The Death," "The Return," "The Hunt Supper," and "At the Three Pigeons." Reportedly, "Deldare" items featuring these scenes were produced only in 1908 and 1909.

Some of the scenes used in the "Ye Olden Days" series were derived from Oliver Goldsmith's book *The Vicar of Wakefield*, and Elizabeth Cleghorn Gaskell's 1853 book *Cranford*. This series included such scenes of English village life as "Ye Village Gossips," "Ye Village Schoolmaster," and "Dancing Ye Minuet." The "Ye Lion

Inn" grouping features scenes of people in 18th-century garb visiting an English tavern of the day. Other than "Ye Lion Inn," few of these pieces are actually titled.

"Emerald Deldare" is a special grouping of Buffalo's "Deldare" wares, and the pieces in this grouping are the most expensive and highly sought after of the lot. Many "Emerald Deldare" pieces feature scenes from a series called the "Tour of Dr. Syntax," which are based on the watercolors of English artist Thomas Richardson, and the accompanying poetic verses of William Combe. These scenes were first reproduced in approximately 1820 by Clews, the English Staffordshire pottery, in blue and white on earthenware pieces. Buffalo turned out some "Dr. Syntax" pieces in 1909, but the scenes did not appear on "Emerald Deldare" wares until about 1911.

"Emerald Deldare" pieces are most easily distinguished by their Art Nouveau-inspired borders and, on pieces lacking "Dr. Syntax" scenes, other Art Nouveau-style design elements. These pieces are also marked "Emerald Deldare" on their backs, just as the regular pieces are signed "Deldare." In addition, pieces of Buffalo Pottery are usually dated, a fact that greatly pleases most collectors.

Another Buffalo art line is "Abino Ware," named for Point Abino, which juts into Lake Erie to form a shallow bay that is a mecca for boaters. Typically, "Abino" wares feature seascapes, nautical themes, and images of windmills based on another historic landmark associated with Buffalo-area history. Exceptions do exist, however, and some "Abino" pieces feature pastoral landscapes or even exotic desert scenes, complete with camels and pyramids. "Abino Ware" pieces were largely made between 1911 and 1913, and should be marked with this name and be dated.

By 1908, Buffalo Pottery was not just making wares for Larkin; it had also acquired selling agents throughout the United States and, by 1911, was selling its wares to more than 25 countries around the world. In 1915, the company changed from making semiporcelain to making vitrified wares, and it started marking its wares "Buffalo China" instead of "Buffalo Pottery."

During World War I, Buffalo Pottery turned to making items for the U.S. military, and virtually ceased making products for Larkin and the public in general. By the late 1920s, Larkin was once again buying its pottery and porcelain premiums from overseas, and Buffalo was concentrating on making and marketing hotel wares, dinnerware for both institutional and home use, and items for the consumer market. The company is still in business.

"Deldare"

"Fallowfield Hunt"

Cup and saucer	$ 250–300
Bowl, *punch*	$ 7,500–7,800
Bowl, *round, 9 inches*	$ 575–625
Bowl, *round, 12 inches*	$ 1,000–1,100
Bowl, *soup, 9 inches*	$ 300–350
Bowl, *sugar, open*	$ 350–400
Dish, *relish, 12 by 6^1/$_2$ inches*	$ 500–550
Jug, *octagon, 8 inches*	$ 725–775
Jug, *octagon, 10 inches*	$ 850–900
Jug, *tankard, 12^1/$_2$ inches*	$ 1,200–1,300
Mug, *2^1/$_2$ inches*	$ 525–575
Mug, *3^1/$_2$ inches*	$ 475–525
Mug, *4^1/$_2$ inches*	$ 400–450
Plaque, *12^1/$_2$ inches*	$ 825–875
Plate, *chop, 14 inches*	$ 725–775
Plate, *dinner, 9^1/$_4$ inches*	$ 225–275
Plate, *dinner, 10 inches*	$ 275–325
Plate, *luncheon, 8^1/$_2$ inches*	$ 175–225
Plate, *salad, 6^1/$_2$ inches*	$ 150–200
Tray, *calling card, 7^3/$_4$ inches*	$ 400–450

"Ye Olden Days"

Scenes depicted in this series:

> "Scenes of Village Life in Ye Olden Days"
> "Traveling in Ye Olden Days"
> "Heirlooms"
> "Ye Village Gossips"
> "Dancing Ye Minuet"
> "Ye Village Streets"
> "Ye Olden Days"
> "Ye Olden Times"
> "Ye Town Cryer"

"Deldare" pitcher, "Ye Olden Days,"
"Scenes of Village Life," 9 inches,
$800–$850.
Item courtesy of Kemble's, Norwich, Ohio.

"Ye Village Tavern"
"Ye Village Parson"
"Ye Evening at Ye Lion Inn"
"Vicar of Wakefield"

Ashtray/matchbox holder	$ 575–625
Bowl, *fern, 8 inches*	$ 625–675
Bowl, *nut, 8 inches*	$ 575–625
Bowl, *salad or fruit, 9-inch diameter*	$ 625–675
Bowl, *vegetable, 8$^{1}/_{2}$ by 6$^{1}/_{2}$ inches*	$ 525–575
Candleholder, *shield back, 7 inches tall*	$ 2,000–2,200
Candleholder/matchbox holder, *with finger ring, 5$^{1}/_{2}$ inches*	$ 725–775
Candlestick, *9$^{1}/_{2}$ inches tall*	$ 775–825
Chocolate cup and saucer	$ 250–300
Chocolate pot	$ 2,750–3,000
Creamer	$ 250–300
Cup and saucer, *coffee or tea*	$ 275–325

Dish, *relish, 12 by 6^1/$_2$ inches*	$ 500–550
Hair receiver	$ 450–500
Humidor, *octagonal, 7 inches*	$ 1,400–1,500
Jug, *octagonal, 6 inches*	$ 500–550
Jug, *octagonal, 7 inches*	$ 550–600
Jug, *octagonal, 8 inches*	$ 575–625
Jug, *octagonal, 9 inches*	$ 625–675
Jug, *octagonal, 10 inches*	$ 775–825
Jug, *tankard, 12^1/$_2$ inches*	$ 1,200–1,300
Mug, *3^1/$_2$ inches*	$ 425–475
Mug, *4^1/$_2$ inches*	$ 375–425
Mug, *tankard, 6^3/$_4$ inches*	$ 875–925
Plaque, *wall, 12 inches*	$ 675–725
Plate, *6^1/$_4$ inches*	$ 150–200
Plate, *7^1/$_4$ inches*	$ 175–225
Plate, *8^1/$_4$ inches*	$ 200–250
Plate, *9^1/$_2$ inches*	$ 225–275
Plate, *10 inches*	$ 275–325
Plate, *cake, pierced tab handles, 10 inches*	$ 575–625
Plate, *chop, 14 inches*	$ 775–825
Powder jar	$ 425–475
Sugar bowl	$ 300–350
Tea tile, *6 inch*	$ 425–475
Teapot, *2-cup*	$ 425–475
Teapot, *4-cup*	$ 575–625
Tray, *calling card, round, tab handles, 7^3/$_4$ inches*	$ 475–525
Tray, *dresser, 12 by 9 inches*	$ 775–825
Tray, *pin, 6^1/$_4$ by 3^1/$_2$ inches*	$ 275–325
Vase, *broad bottom, 8^1/$_2$ inches*	$ 1,500–1,600
Vase, *pinched waist, 9 inches*	$ 1,200–1,300
Vase, *urn shape, 8 inches*	$ 1,650–1,750

"Emerald Deldare" charger, "The Landing," 12-inch diameter, $2,800–$3,000.
Item courtesy of Tony McCormack, Sarasota, Florida.

"Emerald Deldare"

Scenes depicted in this series:

"A Noble Hunting Party"
"The Garden Trio"
"Misfortune at Tulip Hall"
"Dr. Syntax Stopped by Highwaymen"
"Dr. Syntax Sketching the Lake"
"Dr. Syntax Soliloquizing"
"Dr. Syntax Setting Out to the Lakes"
"Dr. Syntax Entertaining at College"
"Dr. Syntax Mistakes a Gentleman's House for an Inn"
"Dr. Syntax Robbed of His Property"
"Dr. Syntax Made Free of the Cellar"
"Dr. Syntax in the Wrong Lodging House"
"Dr. Syntax with the Maid"
"Dr. Syntax Copying the Wit of the Widow"
"Dr. Syntax Reading His Tour"
"Dr. Syntax Taking Possession of His Living"
"Dr. Syntax at Liverpool"
"Dr. Syntax and the Bookseller"

"Dr. Syntax Returned Home"
"Dr. Syntax Bound to a Tree by a Highwayman"
"Dr. Syntax Making a Discovery"
"Dr. Syntax Sells Grizzle"
"Dr. Syntax Star Gazing"

Chocolate pot, *Art Nouveau design*	$ 3,500–3,750
Plaque, *12-inch diameter, round*	$ 2,000–2,200
Plaque, *13¹/₂-inch diameter, round*	$ 2,500–2,700
Plaque, *16¹/₂ inches*	$ 7,500–8,000
Plate, *7¹/₄ inches, Dr. Syntax*	$ 1,400–1,500
Plate, *8¹/₂ inches, Art Nouveau*	$ 825–875

Jugs and Pitchers

Art Nouveau, *spelled "Art Neveau," 1908, 8¹/₂ inches*	$ 1,200–1,300
Buffalo Hunt, *6 inches*	$ 375–425
Cinderella, *1907, 6 inches*	$ 725–775
Dutch (windmill), *6¹/₂ inches*	$ 575–625
Fox Hunt ("Whirl of the Town"), *1907, 7 inches*	$ 675–725
George Washington/Mt. Vernon, *blue and white, 7¹/₂ inches*	$ 675–725
Gloriana, *blue and white, 9 inches*	$ 875–925
Gloriana, *multicolor with gold, 9 inches*	$ 1,000–1,100
Gunner, *w/gold trim*	$ 525–575
Holland (Dutch children), *1907, 6 inches*	$ 725–775
Hounds and Stag (Deer Hunt)	$ 625–675
Imperial, *6³/₄ inches*	$ 325–350
John Paul Jones/Bonhomme Richard, *1908, 9¹/₄ inches*	$ 1,100–1,200
Landing of Roger Williams/Betsey Williams' Cottage, *1907, 6 inches*	$ 725–775
Mason, *beige and green, 1907, 8¹/₂ inches*	$ 1,200–1,300
Melon-shaped, *1909, 8³/₄ inches*	$ 1,000–1,100
Nautical pitcher, *two sailors, sailing ships, lighthouse, 1906, 9¹/₄ inches*	$ 1,200–1,300

New Bedford Whaler (sperm whales, whaling ship "The Niger"), *6 inches*	$ 875–925
Old Mill, *6 inches*	$ 775–825
Orchid spray, *6 inches*	$ 425–475
Pilgrims (Miles Standish/John and Priscilla Alden), *1908, 9 inches*	$ 1,000–1,100
Poppies, *with lid, blue monochrome, 6 inches*	$ 475–525
Rip Van Winkle/Joseph Jefferson, *1906, 9^{1}/$_4$ inches*	$ 925–975
Robin Hood, *1906, 8^{1}/$_4$ inches*	$ 575–625
Roosevelt Bears, *8^{1}/$_4$ inches*	$ 3,250–3,500
Sailors/Lighthouse (marine jug), *1906–07, 9^{1}/$_4$ inches, blue and white*	$ 1,000–1,200
Sailors/Lighthouse (marine jug), *1906–07, 9^{1}/$_4$ inches, brown monochrome*	$ 1,000–1,100
Vienna, *6^{3}/$_4$ inches*	$ 300–350
Wild Duck/Dog ("Major"), *6 inches*	$ 525–575

Dinnerware

"Blue Bird"

Pieces feature a red-breasted bluebird in flight, similar to products made in Austria at the time. This line was first produced in 1919.

Creamer	$ 175–200
Cup and saucer	$ 125–145
Pitcher, *7 inches*	$ 350–400
Plate, *dessert*	$ 50–75
Sugar bowl	$ 175–225

"Blue Willow"

Pieces in this line feature a blue-and-white transfer print in the typical English "Blue Willow" style, and were first produced in 1905. There were two grades: institutional grade, which is made for restaurants, and home grade, which is lighter. It should be noted that collectors prefer "Blue Willow" pieces marked "Buffalo Pottery" to those marked "Buffalo China," and will pay more for the former than for the latter. Pieces produced during the first year of manufacture in 1905 were marked "First Old Willow Ware Manufactured in America, 1905." Examples so marked can bring premium prices as much as double the prices listed below. Production of Buffalo "Blue Willow" stopped in 1917.

Home Grade

Bowl, *cereal*	$ 40–50
Bowl, *cream soup with saucer*	$ 125–145
Bowl, *individual fruit*	$ 20–30
Bowl, *salad, square, 9¼ inches*	$ 275–325
Bowl, *vegetable, oval, 8 inches*	$ 85–110
Bowl, *vegetable, oval, 8½ inches*	$ 100–125
Bowl, *vegetable, round, 9 inches*	$ 125–175
Bowl, *vegetable, oval, 10 inches*	$ 110–135
Bowl, *vegetable, covered, square*	$ 425–475
Butter pat	$ 25–35
Creamer	$ 85–110
Cup and saucer	$ 60–75
Cup and saucer, *demitasse*	$ 60–75
Gravy boat, *no underliner*	$ 160–180
Pitcher, *wash set*	$ 775–825
Plate, *chop, 11-inch diameter*	$ 250–300
Plate, *cake, 11-inch diameter, handled*	$ 165–180
Plate, *dessert, 7-inch diameter*	$ 25–35
Plate, *dinner, 10-inch diameter*	$ 75–85
Plate, *luncheon, 9-inch diameter*	$ 25–35
Plate, *salad, 8½-inch diameter*	$ 30–40
Platter, *oval, 9 inches*	$ 110–130
Platter, *oval, 10 inches*	$ 110–130
Platter, *oval, 11 inches*	$ 125–140
Platter, *oval, 12 inches*	$ 140–160
Platter, *oval, 14 inches*	$ 175–225
Platter, *oval, 16 inches*	$ 275–300

Platter, *oval, 18 inches*	$ 325–375
Ramekin	$ 75–90
Teapot, *square, 2-pint*	$ 350–400

Institutional (or Heavy) Grade

Bowl, *cereal, $6^1/_2$ inches*	$ 10–14
Bowl, *individual fruit*	$ 8–12
Bowl, *soup*	$ 15–18
Bowl, *soup, 9 inches*	$ 15–18
Creamer	$ 38–42
Cup and saucer	$ 18–22
Custard cup	$ 8–12
Plate, *dessert, 8-inch diameter*	$ 8–12
Plate, *dinner, 10-inch diameter*	$ 20–30
Plate, *luncheon, 9-inch diameter*	$ 15–18
Plate, *salad, 8-inch diameter*	$ 12–15
Platter, *oval, $12^1/_2$ inches*	$ 35–45
Tray, *two-tier, serving*	$ 50–60

"Gaudy Willow"

First introduced in 1905, this is the standard "Willow" pattern in shades of rust, blue, green, and brown, accented with gold. The colors in this pattern were hand-applied both over and under the glaze, and the pattern was thus more expensive to make than the more common "Blue Willow" pattern. "Gaudy Willow" pieces are much rarer than standard "Blue Willow" pieces, and are eagerly sought after by collectors.

Creamer	$ 125–175
Cup and saucer	$ 150–200
Bone dish	$ 225–275
Butter dish with insert	$ 675–725
Plate, *cake, two handles, 10-inch diameter*	$ 425–475
Plate, *dessert*	$ 90–100
Plate, *dinner, $10^1/_2$-inch diameter*	$ 175–225

Platter, *oval, 18 inches*	$ 875–925
Sugar bowl	$ 425–475

"Lamare"

"Lamare" pieces were first offered in the 1904 Larkin catalog: a 100-piece set was available for free with a $16 purchase. Pieces made with this pattern feature a lush floral swag around the edge, with shades of Dove Gray, dark blue, green, or brown.

Bowl, *individual fruit*	$ 16–20
Bowl, *vegetable, round, 9 inches*	$ 70–80
Bowl, *soup*	$ 25–35
Butter dish, *round, covered*	$ 125–145
Gravy boat	$ 110–130
Plate, *dinner, 10-inch diameter*	$ 30–40
Pate, *luncheon, 9-inch diameter*	$ 20–24
Plate, *salad, 8-inch diameter*	$ 16–20
Platter, *12 inches*	$ 85–100
Sugar bowl	$ 60–75
Tureen with lid	$ 350–400

CALIFORNIA CLEMINSONS

HAND PAINTED

One of the marks used on pottery made by the *California Cleminsons.*

This company began in a garage in Monterey Park in 1941. Betty Cleminson, with the help of her husband, George, began hand-making a variety of ceramic pieces that very quickly found favor with the buying public. Until 1943, the enterprise was called "Cleminson Clay," but the orders came in so fast that the couple had to move out of their garage and set up a manufacturing facility in El Monte, California, where they changed the company's name to "California Cleminsons."

Eventually the company employed as many as 170 people to slip-paint novelties, cookie jars, and art wares. Sadly, however, Japanese competition and the high cost of doing everything by hand caused the Cleminsons to cease production in 1963. Some of the company's pieces are unmarked, but most are stamped "The California Cleminsons" or "bc" for "Betty Cleminson."

Cookie Jars

Card King, *crowned head with bead, marked*	$ 575–625
Cookie House, *in the form of a contemporary dwelling, marked*	$ 175–225
Gingerbread house, *marked*	$ 175–225

Pig, *marked*	$ 300–350
Potbellied stove, *painted like a face, marked*	$ 325–375
"Way to a Man's Heart," *marked*	$ 175–225

Miscellany

Cleanser shaker in the form of a woman with a full, floor length skirt, *marked*	$ 60–75
Covered cup, *grimacing clown's head with ice pack as lid, marked*	$ 75–90
Laundry sprinkler in the form of a Chinaman, *9 inches, marked*	$ 100–120
Pie bird in the form of a crowing rooster, *4¹/₂ inches, signed "bc"*	$ 90–110
Plaque, "No Matter Where I Place My Guests They Always Like My Kitchen Best," *signed*	$ 35–45

CALIFORNIA ORIGINALS

Established by Bill Bailey in Torrance, California, in 1944, this company was originally called "Heirlooms of Tomorrow," and reportedly used "California Originals" as a trade name. The name of the company was officially changed to "California Originals" in 1955, and the company remained in business until 1982.

California Originals is known primarily for its cookie jars, shakers, cigarette boxes, ashtrays, wall pockets, figures, planters, lazy Susans, bowls, and vases. The company had contracts with both Disney and *Sesame Street*, and sold items to a number of mass marketers including KMart, Montgomery Ward, J.C. Penney, and Sears. Some pieces were marked with paper labels; others were incised with either "Cal. Orig USA" and a model number, or a model number above the mark "USA Calif Orig."

Cookie Jars and Related Items

Airplane, *pilot finial (Red Baron)*, *#2629*	$ 600–650
Apple, *11 inches,* *#8214*	$ 100–125
Bakery, *cookies on roof,* "*Cookie Bakery,*" *all variations,* *#863*	$ 100–125
Basket of carrots, *rabbit finial,* *#703*	$ 200–225

Bear, *brown, hands on tummy, 12 inches, #405*	$ 75–95
Bear, *in sweater and tie, brown, #2648*	$ 150–175
Bear, *in sweater and tie, underglaze painted, #2648*	$ 125–150
Bear, *Koala, 10 inches, dark brown with white face, #885*	$ 400–450
Bear, *Koala, 10 inches, unmarked, gray fur*	$ 250–275
Bear, *Panda, 11 inches, #889*	$ 175–200
Boy, *with baseball bat, #875*	$ 75–95
Bull (Ferdinand), *#870, brown*	$ 75–95
Bull (Ferdinand), *#870, red*	$ 150–165
Cat, *embossed flowers, 12 inches long, #884*	$ 150–165
Caterpillar, *with hat and tie, butterfly finial, #853*	$ 375–400
Christmas Tree, *#873*	$ 475–525
Circus Wagon, *#2631*	$ 175–200
Clock, *Alarm, smiling face, "Cookie Time," 13¹/₂ inches, #860*	$ 150–175
Clown, *full-figured, arms up, 12¹/₂ inches, #862*	$ 200–225
Clown, *full-figured, hand to hat, #213, white face*	$ 110–125
Clown, *full-figured, hand to hat, #213, brown tones*	$ 75–95
Clown, *full-figured, juggling three balls, #876, full color*	$ 150–175
Clown, *full-figured, juggling three balls, #876, mainly brown*	$ 85–100
Clown, *head, 12¹/₂ inches, #859*	$ 275–300
Coffee Grinder, *#861*	$ 150–175
Crocodile in jar, *"I Am a Cookie Crock," #662*	$ 350–400
Dog, *Cocker Spaniel, sitting, tongue out, #458*	$ 75–95
Dog, *Schnauzer, #905*	$ 225–250
Dog, *Yorkshire Terrier, #937*	$ 125–150
Duck, *#857*	$ 125–150
Duckbill Platypus, *#790*	$ 225–250
Elephant, *with clown on lid, #896*	$ 175–200
Elephant, *with hat and suspenders, #2643*	$ 150–175
Elf, *head*	$ 200–225
Elf's School House	$ 175–200

Engine, *#2628*	$ 200–225
Fire Truck, *"Fire," 11¹/₂ inches long, #841*	$ 300–325
Frog, *sitting, #884*	$ 175–200
Frog, *sitting, with bow tie, #2645*	$ 150–175
Frog, *with bow tie, leaning on stone wall, #877*	$ 175–200
Gingerbread House, *11¹/₂ inches, #857*	$ 225–250
Girl, *holding bowl of cookies*	$ 450–475
Gramophone, *#891*	$ 500–525
Gumball Machine, *"1 cent each," all variations, #890*	$ 200–225
Hen, *8¹/₂ inches, #1127*	$ 85–100
Hippopotamus, *with embossed flowers, 14 inches long, #883*	$ 325–350
Humpty-Dumpty, *on wall, unpainted nose, cheeks, and mouth, #882*	$ 175–200
Humpty-Dumpty, *on wall, painted nose, cheeks, and mouth, #882*	$ 300–325
Indian, *licking lollipop, #738*	$ 125–150
Lemon, *11 inches, #8497-S*	$ 100–110
Liberty Bell, *"Liberty Throughout All the Land 1776–1976," #889*	$ 100–120
Lion, *with lollipop, bow on head, #866*	$ 200–225
Lioness, *yawning, with cub, #739*	$ 125–150
Little Red Riding Hood, *#320*	$ 600–650
Man in barrel, *"Down to the Last Cookie," #873*	$ 350–375
Monkey, *sitting with banana, #884*	$ 225–275
Mouse, *#2630*	$ 145–175
Noah's Ark, *#881*	$ 325–375
Orange, *#8218*	$ 150–175
Owl, *winking, #2751*	$ 75–95
Owl, *wing raised, in overalls, winking, #856, all variations*	$ 90–110
Pack Mule, *#2653*	$ 425–475
Pear, *#8217*	$ 100–120
Pelican, *small pelican finial*	$ 145–175

Penguin, *in vest and pants, wing up, 12 inches*	$ 175–200
Rabbit, *eating cookie*	$ 125–150
Radio, *Cathedral model, "Tune in a Cookie," #888*	$ 135–160
Raggedy Andy, *sitting on barrel, #860*	$ 350–375
Raggedy Ann, *sitting on barrel, #859*	$ 350–375
Riverboat, *"Southern Belle Cookie Jar," 14¹/₂ inches, #868*	$ 250–275
Roly Poly, *turnabout lid, happy and sad face, embossed flowers, #858*	$ 325–375
Safe, *cat-with-arched-back finial, #2630-1-2*	$ 200–225
Safe, *cat sitting, #2630-1-2*	$ 150–175
Safe, *rabbit-with-cookie final, #2630*	$ 150–175
Santa Claus, *#871*	$ 850–900
Scarecrow, *with pumpkin, #871*	$ 350–400
Schoolhouse, *"Li'l Old School House," #869*	$ 275–325
Sheriff, *with hole in hat, 12 inches, #869*	$ 85–100
Shoe House, *tile roof, 12¹/₄ inches, #2637*	$ 100–125
Shoe House, *shingle roof, 12³/₄ inches, #874*	$ 100–125
Snail, *13 inches, #854*	$ 300–350
Snowman, *#872*	$ 500–550
Store, *"Cookie Bakery," green roof, #863*	$ 110–125
Stove, *potbellied, #743*	$ 125–150
Strawberry, *8³/₄ inches, #8413-C*	$ 100–125
Strawberry, *11 inches, #821*	$ 125–150
Stump, *bear-and-beehive finial, #2622*	$ 110–135
Stump, *mouse finial, #891–92*	$ 100–125
Stump, *mushroom finial*	$ 75–100
Stump, *owl finial, #2624*	$ 100–125
Stump, *puppy finial, #2623*	$ 100–125
Stump, *rabbit finial, #2621*	$ 110–135
Stump, *squirrel finial, small size, 12¹/₂ inches, #2620*	$ 100–125
Stump, *squirrel finial, large size, 14 inches, #2620–23*	$ 125–150

Taxicab, *yellow, 10³/₄ inches long, #501*	$ 300–350
Teapot, *with embossed flowers, brass handle, #737*	$ 90–110
Treasure Chest, *with octopus on lid, #876*	$ 325–375
Turtle, *on back, #2637*	$ 150–200
Turtle, *"Tortoise and the Hare," rabbit with carrot on lid, 12¹/₂ inches, #728*	$ 75–100
Turtle, *rabbit with cookie on lid, #2728*	$ 60–85
Turtle, *sitting, feet out, 12¹/₄ inches, #2635*	$ 75–100
Turtle, *sitting with flowers, 11¹/₂ inches, #842*	$ 110–135
Van, *red, 10 inches long, #843*	$ 300–350
Volkswagen Beetle, *with windup key, 7 inches, #2632*	$ 325–375

Cookie Jars—Cartoon and *Sesame Street* Themes

Cartoons

Superman, *in telephone booth, #846, monochrome finish*	$ 425–475
Superman, *in telephone booth, #846, multicolored, brown booth*	$ 425–475
Superman, *in telephone booth, #846, multicolored, silver booth*	$ 750–800
Wonder Woman, *roping safe and robber, #847*	$ 1,400–1,500
Woody Woodpecker, *monochrome, #980*	$ 850–900
Woody Woodpecker, *multicolored, #980*	$ 950–1,000

Sesame Street

Bert and Ernie, *"Ernie and Bert Fine Cookies," #977*	$ 600–650
Big Bird, *"Cookie," #971*	$ 200–250
Cookie Monster, *#970*	$ 175–225
Cookie Monster, *cylinder, "wanted" poster, #505*	$ 175–225
Cookie Monster, *cylinder, in chef's hat, #505*	$ 175–225
The Count, *#975*	$ 1,400–1,500
Ernie, *#973*	$ 150–200
Oscar the Grouch, *#972*	$ 150–200

CAMARK POTTERY, INC.

One of the paper labels used by *Camark Pottery, Inc.*

USA

Camark

846 R

One of the marks found on *Camark* pottery.

Founded by Samuel F. "Jack" Carnes in 1926 as the Camden Art and Tile Company in Camden, Arkansas, this company had laudable ambitions at an inauspicious time. Carnes wanted to produce handmade art wares, and he hired John Lessell, who had designed the "LaSa" line for Weller Pottery in Zanesville, Ohio, to be the art director. Lessell designed a line similar to "LaSa" and to other lines of metallic luster ware made at both Weller and Owens. The line was called, and eventually marked, "Le-Camark" ("Camark" was a name formed from the first three letters of "Camden" and the first three letters of "Arkansas").

Unfortunately, Lessell died in 1926, and Lessell's wife and stepdaughter took over in his stead. They oversaw the production of Le-Camark during 1927 but, by 1928, the company's emphasis had shifted to more traditional lines requiring less-demanding glazes: the family was simply trying to survive. There was not a strong market for handmade art pottery, and the company was sold in 1928 and renamed the "Camark Art Pottery." The new owners began making less-expensive commercial art wares (molded) for florists and gift shops, but Japanese competition during the late 1950s caused them to sell the company. It was then renamed "Camark Potteries, Inc."

Camark stopped producing in the early 1960s, but remained open to sell existing inventory. There was an attempt to reopen the pottery in the 1980s, but there are no reports of pottery actually having been made at this time. Collectors are very interested in the "Le-Camark" pieces, but there are too few pieces sold to price them accurately. Collectors are also interested in the figural pieces, pitchers with figural handles, and the "Aquaria" pieces, which are figural pieces of pottery designed to hold a glass fishbowl. Blown-glass bowls made in Mexico were included with the "Aquaria" pieces.

"Aquaria"

Balancing Seal, *13¹/₂ inches, #552*	$ 100–125
Bear, *on his back, 10 inches, #870*	$ 125–150
Pensive Bird, *7¹/₂ inches, #901*	$ 100–125
Seals (three), *large, 16³/₄ inches, #802*	$ 125–150
Tropical Fish, *8¹/₂ inches, #200*	$ 225–250
Wistful Kitten, *8¹/₂ inches (most commonly found example)*	$ 85–100

Early Wares

Vase, *signed "Lessell" in the style of Weller "LaSa," landscape with mountains and trees, 12¹/₂ inches tall*	$ 1,600–1,750
Vase, *signed "LeCamark" in the style of Weller "La Sa," palm tree*	$ 850–900
Vase, *signed "LeCamark" in the style of Weller "Lamar," palm trees against a crimson ground*	$ 1,200–1,300
Vase, *signed "Camark" in the style of Weller "Maringo," stylized orange trees and mountains, "Old English Ivory," 8¹/₂ inches high*	$ 750–800
Vase, *signed "Camark," green ground with coralline (beaded) decoration in imitation of Victorian glass*	$ 1,100–1,200

Figures

Cat, *climbing, two models (one heads left, the other right), 16 inches, #058*	$ 85–100
Cat, *climbing, 10 inches, unmarked*	$ 75–95
Cat, *tail up, 12 inches, black glaze, unmarked*	$ 225–250

Dog, *wide collar, head down, "S"-shaped tail in air, brown glaze, 10^1/$_2$ inches, unmarked*	$ 350–375
Ducks, *on base, two birds with wings outspread, 9 by 6 inches, unmarked*	$ 350–375
Elephant, *on base with trunk raised, yellow matte glaze, unmarked, 2^1/$_4$ inches*	$ 20–30
Hog, *razorback, on base labeled "Razorback," burgundy glaze, 4^1/$_4$ inches, marked "117 USA"*	$ 20–30
Horse, *ink-stamped "Camark," sitting down, Art Deco-esque styling, on base, 9 by 8^1/$_4$ inches, ivory glaze*	$ 250–300
Horse, *on base, prancing, marked "567," 10 by 8 inches*	$ 150–200
Lion, *12 inches long, paper label*	$ 200–250
Squirrel, *9 inches, unmarked, brown glaze, squirrel appears to be climbing*	$ 60–70

Miscellany

Bank, *pig-shaped, handle on back, black, 3^3/$_4$ inches, unmarked*	$ 80–90
Bowl, *canoe with oval flower frog, orange with green drip, canoe is 11 by 3^1/$_4$ inches and has an ink stamp mark*	$ 175–225
Bowl and pitcher set, *pitcher is 9^3/$_4$ inches tall, bowl is 7^1/$_4$ inches in diameter, flower-decorated, signed*	$ 150–200
Cake plate, *rattan-covered handles on either side, 12^3/$_4$ inches, ring pattern in center, royal blue*	$ 80–90
Candlesticks, *dolphins in the form of the glass examples made at Boston and Sandwich and elsewhere, 6^3/$_4$ inches, paper label, yellow matte, pair*	$ 60–70
Candlestick, *green matte, three cornucopias, unmarked*	$ 75–85
Cup and saucer, *shaped like a lotus blossom, burgundy, 2^1/$_4$ by 4^1/$_4$ inches, marked*	$ 25–35
Flower frog, *fish on a wave mound, 3^1/$_2$ inches, marked*	$ 70–80
Pitcher, *batter, pinch spout, parrot handle, marked "200"*	$ 135–155
Planter, *swan, 4^3/$_4$ inches, royal blue, unmarked*	$ 20–30
Planter, *swan, 3^3/$_4$ inches, Delphinium Blue, unmarked*	$ 15–25
Planter, *swan, 3 inches, yellow matte, unmarked*	$ 10–20
Planter, *majolica glaze, leaves and flowers, footed, 17^1/$_4$ by 7 inches, unmarked*	$ 375–425

Camark tankard pitcher, majolica glaze, 12 inches, green with white flowers, $200–$250.
Item courtesy of Richard H. Crane, Knoxville, Tennessee.

Camark bowl with bird-shaped flower frog, bowl is 10½ inches in diameter, $65–$80.
Item courtesy of Needful Things, Hendersonville, North Carolina.

Camark vase, white glaze, #110, 10 inches tall, $60–$75.
Item courtesy of Needful Things, Hendersonville, North Carolina.

Salt and pepper shakers, *ball jug shaped with "S" and "P" handles, Delphinium Blue, paper label*	$ 30–40
Shelf sitter, *Humpty-Dumpty, 6¹/₂ inches, unmarked*	$ 175–225
Vase, *gunmetal glaze with green drips, 8 inches tall, paper label*	$ 275–325
Vase, *ivory matte with very distinct crackle, pinch sides, 9¹/₂ inches tall, unmarked*	$ 575–625
Vase, *orange matte with heavy crackle in black, 7 inches tall, unmarked*	$ 350–400

CANONSBURG POTTERY COMPANY

THE HALLMARK

OF QUALITY

Mark often found on products made by the Canonsburg Pottery Company.

This company began operations in Canonsburg, Pennsylvania, in 1901 as the Canonsburg China Company. One of its principal founders was W. S. George, who operated the East Palestine Pottery Company in East Palestine, Ohio, which became the W. S. George Pottery Company in 1909. Canonsburg specialized in making semiporcelain dinnerware, as well as toilet sets and assorted other items. In 1909, the company was purchased by a corporation and the name was changed to the Canonsburg Pottery Company. John George, who was W. S. George's brother, was president. After a fire in 1975, production at Canonsburg came to an end.

"Modern Priscilla"

Despite its name, this pattern is not part of the "Priscilla" or "Washington Colonial" lines discussed below. Instead, pieces in this line are decal-decorated, with sprays of pink roses around their rims and a smaller pink rose in the center of the plates.

Bowl, *individual fruit*	$ 8–10
Bowl, *vegetable, round, 8³/₄ inches*	$ 30–40
Creamer	$ 25–30
Cup and saucer	$ 20–25

Plate, *bread and butter, 6¹/₄-inch diameter*	$ 6–8
Plate, *dessert, 7¹/₄-inch diameter*	$ 7–10
Plate, *dinner, 10-inch diameter*	$ 18–22
Platter, *oval, 11¹/₂ inches*	$ 40–44
Platter, *oval, 15³/₄ inches*	$ 70–80
Sugar bowl and lid	$ 38–42

"Priscilla"/"Washington Colonial"

This line was introduced in 1931 and was originally called "Priscilla," but by early 1932 its name had become "Washington Colonial." Later, this line became known as "American Traditional," and its pieces were marked accordingly. The pattern is distinguished by a heavily embossed rim (on flatware) or band (on hollowware) composed of rococo basketweave motifs, with sections periodically divided by twining "C" scrolls. Dinnerware was often decal-decorated, but was also produced in solid colors—white, ivory, pink, green, and yellow.

Bowl, *salad serving, 12 inches*	$ 40–45
Bowl, *soup, 9¹/₄-inch diameter*	$ 10–12
Bowl, *vegetable, oval, 9³/₄ inches*	$ 22–26
Bowl, *vegetable, round, 9 inches*	$ 22–26
Butter dish, *¹/₄-pound, covered*	$ 32–36
Creamer	$ 10–14
Cup and saucer	$ 12–16
Gravy boat and underliner	$ 35–38
Plate, *dinner, 10¹/₂ inches*	$ 18–22
Plate, *luncheon, 9-inch diameter*	$ 12–16
Plate, *salad, 6-inch diameter*	$ 4–6
Platter, *oval, 13¹/₂ inches*	$ 38–42
Teapot, *3-cup*	$ 85–95

"Regency"

This is a line of solid-color ware most commonly found in green, but also available in gold. The pattern is distinguished by an embossed rim on the flatware in the neoclassical style, with urns, flower garlands, and gadrooning around the edge. The prices quoted below are for pieces in green; gold pieces are approximately 20 percent more valuable.

Bowl, *individual fruit*	$ 6–8
Bowl, *cereal, 6¼ inches*	$ 8–10
Butter, *¼-pound, covered*	$ 28–32
Coffeepot and lid	$ 55–65
Creamer	$ 14–16
Cup and saucer	$ 12–14
Gravy boat and underliner	$ 35–45
Pitcher, *48-ounce*	$ 55–65
Plate, *dinner, 10-inch diameter*	$ 12–16
Plate, *salad, 7¼-inch diameter*	$ 6–8
Platter, *oval, 12 inches*	$ 26–30
Platter, *oval, 13 inches*	$ 36–40
Salt and pepper shakers, *set*	$ 16–20
Sugar bowl and lid	$ 16–20

"Rose Point"

This line was originated by the Pope-Gosser China Company of Coshocton, Ohio. The molds were bought by the Steubenville Pottery of Steubenville, Ohio, and, when Steubenville went out of business in 1959, the molds were sold to Barium Chemical, which in turn sold them to Canonsburg. Canonsburg then produced "Rose Point" for a number of years. "Rose Point" pieces are all-white, with notched edges and raised decorations of roses around the rims.

Bowl, *cereal, 7-inch diameter*	$ 15–19
Bowl, *individual fruit, 6-inch diameter*	$ 8–12
Bowl, *soup, 8-inch diameter*	$ 18–22
Bowl, *vegetable, oval, 9¾ inches*	$ 26–30
Bowl, *vegetable, round, 8¾-inch diameter*	$ 32–36
Bowl, *vegetable, round, covered*	$ 90–100
Coffeepot, *5-cup*	$ 125–130
Creamer	$ 16–22

Cup and saucer	$ 8–10
Gravy boat, *no underliner*	$ 32–36
Plate, *bread and butter, 6^1/$_2$-inch diameter*	$ 6–8
Plate, *dinner, 10^1/$_2$-inch diameter*	$ 15–18
Plate, *luncheon, 9^1/$_2$-inch diameter*	$ 16–19
Platter, *oval, 11 inches*	$ 38–42
Platter, *oval, 13 inches*	$ 48–52
Snack plate and cup set	$ 18–22
Sugar bowl with lid	$ 30–34

CARDINAL CHINA COMPANY

Located in Carteret, New Jersey, this company began operations in 1946 as the Carteret China Company. Initially, it performed contract work in the lamp and giftware trade. When it started selling its own products, it adopted the trade name "Cardinal China" in order not to compete with its existing customers. The company is still in business, and collectors are most interested in its cookie jars.

Cookie Jars

Boy, *head with mortarboard, sometimes called "Professor"*	$ 250–300
Bus, *"Cookie Bus," #308*	$ 400–450
Castle, *#307*	$ 450–500
Clown, *head, crying, "I Want Some Cookies"*	$ 250–300
French Chef, *head, "Petite Gateaux Cookies," #305*	$ 275–325
Garage, *"Free Parking for Cookies," #306*	$ 125–150
Girl, *head, sometimes called "Cookie Kate," #301*	$ 300–350

Pig, *head, sometimes called "Porky Pig," "Go Ahead, Make a Pig of Yourself,"* #304	$ 135–160
Sack, *"Cookies"*	$ 125–150
Safe, *"Cookie Safe,"* #309	$ 150–175
Soldier, *full figure,* #312	$ 450–500

CASTLETON CHINA

Anticipating the onset of World War II, Louis Hellman brought the shapes and patterns of the famous Rosenthal China Company to New Castle, Pennsylvania, and the Shenango Pottery Company in 1939. Shenango invested $25,000, and production of Castleton china began in 1940. The company made high-quality porcelain dinnerware in the European style. Castleton China prospered and, in 1951, Shenango bought all the Castleton stock from Hellman and took over manufacturing and sales.

The quality of Castleton china is evident from the company's list of distinguished patrons: in 1955, Mamie Eisenhower ordered new gold-rimmed service plates to be used in the White House dining room, and in 1968 Lyndon Johnson ordered an enormous state dinner service consisting of 216 ten-piece place settings and centerpiece bowls.

In 1968, Castleton China and its parent company, Shenango, were sold to the Interpace Corporation, which already owned Gladding, McBean & Company and made "Franciscan" dinnerware. Unfortunately, Castleton china was expensive to produce, and production is said to have stopped around 1970, though no exact date is available.

"Alberta"

Each piece in this line is decorated with a green and gold band. On flatware, the band appears around the rim.

Bowl, *cream soup with saucer*	$ 55–65
Bowl, *vegetable, oval, 11 inches*	$ 100–115
Coffeepot and lid, *6-cup*	$ 225–250
Creamer	$ 50–60
Cup and saucer	$ 35–45
Cup and saucer, *demitasse*	$ 30–40
Plate, *bread and butter, 6¹/₄ inches*	$ 12–18
Plate, *dinner, 10¹/₂-inch diameter*	$ 30–35
Plate, *luncheon, 9-inch diameter*	$ 25–30
Plate, *salad, 8¹/₂ inches*	$ 20–25
Platter, *oval, 13 inches*	$ 110–120
Platter, *oval, 15¹/₂ inches*	$ 140–150
Platter, *oval, 18¹/₂ inches*	$ 210–220
Teapot and lid, *4-cup*	$ 210–220
Sugar bowl and lid	$ 70–80

"Ascona"

This pattern has a pearl edge (tiny beads like pearls around the rim), and decoration consisting of a large off-center grouping of flowers, with scattered flowers around the rim.

Bowl, *soup, 8-inch diameter*	$ 65–75
Cake stand, *with metal pedestal*	$ 65–75
Cheese plate, *footed, with dome*	$ 50–60
Coffeepot and lid, *6-cup*	$ 375–425
Cup and saucer, *demitasse*	$ 50–60
Cup and saucer, *coffee or tea*	$ 40–50
Cup only, *coffee or tea*	$ 38–45
Gravy boat, *with attached underliner*	$ 175–210

Plate, *bread and butter, 6¹/₂ inches*	$ 24–28
Plate, *dinner, 10¹/₂-inch diameter*	$ 36–40
Plate, *luncheon, 9¹/₂-inch diameter*	$ 34–38
Plate, *salad, 8-inch diameter*	$ 32–36
Plate, *serving, center handle*	$ 100–110
Platter, *oval, 13¹/₂ inches*	$ 175–200
Platter, *oval, 16 inches*	$ 275–300

"Belrose"

Pieces bearing this pattern are decorated with a center grouping of gray and pink flowers, with floral garland around the rim.

Bowl, *cream soup, with saucer*	$ 35–40
Bowl, *individual fruit, 5¹/₂-inch diameter*	$ 30–34
Bowl, *vegetable, oval, 10 inches*	$ 110–120
Bowl, *vegetable, oval, 11 inches*	$ 120–130
Bowl, *vegetable, round, covered*	$ 275–300
Cake stand, *metal pedestal*	$ 45–50
Creamer	$ 60–65
Cup and saucer	$ 25–30
Cup and saucer, *demitasse, both styles*	$ 34–38
Gravy boat with attached underliner	$ 110–120
Plate, *bread and butter, 6¹/₄-inch diameter*	$ 10–14
Plate, *cheese, footed, with dome*	$ 40–45
Plate, *dinner, 10¹/₂-inch diameter*	$ 25–30
Plate, *luncheon, 9-inch diameter*	$ 26–30
Plate, *salad, 8¹/₂-inch diameter*	$ 26–30
Plate, *serving, center handle*	$ 40–50
Platter, *oval, 13 inches*	$ 125–135
Platter, *oval, 15¹/₂ inches*	$ 140–150
Sugar bowl and lid	$ 60–70
Tray, *serving, two-tier*	$ 60–70
Tray, *serving, three-tier*	$ 60–70

"Caprice"

On pieces bearing this pattern, gray and blue flowers are spaced around the rim and over the verge, where they terminate at a gold-banded circle.

Bowl, *cream soup with saucer*	$ 30–35
Bowl, *individual fruit, 5¹/₂-inch diameter*	$ 26–30
Bowl, *vegetable, oval, 10 inches*	$ 85–95
Bowl, *vegetable, oval, 11 inches*	$ 85–95
Bowl, *vegetable, round, 10 inches*	$ 125–135
Bowl, *vegetable, round, covered*	$ 275–285
Cake stand with metal pedestal	$ 45–55
Coffeepot and lid, *6-cup*	$ 275–300
Creamer	$ 55–60
Cup and saucer, *coffee or tea*	$ 25–30
Cup and saucer, *demitasse*	$ 25–30
Gravy boat with attached underliner	$ 110–120
Plate, *bread and butter, 6¹/₄-inch diameter*	$ 8–12
Plate, *cheese, footed and domed*	$ 35–40
Plate, *chop, round, 13-inch diameter*	$ 130–140
Plate, *dinner, 10³/₄-inch diameter*	$ 25–30
Plate, *luncheon, 9-inch diameter*	$ 24–28
Plate, *salad, 8¹/₂-inch diameter*	$ 15–18
Plate, *serving, with central handle*	$ 40–45
Platter, *oval, 13 inches*	$ 100–110
Platter, *oval, 15¹/₂ inches*	$ 125–135
Platter, *oval, 19 inches*	$ 175–200
Sugar bowl and lid	$ 50–60
Teapot and lid, *4-cup*	$ 230–240
Tidbit server, *two-tier*	$ 130–140

"Castleton Bouquet"

Pieces bearing this lovely pattern have a pearl edge and small clusters of flowers scattered around the rim. The pearl edge is gilded, and there is a gilded ring around the verge.

Bowl, *cream soup, with saucer*	$ 50–60
Bowl, *soup, 8-inch diameter*	$ 45–50
Bowl, *vegetable, oval, 10-inch diameter*	$ 80–90
Bowl, *vegetable, oval, 11-inch diameter*	$ 110–120
Cake stand with metal pedestal	$ 60–70
Creamer	$ 55–65
Cup and saucer	$ 35–40
Cup and saucer, *demitasse*	$ 35–40
Gravy boat with attached underliner	$ 135–150
Plate, *bread and butter, 6^1/$_2$-inch diameter*	$ 12–16
Plate, *dinner, 11-inch diameter*	$ 40–45
Plate, *luncheon, 9^1/$_2$-inch diameter*	$ 34–38
Plate, *salad, 8-inch diameter*	$ 20–24
Plate, *serving, with center handle*	$ 55–60
Platter, *oval, 13^1/$_2$ inches*	$ 125–135
Platter, *oval, 16 inches*	$ 175–185
Platter, *oval, 19 inches*	$ 225–250
Sugar bowl and lid	$ 85–90
Tray, *serving, two-tier*	$ 85–90
Tray, *serving, three-tier*	$ 100–110

"Castleton Rose"

This pattern is somewhat similar to "Castleton Bouquet." Pieces bearing this pattern feature the same small clusters of flowers around the rim of the flatware, the same gilded pearl edge, and the same gold ring around the verge. However, this pattern also features a large bouquet of flowers at its center. Prices for this pattern are generally a little higher than they are for "Castleton Bouquet."

Bowl, *cream soup, with saucer*	$ 55–60
Bowl, *individual fruit, 5^1/$_2$-inch diameter*	$ 35–40
Bowl, *soup, 8-inch diameter*	$ 55–60
Bowl, *vegetable, oval, 10 inches*	$ 130–140
Bowl, *vegetable, oval, 11 inches*	$ 130–140

Cake stand with metal pedestal	$ 60–70
Creamer	$ 60–70
Cup and saucer, *coffee or tea*	$ 35–40
Cup and saucer, *demitasse*	$ 35–40
Gravy boat with attached underliner	$ 160–170
Plate, *bread and butter, 6^1/$_2$-inch diameter*	$ 15–18
Plate, *dinner, 10^1/$_2$-inch diameter*	$ 45–50
Plate, *luncheon, 9^1/$_2$-inch diameter*	$ 38–42
Plate, *salad, 8-inch diameter*	$ 24–26
Plate, *serving, with center handle*	$ 60–65
Platter, *oval, 13^1/$_2$ inches*	$ 125–130
Platter, *oval, 16 inches*	$ 170–180
Sugar bowl with lid	$ 100–110
Tidbit server, *two-tier*	$ 95–100
Tidbit server, *three-tier*	$ 110–120

"Dolly Madison"

Pieces bearing this pattern have the distinctive pearl edge that is scalloped, a gold ring around the edge and verge, and a full-blown pink rose with green leaves in the center.

Bowl, *cream soup, with saucer*	$ 60–70
Bowl, *individual fruit, 5^1/$_2$-inch diameter*	$ 35–40
Bowl, *soup, 8-inch diameter*	$ 50–60
Bowl *vegetable, oval, 10 inches*	$ 100–110
Bowl, *vegetable, oval, 11 inches*	$ 110–120
Bowl, *vegetable, round, covered*	$ 375–385
Cake stand with metal pedestal	$ 50–60
Creamer	$ 60–70
Cup and saucer, *coffee or tea*	$ 35–40
Cup and saucer, *demitasse*	$ 35–40
Plate, *bread and butter, 6^1/$_2$-inch diameter*	$ 18–22

Plate, *cheese, footed and domed*	$ 40–45
Plate, *dinner, 10¹/₂-inch diameter*	$ 35–40
Plate, *salad, 8-inch diameter*	$ 18–22
Plate, *serving, center handle*	$ 50–60
Platter, *oval, 13¹/₂ inches*	$ 175–185
Platter, *oval, 16 inches*	$ 185–200
Platter, *oval, 19 inches*	$ 325–350
Tidbit server, *two-tier*	$ 80–90
Tidbit server, *three-tier*	$ 100–110

"Empire"

This pattern is distinguished by a pearl edge and gilded ring around the verge. A blue neoclassical wreath appears in the center of the flatware.

Bowl, *cream soup, with saucer*	$ 50–55
Bowl, *individual fruit, 5¹/₂-inch diameter*	$ 30–35
Bowl, *soup, 8-inch diameter*	$ 75–80
Bowl, *vegetable, oval, 11 inches*	$ 140–150
Bowl, *vegetable, round, covered*	$ 375–400
Creamer	$ 70–80
Cup and saucer, *coffee and tea*	$ 40–45
Cup and saucer, *demitasse*	$ 35–40
Gravy boat with attached underliner	$ 150–160
Plate, *bread and butter*	$ 15–20
Plate, *cake, handled*	$ 130–140
Plate, *dinner, 10¹/₂-inch diameter*	$ 40–50
Plate, *salad, 8-inch diameter*	$ 25–30
Platter, *oval, 13¹/₂ inches*	$ 150–160
Platter, *oval, 16 inches*	$ 230–240
Sugar bowl and lid	$ 90–100
Tidbit server, *two-tier*	$ 90–100
Tidbit server, *three-tier*	$ 110–120

Castleton China "Gloria" pattern dinner plate, 10½-inch diameter, $25–$30.
Item courtesy of Patty Tower, Old School Antique Mall, Sylva, North Carolina.

"Gloria"

This is a bold pattern with taupe roses and a pearl edge. The decoration consists of two large blossoms, with leaves that take up most of the surface of the flatware.

Bowl, *cream soup, with saucer*	$ 30–40
Bowl, *individual fruit bowl, 5½-inch diameter*	$ 20–25
Bowl, *soup, 8-inch diameter*	$ 44–48
Bowl, *vegetable, oval, 10 inches*	$ 90–100
Bowl, *vegetable, oval, 11 inches*	$ 90–100
Bowl, *vegetable, round, covered*	$ 325–335
Cake stand, *metal pedestal*	$ 40–50
Creamer	$ 50–60
Cup and saucer, *coffee and tea*	$ 30–35
Cup and saucer, *demitasse*	$ 25–30
Gravy boat, *faststand*	$ 120–130
Plate, *bread and butter, 6½ inches*	$ 10–14

Plate, *chop, 13-inch diameter*	$ 160–170
Plate, *dinner, 10$\frac{1}{2}$-inch diameter*	$ 25–30
Plate, *luncheon, 9$\frac{1}{2}$-inch diameter*	$ 25–30
Plate, *salad, 8-inch diameter*	$ 15–20
Plate, *serving, with center handle*	$ 45–55
Platter, *oval, 13$\frac{1}{2}$ inches*	$ 125–135
Platter, *oval, 16 inches*	$ 150–160
Snack set, *cup and plate*	$ 35–45
Sugar bowl and lid	$ 65–75
Tidbit server, *two-tier*	$ 65–75
Tidbit server, *three-tier*	$ 80–90

"Ma-Lin"

This pattern features Asian-inspired flowers in orange red, yellow, and blue. Pieces in this line are decorated with green leaves, and a large spray of flowers that extends from one edge to the center, and is surrounded by single blossoms around the rim.

Bowl, *cream soup, with saucer*	$ 70–85
Bowl, *individual fruit, 5$\frac{1}{2}$ inch diameter*	$ 30–40
Bowl, *soup, 8-inch diameter*	$ 50–60
Bowl, *vegetable, oval, 10 inches*	$ 120–135
Bowl, *vegetable, oval, 11 inches*	$ 140–160
Bowl, *vegetable, round, 10-inch diameter*	$ 230–250
Bowl, *vegetable, round, covered*	$ 350–375
Cake stand with metal pedestal	$ 70–85
Coffee pot and lid, *6 cups*	$ 380–425
Creamer	$ 70–85
Cup and saucer, *coffee or tea*	$ 35–45
Cup and saucer, *demitasse*	$ 30–40
Gravy boat with attached underliner	$ 120–160
Plate, *bread and butter*	$ 14–18
Plate, *cake, handled*	$ 150–175

Plate, *cheese, footed with dome*	$ 50–60
Plate, *chop, 13-inch diameter*	$ 220–240
Plate, *dinner, 10^{1}/$_{2}$-inch diameter*	$ 50–60
Plate, *luncheon, 9-inch diameter*	$ 40–50
Plate, *salad, 8^{1}/$_{2}$-inch diameter*	$ 25–30
Plate, *serving, center handle*	$ 65–80
Platter, *oval, 13 inches*	$ 160–175
Platter, *oval, 15^{1}/$_{2}$ inches*	$ 200–225
Platter, *oval, 18^{1}/$_{2}$ inches*	$ 300–325
Sugar bowl and lid	$ 90–110
Teapot and lid, *4 cups*	$ 340–375

"Museum"

This pattern reportedly features the first modern, free-form shape used on American china. It was designed for Castleton by Eva Zeisel, and created under the auspices of the Museum of Modern Art in New York City. It was made by special order, and was entirely handmade. Prices listed below are for all-white pieces.

Bowl, *cream soup with saucer*	$ 70–85
Bowl, *vegetable, round, 8^{1}/$_{2}$-inch diameter*	$ 110–125
Bowl, *vegetable, round, 9-inch diameter*	$ 110–125
Cake stand with metal pedestal	$ 70–85
Creamer	$ 90–110
Cup and saucer	$ 38–45
Gravy boat with attached underliner	$ 170–185
Plate, *bread and butter, 6^{1}/$_{4}$ inches*	$ 18–22
Plate, *dinner, 10^{1}/$_{2}$-inch diameter*	$ 50–65
Plate, *salad, 8 inches*	$ 30– 40
Plate, *serving, with central handle*	$ 65–75
Platter, *oval, 14^{3}/$_{4}$ inches*	$ 190–225
Tray, *serving, three-tier*	$ 120–140

"Venetian"

This pattern features an exotic bird with long tail feathers flying above a grouping of flowers. There is a gold ring around the verge, and scattered flowers around the rim of the flatware.

Bowl, *cream soup with saucer*	$ 50–65
Bowl, *individual fruit, 5¹/₂-inch diameter*	$ 22–28
Bowl, *vegetable, oval, 11 inches*	$ 125–150
Bowl, *vegetable, round, covered*	$ 300–350
Creamer	$ 70–85
Cup and saucer, *coffee or tea*	$ 42–55
Cup and saucer, *demitasse*	$ 26–32
Gravy boat with attached underliner	$ 140–160
Plate, *dinner, 10³/₄-inches in diameter*	$ 37–45
Plate, *luncheon, 9-inch diameter*	$ 26–32
Plate, *salad, 8¹/₂-inch diameter*	$ 12–16
Plate, *serving, with central handle*	$ 55–65
Platter, *oval, 13 inches*	$ 135–150
Platter, *oval, 18¹/₂ inches*	$ 240–260
Sugar bowl and lid	$ 75–90
Tray, *serving, two-tier*	$ 80–95
Tray, *serving, three-tier*	$ 95–110

CATALINA ISLAND POTTERY

One of the marks found on pieces made by the *Catalina Island Pottery.*

In the 1920s, William Wrigley, Jr., of chewing-gum fame, was very much involved with the development of Catalina Island, which is located off the coast of Southern California. Wrigley actually owned the island, and he wanted to provide year-round jobs for the residents, as well as clay building products for a tourist attraction he was building at Avalon. To do this, he established the Clay Products Division of the Catalina Island Company to make roofing and patio tiles and bricks from the clay found on the island. This worked very well, and in 1930 dinnerware was added to the company's output. The dinnerware produced was arguably the first solid-color dinnerware made in America. It was called "Rancho" ware, and is priced in the "Gladding, McBean & Company" section of this book.

Art pottery was added to the company's repertoire in 1931, and continued to be made until 1937. Success was the undoing of Catalina Island pottery, however, because as production increased, clay had to be imported from the mainland. This was simply too expensive, and the operation was sold to Gladding, McBean & Company. Along with everything else, Gladding, McBean bought the right to use the Catalina name for ten years, and for a time produced items similar to those made on the island, although all production had been moved to the mainland.

Marks on pieces produced before the company was sold to Gladding, McBean tend to include the words "Catalina" or "Catalina Island." Pieces produced after the company's sale are ink-stamped, which they never were originally, and usually read "Catalina Pottery." Collectors generally prefer items produced during the pre-Gladding, McBean era of the company's history.

Ashtray, *shape of cowboy hat, common colors*	$ 175–200
Ashtray, *shape of cowboy hat, uncommon colors*	$ 375–425
Ashtray, *shape of starfish, 5 inches, white*	$ 225–250
Ashtray caddy, *round container holding four small ashtrays, raised Art Deco-style flowers, yellow glaze*	$ 425–475
Bookends, *frog, green glaze, 4 inches by 4 inches*	$ 2,250–2,400
Bookends, *monk, blue glaze*	$ 1,200–1,300
Bowl, *cactus, red-orange glaze*	$ 125–175
Bowl, *shell-shaped, 9 inches, pink glaze*	$ 125–175
Box in the form of a treasure chest, *blue glaze*	$ 2,250–2,400
Candleholder, *in form of cactus ear, raised thorns, 6$^{1}/_2$ inches tall, green glaze, pair*	$ 1,800–2,000
Chamberstick, *handled, 4-inch diameter*	$ 150–175
Coaster, *native bird, painted, 4-inch diameter, yellow ground*	$ 125–150
Flower frog, *crane, white, 7 inches tall*	$ 650–700
Flower frog, *pelican, green, 5$^{1}/_2$ inches tall*	$ 700–750
Flower frog, *plain, four-legged, 8-inch diameter, yellow glaze*	$ 200–225
Lamp base, *raised "Fishnet" or "Rope" pattern, green glaze*	$ 1,750–1,850
Lamp base, *two "elephant trunk" handles, seafoam glaze*	$ 2,800–3,000
Lamp base in form of kerosene lamp, *tall chimney, red glaze*	$ 500–550
Planter, *39 inches tall*	$ 175–200
Planter, *in the shape of a nautilus shell, yellow glaze*	$ 750–800
Plate, *"Arches of Mission, San Juan Capistrano," 10-inch diameter, artist-signed*	$ 650–700
Plate, *sailboat and seagull, painted, 10-inch diameter, artist-signed*	$ 1,000–1,100
Plate, *wall, seahorses, blue ground, 12$^{1}/_2$-inch diameter*	$ 1,000–1,100

Plate, *"Undersea Garden," colorful fish swimming among plants, blue ground, 13-inch diameter*	$ 1,200–1,400
Salt and pepper shakers, *señor and señorita*	$ 275–300
Tile, *red-brick clay, relief image of pelican, 5¹/₂-inch square*	$ 225–250
Urn, *cigarette, in form of bear, brown glaze*	$ 750–800
Vase, *Chinese-style handles, blue*	$ 125–150
Vase, *cornucopia, 5 inches, green glaze*	$ 450–500
Vase, *fan, 9 inches tall, red glaze*	$ 375–400
Vase, *globular with raised collar neck, 13 inches tall, solid green glaze*	$ 525–575
Vase, *raised floral design (blossom, stem, and leaves), 13 inches, two handles, solid-color glaze*	$ 1,200–1,400

CERAMIC ARTS STUDIO

When World War II cut off the supply of Japanese ceramic giftware to the United States, American manufacturers attempted to fill the gap. The Ceramic Arts Studio of Madison, Wisconsin, had been founded sometime prior to 1940 to make flowerpots and vases, but in 1941 its emphasis shifted to production of the kinds of novelty items and figures that previously had been supplied in great numbers by the Japanese. Some of the best examples of these pieces were modeled by Betty Harrington, but the company also employed other designers, such as Ulli Rebus and Ruth Planter. The factory stopped production in 1955, but the owner, Ruben Sand, took some of the molds and began producing a line of items that was much the same as the earlier line. Production lasted for only a short time, however, until the pieces previously made in the United States were discontinued and new designs were created.

Pieces made in Japan are often marked "Ceramic Arts Studio" in either red or blue, but the location "Madison, Wisconsin" is omitted from these marks. Unfortunately, many of the pieces made by the Ceramic Arts Studio in the United States were never marked. When such pieces are marked, however, the marks will include the location, and will never be in blue or red.

This company is not to be confused with the Ceramic Art Company, which is discussed in the section of this book entitled "Lenox, Inc. and the Ceramic Art Company."

Animal Figures

Bird, *Bird of Paradise*	$ 225–250
Bird, *Canary, left, shelf sitter*	$ 100–125
Bird, *Canary, right, shelf sitter*	$ 100–125
Bird, *Parrot, "Pete," shelf sitter, 7¹/₂ inches*	$ 130–140
Bird, *Parrot, "Polly," shelf sitter, 7¹/₂ inches*	$ 130–140
Bird, *Swan, black, large*	$ 225–250
Bird, *Swan, small, black or white*	$ 150–175
Cat, *ancient*	$ 125–150
Cat, *Kitten, ancient*	$ 110–125
Cat, *Calico, 3 inches, #A34*	$ 65–75
Cat, *with bow, sitting, "Bright Eyes," 3 inches*	$ 75–90
Cat, *Persian, shelf sitter, mother, "Fluffy," #109*	$ 125–150
Cat, *Persian, shelf sitter, father, "Tuffy," #208*	$ 125–150
Deer, *Doe, stylized, 3³/₄ inches*	$ 135–160
Deer, *Fawn, stylized, 2 inches*	$ 110–125
Donkey, *"Daisy," beflowered, 4³/₄ inches, #189*	$ 165–185
Donkey, *"Dem," 4¹/₂ inches*	$ 145–165
Dog, *Boxer, "Billy," 2 inches, #A90*	$ 100–125
Dog, *Boxer, "Butch," 3 inches, #A89*	$ 100–125
Dog, *Cocker Spaniel, "Honey," 5³/₄ inches*	$ 235–250
Dog, *Cocker Spaniel, "Sonny," 5³/₄ inches*	$ 235–250
Dog, *Collie, mother, shelf sitter, 5 inches, #152*	$ 100–125
Dog, *Collie, modern, stylized*	$ 600–650
Dog, *Gingham, 2³/₄ inches, #A35*	$ 65–75
Dog, *Pekingese, sitting up, 3¹/₂ inches, #207*	$ 110–125
Dog, *Poodle, "Fifi," 3 inches, #A55*	$ 95–110
Dog, *Scotties, two puppies, one piece*	$ 150–175

Donkey, *"Daisy"*	$ 125–150
Duck, *mother*	$ 80–100
Elephant, *"Annie," mother, trunk up, 3³/₄ inches, #141*	$ 100–125
Elephant, *"Benny," baby, trunk up, 3¹/₄ inches, #142*	$ 100–125
Elephant, *"Elsie"*	$ 125–150
Elephant, *"Tembo," tusked with raised trunk*	$ 275–300
Elephant, *"Tembino," baby elephant*	$ 225–250
Fish, *"Swirl," straight-tail, on stomach, 3 inches*	$ 90–110
Fish, *"Swish," twist-tail, on stomach, 2¹/₂ inches*	$ 90–110
Giraffe, *mother, 6¹/₂ inches, #324*	$ 125–150
Giraffe, *young, 5¹/₂ inches, #325*	$ 125–150
Goat, *"Ralph the Goat," with flower*	$ 275–300
Goat, *"Ralph the Goat," without flower*	$ 125–150
Horse, *"Balky," colt, 3³/₄ inches, #293*	$ 150–175
Horse, *"Frisky," colt, 3³/₄ inches, #292*	$ 150–175
Horse, *"Lightning," fighting stallion, #377*	$ 200–225
Horse, *"Thunder," fighting stallion, #378*	$ 200–225
Horse, *"Toby"*	$ 110–125
Jaguar, *stylized, 5 inches*	$ 200–250
Lamb, *with garlands on head and around two ankles*	$ 250–300
Leopard, *fighting, small size, 3¹/₂ inches, #357*	$ 150–175
Leopard, *fighting, small size, 6¹/₄ inches, #358*	$ 150–175
Leopard, *fighting, large size, 6 inches*	$ 550–600
Leopard, *fighting, large size, 8¹/₂ inches tall*	$ 550–600
Lion, *with small crown on head*	$ 425–475
Monkey, *Mr. or Mrs., each*	$ 150–175
Monkey, *baby*	$ 150–175
Rabbit, *mother, running*	$ 50–60
Rabbit, *baby, running, 2¹/₄ inches*	$ 50–60
Rabbit, *Peter*	$ 125–145
Skunk, *Mr. or Mrs., each*	$ 75–95

Skunk, *baby*	$ 50–60
Squirrel, *"Miss Squeaky," with necklace, 3$^{1}/_{4}$ inches, #144*	$ 100–120
Squirrel, *"Saucy," wearing a jacket*	$ 210–230
Squirrel, *"Saucy," not wearing a jacket*	$ 350–400
Squirrel, *wearing jacket, 2$^{1}/_{4}$ inches, #278*	$ 125–145
Tortoise, *crawling, in top hat*	$ 200–225
Tortoise, *carrying a cane*	$ 150–175
Zebra, *black and white, 5 inches, #338*	$ 425–475
Zebra, *unusual color scheme*	$ 475–525

Childhood Favorites

Alice in Wonderland	$ 225–250
Boy Doll	$ 1,600–1,700
Cinderella	$ 50–60
Hansel and Gretel, *one piece*	$ 175–200
Jack and Jill, *shelf sitters, each*	$ 75–90
Lady Doll	$ 1,600–1,700
Little Black Sambo	$ 400–425
Little Black Sambo, *umbrella, 3$^{1}/_{2}$ inches*	$ 400–425
Little Bo Peep	$ 50–60
Little Boy Blue	$ 50–60
Little Jack Horner, *shelf sitter*	$ 85–100
Little Jack Horner	$ 110–125
Little Lamb (from "Mary Had a Little Lamb")	$ 70–85
Little Miss Muffet	$ 85–100
March Hare (from *Alice in Wonderland*)	$ 300–325
Mary (from "Mary Had a Little Lamb")	$ 55–65
Mary Quite Contrary	$ 200–225
Paul Bunyan	$ 175–200
Peter Pan or Wendy, *on leaf base, 5$^{1}/_{4}$ inches each*	$ 150–175
Pied Piper, *6$^{1}/_{4}$ inches*	$ 250–275

Pixie, *"Toadstool Pixie"*	$ 60–70
Pixie, *"Riding Pixie"*	$ 60–70
Pixie, *"Peek-a-boo Pixie"*	$ 60–70
Prince Charming	$ 50–60
Santa Claus, *2¹/₄ inches*	$ 150–175
Tiger (from "Little Black Sambo")	$ 350–375
Wendy, *on leaf base, 5¹/₄ inches, #214*	$ 150–175

St. George Group

Archibald the Dragon, *8 inches, #369*	$ 450–475
Charger	$ 550–575
Lady Rowena on charger	$ 350–375
St. George on charger, *8¹/₂ inches, #370*	$ 350–375

Couples and Trios

Bedtime Boy and Girl, each	$ 100–120
Belles (woman with bell inside skirt), *"Summer Belle"*	$ 125–150
Belles (woman with bell inside skirt), *"Winter Belle"*	$ 100–120
Belles (woman with bell inside skirt), *"Lillibelle"*	$ 100–120
Bride and Groom, *each*	$ 175–200
Colonial Boy	$ 145–165
Colonial Girl	$ 145–165
Colonial Man	$ 90–110
Colonial Woman	$ 90–110
Cowboy	$ 175–200
Cowgirl	$ 175–200
Cupid, *standing with wings, black*	$ 600–650
Cupid, *standing with wings, flesh tones*	$ 350–375
Cupids, *sleeping and praying angels, flowered base*	$ 275–300
Farmer Boy	$ 60–75
Farmer Girl	$ 60–75

Fireman	$ 300–325
Firewoman	$ 300–325
Gay '90s Man, *"Harry"*	$ 65–75
Gay '90s Woman, *"Lillibeth"*	$ 65–75
Hunter, *"Al" and his English Setter, "Kirby"*	$ 225–250
Hunter's dog, *English Setter, "Kirby"*	$ 200–225
Mermaid, *sitting on a rock*	$ 200–225
Mermaid, *sitting baby*	$ 225–250
Mermaid, *diving baby*	$ 200–225
19th-Century Man, *in a cape*	$ 350–375
19th-Century Woman, *carrying a parasol*	$ 350–375
Pioneer Sam, *with pig and sack of grain*	$ 60–75
Pioneer Susie, *wearing apron, holding broom*	$ 60–75
Promenade Couple, *male*	$ 175–200
Promenade Couple, *female*	$ 175–200
Shepherd	$ 125–150
Shepherdess	$ 125–150
Southern gentleman, *"Colonel Jackson"*	$ 65–75
Southern lady, *"Miss Lucindy"*	$ 65–75
Square Dance Boy	$ 150–175
Square Dance Girl	$ 150–175
Water Man	$ 225–250
Water Woman	$ 225–250

Couples—Foreign Nationalities

Balinese Dancer, *Male*	$ 150–175
Balinese Dancer, *Female*	$ 150–175
Burmese Lady, *white bisque*	$ 175–200
Burmese Man, *white bisque*	$ 175–200
Burmese Lady, *fully colored costume*	$ 225–250
Burmese Man, *fully colored costume*	$ 225–250

Chinese Boy, *on bamboo planter*	$ 45–55
Chinese Girl, *on bamboo planter*	$ 45–55
Chinese Boy, *"Sun-Li," shelf sitter, 5¹/₂ inches, #294*	$ 60–75
Chinese Girl, *"Su-Lin," shelf sitter, 5¹/₂ inches, #295*	$ 60–75
Chinese Boy, *"Smi-Li," 6 inches, #296*	$ 75–90
Chinese Girl, *"Mo-Pi," 6 inches, #297*	$ 75–90
Chinese Musician, *"Lu-Tang" (male), on bamboo vase*	$ 60–75
Chinese Musician, *"Wing-Sang" (female), on bamboo vase*	$ 60–75
Chinese Musician, *"Lu-Tang" (male), without bamboo vase*	$ 70–85
Chinese Musician, *"Wing-Sang" (female), without bamboo vase*	$ 70–85
Cuban Girl, *"Carmelita"*	$ 175–200
Cuban Woman, *"Carmen"*	$ 250–275
Dutch Boy, *dancing, arms out, foot up, "Hans," 5¹/₂ inches, #167*	$ 275–300
Dutch Girl, *dancing, arms out, foot up, "Katrina," 5¹/₄ inches, #168*	$ 275–300
Dutch Boy, *kissing*	$ 80–95
Dutch Girl, *kissing*	$ 80–95
Egyptian Man, *9¹/₂ inches*	$ 850–900
Egyptian Woman, *9¹/₂ inches*	$ 850–900
Gypsy Man, *6¹/₂ inches, with violin, #258*	$ 110–125
Gypsy Woman, *6¹/₂ inches*	$ 110–125
Kabuki Man, *Japanese*	$ 1,200–1,400
Kabuki Woman, *Japanese*	$ 1,000–1,200
Pan-American Boy, *"Poncho"*	$ 125–150
Pan-American Girl, *"Pepita"*	$ 90–110
Russian Boy, *"Petrov"*	$ 90–110
Russian Girl, *"Petrushka"*	$ 90–110
Swedish Man and Lady, *each*	$ 125–150
Wee Chinese Boy, *3 inches, #A11*	$ 40–50
Wee Chinese Girl, *3 inches, #A12*	$ 40–50

Zulu Man, *5¹/₂ inches*	$ 325–350
Zulu Woman, *5¹/₂ inches*	$ 325–350

Head Vases

African man	$ 185–200
African woman	$ 185–200
Barbie, *in bonnet*	$ 200–225
Becky, *pigtails*	$ 175–200
Bonnie, *with high collar*	$ 200–225
Lotus, *Asian woman*	$ 150–175
Manchu, *Asian man*	$ 150–175
Mei Ling, *Chinese woman*	$ 225–250
Svea, *Swedish girl*	$ 250–275
Sven, *Swedish boy*	$ 250–275
Tony the Barber	$ 150–175

Performing-Themed Figures

The All-Children's Orchestra

Accordion Boy	$ 200–225
Banjo Girl	$ 175–200
Bass Viol Boy	$ 150–175
Drum Girl	$ 200–225
Drum Girl, *bank*	$ 275–300
Flute Girl	$ 175–200
Guitar Boy	$ 175–200
Harmonica Boy	$ 150–175
Saxophone Boy	$ 175–200

The Adult Orchestra

Accordion Lady	$ 700–750
Cellist Man	$ 700–750
Flute Lady	$ 700–750

French Horn Man	$ 700–750
Guitar Man	$ 700–750
Violin Lady	$ 700–750

Ballerina Quartet

Daisy	$ 325–350
Pansy	$ 350–375
Rose	$ 325–350
Violet	$ 275–300

Miscellaneous Performers

Ballerina, *sitting, adult*	$ 575–600
Ballerina, *en pose*	$ 225–250
Ballerina, *stretching*	$ 450–475
Ballet dancers, *Greg and Grace, shelf sitters, each*	$ 90–100
Comedy and Tragedy, *one black gown, other white, each*	$ 125–145
Comedy and Tragedy, *more angular than above, highly decorated gowns, 1980s, each*	$ 275–300
Commedia dell'Arte figure, *Columbine*	$ 1,000–1,100
Commedia dell'Arte figure, *Harlequin*	$ 1,000–1,100
Dance Moderne, *couple, each*	$ 125–150
Dancer, *Beth*	$ 65–75
Dancer, *Bruce*	$ 65–75
Dancer, *Adonis, clothed*	$ 350–375
Dancer, *Aphrodite, clothed*	$ 350–375
Dancer, *Macabre Dance Man, similar to Adonis except unclothed*	$ 1,200–1,300
Dancer, *Macabre Dance Woman, similar to Aphrodite except unclothed*	$ 1,200–1,300
Dancer, *robed, nude underneath*	$ 1,850–2,000
King's Jester, *flutist*	$ 250–275
King's Jester, *lutist*	$ 250–275
Pierrot and Pierette, *each*	$ 125–150

| Rumba dancers, *man and woman, each* | $ 75–90 |
| Temple dancers, *Asian, man and woman, each* | $ 600–650 |

Plaques and Wall Pockets

Arabesque, *ballerina*	$ 65–75
Attitude, *ballerina*	$ 65–75
Chinese Lantern Man and Woman, *in white, each piece*	$ 85–95
Chinese Lantern Man and Woman, *in color, each piece*	$ 145–165
Cockatoo, *each*	$ 125–135
Dancers, *ballet, Greg and Grace, each*	$ 50–60
Dancers, *Zor and Zorina, each*	$ 125–135
Deer, *stylized, on leaf background*	$ 1,400–1,500
Dutch Boy and Girl, *will hold hands, each*	$ 90–100
Fish	$ 550–600
Harlequin and Columbine, *each*	$ 85–95
Lotus, *Asian head, wall pocket, female*	$ 275–300
Manchu, *Asian head, wall pocket, male*	$ 275–300
Masks, *comedy and tragedy, each*	$ 125–135
Masquerade Man and Woman, *pair*	$ 2,500–2,600
Mermaid	$ 475–500
Neptune, *trident and tail*	$ 475–500
Sprite, *mermaid, holding fish down*	$ 425–475
Sprite, *mermaid, holding fish up*	$ 425–475
Zulu Man and Woman, *each*	$ 950–1,000

Religious Figures

Angel, *in the clouds, candleholders, each*	$ 125–135
Angels, *shelf sitters, "Sleeping," "Praying," each*	$ 175–200
Devil Imp, *"Gleeful Imp," sitting and smiling*	$ 600–650
Devil Imp, *"Happy Imp," reclining and smiling*	$ 600–650
Devil Imp, *"Sad Imp," standing and frowning*	$ 600–650

Isaac *(paired with Rebekah, listed below)*	$ 125–135
Madonna, *in white*	$ 750–800
Madonna, *in color*	$ 550–600
Madonna and child	$ 250–275
Madonna with bible	$ 400–450
Our Lady of Fatima	$ 325–375
Rebekah (paired with Isaac, *above*)	$ 125–135
Salome, *with John the Baptist's head on a platter*	$ 2,250–2,500
St. Agnes, *holding lamb*	$ 300–325
St. Francis, *birds on outstretched arms*	$ 250–275
St. Francis, *bird in crook of arm*	$ 225–250
St. Francis, *bird in crook of arm, with birdbath*	$ 300–350

Sets

Babies, *"Wally," "Willy," "Winney," or "Woody," each*	$ 275–300
Babies, *brown, "Berty," "Betty," "Billy," or "Bobby," each*	$ 300–325

Balinese Dance Suite

Bali Boy	$ 275–300
Bali Girl	$ 275–300
Bali-Gong	$ 165–185
Bali-Hai	$ 125–135
Bali-Kris	$ 165–185
Bali-Lao	$ 125–135

Four Seasons

Autumn Andy	$ 200–225
Spring Sue	$ 175–200
Summer Sally	$ 150–175
Winter Willie	$ 125–135

Harem Group

Harem girl, *sitting*	$ 150–175
Harem girl, *reclining*	$ 150–175
Sultan on pillow	$ 175–200

Snugglers/Lap Sitters

Two figures that fit together are called "snugglers." The first of these was "Mother Bear and Baby," which was first made in 1951. Snugglers often come in the form of salt-and-pepper sets.

Clown and Dog, *clown*	$ 110–125
Clown and Dog, *dog*	$ 125–135
Cow and Calf, *brown tones, each piece*	$ 90–100
Cow and Calf, *purple tones, each piece*	$ 175–200
Kangaroo Baby	$ 110–125
Kangaroo Mother	$ 95–110
Monkey and Baby, *each piece*	$ 40–50
Mother Bear and Baby, *each piece*	$ 35–45
Mouse and Cheese, *each piece*	$ 20–30
Native Boy on Crocodile, *boy*	$ 200–225
Native Boy on Crocodile, *crocodile*	$ 100–120
Sabu and Elephant, *elephant*	$ 85–100
Sabu and Elephant, *Sabu*	$ 175–200
Sea Horse and Coral, *each piece*	$ 80–95

Miscellany and Nonfigural

Ballerina, *ewer, relief decoration*	$ 100–110
Bank, *Paisley Pig*	$ 425–450
Bowl, *"Space Bowl," 1950s, modernistic*	$ 200–225
Buddha, *teapot/pitcher, relief decoration*	$ 160–175
Ewer, *with Statue-of-Liberty-type figure: "Miss Forward" (based on figure from Wisconsin State Capitol Building), elaborate handle, relief decoration*	$ 300–325

Fox and Hounds, *tankard, figural fox handle, relief decoration*	$ 350–375
George Washington, *pitcher, relief decoration*	$ 110–125
Hippo, *ashtray*	$ 135–150
Horse Head, *gravy boat, relief decoration*	$ 110–125
Lamp, *St. George and Lady Rowena, castle*	$ 850–900
Mug, *barbershop quartet*	$ 850–900
Mug, *devil's head*	$ 1,000–1,100
Mug, *Toby, seated man with mug*	$ 110–125
Pitcher, *pine cone*	$ 100–110
Vase, *conical bud, spiral*	$ 425–450
Vase, *mermaid and fish*	$ 1,200–1,300
Vase, *raised relief, Chinese-style decoration*	$ 100–120
Vase, *"Rooster/Hen," cubistic modern design*	$ 1,200–1,300

CLEWELL METAL ART

Mark found on *Clewell* vase pictured in photograph below.
Courtesy of Richard Hatch and Associates, Hendersonville, North Carolina.

One of the marks found on *Clewell* pottery.

While on a visit to the Wadsworth Athenaeum in Hartford, Connecticut, Charles Walter Clewell of Canton, Ohio, happened to see a small Roman bronze jug that had developed a beautiful variegated patina of blues with accents of green, brown, and black. After much experimentation, Clewell learned how to deposit a metal skin on a ceramic body, and a process by which he could chemically induce a patina similar to one he had seen on the ancient jug. Clewell was not a potter *per se,* and he bought undecorated bodies from such companies as Roseville, Weller, and Knowles, Taylor & Knowles. He then coated these pieces with copper, bronze, or silver, patinated them, and offered them for sale to the public as art pottery. Clewell Metal Art was essentially a one-man operation, and Clewell worked from 1906 to about 1955. He died in 1965.

Basket, *5 inches tall, embossed squiggly lines around top with arrowhead drop pendant, brown patina*	$ 700–800
Bowl, *covered, 6½-inch diameter, good variegated patina, green and brown*	$ 1,600–1,800
Mug, *4³/8 inches tall, riveted side*	$ 145–175
Vase, *4 inches tall, globular form with red, green, and brown patina*	$ 850–1,000

Clewell vase, good patina, 5¾ inches tall, dated 1931, $1,000–$1,200.
Item courtesy of Richard Hatch and Associates, Hendersonville, North Carolina.

Vase, *7 inches tall, bulbous globular shape with foot, good patina* $ 1,100–1,250

Vase, *12 inches tall, bulbous form with elaborately embossed grapes and vines* $ 1,600–2,000

CONTINENTAL KILNS

Continental Kilns was founded in Chester, West Virginia, in 1944 by owners with high ambitions who planned to produce a Belleeklike bone china that would be finely crafted and hand-painted. There is no evidence that such a product was ever made, and all of the company's products that have been found are semiporcelain with hand-painted decoration. Continental Kilns closed in 1957.

"Square"

This is the most common type of piece made by Continental Kilns. Pieces in this line have a squared or oblong shape with a notch in each corner. They are usually decorated with designs that suggest tropical themes. Examples of such designs include "Bali-Hai" (large red flower with green leaves on a gray ground), "Tahiti" (brown and green palm trees on a chartreuse ground), and "Woodleaf" (green leaves with brown stems on a white background). Most of these patterns originated around 1952. Of these, "Woodleaf" is generally the least expensive, with "Bali-Hai" and "Tahiti" pieces generally being priced about 30 percent higher. Prices quoted are for "Woodleaf" pieces.

Bowl, *individual fruit*	$ 9–11
Bowl, *soup, 7¹/₄ inches*	$ 14–16

Butter, *¹/₄-pound*	$ 37–40
Cup and saucer	$ 18–20
Gravy boat with attached underliner	$ 47–50
Plate, *bread and butter, 6³/₄-inch diameter*	$ 4–6
Plate, *dinner, 10-inch diameter*	$ 14–16
Plate, *salad, 8¹/₂-inch diameter*	$ 8–10
Platter, *oval, 11¹/₂ inches*	$ 25–28
Shakers, *salt and pepper, set*	$ 24–26
Sugar bowl and lid	$ 24–26
Tumbler, *tall, 4¹/₄ inches*	$ 15–18

COWAN POTTERY

Typical mark found on most *Cowan* pottery.

The mark of the *Cowan Pottery*, as seen on a strawberry jar. *Courtesy of Tony McCormack, Sarasota, Florida.*

R. Guy Cowan was born to a family of potters in East Liverpool, Ohio, in 1884. He was trained as a potter from an early age, and then studied at the prestigious New York State School of Claywork at Alfred University. For a while after that, Cowan taught in Cleveland, Ohio, and established a reputation as an artist on the rise.

In 1913, with the sponsorship of the Cleveland Chamber of Commerce, Cowan established a small pottery where he worked making tiles and art pottery. His first wares had red-clay bodies, and Cowan worked to perfect glazes that would cover and conceal this material effectively. World War I interrupted Cowan's rising career, but in 1919 he returned to Cleveland and went back to work at his old facilities.

In 1920, when his old facilities became inadequate, Cowan opened up a new pottery in Rocky River, Ohio, and changed the material he used to craft his pottery from red clay to a white porcelain made from English clay. The next year, Cowan began producing commercial art wares that could be produced in large quantities and sold at an affordable price. Individually made pieces were largely a thing of the past, but Cowan believed that well-designed molded pieces had a certain amount of validity as art and did not necessarily compromise his aesthetic integrity.

Some of the most important figures in early 20th-century American ceramics designed pieces for Cowan, including Waylande Gregory, who modeled figures for Cowan, Victor Schreckengost, Arthur Baggs (see the section in this book on Marblehead pottery), Thelma Frazier Winter, and Paul Bogatay. Collectors are most interested in Cowan's sculptural pieces such as "Russian Dancers," art pieces made in small editions, and artistic pieces that are very Art Deco in design.

Cowan's commercial wares and the wares he made for florists (called "Lakeware") are abundant, and are of less interest to serious collectors of Cowan pottery. During the late 1920s, Cowan was doing well and had plans to expand, but the stock market crash of 1929 and the ensuing Great Depression caused him to close his pottery in the latter part of 1931.

Rare Cowan colors and glazes such as "Feu Rouge" (a glossy red), Black (gunmetal), Flambé (drip glaze), or Crystalline may cause the prices listed below to rise considerably, while examples of Cowan pottery with common glazes will be at the lower end of the price range.

Figural Items

Bookends, *doves, 4³/₄ inches, pair*	$ 500–650
Bookends, *elephants, 7¹/₄ inches, pair, #E-2*	$ 2,250–2,500
Bookends, *rams, 7¹/₂ inches, pair, #E-3*	$ 2,750–3,000
Bookends, *unicorns, 7 inches, pair, #961*	$ 1,100–1,200
Burlesque Dancer, *17³/₄ inches, limited edition*	$ 3,500–4,000
Candelabra, *"Dawn," three nude figures, 10 inches*	$ 1,200–1,500
Candlestick, *Byzantine angels flanking a central figure, 9 inches*	$ 300–400
Candlestick, *nude with drape, two candle cups, ivory glaze, 8 inches, #745*	$ 1,250–1,400
Candlestick, *seminude, standing in front of branches, 12¹/₂ inches, #744-R*	$ 1,100–1,250
Dancer, *Russian peasant, 11 inches*	$ 1,200–1,400
Dancer, *Spanish, female, white glaze, #793*	$ 950–1,100
Dancer, *Spanish, male, white glaze, #793*	$ 950–1,000
Decanter, *"Queen of Hearts," black and gold, 10¹/₂ inches, #E-5*	$ 750–950
Europa, *nude with drape, Oriental Red, 15¹/₂ inches*	$ 3,000–3,250
Flower frog, *scarf dancer, ivory, 7 inches, #686*	$ 400–500

Unusual Cowan Pottery strawberry jar, 11⅛ inches, $495–$525.

Flower frog, *Pan on a toadstool, 9 inches, #F-9*	$ 850–950
Heron, *13¼ inches tall, #D-7*	$ 900–1,000
Persephone, *nude figure with drape, ivory, 15 inches, #D-16*	$ 3,700–4,000
Pierette, *8¼ inches, ivory, #792*	$ 700–850
Pierrot, *8¼ inches, ivory, #791*	$ 700–850
Russian Peasant, *balalaika player, 11½ inches, #52*	$ 1,100–1,200
Russian Peasant, *tambourine player, 9 inches, #757–760*	$ 1,100–1,200
Three Marys, *three figures of the Virgin Mary, ivory*	$ 325–450
Torso, *17½ inches*	$ 2,200–2,500

Nonfigural Pieces

Bowl, *ribbed, black exterior, yellow interior, 10-inch diameter, #845-A*	$ 145–175
Bowl, *"Jazz," 11⅜ inches high by 16½ inches in diameter, limited edition, turquoise and black, circa 1931*	$65,000–75,000

Bowl, *punch, "Jazz," 9 inches high by 16³/₄ inches in diameter, turquoise and black*	$ 18,000–20,000
Centerpiece with pierced lid as flower frog, *bowl is fluted, 10 inches, shades of green, #B-17*	$ 225–275
Compote, *seahorse, 6 inches, ivory and green, #724*	$ 80–100
Jar, *ginger, with lid, drip glaze, black and orange, 12 inches*	$ 2,000–2,500
Jar, *strawberry, with saucer, green, 11¹/₂ inches, #SJ-3*	$ 300–400
Plate, *"The Hunt," 11¹/₄-inch diameter, raised decoration of horses, hunters, dogs, green, #X-44*	$ 900–1,000
Plate, *decorated with representations of sea life, designed by Thelma Frazier Winter, shades of blue, 11¹/₂-inch diameter*	$ 1,200–1,600
Urn, *covered, neoclassical ram's head, two handles, turquoise, 13¹/₄ inches, #V-88*	$ 225–275
Vase, *"Artichoke," limited edition, 12¹/₄ inches, #V-100*	$ 1,800–2,000
Vase, *drop glaze, black and orange, handled, 7 inches, #652-A*	$ 110–150
Vase, *"Lakeware," blue, 5¹/₂ inches, #V-72*	$ 100–125
Vase, *"Logan," handled, floral detail, speckled glaze, 8¹/₂ inches, #649-B*	$ 175–225
Vase, *"Logan," handled, floral detail, Lakespur Blue, 8¹/₂ inches, #649-B*	$ 125–150
Vase, *ribbed, 11¹/₂ inches tall, ivory, #V-97*	$ 200–250
Vase, *fan, seahorse, 6 inches, #715-X*	$ 75–100

COXON BELLEEK POTTERY

The *Coxon* "Belleek" mark.

In 1926, Frederick Coxon established the Coxon Pottery Company in Wooster, Ohio, to compete with the Lenox Company. Ironically, Frederick's father, Jonathan Coxon, had founded the Ceramic Art Company with Walter Lenox in 1889, and it was this company that evolved into Lenox, Inc.

Primarily, Coxon Belleek made high-quality porcelain dinnerware that was decorated with decals instead of hand-painting, but was enhanced with some handwork and rich gold accents. Coxon Belleek was sold as upper-end ware, and many upscale brides during the late 1920s chose Coxon Belleek dinnerware as their wedding china. Unfortunately, the stock market crash of 1929 and the ensuing Great Depression caused Coxon Belleek to close in 1930 after just four years of production.

"Boulevard"

This pattern features a blue border with a cluster of yellow, blue, and rust flowers in the center, and a band containing similar flowers around the verge.

Bowl, *cream soup, and saucer*	$ 60–70
Bowl, *individual fruit, 6-inch diameter*	$ 24–28

Coxon Belleek table setting, three pieces: dinner plate,
$50–$60; bread and butter plate, $25–$30; and regular
cup and saucer, $75–$85.
Item courtesy of Richard Crane, Knoxville, Tennessee.

Bowl, *soup, 8¹/₂-inch diameter*	$ 32–40
Bowl, *vegetable, round, covered*	$ 250–275
Coffeepot	$ 250–275
Creamer	$ 75–85
Cup and saucer	$ 60–70
Plate, *bread and butter, 6³/₄-inch diameter*	$ 20–25
Plate, dinner, *10¹/₂-inch diameter*	$ 42–52
Plate, salad, *7¹/₄-inch diameter*	$ 25–32
Platter, *oval, 13 inches*	$ 130–145
Sugar bowl	$ 100–120

"Floral Bouquet" (also called "Bouquet")

Pieces bearing this very-famous Coxon pattern are decorated with clusters of flowers around the rim and a large cluster in the center. The rim and verge are accented
with a heavy band of gold.

Bowl, *cream soup, with saucer*	$ 75–85
Bowl, *individual fruit, 6-inch diameter*	$ 32–36
Bowl, *vegetable, oval, 9^1/$_2$ inches*	$ 135–150
Bowl, *vegetable, oval, 10 inches*	$ 150–165
Cup and saucer	$ 75–85
Cup and saucer, *demitasse*	$ 55–65
Gravy boat, *faststand*	$ 225–250
Plate, *bread and butter, 6-inch diameter*	$ 25–30
Plate, *cake-serving, square, handled*	$ 150–165
Plate, *dinner, 10^1/$_2$-inch diameter*	$ 50–60
Plate, *luncheon, 9-inch diameter*	$ 35–42
Plate, *salad, 7^1/$_2$-inch diameter*	$ 32–36
Platter, *oval, 15 inches*	$ 200–220
Relish, *8^1/$_4$ inches*	$ 60–70

CROOKSVILLE CHINA COMPANY

One of the marks used by the *Crooksville China Company.*

When the Crooksville China Company opened for business in Crooksville, Ohio, in 1902, it had 125 employees. When it went out of business in 1959, it had 300 employees. Crooksville specialized in making a very good grade of semiporcelain earthenware that, at its best, appears to be vitrified porcelain. The company's finest, thinnest dinnerware products were often marked "Stinthal China," with no overt mention of Crooksville except for the initials "C. C. Co," which sometimes appear below the mark. Crooksville is known for its fine decaled decorations, and several of these attract current collector attention.

"Dairy Maid"

Pieces in this line feature a charming decaled decoration in the Pennsylvania Dutch tradition. The center shows two figures standing facing each other. The woman is churning butter and the man is holding a cane under his arm. The two figures are surrounded by flowers, and behind the woman a bird perches on one of the blossoms. Below this image is a heart, and the border is decorated with floral sprays.

Bowl, *individual fruit*	$ 13–15
Bowl, *soup, 8-inch diameter*	$ 20–24
Bowl, *vegetable, oval, 9½ inches*	$ 40–45

Mixing bowl, Crooksville China Company, 11-inch
diameter, $30–$45.
*Item courtesy of Kingston Pike Antique Mall, Knoxville,
Tennessee.*

Creamer	$ 30–35
Cup and saucer	$ 26–30
Dish, *relish*	$ 11–14
Plate, *dinner, 10-inch diameter*	$ 18–22
Plate, *salad, 7^1/$_4$-inch diameter*	$ 10–12
Platter, *oval, 13^1/$_2$ inches*	$ 50–55

"Petit Point House," "House," or "Cottage"

These are three names given to a charming decal design that appears on several different Crooksville shapes. This pattern features the image of a cottage and colorful garden that looks like it has been rendered in petit point stitchery. Pieces are accented with a red ring around the design or, in some cases, around both the design and the item's outer edge. "Petit Point House" is a pattern that was used mainly in the late 1930s and 1940s.

Bowl, *individual fruit, 5-inch diameter*	$ 12–15
Bowl, *vegetable, round, 8^1/$_2$-inch diameter*	$ 50–55

Cookie jar	$ 100–110
Creamer	$ 40–45
Cup and saucer	$ 28–32
Jug, *batter, with lid*	$ 125–135
Plate, *bread and butter, 6-inch diameter*	$ 9–12
Plate, *dinner, 9³/₄-inch diameter*	$ 25–30
Plate, *pie serving, 10¹/₈ inches*	$ 80–90
Plate, *salad, 7-inch diameter*	$ 17–20
Platter, *oval, 11¹/₂ inches*	$ 65–70
Platter, *oval, 13¹/₂ inches*	$ 80–85

"Silhouette"

This decoration is similar to Hall's "Taverne" pattern, except this design shows two figures sitting in chairs at a table with a dog begging at their feet. Some collectors have speculated that one of these figures is a female, but this is doubtful since both figures are showing too much leg in their colonial-style garb, with absolutely no skirts in sight. "Silhouette" was first made at Crooksville in the early 1930s, and is usually found on pieces with a pale-yellow background with a black-line border around the edge or rim. There are reports of "Silhouette" being found on a pink body, and it can be found on several different Crooksville shapes.

Bowl, *mixing, 8-inch diameter*	$ 35–40
Bowl, *mixing, 9-inch diameter*	$ 50–55
Bowl, *soup, 7¹/₄-inch diameter*	$ 25–30
Casserole, *individual, 4- or 6-inch diameter*	$ 65–70
Coffeepot with china drip	$ 175–200
Creamer	$ 20–25
Cup and saucer	$ 20–25
Mug, *tankard style*	$ 70–75
Plate, *10-inch diameter*	$ 20–25
Plate, *9-inch diameter*	$ 18–22
Plate, *8-inch diameter*	$ 15–20
Platter, *oval, 11¹/₂ inches*	$ 35–40
Teapot, *footed*	$ 125–150

CRONIN CHINA COMPANY

One of the marks
commonly found on
products made by the
Cronin China Company.

The Cronin China Company began operating in New Cumberland, West Virginia, in about 1928. In 1934, it purchased the old Owens China Company in Minerva, Ohio. In this facility, the company manufactured semiporcelain dinnerware and kitchenware until it closed in 1956. Cronin also made kitchenware and cookie jars for Block China Company, which were marketed under the "Pottery Guild" name (see the "Pottery Guild" section of this book).

"Tulip"

This pattern was reportedly made for the A & P grocery store chain. The most commonly found color scheme is dark blue tulips against a light-blue ground. Yellow with brown tulips can also be found; pink with blue tulips is rare. Prices listed below are for the blue-on-blue pieces.

Bean pot, *7 inches*	$ 75–85
Bowl, *batter*	$ 34–42
Casserole, *individual, with lid, stick, or lug handle*	$ 30–38
Casserole, *French, with spout, 6¹/₂ inches*	$ 28–35
Creamer	$ 12–18
Jug, *7 inches*	$ 45–55

Jug, *ball*	$ 65–75
Relish, *three-section, oval with handle, 13 inches*	$ 22–30
Skillet, *open*	$ 18–24
Sugar bowl	$ 30–36
Teapot	$ 60–70

"Zephyr"

This pattern can be found on both solid-color and decal-decorated pieces. Pieces bearing this pattern are lightly banded, and the handles are angular. The pattern originated in 1938, and can be found in Mango Red, Medium Blue, Medium Green, maroon, turquoise, and yellow. Prices below are for solid-color ware in the more easily found shades.

Bowl, *individual fruit, 5^1/$_2$-inch diameter*	$ 12–18
Creamer	$ 10–14
Cup and saucer	$ 15–20
Plate, *bread and butter, 6^1/$_4$ inches*	$ 7–10
Plate, *chop, lug handles, 10 inches*	$ 18–25
Plate, *chop, lug handles, 11^1/$_2$ inches*	$ 22–30
Plate, *chop, 14 inches*	$ 28–35
Plate, *luncheon, 9-inch diameter*	$ 13–20
Platter, *11^1/$_2$ inches*	$ 20–30
Sugar bowl	$ 18–24

DEDHAM POTTERY

The famous rabbit mark found on most examples of *Dedham* dinnerware.

Alexander Robertson began making brown-glazed red-ware in Chelsea, Massachusetts, just after the end of the Civil War. When his brother Hugh joined him in this enterprise in 1868, the company shifted its emphasis from producing brown ware to making a variety of flowerpots and other useful wares. It is said that in that same year the Robertsons tried their hand at making one piece of art pottery, but it did not appeal to their customers, and the project was abandoned.

Then, in 1872, James Robertson, who until this time had been working for other pottery companies, joined forces with his sons—George, Alexander, and Hugh—to form the Chelsea Keramic Art Works in the same building where Alexander and Hugh had been working previously. There is no question that this company was extremely important to the development of American Art Pottery: its building was one of the two places where the movement supposedly got its start.

The first Chelsea-made art wares were derived from ancient Greek redware pieces and were made available to the public in about 1875. They were not well received, and the company discontinued production of these wares by 1878. In 1877, the company introduced its faience wares, which used solid-colored glazes on pieces with buff-colored bodies. These were the pieces that caught the eye of the art-buying public, who were also interested in Chelsea-made pieces whose surfaces had been hammered to make them look like hand-hammered metal.

Chelsea also produced some pottery pieces that were called "Bourg-la-Reine," which was the company's interpretation of the French "Haviland" wares that the Robertsons had seen at the Philadelphia Centennial Exposition. Decoration on these pieces consisted of colored slip designs painted underglaze on backgrounds that were usually blue or green. The Robertsons were also noted for their production of fine Chinese-style glazes, including "Oxblood," which at its best was said to resemble "arterial blood" with a golden luster. Again, the Robertsons had seen this type of ware at the Philadelphia Exposition, and many experimental pieces were fired before Hugh Robertson managed to perfect a glaze that emulated what he had seen. Indeed, creation of this glaze was so difficult that the pottery dubbed it "Robertson's Blood." Supposedly only 300 examples of the true "Oxblood" (or "sang-de-boeuf") pieces were produced.

Chelsea also perfected Chinese-style glazes in turquoise, apple green, mustard yellow, peachblow (think crushed strawberries), and sea green, as well as a Chinese-style crackle glaze that would become very important in the company's later history. Unfortunately, the Chelsea Keramic Art Works was never a financial success, and it closed in 1889.

The company came back to life in 1891 with Hugh Robertson as the manager, and this time he wanted to avoid the quagmire of making expensive art pottery. Hugh remembered the Chinese crackle ware, and decided to produce tableware that was in greater demand with the general public. The result was a gray stoneware with a crackle glaze that was decorated under the glaze with blue designs.

The new product was a success, but the location of the pottery was unsatisfactory because it was located at the edge of a marsh, and the kilns thus sat on damp ground. A decision was made to relocate to nearby Dedham, Massachusetts, and Dedham Pottery began operations in 1896. This company had two kilns, one to make the "Crackleware" and the other to make art wares that are known to collectors as "volcanic ware." These highly desired pieces had thick glazes that ran, in a manner reminiscent of the lava flows associated with volcanoes. They required as many as twelve firings to achieve this effect, and were multicolored.

"Crackleware," however, is the product most associated with the Dedham Pottery. "Crackleware" generally consists of flatware pieces with rims decorated with a design painted in cobalt blue, and hollowware items with bands or rims of designs, also painted in cobalt blue. One exception is the "Night and Morning" pitcher, which has an allover design featuring a rooster crowing at the sun on one side, and a moon and owl on the other side.

Examples of Dedham "Crackleware" feature a number of patterns, but pieces bearing images of rabbits parading around their edges are the most famous and the most common. On early pieces, these rabbits are facing left, but on later examples they face right. Pieces with left-facing rabbits are more desired by collectors, and bring about 20 percent more than the items with right-facing bunnies.

Other border patterns found on Dedham "Crackleware" feature apples, lobsters, crabs, birds on potted orange trees, butterflies, butterflies with flowers, cats, cherries, chicks, ducks, dolphins, magnolias, peacocks, polar bears, snow trees, strawberries, swans, turkeys, turtles, wild roses, water lilies, grapes, and others, plus variations. It should also be noted that there were lobster and crab patterns that were not border designs; instead, these patterns featured the crustaceans represented in much larger format, usually as a single animal instead of a series of animals.

Unfortunately for Dedham, Hugh Robertson died in 1908 (many speculate that he died from lead poisoning incurred during his exhaustive experimentation with glazes). Hugh's son William succeeded him, but William's hands had been severely damaged during a kiln explosion, and he was unable to continue the developmental work that had made his father famous. Dedham Pottery closed in 1943.

Chelsea Keramic Art Works

Cup and saucer, *embossed design of berries, yellow glaze*	$ 300–350
Salt dip in the form of a walnut on a leaf, *realistic molding, bisque finish*	$ 550–650
Shoe, *6 inches, floral painting on brown ground, repaired*	$ 800–900
Tazza, *11^1/$_4$-inch diameter, on low foot, by Hugh C. Robertson, incised nature study with rabbits in a field, blue/gray high-gloss glaze, chips to base*	$ 3,500–4,000
Vase, *flat moon, flask-style, 7^1/$_2$ inches, painted Oriental poppies on brown and green mottled background*	$ 1,000–1,200

"Crackleware"

Originally a product of the Chelsea Pottery, this line became the mainstay of the Dedham Pottery throughout its existence. Its patterns are many and varied, but the rabbit design is by far the most common.

Bowl, *4-inch diameter, rabbit pattern*	$ 175–225
Bowl, *4^1/$_2$-inch diameter, adult elephants with baby*	$ 1,000–1,200
Bowl, *5-inch diameter, lotus design*	$ 750–800

Dedham salad serving bowl, 12-inch diameter, rabbit pattern, $1,200–$1,500. *Item Courtesy of Kingston Pike Antique Mall, Knoxville, Tennessee.*

Dedham rabbit-pattern child's mug, $800–$850. *Item courtesy of Richard Hatch and Associates, Hendersonville, North Carolina.*

Bowl, *oval, 10³/₄ inches, rabbit design*	$ 500–600
Bowl, *12-inch diameter, rabbit design*	$ 1,200–1,500
Compote, *6-inch diameter, two handles, rabbit design*	$ 450–500
Cup and saucer, *adult elephants with baby*	$ 1,200–1,400
Cup and saucer, *polar bear*	$ 750–800
Cup and saucer, *rabbit*	$ 325–375
Dish, *child's, 8-inch diameter, elephant*	$ 3,800–4,000
Dish, *pickle, 10 inches long*	$ 1,500–1,650
Dish, *pentagon-shaped, azalea pattern*	$ 800–900
Egg cup, *covered, adult elephant with baby*	$ 4,500–5,000
Mug, *5 inches tall, rabbit pattern*	$ 600–650
Mug, *child's, 3¹/₂ inches, rabbit*	$ 800–850
Pitcher, *4³/₄ inches tall, rabbit design*	$ 650–750
Pitcher, *5 inches tall, adult elephants with baby*	$ 2,250–2,500

Dedham rabbit-pattern plate, 8 inch diameter,
$275–$300.
*Item courtesy of Kingston Pike Antique Mall, Knoxville,
Tennessee.*

Pitcher, *5 inches tall, "Night and Morning," sun and rooster crowing on one side, owl on other*	$ 1,000–1,200
Plate, *6 inches, butterfly design*	$ 750–825
Plate, *6-inch diameter, lobster design*	$ 750–825
Plate, *6-inch diameter, bird in potted orange tree*	$ 1,000–1,200
Plate, *6 inches, moth*	$ 650–750
Plate, *6 inches, turkey pattern*	$ 600–675
Plate, *7^1/$_2$-inch diameter, azalea design*	$ 250–275
Plate, *8-inch diameter, azalea design*	$ 275–300
Plate, *8-inch diameter, rabbit design*	$ 250–300
Plate, *8^1/$_4$-inch diameter, iris design*	$ 350–425
Plate, *8^1/$_2$-inch diameter, dove*	$ 2,000–2,200
Plate, *8^1/$_2$-inch diameter, lobster*	$ 1,200–1,400
Plate, *8^1/$_2$-inch diameter, snowtree pattern*	$ 250–300
Plate, *8^3/$_4$-inch diameter, grape pattern*	$ 350–400

Plate, *10-inch diameter, rabbit design*	$ 500–550
Plate, *10-inch diameter, French mushroom design*	$ 900–1,000
Plate, *10-inch diameter, pond lily pattern*	$ 350–400
Plate, *10¼-inch diameter, snow tree*	$ 800–850
Plate, *chop, 12-inch diameter, adult elephants and one baby*	$ 4,500–4,800
Platter, *oval, 18 inches, lobster design*	$ 3,000–3,500
Sugar bowl, *lidded, rabbit design*	$ 350–400
Tile, *5¾ inches square, turkey design*	$ 1,200–1,400

KAY FINCH

KAY FINCH
CALIFORNIA

One of the marks used by
Kay Finch Ceramics.

Kay Finch
CALIFORNIA

A mark used by *Kay Finch
Ceramics.*

Born in El Paso, Texas, in 1903, Kay Finch was interested in modeling clay, and as a child sculpted images of the animals that wandered into her family's backyard. She studied art at Belmont College in Nashville, Tennessee, and continued her art education at Scripps College in Claremont, California, after moving to California with her husband, Brandon, in 1926. At Scripps she showed a great aptitude for clay modeling, and her teacher, William Manker, encouraged her to do more with her skills.

After an around-the-world trip in which she studied native ceramics, Finch returned to California and decided to go into commercial production. Her husband, who was a newspaper editor and publisher, bought her a used kiln in 1938, and installed it in a ramshackle building behind their Santa Ana, California, home. Later, Finch's husband quit his job to manage the business end of his wife's ceramics enterprise. In 1939, the Finches moved to Corona del Mar and set up a studio next to their home. The studio was such a success that, in 1940, the Finches had to open a new studio with retail space on the Pacific Coast Highway.

Finch's specialty was hand-modeled and hand-decorated figures—especially animals. She became a dog breeder in the 1940s, and when her husband died in 1963, she closed the pottery and devoted herself to her champion show dogs.

Animals

Birds, *doves, tail up or tail down, 8 inches by 5 inches*	$ 125–150
Bird, *"Mr. Bird," 4¹/₂ inches*	$ 110–125
Bird, *"Mrs. Bird," 3 inches*	$ 110–125
Bird, *Owl, "Hoot," 8³/₄ inches*	$ 225–250
Bird, *Owl, "Toot," 5³/₄ inches*	$ 110–125
Bird, *Owl, "Tootsie," 3³/₄ inches*	$ 65–75
Cat, *"Ambrosia," Persian, 10³/₄ inches*	$ 525–550
Cat, *"Hannibal," angry, 10¹/₄ inches*	$ 450–475
Cat, *"Jezebel," contented, 6 inches*	$ 275–300
Cat, *"Mehitabel," playful, 8¹/₂ inches*	$ 400–425
Cat, *"Muff," sleeping kitten, 3¹/₄ inches*	$ 125–150
Cat, *"Puff," playing kitten, 3¹/₄ inches*	$ 110–125
Chicken, *Hen, "Biddy," 8¹/₄ inches*	$ 125–150
Chicken, *Rooster, "Butch," 8¹/₄ inches*	$ 125–150
Chicken, *Rooster, "Chanticleer," 10³/₄ inches*	$ 325–350
Dog, *Boxer, 5 inches*	$ 600–650
Dog, *Cocker Spaniel, sitting*	$ 400–425
Dog, *Cocker Spaniel, "Vicki," sitting, 11 inches*	$ 1,200–1,300
Dog, *Pekingese, "Peke," 14 inches*	$ 550–600
Dog, *Pomeranian, "Mitzi," 10 inches*	$ 800–850
Duck, *"Jeep"*	$ 60–75
Duck, *"Peep"*	$ 60–75
Elephant, *"Popcorn," trunk down, 6³/₄ inches*	$ 125–150
Elephant, *"Peanuts," trunk up, 8³/₄ inches*	$ 225–250
Elephant, *"Violet (Queen of the Circus)," 17 inches*	$ 3,000–3,200
Lamb, *prancing, with floral collar, 10¹/₂ inches*	$ 575–625
Lamb, *life-size, with floral collar, 20 inches*	$ 3,500–3,750
Penguin, *"Pee Wee," 3¹/₄ inches*	$ 75–90
Penguin, *"Pete," 7¹/₂ inches*	$ 350–400
Penguin, *"Polly," 4¹/₂ inches*	$ 175–200

Pig, *"Grandpa," 10^1/$_2$ inches by 16 inches*	$ 450–500
Pig, *"Grumpy," 6 inches*	$ 250–275
Pig, *"Sassy," 3^1/$_2$ inches*	$ 110–125
Pig, *"Smiley," 6^3/$_4$ inches*	$ 200–225
Pig, *"Winkie," 3^3/$_4$ inches*	$ 110–125

People

Angel, *three styles, 4^1/$_4$ inches*	$ 65–75
Bride, *6^1/$_2$ inches*	$ 275–300
Cherub, *head, with wings, 2^3/$_4$ inches*	$ 75–95
Choirboy, *kneeling, 5^1/$_2$ inches*	$ 90–110
Choirboy, *standing, 7^1/$_2$ inches*	$ 125–150
Godey Lady, *9^1/$_2$ inches*	$ 110–125
Godey Man, *9^1/$_2$ inches*	$ 110–125
Groom, *6^1/$_2$ inches*	$ 275–300
Mermaid, *6^1/$_2$ inches*	$ 550–550
Peasant, *boy, 6^3/$_4$ inches*	$ 60–75
Peasant, *girl, 6^3/$_4$ inches*	$ 60–75

FLORENCE CERAMICS

One of the identifying marks used by the *Florence Ceramics Company.*

When Florence Ward's son died in the early 1940s, she began dabbling with ceramics as a hobby to keep her mind off her tragic loss. While her husband and surviving son were away fighting World War II, she set up shop in her garage in Pasadena, California, and commercial production began in 1942. Both men joined the business when they returned from the war, and the company had to move to larger quarters in 1946. In 1949, still growing, Florence Ceramics once again moved—this time to one of the most modern ceramics plants in the state of California.

Florence Ceramics is especially known for its figures, but the company also made flower holders, frames, lamps, plaques, bowls, and other accessory items. Pieces were semiporcelain with overglaze decoration. Florence Ceramics was sold to Scripto Corporation in 1965, but while Scripto continued making ceramics using the Florence name, it did not make the figures. The plant closed altogether in 1977.

Fashions in Brocade

These pieces were hand-fashioned with brocade dresses, and are considered to be some of Florence Ceramics' best pieces. The hands and faces are carefully detailed, and some pieces have genuine feather hair ornaments.

Amelia, *"Godey Lady," brocade dress, 12 inches tall*	$ 2,200–2,400
Anita, *gold-brocade long dress, 10 inches*	$ 2,200–2,400
Caroline, *15 inches*	$ 5,000–5,500
Georgia, *12 inches, hands lifting gown*	$ 2,200–2,400
Lillian Russell, *long "Gay Nineties" gown, 15 inches tall*	$ 2,750–3,000
Marlene, *10 inches*	$ 2,200–2,500

People, Real and Mythical

Although all the Florence figures were hand-painted, some pieces are of higher quality than others. There was, for example, an economy grouping of figures that was sold in a limited range of colors and with less detail work, along with a higher-end grouping in which the figures were richly detailed with articulated fingers. The colors used on these higher-end figures include gray, beige, maroon, aqua, Royal Red, royal purple, rose, yellow, white, blue, and several shades of green. Colors used on the economy figures include gray, beige, maroon, green, or aqua. Yellow is a rare color on Florence figures.

A number of Florence figures were made to go together. These include: John Alden and Priscilla, Blue Boy and Pinkie, Blynken and Wynken, Companion and Spring Revelry, Douglas and the smaller Godey Girls, Edward with Elizabeth and Victoria, Leading Man and Prima Donna, Mme Pompadour and Louis XV, Marie Antoinette and Louis XVI, and Scarlett, Rhett, Melanie, and Sue Ellen.

Abigail, *in Godey-style dress, 8 inches*	$ 165–185
Adeline, *9 inches*	$ 350–400
Alden, *John, 9^{1}/$_{4}$ inches*	$ 225–250
Amber, *with parasol, 9^{1}/$_{4}$ inches*	$ 525–550
Amelia, *in Godey-style dress, 8^{1}/$_{4}$ inches*	$ 275–300
Angel, *7 inches*	$ 100–125
Ann, *6 inches tall*	$ 100–125
Annabel, *in Godey-style dress, 8 inches, articulated fingers, carrying a basket*	$ 550–600
Annabel, *in Godey-style dress, 8 inches, articulated fingers, card in hand*	$ 475–500
Barbara, *American colonial-era costume, 8^{1}/$_{2}$ inches*	$ 700–750
Bea, *6 inches*	$ 150–175

Beth, *7¹/₄ inches*	$ 200–225
Blossom Girl, *8¹/₄ inches*	$ 175–200
Blue Boy, *12 inches*	$ 500–550
Blynken, *5¹/₂ inches*	$ 250–275
Boy with ice cream cone, *7¹/₂ inches*	$ 325–350
Boy with life preserver, *7 inches*	$ 325–350
Bride, *lace veil, 8¹/₂ inches*	$ 1,800–2,000
Bride, *ceramic veil, 8¹/₂ inches*	$ 1,400–1,500
Bryan, *10¹/₂ inches*	$ 3,000–3.500
Camille, *8¹/₂ inches, one hand showing*	$ 325–350
Camille, *8¹/₂ inches, two hands showing*	$ 425–475
Carmen with red lace, *12 inches*	$ 1,400–1,500
Carol, *girl, 7³/₄ inches*	$ 300–325
Carol, *woman, 10 inches tall*	$ 700–750
Catherine, *seated, with hat, 7³/₄ inches by 6³/₄ inches*	$ 700–750
Catherine, *seated, no hat, 7³/₄ inches by 6³/₄ inches*	$ 800–850
Charles, *8¹/₂ inches*	$ 225–250
Charmaine, *8¹/₂ inches*	$ 250–275
Charmaine, *articulated hands, 8¹/₂ inches*	$ 400–425
Chinese Boy, *7³/₄ inches*	$ 165–185
Chinese Girl, *7³/₄ inches*	$ 165–185
Choir Boys, *three poses, 6 inches, set*	$ 300–325
Cinderella and Prince Charming, *dancing, one piece,* *11³/₄ inches*	$ 2,500–2,750
Cindy, *8 inches*	$ 350–375
Clarissa, *7³/₄ inches*	$ 200–225
Clarissa, *articulated hand, 7³/₄ inches*	$ 275–300
Claudia, *no hands showing, 8¹/₄ inches*	$ 250–275
Claudia, *articulated hand, lace shawl, 8¹/₄ inches*	$ 350–375
Claudia, *articulated hand, no lace shawl, 8¹/₄ inches*	$ 300–325
Colleen, *two hands to the front, 8 inches*	$ 325–350

Colleen, *one hand behind back, 8 inches*	$ 250–275
Cynthia, *9¹/₄ inches*	$ 600–650
Darlene, *8¹/₄ inches*	$ 750–800
David, *7¹/₂ inches*	$ 125–145
Dear Ruth, *7³/₄ inches*	$ 1,200–1,300
Deborah, *9¹/₂ inches*	$ 850–900
Delia, *7³/₄ inches*	$ 125–145
Denise, *articulated fingers, 10 inches*	$ 750–800
Diane, *8 inches*	$ 275–300
Diane, *articulated hands, 8 inches*	$ 350–375
Dolores, *8¹/₂ inches*	$ 650–700
Doralee, *9¹/₂ inches*	$ 1,000–1,100
Douglas, *8¹/₄ inches*	$ 200–225
Edith, *7¹/₂ inches*	$ 400–450
Edward, *7 inches*	$ 300–325
Elaine, *6 inches*	$ 100–125
Elizabeth, *gray sofa, 8¹/₄ inches by 7 inches*	$ 400–450
Elizabeth, *white sofa, 8¹/₄ inches by 7 inches*	$ 1,600–1,750
Ellen, *7 inches*	$ 200–225
Ethel, *7 inches*	$ 300–325
Eugenia (Eugenie), *9 inches*	$ 350–375
Eve, *8¹/₂ inches*	$ 275–300
Fair Lady, *11¹/₂ inches*	$ 2,250–2,500
Fall, *6¹/₂ inches*	$ 125–145
Gary, *8¹/₂ inches*	$ 300–325
Genevieve, *8 inches*	$ 250–275
Grace, *7³/₄ inches*	$ 200–225
Grandmother and I, *two figures across a tea table*	$ 2,800–3,000
Her Majesty, *7 inches*	$ 250–275
Irene, *6 inches*	$ 100–120
Jeanette, *in Godey-style dress*	$ 200–225

Jeanette, *in Godey-style dress, articulated hands*	$ 250–275
Jennifer	$ 275–300
Jim, *6¹/₂ inches*	$ 100–120
Josephine, *9 inches*	$ 300–325
Joy, *6 inches*	$ 100–120
Joyce, *8¹/₂ inches*	$ 400–450
Juliette	$ 2,500–2,750
Karen, *8¹/₂ inches*	$ 1,500–1,650
Karla, *ballerina, 9³/₄ inches*	$ 250–275
Kay, *6³/₄ inches*	$ 85–100
Lady Diana, *10 inches*	$ 650–700
Lantern Boy, *8¹/₄ inches*	$ 150–175
Laura, *7¹/₂ inches*	$ 175–200
Leading Man, *10¹/₄ inches*	$ 400–450
Lillian, *7 inches*	$ 150–175
Linda Lou, *7³/₄ inches*	$ 165–185
Lisa, *ballerina, 7¹/₄ inches*	$ 225–250
Lorry, *8 inches*	$ 500–550
Louis XV, *12¹/₂ inches*	$ 700–750
Louis XVI, *10 inches*	$ 500–550
Love Letter, *12 inches high*	$ 2,000–2,250
Madonna, *no child, 10 inches*	$ 150–175
Madonna, *child, 10¹/₂ inches*	$ 200–225
Marc Anthony, *13 inches*	$ 1,200–1,400
Marie Antoinette, *small skirt, 10 inches*	$ 300–325
Marie Antoinette, *large skirt, 10 inches*	$ 400–450
Mary, *picture hat, 7¹/₂ inches*	$ 700–750
Mary, *feathered hat, 7¹/₂ inches*	$ 625–675
Masquerade, *holding black mask*	$ 850–900
Master David, *8 inches*	$ 600–650
Matilda, *in Godey-style dress, 8¹/₂ inches*	$ 175–200

Melanie, *in Godey-style dress, 7¹/2 inches*	$ 150–175
Memories, *5¹/4 inches by 6¹/2 inches*	$ 750–800
Mikado, *13¹/2 inches*	$ 400–450
Mike, *6¹/4 inches*	$ 125–150
Mimi	$ 100–125
Ming	$ 100–125
Mme Pompadour, *12¹/2 inches*	$ 850–875
Musette, *8³/4 inches*	$ 375–400
Nancy, *6³/4 inches*	$ 125–150
Nell Gwyn, *12 inches*	$ 1,800–2,000
Our Lady of Grace, *10³/4 inches*	$ 250–275
Pamela, *bonnet and basket of flowers, 7¹/4 inches*	$ 550–600
Pat, *6 inches*	$ 100–125
Patrice	$ 165–185
Peter, *adult, 9¹/4 inches*	$ 300–350
Peter, *youth, 5¹/2 inches*	$ 150–175
Pinkie, *12 inches*	$ 475–525
Prima Donna, *10 inches*	$ 700–750
Princess, *10¹/4 inches*	$ 600–650
Priscilla, *7³/4 inches*	$ 225–250
Prom Boy, *9 inches*	$ 250–275
Prom Girl, *9 inches*	$ 325–375
Rhett, *stone wall, 9 inches*	$ 200–225
Rhett, *wooden wall, 9 inches*	$ 250–275
Roberta, *8¹/2 inches*	$ 275–300
Rosalie, *9¹/2 inches*	$ 675–725
Rosemarie, *9¹/2 inches*	$ 650–700
Sally, *6³/4 inches*	$ 175–200
Sarah, *7¹/2 inches*	$ 150–175
Scarlett, *hands not showing, 8³/4 inches*	$ 150–175
Scarlett, *articulated hands showing, 8³/4 inches*	$ 350–375

Shen, *7¹/₂ inches*	$ 125–150
Sherri, *8¹/₂ inches*	$ 300–350
Spring Revelry, *holding bird's nest, 12 inches*	$ 1,500–1,750
Stephen, *8³/₄ inches*	$ 275–300
Story Hour, *mother and girl, 8 inches by 6³/₄ inches*	$ 900–1,000
Story Hour, *mother, girl, and boy, 8 inches by 6³/₄ inches*	$ 1,200–1,400
Sue, *6 inches*	$ 75–100
Sue Ellen, *8¹/₄ inches*	$ 175–200
Susan/Susann, *9 inches*	$ 450–500
Tess, *lace ruffle, 7¹/₄ inches*	$ 350–400
Tess, *no lace ruffle, 7¹/₄ inches*	$ 300–350
Toy, *8¹/₂ inches*	$ 175–200
Victor, *9¹/₄ inches*	$ 250–275
Victoria, *bonnet, 7 inches*	$ 350–400
Victoria, *no bonnet, 7 inches*	$ 400–450
Virginia, *lace at collar, 9 inches*	$ 2,000–2,250
Virginia, *no lace at collar, 9 inches*	$ 1,200–1,400
Wynken, *5¹/₂ inches*	$ 250–275
Yvonne, *8³/₄ inches*	$ 250–275
Yvonne, *articulated hands, 8³/₄ inches*	$ 350–400

Flower Holders

These are figures meant to hold flowers. In old catalogs, they are also referred to as "flower containers."

Ava, *10¹/₂ inches*	$ 165–185
Bea	$ 80–100
Belle, *7¹/₂ inches*	$ 80–100
Beth, *7¹/₂ inches*	$ 80–100
Blossom Girl, *8¹/₂ inches*	$ 80–100
Chinese Boy, *holder in back, 7³/₄ inches*	$ 60–75
Chinese Girl, *holder in back, 7³/₄ inches*	$ 60–75

Chinese Boy, *bamboo-style holder at side, 7 inches*	$ 150–175
Chinese Girl, *bamboo-style holder at side, 7 inches*	$ 150–175
Dutch Girl, *small*	$ 60–75
Dutch Girl, *large*	$ 75–95
Emily, *8 inches*	$ 60–75
Fern, *bust (head vase), 7 inches*	$ 175–200
June, *6 inches*	$ 60–75
Kay, *7 inches*	$ 60–75
Lantern Boy, *8^1/4 inches*	$ 85–100
Lea, *6 inches*	$ 50–65
Lyn, *6 inches*	$ 50–65
May, *5^1/2 inches*	$ 50–65
Mimi, *6 inches*	$ 50–65
Molly, *6^1/2 inches*	$ 50–65
Patsy, *6 inches*	$ 50–65
Peasant Man, *large, with flower cart*	$ 225–250
Peg, *7^1/2 inches*	$ 50–65
Suzette, *7 inches*	$ 75–95
Violet, *bust (head vase), 7 inches tall*	$ 175–200

FRANKOMA POTTERY

A *Frankoma Pottery* mark that generally appears on early, desirable examples.

Embossed mark of the *Frankoma Pottery Company.*

In 1927, John Frank became an instructor in the new ceramics department at the University of Oklahoma at Norman. In 1933, while still working at the university, he founded the Frank Pottery in Norman, where he produced wares using a light-colored clay that came from a deposit near the town of Ada, Oklahoma. The name of the pottery was changed to "Frankoma Potteries" in 1934, and in 1936 John Frank left the University of Oklahoma to work at the pottery full-time. Two years later, in 1938, the company was moved to Sapulpa, Oklahoma, and at this time its name became "Frankoma Pottery."

Frankoma used the light-colored clay from Ada until 1953, when it was replaced by a brick-red clay that was found near the plant. Collectors are particularly interested in Frankoma wares made with the light-colored Ada clay, and will generally pay as much as double the price they would be willing to pay for the same piece with a more-common brick-red body. Frankoma was owned and operated by the Frank family until 1990, when it filed for Chapter 11 bankruptcy. The company was later sold.

Very early pieces made by John Frank and his company are marked "John Frank," "Frank Pottery," or "Frank Potteries," but most pieces found on today's market will have an impressed or ink-stamped mark reading "Frankoma" or

"Frankoma Pottery." The company made novelties, Christmas cards and plates, plaques, bookends, figures, and dinnerware.

Dinnerware

"Lazybones"

This line was introduced in 1953 and has been discontinued. Pieces from this line bear a very simple pattern, with each piece of flatware featuring spiral lines radiating from its center that appear almost to form the "yin and yang" symbol. The pattern was produced in a variety of colors, including Prairie Green, Desert Gold, Autumn Yellow, Robin's Egg Blue, Flame, Woodland Moss, and Brown Satin. Of these, Flame is the most highly desired color, and prices for pieces featuring this hue can be up to 50 percent higher than prices for pieces featuring less-coveted colors.

Bean pot, *individual/custard*	$ 8–12
Bowl, *individual fruit, 6-ounce*	$ 10–12
Bowl, *soup, 6-inch diameter, tab handle*	$ 12–15
Bowl, *vegetable, oval, $7^1/_2$ inches*	$ 35–40
Bowl, *vegetable, oval, $10^1/_2$ inches*	$ 40–45
Bowl, *vegetable, oval, divided*	$ 50–65
Bowl, *vegetable, round, 8-inch diameter*	$ 35–45
Butter dish, *$^1/_4$-pound, covered*	$ 20–40
Casserole, *round, covered, 3-quart*	$ 135–145
Creamer	$ 20–35
Cup and saucer	$ 15–25
Gravy boat	$ 40–55
Jug, *2-quart*	$ 20–30
Mug, *18-ounce*	$ 15–25
Plate, *bread and butter, 7-inch diameter*	$ 5–10
Plate, *dinner, 10-inch diameter*	$ 15–25
Platter, *oval, 13 inches*	$ 40–55
Salt and pepper shakers, *set*	$ 20–30
Spoon holder	$ 20–35
Sugar bowl	$ 30–45
Tumbler, *12-ounce*	$ 15–20

"Mayan/Aztec"

This line was first introduced in 1945. Its pieces are decorated with raised designs that are supposed to suggest Mesoamerican hieroglyphs or runes. Some pieces in this pattern were available in as many as eight colors, but Prairie Green, Desert Gold, and White Sand are the most common. White Sand and Prairie Green pieces are generally priced at the top end of the price ranges listed below, with Flame pieces generally priced a bit higher.

Bowl, *individual fruit, 4¹/₂-inch diameter*	$ 5–11
Bowl, *vegetable, round, 8-inch diameter*	$ 15–35
Butter dish, *¹/₄-pound, covered*	$ 25–40
Casserole, *individual*	$ 18–35
Creamer	$ 14–26
Cup and saucer	$ 14–24
Plate, *bread and butter, 7-inch diameter*	$ 6–8
Plate, *dinner, 10-inch diameter*	$ 15–20
Platter, *13 inches*	$ 35–55
Salt and pepper shakers, *set*	$ 15–25
Spoon holder	$ 20–40
Sugar bowl	$ 20–38

"Plainsman"

This pattern was initially named "Oklahoma." It is a solid-color pattern with a brown edge (in most cases), with some pieces available in eight colors. Most items, however, were made in Prairie Green, Desert Gold, Brown Satin, Woodland Moss, and Autumn Yellow. Flatware pieces in this pattern have a simple notched edge with four indentions. Some hollowware items such as the mug have embossed geometric designs, and the trivet has an embossed floral decoration. Once again, pricing is color-dependent.

Bowl, *cereal, 5³/₄-inch diameter*	$ 8–15
Bowl, *individual fruit, 5-inch diameter*	$ 6–12
Bowl, *vegetable, oval, 12 inches*	$ 30–50
Bowl, *vegetable or salad, square, 9 inches*	$ 30–45
Bowl, *vegetable, rectangular, divided, 13 inches*	$ 60–80
Butter, *covered, ¹/₄-pound*	$ 40–60

Casserole, *individual*	$ 30–45
Creamer, *large*	$ 7–12
Creamer, *small, individual*	$ 13–22
Cup and saucer	$ 12–18
Cup and saucer, *demitasse*	$ 12–20
Gravy boat	$ 60–85
Jug, *3-quart*	$ 30–45
Mug, *12-ounce*	$ 7–14
Pitcher and bowl set, *small*	$ 100–140
Plate, *bread and butter, 6^1/$_2$-inch diameter*	$ 5–10
Plate, *dinner, 10-inch diameter*	$ 20–35
Plate, *luncheon, 9-inch diameter*	$ 8–12
Plate, *salad, 7-inch diameter*	$ 10–15
Platter, *rectangular, 9 inches*	$ 35–55
Platter, *rectangular, 13 inches*	$ 22–40
Salt and pepper shakers, *set*	$ 15–25
Spoon holder	$ 18–28
Sugar bowl	$ 15–25
Trivet	$ 15–22
Tumbler, *juice, 6-ounce*	$ 10–16
Tumbler, *12-ounce*	$ 14–20
Tureen, *covered with ladle*	$ 230–275

"Wagon Wheels"

This distinctive pattern, based on a wagon wheel in high relief, was made from 1941 until 1983. Pieces are found primarily in Prairie Green and Desert Gold. The range of prices is color-dependent, with Desert Gold pieces being the most expensive.

Bowl, *individual fruit, 4-inch diameter*	$ 10–14
Bowl, *vegetable, 10^1/$_2$ inches*	$ 30–40
Creamer, *large*	$ 24–28
Creamer, *small*	$ 12–16
Cup and saucer	$ 14–20

Frankoma "Wagon Wheel" vase, 7 inches, green, $50–$65.
Item courtesy of Kingston Pike Antique Mall, Knoxville, Tennessee.

Plate, *bread and butter, 6¹/₂-inch diameter*	$ 8–10
Plate, *dinner, 10-inch diameter*	$ 18–22
Plate, *luncheon, 9-inch diameter*	$ 13–16
Plate, *salad, 7-inch diameter*	$ 8–10
Platter, *rectangular, 13 inches*	$ 50–60
Salt and pepper shakers	$ 25–30
Teapot, *2-cup*	$ 40–50
Tumbler, *6-ounce*	$ 10–12
Tumbler, *12-ounce*	$ 14–18
Sugar bowl, *open*	$ 10–15
Vase, *7 inches*	$ 50–65

"Westwind"

Pieces in this solid-color line (some pieces have a brown edge) came in Prairie Green, Autumn Yellow, Robin's Egg Blue, White Sand, Woodland Moss, Desert Gold, Peach Glow, and Flame. Newer production pieces were made in Navy, Teal, and

Frankoma cookie jar, 8³/₄ inches, Sapulpa clay, #25K, $50–$65.
Item courtesy of Richard Crane, Knoxville, Tennessee.

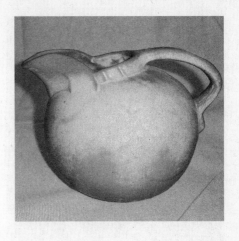

Frankoma pitcher, #30A, Sapulpa clay, 5¹/₂ inches, $25–$40.
Item courtesy of Needful Things, Hendersonville, North Carolina.

Cabernet. Prices are color-dependent, with White Sand and Flame generally occupying the higher end of the price range, and newer colors and Prairie Green occupying the lower part of the price range.

Bowl, *individual fruit, 5-inch diameter*	$ 6–12
Bowl, *cereal, 5³/₄-inch diameter*	$ 9–15
Butter, *¹/₄-pound, with lid*	$ 30–48
Casserole, *2¹/₂-quart*	$ 80–110
Casserole/candy dish, *18-ounce*	$ 35–45
Creamer	$ 12–26
Cup and saucer	$ 14–28
Gravy boat	$ 40–75
Jug, *1-quart*	$ 14–28
Jug, *2-quart*	$ 22–55
Plate, *dinner, 10-inch diameter*	$ 13–22
Plate, *salad, 7-inch diameter*	$ 5–10

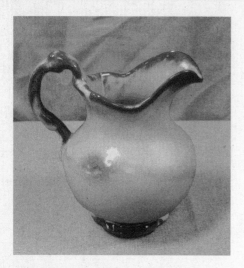

Frankoma creamer, typical green-and-brown glaze,
Sapulpa clay, $18–$25.
Item courtesy of Richard Crane, Knoxville, Tennessee.

Salt and pepper shakers, *set*	$ 16–30
Spoon rest	$ 25–40
Sugar bowl	$ 20–40
Teapot, *2-cup*	$ 42–55
Teapot, *6-cup*	$ 55–75
Tumbler, *juice, 6-ounce*	$ 10–15
Tumbler, *12-ounce*	$ 12–18
Tureen, *with lid and ladle*	$ 150–200

Bookends

Boot, *Sapulpa red clay, pair*	$ 60–75
Bucking Bronco, *5$^{1}/_{2}$ inches, Prairie Green, pair*	$ 600–650
Deco Lady, *Ada clay, pair*	$ 1,100–1,200
Dreamer Girl, *early Norman mark*	$ 750–800
Mallard Head, *wooden base, pair*	$ 1,400–1,500

Panther, *walking, 7 inches long, similar to the panther used on the early Frankoma mark, black glaze, pair*	$ 1,500–1,750
Seahorse, *pair*	$ 1,800–2,000
Seated figure, *ivory glaze, 5³/₄ inches, pair*	$ 1,200–1,400
Setter, *wooden base, pair*	$ 300–350

Figures

Animals

Bucking Bronco	$ 600–650
Buffalo, *large and small version, 4 or 3¹/₂ inches, early mark*	$ 3,200–3,400
Camel, *6 inches tall, early mark*	$ 2,750–3,000
Charging Tiger, *12¹/₂ inches long, early mark*	$ 2,500–2,650
Circus Horse, *4¹/₂ inches tall, early mark*	$ 500–550
Circus Horse, *Sapulpa red clay*	$ 100–125
Deer group, *three deer, 8 inches by 9¹/₄ inches, early mark*	$ 3,500–3,750
Gannet (bird), *9 inches tall, early mark*	$ 3,500–3,750
Greyhound, *8¹/₂ inches long, Sapulpa clay*	$ 500–550
Hound Dog, *5¹/₂ inches, early mark*	$ 1,600–1,800
Pekingese Dog, *7³/₄ inches*	$ 3,250–3,500
Puma with Prey, *11¹/₂ inches long, early mark*	$ 3,300–3,500
Rearing Clydesdale, *black glaze, 7¹/₄ inches, early mark*	$ 800–850
Rearing Clydesdale, *Sapulpa red clay, 6¹/₄ inches*	$ 95–125
Sleeping Cocker Spaniel, *8¹/₂ inches long, Ada clay*	$ 500–550

Miniature Animals

Bull, *2 inches, Ada clay*	$ 500–550
Cat, *3 inches, Ada clay*	$ 175–200
Donkey, *3 inches, Ada clay*	$ 600–650
Elephant, *2³/₄ inches, Ada clay*	$ 200–225
Elephant, *3¹/₈ inches, Ada clay*	$ 225–250
Setter (English), *3 inches, Ada clay*	$ 250–275

Swan, *3 inches, Ada clay*	$ 175–200
Swan, *3 inches, Sapulpa clay*	$ 90–110
Terrier, *3 inches, Ada clay*	$ 600–650
Trojan Horse, *2¹/₂ inches, Ada clay*	$ 150–175
Trojan Horse, *2¹/₂ inches, Sapulpa clay*	$ 110–125

People

Cowboy, *7³/₄ inches tall, early mark*	$ 1,500–1,650
Fan Dancer, *Norman mark, 8¹/₂ inches*	$ 1,750–2,000
Fan Dancer, *Sapulpa clay*	$ 500–550
Fan Dancer, *1997 reissue*	$ 65–80
Harlem Hoofer, *13¹/₂ inches tall, early mark*	$ 4,000–4,500
Indian Bowl Maker, *8 inches tall, early mark*	$ 750–800
Indian Bowl Maker, *8 inches tall, Sapulpa clay*	$ 65–80
Madonna, *5³/₄ inches, Ada clay*	$ 700–750
Medicine Man, *9¹/₂ inches, Ada clay*	$ 800–850
Medicine Man, *1996 reissue*	$ 65–80
Taos Indian Squaw, *8 inches tall, gunmetal glaze*	$ 2,200–2,400
Torch Singer, *13¹/₂ inches tall*	$ 4,000–4,500
Will Rogers, *Ada clay, 6³/₄ inches*	$ 1,400–1,600

Flower Frogs

Fish, *4¹/₂ inches, early mark*	$ 2,250–2,500
Nonfigural, *oval block, 5¹/₂ inches, Ada clay*	$ 75–90
Swan, *4 inches*	$ 900–950

Masks, *Plaques, and Wall Pockets*

Acorn wall pocket, large, 1960s	$ 95–110
African man, *mask, large, 7¹/₄ inches by 5 inches, Ada clay*	$ 200–225
African man, *mask, large, 7¹/₄ inches by 5 inches, Sapulpa clay*	$ 150–175
African woman, *mask, large, 7¹/₂ inches by 4¹/₂ inches, Ada clay*	$ 200–275

African woman, *mask, large, 7^1/$_2$ inches by 4^1/$_2$ inches, Sapulpa clay*	$ 150–175
Asian man, *mask, 5^1/$_2$ inches, Ada clay*	$ 600–650
Asian woman, *mask, Ada clay*	$ 600–650
Billiken, *wall pocket, Ada clay*	$ 225–250
Billiken, *wall plaque, Sapulpa clay*	$ 150–175
Buffalo, *wall plaque, Ada clay*	$ 60–75
Horseshoe-shaped wall plaque, *rearing horse, "Silver Squirrel"*	$ 500–550
Indian, *mask, 5 inches, Ada clay*	$ 175–200
Indian maiden, *mask, 4^1/$_8$ inches, Ada clay*	$ 175–200
Leaf, *wall pocket, 13 inches by 10^1/$_2$ inches, Sapulpa clay*	$ 250–275
Peter Pan, *mask, Ada clay*	$ 200–225
Peter Pan, *mask, Sapulpa clay*	$ 75–90
Phoebe, *wall pocket, 7^1/$_2$ inches by 5^1/$_4$ inches, Sapulpa clay*	$ 150–175
Ram's head, *wall pocket, Ada clay*	$ 300–325
Smiling Indian, *mask, Ada clay*	$ 1,000–1,100
Terpsichore, *Goddess of Dance, wall plaque, 1950s*	$ 75–90
Wagon Wheel, *wall pocket*	$ 100–125
Will Rogers, *wall plaque, 1879–1935, round, 6-inch diameter*	$ 400–450

Planters

Cork Bark, *11^1/$_2$ inches long, Sapulpa clay*	$ 35–45
Duck, *9^1/$_2$ inches, Sapulpa clay, yellow, #208A*	$ 40–50
Log, *10 inches long, Ada clay*	$ 40–50
Swan, *large, 12 inches long, Ada clay*	$ 250–300

Vases

Cactus, *disk with raised cactus, Ada clay*	$ 60–75
Cactus, *disk with raised cactus, Sapulpa clay*	$ 35–45
Crocus, *bud, 8 inches tall, early mark*	$ 110–125
Crocus, *bud, 8 inches tall, Sapulpa clay*	$ 15–25
Low-ringed, *3 inches tall, early mark*	$ 175–200

Frankoma duck planter, #208A, 9½ inches,
yellow glaze, Sapulpa clay, $40–$50.
*Item courtesy of Kingston Pike Antique Mall,
Knoxville, Tennessee.*

Frankoma GOP elephant mug, 1983,
$30–$40.
*Item courtesy of Bill Brooker, Old School
Antique Mall, Sylva, North Carolina.*

Low-ringed, *3 inches tall, Ada clay*	$ 100–125
Nautilus, *6 inches tall, Ada clay*	$ 60–75
Nautilus, *6 inches tall, Sapulpa clay*	$ 25–35
Pillow, *7¹/₄ inches tall, Ada clay*	$ 50–65
Pillow, *7¹/₄ inches tall, Sapulpa clay*	$ 25–35
Pinnacle, *raised architectural design, 6³/₄ inches, early mark*	$ 450–500
Silver overlay, *floral, two-handled, 1940s*	$ 750–800
Snail vase, *bud, 6 inches tall, Ada clay*	$ 50–65
Snail vase, *bud, 6 inches tall, Sapulpa clay*	$ 10–15
Spire, *6¹/₂ inches tall, Ada clay*	$ 110–125

FULPER POTTERY/STANGL POTTERY

Mark found on art pottery made by *Fulper Pottery*.

There is some debate as to the exact year in which work began at the Flemington, New Jersey, location that would later become Fulper Pottery and, later still, Stangl Pottery. Some sources say it was 1805; others say it was 1814. The owner was Samuel Hill and, at the time work first began, the company's main product was utilitarian drain tiles. Hill died in 1858, and some say the pottery was bought by Abraham Fulper in that year, while others say the surviving family sold it to him in 1860.

Typical *Fulper* oval mark with impressed style number.

Fulper continued making drain tiles, but he also made other utilitarian objects such as beer mugs, vinegar containers, and pickling jars. Fulper died in 1881, and his four sons took over the business. The name of the enterprise changed several times before it was incorporated as the Fulper Pottery Company in 1899.

Fulper impressed mark without the usual oval surrounding the mark.

In 1909, after much experimentation, Fulper introduced a line of art wares called "Vasekraft," which current collectors strongly associate with the American Arts and Crafts movement. Pieces in this line featured the same body Fulper used on its more utilitarian wares such as water filters and crocks. While the bodies were ordinary, however, the shapes and glazes were not. The palette of glaze colors was particularly extensive, and included such hues as Elephant Breath (gray), Mission Matte (brown/black), Mustard

Matte, Verte Antique (rich green), Leopard Skin (a spotted luster glaze with crystalline formations on a slate or mauve background), Cucumber Green, and Famille Rose.

This latter glaze is perhaps the most expensive produced by Fulper, and supposedly recreated the pink color that Europeans had introduced to the Chinese palette in the late 17th century. It was actually a range of colors that ran the gamut from Apple Blossom and Ashes of Roses to Deep Rose and True Rose. It has been reported that at the time they were made, pieces with the Famille Rose glaze were ten times more expensive than other "Vasekraft" pieces of similar size and shape.

In 1910, Martin Stangl became Fulper's ceramics engineer and plant superintendent, but he left in 1914 to work for the Haeger Pottery in Dundee, Illinois. Stangl returned to Fulper in 1920 as general manager, and he became president of the company in 1928. The next year, the old Fulper Pottery in Flemington burned down, and the company moved the majority of its operations to the facilities of the old Anchor Pottery Company in Trenton, New Jersey, which had been acquired by Fulper in 1926. Art pottery continued to be made on a somewhat reduced level at a secondary location in Flemington until 1935, when that operation was completely shut down.

Martin Stangl bought the Fulper pottery in 1930, and changed the emphasis of the company's production. Fulper produced the first American solid-color dinnerware in 1920, but the only color available was green until the 1930s, when other hues were added. The mark "Stangl Pottery" was used on dinnerware as early as the late 1920s, but was not adopted officially until 1955.

Stangl is perhaps best known for its figures of birds taken from the works of John James Audubon, and for its hand-painted dinnerware on red-clay bodies, which was first made in 1942. To make a piece of this dinnerware, Stangl covered the top surface of a red-clay body with a white engobe coating. The pattern was then stenciled on and subsequently carved into the piece's surface. After a firing, the design was hand-colored, covered with a clear glaze, and fired again. Most Stangl dinnerware pieces are marked with the Stangl name and the name of the applicable pattern.

Stangl closed in 1978, ending the long history of the Fulper Pottery Company. It should be noted that some fine Fulper pieces are marked "Prang," which was the name of the company that supplied Fulper with pigments. It is thought that this mark was applied to pieces that Prang used to demonstrate its products.

Fulper bowl, 9½ inches by 4 inches, purple splotches on green, $500–$600.
Item courtesy of Richard Hatch and Associates, Hendersonville, North Carolina.

Fulper compote, 11½ inches by 5 inches, two shades of green, $450–$550.
Item courtesy of Richard Hatch and Associates, Hendersonville, North Carolina.

Fulper mushroom-shaped flower frog, 4-inch diameter, $145–$165.
Item courtesy of Tony McCormack, Sarasota, Florida.

Fulper urn, two handles, 7¼ inches, $475–$525.
Item courtesy of Tony McCormack, Sarasota, Florida.

Fulper Art Pottery

Bookends, 7¼ inches tall, figures of ladies with hats, blue dress, pair	$ 350–400
Bowl, 7½-inch diameter, footed with flared lip, mottled mauve glaze, slight damage to glaze	$ 250–300
Bowl, 8-inch diameter, shallow, surmounted with a handle twisted into a loop, blue and cream glaze on interior, green outer glaze, circa 1910	$ 575–650

175

Fulper vase, 4³/₄ inches, tan to pale blue,
$225–$275.
*Item courtesy of Tony McCormack, Sarasota,
Florida.*

Fulper vase, 4³/₄ inches, two handles,
crystalline glaze, $300–$375.
*Item courtesy of Patty Tower, Old School
Antique Mall, Sylva, North Carolina.*

Fulper vase, 9 inches tall, ribbed,
crystalline glaze, $750–$800.
*Item courtesy of Tony McCormack, Sarasota,
Florida.*

Flower frog, *in the shape of a mushroom, 4-inch diameter*	$ 145–165
Fulper bowl, *9¹/₂-inch diameter, purple splotches on green, green interior, "Colonial Revival"*	$ 500–600
Fulper compote, *green and avocado, 11¹/₂ inches by 5 inches*	$ 450–550
Pitcher, *tankard, 12 inches, brown glaze, circa 1915*	$ 350–400
Urn, *7¹/₄ inches, classical shape with two handles on bulbous base, flared and fluted top, butterscotch flambé*	$ 475–525
Vase, *4³/₄ inches, tan to pale blue*	$ 225–275

Vase, $4^3/4$ inches, two handles, crystalline glaze	$ 300–375
Vase, 7 inches, bulbous, two handles from mid-body to lip, mottled blue-matte shading from light at bottom to dark at top	$ 425–475
Vase, $7^1/2$ inches, globular form with three small handles from shoulder to lip, blue crystalline glaze	$ 425–500
Vase, $7^1/2$ inches, ovoid cylinder-shaped, olive-green to brown glaze	$ 375–425
Vase, $8^1/2$ inches, Mustard Matte on bulbous base, shaded to Elephant's Breath (dark gray) at top, two handles from upper shoulder to lip	$ 450–500
Vase, $8^3/4$ inches, long neck with small bulbous base, blue crystalline glaze	$ 450–500
Vase, 9 inches, ribbed, crystalline glaze	$ 750–800
Vase, 9 inches tall, trumpet-shaped, blue flambé glaze	$ 250–300
Vase, $9^1/4$ inches tall, baluster-shaped with flared lip, blue-glaze shading from light at the bottom to dark at the top	$ 275–325
Vase, $9^1/2$ inches, unusual multicolor glaze with shades of brown, blue, green, and lavender, matte glaze at bottom, high gloss at top	$ 650–700
Vase, $10^1/2$ inches tall, crystalline glaze of tan and green	$ 350–400
Vase, $10^1/2$ inches tall, urn-shaped with two handles, glaze shaded from matte to high gloss in shades of lavender, rose, and blue	$ 600–650
Vase, $11^1/2$ inches, two handles, bulbous body, tall narrow neck, thick gray/green drip glaze on neck, shades to brown and then to Mustard Matte	$ 850–925

Stangl Birds

Largely based on John James Audubon's *Birds of America,* the Stangl figures of birds were made from 1939 to approximately 1978. These pieces were modeled by John Tierney and August Jacob, and Jacob's name can be found molded into the base of the #3584 Large Cockatoo. It is thought that Jacob received a royalty on each bird Stangl sold, but when his contract ran out, Stangl had Jacob's name removed from the mold. Collectors are particularly interested in the birds glazed with Antique Ivory or Turquoise Crackled, as well as those glazed with the Terra Rose art glaze. These pieces were produced early in the company's history, and are difficult to find. There are many color variations found on Stangl birds, and these variations can greatly affect the value of the pieces.

Mark used by *Stangl Pottery*.

3250A Standing Duck, *3¹/₂ inches, Antique Ivory or Turquoise*	$ 150–175
3250A Standing Duck, *3¹/₂ inches, brushed gold*	$ 65–85
3250B Preening Duck, *2³/₄ inches*	$ 110–135
3250B Preening Duck, *Terra Rose glaze, 2³/₄ inches*	$ 95–110
3250C Feeding Duck, *1³/₄ inches*	$ 110–135
3250D Gazing Duck, *3³/₄ inches*	$ 125–150
3250E Drinking Duck, *1¹/₂ inches*	$ 110–135
3250F Quacking Duck, *3¹/₄ inches*	$ 125–150
3273 Rooster, *5³/₄ inches*	$ 600–700
3274 Penguin, *black and white, 6 inches*	$ 525–600
3275 Turkey, *3¹/₂ inches, Antique Ivory or Turquoise*	$ 575–650
3276S Bluebird, *single, 5 inches, 1939-style*	$ 225–250
3276S Bluebird, *single, 5 inches, restyled*	$ 125–150
3276D Bluebird, *double, 8¹/₂ inches, early version*	$ 300–350
3276D Bluebird, *double, 8¹/₂ inches, restyled*	$ 225–275

3400 Love Bird, *single, 4 inches, original version, unmarked*	$ 165–185
3400 Love Bird, *single, 4 inches, restyled version, marked*	$ 120–145
3401S Wren, *single, 3¹/₂ inches, original, head up*	$ 325–375
3401S Wren, *single, 3¹/₂ inches, restyled, head down*	$ 85–100
3401D Wren, *double, 8 inches, original*	$ 650–700
3401D Wren, *double, 8 inches, restyled*	$ 175–200
3402S Oriole, *single, original version, head down, 3¹/₄ inches*	$ 175–200
3402S Oriole, *single, restyled, head up, 3¹/₄ inches*	$ 175–200
3402D Oriole, *double, original, 5¹/₂ inches*	$ 400–450
3402D Oriole, *double, restyled, 5¹/₂ inches*	$ 150–175
3404D Love Birds (parakeets), *double, original, 5¹/₂ inches*	$ 475–525
3404D Love Birds (parakeets), *double, restyled, 5¹/₂ inches*	$ 200–225
3405S Cockatoo (originally called "Parrot"), *single, original, brightly multicolored, 6 inches*	$ 850–950
3405S Cockatoo, *original, Antique Ivory or Turquoise, single, 6 inches*	$ 200–235
3405S Cockatoo, *original, white with colored accents and red crest, single, 6 inches*	$ 750–850
3405S Cockatoo, *restyled, single, 6 inches*	$ 100–150
3405D Cockatoo, *double, original, 6 inches*	$ 275–325
3405D Cockatoo, *double, restyled, 6 inches*	$ 200–250
3406S Kingfisher, *single, 3¹/₂ inches, original*	$ 175–200
3406S Kingfisher, *single, 3¹/₂ inches, restyled*	$ 110–125
3406D Kingfisher, *double, 5 inches, original*	$ 275–325
3406D Kingfisher, *double, 5 inches, restyled*	$ 200–250
3407 Owl, *4 inches, original, brown*	$ 550–650
3407 Owl, *4 inches, original, white with black*	$ 650–700
3408 Bird of Paradise, *5¹/₂ inches, Antique Ivory, Turquoise, or Terra Rose*	$ 400–450
3408 Bird of Paradise, *multicolored*	$ 150–175
3430 Duck, *22 inches*	$ 10,000–12,000
3431 Duck, *standing, 8 inches, white and black*	$ 1,400–1,600

3431 Duck, *standing, 8 inches, brown and green*	$ 850–950
3432 Duck, *running, 5 inches, white and black*	$ 850–950
3432 Duck, *running, 5 inches, brown and green*	$ 800–900
3433 Rooster, *16 inches*	$ 5,000–6,000
3443 Flying Duck, *9 inches, multicolored, airbrushed*	$ 850–950
3443 Flying Duck, *9 inches, green*	$ 300–350
3443 Flying Duck, *9 inches, gray or Antique Gold*	$ 400–450
3444 Cardinal, *female, pinecones, 6^1/$_2$ inches, original*	$ 200–250
3444 Cardinal, *female, pine cones, 6^1/$_2$ inches, restyled*	$ 120–150
3445 Rooster, *9 inches, gray*	$ 350–400
3445 Rooster, *9 inches, yellow*	$ 250–300
3446 Hen, *7 inches, gray*	$ 350–400
3446 Hen, *7 inches, yellow*	$ 225–250
3447 Yellow Warbler, *5 inches, yellow and green*	$ 110–135
3448 Blue-Headed Vireo, *4^1/$_4$ inches, multicolored*	$ 110–135
3449 Parakeet, *5^1/$_2$ inches, multicolored*	$ 200–250
3450 Passenger Pigeon, *marked "American Way,"* *Russel Wright, 18 inches by 9 inches*	$ 2,500–2,700
3450 Passenger Pigeon, *marked "Stangl," 18 inches by 9 inches*	$ 2,000–2,200
3451 Willow, *Ptarmigan, 11 inches by 11 inches,* *marked "American Way," Russel Wright*	$ 4,500–5,000
3451 Willow, *Ptarmigan, 11 inches by 11 inches, marked* *"Stangl"*	$ 3,250–3,500
3452 Painted Bunting, *5 inches*	$ 125–150
3453 Mountain Bluebird, *marked "American Way,"* *Russel Wright, 6^1/$_8$ inches*	$ 2,000–2,250
3453 Mountain Bluebird, *marked "Stangl," 6^1/$_8$ inches*	$ 1,400–1,600
3454 Key West Quail Dove, *marked "American Way,"* *Russel Wright, 9 inches*	$ 850–950
3454 Key West Quail Dove, *marked "Stangl," 9 inches*	$ 300–350
3454 Key West Quail Dove, *renumbered #5071, two wings up,* *bright multicolored, 9 inches*	$ 1,850–2,000

Stangl bird, American redstarts, double, 9 inches, #3490, pale wartime colors, $275–$300.
Item courtesy of Richard Hatch and Associates, Hendersonville, North Carolina.

Stangl bird, cock pheasant, 11 inches, #3492, $250–$300.
Item courtesy of Tony McCormack, Sarasota, Florida.

3455 Shoveler, *12¹/₄ inches by 14 inches, marked "American Way," Russel Wright*	$ 3,750–4,000
3455 Shoveler, *12¹/₄ inches by 14 inches, marked "Stangl"*	$ 2,600–2,750
3456 Cerulean Warbler, *4¹/₄ inches, multicolored*	$ 100–120
3457 Pheasant, *7¹/₄ inches by 15 inches*	$ 5,250–5,500
3458 Quail, *7¹/₂ inches*	$ 2,000–2,250
3459 Fish Hawk, *9¹/₂ inches*	$ 7,500–8,250
3490 American Redstarts, *double, 9 inches, pale wartime colors*	$ 275–300
3491 Hen Pheasant, *11 inches by 6¹/₄ inches*	$ 200–235
3492 Cock Pheasant, *11 inches by 6¹/₄ inches*	$ 250–300
3518D White-Headed Pigeon, *double, 12¹/₂ inches by 7¹/₂ inches*	$ 1,250–1,400
3580 Cockatoo, *medium, 8⁷/₈ inches, lighter multicolor*	$ 225–250
3580 Cockatoo, *medium, 8⁷/₈ inches, darker multicolor*	$ 200–225

3581 Chickadees, *group, three, 5¹/₂ inches by 8¹/₂ inches, brown and white*	$ 200–250
3582 Parakeets, *double, 7 inches, green*	$ 250–300
3582 Parakeets, *double, 7 inches, blue*	$ 325–375
3583 Parula Warbler, *4¹/₄ inches*	$ 85–100
3584 Cockatoo, *large, 11¹/₂ inches*	$ 225–275
3584 Cockatoo, *large, signed "Jacob," 11¹/₂ inches*	$ 325–350
3584 Cockatoo, *large, white with pastel colors, 11¹/₂ inches*	$ 1,000–1,100
3585 Rufous Hummingbird, *3 inches*	$ 85–100
3586 Pheasant, *"Della Ware" line, 15¹/₂ inches by 9 inches, multicolored*	$ 1,450–1,600
3589 Indigo Bunting, *3¹/₄ inches*	$ 100–120
3590 Chat (Carolina Wren), *4¹/₂ inches*	$ 200–225
3591 Brewer's Blackbird, *3¹/₂ inches*	$ 225–250
3592 Titmouse, *2¹/₂ inches*	$ 80–100
3593 Nuthatch, *2¹/₂ inches*	$ 100–120
3594 Red-faced Warbler, *3 inches*	$ 120–135
3595 Bobolink, *4³/₄ inches*	$ 200–225
3596 Gray Cardinal (Pyrrhuloxia), *4³/₄ inches*	$ 120–135
3597 Wilson Warbler, *3¹/₂ inches*	$ 75–85
3598 Kentucky Warbler, *3 inches*	$ 75–85
3599 Hummingbirds, *double, 10¹/₂ inches by 8 inches*	$ 400–450
3625 Bird of Paradise, *13¹/₂ inches*	$ 3,000–3,250
3626 Broadtail Hummingbird, *blue flower, 6 inches*	$ 200–225
3627 Rivoli Hummingbird, *pink flower, 6 inches*	$ 200–225
3628 Rieffers Hummingbird, *4¹/₂ inches*	$ 200–225
3629 Broadbill Hummingbird, *4¹/₂ inches*	$ 200–225
3634 Allen Hummingbird, *3¹/₂ inches*	$ 125–150
3635 Goldfinches, *group of four, 11¹/₂ inches by 4 inches*	$ 250–300
3715 Blue Jay, *peanut, 10¹/₄ inches*	$ 850–950
3716 Blue Jay, *leaf, 10¹/₄ inches*	$ 750–825
3717 Blue Jay, *double, 12¹/₂ inches*	$ 4,250–4,500

3746 Canary, *right, rose flower, 6^1/$_4$ inches*	$ 275–325
3747 Canary, *left, blue flower, 6^1/$_4$ inches*	$ 275–325
3749S Scarlet Tanager, *pink body, 4^3/$_4$ inches*	$ 425–475
3749S Western Tanager, *red matte body, 4^3/$_4$ inches*	$ 450–500
3750D Scarlet Tanager, *double, pink body, 8 inches*	$ 600–650
3750D Western Tanager, *red matte body, double, 8 inches*	$ 650–700
3751S Red-Headed Woodpecker, *6^1/$_4$ inches, pink glossy*	$ 400–425
3751S Red-Headed Woodpecker, *6^1/$_4$ inches, red matte*	$ 550–600
3752D Red-Headed Woodpecker, *double, 7^3/$_4$ inches, pink glossy*	$ 600–650
3752D Red-Headed Woodpecker, *double, 7^3/$_4$ inches, red matte*	$ 650–700
3753S White Wing Crossbill, *3^1/$_2$ inches, pink glossy*	$ 3,200–3,400
3754D White Wing Crossbill, *8^3/$_4$ inches, double, pink glossy*	$ 600–650
3754D White Wing Crossbill, *8^3/$_4$ inches, double, red matte*	$ 800–850
3755S Audubon Warbler, *4^1/$_4$ inches, black head and tail*	$ 450–500
3755S Audubon Warbler, *4^1/$_4$ inches, blue head and tail*	$ 550–600
3756D Audubon Warbler, *7^3/$_4$ inches, double*	$ 650–700
3757 Scissor-Tailed Flycatcher, *11 inches*	$ 1,200–1,300
3758 Magpie Jay, *10^3/$_4$ inches*	$ 1,500–1,600
3810 Blackpoll Warbler, *3^1/$_2$ inches*	$ 225–250
3811 Chestnut-Backed Chickadee, *5 inches*	$ 175–200
3812 Chestnut-Sided Chickadee, *5 inches*	$ 175–200
3813 Evening Grosbeak, *5 inches*	$ 200–275
3814 Black-Throated Green Warbler, *3^1/$_8$ inches*	$ 200–225
3815 Western Bluebird, *7 inches*	$ 550–600
3848 Golden Crowned Kinglet, *4^1/$_8$ inches*	$ 140–160
3849 Goldfinch, *4 inches*	$ 175–200
3850 Yellow Warbler, *4 inches*	$ 200–225
3851 Red-Breasted Nuthatch, *3^3/$_4$ inches*	$ 125–145
3852 Cliff Swallow, *3^3/$_4$ inches*	$ 175–200
3853 Golden-Crowned Kinglets, *group, 5 inches by 5^1/$_2$ inches*	$ 900–1,000

3868 Summer Tanager, *4 inches*	$ 900–1,000
3921 Yellow-Headed Verdin, *4¹/₂ inches*	$ 1,600–1,750
3922 European Finch, *4¹/₂ inches*	$ 1,600–1,750
3923 Vermillion Flycatcher, *5³/₄ inches*	$ 1,750–2,000
3924 Yellow-Throated Warbler	$ 850–950
3925 Magnolia Warbler	$ 3,000–3,250

Miscellaneous Bird-Related Items

Bird on Gourd ashtray, *white gourd*	$ 275–300
Bird on Gourd ashtray, *green gourd*	$ 325–350
Deviled-egg plate with duck in center	$ 275–300
Deviled-egg plate with hen in center	$ 165–180

Animal Figures

In late 1937, Stangl began producing small figures of animals. The early animals in the 3178 series were fairly monochromatic (sometimes they were decorated with polka dots and colored glazes), and extensively hand-painted animal figures were not produced until approximately 1939. Production of these animals ceased in 1978.

3178A Elkhound, *4 inches, black and white*	$ 275–300
3178A Elkhound, *4 inches, polka dots*	$ 425–450
3178B Pony, *3¹/₂ inches, black and white*	$ 300–325
3178B Pony, *3¹/₂ inches, polka dots*	$ 425–450
3178C Burro, *3¹/₂ inches, black and white*	$ 425–450
3178C Burro, *3¹/₂ inches, polka dots*	$ 475–500
3178D Mule, *3¹/₂ inches, black and white*	$ 375–400
3178D Mule, *polka dots*	$ 475–500
3178E Giraffe, *3¹/₂ inches, black and white*	$ 425–450
3178E Giraffe, *3¹/₂ inches, polka dots*	$ 475–500
3178F Percheron, *3 inches, black and white*	$ 225–250
3178F Percheron, *3 inches, polka dots*	$ 350–400
3178G Elephant, *2¹/₂ inches, black and white*	$ 275–300
3178G Elephant, *2¹/₂ inches, polka dots*	$ 375–400

3178H Squirrel, *3 inches, black and white*	$ 325–350
3178H Squirrel, *3 inches, polka dots*	$ 375–400
3178I Scottie, *3¹/₂ inches, black and white*	$ 450–500
3178I Scottie, *3¹/₂ inches, polka dots*	$ 500–575
3178J Gazelle, *3¹/₂ inches, black and white*	$ 275–325
3178J Gazelle, *3¹/₂ inches, polka dots*	$ 325–375

Hand-Painted Animals

Prices listed below are for standard glazed pieces. Pieces with marbling or unusual glazes such as Terra Rose (mottled green, mauve, or blue), Antique Ivory Crackled, or Turquoise Crackle can, in some instances, bring significantly higher prices.

3243 Wire-Haired Terrier, *3¹/₄ inches*	$ 350–400
3244 Clydesdale ("Draft Horse"), *3 inches*	$ 200–250
3245 Running Rabbit, *2 inches*	$ 350–400
3246 Buffalo, *2 inches*	$ 475–525
3247 Gazelle, *3³/₄ inches*	$ 325–350
3248 Giraffe, *3¹/₂ inches*	$ 750–850
3249 Elephant, *3 inches*	$ 275–325
3272 Airedale Terrier, *2¹/₄ inches*	$ 650–750
3277 Colt, *5 inches*	$ 1,750–1,850
3278 Goat, *5 inches*	$ 1,750–1,850
3279 Calf, *3¹/₂ inches*	$ 900–1,100

Ashtrays

These very collectible items were intended to appeal to sportsmen: they featured images related to golfing, fishing, and hunting. Examples usually feature a gray engobe background, but white was used occasionally, and the pieces with white backgrounds are generally (but not always) more valuable. These ashtrays were part of the "Sportsman Giftware" line that was introduced in 1955 and discontinued in the mid-1970s.

Square Ashtrays

Canvasback duck on gray engobe background, *9¹/₄ inches*	$ 60–85
Canvasback duck on white engobe background, *9¹/₄ inches*	$ 125–150

Stangl square ashtray, Caribbean pattern,
#3915, $110–$135.
*Item courtesy of Richard H. Crane, Knoxville,
Tennessee.*

Stangl square ashtray, rare pink-elephant
decoration, $325–$375.
*Item courtesy of Richard H. Crane, Knoxville,
Tennessee.*

Caribbean, *tropical fish and sea life, #3915*	$ 110–135
Elephant, *pink, extremely rare*	$ 325–375
Golf Course, *with golf ball in center well, $9^1/_4$ inches*	$ 175–200
Mallard Duck, *flying*	$ 60–85
Porpoise, *jumping, $9^1/_4$ inches*	$ 110–135
Rainbow Trout, *$9^1/_4$ inches*	$ 150–175

Oval Ashtrays

California Quail	$ 140–160
Canadian Goose	$ 30–45
Deer	$ 50–65
Golf Course	$ 150–175
Partridge	$ 125–150
Pheasant	$ 35–45

Stangl oval ashtray, Canadian goose,
#3926, $30–$45.
*Item courtesy of Richard H. Crane, Knoxville,
Tennessee.*

Stangl oval ashtray, deer decoration,
#3962, $50–$65.
*Item courtesy of Richard H. Crane, Knoxville,
Tennessee.*

Stangl oval ashtray, sailfish decoration,
$75–$95.
*Item courtesy of Richard H. Crane, Knoxville,
Tennessee.*

Sailfish, *white engobe*	$ 75–95
Snow Goose	$ 300–350
Striped Bass	$ 165–185
Woodcock	$ 135–165

Amoeba-Shaped Ashtrays

Pinecone	$ 50–70
Tropical Fish	$ 75–100

Stangl round ashtray, 8-inch diameter, hunting dog, $60–$75.
Item courtesy of Kingston Pike Antique Mall, Knoxville, Tennessee.

Round Ashtrays

This list includes both 8-inch diameter windproof ashtrays and large 10-inch diameter ashtrays that collectors often refer to as "flying saucers."

Canvasback Duck, *10-inch diameter*	$ 150–175
Hunting Dog, *8-inch diameter, windproof*	$ 60–75
Marlin, *10-inch diameter*	$ 175–210
Pheasant, *10-inch diameter*	$ 150–175
Sailboat, *10-inch diameter*	$ 190–225
Seagull, *10-inch diameter*	$ 190–225

Figural Salt and Pepper Shakers

Bluebirds, *set*	$ 225–250
Cherubs, *multicolored*	$ 160–190
Cowboy and Cowgirl ("Ranger"), *multicolored, set*	$ 700–800
Cowboy and Cowgirl ("Ranger"), *solid-color, set*	$ 325–400

Daisy, *solid-color, set*	$ 140–165
Fish, *solid-color, set*	$ 185–225
Golf balls, *set*	$ 75–100
Hurricane lamps, *yellow and green*	$ 130–160
Lemons, *solid-color, set*	$ 110–140
Pigs, *set*	$ 150–180
Sailor and Sailor Girl, *hand-painted, set*	$ 600–675
Sailor and Sailor Girl, *solid-color, set*	$ 300–350

Dinnerware

The dinnerware lines most often associated with Stangl were introduced in 1942. Pieces generally featured red-clay bodies with hand-incised and hand-painted decorations. To make the vast majority of these items, red-clay blanks were covered with white engobe, and patterns were stenciled and then carved into the stenciled outlines. The pieces then went through their first firing. After that, the items were painted, covered with a clear glaze, and fired a second time.

"Amber Glo"

This is an unusual pattern designed by Kay Hackett. On pieces featuring this pattern, wavy lines enclose stick-figure trees with dots and commalike dashes.

Bowl, *individual fruit*	$ 10–14
Bowl, *individual soup, lug handle, 5^1/$_2$-inch diameter*	$ 15–18
Bowl, *individual soup, coupe shape, 7^1/$_2$-inch diameter*	$ 16–20
Bowl, *vegetable, oval, divided, 10 inches*	$ 50–60
Bowl, *vegetable, round, 8 inches*	$ 35–40
Butter dish, *^{1}/$_4$-pound, covered*	$ 45–55
Casserole, *individual, lidded*	$ 38–44
Coffeepot	$ 75–85
Creamer	$ 22–28
Cup and saucer	$ 14–18
Dish, *pickle*	$ 28–32
Dish, *relish*	$ 18–22
Gravy boat and underliner	$ 45–55

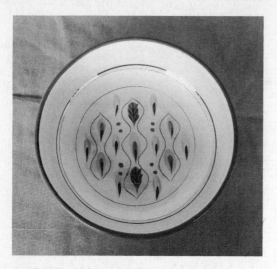

Stangl "Amber Glo" vegetable bowl, 8-inch diameter,
$35–$40.
Item courtesy of Richard H. Crane, Knoxville, Tennessee.

Jug, *32-ounce*	$ 38–44
Plate, *bread and butter, 6-inch diameter*	$ 4–6
Plate, *chop, 12-inch diameter*	$ 60–70
Plate, *dinner, 10-inch diameter*	$ 22–28
Plate, *luncheon, 9-inch diameter*	$ 15–18
Plate, *salad, 8-inch diameter*	$ 10–14
Platter, *oval, 13 inches*	$ 48–56
Salt and pepper shakers, *set*	$ 25–35
Skillet, *open*	$ 45–55
Sugar bowl	$ 35–40
Tray, *bread*	$ 35–45

"Apple Delight"

This pattern features a cluster of red apples with a green border.

Bowl, *cereal*	$ 22–26
Bowl, *individual soup, lug handle*	$ 22–26

Bowl, *vegetable, oval, divided, 10 inches*	$ 48–55
Bowl, *vegetable, round, 9-inch diameter*	$ 38–44
Cup and saucer	$ 14–18
Jug, *24-ounce*	$ 45–55
Plate, *bread and butter, 6^{1}/$_{2}$-inch diameter*	$ 6–10
Plate, *dinner, 10-inch diameter*	$ 18–22
Platter, *oval, 13^{3}/$_{4}$ inches*	$ 65–75
Platter, *oval, 15 inches*	$ 75–85

"Blueberry"

This pattern was designed by Kay Hackett. Flatware pieces in this line have yellow rims around the outside, with a cluster of blueberries and leaves in the center.

Bowl, *cereal*	$ 25–32
Bowl, *individual fruit*	$ 24–30
Bowl, *individual soup, lug handle, 5^{1}/$_{2}$-inch diameter*	$ 25–32
Bowl, *individual soup, coupe shape, 7^{1}/$_{2}$-inch diameter*	$ 32–40
Bowl, *vegetable, oval, divided, 10 inches*	$ 55–65
Bowl, *vegetable, round, 8-inch diameter*	$ 45–55
Casserole, *individual, lidded*	$ 35–45
Casserole, *1^{1}/$_{2}$-quart, lidded*	$ 140–160
Coffeepot	$ 110–125
Creamer	$ 35–42
Cup and saucer	$ 18–25
Dish, *pickle*	$ 45–55
Gravy boat and underliner	$ 65–75
Plate, *bread and butter, 6^{1}/$_{2}$-inch diameter*	$ 12–16
Plate, *chop, 12-inch diameter*	$ 65–75
Plate, *chop, 14-inch diameter*	$ 90–110
Plate, *dinner, 10-inch diameter*	$ 55–65
Plate, *luncheon, 9-inch diameter*	$ 35–45
Plate, *salad, 8-inch diameter*	$ 32–36

Salt and pepper shakers, *set*	$ 38–45
Skillet, *open*	$ 55–65
Skillet, *open, small*	$ 45–55
Sugar bowl, *lidded*	$ 45–55
Tidbit server, *two-tier*	$ 100–115

"Bittersweet"

Pieces bearing this design feature an orange band with orange flowers and green leaves.

Bowl, *cereal*	$ 10–14
Bowl, *salad, serving*	$ 44–50
Bowl, *vegetable, oval, divided, 10 inches*	$ 35–45
Bowl, *vegetable, round, 8-inch diameter*	$ 22–28
Butter dish, *1/4-pound, covered*	$ 35–45
Cup and saucer	$ 12–16
Dish, *relish*	$ 16–20
Gravy boat and underliner	$ 45–55
Plate, *bread and butter, 6 1/2-inch diameter*	$ 5–7
Plate, *chop, 12-inch diameter*	$ 42–50
Plate, *dinner, 10-inch diameter*	$ 15–19
Plate, *salad, 8-inch diameter*	$ 7–10
Platter, *oval, 14 inches*	$ 40–50
Skillet, *open*	$ 45–55
Snack set, *cup and plate*	$ 16–20
Sugar bowl, *lidded*	$ 22–28
Tidbit server, *two-tier*	$ 65–75
Tray, *bread, 15 inches*	$ 35–45

"Caughley" or "Town and Country"

This pattern was in production from 1964 to 1978, and was designed to look like the spatter-decorated items associated with 19th-century enamelware. Pieces in this line were produced in blue, black, brown, green, honey, pink, and yellow. Crimson pieces were reportedly made as well, but examples have not been found. Honey was

Stangl pitcher, "Caughley" or "Town and Country" pattern, yellow spatter, 11 inches tall, $100–$115.

added to the line's color palette in 1977, and is probably the least desirable of the various colors.

Bean pot, *blue*	$ 35–45
Bean pot, *green, pink, or yellow*	$ 30–40
Cup and saucer, *blue*	$ 35–45
Cup and saucer, *green, pink, or yellow*	$ 20–30
Dessert mold, *Turk's head, 7¹/₂ inches, blue*	$ 65–75
Dessert mold, *Turk's head, 7¹/₂ inches, green, pink, or yellow*	$ 45–55
Pitcher, *11 inches tall, yellow*	$ 100–115
Plate, *bread and butter, 6¹/₂-inch diameter, blue*	$ 14–18
Plate, *bread and butter, 6¹/₂-inch diameter, green, pink, or yellow*	$ 8–12
Plate, *dinner, 10-inch diameter, blue*	$ 55–65
Plate, *dinner, 10-inch diameter, green, pink, or yellow*	$ 25–35
Plate, *salad, 8-inch diameter, blue*	$ 32–42
Plate, *salad, 8-inch diameter, green, pink or yellow*	$ 22–28

"Chicory"

This pattern was designed by Kay Hackett, and is decorated with blue flowers with long brown stems.

Bowl, *cereal*	$ 26–34
Bowl, *individual fruit*	$ 22–30
Bowl, *oval, vegetable, divided, 10 inches*	$ 75–85
Bowl, *vegetable, round, 10-inch diameter*	$ 60–68
Casserole, *individual, lidded*	$ 40–50
Creamer	$ 28–35
Cup and saucer	$ 16–22
Gravy boat and underliner	$ 75–85
Plate, *bread and butter, 6^1/$_2$-inch diameter*	$ 12–16
Plate, *chop, 12-inch diameter*	$ 65–75
Plate, *dinner, 10-inch diameter*	$ 35–45
Plate, *luncheon, 9-inch diameter*	$ 22–30
Plate, *salad, 8-inch diameter*	$ 22–30
Salt and pepper shakers, *set*	$ 32–40
Skillet, *open*	$ 42–48
Sugar bowl, *lidded*	$ 40–48

"Country Garden"

This pattern was designed by Kay Hackett. Flatware pieces in this line have a cluster of colorful flowers—yellow jonquils, bluebells, and buttercups—in their centers. "Country Garden" pieces were produced both with typical red (or brown) bodies and with white bodies. The white body is rarer, and pieces made with white bodies are about 25 percent more valuable than is indicated by the prices listed below.

Bowl, *cereal*	$ 22–30
Bowl, *individual soup, lug handle, 6-inch diameter*	$ 24–32
Bowl, *salad, serving, 10-inch diameter*	$ 55–65
Bowl, *salad, serving, 12-inch diameter*	$ 75–85
Bowl, *vegetable, divided, 10 inches*	$ 30–40

Casserole, *individual, lidded*	$ 55–65
Casserole, *1^1/$_4$-quart*	$ 150–160
Cup and saucer	$ 12–18
Creamer	$ 18–22
Dish, *relish*	$ 25–32
Dish, *nut, footed*	$ 40–46
Gravy boat and underliner	$ 40–50
Plate, *bread and butter, 6^1/$_2$-inch diameter*	$ 8–12
Plate, *dinner, 10-inch diameter*	$ 22–30
Plate, *chop, 12-inch diameter*	$ 40–48
Plate, *chop, 14-inch diameter*	$ 80–90
Plate, *luncheon, 9-inch diameter*	$ 20–28
Platter, *oval, 14 inches*	$ 55–65
Snack set, *cup and plate*	$ 15–22
Skillet, *open*	$ 80–90
Sugar bowl, *lidded*	$ 36–44
Teapot	$ 90–110
Tidbit server, *two-tier*	$ 75–85
Tray, *bread, 15 inches*	$ 55–65

"Country Life"

This is a charming pattern, designed by Kurt Weis and adapted by Kay Hackett, featuring depictions of farm animals and farm life. One 10-inch diameter plate, for example, depicts a farmer's wife harvesting carrots while another more common 10-inch dinner plate features the image of a rooster. In addition, there were images of ducks, chickens, farmhouses, barns, pigs, colts, calves, and mallard ducks.

Bowl, *individual soup, mallard, 8-inch diameter*	$ 115–125
Bowl, *individual soup, mallard diving for food, 8-inch diameter*	$ 240–250
Cup and saucer (hen on cup, three eggs on saucer)	$ 70–80
Plate, *bread and butter, 6^1/$_2$-inch diameter*	$ 25–35
Plate, *chop, 12-inch diameter, barn*	$ 400–425
Plate, *chop, 12-inch diameter, barn with personalized name of a farm*	$ 500–525

Stangl "Country Life" 8-inch diameter plate, $90–$110.
*Item courtesy of Kingston Pike Antique Mall, Knoxville,
Tennessee.*

Plate, *dinner, rooster, 10-inch diameter*	$ 115–125
Plate, *dinner, farmer's wife harvesting carrots, 10-inch diameter*	$ 220–230
Plate, *salad, 8-inch diameter, pig at fence*	$ 90–110

"Fruit"

This pattern was designed by Kay Hackett and went into production about 1945. The decoration consists of various colorful depictions of fruit, including plums, cherries, apples, grapes, peaches, and pears. The original production had a yellow border with a brown edge, but late examples do not have the brown accent.

Bean pot	$ 190–200
Bowl, *individual fruit*	$ 18–22
Bowl, *cereal*	$ 32–36
Bowl, *oval, divided, 10-inch diameter*	$ 35–45
Bowl, *round, 9-inch diameter*	$ 45–55
Bowl, *round, 10-inch diameter*	$ 65–75
Butter dish, *¹/₄-pound, covered*	$ 90–100

Casserole, $1^1/_2$-quart	$ 130–140
Coffeepot	$ 150–160
Creamer	$ 25–30
Cup and saucer	$ 18–22
Dish, *pickle*	$ 40–48
Dish, *relish*	$ 32–38
Gravy boat and underliner	$ 45–55
Plate, *bread and butter, 6$^1/_2$-inch diameter*	$ 10–14
Plate, *chop, 13-inch diameter*	$ 55–65
Plate, *dinner, 10-inch diameter*	$ 40–46
Plate, *luncheon, 9-inch diameter*	$ 38–44
Plate, *salad, 8-inch diameter*	$ 18–22
Platter, *oval, 14 inches*	$ 40–50
Platter, *oval, 14$^3/_4$ inches*	$ 75–85
Platter, *oval, 15 inches*	$ 90–100
Sugar bowl, *lidded*	$ 28–34

"Fruit and Flowers"

This pattern is yet another designed by Kay Hackett. Flatware bearing this pattern features green and blue bands around its outer edge, and is decorated with a profusion of fruit and flowers with leaves.

Bowl, *cereal*	$ 28–32
Bowl, *individual fruit, 5$^1/_2$-inch diameter*	$ 22–28
Bowl, *individual soup*	$ 25–32
Bowl, *vegetable, oval, divided, 10 inches*	$ 65–75
Bowl, *vegetable, round, 8-inch diameter*	$ 60–70
Creamer	$ 30–35
Cup and saucer	$ 18–22
Dish, *nut, footed*	$ 50–60
Dish, *relish*	$ 32–38
Gravy boat with underliner	$ 85–95

Plate, *bread and butter, 6^1/$_2$-inch diameter*	$ 12–16
Plate, *dinner, 10-inch diameter*	$ 38–44
Plate, *salad, 8-inch diameter*	$ 22–28
Salt and pepper shakers, *set*	$ 45–52
Sugar bowl	$ 40–48
Teapot	$ 180–200
Tidbit server, *two-tier*	$ 80–90
Tidbit server, *three-tier*	$ 90–100

"Garden Flower"

Yet another Kay Hackett design, this pattern features a yellow edge with a decoration of various flowers and leaves. Among the different flowers depicted are blue balloon flowers, purple campanula, yellow campanula, blue flax, blue morning glory, pink phlox, yellow sunflowers, and yellow tiger lilies.

Bowl, *individual fruit, calendula*	$ 16–20
Bowl, *vegetable, round, 8-inch diameter, phlox*	$ 50–60
Creamer, *calendula or morning glory*	$ 35–40
Creamer, *small individual, rose*	$ 30–35
Cup and saucer, *rose on cup, leaves on saucer*	$ 18–22
Pitcher, *2-quart, sunflower*	$ 75–85
Plate, *bread and butter, 6^1/$_2$-inch diameter, balloon flower*	$ 10–15
Plate, *chop, 12-inch diameter, tiger lily or balloon flower*	$ 70–80
Plate, *dinner, 10-inch diameter, rose*	$ 35–45
Plate, *luncheon, 9-inch diameter, tiger lily*	$ 25–32
Plate, *salad, 8-inch diameter, bleeding heart*	$ 22–28
Plate, *service, 11-inch diameter, sunflower*	$ 50–60
Salt and pepper shakers, *set*	$ 35–45
Teapot, *sunflower*	$ 100–110
Tidbit server, *two-tier*	$ 80–90
Tidbit server, *three-tier*	$ 80–100

Stangl 2-quart pitcher in the "Garden Flower" pattern, sunflower, $75–$85.
Item courtesy of Hank and Mary J. Clemens, Old School Antique Mall, Sylva, North Carolina.

"Golden Harvest"

This pattern is very similar to "Magnolia." It has a gray background with white and tan flowers.

Bowl, *individual fruit, 5¹/₂-inch diameter*	$ 12–16
Bowl, *salad, serving, 10-inch diameter*	$ 45–55
Bowl, *soup, lug-handled, 6-inch diameter*	$ 20–26
Bowl, *vegetable, oval, divided, 10³/₄ inches*	$ 32–38
Bowl, *vegetable, round, 8-inch diameter*	$ 30–35
Casserole, *individual, lidded*	$ 35–45
Creamer	$ 16–22
Cup and saucer	$ 12–16
Dish, *relish, 11¹/₄ inches*	$ 15–20
Gravy boat	$ 28–34
Plate, *bread and butter, 6-inch diameter*	$ 5–8
Plate, *chop, 14-inch diameter*	$ 65–75

Stangl teapot, "Golden Harvest" pattern, $85–$100.
Item courtesy of Hank and Mary J. Clemens, Old School Antique Mall, Sylva, North Carolina.

Plate, *dinner, 10-inch diameter*	$ 20–26
Plate, *service or place, 11¹/₂-inch diameter*	$ 28–32
Skillet, *open*	$ 45–55
Sugar bowl, *lidded*	$ 28–32
Teapot	$ 85–100
Tray, *bread, 15¹/₄ inches*	$ 35–45

"Lyric"

This is a very unusual pattern for Stangl, and few people recognize it as either a Stangl product or a Kay Hackett design without first looking on the back of a piece and seeing the mark. "Lyric" features abstract, stylized musical notes (that look a bit like Alexander Calder mobiles) painted in black and brown on a white background.

Cup and saucer	$ 22–28
Plate, *bread and butter, 6-inch diameter*	$ 18–24
Plate, *dinner, 10-inch diameter*	$ 45–55
Plate, *salad, 8-inch diameter*	$ 30–40

"Magnolia"

This common pattern consists of rust and white flowers with green leaves on a gray-green background and, like so many other Stangl patterns, was designed by Kay Hackett.

Bowl, *individual fruit*	$ 12–18
Bowl, *individual soup, lug handles*	$ 22–26
Bowl, *individual soup, coupe shape, $7^{1}/_{2}$-inch diameter*	$ 35–45
Bowl, *salad, serving, 10-inch diameter*	$ 45–55
Bowl, *vegetable, oval, divided, 10 inches*	$ 32–38
Bowl, *vegetable, round, 8-inch diameter*	$ 34–40
Casserole, *individual, covered*	$ 35–45
Casserole, *$1^{1}/_{4}$-quart, covered*	$ 55–65
Creamer	$ 18–24
Dish, *relish*	$ 15–20
Plate, *bread and butter, $6^{1}/_{2}$-inch diameter*	$ 6–10
Plate, *chop, 12-inch diameter*	$ 35–45
Plate, *chop, 14-inch diameter*	$ 65–75
Plate, *dinner, 10-inch diameter*	$ 22–28
Plate, *luncheon, 9-inch diameter*	$ 10–14
Plate, *salad, 8-inch diameter*	$ 12–16
Salt and pepper shakers, *set*	$ 25–30
Skillet, *open*	$ 45–55
Sugar bowl, *covered*	$ 28–34
Teapot	$ 90–100

"Thistle"

This charming pattern features pink thistle blooms with two shades of green leaves. Designed by Kay Hackett, this pattern was copied by the Japanese, but the copies are easily recognized because the Japanese patterns were applied as a decal with no hand-incising or hand-painting. The copies are also marked "Japan."

Bowl, *cereal, $5^{3}/_{4}$-inch diameter*	$ 28–35
Bowl, *individual fruit*	$ 15–20
Bowl, *individual soup, $7^{3}/_{4}$-inch diameter*	$ 35–42

Stangl coffeepot in the "Thistle" pattern, $100–$125.
Item courtesy of Charles Seagrove and Don Griffin, Old School Antique Mall, Sylva, North Carolina.

Bowl, *salad, serving, 9-inch diameter*	$ 62–72
Bowl, *salad, serving, 12-inch diameter*	$ 75–85
Bowl, *vegetable, oval, 10 inches, divided*	$ 35–45
Bowl, *vegetable, round, 8-inch diameter*	$ 35–42
Bowl, *vegetable, round, 9³/₄-inch diameter*	$ 50–60
Box, *cigarette*	$ 35–45
Butter dish, *¹/₄-pound, covered*	$ 55–65
Casserole, *individual, covered*	$ 35–45
Coffeepot	$ 100–125
Creamer	$ 25–30
Cup and saucer	$ 12–16
Plate, *bread and butter, 6¹/₂-inch diameter*	$ 5–8
Plate, *chop, 12-inch diameter*	$ 75–85
Plate, *dinner, 10-inch diameter*	$ 22–28
Plate, *luncheon, 9-inch diameter*	$ 25–32

Plate, *salad, 8-inch diameter*	$ 15–20
Platter, *oval, 14 inches*	$ 60–70
Salt and pepper shakers, *set*	$ 26–32
Sugar bowl, *lidded*	$ 32–40
Tidbit tray, *two-tier*	$ 60–68
Tidbit tray, *three-tier*	$ 68–75

"Tulip"

Yellow tulips dominate this Kay Hackett design, but it should be noted that the same pattern in blue was made exclusively for Chicago's Marshall Field Department Store. Prices for the two colors are comparable.

Bowl, *cereal*	$ 14–18
Bowl, *individual fruit*	$ 12–16
Bowl, *salad, serving, 11-inch diameter*	$ 60–75
Bowl, *vegetable, round, 9-inch diameter*	$ 45–52
Casserole, *individual, with lid*	$ 35–42
Casserole, *1¹/₂-quart, covered*	$ 110–120
Creamer	$ 25–30
Cup and saucer	$ 18–22
Plate, *bread and butter, 6¹/₂ inches*	$ 6–10
Plate, *chop, 14-inch diameter*	$ 65–75
Plate, *dinner, 10-inch diameter*	$ 30–38
Plate, *luncheon, 9-inch diameter*	$ 18–24
Plate, *salad, 8-inch diameter*	$ 16–22
Plate, *service, 11-inch diameter*	$ 28–34
Sugar bowl, *covered*	$ 35–45

"Wild Rose"

Designed by Kay Hackett, this pattern features pink, full-blown roses nestled amid green leaves.

Bowl, *individual fruit*	$ 12–16
Bowl, *individual soup*	$ 25–30

Set of three pitchers in graduated sizes, "Terra Rose" line, "Yellow Tulip" pattern, $125–$150.
Item courtesy of Needful Things, Hendersonville, North Carolina.

Stangl cake stand in "Orchard Song" pattern, 10-inch diameter, $40–$50.
Item courtesy of Richard Hatch and Associates, Hendersonville, North Carolina.

Stangl "Provincial" pattern dinner plate, 10-inch diameter, $20–$25.
Item courtesy of Kingston Pike Antique Mall, Knoxville, Tennessee.

Bowl, *salad, serving, 10-inch diameter*	$ 50–60
Bowl, *salad, serving, 12-inch diameter*	$ 60–70
Bowl, *vegetable, oval, divided, 10 inches*	$ 40–48
Cup and saucer	$ 18–22
Gravy boat and underliner	$ 38–45
Plate, *bread and butter, $6^{1}/_{2}$-inch diameter*	$ 8–12
Plate, *chop, 12-inch diameter*	$ 55–65

Plate, *chop, 14-inch diameter*	$ 65–75
Plate, *dinner, 10-inch diameter*	$ 25–32
Plate, *luncheon, 9-inch diameter*	$ 22–26
Plate, *salad, 8-inch diameter*	$ 18–22
Skillet, *open*	$ 40–48
Tray, *bread*	$ 45–52

W. S. GEORGE POTTERY COMPANY

W. S. George

One of the marks used by the *W. S. George Pottery Company.*

The long and convoluted history of this company begins with the East Palestine Pottery Company of East Palestine, Ohio, which was founded in 1880 (though it was not given this name until 1884). The East Palestine Pottery Company made yellowware and pieces with a "Rockingham" glaze—in the United States, a brown mottled glaze that may feature streaks and blotches of color—and for years was teetering on the brink of bankruptcy. George Sebring improved the financial condition of the enterprise when he became manager in 1893, but after he left in 1896, the story becomes somewhat vague. It is unclear whether William Shaw George leased the company in 1898 or went to work for the Sebring brothers as its manager. Whichever it was, George owned the company by 1903 or 1904, and changed its name to the W. S. George Pottery Company.

After recovering from some health problems, George began an expansion program that added two pottery plants in Pennsylvania and another in East Palestine. The W. S. George Pottery Company produced large quantities of hotel ware, toilet ware, and semiporcelain dinnerware. The company closed sometime around the late 1950s.

This W. S. George teapot features an "Orange Poppy" decal that should not be confused with the more widely known "Orange Poppy" design used by the Hall China Company. $45–$65.
Item courtesy of Kingston Pike Antique Mall, Knoxville, Tennessee.

Dinnerware

"Basketweave"

As the name suggests, this W. S. George shape is distinguished by a broad band of basketweave around the edges of the flatware, the rim of the pitchers, and the bodies of the other hollowware pieces. This design was introduced in 1930, and can be found in solid colors of blue, brown, green, Maple Bisque, and yellow. Decal decoration was usually applied either to the yellow or green colors.

In 1938, the "Pastels Plus" line was introduced. Its pieces resembled pieces from the "Basketweave" line, with colored rims and decal decorations such as "Dallas" (bluebonnets arranged to form a five-pointed star, "Fresno" (a "Willow"-style pattern), "Lancaster" (a pattern featuring ladies in 19th-century style fashions), "Omaha" (stylized wheat), and Taos (basket of flowers).

Bowl, *vegetable, oval, 9³/₈ inches*	$ 30–40
Casserole, *with lug handles*	$ 35–45
Creamer	$ 8–12
Cup and saucer	$ 12–18

Egg cup	$ 20–25
Gravy boat	$ 25–32
Plate, *dinner, 9¹/₈-inch diameter*	$ 14–20
Plate, *grill, 10-inch diameter*	$ 18–24
Platter, *oval, 11 inches*	$ 20–25
Sugar bowl	$ 18–24
Teapot	$ 65–80

"Breakfast Nook" or "Springtime"

This charming decal design features a flower-bedecked fence in front of an open lat-ticework window with a birdcage and flowerpot. On plates, this romantic image is set off to one side near the edge, and conjures the image of a stage setting where a mid-20th-century Snow White will soon appear—looking very much like June Cleaver of *Leave It to Beaver* fame. This pattern is associated with W. S. George's "Lido" and "Rainbow" shapes, and was introduced in the early 1930s. It can also be found on pieces in the "Argosy" line, which features both round and square (i.e., rounded-corner) plates. This pattern was promoted as "Springtime" by the Chicago department store Daniel Low & Company.

Bowl, *cereal, 6¹/₂-inch diameter*	$ 18–24
Bowl, *individual fruit, 5¹/₂-inch diameter*	$ 10–14
Bowl, *vegetable, covered, round*	$ 125–150
Casserole, *9¹/₂ inches*	$ 35–45
Creamer	$ 38–45
Cup and saucer	$ 15–25
Gravy boat	$ 70–85
Plate, *6¹/₂-inch diameter*	$ 9–10
Plate, *10-inch diameter*	$ 18–30
Platter, *oval, 13 inches*	$ 60–75
Platter, *oval, 15¹/₂ inches*	$ 90–110
Sugar bowl	$ 50–60

"Bolero"

Introduced in 1933, the "Bolero" line is distinguished by the elegant fluted shapes of its pieces. Early pieces in this line included an oval teapot, casserole, sugar, and creamer, but these pieces were restyled in the late 1930s into round forms. The earlier oval forms are much more desired by collectors than the later round ones.

"Bolero" pieces were decorated with a number of different decal designs, including "Flight" (flying geese), "Pals" (two fish), "Cherry Blossom," and "Gracia" (a Mexican-style pattern with flowers and pots on a serape). In 1934, "Bolero Faience" was introduced, which was a line featuring solid-color versions of the "Bolero" shapes. Officially, pieces in this line were produced in lemon yellow, alabaster, and turquoise. Cobalt blue and brown, however, are the only colors that have actually been found.

Bowl, *cereal, 6¹/₄-inch diameter*	$ 10–14
Bowl, *individual fruit, 5-inch diameter*	$ 5–7
Bowl, *soup, 7³/₄-inch diameter*	$ 8–10
Bowl, *vegetable, round, 9-inch diameter*	$ 30–35
Creamer	$ 18–22
Cup and saucer	$ 14–18
Dish, *pickle*	$ 18–25
Gravy boat, *double lip, round, handled*	$ 35–45
Plate, *bread and butter, 6¹/₄-inch diameter*	$ 4–6
Plate, *dinner, 9¹/₄-inch diameter*	$ 14–18
Plate, *luncheon, 8-inch diameter*	$ 8–12
Platter, *oval, 11³/₄ inches*	$ 30–35
Salt and pepper shakers, *pair*	$ 24–30
Sugar bowl, *oval*	$ 22–28
Sugar bowl, *round*	$ 18–25
Teapot, *oval*	$ 90–125
Teapot, *round*	$ 80–110

"Elmhurst"

Introduced in 1936, this is a paneled shape with a slight scallop to the rim. "Elmhurst" pieces can be found in pastel solid colors, which were introduced in 1939 and feature shades of Apple Green, blue, Maple Sugar, pink, turquoise, and yellow. Decal decorations found on pieces in this line include "Harvest" (stylized wheat), "Tasket" (a basket of flowers), and "Wing" (birds perched on a flower trellis).

Bowl, *lug soup*	$ 18–22
Bowl, *vegetable, oval, 9 inches*	$ 40–50
Bowl, *vegetable, round, 9-inch diameter*	$ 40–50
Creamer	$ 8–12
Cup and saucer	$ 15–20
Egg cup	$ 20–25
Gravy boat	$ 25–32
Plate, *bread and butter, 6-inch diameter*	$ 3–5
Plate, *dessert, 7-inch diameter*	$ 8–10
Plate, *dinner, 10-inch diameter*	$ 20–25
Plate, *luncheon, 9-inch diameter*	$ 14–18
Plate, *salad, 8¹/₄-inch diameter*	$ 8–10
Platter, *11 inches*	$ 20–25
Platter, *13 inches*	$ 25–35
Sugar bowl	$ 15–22
Teapot	$ 50–60

"Georgette" or "Petal"

First produced in 1933, flatware pieces in this shape have flat panels that look like petals surrounding a flower's center—thus "Petal" is the popular nickname for this line. Initially, "Georgette" pieces were decorated with a wide range of decals including "Federal" (stars and an eagle), "Jolly Roger" (ships depicted in black silhouette), and "Peasant" (a woman in a polka-dotted apron and a man in a field). The solid-color line originated in 1947 and came in shades of aqua, dark green, chartreuse, gray, light green, maroon, medium blue, pink, and yellow. Prices listed below are for solid-color "Georgette" pieces. Since there is little variation in price between the various colors (seldom more than two to five dollars per piece at most), only one value will be given for each item instead of a range.

Bowl, *cereal, 6-inch diameter*	$ 15
Bowl, *individual fruit*	$ 15
Bowl, *vegetable, oval, 9 inches*	$ 40
Bowl, *vegetable, round, 9 inches*	$ 50
Creamer	$ 32
Cup and saucer	$ 25

Plate, *bread and butter, 6¹/₂-inch diameter*	$ 8
Plate, *dinner, 10¹/₄-inch diameter*	$ 20
Plate, *salad, 8¹/₂-inch diameter*	$ 20
Platter, *oval, 13 inches*	$ 28
Salt and pepper shakers, *set*	$ 33
Sugar bowl	$ 42

"Rainbow"

Introduced in 1934, this line was decorated with a number of different decals such as "Iceland Poppy," "Reflections" (a weeping willow and its reflection), "Hollyhock" (six groups of blossoms in shades of orchid, blue, and yellow), and "Fantasy" (blue bowls filled with arrangements of poppies). A special solid-color line called "Rainbow Petitpoint" featured embossed decoration with the look of needlework depicting a tuliplike flower inside a hexagon. The "Rainbow Petitpoint" line was introduced in 1935, and pieces were produced in cobalt blue, light green, yellow, and chocolate brown. Chocolate brown is the hardest "Rainbow Petitpoint" color to find. Regular solid-color "Rainbow" pieces came in shades of blue, green, pink, tan, and yellow. Prices listed below are for regular "Rainbow" pieces; "Rainbow Petitpoint" pieces are less valuable.

Candleholders, *pair*	$ 25–35
Creamer	$ 15–20
Cup and saucer	$ 12–18
Egg cup	$ 20–25
Gravy boat, *round or oval*	$ 18–25
Plate, *dinner, 9-inch diameter*	$ 14–20
Plate, *salad, 7¹/₄ inches*	$ 10–12
Platter, *oval, 10 inches*	$ 20–25
Platter, *oval, 11¹/₄ inches*	$ 25–32
Platter, *oval, 13 inches*	$ 30–35
Sugar bowl	$ 15–20

"Ranchero"

Designed by Simon Slobodkin in 1938, pieces in this line have a plain coupe shape. Pieces were decorated with such decals as "Fruit Fantasy" (multicolored fruit), "Indian Corn" (a realistic ear of corn), "Rosita" (clusters of red roses), "Shortcake" (strawberries), and Tom Tom (drum and drumsticks). "Ranchero" can also be found in solid colors such as pink, gray, apricot, green, and ivory.

Bowl, *individual fruit, 5¹/₂ inches*	$ 7–10
Bowl, *soup, 8-inch diameter*	$ 16–20
Bowl, *vegetable, oval, 9¹/₂ inches*	$ 26–30
Bowl, *vegetable, round, 9-inch diameter*	$ 42–48
Creamer	$ 28–32
Cup and saucer	$ 18–22
Plate, *bread and butter, 6¹/₄-inch diameter*	$ 5–7
Plate, *dinner, 10-inch diameter*	$ 18–22
Plate, *luncheon, 9-inch diameter*	$ 13–16
Plate, *salad, 7-inch diameter*	$ 9–12
Platter, *oval, 13 inches*	$ 40–45
Sugar bowl	$ 35–42

GILNER POTTERY

Cookie jar, *Gilner Pottery,* 10 inches tall, $100–$125. *Item courtesy of Kingston Pike Antique Mall, Knoxville, Tennessee.*

There is very little information available on the Gilner Pottery, which was located in Culver City, California. Most of its products have the look of pieces from the late 1940s and 1950s, and the earliest date associated with a piece from this company is 1951. The Gilner Pottery is most famous for its "Mammy" cookie jar, which has been widely reproduced, and for its pieces featuring a "pixie" or "native" boy or girl theme. Besides cookie jars, the company made novelties such as ashtrays, dishes, and planters to be placed on the tops of television sets. The plant burned down in 1957, and many of Gilner's products reportedly came to be manufactured by California Originals.

Mother Goose cookie jar, *marked*	$ 400–450
"Peter, Peter Pumpkin Eater" cookie jar, *marked*	$ 425–475

GLADDING, McBEAN & COMPANY

One of the marks used on *Gladding, McBean & Company's* "Franciscan Ware."

This company began operating in Lincoln, California, in 1875. The placement of the firm in this rather out-of-the-way location was the result of a purely serendipitous decision to straighten an existing road by cutting through a low ridge. Not ten feet into the job, workmen struck a deposit of kaolin clay, and further investigation turned up other types of clay and coal.

Charles Gladding of Chicago, Illinois, read about the discovery in the newspaper and traveled to California to see the clay for himself. He shipped samples of the newfound material back to Chicago, and to a friend in Akron, Ohio, who made vitrified sewer pipe. The friend opined that Gladding's clay would be perfect for making this type of product and, on May 1, 1875, the Gladding McBean Company was founded to make vitrified pipe.

The principals in this new business were three friends: Charles Gladding, Peter McGill McBean, and George Chambers. The first shipment of pipe went to San Francisco in August, 1875, and it is said that the discovery of clay near Lincoln was more important to the development of California than the discovery of gold. This was because building products made from clay were bulky and heavy, and therefore very expensive to ship from the East to the West Coast around the horn of South America. With the development of a clay building-products industry in California, development of this region became much more practical and somewhat less expensive.

The Gladding McBean Company began making architectural terra cotta in 1884, and in 1886 the firm was incorporated as Gladding, McBean & Company. Over the years, Gladding, McBean acquired a number of California potteries, including Tropico Pottery, Catalina Pottery, and the West Coast operations of the American Encaustic Tiling Company of Zanesville, Ohio.

In about 1932, Gladding, McBean began making preparations to manufacture dinnerware. At that time, three other California potteries were making solid-color dinnerware and, after testing the other companies' products, Gladding, McBean decided that these products were made from inferior bodies that were too fragile, and were therefore susceptible to crazing. Gladding, McBean decided to use a sturdy, noncrazing body invented by Dr. Andrew Malinovsky in 1928. The material used to make these bodies contained talc rock—the same substance from which ordinary talcum powder is made.

The first dinnerware lines were produced in 1934. Gladding, McBean chose the trade name "Franciscan" to apply to a wide variety of both art wares and dinnerwares, because they felt the name symbolized California. In 1941, however, the company decided to use the designation "Franciscan Ware" for its tableware and "Catalina Ware" for its art pottery lines.

Gladding, McBean merged with the Lock Joint Company in 1962, which was incorporated as the Interpace Corporation in 1963. In 1979, Gladding, McBean was sold to the famous Wedgwood Company of Barlaston, England. Wedgwood continued to manufacture "Franciscan" products at Gladding, McBean's plant in Glendale, California, until 1984, when all operations were transferred to England and the American facilities closed. "Franciscan" ware is still being made, though not in the United States. Current collectors prefer "Franciscan" ware with American rather than English marks, and prices quoted below thus refer to American-made examples.

Art Ware

"Catalina"

Introduced in 1939, this line featured a wide variety of shapes and was not discontinued until 1942. Most of the "Catalina" art ware pieces were made in molds acquired from Catalina, but others were originated at Gladding, McBean. The most important of these was the #C801, which was the bust of a peasant girl wearing a kerchief, with her hands raised beside her head. Gladding, McBean actually patented this design and produced it with a number of different glaze configurations, including "Terra Cotta," which was a special stain added to Malinite bodies to produce a finish resembling true terra cotta. Pieces made in this way were a part of Gladding, McBean's "Terra Cotta Specialties" line, examples of which can command a premium over "Catalina" pieces made with regular glazes.

Bird, *planter, not on base, satin ivory glaze, #C802*	$ 150–175
Bird, *planter, not on base, Terra Cotta glaze, #C802*	$ 225–275
Bird on base, *satin ivory glaze, #C806*	$ 200–225
Bird on base, *Terra Cotta glaze, #C806 (see also #C806 under* "Ox-Blood")	$ 325–375
Bust of lady with corsage, *satin ivory glaze, #C814*	$ 150–175
Bust of lady with corsage, *Terra Cotta glaze, #C814*	$ 225–275
Girl with fan, *satin ivory glaze, #C803*	$ 100–135
Girl with fan, *Terra Cotta glaze, #C803*	$ 150–175
Lady with hat, *satin ivory glaze, #C805*	$ 250–300
Lady with hat, *Terra Cotta glaze, #C805*	$ 325–375
Large girl's head, *satin ivory glaze, #C804*	$ 175–225
Large girl's head, *Terra Cotta glaze, #C804*	$ 250–300
Malayan Woman, *turbaned head, satin white glaze, #C809*	$ 350–425
Malayan Woman, *turbaned head, Terra Cotta glaze, #C809*	$ 400–475
Mermaid, *satin white glaze, #C813*	$ 350–425
Samoan Girl, *reclining, satin ivory glaze, #C813*	$ 175–225
Samoan Girl, *reclining, Terra Cotta glaze, #C813*	$ 250–300
Samoan Mother and Child, *satin ivory glaze, #C807*	$ 175–225
Samoan Mother and Child, *Terra Cotta glaze, #C807*	$ 250–300
Table ornament, grapes, *satin ivory glaze, #C810*	$ 150–200
Table ornament, *fruit and nut, satin ivory glaze, #C812*	$ 150–200

"Ox-Blood"

This art ware line was based on the Chinese "Sang de Boeuf" or "Ox-blood" glaze. Produced from copper, this glaze is a rich red color that shades to a whitish-green on rims, on the interiors of vases, and in places where the copper-red glaze runs thin. The glaze was available at Gladding, McBean as early as 1935, but the "Ox-Blood" art ware line was not made until 1938, and continued to be produced until 1942. Pieces are marked either "Catalina Pottery" or "Franciscan Ware." A "C" prefix before a piece's style number indicates that the piece is from a mold that originated at the Catalina Pottery.

Bowl, *round, small, #16*	$ 150–175
Bowl, *square, low, 7¹/₂ inches, #282*	$ 275–325
Bowl, *round, same shape as #16, #79*	$ 250–300
Bowl, *round, 10 inches, #C283*	$ 325–375
Bowl, *round, 16 inches, #287*	$ 425–500
Figure of a bird, *French Pheasant, planter, #C806*	$ 425–475
Vase, *cylindrical base with flared mouth, #288*	$ 300–350
Vase, *low, bowl-shaped, footed, #140*	$ 225–275
Vase, *small, 4¹/₂ inches, #104*	$ 225–275
Vase, *round, low, 4¹/₂ inches, #C277*	$ 325–375
Vase, *round, 4¹/₂ inches, #132*	$ 175–225
Vase, *square, 4¹/₂ inches, #C279*	$ 275–325
Vase, *small, 5 inches, #C300*	$ 125–150
Vase, *round, 5¹/₂ inches, #C293*	$ 300–350
Vase, *bottle-shaped, 6 inches, #105*	$ 200–250
Vase, *footed, #C281*	$ 225–275
Vase, *Japanese, with flaring top, #C278*	$ 375–425
Vase, *beaker, 7¹/₂ inches, #141*	$ 275–325
Vase, *8³/₄ inches, #C284*	$ 350–400
Vase, *flaring top, 8³/₄ inches, #114*	$ 325–375
Vase, *flaring top in the Japanese manner, 9 inches, #C285*	$ 900–1,000
Vase, *flared top, 9 inches, #C289*	$ 400–450
Vase, *9¹/₂ inches, #122*	$ 450–500
Vase, *bottle-shaped, 9¹/₂ inches*	$ 275–325
Vase, *10¹/₂ inches, #115*	$ 275–325
Vase, *11 inches, #C290*	$ 325–375
Vase, *flaring, 11 inches, #C286*	$ 900–1,000
Vase, *large, 11 inches, #123*	$ 525–600

"Polynesian"

This is one of the most sought-after Gladding, McBean art lines. The decorations are embossed and hand-painted, in much the same manner as decorations in the company's embossed dinnerware lines, such as "Apple" and "Desert Rose." The shapes for this line came from the "Encino" art ware pieces, and the raised florals with a "South Sea" flavor were painted using the "Desert Rose" color palette.

Bowl, *shallow, 14 inches, floral decoration, #388*	$ 300–350
Box, *cigarette, solid-color base with embossed floral decoration on the top in pink and green, #375*	$ 225–275
Vase, *cylindrical, 9 inches tall, decorated with bamboo and leaves, #387*	$ 300–350
Vase, *oval, 5 inches by 4 inches, floral-decorated, #382*	$ 225–275
Vase, *round, 6³/₄ inches tall, decorated with flowers and leaves, #385*	$ 325–375

Dinnerware

"Apple"

This pattern, with its raised (or embossed) apple motifs, was first introduced in 1940 and was copied from the "Zona" pattern made by the Weller Pottery Company of Zanesville, Ohio. Pieces with lids have apple-shaped finials. The decoration is embossed, and is hand-painted under the glaze.

Ashtray, *individual, apple-shaped*	$ 12–15
Ashtray, *oval, 9 inches*	$ 65–75
Ashtray, *square*	$ 250–300
Baker, *1-quart, 9¹/₂ inches by 8³/₄ inches*	$ 175–200
Baker, *1¹/₂-quart, 14 inches by 9 inches*	$ 235–250
Baker, *apple-shaped*	$ 125–150
Bowl, *batter*	$ 425–475
Bowl, *cereal, 6-inch diameter*	$ 14–18
Bowl, *individual fruit, 5¹/₂-inch diameter*	$ 11–14
Bowl, *mixing, 6-inch diameter*	$ 125–135
Bowl, *mixing, 7¹/₂-inch diameter*	$ 135–145
Bowl, *mixing, 9-inch diameter*	$ 175–190
Bowl, *porringer, 6-inch diameter*	$ 30–35
Bowl, *salad, scalloped, 10-inch diameter*	$ 110–120

Bowl, *soup, 8$^1/_2$-inch diameter*	$ 24–30
Bowl, *vegetable, oval, divided, 10$^3/_4$ inches*	$ 30–40
Bowl, *vegetable, round, 8-inch diameter*	$ 25–29
Bowl, *vegetable, round, 9-inch diameter*	$ 48–55
Bowl, *vegetable, round, covered*	$ 58–65
Box, *cigarette*	$ 155–175
Butter dish, *$^1/_4$-pound, covered*	$ 48–54
Candleholder	$ 55–65
Casserole, *individual, with lid*	$ 60–70
Coaster, *3$^3/_4$-inch diameter*	$ 38–45
Coffeepot, *8-cup*	$ 120–140
Cookie jar	$ 300–325
Creamer, *after-dinner size*	$ 11–14
Cup and saucer	$ 25–30
Cup and saucer, *after-dinner*	$ 40–45
Egg cup	$ 32–36
Gravy boat, *faststand*	$ 38–42
Jam jar	$ 130–145
Jug, *syrup, 1-pint*	$ 75–85
Jug, *1-quart*	$ 78–85
Jug, *2$^1/_2$-quart*	$ 150–165
Mug, *7-ounce*	$ 28–32
Mug, *12-ounce*	$ 50–57
Napkin ring	$ 55–65
Pepper mill, *bulbous base*	$ 175–185
Pepper mill, *cylindrical*	$ 200–225
Plate, *bread and butter, 6$^1/_2$-inch diameter*	$ 5–8
Plate, *chop, 12-inch diameter*	$ 45–50
Plate, *child's, 3-part, 9 inches by 7$^1/_4$ inches*	$ 135–150
Plate, *chop, 14-inch diameter*	$ 85–95
Plate, *dinner, 10$^1/_2$-inch diameter*	$ 20–25

Gladding, McBean & Company's "Franciscan" "Apple"
platter, 14 inches, $38–$44.
*Item courtesy of Kingston Pike Antique Mall, Knoxville,
Tennessee.*

Plate, *luncheon, 9¹/₂-inch diameter*	$ 22–27
Plate, *grill/buffet, round, divided, 11-inch diameter*	$ 115–125
Plate, *party, 10¹/₂ inches*	$ 120–130
Plate, *salad, 8¹/₂-inch diameter*	$ 12–15
Plate, *salad, crescent, 8 inches*	$ 30–35
Plate, *steak, oval, 11 inches, coupe shape*	$ 175–200
Plate, *television, with cup well, oval, 14 inches*	$ 100–110
Platter, *oval, 12 inches*	$ 32–36
Platter, *oval, 14 inches*	$ 38–44
Platter, *oval, 19 inches*	$ 245–275
Relish, *three-part, 12 inches by 9¹/₂ inches*	$ 32–36
Salt and pepper shakers, *small, pair*	$ 25–30
Salt and pepper shakers, *large, pair*	$ 85–95
Sherbet	$ 15–18
Sugar bowl	$ 42–47

Teapot, *6-cup*	$ 125–140
Tea tile, *square, 6 inches*	$ 100–115
Tea tile, *round, 6-inch diameter*	$ 125–145
Tidbit tray, *two-tier*	$ 100–110
Tidbit tray, *three-tier*	$ 135–145
Tumbler, *6-ounce*	$ 55–65
Tumbler, *10-ounce*	$ 22–26
Tureen, *covered, footed*	$ 475–525
Tureen, *covered, flat-bottomed*	$ 475–525
Tureen, *covered, three feet*	$ 550–650

"Colorado"

Also called "Swirl," this pattern was made between 1934 and 1954. "Colorado" pieces came in a variety of colors and in two glaze finishes: a satin (or matte) finish and a high-gloss (or shiny) finish. The matte grouping was produced in shades of ivory, green, blue, white, gray, turquoise, and yellow. The high-gloss grouping features shades of turquoise, copper, coral, maroon (or burgundy), light yellow, Apple Green, ruby, and white. In general, the high-gloss "Colorado" pieces are the most highly desired by collectors and are rarer than examples with matte glazes. Of the high-gloss colors, coral is the least valuable, while copper, gray, and maroon (burgundy) are priced at the upper end of the ranges listed below. High-gloss Apple Green, ruby, and white were available only as special-order colors, and their value is thus 20 to 25 percent greater than is indicated by the price ranges listed below.

Ashtray, *oval, 4¹/₂ inches*	$ 7–12
Bowl, *cream soup, with saucer*	$ 22–34
Bowl, *individual fruit, 6-inch diameter*	$ 10–18
Bowl, *salad, large, 10-inch diameter*	$ 45–65
Bowl, *soup, 8-inch diameter*	$ 16–22
Bowl, *vegetable, oval, 10 inches*	$ 30–40
Bowl, *vegetable, round, 9-inch diameter*	$ 20–25
Casserole, *individual, with lid*	$ 28–40
Creamer	$ 20–30
Cup and saucer	$ 12–22
Cup and saucer, *after-dinner*	$ 18–40

Gravy boat, *faststand*	$ 28–50
Plate, *bread and butter, 6¹/₂-inch diameter*	$ 4–8
Plate, *chop, 12¹/₂-inch diameter*	$ 35–50
Plate, *dinner, 10¹/₂-inch diameter*	$ 18–40
Plate, *luncheon, 9¹/₄-inch diameter*	$ 10–18
Plate, *salad, 8-inch diameter*	$ 10–18
Platter, *oval, 13 inches*	$ 28–40
Platter, *oval, 15 inches*	$ 80–110
Relish, *oval, 9¹/₄ inches*	$ 20–30
Shaker, *salt or pepper, each*	$ 13–15
Sugar bowl	$ 25–38
Teapot, *6-cup, flat*	$ 80–130

"Desert Rose"

First produced in 1941, "Desert Rose" is said to be one of the most popular American dinnerware patterns ever made. This design features raised (embossed) roses that are hand-painted, and items with lids have finials in the shape of rosebuds. "Desert Rose" has been in continuous production since its inception. The popularity of this pattern means that there are vast quantities available, many examples of which were produced quite recently.

Ashtray, *small, square*	$ 100–110
Ashtray, *small, rose-shaped*	$ 13–16
Baker, *1-quart*	$ 135–150
Baker, *1¹/₂-quart*	$ 235–250
Bell	$ 120–130
Bowl, *individual fruit, 5¹/₄-inch diameter*	$ 10–13
Bowl, *mixing, 6-inch diameter*	$ 145–160
Bowl, *mixing, 7¹/₂-inch diameter*	$ 135–150
Bowl, *mixing, 9-inch diameter*	$ 190–210
Bowl, *oatmeal, 5¹/₂ inches*	$ 25–30
Bowl, *porringer, 6 inches*	$ 155–175
Bowl, *salad, large, scalloped, 10-inch diameter*	$ 90–110

"Franciscan" "Desert Rose" regular tea- or coffee cup and saucer, $10–$15.
Item courtesy of Kingston Pike Antique Mall, Knoxville, Tennessee.

Bowl, *soup, 8¹/₂ inches*	$ 20–25
Bowl, *vegetable, oval, divided*	$ 32–38
Bowl, *vegetable, round, 9-inch diameter*	$ 24–28
Butter dish, *¹/₄-pound, covered*	$ 45–50
Candleholder	$ 40–48
Canister, *tea*	$ 325–350
Casserole, *covered, 1¹/₂-quart*	$ 120–140
Casserole, *covered, 2¹/₂-quart*	$ 135–150
Coffeepot, *8-cup*	$ 120–140
Compote, *8 inches*	$ 75–85
Cookie jar	$ 295–325
Creamer	$ 15–19
Cup and saucer, *after-dinner, demitasse*	$ 42–50
Cup and saucer, *tea or coffee*	$ 10–15
Cup and saucer, *jumbo*	$ 50–65

Egg cup	$ 32–38
Gravy boat, *faststand*	$ 42–50
Jam jar	$ 135–150
Jug, *1-quart*	$ 62–75
Jug, *2¹/₂-quart*	$ 120–135
Mug, *7-ounce*	$ 20–24
Mug, *12-ounce*	$ 42–48
Napkin ring	$ 40–48
Pickle dish, *11 inches*	$ 145–160
Plate, *bread and butter, 6¹/₂-inch diameter*	$ 5–8
Plate, *dinner, 10¹/₂-inch diameter*	$ 16–22
Plate, *chop, 12-inch diameter*	$ 40–46
Plate, *chop, 14-inch diameter*	$ 100–120
Plate, *grill/buffet, round, divided, 11-inch diameter*	$ 80–90
Plate, *heart-shaped, 5³/₄ inches by 5¹/₂ inches*	$ 95–110
Plate, *luncheon, 9¹/₂-inch diameter*	$ 18–24
Plate, *salad, 8¹/₂-inch diameter*	$ 11–14
Plate, *salad, crescent, 8 inches*	$ 22–28
Plate, *steak, oval, 11 inches*	$ 115–125
Plate, *television, oval, cup well, 14 inches*	$ 100–115
Platter, *oval, 12 inches*	$ 34–40
Platter, *oval, 14 inches*	$ 40–48
Platter, *oval, 17 inches*	$ 245–275
Relish, *three-part, 12 inches by 9¹/₂ inches*	$ 50–65
Salt and pepper shakers, *small, set*	$ 25–30
Salt and pepper shakers, *large, set*	$ 80–90
Sherbet	$ 15–18
Sugar bowl	$ 30–35
Teapot, *6-cup*	$ 110–125
Tidbit, *two-tier*	$ 100–110
Tidbit, *three-tier*	$ 80–100

Tile, *square, 6 inches*	$ 80–100
Tile, *round, 6-inch diameter*	$ 125–150
Toast cover	$ 225–250
Trivet, *round, fluted*	$ 115–125
Tumbler, *6-ounce*	$ 42–48
Tumbler, *10-ounce*	$ 27–32
Tureen, *covered*	$ 700–750

"El Patio"

This was the first "Franciscan" dinnerware line made by Gladding, McBean & Company. It was introduced in 1934 and discontinued in 1953. Initially, this solid-color ware was produced in just eight colors: white, Golden Glow, Redwood, Glacial Blue, Mexican Blue, Tahoe Green, Flame Orange, and yellow. Eventually, however, the ware was made in either 19 or 20 shades (depending on what shades are counted), and more than 100 different shapes. Rare colors in the "El Patio" line include Celestial White, Ruby, Clear Glaze, dark green, black, and Eggplant, which is rare and extremely desirable to collectors. Pieces in the "El Patio" series featured either a matte or glossy finish.

For a very short time in 1935 and 1936, the company produced an offshoot line called "El Patio Nuevo." Like the original "El Patio," the "El Patio Nuevo" line featured solid-color wares, but the pieces were two-toned, with one color on the interior and another on the exterior. Prices listed below are for colors other than Eggplant or Ruby, which can cost twice what is indicated by the price ranges listed below. Of the two colors, Ruby is generally the more valuable.

Bowl, *cereal, 6-inch diameter*	$ 12–18
Bowl, *cream soup, and saucer*	$ 28–34
Bowl, *individual fruit*	$ 10–14
Bowl, *salad, large serving, 11 inches*	$ 70–85
Bowl, *vegetable, oval, 9 inches*	$ 33–40
Bowl, *vegetable, round, 8¹/₂ inches*	$ 33–40
Butter, *¹/₄-pound, covered*	$ 40–55
Candleholder	$ 17–24
Carafe, *lid*	$ 80–100
Casserole, *individual, with lid*	$ 25–32

Coffeepot	$ 70–85
Creamer	$ 23–30
Cup and saucer	$ 12–26
Cup and saucer, *jumbo*	$ 20–28
Gravy boat, *faststand*	$ 35–80
Jar, *jam*	$ 17–25
Jug, *syrup, lidded*	$ 40–50
Plate, *bread and butter, 6^1/$_2$-inch diameter*	$ 5–8
Plate, *chop, 12-inch diameter*	$ 44–67
Plate, *chop, 14-inch diameter*	$ 60–72
Plate, *dinner, 10^1/$_2$-inch diameter*	$ 16–25
Plate, *luncheon, 9-inch diameter*	$ 9–14
Plate, *salad, 8-inch diameter*	$ 10–15
Platter, *oval, 11^1/$_2$ inches*	$ 37–45
Platter, *oval, 13 inches*	$ 48–60
Relish, *two-part*	$ 15–22
Relish, *three-part, center handle*	$ 30–37
Salt and pepper shakers, *set*	$ 25–32
Sherbet	$ 15–20
Sugar bowl	$ 27–40
Teapot, *5-cup*	$ 70–90
Toby jug, *in the shape of a monk*	$ 100–125
Tumbler, *juice*	$ 14–18
Tumbler, *tall*	$ 17–22

"Fruit"

This Gladding, McBean pattern appears on "Montecito" shapes, which are decorated with bold decals of fruit and flowers. Pieces in this line are banded in dark blue with a lighter blue overglaze, and the fruit is rendered in blue to match the dark-blue bands. "Fruit" pieces were also reportedly produced in brown with a clear overglaze, but examples are rare. A limited number of pieces were produced, and the line was discontinued in 1942.

Bowl, *vegetable, oval, divided, 11 inches*	$ 30–36
Bowl, *vegetable, round, 7^1/$_2$-inch diameter*	$ 35–40
Bowl, *vegetable, round, 9^1/$_2$-inch diameter*	$ 38–42
Butter, *^{1}/$_4$-pound, covered*	$ 32–38
Creamer	$ 20–25
Cup and saucer	$ 15–20
Plate, *bread and butter, 7-inch diameter*	$ 5–7
Plate, *dinner, 10^1/$_2$-inch diameter*	$ 15–20
Plate, *salad, 8^1/$_2$-inch diameter*	$ 22–28
Platter, *oval, 11^1/$_2$ inches*	$ 25–30
Platter, *oval, 13^1/$_2$ inches*	$ 36–40
Salt and pepper shakers, *set*	$ 25–30
Sugar bowl	$ 26–32
Teapot, *6-cup*	$ 75–90

"Small Fruit"

Bowl, *individual fruit*	$ 40–50
Bowl, *salad, serving, large, 11-inch diameter*	$ 300–325
Bowl, *soup, 8^1/$_2$-inch diameter*	$ 100–115
Bowl, *vegetable, oval, 10^1/$_2$ inches*	$ 125–140
Bowl, *vegetable, round, 8^1/$_2$-inch diameter*	$ 115–125
Casserole, *covered, round, 1^1/$_2$-quart*	$ 165–175
Compote	$ 325–375
Creamer	$ 95–110
Cup and saucer	$ 35–45
Gravy boat, *faststand*	$ 150–175
Plate, *bread and butter, 6^1/$_2$-inch diameter*	$ 16–20
Plate, *chop, 12-inch diameter*	$ 185–200
Plate, *dinner, 10^1/$_2$-inch diameter*	$ 70–80
Plate, *luncheon, 9-inch diameter*	$ 70–80
Plate, *salad, 8-inch diameter*	$ 42–50

Sugar bowl	$ 85–95
Tidbit, *two-tier*	$ 135–150
Tumbler, *10-ounce*	$ 150–175

† *There is another Gladding, McBean "Fruit" pattern, sometimes called "Small Fruit" by collectors. Instead of large, bold representations of fruit in the centers of flatware pieces, this line is characterized by rings of small fruit placed around the edges of plates and bowls. Trimmed in yellow, the fruits depicted on these pieces include apples, oranges, grapes, and lemons.*

"Ivy"

This is the third embossed line of the "Franciscan Classics" series, which also included "Apple" and "Desert Rose." Like pieces in the other two lines, "Ivy" pieces feature embossed patterns that are hand-painted underglaze. The line was initially produced in 1948, and is less well known than the other two "Franciscan Classics."

Ashtray, *leaf-shaped*	$ 25–30
Bowl, *individual fruit, 5$1/4$-inch diameter*	$ 11–14
Bowl, *salad, serving, large, 11$1/4$-inch diameter*	$ 150–165
Bowl, *soup, 8$1/2$-inch diameter*	$ 30–35
Bowl, *vegetable, round, 7$1/4$-inch diameter*	$ 25–30
Bowl, *vegetable, round, 8$1/4$-inch diameter*	$ 27–32
Bowl, *vegetable, oval, divided, 12$1/4$ inches*	$ 42–46
Butter dish, *$1/4$-pound, covered*	$ 85–100
Casserole, *1$1/2$-quart, covered, round*	$ 120–130
Coffeepot, *8-cup*	$ 325–350
Compote, *8 inches*	$ 110–125
Creamer	$ 26–30
Cup and saucer, *coffee or tea*	$ 18–22
Cup and saucer, *jumbo*	$ 150–165
Dish, *cereal, 6-inch diameter*	$ 18–22
Gravy boat, *faststand*	$ 45–55
Jug, *2$1/2$-quart*	$ 175–195
Mug, *12-ounce*	$ 78–85
Plate, *bread and butter, 6$1/2$-inch diameter*	$ 5–8

"Franciscan" "Ivy" salad plate with salt
and pepper shakers. Plate, $22–$26;
shaker set, $45–$55.
Item courtesy of Aileen and John Willis.

"Franciscan" "Ivy" pattern, individual
tureen or "tureenette," $85–$100.
*Item courtesy of Richard H. Crane, Knoxville,
Tennessee.*

Plate, *cake, 13-inch diameter*	$ 100–110
Plate, *chop, 12-inch diameter*	$ 52–58
Plate, *chop, 14-inch diameter*	$ 52–58
Plate, *dinner, $10^1/_2$-inch diameter*	$ 28–32
Plate, *luncheon, $9^1/_2$-inch diameter*	$ 28–32
Plate, *salad, $8^1/_2$-inch diameter*	$ 22–26
Plate, *salad, crescent-shaped*	$ 46–50
Platter, *oval, $11^1/_4$ inches*	$ 38–43
Platter, *oval, 13 inches*	$ 50–65
Platter, *oval, 19 inches*	$ 265–280
Relish, *divided*	$ 40–48
Relish, *divided, three-part*	$ 100–110
Salt and pepper shakers, *set*	$ 45–55
Sherbet	$ 42–46
Sugar bowl	$ 26–30

Teapot, *6-cup*	$ 325–350
Tidbit, *two-tier*	$ 80–95
Tidbit, *three-tier*	$ 100–110
Tile, *square, 6 inches*	$ 90–100
Tumbler, *10-ounce*	$ 38–44
Tureen, *individual, 4¹/₂ inches, lidded*	$ 85–100
Tureen, *lidded*	$ 875–950

"Metropolitan"

This line was created by Marc Sanders in 1940 for an exhibition held at New York City's Metropolitan Museum of Art. It was discontinued in 1942. Pieces in the "Metropolitan" line are either square or rectangular-shaped with rounded corners. The standard color scheme is two-toned, with Matte Ivory on the interiors of pieces and Satin (or Matte) Coral, turquoise, gray, mauve, or yellow on the exteriors. Solid-color pieces were also produced in Matte Ivory and Shell Pink Buff, with the latter color being the rarest. The pieces exhibited at the Metropolitan Museum were decal-decorated, but these pieces never went into production.

The "Metropolitan" shapes were reused from 1949 to 1954 for a line called "Tiempo," which featured such colors as Copper (reddish-brown), Hot Chocolate (dark brown), Leaf (dark green), Mustard (yellow), Pebble (light brown), Sprout (light green), and Stone (gray). From 1954 to 1957, a three-leaf decal called "Trio" was used on "Metropolitan" shapes. Sprout is the least-expensive color for pieces in the "Tiempo" line.

Solid Ivory pieces are priced near the top of the price ranges listed below; more common colors are generally less valuable.

Bowl, *cream soup, and saucer*	$ 18–25
Bowl, *individual fruit, 5 inches*	$ 10–14
Bowl, *salad, rectangular, 10 inches*	$ 40–60
Bowl, *vegetable, rectangular*	$ 30–45
Butter, *¹/₄-pound, covered*	$ 45–65
Casserole, *covered vegetable*	$ 75–90
Coffeepot, *6-cup*	$ 70–100
Cup and saucer, *tea or coffee*	$ 15–22
Gravy boat and underplate	$ 60–75

Plate, *bread and butter, 6 inches*	$ 5–8
Plate, *chop, 13 inches*	$ 30–50
Plate, *dinner, 10 inches*	$ 18–25
Plate, *salad, 8 inches*	$ 9–12
Platter, *14 inches*	$ 45–60
Salt and pepper shakers, *pair*	$ 25–35
Sugar bowl	$ 25–40
Teapot, *6-cup*	$ 70–100

"Montecito" and "Del Oro"

The solid-color "Montecito" line was first introduced in 1937, and was promoted in Gladding, McBean's "Franciscan" advertising as a suave and formal line with beautiful contours and coloring. The initial line featured such colors as Eggplant (maroon/purple), Turqoise, and light yellow (all in gloss), and Coral, Celadon Green, gray, and ivory (all in matte). Later, around 1942, a gloss Ruby (or "Chinese Red") was added. This is by far the rarest of the "Montecito" colors, and is valued at as much as four times the price of the other colors.

The "Montecito" shapes were also used for Gladding, McBean's "Del Oro" line, examples of which came in two-toned shades of Chinese Yellow and White. Flatware pieces in this line feature brilliant yellow centers with a band of white around the edge, which gives the impression of an intense sunrise.

Prices for Eggplant pieces are about 20 percent higher than the prices listed below, prices for Ruby pieces are about four times higher than those listed below, and prices for two-tone "Montecito" pieces (featuring such colors as Celadon Green and Coral) are approximately 20 percent higher than those listed below.

Bowl, *cereal, 7-inch diameter*	$ 12–16
Bowl, *individual fruit*	$ 12–15
Bowl, *salad serving, 11-inch diameter*	$ 48–60
Bowl, *vegetable, round, 7$^{1}/_{2}$ inches*	$ 28–36
Cup and saucer	$ 18–25
Gravy boat, *faststand*	$ 70–85
Plate, *bread and butter, 7$^{1}/_{2}$-inch diameter*	$ 5–8
Plate, *dinner, 10$^{1}/_{2}$-inch diameter*	$ 18–25
Plate, *chop, 14-inch diameter*	$ 60–80

Plate, *luncheon, 9¹/₂-inch diameter*	$ 12–16
Plate, *salad, 8¹/₂-inch diameter*	$ 9–13
Platter, *oval, 13 inches*	$ 55–70
Platter, *oval, 16 inches*	$ 80–95
Salt and pepper shakers, *set*	$ 25–30
Sugar bowl	$ 37–45
Teapot	$ 80–100

"Padua I" and "Padua II"

"Padua I" was Gladding, McBean's first hand-painted line, and to make it the company had to buy new machinery and hire more help. The new "machinery" was essentially a table on which objects were placed to have circular lines painted on them. Each flatware piece in the "Padua I" line features a clear overglaze on a cream or buff-colored body, decorated with concentric circles of brown and yellow and a stylized flower in the center.

"Padua II" originated in 1939, and its pieces feature the same hand-painted design as those in the "Padua I" line. The only difference is that "Padua II" pieces feature a Celadon Green overglaze instead of the clear one found on the original pieces. Both styles of "Padua" were carried by Barker Brothers Department Stores, which renamed them "Freesia." In addition, both patterns were made using "El Patio" shapes, although "Padua" pieces were initially made using only a few of these forms. Many more shapes were added to the line in January, 1942, but both "Padua I" and "Padua II" were discontinued later that same year.

"Padua II" is somewhat rarer than "Padua I," and these two very similar patterns will be priced separately below.

"Padua I"

Bowl, *individual fruit*	$ 14–18
Bowl, *individual salad*	$ 18–22
Bowl, *salad, serving*	$ 75–100
Carafe with lid	$ 100–120
Creamer	$ 32–38
Cup with metal holder and handle	$ 38–45
Cup and saucer	$ 20–28
Plate, *chop, 12-inch diameter*	$ 110–130

Plate, *dinner, 10¹/₂-inch diameter*	$ 26–32
Plate, *luncheon, 9¹/₂-inch diameter*	$ 18–22
Sugar bowl	$ 38–45

"Padua II"

Creamer	$ 38–50
Cup and saucer	$ 30–40
Plate, *bread and butter*	$ 8–10
Plate, *chop, 12-inch diameter*	$ 125–165
Plate, *dinner, 10¹/₂-inch diameter*	$ 35–45
Plate, *luncheon, 9¹/₂-inch diameter*	$ 18–22
Plate, *salad, 7¹/₂-inch diameter*	$ 16–20

"Palomar"

Gladding, McBean added fine porcelain dinnerware to its line in 1942, and continued to produce it until 1977. More than 150 different patterns were produced, and all are priced about the same, except for the "Renaissance" pattern pieces.

"Palomar" is one of the standard fine china lines. Pieces in this line came in solid colors such as Jasper Green (light green), Jade Green (dark green), Dove Grey, Robin's Egg Blue, Cameo Pink, and Primrose Yellow. Flatware pieces feature white centers with these colors around their rims, and hollowware pieces have colored exteriors with white interiors. Generally, finials and bases are also white. Some "Palomar" pieces came with either gold or platinum trim; the pieces with platinum trim are generally 10 to 15 percent more expensive than the ones with gold. Of the colors, Primrose Yellow and Dove Grey are the most valuable.

Bowl, *cream soup, with saucer*	$ 47–70
Bowl, *individual fruit*	$ 22–30
Bowl, *soup, 8-inch diameter*	$ 28–60
Bowl, *vegetable, oval, 9¹/₂ inches*	$ 80–95
Bowl, *vegetable, oval, 10 inches*	$ 80–95
Coffeepot	$ 150–200
Creamer	$ 50–65
Cup and saucer, *after-dinner demitasse*	$ 25–35
Cup and saucer	$ 37–50

Gravy boat, *faststand*	$ 110–140
Plate, *bread and butter, 6¹/₂-inch diameter*	$ 15–20
Plate, *chop, 13-inch diameter*	$ 130–150
Plate, *dinner, 10¹/₂-inch diameter*	$ 32–60
Plate, *luncheon, 9-inch diameter*	$ 22–35
Plate, *salad, 8¹/₂-inch diameter*	$ 20–30
Platter, *oval, 12¹/₂ inches*	$ 85–110
Platter, *oval, 16 inches*	$ 130–170
Salt and pepper shakers, *set*	$ 50–65
Sugar bowl	$ 50–70
Tidbit server, *two-tier*	$ 76–110
Tidbit server, *three-tier*	$ 90–120

"Rancho"

Like many other makers of pottery in America, Gladding, McBean was hit hard by the Great Depression. By 1937, however, the company was turning a profit once again, and in April of that year it purchased Catalina Pottery (a division of the Santa Catalina Island Company), along with the Catalina Pottery name, its molds, and all of its existing inventory.

After this acquisition, Gladding, McBean continued to make many of the old Catalina products. In the case of dinnerware, however, Gladding, McBean's products were different. Catalina had used a two-fire system to produce its dinnerware line, a process that left its products subject to damage such as chipping and crazing. When the line was revamped by Gladding, McBean, the company employed a one-fire process using Malinite bodies, which had a high talc content and were invented by Dr. Andrew Malinovsky in 1928 for use in making tiles. The resulting "Rancho" ware was much more durable and not subject to the problems that had plagued Catalina's dinnerware.

"Rancho" was a solid-color line, and the Catalina colors used by Gladding, McBean included dark blue, red, sand, red-brown, turquoise, and green. Other colors introduced by Gladding, McBean include dark yellow, Satin Coral, Gloss Coral, Transparent, Pastel Green, and Ivory White. Most pieces of "Rancho" are rather plain, and the flatware pieces tend to be coupe shaped. However, shell-shaped pieces, pieces with tab handles, gourd-shaped pieces, and pieces with numerous lobes (like the petals on a daisy) do exist. Examples of "Rancho" ware are marked with an ink stamp reading "Catalina Rancho" or "Catalina Rancho Ware," both with patent numbers between the words "Catalina" and "Rancho." This line was discontinued in 1941.

Bowl, *cereal/soup, table handles*	$ 20–26
Bowl, *chowder, shaped like a shell, shape C-44*	$ 110–175
Bowl, *salad, fluted*	$ 50–65
Bowl, *vegetable, round, 7-inch diameter*	$ 40–50
Casserole, *individual, lidded*	$ 45–55
Coffee carafe with wooden handle	$ 55–70
Creamer	$ 15–20
Cup and saucer	$ 25–35
Jug, *flat-bottomed*	$ 70–85
Pitcher, *lidded, shape C-30*	$ 100–150
Plate, *bread and butter, 6$^1/_2$-inch diameter*	$ 10–15
Plate, *chop, 13-inch diameter*	$ 70–85
Plate, *dinner, 10$^1/_2$-inch diameter*	$ 28–36
Plate, *salad, 8$^1/_2$-inch diameter*	$ 15–20
Relish	$ 18–24
Salt and pepper shakers, *gourd shape, pair*	$ 30–40
Salt and pepper shakers, *tulip shape*	$ 30–40
Sugar bowl	$ 25–32
Teapot, *shape C-24*	$ 175–250

† *In mid-1939, a two-tone color scheme was added to the "Rancho" line. The new line was called "Duo-Tone," and its pieces featured Satin Ivory on the exterior with interior colors of coral, blue, green, or yellow. This line is rather rare, and prices are 40 to 60 percent higher than the prices listed for regular "Rancho" pieces.*

"Renaissance"

Pieces in this premium fine china grouping feature a very rich design of rococo-style leaves and flower tendrils against a solid-color background. Colors in this line include green, gray, gold, and Renaissance Royal (cobalt blue). Note that there are differences in price between pieces of various colors and between pieces with platinum or gold trim (platinum is generally a bit more expensive).

Bowl, *cream soup, with saucer*	$ 100–140
Bowl, *individual fruit*	$ 50–65
Bowl, *soup/cereal, 8$^1/_4$-inch diameter*	$ 90–150

Bowl, *vegetable, oval, 9 inches*	$ 200–269
Creamer	$ 100–120
Cup and saucer	$ 40–52
Cup and saucer, *after-dinner demitasse*	$ 50–65
Gravy boat, *faststand*	$ 235–275
Plate, *bread and butter, 6¹/₂-inch diameter*	$ 25–32
Plate, *chop, 13-inch diameter*	$ 185–270
Plate, *dinner, 10¹/₂-inch diameter*	$ 50–80
Plate, *salad, 8¹/₂-inch diameter*	$ 35–42
Platter, *oval, 15¹/₂ inches*	$ 250–275
Sugar bowl	$ 140–165
Tidbit server, *two-tier*	$ 100–150
Tidbit server, *three-tier*	$ 130–175

"Starburst"

This line was designed by George James, and was first available in 1954. Pieces in this line were created using Gladding, McBean's "Eclipse" shapes, and feature a transfer-printed pattern of stars in shades of aqua, green, and yellow. Shapes in the "Eclipse" line are very reminiscent of the 1950s, as is the "Starburst" pattern itself. Pieces include candleholders with arched tripod bases, casseroles with pinch-grip handles on the lids, and a barrel-shaped canister set (flour, sugar, tea, and coffee) that is now very valuable. Other Gladding, McBean transfer decorations on "Eclipse" shapes include "Oasis" (1955, blue and gray with stars and lines that form squares) and "Duet" (1956, two pink roses with gray stems that are crossed at the lower end). Pieces featuring these two patterns are priced between 10 and 20 percent less than pieces featuring "Starburst," with "Duet" pieces being the least valuable. Prices listed below are for pieces in the "Starburst" line.

Bowl, *individual fruit*	$ 17–22
Bowl, *salad, serving, 12-inch diameter*	$ 110–125
Bowl, *soup/cereal, 7-inch diameter*	$ 35–42
Bowl, *vegetable, oval, 8¹/₂ inches*	$ 27–35
Bowl, *vegetable, round, divided, 8¹/₂-inch diameter*	$ 15–20
Canister, *flour (doubles as cookie jar)*	$ 400–450
Canister, *sugar*	$ 350–375

Canister, *coffee*	$ 275–300
Canister, *tea*	$ 265–290
Casserole, *individual, 5³/₄-inch diameter*	$ 100–225
Creamer	$ 18–22
Cup and saucer	$ 11–15
Egg cup	$ 85–95
Gravy boat, *faststand*	$ 35–42
Jelly dish with handle	$ 25–32
Mug, *small*	$ 100–120
Mug, *large*	$ 90–110
Plate, *bread and butter, 6¹/₂-inch diameter*	$ 5–8
Plate, *chop, 13-inch diameter*	$ 42–50
Plate, *dinner, 10¹/₂-inch diameter*	$ 18–24
Plate, *luncheon, 9¹/₂-inch diameter*	$ 42–50
Plate, *salad, 8-inch diameter*	$ 17–22
Platter, *oval, 13 inches*	$ 35–42
Platter, *oval, 15 inches*	$ 45–52
Relish, *three-part*	$ 65–75
Salt and pepper shakers, *set*	$ 32–38
Sugar bowl	$ 40–50
Tidbit server, *three-tier*	$ 60–75
Vinegar and oil set	$ 200–225

"Wildflower"

This is a very attractive pattern that features embossed (raised) depictions of Mariposa Lilies, California Poppies, Shooting Stars, and Desert Lupin. Pieces are hand-colored in shades of yellow, red, blue, and green. This very short-lived line was introduced in 1942, and was discontinued that same year.

Ashtray, *Mariposa Lily*	$ 100–125
Ashtray, *Poppy*	$ 100–125
Bowl, *salad, serving, 10¹/₂-inch diameter*	$ 700–800
Cup and saucer	$ 90–125

Gladding, McBean & Company Toastmaster jam set with toast plate. In the late 1930s, the Toastmaster Division of McGraw Edison commissioned Gladding, McBean to produce accessory items to complement its toasters. This jam set with toast plate underliner is yellow and dark green, but was photographed with the lids positioned incorrectly: the dark-green base should be paired with the yellow lid, and vice versa, for a harlequin effect. $35–$45. *Item courtesy of Kingston Pike Antique Mall, Knoxville, Tennessee.*

Cup and saucer, *after-dinner, demitasse*	$ 300–325
Plate, *bread and butter, 6¹/₂-inch diameter*	$ 50–65
Plate, *chop, 12-inch diameter*	$ 325–360
Plate, *dinner, 10¹/₂-inch diameter*	$ 150–175
Plate, *luncheon, 9¹/₂-inch diameter*	$ 115–135
Plate, *salad, 8-inch diameter*	$ 65–80
Platter, *oval, 14 inches*	$ 375–400
Relish	$ 310–340
Sugar bowl	$ 175–200
Tidbit server, *two-tier*	$ 240–265
Tidbit server, *three-tier*	$ 300–330
Tumbler, *10-ounce*	$ 225–260

GLIDDEN POTTERY

One of the marks used by the *Glidden Pottery*.

This pottery was founded in Alfred, New York, in 1940 by Glidden Parker, who did his graduate work at the prestigious New York State College of Ceramics at Alfred University. The company used fine stoneware bodies and beautiful glazes to produce dinnerware and art wares that are the embodiment of mid-20th-century style. Glidden was very successful for a while, and even sold its products internationally, but the company closed in 1957 after Parker decided to switch his artistic focus to making stained glass.

Art Ware

Dinnerware

"FEATHER"
This pattern features a large stylized feather with a curlicued end. Flatware shapes are generally oval or square.

Casserole, *individual, lidded*	$ 60–75
Creamer	$ 50–65
Cup and saucer	$ 36–40
Plate, *bread and butter, 6 inches, oval*	$ 11–15
Plate, *dinner, oval, 10 inches*	$ 34–40

 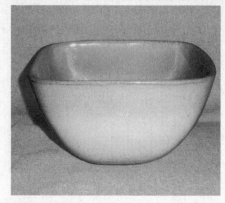

Pair of poodle-decorated square dishes,
5½ inches, Glidden, $60–$85.
*Item courtesy of Richard Hatch and
Associates, Hendersonville, North Carolina.*

Glidden Pottery bowl, blue, 7¼ inches in
diameter, $35–$45.
*Item courtesy of Richard H. Crane, Knoxville,
Tennessee.*

Plate, *luncheon, 8 inches*	$ 22–28
Plate, *salad, oval, 7 inches*	$ 20–25
Plate, *salad, square, 7 inches*	$ 18–22
Relish	$ 32–45

GONDER CERAMIC ART COMPANY

Impressed *Gonder* mark.

On December 8, 1941, Lawton Gonder purchased the old Peters and Reed plant in Zanesville, Ohio, which had last been used by the Zane Pottery. Gonder specialized in making high-quality commercial art wares, often with exotic glazes that are much prized by current collectors. Gold Crackle is the most desired of the Gonder special glazes, followed by the Flambé glaze (red with streaks of yellow), which Gonder is said to have perfected for commercial purposes. Also in demand are the Chinese Crackle glazes, which were produced in shades of turquoise, white, or yellow, as well as Ming Blue and Ming Yellow.

Impressed *Gonder* mark.

Initially Gonder was very successful, and in 1946 another plant was built to manufacture lamps. This entity was named "Elgee Pottery," a reference to Lawton Gonder's initials ("L. G."). The Elgee Pottery factory burned down in 1954 and, to replace its production capacity, Gonder's main factory was enlarged. Unfortunately, however, competition from foreign imports caused Gonder to stop making commercial art wares, and production stopped in 1957.

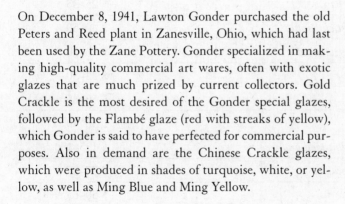

A mark used by *Gonder Ceramic Arts, Inc.*

Cookie Jars and Related Items

Pirate with pistol, *unmarked*	$ 2,000–2,200
Round, *with swirls, plain lid, #P24*	$ 100–125

Round, *with swirls, sleeping dog on lid*	$ 135–150
Sheriff bank	$ 600–700
Sheriff reaching for guns, *marked, flesh-toned face, #950*	$ 1,750–2,000

Dinnerware

"La Gonda"

Introduced in 1947, "La Gonda" is a line of solid-color dinnerware in shades of blue, brown, gray, green, pink, and yellow. Sometimes these colors are augmented with a drip glaze. "La Gonda" shapes are largely square and rectangular, and the line was initially very popular. Unfortunately, its pieces chipped easily, and sales dropped off so much as a result of this that the line was discontinued in the early 1950s.

Bowl, *individual fruit, 4¹/₂ inches square*	$ 20–30
Bowl, *covered, casserole or vegetable*	$ 110–130
Candleholders, *cubic, pair*	$ 25–35
Casserole, *individual, stick handle*	$ 40–50
Creamer and sugar set, *stacked*	$ 40–50
Cup and saucer	$ 22–30
Jug, *ice lip*	$ 50–65
Plate, *8¹/₂ inches*	$ 30–40
Platter, *chop, rectangular, well and tree*	$ 125–150
Salt and pepper shakers, *set*	$ 25–35
Snack set, *cup and plate*	$ 50–65
Teapot, *6-cup*	$ 80–100

Figures

† *Prices listed below are for pieces featuring a range of glaze colors. The rarest Gonder hues are the crackles—Gold Crackle, Chinese White Crackle, Chinese Turquoise Crackle, and Chinese Yellow Crackle—as well as the Flambé glaze, Ming Blue, and Ming Yellow. The wide range in prices listed below is due to the differences in value between pieces with common glaze colors and those with rarer glaze treatments. Pieces found in certain rare colors may command prices that are even higher than the highest prices listed below.*

Animals

| Cat, *"Modern" or "Imperial," 12¹/₄ inches* | $ 290–375 |
| Deer, *doe, 10¹/₂ inches tall, #213* | $ 60–75 |

Deer, *running, two animals, 6 inches tall, #690*	$ 110–145
Elephant, *7¹/₂ inches by 10 inches, #108*	$ 500–600
Elephant, *trunk raised, 8¹/₂ inches by 11¹/₂ inches, #207*	$ 100–125
Elephant, *trunk raised, 6¹/₂ inches by 8 inches, #209*	$ 85–110
Goose, *head down, #B-14*	$ 50–65
Goose, *head up, #B-15*	$ 50–65
Hen pecking at worm, *6³/₄ inches tall, #525*	$ 165–200
Horse head, *racing, 7 inches tall, #872*	$ 200–275
Panther, *reclining, 19 inches long, #210*	$ 275–325
Panther, *stalking, 19 inches long, #206*	$ 150–225
Rooster, *stylized, 10¹/₂ inches tall, #212*	$ 200–225
Rooster, *10¹/₂ inches tall, #525*	$ 200–250

People

Asian figure in conical hat, *kneeling, 6 inches, #547*	$ 25–60
Asian man, *formed as though carved from ivory tusk, 6³/₄ inches*	$ 70–85
Asian man with beard, *8¹/₂ inches tall, #775*	$ 70–85
Asian man, *carrying two water buckets, 10¹/₂ inches, #777*	$ 85–110
Balinese water bearer, *man, 14 inches, #763*	$ 75–95
Balinese water bearer, *woman, 14 inches, #763*	$ 75–95
Chair bearer, *Asian figures bearing a chair-shaped planter, 12 inches, #765*	$ 200–250
Gay '90s water bearer, *man, 13 inches*	$ 200–250
Gay '90s water bearer, *woman, 13 inches*	$ 200–250
Head of Asian man, *in conical hat, 11¹/₂ inches, #541*	$ 500–700
Head of woman, *9¹/₄ inches tall, #587*	$ 165–200
Head of woman, *roses in hair, 12 inches, #588*	$ 200–250
Jester, *bust, 13³/₄ inches*	$ 500–600
Madonna, *base inscribed "Mariae Virginis De Fatima," with original rosary, 9¹/₂ inches, #772*	$ 110–125
Madonna, *no inscription, 9¹/₄ inches, #549*	$ 75–135

Porters, *Asian, two figures bearing an urn suspended on a pole, 12$^1/_4$ inches, #764*	$ 195–225
St. Francis, *17$^1/_2$ inches tall*	$ 500–600
Woman figure with rings around neck and flowers at bodice, *carrying a ringed planter on head, #762*	$ 85–110

Console Sets (Center Bowl and Two Candlesticks)

Crescent moon, *#J-55 (bowl) and #J-56 (candlesticks)*	$ 110–130
Freeform, *#520 (bowl) and #520C (candlesticks)*	$ 120–140
Shell, *#505 (bowl) and #506 (candlesticks)*	$ 120–140

Miscellaneous

Ashtray, *boomerang, #223*	$ 45–60
Ashtray, *fish, #224*	$ 70–85
Ashtray, *foot, #586*	$ 35–45
Ashtray, *horse head, 6 inches, #548*	$ 60–75
Basket, *fluted, 9 inches, #L-19*	$ 50–65
Bell, *lady in bonnet*	$ 110–135
Bookends, *Grecian horses, #211*	$ 150–200
Bookends, *Roman horse heads, #220*	$ 175–225
Bowl, *lobed, 8 inches, #H-29*	$ 40–50
Cigarette box, *2$^1/_2$ inches by 3$^1/_2$ inches, "Sovereign," #806*	$ 85–100
Cigarette urn, *footed, "Sovereign," 3$^1/_2$ inches tall, #802*	$ 70–85
Ewer, *11 inches tall, #J-25*	$ 60–75
Flower frog, *three-tier, #250*	$ 110–130
Jar, *covered, dragons, 7$^3/_4$ inches, #533*	$ 135–200
Lamp, *table, cactus, 15$^1/_2$ inches*	$ 125–175
Lamp, *table, large elephant, 9 inches, #207*	$ 165–225
Lamp, *table, lyre, 10 inches*	$ 75–100
Lamp, *TV, crowing rooster, 14 inches, #1902*	$ 130–160
Lamp, *TV, old mill, 8$^1/_2$ inches*	$ 110–150
Lamp, *TV, ship, 13 inches, #1903*	$ 80–100

Gonder Ceramic Art bowl, lobed, 8
inches in diameter, $40–$50.
*Item courtesy of Richard Hatch and
Associates, Hendersonville, North Carolina.*

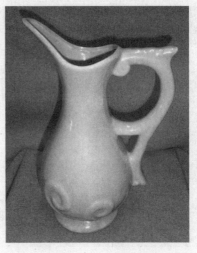

Gonder Ceramic Art ewer, 11 inches tall,
#J-25, $60–$75.
*Item courtesy of Bill Brooker, Old School
Antique Mall, Sylva, North Carolina.*

Pitcher, *shell and starfish, #400*	$ 200–275
Tray, *8 sections, #100*	$ 225–300

Planters

Conch Shell, *#793*	$ 275–325
Covered Wagon, *#802*	$ 130–160
Flying Horse, *#553*	$ 95–110
Gondola, *14 inches*	$ 100–125
Masks of Comedy and Tragedy, *#519*	$ 110–135
Nude and Running Deer, *#593*	$ 350–425
Sampan, *#550*	$ 25–40
Swan, *small, #E-44*	$ 20–30
Swan, *medium, #J-31*	$ 50–65
Swan, *large, #L-14*	$ 80–100
Winged Horse, *#553*	$ 100–125

Gonder Ceramic Art planter, flying or winged horse, #553,
$95–$110.
*Item courtesy of Bill Brooker, Old School Antique Mall,
Sylva, North Carolina.*

Vases

#215 Jumping gazelle vase, *round or moon-shaped*	$ 90–125
#216 Double horn vase	$ 75–125
#365 Ewer, *with handle shaped like a "3"*	$ 30–45
#380 Cornucopia, *with "pretzel" handle*	$ 50–75
#401 Rectangular, *with raised lines in a maze configuration*	$ 60–85
#410 Ewer	$ 40–65
#505 Leaf fan	$ 70–90
#507 Pinecone	$ 100–140
#508 Tall shell and starfish with handle	$ 100–150
#509 Double cornucopia	$ 175–250
#518 Doe head	$ 90–125
#519 Asian figure in conical hat	$ 30–60
#524 Seahorse	$ 225–325
#526 Pegasus	$ 200–325

Vase with scroll foot by Gonder Ceramic
Art, #E-4, 7 inches tall, $50–$60.
*Item courtesy of Bill Brooker, Old School
Antique Mall, Sylva, North Carolina.*

Vase with gray-on-pink pearlized glaze by
Gonder Ceramic Art, #H-5, $45–$60.
*Item courtesy of Bill Brooker, Old School
Antique Mall, Sylva, North Carolina.*

#527 Bottle vase, *with base, Asian influence*	$ 110–200
#530 Swan	$ 150–225
#531 Stick vase	$ 200–350
#534 Square, *Chinese-style*	$ 85–120
#539 Plumes	$ 85–110
#599 Leaves and twigs	$ 150–250
#710 Small cylinder, *with drip glaze*	$ 25–40
#711 Medium cylinder, *with drip glaze*	$ 30–45
#712 Large cylinder, *with drip glaze*	$ 45–60
#720 Chinese-style, *with offset handle and pinched waist, drip glaze*	$ 110–145
#876 Trumpet flower	$ 200–250
E-4 Vase, *7 inches tall*	$ 50–60
H-5 Twist handles	$ 45–60
H-47 Swan	$ 35–65

H-67 Triple leaf	$ 30–55
H-76 Crane	$ 65–100
H-401 Shell and coral	$ 110–140
H-605 Tied-back curtains	$ 80–100
H-607 Double gourd	$ 150–185
J-57 Lyre	$ 110–140
J-66 Cornucopia	$ 50–70
K-15 Feather fan	$ 150–200
K-25 Swallows	$ 210–250
M-8 Vine, *leaf, and flower*	$ 110–150

GRUEBY FAIENCE COMPANY/
GRUEBY POTTERY

The mark most commonly found on pottery made by the *Grueby Faience Company*.

The early history of William Henry Grueby, the man responsible for the eventual founding of the Grueby Faience Company, is far from clear. Grueby was born in 1867 and reportedly went to work for the Low Art Tile Company of Chelsea, Massachusetts, at the age of either 13 or 15. How long he stayed there is a matter of some debate, but it is believed that he founded his own company in Revere, Massachusetts, in 1890 to make architectural faience in partnership with Eugene R. Atwood.

The company was initially called "Atwood and Grueby," but this relationship collapsed very quickly and the company was renamed the Grueby Faience Company in 1894. At first the company focused on making architectural ornaments (mostly tiles and glazed bricks), but even at this early date the company was also experimenting with the production of art pottery.

Grueby had been influenced by French pottery that he had seen at the Chicago World's Fair in 1893. After much trial and error, Grueby developed a matte glaze that was similar to a French glaze he had seen in Chicago. He used the same type of earthenware body that he employed to make his architectural tiles, dipping the body in an opaque enamel and firing until vitrification occurred. The glaze on these pieces

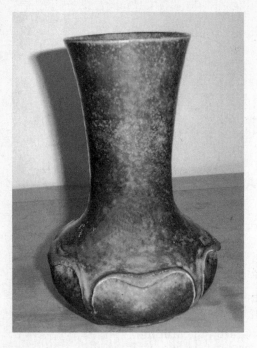

Vase by Grueby Faience, 7 inches tall, typical dark-green glaze, artist-initialed: "HP," $3,750–$4,000.
Item courtesy of B and D Antiques and Art Pottery.

is very thick, and it sometimes ran and obscured the marks that were placed on the bottoms of the pottery.

The vast majority of all Grueby pieces that collectors find today have a green matte glaze that resembles the skin of a cucumber or the rind of a watermelon. Yellow, gray, brown, purple, blue, cream, and pink glazes can also be found, and any piece covered with one of these shades or with two or more colors on its surface is considered rare and potentially valuable.

The decorations found on Grueby pottery are usually very naturalistic, with depictions of leaves and flowers being the most common. Most Grueby products were handmade by young men and women hired from local Boston art schools, but some pieces (such as the company's famous scarab paperweight) were molded.

Grueby first exhibited its art pottery in 1897, and in 1900 it sent 100 pieces to the Paris Universal Exposition, where it won two gold metals and a silver, defeating several better-known American potteries such as Rookwood. In 1901, Grueby won a second gold metal in Saint Petersburg, Russia, and the company was awarded the Grand Prize at the 1904 St. Louis World's Fair.

In 1907, the company divided into two parts: the Grueby Pottery Company and the separate Grueby Faience and Tile Company. Unfortunately, the new Grueby Pottery Company only stayed in business until 1911, when the last Grueby art pottery was made. Despite a disastrous fire in 1913, the Grueby Faience and Tile Company continued to make architectural tiles until about 1920, when the company was sold to the C. Pardee Works of Perth Amboy, New Jersey.

Grueby pottery is usually marked with a clear impression containing the name of the company and the location. Usually the mark is circular, with a lotus blossom in the center surrounded by the company designation. Pieces marked "Grueby Faience" were produced earlier than those marked "Grueby Pottery." Most pieces made after 1905 will have the "Grueby Pottery" mark. It should also be noted that Grueby occasionally used paper labels, many of which have been removed over the years.

Jar, *covered, 6^1/$_2$ inches tall, typical green matte glaze*	$ 4,100–4,250
Paperweight, *round, 2^1/$_4$-inch diameter, scarab beetle, two-toned green matte glaze*	$ 550–650
Tile, *4 inches square, lion decoration, artist-signed*	$ 1,200–1,400
Tile, *6 inches square, image of putti carrying a cornucopia, mustard yellow and brownish red*	$ 500–550
Tile, *6 inches square, images of grape, leaves, and vine, four colors, chip to underside corner*	$ 725–775
Vase, *4^1/$_2$ inches tall, matte blue glaze, no decoration*	$ 825–900
Vase, *5 inches, matte green glaze, bulbous base tapers to mouth*	$ 1,200–1,500
Vase, *6^1/$_2$ inches tall, cylinder with tapered mouth, matte green glaze, good color*	$ 1,950–2,200
Vase, *7 inches, thick and very dark green matte glaze, tooled and applied leaves, exceptional quality, artist-signed*	$ 3,900–4,200
Vase, *7^1/$_4$ inches, matte blue/green glaze, tapered cylinder, plain*	$ 825–925
Vase, *7^1/$_4$ inches, broad leaves run vertically to ruffled edge, two-toned matte green glaze*	$ 4,200–4,500
Vase, *7^1/$_2$ inches, applied leaves on body to waisted shoulder, good matte dark-green glaze*	$ 4,000–4,500
Vase, *8 inches, mottled matte green glaze, no decoration*	$ 1,575–1,650
Vase, *8^1/$_2$ inches, leaves around base, two-toned matte green drip glaze*	$ 5,500–6,000
Vase, *10^1/$_2$ inches, signed by artist Gertrude Priest, mottled green matte glaze, leaves around base with oval bud details above the leaves, excellent quality*	$ 8,500–9,000

Vase, *11 inches, modeled by Wilhelmina Post, carved leaves, golden-brown matte glaze*	$ 10,000–12,000
Vase, *12 inches, modeled by Wilhelmina Post, exquisite hand-tooled leaves on base with more leaves around mouth*	$ 32,000–35,000
Vase, *14¹/₂ inches, modeled by Wilhelmina Post, two-color, yellow to matte green, bulbous bottom tapering to a long neck, top surrounded by yellow flower blossoms, base has green leaves and stems, important piece with a few chips around neck*	$ 32,000–35,000

HAEGER POTTERIES

One of the paper labels found on *"Royal Haeger"* pottery.

Haeger was founded in Dundee, Illinois, in 1871 by Henry David Haeger. It was a brickyard, and it was reportedly Haeger brick that rebuilt Chicago after the great fire of 1871. Haeger died in 1900, and management of the company passed to his sons. Around 1912, the company began slowly to diversify and add new products to its lines. At first it produced simple flowerpots, which is a logical first step after brickmaking, but the company began adding glazed products to its repertoire around 1914, and by the beginning of World War I it was making commercial art wares.

Over the years, Haeger hired a number of talented designers to produce prototypes for its art wares. One of the most influential of these was Royal Arden Hickman. Hickman was born in 1893, and although he was trained in art he began his career doing construction work on the Panama Canal. Sunstroke in the brutal tropical climate nearly killed him, and while he was recovering in California, he began working with clay.

Soon he was professionally designing both dinnerware and crystal, and in 1938 he joined the Haeger Pottery Company. There he began creating a premium line of commercial art wares known as "Royal Haeger," a name that combined the designer's first name with that of the company. The "Royal Haeger" line sold very well, and the company had to build

Haeger lighter, #813H, gold/orange to green, 11 inches, $35–$45.
Item courtesy of Kingston Pike Antique Mall, Knoxville, Tennessee.

another kiln to process all the orders. In 1944, Hickman left Haeger and worked with other important companies such as Heisey Glass and Vernon Kilns, but he also established his own company, which he named "Royal Hickman Industries." Haeger continued to make the prestigious "Royal Haeger" line, and is still in business today.

Ashtrays

"Century of Progress," *1934, figure of elephant*	$ 75–100
"Century of Progress," *1934, arch with cityscape*	$ 60–80
"Century of Progress," *1934, rectangular, two receptacles*	$ 60–80
"Century of Progress," *1934, round*	$ 60–80
134 Palm leaf, *19 inches long*	$ 35–50
175 "Sands of Time," *footprints*	$ 24–30
R-449 Leaf	$ 20–25
R-668 Elephant	$ 45–60
R-873 Free-form	$ 22–28

R-1095 Lincoln, *1818–1968, in shape of state of Illinois*	$ 40–50
R-1441 Poodle	$ 100–125
R-1718 Boomerang	$ 22–28
R-1755 "Executive Ashtray"	$ 30–40

Bookends

R-132 Rams, *9 inches, pair*	$ 175–200
R-475 Calla lilies, *pair*	$ 85–125
R-638 Panthers, *pair*	$ 150–175
R-641 Stallion heads, *8¹/₂ inches, pair*	$ 75–100
R-718 Ram's heads, *pair*	$ 75–100
R-1144 Water lilies, *pair*	$ 35–45

Bowls

329-H Pheasant	$ 65–75
R-112 Leaf-edged	$ 85–100
R-224 Daisy	$ 60–70
R-277 Spiral Plume	$ 45–50
R-297 Shell	$ 40–45
R-328 Bowl with plume feet	$ 75–90
R-370 "Dutch Cup" bowl	$ 55–70
R-373 Bowl with applied flowers	$ 95–110
R-421 Bowl with clusters of fruit	$ 80–95
R-442 Bowl with embossed floral decoration	$ 100–125
R-481 Shell-shaped bowl with seashells on base	$ 100–125
R-484 Garden bowl	$ 35–40

Candleholders

R-203 Fish, *standing, pair*	$ 85–110
R-220 Ball-shaped, *with two birds, pair*	$ 65–85
R-304 Fish, *pair*	$ 60–75

R-312 Cornucopia, *pair*	$ 40–50
R-473 Tall twin stalks, *not marked, rococo, pair*	$ 175–200
R-433 Triple plume, *pair*	$ 70–85
R-516 Swans, *pair*	$ 75–90
R-579 Two blocks, *pair*	$ 50–60
R-622 Chinese figures, *pair*	$ 40–50
R-1206 Apple, *pair*	$ 35–45
R-1208 Butterfly, *pair*	$ 45–55

Candy Dishes

R-431 Calla Lily, *covered*	$ 75–90
R-512 Dolphin	$ 100–125
R-631 Leopard	$ 100–125
R-1730 Urn-shaped, *covered*	$ 25–30

Cigarette Boxes

R-631 Leopard	$ 100–125
R-685 Three horse heads	$ 95–115

Figures

683 Panther stalking	$ 85–100
837 Girl's head	$ 90–110
838 Boy's head	$ 100–125
R-103 Horse, *8 inches*	$ 45–55
R-130 Pheasant	$ 40–50
R-138 Flying Fish	$ 125–150
R-164 Pheasant Hen	$ 25–30
R-165 Pheasant Cock	$ 30–40
R-166 Greyhound, *head down*	$ 85–100
R-167 Greyhound, *head up*	$ 85–100
R-180 Bird, *Parrot/Macaw*	$ 95–110

R-218 Giraffe	$ 125–150
R-233 Bird, *Pouter Pigeon*	$ 80–100
R-237 Ducks, *wings down*	$ 60–70
R-287 Birdhouse with two birds	$ 125–150
R-313 Tigress	$ 145–175
R-314 Tiger	$ 145–175
R-318 Russian Wolfhound	$ 85–100
R-375 A Polar Bear Cub	$ 55–65
R-375 B Polar Bear, *sitting, large*	$ 95–110
R-376 A Polar Bear Cub, *standing*	$ 55–65
R-379 Bull, *with base*	$ 325–375
R-382 Peasant Man	$ 150–175
R-383 Peasant Woman	$ 150–175
R-402 Horse	$ 50–60
R-412 Standing Fawn	$ 60–70
R-413 Sitting Fawn	$ 50–60
R-424 Cowboy on Bucking Horse	$ 225–275
R-434 Hen Pheasant	$ 55–65
R-435 Rooster Pheasant	$ 55–65
R-451 Horse, *Mare and Foal*	$ 200–250
R-479 Prospector with Burros	$ 200–250
R-502 Bullfighter	$ 160–185
R-624 Deer, *two does*	$ 75–95
R-648 Panther, *on pedestal*	$ 55–65
R-649 Leopard, *lying down*	$ 55–65
R-694 Buddha	$ 100–125
R-711 Man, *Chinese musician*	$ 50–65
R-721 Indian, *on horse with cactus*	$ 225–250
R-734 Dog, *Collie*	$ 100–125
R-736 Dog, *Dachshund*	$ 100–125
R-777 Cocker Spaniel	$ 65–75

Haeger head of a boy, white glaze, 6 inches, $100–$125.
Item courtesy of Richard H. Crane, Knoxville, Tennessee.

R-780 Mister Scot	$ 60–70
R-781 Dog, *Miss Peke*	$ 60–70
R-784 Elephant	$ 50–65
R-975 Running Deer	$ 45–60
R-1131 Leopard	$ 90–110
R-1177 Neptune on Sailfish	$ 275–300
R-1178 Mermaid on Sailfish	$ 275–300
R-1179 Garden Girl	$ 60–70
R-1224 Gypsy with two baskets	$ 125–150
R-1301 Giraffe and young	$ 100–125
R–1762 Rooster	$ 125–150

Flower Frogs

#86 Mermaid with child	$ 250–300
R-125 Bird, *flying*	$ 175–200

"Royal Haeger" basket-shaped planter in a metal handle and base, #R-1540-S, $80–$100.
Item courtesy of Richard Hatch and Associates, Hendersonville, North Carolina.

"Royal Haeger" planter, figure of a boy with a basket, 12 inches, $90–$110.
Item courtesy of Needful Things, Hendersonville, North Carolina.

Haeger planter in the form of a pouter pigeon, #R-108, Mauve Agate glaze, $160–$185.
Item courtesy of Elaine Delcuze, Old School Antique Mall, Sylva, North Carolina.

R-169B Trout, *leaping*	$ 110–135
R-359 Birds, *two*	$ 100–125
R-360 Fish, *tropical*	$ 140–160
R-363 Nude on Fish	$ 150–175
R-364 Nude with Seal	$ 110–135
R-772 Stag	$ 95–110
R-788 Jockey	$ 150–165

R-820 Bird	$ 80–95
R-838 Frog	$ 90–110

Table Lamps

#1138 Horse on top of cylinder	$ 200–225
#3003 Lady's head	$ 350–400
#4172 Cabbage rose with three-dimensional flowers	$ 175–200
#5024 Plume on square base	$ 150–175
#5051 Mushroom (or Toadstool) lamp	$ 300–350
#5171 Bison, *bird finial*	$ 325–375
#5190 Bucking bronco	$ 300–350
#5195 Fawn	$ 200–225
#5202 Parrot on tree	$ 250–300
#5205 Girl on turtle's back	$ 300–350
#5292 Plume	$ 150–175
#5349 Acanthus leaf	$ 150–175
#5398 Mermaid	$ 275–325
#6204 Stallion head	$ 250–300
R-115 Gazelle head	$ 125–150
R-869 Gazelle with planter base	$ 140–160
Duck, flying	$ 200–250
Fish on wave	$ 150–175

Television Lamps

#5473 Deer, *abstract*	$ 200–250
#6051-TV Panther	$ 100–125
#6140 Sailfish	$ 85–100
#6424S-TV Fish	$ 100–125
R-1262 Prancing horse	$ 85–100
Gazelle, *leaping*	$ 100–125
Horses racing	$ 125–150

Haeger Centennial vase, #2688, Gold
Tweed glaze, $30–$45.
*Item courtesy of Needful Things,
Hendersonville, North Carolina.*

"Royal Haeger" snail vase, #R-299,
$50–$65.
*Item courtesy of Old School Antique Mall,
Sylva, North Carolina.*

Masks, *Comedy and Tragedy*	$ 100–125
Peacock	$ 100–125

Vases

#2688 Haeger Centennial, *1871–1971*	$ 30–45
#3053 Donkey vase	$ 95–110
#3105 Girl dancing in front of disk	$ 40–50
#3220 Rooster	$ 95–110
#3227 Double shell	$ 95–110
#3270 Leaf	$ 45–60
#3531 Ballerina and lily	$ 45–60
R-36 Swan	$ 65–80
R-131 Basket of flowers	$ 65–75
R-182 Swan	$ 35–50
R-186 Bird of Paradise	$ 85–100

R-208 Seagulls, *three, wings up*	$ 200–250
R-246 Double cornucopia	$ 60–75
R-299 Snail	$ 50–65
R-303 Laurel wreath and bow	$ 95–110
R-320 Elm leaf	$ 45–55
R-386 Basket of flowers, *fan-shaped*	$ 95–110
R-393 Pegasus (horse head)	$ 125–150
R-422 Butterfly	$ 50–65
R-426 Cornucopia with nude	$ 50–65
R-441 Disk vase, *Deco-style*	$ 225–250
R-441 Disk vase, *Deco-style, silver overlay decoration*	$ 450–525
R-453 Peacock	$ 100–125
R-482 Plume, *three feathers*	$ 95–110
R-646 Tulip	$ 40–50
R-647 Sunflower	$ 40–50
R-701 Seashell	$ 75–90
R-706 Running deer	$ 50–65
R-707 Standing deer	$ 50–65
R-888 Chinese-style bird on branch	$ 45–60
R-917 Peter Pan	$ 80–100
R-1189 Pinecone, *9 inches*	$ 40–50
R-1190 Pinecone, *12 inches*	$ 45–55
R-1215 Ballet dancer, *male*	$ 75–85
R-1216 Ballet dancer, *female*	$ 75–85

Miscellany

Bank in the form of a Harley Davidson "hog," 1982	$ 300–350
Bank in the form of a winking poodle, *#8034*	$ 100–110
Basket, *tall and slender, 21 inches tall*	$ 110–125
Clock in the shape of a pagoda	$ 200–250
Cookie jar, *Keebler Tree House*	$ 125–150

"Royal Haeger" basket, 21 inches tall,
$110–$125.
Item courtesy of Richard Hatch and
Associates, Hendersonville, North Carolina.

Haeger "Earth Wrap" pitcher, #8177,
$150–$175.
Item courtesy of Tony McCormack, Sarasota,
Florida.

Haeger display sign in the shape of a crown	$ 400–450
Haeger display sign, *rectangular, "Haeger" spelled out*	$ 75–90
Lavabo, *lion mask, two pieces*	$ 200–250
Pitcher, *"Earth Wrap," 8¹/₂ inches, #8177*	$ 150–175

HAGEN-RENAKER

Paper label found on
Hagen-Renaker pottery.

This company is not yet a household name among collectors, but for those who are interested in California ceramics in general and miniature in particular, the name Hagen-Renaker is very important indeed. Some sources say that John and Maxine Renaker founded this business in their garage in Culver City, California, in 1945, and moved it to a factory in Monrovia, California, in 1946. Most references, however, omit the Culver City beginnings. "Hagen" is Maxine Renaker's maiden name and, since her father reportedly financed the company and built the factory in Monrovia, she perhaps wished to include him in the company name—hence the name "Hagen-Renaker." The firm moved to San Dimas, California, in 1962, and is still in business making figures of dogs, horses, and other animals.

During the 1950s, figures of some Walt Disney characters were manufactured under license from the Disney Company, and these are some of the most desired items made by Hagen-Renaker. Some of these items are less than one inch tall, and others are somewhat larger, but $9^{1}/_{2}$ inches is about the maximum size for one of the company's figures. In many instances the Hagen-Renaker animals were too small to mark, and some items thus came with hang tags or paper labels (the early ones were black and gold, while later ones were green and gold). Other pieces are marked with the name of the company or the initials "H-R."

Current production pieces of Hagen-Renaker's work can be fairly inexpensive but some earlier pieces command prices of over $1,000, with the most valuable piece being the evil witch "Malificent" from *Sleeping Beauty*. This very rare piece is just $1^1/_2$ inches tall, but should be valued at more than $1,200 (though no firm prices are available).

Adelaide, *jenny donkey, 5¹/₂ inches*	$ 175–200
Amir, *Arabian stallion, 6⁷/₈ inches tall, paper label*	$ 225–250
Buffalo, *1³/₄ inches, on card, circa 1995*	$ 15–20
Clover, *Morgan foal, 2¹/₂ inches tall*	$ 250–275
Mickey, *Pomeranian, 3¹/₂ inches tall*	$ 60–75
Ming Toy, *Pekingese, 3 inches*	$ 50–60
Pixie, *Millesan Drew Leaping Pixie, 5¹/₄ inches*	$ 70–80
Sparkle, *cat, 2¹/₂ inches*	$ 30–35
Spooky, *Dalmatian, Pedigreed Dog*	$ 150–175
Terrang, *Designer's Workshop Thoroughbred Horse, 6¹/₄ inches*	$ 215–225

HALDERMAN POTTERIES

Virgil K. Halderman graduated from the University of Illinois in 1923 with a degree in Ceramic Engineering. After working for a firm in Pennsylvania, Halderman moved to Southern California in 1927 and went to work for Santa Catalina Clay Products. There he was both a ceramics engineer and the plant manager, but he quit in 1933 to establish the Halderman Pottery in Burbank, California. Halderman created glazes for an extensive line known as "Caliente," which included such items as shallow bowls for floating flowers, figures of dancing women in the Art Deco style, and a wide variety of other figures and giftware. Interstate construction forced the firm to move to Calabasas in 1951, and the company closed shortly thereafter in 1953. Pieces of Halderman's "Caliente" pottery were often marked with paper labels that did not survive the years, leaving most examples largely unmarked except for an incised or raised "Made In California" or, very rarely, an incised "Halderman California" written in script.

Bowl for floating flowers, *quatrefoil, green interior, creamy-white exterior, embossed florals, 12 inches*	$ 60
Figure of a dancing woman, *arms outstretched with each hand holding the hem of her full skirt, model 408*	$ 135

Figure of a dancing woman, *one hand holding hem of dress as she raises one bent leg, model 408*	$ 150
Figure of a shorebird, *long legs and beak, 6^1/$_8$ inches tall*	$ 75
Flower frog in the form of a sailboat, *burgundy glaze, 6^3/$_4$ inches high*	$ 80
Vase, *green glaze, small handles at neck, 9 inches tall*	$ 250

HALL CHINA COMPANY

Mark commonly found on the "Autumn Leaf" pattern made by Hall China for the Jewel Tea Company.

Hall printed mark.

In 1903, Robert Hall bought the old East Liverpool Pottery Company of East Liverpool, Ohio, and renamed it the Hall China Company. At first, Hall continued to make the same semiporcelain products that had been the original company's specialty, but after Hall's death in 1904, his son began trying to develop a vitrified ceramic body that required only one firing for both the glaze and the pottery.

The problem was finding a glaze that could withstand the intense heat of the bisque firing process. Hall also wanted the glaze to be lead-free, craze-proof, and nonporous. A single-fire process had been used by the Chinese during the Ming Dynasty, and Hall finally managed to unlock the secret of this process in 1911. Appropriately, the company called it the "Secret Process," and the process is reportedly still in use today.

During the early 20th century, Hall specialized in making such items as teapots and casseroles for use by institutions and businesses such as hotels and restaurants. The company's cookware line became very successful, and in 1919 it purchased the Goodwin Pottery plant in East Liverpool just to make decorated teapots. Hall launched a program to teach Americans how to brew tea using the Hall teapot, and soon the company became the world's largest manufacturer of this type of vessel.

Hall began making decal-decorated dinnerware and kitchenware around 1931, and these items were made available to the public through trading-stamp companies, mass merchandisers, department stores, and companies that offered the dinnerware as premiums for buying their products. The best example of such a company was the Jewel Tea Company, which used pieces from Hall's "Autumn Leaf" and "Cameo Rose" lines as premiums.

Hall is still in business today, and is an important name to many collectors.

Dinnerware

"Autumn Leaf"

The Hall China Company first produced pieces in this legendary line in 1933 for use as premiums by the Jewel Tea Company, which was headquartered in Barrington, Illinois, just a few miles northwest of Chicago. Most of the marks found on "Autumn Leaf" pieces read "Tested and Approved by Mary Dunbar Jewel Homemakers Institute." Mary Dunbar was the maiden name of Mrs. Mary Reed Hartson, who became known as the "Jewel Lady" after she began answering questions about home cooking from Jewel Tea customers in 1925. The number of different items that Hall made with the "Autumn Leaf" decal is truly mind-boggling, and every now and then a previously unrecorded form will turn up. Such pieces can be rather valuable. The "Autumn Leaf" design was also applied to a wide variety of ancillary items, from playing cards and cleanser cans to tablecloths and blankets (though these items are not within the scope of this book), and collectors of the dinnerware are often very interested in these items as well. "Autumn Leaf" was officially discontinued in 1978, but reissues and limited-edition items have been produced since that time.

It should be noted that Hall was not the only company to use the famous "Autumn Leaf" decal on its dinnerware and accessory items, though it was the only company to use it on premiums for the Jewel Tea Company. Other companies that used this decal include Crown Pottery, W. S. George, Columbia Chinaware (a division of the more well-known Harker Pottery), Vernon Kilns, and Paden City.

Baker, *round, 6-inch diameter*	$ 175–190
Baker, *round, 7-inch diameter*	$ 25–30
Bean pot, *covered, two handles*	$ 350–375
Bean pot, *covered, one handle*	$ 1,000–1,200
Bowl, *cereal, 6-inch diameter*	$ 14–18
Bowl, *cream soup, and saucer*	$ 40–45
Bowl, *individual fruit, $5^{1}/_{2}$-inch diameter*	$ 3–5

Rare clock in Hall China Company's "Autumn Leaf" pattern, which was made for the Jewel Tea Company. The "Autumn Leaf" clock came in both electric and battery-powered models, with the electric examples being much more valuable than the later pieces that ran on batteries. This is the electric model. $850–$950.
Item courtesy of Chris Paddleford.

"Autumn Leaf" round warmer base, fits the 8-cup drip percolator, manufactured between 1956 and 1960, $175–$190.
Item courtesy of Chris Paddleford.

Bowl, *salad, serving, 9-inch diameter*	$ 22–28
Bowl, *soup, $8^1/_2$-inch diameter*	$ 14–18
Bowl, *vegetable, oval, $10^1/_2$ inches*	$ 18–22
Bowl, *vegetable, oval, covered*	$ 55–65
Butter, *covered, $^1/_4$-pound*	$ 320–340
Butter, *$^1/_4$-pound, winged or "butterfly" finial*	$ 1,800–2,200
Butter, *covered, square*	$ 600–650
Butter, *covered, 1-pound, bud-ray lid*	$ 3,200–3,500
Cake plate, $9^1/_2$ *inches*	$ 25–30
Cake stand with metal base, *$9^1/_2$-inch diameter*	$ 600–700
Casserole, *covered, round, 2-quart*	$ 42–48
Clock, *electric*	$ 850–950
Clock, *battery*	$ 450–500
Coffeepot, *8-cup*	$ 65–75
Coffeepot, *electric, 6-cup*	$ 375–425

"Autumn Leaf" round bud vase,
$250–$300.
Item courtesy of Chris Paddleford.

"Autumn Leaf" wall pocket, a reissue of the famous
design made by China Specialties, original price
was $39.95. $75–$90.
*Item courtesy of Needful Things, Hendersonville,
North Carolina.*

Mark found on the wall pocket made by
China Specialties.

Cookie jar, *rayed lid*	$ 325–375
Creamer	$ 20–25
Cup and saucer, *regular*	$ 9–12
Cup and saucer, *"St. Denis" shape*	$ 38–42
Cup, *Irish coffee*	$ 120–130
Custard cup	$ 5–8
Dish, *candy, open*	$ 625–700

Dish, *soufflé, individual*	$ 42–46
Dish, *pickle*	$ 38–44
Mug	$ 75–85
Pitcher, *ball, 5 1/2 inches*	$ 35–40
Plate, *bread and butter, 6-inch diameter*	$ 6–8
Plate, *dessert, 7 1/4-inch diameter*	$ 8–10
Plate, *dinner, 10-inch diameter*	$ 30–34
Plate, *luncheon, 9-inch diameter*	$ 12–15
Plate, *salad, 8 1/4-inch diameter*	$ 15–18
Platter, *oval, 11 1/2 inches*	$ 25–30
Ramekin	$ 15–18
Salt and pepper shakers, *range set*	$ 42–50
Stack set, *"MaryLou," three bowls and lid*	$ 150–175
Teapot, *"Aladdin" shape*	$ 85–95
Teapot, *"Newport" shape*	$ 350–400
Tidbit server, *two-tier*	$ 70–80
Tidbit server, *three-tier*	$ 135–150
Vase	$ 250–300
Warmer base, *round*	$ 175–190
Warmer base, *oval*	$ 215–245

"Blue Bouquet"

Though the name of this pattern refers only to one color, pieces decorated with "Blue Bouquet" feature a bouquet of various-colored flowers (red, yellow, and blue) against a band of latticework that surrounds their edge (in the case of flatware items) or extends from their center to their top (in the case of hollowware pieces). The pattern was produced from the early 1950s until the mid-1960s for the Standard Coffee Company of New Orleans, Louisiana.

Baker, *"French," fluted*	$ 30–35
Bean pot, *"New England," #4*	$ 240–260
Bowl, *batter, "Sundial"*	$ 2,400–2,600
Bowl, *individual fruit, 5 1/2-inch diameter*	$ 12–14

Bowl, *cereal, 6-inch diameter*	$ 24–28
Bowl, *salad, serving, 9-inch diameter*	$ 40–45
Bowl, *soup, 8¹/₂-inch diameter*	$ 34–38
Bowl, *vegetable, 9¹/₄-inch diameter*	$ 50–55
Coffeepot, *drip,* "*Kadota,*" *all china*	$ 600–650
Coffeepot, "*Terrace*"	$ 145–160
Creamer	$ 30–35
Cup and saucer	$ 30–35
Dish, *leftover, rectangular*	$ 135–150
Dish, *leftover, square*	$ 175–200
Gravy boat	$ 70–80
Jar, *pretzel*	$ 300–325
Jug, *ball, #3*	$ 170–180
Plate, *bread and butter, 6-inch diameter*	$ 8–10
Plate, *dessert, 7¹/₄-inch diameter*	$ 12–14
Plate, *dinner/luncheon, 9-inch diameter*	$ 25–30
Plate, *salad, 8¹/₄-inch diameter*	$ 14–18
Platter, *oval, 11¹/₄ inches*	$ 35–40
Platter, *oval, 13¹/₄ inches*	$ 55–60
Salt and pepper shakers, *set, handled*	$ 50–60
Sugar bowl, *lidded*	$ 45–50
Teapot, "*Aladdin*"	$ 200–225
Teapot, "*Boston*"	$ 250–275
Tureen, *soup, lidded*	$ 325–450

"Cameo Rose"

This is another Hall dinnerware pattern, examples of which were made to be used as premiums by the Jewel Tea Company. It was introduced in 1951, and continued to be offered until the early 1970s. The pattern consists of a white rose surrounded by buds and leaves, with a leaf-and-bud garland around the edge of the flatware pieces. It appears on Hall's "E"-shaped pieces, which can also be found decorated with other designs such as "Monticello" and "Mt. Vernon."

Bowl, *individual fruit, 5¹/₄-inch diameter*	$ 8–10
Bowl, *cereal, 6¹/₄-inch diameter*	$ 20–25
Bowl, *soup, 8-inch diameter*	$ 20–24
Bowl, *vegetable, oval, 10¹/₂ inches*	$ 22–26
Bowl, *vegetable, round, 9-inch diameter*	$ 30–35
Butter dish, *¹/₄-pound*	$ 600–700
Butter dish, *¹/₄-pound, "wings top"*	$ 1,250–1,400
Creamer	$ 17–22
Cup and saucer	$ 17–22
Gravy boat and underliner	$ 50–60
Plate, *bread and butter, 6¹/₄-inch diameter*	$ 6–8
Plate, *dinner, 10¹/₄-inch diameter*	$ 28–32
Plate, *luncheon, 9-inch diameter*	$ 13–16
Platter, *oval, 11¹/₂ inches*	$ 38–42
Platter, *oval, 13 inches*	$ 38–42
Platter, *oval, 15¹/₂ inches*	$ 65–75
Salt and pepper shakers, *set*	$ 40–45
Sugar bowl	$ 27–32
Teapot	$ 120–135
Tidbit server, *three-tier*	$ 85–100

"Crocus"

Considered the most popular of all the Hall dinnerware patterns that had an ivory-colored background, "Crocus" was first produced in 1938. The design features bell-shaped, stylized flowers and leaves. Pieces featuring this pattern were popular premiums for gas stations, tea companies (other than Jewel Tea), and other types of stores, and were also sold at retail.

Baker, *"French," fluted*	$ 50–65
Bean pot, *covered, one handle*	$ 450–500
Bowl, *individual fruit*	$ 20–24
Bowl, *salad, serving, 9-inch diameter*	$ 60–70
Bowl, *soup, 8¹/₂-inch diameter*	$ 32–38

Bowl, *vegetable, oval, 10 inches*	$ 68–75
Bowl, *vegetable, round, 9-inch diameter*	$ 60–70
Butter dish, *¼-pound, "Zephyr" style*	$ 1,200–1,400
Casserole, *round, covered, 1½-quart*	$ 65–75
Coffeemaker, *drip, "Kadota" shape*	$ 500–550
Coffeemaker, *drip, "Waverly" shape*	$ 90–100
Coffeepot, *"Terrace" shape*	$ 85–100
Creamer, *old-style*	$ 40–46
Creamer, *Art Deco*	$ 50–55
Cup and saucer	$ 32–38
Cup, *"St. Denis"*	$ 45–55
Dish, *leftover, rectangular, covered*	$ 110–125
Dish, *leftover, square, covered*	$ 140–160
Flagon mug	$ 90–100
Gravy boat	$ 85–95
Jug, *ball-shaped*	$ 225–250
Plate, *bread and butter, 6⅛ inches*	$ 20–24
Plate, *dinner, 10-inch diameter*	$ 70–90
Plate, *luncheon, 9-inch diameter*	$ 26–32
Plate, *salad, 8¼-inch diameter*	$ 25–30
Platter, *oval, 11½ inches*	$ 50–60
Platter, *oval, 13½ inches*	$ 80–90
Pretzel jar, *covered*	$ 300–350
Salt and pepper shakers, *handled, pair*	$ 75–85
Shakers, *sugar or flour, each*	$ 50–65
Stack set, *"Radiance"*	$ 400–450
Teapot, *"Aladdin," 6-cup*	$ 400–475
Teapot, *"Colonial," 6-cup*	$ 100–125
Teapot, *"Medallion," 8-cup*	$ 135–150
Teapot, *"Donut"*	$ 2,200–2,400
Teapot, *"New York," 2-cup*	$ 200–250

Teapot, *"New York,"* 6-cup	$ 175–225
Teapot, *"New York,"* 8-cup	$ 250–300
Teapot, *"New York,"* 12-cup	$ 275–325
Tidbit server, *three-tier*	$ 110–125
Tureen with lid, *"Clover"*	$ 500–550

"Hallcraft"

While working as a teacher at the Pratt Institute in Brooklyn, New York, Eva Zeisel also worked as a designer for Hall China. In the early 1950s, she designed two modernistic shapes for Hall: "Century" and "Tomorrow's Classic." "Hallcraft" pieces are clearly marked with a fancy "H C" monogram and the words "Hallcraft by Eva Zeisel Made in the U. S. A. by Hall China." The "Century" shape was essentially an elongated oval, with points at the ends that arched slightly downward to be used as handles. "Tomorrow's Classic" shapes are similar to those of the "Century" line, but the oval shapes lack the elongated points that distinguish "Century" items. In 1952, nine decal designs were introduced, but these lines can also be found in plain, high-gloss white and satin black.

"Century Fern"

This decal design has rather dainty green, burgundy, and pastel-blue leaves against a textured gray ground.

Bowl, *individual fruit, 5³/₄ inches*	$ 8–12
Bowl, *salad, serving, 11³/₄ inches*	$ 35–45
Bowl, *soup or cereal, 8 inches*	$ 10–14
Bowl, *vegetable, 10¹/₂ inches*	$ 25–30
Bowl, *vegetable, divided*	$ 35–45
Butter dish, *¹/₄-pound, covered*	$ 140–160
Casserole, *covered*	$ 75–85
Creamer	$ 14–18
Cup and saucer	$ 10–14
Gravy boat	$ 35–45
Jug	$ 40–50
Plate, *bread and butter, 6 inches*	$ 6–9
Plate, *dinner, 10¹/₄ inches*	$ 15–20

Plate, *salad, 8 inches*	$ 10–14
Platter, *13³/₄ inches*	$ 32–42
Platter, *15 inches*	$ 40–50
Salt and pepper shakers, *set*	$ 35–45
Teapot, *6-cup*	$ 200–225

"Century Sunglow"

This pattern depicts a slender tree with lemon-yellow leaves, with larger yellow leaves scattered around its surface. Interiors of jugs and cups are solid yellow, as are the tops of casseroles, teapots, and sugar bowls.

Bowl, *individual fruit, 5³/₄ inches*	$ 12–15
Bowl, *soup or cereal, 8 inches*	$ 15–20
Bowl, *salad, serving, 11³/₄ inches*	$ 40–50
Bowl, *vegetable, divided*	$ 65–75
Creamer	$ 15–20
Cup and saucer	$ 12–15
Gravy boat	$ 50–60
Jug	$ 55–65
Plate, *bread and butter*	$ 7–10
Plate, *dinner, 10¹/₄ inches*	$ 20–25
Plate, *salad, 8 inches*	$ 12–15
Platter, *13³/₄ inches*	$ 55–65
Platter, *15 inches*	$ 65–75
Salt and pepper shakers, *set*	$ 40–50
Sugar bowl, *lidded*	$ 28–35
Teapot, *6-cup*	

"Tomorrow's Classic Arizona"

Baker, *11-ounce*	$ 30–35
Bowl, *cereal, 6 inches*	$ 15–19
Bowl, *individual fruit, 5³/₄ inches*	$ 8–12
Bowl, *onion soup, cover*	$ 65–75

Bowl, *salad, serving, 14¹/₂ inches*	$ 45–55
Bowl, *vegetable, square, 8³/₄ inches*	$ 45–55
Bowl, *soup, 9 inches*	$ 15–20
Butter dish, *¹/₄-pound, covered*	$ 225–250
Casserole, *1¹/₄-quart, covered*	$ 45–55
Casserole, *2-quart, covered*	$ 70–80
Creamer	$ 15–20
Cruet, *vinegar*	$ 125–150
Cup and saucer	$ 18–24
Cup and saucer, *demitasse*	$ 25–30
Dish, *celery*	$ 32–38
Egg cup	$ 75–85
Gravy boat	$ 70–80
Jug, *1¹/₄-quart*	$ 45–55
Jug, *2-quart*	$ 55–65
Plate, *bread and butter, 6 inches*	$ 5–9
Plate, *dinner, 11 inches*	$ 15–20
Platter, *12¹/₄ inches*	$ 30–40
Platter, *15 inches*	$ 60–70
Platter, *17 inches*	$ 65–75
Salt and pepper shakers, *set*	$ 50–60
Sugar bowl, *lidded*	$ 25–32
Teapot, *6-cup*	$ 225–250
Vase	$ 110–125

"Tomorrow's Classic Bouquet"

This is one of the most popular of Eva Zeisel's decals, and it is also one of the most available. As the name suggests, flatware pieces bearing this pattern have a lavish bouquet of flowers in their centers; other pieces may simply have sprigs of individual flowers. In addition, the "Bouquet" decal appears on another Hall shape known to collectors as "M. J."

Baker, *11-ounce*	$ 50–58
Bowl, *cereal, 6 inches*	$ 28–32
Bowl, *individual fruit, 5³/₄ inches*	$ 12–16
Bowl, *salad, serving, 14¹/₂ inches*	$ 85–95
Bowl, *soup, 9 inches*	$ 30–35
Bowl, *vegetable, square, 8³/₄ inches*	$ 42–48
Butter dish, *¹/₄-pound, covered*	$ 325–375
Casserole, *1¹/₄-quart, covered*	$ 115–125
Casserole, *1¹/₄-quart*	$ 75–85
Casserole, *2-quart*	$ 100–120
Coffeepot, *6-cup*	$ 190–210
Creamer	$ 25–32
Cruet, *vinegar*	$ 115–125
Cup and saucer	$ 18–22
Dish, *celery*	$ 40–50
Egg cup	$ 90–110
Gravy boat	$ 32–38
Jug, *1¹/₄-quart*	$ 50–60
Jug, *3-quart*	$ 60–70
Plate, *bread and butter, 6 inches*	$ 6–9
Plate, *dinner, 11 inches*	$ 32–38
Plate, *salad, 8 inches*	$ 18–22
Platter, *oval, 12¹/₄ inches*	$ 50–60
Platter, *oval, 15 inches*	$ 70–80
Platter, *oval, 17 inches*	$ 75–85
Salt and pepper shakers, *set*	$ 65–75
Sugar bowl, *lidded*	$ 35–45
Teapot, *6-cup*	$ 325–375

"Tomorrow's Classic Hi-White" and "Tomorrow's Classic Satin Black"

Baker, *oval, 11$\frac{1}{2}$-ounce*	$ 60–70
Bowl, *individual fruit, 5$\frac{3}{4}$-inch diameter*	$ 18–22
Bowl, *cereal, 6 inches*	$ 20–25
Bowl, *salad, serving, 14-inch diameter*	$ 100–120
Bowl, *soup, 9 inches*	$ 30–35
Bowl, *vegetable, square*	$ 50–60
Butter dish, *$\frac{1}{4}$-pound, covered*	$ 325–375
Casserole, *covered, 1$\frac{1}{4}$-quart*	$ 130–150
Casserole, *covered, 2-quart*	$ 150–175
Coffeepot, *6-cup*	$ 200–250
Creamer	$ 30–35
Cup and saucer	$ 35–40
Dish, *celery*	$ 50–60
Egg cup	$ 100–110
Gravy boat	$ 70–85
Jug, *1$\frac{1}{4}$-quart*	$ 60–70
Jug, *3-quart*	$ 65–75
Plate, *bread and butter, 6 inches*	$ 12–15
Plate, *dinner, 10$\frac{1}{4}$ inches*	$ 40–45
Plate, *salad, 8 inches*	$ 22–28
Platter, *oval, 13$\frac{3}{4}$ inches*	$ 60–70
Platter, *oval, 15 inches*	$ 80–90
Platter, *oval, 17 inches*	$ 90–100
Salt and pepper shakers, *set*	$ 75–85
Sugar bowl	$ 40–45
Teapot, *6-cup*	$ 325–375

"Poppy" or "Orange Poppy"

Hall first produced pieces in the "Poppy" (or "Orange Poppy") line in 1933 for the Great American Tea Company to use as premiums. The beautiful orange-poppy decals were added to shapes from Hall's "C" line, and the line was in production until the 1950s. Each flatware piece features three groupings of poppies spaced like a triangle around its edge.

Baker, *fluted, "French"*	$ 46–52
Bean pot, *covered, one handle, "New England"*	$ 200–225
Bowl, *individual fruit, 5^1/$_2$-inch diameter*	$ 22–28
Bowl, *cereal, 6^1/$_2$-inch diameter*	$ 40–46
Bowl, *salad, serving, 9-inch diameter*	$ 38–44
Bowl, *soup, 8^1/$_2$-inch diameter*	$ 50–57
Casserole, *oval, 1^1/$_2$-quart*	$ 115–125
Casserole, *round, 1^1/$_2$-quart*	$ 150–165
Casserole, *round, 2^1/$_2$-quart*	$ 110–120
Coffeepot, *Great American*	$ 165–180
Cup and saucer	$ 55–65
Custard cup	$ 11–14
Jar, *mustard, with underliner, lidded*	$ 165–185
Jug, *"Sunshine," #5*	$ 55–65
Leftover, *loop handle*	$ 150–175
Plate, *bread and butter, 6^1/$_8$-inch diameter*	$ 22–26
Plate, *cake, serving, 9^1/$_2$-inch diameter*	$ 65–75
Plate, *dinner, 9-inch diameter*	$ 30–35
Plate, *luncheon, 7^1/$_4$-inch diameter*	$ 26–30
Platter, *oval, 11^1/$_4$ inches*	$ 100–110
Platter, *oval, 13^1/$_4$ inches*	$ 100–110
Salt and pepper shakers, *set, handled*	$ 60–70
Sugar bowl, *lidded*	$ 40–50
Teapot, *"Bellevue" shape, 2-cup*	$ 2,000–2,250
Teapot, *"Boston" shape*	$ 350–400
Teapot, *"Donut" shape*	$ 500–550
Teapot, *"Melody" shape*	$ 500–550

Hall "Red Poppy" jug, "Radiance" shape, 6½ inches,
$40–$50.
*Item courtesy of Needful Things, Hendersonville, North
Carolina.*

"Red Poppy"

The "Red Poppy" line was produced for the Grand Union Company from the mid-1940s to the mid-1950s. Unlike "Orange Poppy" pieces, "Red Poppy" pieces were created using Hall's "D" shapes, and the flatware is decorated with only one grouping of red flowers and green leaves. All pieces have an ivory background, except the teapot, which is white.

Baker, *"French," fluted*	$ 60–65
Bowl, *individual fruit*	$ 11–13
Bowl, *cereal, 6¹/₈-inch diameter*	$ 21–25
Bowl, *salad, serving, 9-inch diameter*	$ 50–60
Bowl, *soup, 8¹/₂-inch diameter*	$ 15–18
Bowl, *vegetable, round, 9-inch diameter*	$ 55–62
Casserole, *covered, round, 1¹/₂-quart*	$ 55–65
Coffeepot, *8-cup*	$ 100–110
Creamer	$ 30–35
Cup and saucer	$ 40–45

Dish, *leftover, rectangular*	$ 225–275
Dish, *leftover, square*	$ 275–325
Jug, *"Radiance," 6^1/$_2$ inches*	$ 40–50
Jug, *"Sunshine," #5, 64-ounce*	$ 55–65
Plate, *bread and butter, 6^1/$_4$-inch diameter*	$ 15–18
Plate, *cake, serving, 9^1/$_2$ inches*	$ 50–60
Plate, *dinner, 10-inch diameter*	$ 60–75
Plate, *luncheon, 9^1/$_8$-inch diameter*	$ 15–18
Plate, *pie, serving, 9^1/$_2$-inch diameter*	$ 75–85
Plate, *salad, 7^1/$_4$-inch diameter*	$ 15–18
Platter, *oval, 11^1/$_2$ inches*	$ 60–70
Platter, *oval, 13^1/$_2$ inches*	$ 70–80
Salt and pepper shakers, *set*	$ 50–60
Sugar bowl, *lidded*	$ 30–40

"Rose Parade"

Pieces decorated with this pattern usually have a pink floral decal, but occasionally a blue-and-yellow, blue-and-pink, or pink-and-yellow floral decal will also turn up.

Bean pot, *tab handle*	$ 175–200
Bowl, *salad, serving, 9-inch diameter*	$ 65–75
Casserole, *covered, round, tab handle*	$ 100–115
Creamer, *"Sani-Grid"*	$ 35–45
Jug, *"Sani-Grid," small*	$ 90–100
Jug, *"Sani-Grid," medium*	$ 100–125
Jug, *"Sani-Grid," large*	$ 120–135
Shaker, *"Sani-Grid," handled*	$ 60–70
Teapot, *"Sani-Grid," large, 6-cup*	$ 110–125
Teapot, *"Sani-Grid," small, 3-cup*	$ 90–100

"Silhouette" or "Taverne"

Pieces with this attractive design were used as premiums by the Cook Coffee Company, Hellick's Coffee, and the Standard Coffee Company. Several look-alike patterns were produced by other companies, but the pieces made by Hall are clearly marked. This dinnerware and its accessory pieces were available in the 1930s and 1940s.

Baker, *"French," fluted*	$ 60–70
Bowl, *salad, serving, 9-inch diameter*	$ 85–100
Bowl, *vegetable, 7¹/₂ inches*	$ 45–60
Casserole, *round, 1³/₄ quart, Medallion*	$ 165–180
Coffeemaker, *drip, "Colonial"*	$ 350–400
Coffeepot, *9-cup, "Colonial"*	$ 150–175
Cup and saucer, *footed*	$ 45–50
Cup and saucer, *flat*	$ 25–35
Plate, *bread and butter, 6-inch diameter*	$ 8–10
Plate, *dinner, 10-inch diameter*	$ 45–65
Plate, *luncheon, 9¹/₈-inch diameter*	$ 20–30
Plate, *salad, 8¹/₄-inch diameter*	$ 15–20
Platter, *oval, 11¹/₂ inches*	$ 65–75

"Wildfire"

Pieces featuring this pattern were produced as premiums for the Great American Tea Company. Flatware pieces feature an undulating garland of pink roses and green leaves entwined with a blue ribbon to form ovals around their rims. These pieces have white backgrounds rather than Hall's usual ivory background.

Baker, *"French," fluted*	$ 22–28
Bean pot, *"New England," #4*	$ 175–200
Bowl, *individual fruit, 5¹/₂-inch diameter*	$ 8–10
Bowl, *cereal, 6¹/₈-inch diameter*	$ 15–20
Bowl, *salad, serving, 9-inch diameter*	$ 55–65
Bowl, *soup, 8¹/₂-inch diameter*	$ 20–28
Bowl, *vegetable, round, 9-inch diameter*	$ 28–32
Bowl, *vegetable, oval, 10¹/₄ inches*	$ 35–45
Casserole, *"Medallion"*	$ 55–65
Coffeepot, *"S-Lid," 9-cup*	$ 90–100
Creamer	$ 32–37

Cup and saucer	$ 22–26
Cup and saucer, *"St. Denis"*	$ 50–60
Dish, *leftover, rectangular, covered*	$ 75–85
Dish, *leftover, square, covered*	$ 85–100
Gravy boat	$ 45–55
Jar, *pretzel*	$ 175–200
Jug, *ball, #3*	$ 150–165
Mug	$ 50–60
Plate, *bread and butter, 6¼-inch diameter*	$ 6–9
Plate, *dinner, 10-inch diameter*	$ 40–50
Plate, *luncheon, 9¼-inch diameter*	$ 20–24
Platter, *oval, 11½ inches*	$ 35–45
Platter, *oval, 13½ inches*	$ 45–55
Salt and pepper shakers, *"Five Band,"* set	$ 45–55
Teapot, *"Medallion"*	$ 95–110
Teapot, *"New York"*	$ 275–325

Kitchenware

"Blue Blossom"

Pieces in this easily recognized and highly sought-after line are distinguished by a cobalt blue background with a floral decal. The decal consists of one multicolored blossom with green leaves, a stem, and a red bud. The line was introduced in 1939.

Baker, *rectangular*	$ 300–325
Ball jug, *#1*	$ 175–200
Ball jug, *#2*	$ 185–210
Ball jug, *#3*	$ 175–200
Ball jug, *#4*	$ 210–235
Batter jug	$ 350–400
Bean pot, *"New England,"* #4	$ 250–300
Butter, *1-pound, covered*	$ 800–900
Casserole, *oval, covered*	$ 80–95

Coffeepot, *15-cup*	$ 650–700
Coffeepot, *drip*	$ 600–650
Cookie jar, *"Five Band"*	$ 350–400
Cookie jar, *"Sundial"*	$ 450–500
Creamer	$ 50–60
Jar, *drip or grease, covered*	$ 125–150
Jug, *donut*	$ 350–400
Jug, *1¹/₂-pint*	$ 125–150
Jug, *2-quart*	$ 175–200
Leftover, *loop handle*	$ 175–200
Leftover, *"Zephyr" shape*	$ 250–300
Sugar bowl, *lidded, "New York"*	$ 80–95
Syrup, *"Five Band"*	$ 225–250
Syrup, *"Sundial"*	$ 250–275
Teapot, *"Sundial"*	$ 400–450
Teapot, *"Streamline"*	$ 350–400
Water bottle, *"Zephyr"*	$ 850–1,000

"Five Band"

This line of kitchenware was first introduced in 1936. The most popular colors with collectors are cobalt blue and Chinese Red. Other colors available include ivory, canary yellow, Marine, and Indian Red. Some pieces are decal-decorated.

Bowl, *batter, Chinese Red*	$ 70–80
Bowl, *batter, ivory*	$ 55–65
Bowl, *mixing, 6-inch diameter, cobalt blue*	$ 20–25
Bowl, *mixing, 6-inch diameter, canary yellow*	$ 15–20
Bowl, *mixing, 7¹/₄-inch diameter, cobalt blue*	$ 25–30
Bowl, *mixing, 7¹/₄-inch diameter, Marine*	$ 18–25
Bowl, *mixing, 8³/₄-inch diameter, Chinese Red*	$ 35–40
Bowl, *mixing, 8³/₄-inch diameter, ivory*	$ 30–35
Carafe, *stoppered, Chinese Red*	$ 250–300
Carafe, *stoppered, canary yellow*	$ 200–250

Cookie jar, *cobalt blue*	$ 225–250
Cookie jar, *Chinese Red*	$ 175–200
Cookie jar, *ivory*	$ 150–175
Jug, *5 inches, cobalt blue*	$ 35–42
Jug, *5 inches, canary yellow*	$ 30–35
Jug, *6 1/4 inches, Chinese Red*	$ 50–60
Jug, *6 1/4 inches, ivory*	$ 40–50
Syrup pitcher, *Chinese Red*	$ 85–95
Syrup pitcher, *canary yellow*	$ 75–85

"Medallion"

This was Hall's first kitchenware line. Pieces were first produced in 1932 in ivory and Lettuce Green, though Chinese Red and other colors are also available.

Bowl, *mixing, 5 1/2-inch diameter, Lettuce Green*	$ 15–18
Bowl, *mixing, 5 1/2-inch diameter, Chinese Red*	$ 18–22
Bowl, *mixing, 5 1/2-inch diameter, ivory*	$ 16–20
Bowl, *mixing, 6-inch diameter, Lettuce Green*	$ 16–20
Bowl, *mixing, 6-inch diameter, Chinese Red*	$ 20–24
Bowl, *mixing, 6-inch diameter, ivory*	$ 17–21
Bowl, *mixing, 7 1/4-inch diameter, Lettuce Green*	$ 20–24
Bowl, *mixing, 7 1/4-inch diameter, Chinese Red*	$ 24–28
Bowl, *mixing, 7 1/4-inch diameter, ivory*	$ 20–24
Bowl, *mixing, 8 1/2-inch diameter, Lettuce Green*	$ 24–28
Bowl, *mixing, 8 1/2-inch diameter, Chinese Red*	$ 30–35
Bowl, *mixing, 8 1/2-inch diameter, ivory*	$ 22–26
Bowl, *mixing, 10-inch diameter, Lettuce Green*	$ 35–40
Bowl, *mixing, 10-inch diameter, Chinese Red*	$ 40–45
Bowl, *mixing, 10-inch diameter, ivory*	$ 35–40
Casserole, *covered, Lettuce Green*	$ 50–60
Casserole, *covered, Chinese Red*	$ 60–70
Casserole, *covered, ivory*	$ 40–50

Coffeemaker, *drip, two-part, Lettuce Green*	$ 300–325
Coffeemaker, *drip, two-part, Chinese Red*	$ 450–500
Coffeemaker, *drip, two-part, ivory*	$ 275–300
Creamer, *Lettuce Green*	$ 22–25
Creamer, *Chinese Red*	$ 30–35
Creamer, *ivory*	$ 22–25
Jar, *drip or grease, Lettuce Green*	$ 45–50
Jar, *drip or grease, Chinese Red*	$ 60–70
Jar, *drip or grease, ivory*	$ 40–45
Jug, *ice lip, 4-pint, Lettuce Green*	$ 40–45
Jug, *ice lip, 4-pint, Chinese Red*	$ 50–60
Jug, *ice lip, 4-pint, ivory*	$ 38–42
Jug, *ice lip, 5-pint, Lettuce Green*	$ 55–60
Jug, *ice lip, 5-pint, Chinese Red*	$ 60–70
Jug, *ice lip, 5-pint, ivory*	$ 52–56
Juicer (reamer), *Lettuce Green*	$ 450–500
Juicer (reamer), *Chinese Red*	$ 550–600
Juicer (reamer), *ivory*	$ 650–700
Leftover, *square, Lettuce Green*	$ 75–85
Leftover, *square, Chinese Red*	$ 100–110
Leftover, *square, ivory*	$ 75–85
Stack set, *Lettuce Green*	$ 150–200
Stack set, *Chinese Red*	$ 165–210
Stack set, *ivory*	$ 150–200
Sugar bowl, *lidded, Lettuce Green*	$ 35–40
Sugar bowl, *lidded, Chinese Red*	$ 45–50
Sugar bowl, *lidded, ivory*	$ 30–35
Teapot, *40-ounce, Lettuce Green*	$ 250–275
Teapot, *40-ounce, Chinese Red*	$ 325–350
Teapot, *40-ounce, ivory*	$ 275–300
Teapot, *64-ounce, Lettuce Green*	$ 275–300

Teapot, *64-ounce, Chinese Red*	$ 400–450
Teapot, *64-ounce, ivory*	$ 300–325

"Sani-Grid"

This line was introduced in 1941. Pieces are most commonly found in Chinese Red with white handles and white knobs on lids, though pieces were also made in Cadet (blue) and white. Some pieces of "Sani-Grid" feature decal decorations. Prices listed below are for Chinese Red examples, which are the most plentiful and also the most popular. Examples in Cadet and white are less valuable than those in Chinese Red, sometimes by as much as half, but for common items such as bowls, the differential may be as little as 10 percent.

Bean pot	$ 125–150
Bowl, *mixing, 6-inch diameter*	$ 18–22
Bowl, *mixing, 7$^{1}/_{2}$-inch diameter*	$ 20–25
Bowl, *mixing, 8$^{3}/_{4}$-inch diameter*	$ 25–30
Bowl, *straight-sided, 5$^{1}/_{4}$ inches*	$ 16–20
Bowl, *straight-sided, 6 inches*	$ 18–22
Bowl, *straight-sided, 7$^{1}/_{2}$ inches*	$ 20–24
Bowl, *straight-sided, 9 inches*	$ 25–30
Casserole, *tab-handled, covered*	$ 55–65
Creamer	$ 20–24
Jar, *drip or grease*	$ 40–50
Jug, *5 inches*	$ 30–35
Jug, *6$^{1}/_{2}$ inches*	$ 35–40
Jug, *7$^{1}/_{2}$ inches*	$ 45–50
Sugar bowl, *open*	$ 20–25
Sugar bowl, *lid*	$ 325–350
Teapot, *3-cup*	$ 50–60

"Tri-Tone"

This kitchenware line was designed by Eva Zeisel, and first appeared in the 1950s. It is distinguished by items decorated with straight-line patches in three colors—pink, turquoise, and gray—over a white body, with the pink and turquoise overlapping to form the gray.

Bean pot	$ 325–350
Bowl, *salad, serving*	$ 100–120
Bowl, *mixing, 5-inch diameter*	$ 35–40
Bowl, *mixing, 6-inch diameter*	$ 40–45
Bowl, *mixing, 7-inch diameter*	$ 50–60
Bowl, *mixing, 8-inch diameter*	$ 60–70
Bowl, *mixing, 9-inch diameter*	$ 85–95
Casserole, *individual*	$ 150–175
Casserole, *oval, 3-pint*	$ 150–175
Casserole, *oval, 6-pint*	$ 175–200
Cookie jar	$ 325–350
Creamer	$ 35–45
Jug, *refrigerator*	$ 250–300
Leftover, *covered*	$ 125–150
Salt and pepper shakers, *set*	$ 85–100
Sugar bowl, *lidded*	$ 65–75
Teapot, *6-cup*	$ 300–350
Tureen, *8-pint*	$ 225–250

Refrigerator Ware

General Electric

Hall produced a set of refrigerator ware for General Electric that was given away with the purchase of any G.E. refrigerator. Pieces in this set had gray bodies with yellow tops.

Casserole	$ 50–60
Leftover, *rectangular*	$ 30–40
Leftover, *round, 4-inch diameter*	$ 15–20
Leftover, *round, 7-inch diameter*	$ 35–40
Water pitcher, *covered*	$ 75–90

Hall refrigerator ware, covered water pitcher made for
General Electric, gray body with yellow lid, $75–$90.
Item courtesy of Richard Crane, Knoxville, Tennessee.

Hotpoint

Hall made much more colorful refrigerator ware for Hotpoint than it did for other
companies: pieces in this line came in a variety of shades such as maroon, green, yellow, Chinese Red, Indian Red, dark gray, and dark blue.

Leftover, *rectangular*	$ 30–35
Leftover, *round, 6³/₄-inch diameter*	$ 30–35
Leftover, *round, 7³/₄-inch diameter*	$ 40–50
Leftover, *round, 8³/₄-inch diameter*	$ 60–70
Leftover, *square, 4 inches*	$ 50–60
Leftover, *square, 4³/₄ inches*	$ 40–50
Leftover, *square, 8¹/₂ inches*	$ 60–70
Water pitcher, *with stopper and raised "H" on side*	$ 75–90

Westinghouse

Starting in 1938, Hall made refrigerator ware for Westinghouse in a variety of
shapes. The first was "Phoenix," followed by "General" and "Hercules," with "Ado-
nis" added to the mix in 1952. These pieces came in a variety of colors, including

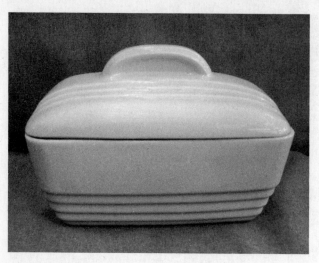

Hall refrigerator dish, casserole, made for Westinghouse, yellow, "Ridged," $30–$40.
Item courtesy of Kingston Pike Antique Mall, Knoxville, Tennessee.

Lettuce Green, Delphinium Blue, tan, cobalt blue, Chinese Red, and Garden Green. The water pitcher in the "Hercules" shape was also made for Toucan Enterprises of Chicago, Illinois, and examples of this piece are marked accordingly.

Baker	$ 25–30
Butter dish, *covered*	$ 60–75
Casserole, *rectangular, covered*	$ 30–40
Leftover, *rectangular*	$ 30–40
Leftover, *round*	$ 15–20
Water pitcher, *covered, "Hercules"*	$ 125–150
Water pitcher, *covered, other shapes*	$ 75–90

Teapots

Hall teapots came in a variety of sizes. The 6-cup size is standard and is priced below, but 2-cup teapots are harder to find and will thus command prices that are higher by 25 to 30 percent. The 4-cup size is slightly lower in value, and the 8-, 10-, and 12-cup teapots are only marginally more valuable.

Airflow—introduced in 1940, ball-shaped:

Black	$ 70–80
Cadet	$ 90–110
Camellia	$ 100–125
Canary	$ 90–110
Chinese Red	$ 175–200
Citrus	$ 250–300
Cobalt blue	$ 125–150
Cobalt blue, *with "French Flower" decoration*	$ 550–600
Dresden	$ 110–135
Emerald	$ 120–140
Golden Glo	$ 200–250
Indian Red	$ 175–225
Ivory	$ 70–80
Marine	$ 150–175
Maroon	$ 125–150
Orchid	$ 450–550
Pink	$ 125–150
Rose	$ 125–150
Silver Luster	$ 185–210
Turquoise	$ 100–125
Warm Yellow	$ 100–125
White, *with "Thornberry Ivy" decal*	$ 100–125

Aladdin—introduced in 1939, shaped like Aladdin's lamp:

Black	$ 60–70
Cadet	$ 85–100
Camellia	$ 95–110
Canary	$ 75–85
Canary, *with "French Flower" decoration*	$ 350–375
Chartreuse	$ 95–110

Chinese Red	$ 200–225
Citrus	$ 400–450
Cobalt blue	$ 150–175
Dresden	$ 110–125
Emerald	$ 85–100
Golden Glo	$ 250–275
Indian Red	$ 275–300
Ivory	$ 75–85
Ivory, *with "Floral Basket" decal*	$ 275–300
Marine	$ 100–120
Maroon	$ 100–120
Orchid	$ 500–600
Orchid, *with "Special Gold" decoration*	$1,000–1,100
Pink	$ 85–100
Rose	$ 120–135
Silver Luster	$ 225–250
Warm Yellow	$ 95–110

† *Prices listed are for items without infusers; add 25 percent for a matching solid-color infuser.*

Albany—introduced in the early 1930s, tall with panels:

Black	$ 60–70
Cadet	$ 75–85
Canary	$ 70–80
Chinese Red	$ 275–325
Cobalt blue	$ 80–90
Dresden	$ 70–80
Emerald	$ 70–80
Maroon	$ 75–85
Warm Yellow	$ 75–85

Automobile—first made in 1938, automobile-shaped:

Black	$ 400–450
Cadet	$ 500–550
Canary	$ 450–500
Chinese Red	$ 700–750
Cobalt blue	$ 650–700
Delphinium	$ 500–550
Dresden	$ 500–550
Emerald	$ 575–625
Indian Red	$ 800–850
Ivory	$ 350–400
Marine	$ 575–625
Maroon	$ 575–625
Orchid	$1,000–1,100
Warm Yellow	$ 500–550

Baltimore—first made in the early 1930s, pieces have a squatty shape:

Black	$ 55–65
Cadet	$ 75–85
Cadet, *standard gold decoration*	$ 100–120
Chinese Red	$ 400–450
Emerald	$ 85–100
Ivory	$ 50–60
Maroon	$ 85–100
Orchid	$ 325–350
Warm Yellow	$ 75–85
Warm Yellow, *with "Minuet" decal decoration*	$ 250–275

Baseball—first made in 1938, circular body with concentric circles around a hemisphere in the center:

Cadet	$ 500–600
Canary	$ 500–600
Chinese Red	$ 700–800
Cobalt blue	$ 675–775
Delphinium	$ 675–775
Dresden	$ 675–775
Emerald	$ 675–775
Indian Red	$ 800–900
Ivory	$ 300–400
Marine	$ 750–850
Maroon	$ 675–775
Pink	$ 675–775
Warm Yellow	$ 550–650

Boston—first made in the 1920s, simple globular shape:

Black	$ 30–40
Black, *with "French Flower" decoration*	$ 175–200
Cadet	$ 40–50
Canary	$ 35–45
Canary, *with standard gold decoration*	$ 60–70
Chartreuse	$ 40–50
Chinese Red	$ 250–300
Cobalt blue	$ 60–75
Dresden	$ 45–55
Emerald	$ 50–60
Golden Glo	$ 200–225
Gray	$ 30–40
Green Luster	$ 50–60
Ivory	$ 30–40
Marine	$ 55–65

Maroon	$ 45–55
Orchid	$ 275–300
Pink	$ 40–50
Rose	$ 40–50
Stock Brown or Green	$ 30–35
Turquoise	$ 45–55
Warm Yellow	$ 45–55

Cleveland—introduced in the late 1930s, flaring cylindrical shape:

Black, *with standard gold decoration on shoulder*	$ 85–100
Cadet	$ 50–60
Canary	$ 65–75
Chinese Red	$ 325–350
Cobalt blue	$ 150–175
Delphinium	$ 90–100
Emerald	$ 90–100
Ivory	$ 35–40
Turquoise	$ 65–75
Warm Yellow	$ 65–75

Donut—introduced in 1938, donut-shaped, with a hole in the middle:

Black	$ 175–200
Cadet	$ 400–450
Camellia	$ 400–450
Canary	$ 400–450
Chinese Red	$ 450–500
Citrus	$ 650–700
Cobalt blue	$ 450–500
Delphinium	$ 400–450
Dresden	$ 400–450
Emerald	$ 450–500

Indian Red	$ 550–600
Ivory	$ 175–200
Marine	$ 450–500
Maroon	$ 450–500
Orchid	$1,000–1,100
Pink	$ 375–425
Warm Yellow	$ 500–550

Football—introduced in 1938, football-shaped, with a lid perched on the side:

Black	$ 550–600
Cadet	$ 650–700
Canary	$ 650–700
Chinese Red	$ 800–900
Citrus	$ 900–1,000
Cobalt blue	$ 750–800
Delphinium	$ 650–700
Dresden	$ 650–700
Emerald	$ 750–800
Indian Red	$ 850–950
Ivory	$ 500–550
Marine	$ 650–700
Maroon	$ 650–700
Pink	$ 650–700
Warm Yellow	$ 750–800

French—introduced in the 1920s, tall globular shape with crescent loop handle, classic design:

Black	$ 35–45
Black, *with gold decoration*	$ 45–55
Cadet	$ 45–55
Canary	$ 45–55

Canary, *with standard gold decoration*	$ 65–75
Chartreuse	$ 40–50
Chinese Red	$ 175–225
Cobalt blue	$ 65–75
Cobalt blue, *"Sycamore" decoration*	$ 200–225
Dresden	$ 45–55
Emerald	$ 50–60
Gray	$ 40–50
Ivory	$ 30–40
Marine	$ 50–60
Maroon	$ 50–60
Pink	$ 50–60
Rose	$ 55–65
Silver Luster	$ 140–160
Stock Brown or Green	$ 30–35
Warm Yellow	$ 45–55

Globe—made with two types of spouts: one standard, the other no-drip, globular-shaped:

Cadet, *regular spout*	$ 110–125
Cadet, *regular spout, with standard gold decoration*	$ 150–175
Cadet, *with no-drip spout*	$ 65–75
Cadet, *with no-drip spout, standard gold decoration*	$ 65–75
Camellia	$ 70–80
Canary, *regular spout*	$ 110–125
Canary, *with no-drip spout*	$ 65–75
Chartreuse, *regular spout*	$ 50–60
Chartreuse, *no-drip spout*	$ 60–70
Chinese Red	$ 450–500
Cobalt blue	$ 275–300
Emerald	$ 165–185

Ivory	$ 50–60
Marine	$ 200–225
Marine, *with standard gold decoration*	$ 145–165
Rose	$ 65–75

Hollywood—rectangular shape with fluted base, introduced in the 1920s:

Black	$ 45–55
Cadet	$ 55–65
Canary	$ 55–65
Chartreuse	$ 50–60
Chinese Red	$ 275–300
Cobalt blue	$ 80–90
Emerald	$ 55–65
Emerald, *with standard gold decoration*	$ 75–85
Golden Glo	$ 250–275
Ivory	$ 45–55
Marine	$ 65–75
Marine, *with standard gold decoration*	$ 110–125
Maroon	$ 55–65
Pink	$ 50–60
Pink, *with standard gold decoration*	$ 80–90
Stock Brown or Green	$ 45–55
Warm Yellow	$ 50–60
Warm Yellow, *with "Christmas" decal*	$ 250–275

Hook—introduced in 1940, named for the hook that secures the lid to the body:

Black	$ 50–60
Cadet	$ 50–60
Cadet, *with standard gold decoration*	$ 55–65
Cadet, *with gold "French Flower" decoration*	$ 325–350

Canary	$ 60–70
Chinese Red	$ 250–300
Cobalt blue	$ 100–110
Delphinium	$ 50–60
Emerald	$ 80–90
Maroon	$ 60–70
Orchid	$ 325–350
Silver Luster	$ 150–175
Warm Yellow	$ 75–85

Illinois—introduced in the 1930s, tall globular shape, crab stock-type handle:

Black	$ 175–200
Black, *standard gold decoration*	$ 225–250
Canary	$ 200–225
Chinese Red	$ 550–600
Cobalt blue	$ 250–300
Cobalt blue, *standard gold decoration*	$ 275–325
Maroon	$ 225–250
Pink	$ 200–225
Stock Brown or Green	$ 145–165

Indiana—distinguished by a heart-shaped design embossed on the body:

Black	$ 325–375
Cadet	$ 350–400
Camellia	$ 350–400
Chinese Red	$ 600–650
Cobalt blue	$ 550–600
Cobalt blue, *with standard gold decoration*	$ 600–650
Ivory	$ 275–300
Maroon	$ 400–450

Maroon, *with standard gold decoration*	$ 500–550
Warm Yellow	$ 425–475

Kansas—oval shape with fluting on base and lid, embossed band around the shoulder:

Black	$ 425–475
Cadet	$ 425–475
Camellia	$ 425–475
Chinese Red	$ 650–700
Emerald	$ 550–600
Ivory	$ 275–325
Ivory, *with standard gold decoration*	$ 450–500
Maroon	$ 375–425
Maroon, *with standard gold decoration*	$ 550–600

Los Angeles—tall teapot with reeded body, introduced in the mid-1920s:

Black	$ 50–60
Cadet	$ 55–65
Canary	$ 55–65
Chinese Red	$ 300–325
Cobalt blue	$ 75–85
Dresden	$ 55–65
Emerald	$ 65–75
Emerald, *with "French Flower" decoration*	$ 250–275
Marine	$ 65–75
Maroon	$ 60–70
Maroon, *with standard gold decoration*	$ 80–90
Pink	$ 60–70
Stock Brown or Green	$ 40–50
Warm Yellow	$ 50–60

Melody—a flared cylindrical shape that first appeared in 1939:

Black	$ 175–200
Cadet	$ 240–260
Camellia	$ 200–225
Canary	$ 200–225
Canary, *with standard gold decoration*	$ 250–275
Chinese Red	$ 300–350
Cobalt blue	$ 300–325
Dresden	$ 200–225
Ivory	$ 100–125
Ivory, *with standard gold decoration*	$ 200–225
Marine	$ 265–285
Maroon	$ 225–250
Warm Yellow	$ 200–225

Moderne—globular shape with embossed triangular sections on shoulder that look something like folded linen:

Black	$ 40–50
Cadet	$ 60–70
Camellia	$ 60–70
Canary	$ 60–70
Canary, *gold floral decoration*	$ 350–400
Chinese Red	$ 175–200
Cobalt blue	$ 75–85
Delphinium	$ 65–75
Dresden	$ 60–70
Emerald	$ 65–75
Indian Red	$ 165–185
Indian Red, *with standard gold decoration*	$ 210–235
Ivory	$ 45–55
Ivory, *with gold floral decoration*	$ 325–350
Marine	$ 60–70

Maroon	$ 75–85
Orchid	$ 275–325
Pink	$ 60–70
Rose	$ 60–70
Warm Yellow	$ 60–70

Nautilus—introduced in 1939, shape resembles a nautilus shell:

Black	$ 250–275
Cadet	$ 275–300
Camellia	$ 275–300
Canary	$ 175–200
Canary, *with standard gold decoration*	$ 225–250
Chinese Red	$ 550–600
Cobalt blue	$ 375–425
Cobalt blue, *with standard gold decoration*	$ 400–425
Emerald	$ 275–300
Ivory	$ 145–165
Maroon	$ 275–300
Warm Yellow	$ 250–275

New York—globular body tapering to a low cylindrical neck, introduced in 1920:

Black	$ 30–35
Cadet	$ 40–45
Canary	$ 35–40
Chartreuse	$ 35–40
Chinese Red	$ 175–200
Cobalt blue	$ 65–75
Dresden	$ 45–50
Emerald	$ 50–55
Ivory	$ 30–35
Ivory, *with standard gold decoration*	$ 50–60

Marine	$ 55–65
Maroon	$ 50–60
Orchid	$ 275–325
Pink	$ 45–50
Rose	$ 45–50
Stock Brown or Green	$ 30–35
Warm Yellow	$ 45–50

Parade—raised crescent shapes run from handle to tip of spout:

Black	$ 40–50
Cadet	$ 60–70
Camellia	$ 60–70
Canary	$ 30–40
Chinese Red	$ 400–450
Cobalt blue	$ 100–125
Delphinium	$ 60–70
Emerald	$ 100–125
Ivory	$ 35–45
Marine	$ 100–125
Maroon	$ 75–85
Pink	$ 70–80
Pink, *with gold "French Flower" decoration*	$ 225–250
Warm Yellow	$ 75–85

Philadelphia—introduced in the 1920s, tall teardrop-shaped body flaring to a low collar rim:

Black	$ 35–45
Cadet	$ 45–55
Canary	$ 40–50
Canary, *with standard gold decoration*	$ 50–60
Chinese Red	$ 200–225
Cobalt blue	$ 90–100

Delphinium	$ 45–55
Dresden	$ 45–55
Dresden, *with "Hearth Scene" decal decoration*	$ 90–100
Emerald	$ 55–65
Indian Red	$ 240–265
Ivory	$ 35–45
Marine	$ 65–75
Maroon	$ 55–65
Pink	$ 40–50
Pink, *with "Minuet" decal decoration*	$ 175–200
Stock Brown	$ 35–45
Stock Green	$ 30–40
Warm Yellow	$ 45–55

Rhythm—introduced in 1939, oval with handle on top and raised crescent lines running horizontally down the body:

Black	$ 125–150
Cadet	$ 150–200
Cadet, *with standard gold decoration*	$ 225–250
Canary	$ 145–165
Chinese Red	$ 300–350
Cobalt blue	$ 200–225
Emerald	$ 140–160
Ivory	$ 100–125
Maroon	$ 150–175
Maroon, *with standard gold decoration*	$ 210–235
Warm Yellow	$ 175–200

Star—named for its standard decoration: gold stars, introduced in 1939:

Black	$ 125–150
Cadet	$ 110–125

Hall "Star" teapot, Cadet color, $110–$125.
Item courtesy of Needful Things, Hendersonville, North Carolina.

Canary	$ 125–150
Chinese Red	$ 600–700
Cobalt blue	$ 175–200
Cobalt blue, *with 1939 World's Fair gold decoration*	$1,000–1,100
Delphinium	$ 110–125
Emerald	$ 110–125
Emerald, *with gold-star decoration*	$ 135–165
Indian Red	$ 600–700
Ivory	$ 100–110
Marine	$ 175–200
Maroon	$ 110–125
Orchid	$ 750–850
Pink	$ 110–125
Pink, *with gold-star decoration*	$ 145–165
Warm Yellow	$ 110–125

Streamline—introduced in 1939, oval loop at end of lid above handle:

Black	$ 60–70
Cadet	$ 75–85
Canary	$ 75–85
Chinese Red	$ 150–200
Citrus	$ 400–450
Cobalt blue	$ 150–200
Delphinium	$ 75–85
Dresden	$ 75–85
Emerald	$ 80–90
Indian Red	$ 300–325
Ivory	$ 55–65
Marine	$ 145–165
Maroon	$ 110–125
Orchid	$ 450–500
Pink	$ 80–90
Warm Yellow	$ 90–100
Warm Yellow, *with standard gold decoration*	$ 110–125

Surfside—introduced in 1937, this line has a nautilus-shell look, but the spiral swirls are cut off at the top and do not complete a full circuit:

Black	$ 140–150
Cadet	$ 175–200
Camellia	$ 175–200
Canary	$ 165–185
Chinese Red	$ 275–325
Cobalt blue	$ 225–275
Delphinium	$ 175–200
Dresden	$ 175–200
Emerald	$ 225–250

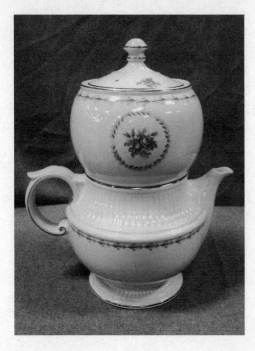

Hall "Harmony House" drip-o-lator,
E-shape, "Mt. Vernon" decal decoration,
$175–$250.
*Item courtesy of Needful Things,
Hendersonville, North Carolina.*

Indian Red	$ 275–300
Ivory	$ 150–175
Maroon	$ 225–250
Pink	$ 175–200
Warm Yellow	$ 200–225
Warm Yellow, *with standard gold decoration*	$ 225–250

Windshield—introduced in 1941, common shape, globular body with a flaring elliptical top that resembles the curved windshield on a racing boat:

Black	$ 55–65
Cadet	$ 65–75
Camellia	$ 70–80
Canary	$ 65–75
Chinese Red	$ 300–350
Cobalt blue	$ 90–100

Dresden	$ 70–80
Emerald	$ 75–85
Indian Red	$ 275–325
Ivory	$ 35–45
Ivory, *with standard gold decoration*	$ 60–70
Marine	$ 75–85
Maroon	$ 70–80
Pink	$ 65–75
Warm Yellow	$ 55–65

HAMPSHIRE POTTERY

Hampshire
Pottery

Hampshire Pottery mark with the "M O" designation.

Impressed mark used by *Hampshire Pottery*.

The Hampshire Pottery was founded by James Taft in Keene, New Hampshire, in 1871. The business got off to a bad start, however, when it burned to the ground before the first piece of pottery could be made and fired. The factory was rebuilt within six weeks, and the company began manufacturing redware and, a little later, stoneware. Its products were strictly utilitarian and included such items as spittoons, molasses jugs, water kegs, and preserve jars.

Around 1880, the company began making a majolica-type ware, which led its owners to realize that a lucrative market existed for decorative pottery. Starting around 1882, the company did some underglaze painting in the style of Rookwood, though its most common decorative wares from this period feature an ivory-colored glaze, reminiscent of a glaze used on wares made by England's Royal Worcester Porcelain Company.

These pieces—mostly souvenir wares showing views of popular tourist spots in the eastern and southern United States—were usually decorated with underglaze transfer prints. In 1904, Cadmon Robertson (no relation to the Robertsons of Dedham and Chelsea Keramic Art Works fame) came to work at Hampshire, and was soon made its superintendent. Robertson was a chemist, and during his tenure at the pottery he formulated more than 900 different glazes. He is especially known for his matte glazes in shades of green, blue, gray, bronze, yellow, and peacock blue. Green is the most common color, and is said to predate by several years the famous matte green produced at Grueby.

Hampshire stopped producing pottery in late 1914, and in 1916 the company was sold to George M. Morton, who began producing many of the same products made by its previous owners. Hampshire was closed once again in 1917, and it reopened in 1919 with a new focus on making mosaic floor tiles. The company closed permanently in 1923.

Not all pieces of Hampshire pottery were marked, and others were marked with paper labels that were easily detached. Other pieces were marked with the name "Hampshire Pottery," and sometimes with a "James Scollay Taft" script signature in the middle of a circle. Collectors often enjoy pieces signed with an "M" inside a circle. This so-called "M O" mark is on pieces designed by Cadmon Robertson; the "M O" is a reference to his wife, Emoretta.

Bowl, *2⅝ inches tall, matte green glaze, embossed organic motifs around shoulder*	$ 575–625
Candleholder, *shield back, green glaze, 7 inches*	$ 200–225
Jardinière, *6 inches tall by 6 inches wide, typical matte green glaze*	$ 425–475
Lamp base, *21 inches tall, matte green glaze, long neck with bulbous base that has Grueby-style leaf panels around the circumference*	$ 1,600–1,850
Stein, *7 inches tall, mottled green glaze*	$ 450–500
Vase, *2½ inches tall, 6 inches wide, squatty bowl-shaped, embossed design on shoulder, matte green glaze with reddish-brown mottling*	$ 525–600
Vase, *3 inches tall by 5 inches wide, melon-ribbed, matte dark-blue glaze*	$ 400–475
Vase, *3¼ inches by 5½ inches, squatty globular form with unusual sea-green/aqua glaze over dark blue, high-gloss cobalt blue interior*	$ 1,250–1,500
Vase, *3½ inches, unusual blue-and-plum mottled glaze*	$ 850–925
Vase, *3¾ inches, panels under shoulder, brown, green, and cream glaze*	$ 350–400

Hampshire shield-back candleholder, green glaze, 7 inches, $200–$225. *Item courtesy of Tony McCormack, Sarasota, Florida.*

Hampshire pottery vase, blue with mottled mauve and green, "M O" mark, 4½ inches, $750–$800. *Item courtesy of B and D Antiques and Art Pottery, Shepherdstown, West Virginia.*

Vase, 4½ inches, "M O" mark, blue with mauve-and-green mottling	$ 750–800
Vase, 5 inches tall, three handles, typical matte green glaze	$ 300–350
Vase, 5½ inches, typical matte green glaze	$ 375–425
Vase, 6¼ inches, matte blue glaze	$ 425–475
Vase, 6 inches, embossed corn ear design with husks, deep-green matte glaze	$ 1,000–1,200
Vase, 6½ inches, mottled green glaze with tan highlights, embossed leaves with stems and buds between each leaf, in the Grueby style	$ 1,200–1,400
Vase, 7 inches tall, mottled blue matte glaze	$ 800–900
Vase, 7¼ inches, embossed broad leaves in the Grueby style, beautiful glaze in aqua/cerulean with dark charcoaling	$ 1,300–1,500
Vase, 7½ inches, embossed swirl band around shoulder, heavily mottled blue glaze	$ 900–1,000

Vase, *7¹/₂ inches, cocoa-brown glaze, ovoid form, semimatte*	$ 500–650
Vase, *8 inches, two small handles between shoulder and neck, unusual blue/green and gray glaze*	$ 1,650–1,750
Vase, *11 inches, unusual shape of bag with tie at neck like a money bag, ruffled edge, green glaze*	$ 1,250–1,400

HARKER POTTERY COMPANY

Mark used by the *Harker Pottery Company* on its "Cameoware" line.

The Harker Pottery Company is a true American success story. In 1839, Benjamin Harker sold everything he had and left England to come to the United States and settle in Ohio, where he bought some land in East Liverpool and built a cabin. Harker had come to America intending to become a farmer, but near his primitive residence he found a hill of clay, which he mined and brought back to his home using a mule to pull the heavy load. He reportedly sold the clay to James Bennett, who had come to East Liverpool just a few weeks after Harker. Bennett bought the clay and started a small pottery, which is thought to be the first pottery ever established in what would become one of the United States' most important pottery-making centers.

According to pottery lore, it did not take long for Harker to realize that, if Bennett could turn clay into finished pottery and make money, he could do the same. Bennett reportedly lent Harker some start-up money, and Harker built a beehive kiln in preparation for the backbreaking work of making pottery. Besides mining the clay, Harker ground it by hand to prepare it for use, and cut the timber used to fire his kiln.

The first utilitarian pottery made by Benjamin Harker went to market in 1840—the start of a family pottery business that would last until 1972. When Harker died in 1844,

Plate, souvenir, "Kroeger Bros. Co.," 1901,
7-inch diameter, $50–$65.
*Item courtesy of Ruben Escayeda, Old School
Antique Mall, Sylva, North Carolina.*

Plate, souvenir, 1911, 7-inch diameter, Native
American on horseback contemplating a biplane
flying overhead, $70–$85.
*Item courtesy of Betty Winston, Old School Antique
Mall, Sylva, North Carolina.*

A number of companies made dinnerware with
floral petit point decal decorations. This version
was made by Harker and is featured on a cake
plate. $25–$35.
*Item courtesy of Kingston Pike Antique Mall, Knoxville,
Tennessee.*

his two sons, Benjamin Jr. and George, took over the business. They called the company "Etruria Pottery" (which rather grandiosely referenced both the ancient Etruscans and England's famous Wedgwood pottery company), and remained in operation until around 1846.

Eventually George and Benjamin Jr. parted ways and, over the years, the brothers formed various other partnerships in order to make pottery. It was George who established the George S. Harker Pottery, the firm that evolved into the Harker Pottery Company familiar to today's collectors.

The Harker Pottery Company was incorporated in July of 1889, and it remained in East Liverpool until 1931. At that time, fearful that the Ohio River would flood, its owners moved the company to the former Edward M. Knowles plant in Chester, West Virginia, located just across the Ohio River from East Liverpool.

Harker reportedly began marketing dinnerware in 1923, and produced a wide variety of patterns until 1972, when the Jeanette Glass Company bought the company and shut down its operations.

"Cameoware"

This ware was first made at the Edwin M. Bennett Pottery in Baltimore, Maryland, around 1935, using a process developed by George Bauer. After Bennett closed in 1936, Bauer moved his process to Harker, and "Cameoware" was added to the dinnerware line in 1941. "Cameoware" was created using an engobe process that used a cloth-covered stamp to create a cameolike design on the surface of the dinnerware. After the stamp was applied to a piece's surface, the piece was dipped in a colored glaze. When the slip was removed, the white below would show through the colored glaze, thus creating the design.

Usually, "Cameoware" pieces feature blue or pink backgrounds, though some pieces were made with yellow backgrounds, and there are unconfirmed reports that black, apricot, and green pieces may also have been produced as experiments. The most common "Cameoware" design is called "Dainty Flower," and consists of a sprig with leaves and two, three, or more blossoms. Collectors sometimes refer to this pattern as "Cameo Rose," though this name can be confusing because there is a Hall pattern with the same name. Another common design was made for Montgomery Ward, but instead of being called "Cameoware," it was named "Carv-kraft." The pattern for "Carv-kraft" is called "White Rose," and the design consists of a single white rose with leaves on either side. Other "Cameoware" designs include vines, pears, apples, maple leaves, tulips, and wheat patterns. Children's dinnerware items were also a part of the "Cameoware" line, and these typically featured patterns of ducks, elephants balancing on a platform, teddy bears with balloons, or a dog or horse pulltoy. Most "Cameoware" items were created using Harker's "Shell Ware" shapes (a swirl design) or the mostly square "Virginia" shapes, but some items were also created using Harker's "Zephyr" shape.

"Shell Ware" Shape (1938)

Bowl, *individual fruit, 5¹/₂-inch diameter*	$ 10–14
Bowl, *salad, serving, 9-inch diameter*	$ 50–60
Creamer	$ 22–26
Cup and saucer	$ 24–30

Plate, *bread and butter, 6¹/₂-inch diameter*	$ 6–10
Plate, *dinner, 9¹/₂-inch diameter*	$ 22–28
Plate, *luncheon, 7¹/₂-inch diameter*	$ 14–18
Platter, *oval, 12 inches*	$ 34–40
Platter, *oval, 12 inches*	$ 40–45
Sugar bowl	$ 30–40

"Virginia" Shape

Ashtray	$ 20–30
Bowl, *individual fruit*	$ 14–18
Bowl, *soup, 7³/₄ inches*	$ 20–25
Cup and saucer	$ 35–42
Pitcher, *lidded, 32-ounce*	$ 72–82
Plate, *bread and butter, 6¹/₂ inches*	$ 8–12
Plate, *cake, handled, square, 12 inches*	$ 50–60
Plate, *dinner, 10¹/₂ inches*	$ 28–35
Plate, *salad, 8¹/₂ inches*	$ 18–22

Miscellaneous

Rolling pin, *15 inches long*	$ 90–110

"White Rose"

Bowl, *cereal, 6³/₄-inch diameter*	$ 18–22
Bowl, *vegetable, round, 8³/₄-inch diameter*	$ 50–60
Cup and saucer	$ 30–35
Plate, *cake, handled, square, 12 inches*	$ 60–70
Plate, *dinner, 10-inch diameter*	$ 40–46
Plate, *pie, serving, 9-inch diameter*	$ 80–90

"Wild Rice Intaglio"

A hard-to-find, grayish-blue-and-white pattern with blue leaves on a cream-colored background. Flatware pieces feature a blue center.

Creamer	$ 40–50
Cup and saucer	$ 35–45

"Colonial Lady," "Colonial Silhouette," "Early American Silhouette," or "Silhouette"

First appearing in the 1930s, items in these lines featured a number of black silhouetted designs, usually on Harker's "Nouvelle" or "Modern Age"-shaped dinnerware. The decaled decorations show a variety of scenes, many of which depict a colonial lady seated in front of a fireplace, a colonial lady seated at a candlestand with a colonial gentleman paying court, two colonial ladies at a piano, or a colonial lady in front of a rose trellis. Other decorations depict a gentleman and his horse among trees, or a couple on horseback under a tree.

Bowl, *cereal, 6-inch diameter*	$ 17–22
Bowl, *individual fruit, 5¹/₂-inch diameter*	$ 14–18
Bowls, *mixing, set of 3, nested*	$ 50–65
Butter dish, *round, covered*	$ 45–60
Creamer	$ 35–45
Cup and saucer	$ 28–35
Gravy boat	$ 30–40
Gravy boat underliner	$ 15–20
Pie lifter	$ 24–30
Plate, *bread and butter, 6¹/₄-inch diameter*	$ 8–12
Plate, *luncheon, 9-inch diameter*	$ 14–20
Plate, *pie, serving*	$ 70–80
Rolling pin, *with cork, 15 inches long*	$ 90–110

"Engraved"

This dinnerware was made in the same manner as "Cameoware," but was produced later, in the 1950s. It is speculated that Harker simply changed the name of the "Cameoware" line, to give the appearance of offering a fresh product to the public. "Engraved" pieces can be found with background colors of Butter Yellow, Celadon Green, Celeste Blue, Coral, and Pink Cocoa (beige). Some of the patterns include "Brown-Eyed Susan" (a scattering of white flowers with brown centers), "Cock-O-Morn" (a crowing rooster with flowers at his feet), "Coronet" (large triangular leaves forming a ring around the edge of the flatware), "Dogwood" (dogwood blossoms with twigs and small leaves), "Ivy Wreath" (white ivy leaves arranged to form a garland), "Petit Fleurs" (a band of five-petal flowers), "Provincial" or "Provincial Tulip" (an interpretation of Pennsylvania Dutch designs), and "Star Lite" (similar to Gladding, McBean's "Starburst"). At the current time, the most popular of these patterns are "Coronet," "Petit Fleurs," and "Provincial," and these patterns will command prices at the top of the ranges listed below.

Bowl, *individual fruit, 5³/₄-inch diameter*	$ 12–15
Bowl, *soup, 7³/₄-inch diameter*	$ 15–20
Bowl, *vegetable, oval, 9 inches*	$ 28–35
Bowl, *vegetable, divided, oval, 10 inches*	$ 55–70
Bowl, *vegetable, round, 8³/₄-inch diameter*	$ 35–42
Bowl, *vegetable, round, covered*	$ 80–95
Butter dish, *covered, ¹/₄-pound*	$ 48–55
Casserole, *covered, round, 7¹/₂-inch diameter*	$ 120–140
Creamer	$ 25–30
Cup and saucer	$ 18–26
Gravy boat	$ 38–48
Mug	$ 15–20
Plate, *bread and butter, 6¹/₂-inch diameter*	$ 8–10
Plate, *dinner, 10-inch diameter*	$ 15–22
Plate, *salad, 7¹/₄-inch diameter*	$ 10–14
Platter, *oval, 11¹/₂ inches*	$ 42–48
Platter, *oval, 13¹/₂ inches*	$ 45–55
Salt and pepper shakers, *set*	$ 24–35
Sugar bowl	$ 30–40

"Pate-sur-Pate"

This is a grouping of several patterns made using the same technique. Classically, the phrase *pâte sur pâte* means "paste on paste," and refers to a technique in which semiliquid clay is carefully and painstakingly built up to create slightly raised decorations on a ceramic surface. American collectors tend to associate this artistic process with fine porcelains made in Europe, particularly by the Minton factory in England. The "Pate-sur-Pate" dinnerware made by Harker, however, was not created using this expensive process. Instead, Harker began with pieces that featured embossed decoration around their rims. The bodies were first covered with a white glaze and fired. A colored glaze was then applied, but was wiped off around the rim of each piece so that the initial white glaze showed through. As a result, the white glaze appeared surrounded by the contrasting color, leaving a white design on a colored ground.

Designs used with this line include "Floral Band" (an attractive band around the rim of pieces, composed of stylized four- and five-petal flowers with leaves and stems), "Gadroon Edge" (a simple raised gadroon pattern around the rim of pieces), and "Laurelton" (a wreath of laurel leaves surrounding each piece's central well). Colors include aqua, beige, celadon, green, teal, blue, and yellow. "Laurelton" and "Gadroon Edge" are the most common patterns, and command prices at the lower end of the ranges listed below.

Bowl, *cereal, 6¹/₄-inch diameter*	$ 9–16
Bowl, *individual fruit, 5¹/₂-inch diameter*	$ 7–14
Bowl, *soup, 8¹/₂-inch diameter*	$ 9–16
Bowl, *vegetable, round, 9-inch diameter*	$ 15–28
Bowl, *vegetable, covered*	$ 65–80
Butter dish, *covered, ¹/₄-pound*	$ 40–50
Coffeepot	$ 70–85
Creamer	$ 18–28
Cup and saucer	$ 14–20
Gravy boat and underliner	$ 38–48
Plate, *bread and butter, 6¹/₄-inch diameter*	$ 3–6
Plate, *cake, serving, handled, 11-inch diameter*	$ 36–45
Plate, *chop*	$ 70–85
Plate, *dinner, 10-inch diameter*	$ 15–22
Plate, *salad, 7¹/₂-inch diameter*	$ 8–12
Platter, *oval, 12 inches*	$ 24–35
Platter, *oval, 14 inches*	$ 55–70
Salt and pepper shakers, *set*	$ 18–25
Snack set, *plate and cup*	$ 16–22

"Royal Gadroon"

This line originated in 1947, and its pieces are distinguished (as the name suggests) by their gadrooned edges. Pieces were produced in solid colors such as celadon

Harker "Royal Gadroon" pattern gravy boat and
underliner, Celeste (sky blue), $77–$105.
Item courtesy of Kingston Pike Antique Mall, Knoxville,
Tennessee.

(grayish green), Celeste (sky blue), charcoal (grayish black), Chesterton (silver gray), Corinthian (teal green), Pink Cocoa (beige), Sun Valley (chartreuse), and Chocolate Brown. Some pieces are marked with the name "Royal Gadroon" under a crowned shield; others are marked with the name of the color in which they were produced: Sun Valley, Chesterton, Avocado, Wedgwood Blue, Pumpkin, or Golden Harvest. "Royal Gadroon" shapes were also decorated with decals such as "Ivy," Bermuda" (blue leaves), "Bouquet" (floral grouping that includes roses and tulips), "Bridal Rose" (a garland of roses), "Magnolia," and "Sweetheart Rose." Of these decals, "Ivy" is the most common, and pieces decorated with "Ivy" thus command prices near the bottom of the ranges listed below.

Ashtray, *4³/4 inches*	$ 7–12
Bowl, *cereal, 6¹/4-inch diameter*	$ 12–17
Bowl, *individual fruit, 5¹/2-inch diameter*	$ 9–14
Bowl, *soup, 8¹/4-inch diameter*	$ 13–18
Bowl, *vegetable, oval, 9¹/2 inches*	$ 46–55
Bowl, *vegetable, round, 8³/4-inch diameter*	$ 20–30
Bowl, *vegetable, round, covered*	$ 130–150

Creamer	$ 20–35
Cup and saucer	$ 16–28
Dish, *relish, 8³/₄ inches*	$ 26–35
Gravy boat	$ 50–70
Gravy boat underliner	$ 27–35
Pie lifter	$ 25–35
Plate, *bread and butter, 6-inch diameter*	$ 5–10
Plate, *cake, serving, 11-inch diameter*	$ 55–70
Plate, *dinner, 10¹/₄ inches*	$ 15–27
Plate, *salad, 7¹/₂-inch diameter*	$ 9–12
Platter, *oval, 12¹/₄ inches*	$ 40–60
Platter, *oval, 13¹/₂ inches*	$ 65–80
Platter, *oval, 16 inches*	$ 70–90
Salt and pepper shakers, *set*	$ 26–35
Snack set, *cup and plate*	$ 20–30
Sugar bowl	$ 40–50
Teapot, *4-cup*	$ 80–100

"White Clover"

This pattern was applied to Harker dinnerware designed by the famous industrial designer Russel Wright. Pieces were made using much the same process used to create Harker's earlier "Cameoware," and the design features sensuous and modern-looking long-stem clovers against a solid-color or speckled background. This was Wright's first line of dinnerware, and it was first produced in 1951. It came in four colors: Golden Spice, Meadow Green, Coral Sand, and Charcoal. Some plates were also made in solid colors, without the clover design. "White Clover" is a very difficult pattern to find, and collectors are most interested in Charcoal and Meadow Green pieces. Charcoal pieces will command prices near the upper end of the price ranges listed below, while Coral pieces will command prices near the lower end.

Bowl, *vegetable, round, 7¹/₂-inch diameter*	$ 30–60
Bowl, *vegetable, round, 8¹/₂-inch diameter*	$ 35–70
Casserole, *covered, 2-quart*	$ 75–150
Cup and saucer	$ 20–40

Pitcher, *covered, 2-quart*	$ 125–250
Plate, *bread and butter*	$ 6–12
Plate, *dinner, 10-inch diameter*	$ 20–40
Plate, *salad, 7³/₄-inch diameter*	$ 14–30
Sugar bowl	$ 35–70

"Wood Song"

This lovely pattern came in two colors: Honey Brown and Sherwood Green. Honey Brown pieces generally command prices about 10 percent higher than those of comparable Sherwood Green items. The pattern consists of engraved maple leaves, which are scattered over the surfaces of the dinnerware pieces. Hollowware items with lids have twig-shaped handles.

Bowl, *individual fruit, 5³/₄-inch diameter*	$ 12–15
Bowl, *soup, 7³/₄ inches*	$ 17–22
Bowl, *vegetable, round, 8³/₄-inch diameter*	$ 40–50
Creamer	$ 28–32
Cup and saucer	$ 20–26
Gravy boat	$ 60–70
Plate, *dinner, 10-inch diameter*	$ 17–22
Plate, *salad, 7¹/₄-inch diameter*	$ 8–12
Platter, *oval, 13¹/₂ inches*	$ 50–60
Salt and pepper shakers, *set*	$ 28–32
Sugar bowl	$ 37–45

HOMER LAUGHLIN CHINA COMPANY

One of the marks used by *Homer Laughlin* on its famous "Fiesta" ware.

There is some disagreement as to when the Homer Laughlin Company was founded. Some say the company began in 1869, when Homer Laughlin formed a partnership with Nathaniel Simms in East Liverpool, Ohio. Others maintain that the company began in 1871, when Laughlin and his brother, Shakespeare, built a small two-kiln pottery near the Ohio River in East Liverpool. Other sources claim that the two brothers first worked together in 1874. In any event, Homer sparked Shakespeare's interest in the pottery business in either 1877 or 1879, and the brothers continued to operate the Laughlin Brothers Pottery until the company was incorporated in 1896.

The next year, Homer Laughlin sold his company to William Erwin Wells and a group of Pittsburgh, Pennsylvania, investors led by the Aaron family (Louis T., Marcus, and Charles). At this time the company was renamed the "Homer Laughlin China Company," even though its namesake had liquidated his interests and was no longer involved in the enterprise.

The new owners began a program of expansion, and by 1903 there were three plants operating on the East Liverpool side of the Ohio River. A new plant was built across the Ohio River in Newell, West Virginia, in 1906, and by 1929 there was a total of five Homer Laughlin manufacturing facilities in Newell. When an eighth plant opened in Newell in 1929, the last Homer Laughlin plant in East Liverpool was shut down. Today, the Homer Laughlin China Company is still in business in Newell.

The Homer Laughlin China Company reportedly produced as much as one third of all the restaurant and home-use dinnerware made in the United States during the 20th century. The company also produced a great deal of pre-1930 dinnerware and "art china," but most of today's collectors are far more interested in the wares it produced during the post-1930 period.

Homer Laughlin products made after the year 1900 are often marked with a date code. Pieces produced between 1900 and 1910 feature a single number to designate the month (1 to 12), another numeral to signify the year (0 to 9), and a third number to indicate the particular plant in which the piece was made. Thus, a piece manufactured in April, 1907 in Plant #1 would be marked with the number "4 7 1."

From 1910 to 1920, the company used a similar dating system, with a two-digit number used to indicate the date of production, and a letter used to indicate the plant in which a piece was produced: "N" (for "Newell") for Plant #4, "N5" for Plant #5, and "L" for the company's East End facility. Thus, a piece produced in June, 1915 in the East End plant would be marked "6 15 L."

From 1921 to 1930, a slightly different marking system was used. In the new system, months were indicated by letters of the alphabet, with "A" used to designate January, "B" used to designate February, and so on. A two-digit number indicated the year of production, and a letter indicated the plant in which the piece was produced. Thus, a piece made in Plant #4 (in Newell) in March of 1925 would be marked "C 25 N."

The dating system used from 1931 to 1940 was much the same, except the plant designations changed slightly. The letter "N" was still used to designate Plant #4, but "R" was now used to designate Plant #5, "C" was used to designate Plants #6 and #7 in Laughlin, and "P" was used to designate Plant #8. Thus, a piece produced in September, 1935, at Plant #5 would be marked "I 35 R."

The dating system was discontinued for some time after 1940, but occasionally the company marked pieces produced after that date with a plain, noncoded date mark (e.g., "1980") below its trademark.

"Americana"

This pattern is sometimes referred to as "Currier and Ives," because the scenes used to decorate pieces in this line were based on Currier and Ives prints. Each piece from this line had a mark on its back giving the name of the scene depicted on the front, plus the phrase "From Currier and Ives Prints Made in U. S. A. by Homer Laughlin." To decorate these pieces, scenes were transfer-printed in red (sometimes described as pink or maroon). Designs included "Home Sweet Home," which depicted a house, trees, a stream, and cattle (10-inch dinner plate), "View of New York" (regular cup and saucer), "On the Mississippi" (5-inch fruit bowl), "Western Farmer's Home" (9-inch luncheon plate), and "View of Harper's Ferry, Virginia" (11^1/$_2$-inch platter). Usually these pieces were accented with a band of leaves around the edge (in the case of flatware) or around the lid (in the case of lidded hollowware). Some rare flatware pieces also feature wide gold bands on either side of the leaf band. This pattern was produced between 1949 and 1956 exclusively for Montgomery Ward, and was available through the store's catalog.

Bowl, *individual fruit, 5-inch diameter*	$ 14–18
Bowl, *soup, 8-inch diameter*	$ 40–50
Bowl, *vegetable, round, covered*	$ 145–160
Creamer	$ 30–40
Cup and saucer, *demitasse (after-dinner)*	$ 65–75
Cup and saucer, *regular*	$ 32–40
Gravy boat	$ 80–100
Plate, *bread and butter, 6^1/$_2$-inch diameter*	$ 10–14
Plate, *dinner, 10-inch diameter*	$ 42–52
Plate, *salad, 7^1/$_2$-inch diameter*	$ 38–45
Platter, *oval, 11^1/$_2$ inches*	$ 60–70
Platter, *oval, 13^3/$_4$ inches*	$ 80–90
Platter, *oval, 15 inches*	$ 100–120
Sugar bowl	$ 45–55

It should also be noted that there were several other Homer Laughlin patterns based on Currier and Ives themes, but these patterns were distinctly different from "Americana." Although decorated with Currier and Ives–type prints, pieces in these lines were decorated in polychrome (multicolored) rather than monochrome red, and feature either a wide or narrow green band around the edge of a blue band. The wide-band pieces are slightly more valuable than the narrow-band examples, but all are less valuable than "Americana" pieces.

Bowl, *individual fruit, 5-inch diameter*	$ 12–14
Bowl, *soup, 8^1/$_4$ inches*	$ 16–22
Creamer	$ 35–45
Cup and saucer	$ 25–32

Plate, *bread and butter, 6¹/₄-inch diameter*	$ 7–12
Plate, *dinner, 10-inch diameter*	$ 22–28
Plate, *luncheon, 9¹/₄-inch diameter*	$ 14–20
Plate, *salad, 7¹/₄- to 8¹/₄-inch diameters*	$ 11–16
Sugar bowl	$ 40–50

"Eggshell"

This name was given to a type of lightweight body with thin, chinalike edges that Homer Laughlin created to appeal to the fine china market. It first appeared in 1937, and was made in four different shapes: "Nautilus," "Swag" (1938), "Theme" (1940), and "Georgian" (1940). (Both the "Nautilus" and "Georgian" shapes were also created using bodies other than "Eggshell.") The various "Eggshell" shapes are decorated with a variety of decals, including "Adobe," "Mexicana," "Prima Donna," and "Briar Rose." All "Eggshell" pieces are clearly marked with the name "Eggshell," as well as with the name of the applicable shape ("Nautilus," "Swag," "Theme," or "Georgian"). Pieces featuring Mexican-themed patterns generally command prices at the upper end of the price ranges listed below.

Bowl, *individual fruit, 5¹/₂-inch diameter*	$ 12–15
Bowl, *soup, 8¹/₄-inch diameter*	$ 18–22
Bowl, *vegetable, oval, 9¹/₂ inches*	$ 40–50
Bowl, *vegetable, oval, covered*	$ 130–150
Bowl, *vegetable, round, 9 inches*	$ 42–50
Creamer	$ 30–40
Cup and saucer	$ 25–35
Egg cup, *"Georgian"*	$ 30–40
Gravy boat	$ 55–65
Plate, *bread and butter, 6¹/₄-inch diameter*	$ 8–12
Plate, *chop, 14-inch diameter*	$ 30–40
Plate, *dinner, 10-inch diameter*	$ 25–35
Plate, *luncheon, 9¹/₄-inch diameter*	$ 14–24
Plate, *salad, 7¹/₄-inch diameter*	$ 10–14
Platter, *oval, 11³/₄ inches*	$ 42–55
Sugar bowl	$ 40–50

Mark used by the Homer Laughlin China Company on its "Eggshell" body in the "Georgian" shape. Note the date code below the "Made in U.S.A." mark, which signifies that the piece was manufactured in March ("C" is the third letter of the alphabet and was thus used to denote the third month of the year) of 1944 in plant number 4.

Homer Laughlin "Eggshell" plate, 9-inch diameter, with a flower bouquet decal, $14–$24.
Item courtesy of Richard H. Crane, Knoxville, Tennessee.

Homer Laughlin "Eggshell" tea set, "Nautilus" shape with gilt floral decal like one found on some Hall China Company pieces, $190–$210.
Item courtesy of Barbara Langston, Old School Antique Mall, Sylva, North Carolina.

"Epicure"

This modern-looking pattern was introduced in 1953, and was designed by the famous Don Schreckengost. Distinguished by their thin, angled rims, pieces in this line were produced in solid colors of charcoal, pink, turquoise, and white.

Bowl, *vegetable, round, 8¹/₂-inch diameter*	$ 52–60
Coffeepot	$ 110–145
Creamer	$ 28–34
Cup and saucer	$ 23–30

Gravy boat and underliner	$ 60–70
Plate, *bread and butter, 6¹/₂-inch diameter*	$ 5–8
Plate, *dinner, 10-inch diameter*	$ 18–22
Platter, *oval, 12³/₄ inches*	$ 56–65
Salt and pepper shakers, *set*	$ 25–30
Sugar bowl	$ 35–45
Tidbit server, *two-tier*	$ 65–75

"Fiesta"

This ware was brightly colored to chase away the "blues"—at least at the dinner table—during the dark days of the Depression. "Fiesta" was designed by Frederick Hurten Rhead, who was a famous English-born ceramist and former art director at the Roseville Pottery Company in Zanesville, Ohio. With its streamlined, earthenware shapes and modern, up-to-the-minute feel, the line was first introduced at the 1936 Pittsburgh Pottery and Glass show. The first pieces came in colors of red (orange), cobalt blue, light green, ivory, and yellow. Turquoise was added in 1937. The red (orange) glaze was made using depleted uranium oxide, and was discontinued during World War II because the United States government needed all available uranium oxide to develop and make the atomic bomb. Despite widespread reports to the contrary, the color was *not* discontinued because of a perceived threat to consumers' health and safety, even though the material from which it was made is slightly radioactive. In 1959, uranium oxide was made available to Homer Laughlin once again, and manufacturing of the harmlessly radioactive red color was resumed. In 1951, light green, ivory, and cobalt blue were dropped from the "Fiesta" line, and forest green, rose, gray, and chartreuse were added. To collectors, these became known as the "fifties colors." In 1959, medium green was added, red was returned to the lineup, and rose, gray, forest green, and chartreuse were discontinued. Currently, the most popular "Fiesta" colors are medium green (the most valuable of all), cobalt blue, and "radioactive" red/orange, with ivory and chartreuse also increasing in popularity.

In 1969, "Fiesta" was redesigned and renamed "Fiesta Ironstone." This line was manufactured in only three colors: Mango Red (a nonradioactive red that replaced the original shade), Turf Green, and Antique Gold. "Fiesta Ironstone" was discontinued in 1973.

To commemorate the 50th anniversary of the introduction of "Fiesta," Homer Laughlin reissued the line in 1986 using new colors including white (1986), black (1986–1997), apricot (1986–1997), chartreuse (1986–1999), yellow (1987–2002), peri-

"Fiesta" 8-inch diameter soup bowl in cobalt blue, $50–$60; and orange/red round vegetable, $50–$65.
Items courtesy of Elaine Tomber Tindell.

"Fiesta" covered casserole, forest green, $250–$300; and 12½-inch oval platter, rose, $75–$85.
Items courtesy of Elaine Tomber Tindell.

"Fiesta" nested set of seven mixing bowls, $2,200–$2,400.
Items courtesy of Lillian Barber, Old School Antique Mall, Sylva, North Carolina.

"Fiesta" relish tray, four compartments, one cobalt blue, one orange/red, one ivory, and one yellow section, $550–$650.
Item courtesy of Lillian Barber, Old School Antique Mall, Sylva, North Carolina.

winkle blue (1989–), turquoise (1988–), Sea Mist Green (1991–), Lilac (1993–1995), Persimmon (1995–), Raspberry (1997–), Sapphire (1997), Pearl Gray (1998–2001), Juniper (2000–2001), Sunshine Yellow (2000), Cinnabar (2001–), Plum (2002–), Shamrock (2003–), and Tangerine (2003–). Currently, Lilac, Raspberry, Sapphire, Juniper, and Sunshine Yellow are the most sought-after colors from the most recent period of production. It should be noted that these were limited-production colors: only 500 Raspberry pieces were produced (all bowls), and Sunshine Yellow was available on only one vase and one dinner plate, both of which were auctioned by the Homer Laughlin China Collectors Association in 2000.

Original Colors

COBALT BLUE AND RED (ORANGE)

Ashtray, *small*	$ 60–70
Bowl, *cream soup, two handles*	$ 55–75
Bowl, *fruit, large, 11^1/$_2$-inch diameter*	$ 340–360
Bowl, *individual fruit, 4^3/$_4$-inch diameter*	$ 30–35
Bowl, *individual fruit, 5^1/$_2$-inch diameter*	$ 32–36
Bowl, *individual fruit, 6-inch diameter*	$ 55–62
Bowl, *mixing, with lid, #2, bowl is 5^7/$_8$ inches in diameter*	$ 800–900
Bowl, *mixing, nested, 5-inch diameter*	$ 275–300
Bowl, *mixing, nested, 7-inch diameter*	$ 150–165
Bowl, *salad, serving, footed, 11^1/$_2$-inch diameter*	$ 600–650
Bowl, *soup, 8-inch diameter*	$ 50–60
Candleholder, *bulb-shaped, each*	$ 60–70
Candleholder, *tripod, each*	$ 350–400
Carafe, *covered*	$ 300–350
Casserole, *covered, round, 1^1/$_4$-quart*	$ 250–275
Casserole, *French (stick handle), covered, cobalt blue*	$ 3,500–4,000
Coffeepot	$ 335–355
Compote, *3^1/$_2$ inches*	$ 125–135
Creamer, *ring handle*	$ 35–42
Creamer, *stick handle*	$ 72–78
Cup and saucer	$ 40–50
Cup and saucer, *demitasse, stick handle*	$ 100–110
Egg cup, *single*	$ 80–90
Jug, *32-ounce*	$ 185–200
Lid, *mixing bowl, 5^1/$_8$-inch diameter*	$ 700–800
Mug, *Tom and Jerry*	$ 120–130
Mustard jar, *lidded*	$ 310–325
Nappy, *8 inches*	$ 55–65
Nappy, *9 inches*	$ 75–85

Onion soup, *covered*	$ 700–850
Plate, *bread and butter, 6^1/$_4$-inch diameter*	$ 12–15
Plate, *chop, 12-inch diameter*	$ 50–60
Plate, *dinner, 10^1/$_2$-inch diameter*	$ 50–60
Plate, *grill, 10^1/$_2$ inches*	$ 60–70
Plate, *grill, 11^1/$_2$ inches*	$ 70–80
Plate, *luncheon, 9^1/$_2$-inch diameter*	$ 18–22
Plate, *salad, 7^1/$_2$-inch diameter*	$ 20–25
Platter, *oval, 12^1/$_2$ inches*	$ 55–65
Salt and pepper shakers, *set*	$ 40–50
Sauce boat	$ 70–80
Syrup pitcher, *with lid*	$ 400–450
Teapot, *4-cup*	$ 275–290
Tidbit server, *two-tier*	$ 100–110
Tidbit server, *three-tier*	$ 110–125
Tray, *under tray for creamer and sugar bowl*	$ 100–125
Tumbler, *juice*	$ 42–50
Tumbler, *8-ounce*	$ 85–95
Vase, *bud, 6 inches*	$ 125–150
Vase, *8 inches*	$ 800–900

IVORY

Bowl, *cream soup, two handles*	$ 55–75
Bowl, *fruit, serving, large, 11^1/$_2$-inch diameter*	$ 335–350
Bowl, *individual fruit, 4^3/$_4$-inch diameter*	$ 20–25
Bowl, *individual fruit, 5^1/$_2$-inch diameter*	$ 25–30
Bowl, *individual fruit, 6-inch diameter*	$ 52–60
Bowl, *mixing, 5-inch diameter, nesting*	$ 180–190
Bowl, *mixing, 7-inch diameter, nesting*	$ 130–140
Bowl, *mixing, 8-inch diameter, nesting*	$ 160–170
Bowl, *mixing, with lid, #3, 7-inch diameter*	$ 950–1,000
Bowl, *soup, 8^1/$_2$-inch diameter*	$ 32–38

Candleholder, *bulb*	$ 90–100
Casserole, *round, covered, 1¹/₄-quart*	$ 180–195
Casserole, *French, stick handle, covered*	$ 550–600
Coffeepot, *after-dinner, 2-cup*	$ 650–700
Creamer, *ring handle*	$ 30–35
Creamer, *stick handle*	$ 70–80
Cup and saucer	$ 40–48
Cup and saucer, *demitasse, stick handle*	$ 100–110
Jug, *32-ounce*	$ 115–125
Marmalade jar	$ 400–425
Mug, *Tom and Jerry*	$ 120–135
Nappy, *8 inches*	$ 50–60
Nappy, *9 inches*	$ 60–70
Onion soup, *covered*	$ 700–850
Pitcher, *disk, water, 2-quart*	$ 160–175
Plate, *bread and butter, 6¹/₂-inch diameter*	$ 6–10
Plate, *chop, 12-inch diameter*	$ 35–42
Plate, *chop, 14-inch diameter*	$ 50–60
Plate, *grill*	$ 45–55
Plate, *dinner, 10¹/₂-inch diameter*	$ 32–38
Plate, *luncheon, 9¹/₂-inch diameter*	$ 12–17
Plate, *salad, 7¹/₂-inch diameter*	$ 10–14
Platter, *oval, 12¹/₂ inches*	$ 35–40
Salt and pepper shakers, *set*	$ 30–40
Sauce boat	$ 60–70
Teapot, *4-cup*	$ 250–265
Teapot, *5-cup*	$ 250–265
Tidbit server, *two-tier*	$ 70–80
Tidbit server, *three-tier*	$ 80–90
Tumbler, *juice*	$ 40–46
Tumbler, *8-ounce*	$ 90–100

Vase, *bud, 6 inches*	$ 135–145
Vase, *8 inches*	$ 800–850
Vase, *10 inches*	$ 1,000–1,100

OTHER ORIGINAL COLORS: LIGHT GREEN, YELLOW, TURQUOISE

Ashtray, *small*	$ 50–60
Bowl, *fruit, large, serving, 11¹/₂-inch diameter*	$ 300–325
Bowl, *individual fruit, 4³/₄-inch diameter*	$ 20–25
Bowl, *individual fruit, 5¹/₂-inch diameter*	$ 20–25
Bowl, *individual fruit, 6-inch diameter*	$ 40–50
Bowl, *individual soup/cereal, 7¹/₂-inch diameter*	$ 90–100
Bowl, *mixing, nesting, 5-inch diameter*	$ 180–200
Bowl, *mixing, nesting, 6-inch diameter*	$ 120–130
Bowl, *mixing, nesting, 7-inch diameter*	$ 130–140
Bowl, *mixing, nesting, 8-inch diameter*	$ 150–160
Bowl, *mixing, nesting, 9-inch diameter*	$ 390–410
Bowl, *mixing, nesting, 10-inch diameter*	$ 380–400
Bowl, *mixing, nesting, 11-inch diameter*	$ 425–440
Bowl, *onion soup, covered, yellow*	$ 650–700
Bowl, *onion soup, covered, turquoise*	$ 7,500–8,500
Bowl, *soup, 8¹/₂-inch diameter*	$ 30–38
Candleholder, *bulb, each*	$ 60–70
Candleholder, *tripod, each*	$ 250–265
Carafe, *lidded*	$ 300–325
Casserole, *round, covered, 1¹/₄-quart*	$ 200–225
Casserole, *French, stick handle, covered, yellow*	$ 300–350
Casserole, *French, stick handle, covered, light green*	$ 600–700
Coffeepot, *2-cup*	$ 600–650
Coffeepot, *5-cup*	$ 210–230
Compote, *3¹/₂ inches*	$ 150–165
Creamer, *ring handle*	$ 23–30

Creamer, *stick handle*	$ 50–60
Cup and saucer	$ 20–25
Cup and saucer, *demitasse, stick handle*	$ 70–80
Egg cup, *single*	$ 60–70
Jug, *32-ounce*	$ 90–100
Lid, *mixing bowl, #4, 7⁷/₈-inch diameter*	$ 1,100–1,300
Marmalade, *lidded*	$ 400–425
Mug, *Tom and Jerry*	$ 52–56
Mustard jar, *lidded*	$ 250–270
Nappy, *8 inches*	$ 25–30
Nappy, *9 inches*	$ 40–45
Pitcher, *juice, 30-ounce*	$ 42–50
Pitcher, *disk, water, 2-quart*	$ 115–125
Pitcher, *64-ounce*	$ 125–140
Plate, *bread and butter, 6¹/₂-inch diameter*	$ 4–7
Plate, *chop, 12-inch diameter*	$ 40–45
Plate, *chop, 14-inch diameter*	$ 55–65
Plate, *grill, 10¹/₂-inch diameter*	$ 40–48
Plate, *grill, 11¹/₂-inch diameter*	$ 60–70
Plate, *dinner, 10¹/₂-inch diameter*	$ 25–35
Plate, *luncheon, 9¹/₂-inch diameter*	$ 10–14
Plate, *salad, 7¹/₂-inch diameter*	$ 8–12
Platter, *oval, 12¹/₂ inches*	$ 35–40
Relish, *lazy Susan, 5 parts (add 15 percent for every cobalt blue, red/orange, or ivory section)*	$ 375–400
Salt and pepper shakers, *set*	$ 35–45
Sauce boat	$ 40–47
Teapot, *4-cup*	$ 165–180
Teapot, *5-cup*	$ 235–250
Tidbit server, *two-tier*	$ 55–65
Tidbit server, *three-tier*	$ 60–70

Tumbler, *juice*	$ 35–40
Tumbler, *8-ounce*	$ 55–65
Vase, *bud, 6 inches*	$ 110–120

CHARTREUSE

Ashtray, *small*	$ 90–100
Bowl, *individual fruit, $4^3/_4$-inch diameter*	$ 25–30
Bowl, *individual fruit, $5^1/_2$-inch diameter*	$ 35–40
Bowl, *individual fruit, 6-inch diameter*	$ 55–65
Bowl, *soup, $8^1/_2$-inch diameter*	$ 65–75
Casserole, *covered, round, $1^1/_4$-quart*	$ 275–290
Creamer, *ring handle*	$ 32–38
Cup and saucer	$ 50–60
Jug, *32-ounce*	$ 165–180
Mug, *Tom and Jerry*	$ 85–95
Nappy, *8 inches*	$ 55–65
Pitcher, *disk, water, 2-quart*	$ 270–280
Plate, *bread and butter, $6^1/_2$-inch diameter*	$ 14–18
Plate, *chop, 12-inch diameter*	$ 100–110
Plate, *chop, 14-inch diameter*	$ 120–130
Plate, *dinner, $10^1/_2$-inch diameter*	$ 80–90
Plate, *luncheon, $9^1/_2$-inch diameter*	$ 25–30
Plate, *salad, $7^1/_2$-inch diameter*	$ 20–25
Platter, *oval, $12^1/_2$ inches*	$ 90–100
Salt and pepper shakers, *set*	$ 70–80
Sauce boat	$ 80–90
Sugar bowl	$ 80–90
Teapot, *4-cup*	$ 375–390

FOREST GREEN

Ashtray, *small*	$ 100–110
Bowl, *individual fruit, $4^3/_4$ inches*	$ 40–50

Bowl, *individual fruit, 5¹/₂ inches*	$ 40–50
Bowl, *individual fruit, 6 inches*	$ 70–80
Bowl, *soup, 8¹/₂-inch diameter*	$ 62–67
Creamer, *ring handle*	$ 40–46
Cup and saucer	$ 45–55
Mug, *Tom and Jerry*	$ 100–110
Nappy, *8 inch*	$ 70–80
Pitcher, *disk, water, 2-quart*	$ 350–370
Plate, *dinner, 10¹/₂-inch diameter*	$ 80–90
Plate, *luncheon, 9¹/₂-inch diameter*	$ 33–40
Platter, *oval, 12¹/₂ inches*	$ 75–85
Salt and pepper shakers, *set*	$ 60–70
Sauce boat	$ 80–90
Teapot, *4-cup*	$ 435–450

1950s Colors

GRAY AND ROSE

Ashtray, small	$ 90–100
Bowl, *individual fruit, 4³/₄-inch diameter*	$ 28–38
Bowl, *individual fruit, 5¹/₂-inch diameter*	$ 30–40
Bowl, *individual fruit, 6-inch diameter*	$ 55–65
Bowl, *soup, 8¹/₂-inch diameter*	$ 45–52
Casserole, *covered, round, 1¹/₄ quart*	$ 180–195
Coffeepot, *5-cup*	$ 600–650
Creamer, *ring handle*	$ 32–38
Cup and saucer	$ 30–35
Egg cup, *single*	$ 150–160
Jug, *32-ounce*	$ 165–175
Mug, *Tom and Jerry*	$ 75–85
Nappy, *8 inches*	$ 55–65

Pitcher, *disk, water, 2-quart*	$ 275–300
Plate, *bread and butter, 6¹/₂-inch diameter*	$ 10–14
Plate, *chop, 12-inch diameter*	$ 80–90
Plate, *grill, 10¹/₂-inch diameter*	$ 65–75
Plate, *dinner, 10¹/₂-inch diameter*	$ 60–70
Plate, *luncheon, 9¹/₂-inch diameter*	$ 20–25
Plate, *salad, 7¹/₂-inch diameter*	$ 20–25
Platter, *oval, 12¹/₂ inches*	$ 65–75
Salt and pepper shakers, *set*	$ 75–85
Teapot, *4-cup*	$ 325–350
Tidbit server, *two-tier*	$ 100–110
Tidbit server, *three-tier*	$ 110–120

MEDIUM GREEN

Bowl, *cream soup, two handles*	$ 5,000–6,000
Bowl, *individual fruit, 4³/₄-inch diameter*	$ 450–500
Bowl, *individual fruit, 5¹/₂-inch diameter*	$ 75–85
Bowl, *individual, salad/cereal*	$ 140–150
Bowl, *soup, 8¹/₂-inch diameter*	$ 140–150
Creamer, *ring handle*	$ 90–100
Cup and saucer	$ 65–75
Pitcher, *disk, water, 2-quart*	$ 1,500–1,750
Plate, *chop, 13-inch diameter*	$ 650–750
Plate, *dinner, 10¹/₂-inch diameter*	$ 200–225
Plate, *luncheon, 9¹/₂ inches*	$ 60–70
Plate, *salad, 7¹/₂ inches*	$ 40–50
Salt and pepper shakers, *set*	$ 250–275
Sugar bowl	$ 200–225
Tidbit server, *two-tier*	$ 250–275
Tidbit server, *three-tier*	$ 280–300

One of a set of two medium green "Fiesta" ball-shaped
salt and pepper shakers, $250–$275 for the set.
Item courtesy of Elaine Tomber Tindell.

Post-1986 Colors

CINNABAR

Bowl, *cereal*	$ 5–7
Bowl, *chili*	$ 6–9
Bowl, *individual fruit, 5¹/₂-inch diameter*	$ 3–5
Bowl, *mixing, 7-inch diameter*	$ 17–22
Bowl, *mixing, 8-inch diameter*	$ 19–24
Bowl, *mixing, 9-inch diameter*	$ 20–25
Bowl, *pasta, 12-inch diameter*	$ 16–10
Bowl, *pedestal, 9¹/₂ inches*	$ 17–20
Bowl, *salad, large serving, 10-inch diameter*	$ 15–20
Bowl, *soup, 7-inch diameter*	$ 6–8
Bowl, *soup, 9-inch diameter*	$ 8–10
Bowl, *vegetable, oval, 12 inches*	$ 22–26
Bowl, *vegetable, round, 8¹/₂-inch diameter*	$ 9–12

"Fiesta" pieces made after 1986 are popular with many collectors, and two of the most desired colors are Lilac and Sapphire Blue. The open carafe on the left is Sapphire Blue and was an exclusive of Bloomingdale's, and is now valued at $100–$110. The 50th Anniversary disk pitcher seen on the right is in Lilac, and came with four tumblers that are not pictured. The set is valued at $150–$200.
Item courtesy of Elaine Tomber Tindell.

Butter dish, *covered, ¹/₄-pound*	$ 18–22
Candleholder, *bulb*	$ 7–9
Cream and sugar set with tray, *3 pieces*	$ 26–30
Creamer	$ 9–12
Cup and saucer	$ 10–14
Cup and saucer, *demitasse*	$ 10–12
Dish, *nut, footed*	$ 25–30
Mug, *pedestal*	$ 15–20
Pitcher, *32-ounce*	$ 14–16
Pitcher, *64-ounce*	$ 20–25
Plate, *bread and butter, 6¹/₂-inch diameter*	$ 4–6
Plate, *cake, serving, handled, 12-inch diameter*	$ 17–20
Plate, *chop, 11-inch diameter*	$ 12–15
Plate, *dinner, 10¹/₂-inch diameter*	$ 7–10
Plate, *luncheon, 9¹/₂-inch diameter*	$ 6–8

Plate, *pie, baking, 6-inch diameter*	$ 5–7
Plate, *pie, baking, 8-inch diameter*	$ 8–10
Plate, *pizza, 15-inch diameter*	$ 20–25
Plate, *salad, 7¹/₂-inch diameter*	$ 5–7
Platter, *oval, 9¹/₂ inches*	$ 7–10
Platter, *oval, 11¹/₂ inches*	$ 10–15
Platter, *oval, 13¹/₂ inches*	$ 15–20
Relish	$ 18–22
Salt and pepper shakers, *set*	$ 10–12
Salt and pepper shakers, *stove top, set*	$ 15–20
Sauce boat	$ 17–20
Spoon rest, *one spoon*	$ 9–12
Sugar bowl	$ 12–15
Sweetener holder	$ 8–10
Teapot, *2-cup*	$ 17–20
Teapot, *5-cup*	$ 25–30
Tidbit server, *two-tier*	$ 33–40
Tidbit server, *three-tier*	$ 40–45
Tray, *bread*	$ 10–12
Trivet	$ 5–7
Tumbler, *6-ounce*	$ 3–5
Utensil holder	$ 25–30
Vase, *7 inches*	$ 25–30
Vase, *9 inches, flared*	$ 30–35

JUNIPER

Bowl, *cereal, 5¹/₂-inch diameter*	$ 12–15
Bowl, *chili*	$ 12–15
Bowl, *soup, 7-inch diameter*	$ 18–22
Bowl, *pasta, 12-inch diameter*	$ 30–35
Bowl, *vegetable, round, 8¹/₂-inch diameter*	$ 20–24
Butter dish, *covered, ¹/₄-pound*	$ 32–36

Candleholder, *tripod*	$ 50–56
Cream and sugar set with tray, *3 pieces*	$ 40–50
Creamer	$ 14–16
Cup and saucer	$ 15–18
Dish, *nut, footed*	$ 30–35
Mug	$ 18–22
Mug, *pedestal*	$ 18–22
Napkin ring	$ 11–13
Plate, *bread and butter*	$ 10–13
Plate, *dinner, 10^1/$_2$-inch diameter*	$ 21–26
Plate, *pie, serving, 10^1/$_4$ inches*	$ 25–30
Plate, *pizza, 15-inch diameter*	$ 40–45
Plate, *salad, 7^1/$_2$-inch diameter*	$ 12–15
Platter, *oval, 13^1/$_2$ inches*	$ 30–35
Relish, *9^1/$_2$ inches*	$ 12–15
Salt and pepper shakers, *set*	$ 20–25
Teapot, *2-cup*	$ 42–48
Teapot, *5-cup*	$ 60–65
Tidbit server, *two-tier*	$ 42–48
Tidbit server, *three-tier*	$ 40–56
Tumbler, *6-ounce*	$ 11–13
Vase, *bud, 6 inches*	$ 11–13
Vase, *7 inches*	$ 50–60
Vase, *9 inches*	$ 60–70

LILAC

Bowl, *chili*	$ 30–40
Bowl, *soup, 7-inch diameter*	$ 50–60
Bowl, *vegetable, round, 8^1/$_4$ inches*	$ 90–100
Butter, *covered, ^{1}/$_4$-pound*	$ 175–190
Candleholder, *tripod*	$ 600–650
Cream and sugar set with tray, *3 pieces*	$ 140–160

Cup and saucer	$ 60–75
Cup, *jumbo*	$ 70–80
Dish, *nut, footed*	$ 70–80
Mug	$ 60–70
Pitcher, *64-ounce*	$ 120–130
Pitcher, *disk, water, 1996, 60th anniversary*	$ 120–130
Plate, *chop, 11-inch diameter*	$ 160–175
Plate, *dinner, 10^1/$_2$-inch diameter*	$ 80–90
Plate, *luncheon, 9^1/$_2$-inch diameter*	$ 60–70
Plate, *pie, serving*	$ 125–135
Plate, *salad, 7^1/$_2$-inch diameter*	$ 60–70
Platter, *oval, 13^1/$_2$ inches*	$ 125–140
Salt and pepper shakers, *set*	$ 100–110
Sauce boat	$ 100–110
Teapot	$ 200–225
Tumbler, *6-ounce*	$ 40–50
Vase, *flared, 9 inches*	$ 400–450

SAPPHIRE BLUE

Carafe, *open*	$ 100–110
Cup and saucer	$ 42–50
Pitcher, *disk, water, 2-quart, 1996, 60th anniversary*	$ 100–110
Pitcher, *64-ounce*	$ 80–90
Plate, *dinner, 10^1/$_2$-inch diameter*	$ 60–70
Tumbler, *6-ounce*	$ 20–25
Vase, *flared, 9 inches*	$ 300–325

"Fiesta Kitchen Kraft"

Cake lifter, *yellow, light green, embossed floral handle*	$ 150–175
Casserole, *individual, lidded, light green*	$ 160–175
Cookie jar, *7-inch diameter, common colors*	$ 275–325
Cookie jar, *8-inch diameter, common colors*	$ 325–375

"Fiesta Ironstone" salad bowl, 10-inch diameter, Antique
Gold, $45–$60.
Item courtesy of Elaine Tomber Tindell.

Fork, *salad, light green*	$ 120–150
Refrigerator storage units, *ivory, cobalt blue*	$ 50–65
Refrigerator storage lids, *ivory, cobalt blue*	$ 85–100
Spoon, *salad, red*	$ 150–175
Spoon, *salad, yellow*	$ 130–150

"Fiesta Ironstone"

Antique Gold

Bowl, *salad, 10-inch diameter*	$ 45–60
Creamer	$ 7–10
Plate, *dinner, 10 1/4-inch diameter*	$ 18–22
Teapot and lid, *4-cup*	$ 40–45

Turf Green

Bowl, *individual fruit, 5 1/2-inch diameter*	$ 11–15
Cup and saucer	$ 20–24

"Harlequin"

Introduced two years after "Fiesta," "Harlequin" was an inexpensive alternative line made on a lighter body and sold only at F. W. Woolworth's. Like "Fiesta," "Harlequin" was designed by Frederick Rhead, and its major design element was concentric rings on streamlined Art Deco-inspired shapes. Unlike the circular handles of "Fiesta" pieces, the handles on "Harlequin" items are triangular. "Harlequin" came in a variety of solid colors; the four original shades were maroon, blue, yellow, and Spruce Green. Later pieces were produced in chartreuse, medium green, light green, gray, forest green, rose, red, and turquoise. "Harlequin" was discontinued in 1964, but was reissued in 1979 as "Harlequin Ironstone" for Woolworth's 100th anniversary. These reissue pieces were made only in turquoise and yellow, and were marked with the Homer Laughlin backstamp, whereas the original "Harlequin" pieces were not marked at all. The most desired colors from the "Harlequin" line are medium green, blue, red, chartreuse, gray, dark green, and Spruce Green.

Medium Green

Bowl, *oatmeal or cereal, 6¹/₂-inch diameter*	$ 40–45
Bowl, *soup, 8¹/₂-inch diameter*	$ 100–120
Bowl, *vegetable, round, 8³/₄-inch diameter*	$ 120–130
Cup and saucer	$ 19–24
Plate, *salad, 7¹/₄-inch diameter*	$ 30–35

Blue, Chartreuse, Gray, Dark Green, Red, Maroon, Spruce

Bowl, *individual fruit, 5¹/₂-inch diameter*	$ 12–18
Bowl, *individual salad, 7¹/₂-inch diameter*	$ 40–45
Bowl, *oatmeal or cereal, 6¹/₂-inch diameter*	$ 26–35
Bowl, *soup, 8¹/₂-inch diameter*	$ 30–43
Bowl, *vegetable, round, 8³/₄-inch diameter*	$ 35–50
Bowl, *vegetable, oval, 9¹/₂ inches*	$ 40–55
Creamer	$ 30–35
Cup and saucer	$ 18–24
Cup and saucer, *demitasse (maroon is at the top of the price range for this particular item)*	$ 80–140
Egg cup, *double*	$ 50–60
Gravy or sauce boat	$ 45–50

"Harlequin" gravy boat, turquoise, $30–$40.
Item courtesy of Needful Things, Hendersonville, North Carolina.

Pitcher, *24-ounce*	$ 75–95
Plate, *bread and butter, 6¹/₄-inch diameter*	$ 10–14
Plate, *dinner, 10-inch diameter*	$ 40–60
Plate, *luncheon, 9¹/₄-inch diameter*	$ 15–20
Plate, *salad, 7¹/₄-inch diameter*	$ 8–12
Platter, *oval, 13¹/₂ inches*	$ 40–45
Salt and pepper shakers, *set*	$ 35–45
Sugar bowl	$ 40–45
Tidbit server, *two-tier*	$ 75–90
Tumbler, *tall*	$ 40–65

Turquoise, Yellow, Rose

Bowl, *individual fruit, 5¹/₂-inch diameter*	$ 11–14
Bowl, *oatmeal or cereal, 6¹/₂-inch diameter*	$ 17–22
Bowl, *salad, individual, 7¹/₂-inch diameter*	$ 30–35

"Harlequin" 3-cup teapot, yellow, $125–$135.
Item courtesy of Elaine Tomber Tindell.

Bowl, *vegetable, round, 8³/₄-inch diameter*	$ 30–35
Bowl, *vegetable, round, covered*	$ 95–130
Bowl, *soup, 8¹/₂-inch diameter*	$ 23–27
Creamer, *regular*	$ 20–25
Creamer, *small, individual*	$ 40–50
Cup and saucer	$ 13–18
Cup and saucer, *demitasse*	$ 65–90
Egg cup, *double*	$ 45–55
Gravy or sauce boat	$ 30–40
Pitcher, *80-ounce*	$ 75–85
Plate, *bread and butter, 6¹/₄-inch diameter*	$ 6–10
Plate, *dinner, 10-inch diameter*	$ 30–40
Plate, *luncheon, 9¹/₄-inch diameter*	$ 13–18
Plate, *salad, 7¹/₄-inch diameter*	$ 11–14

Platter, *oval, 11¹/₄ inches*	$ 28–35
Platter, *oval, 13 inches*	$ 35–42
Sugar bowl	$ 35–40
Teapot, *3-cup*	$ 125–135
Tidbit server, *two-tier*	$ 60–70
Tidbit server, *three-tier*	$ 70–80
Tumbler, *tall*	$ 34–40

"Highland Plaid"

This colorful plaid design came in at least four different color schemes: brown and yellow, monotone green, green and black, and green and brown (called "Dundee Plaid"). This is a DuraPrint line, and can be found on both "Charm House" and "Rhythm" shapes. Only the flatware items in these lines featured the plaid design; the hollowware pieces such as the gravy boat, cup, creamer, sugar bowl, and teapot were all solid colors.

Bowl, *individual fruit, 5¹/₄-inch diameter*	$ 10–14
Bowl, *soup, 8¹/₄-inch diameter*	$ 12–16
Bowl, *vegetable, round, 9-inch diameter*	$ 30–35
Creamer	$ 17–22
Cup and saucer	$ 18–22
Plate, *bread and butter, 6¹/₃-inch diameter*	$ 5–8
Plate, *dinner, 10¹/₄-inch diameter*	$ 14–20
Platter, *oval, 11¹/₂ inches*	$ 35–48
Platter, *oval, 13¹/₂ inches*	$ 44–58
Sugar bowl	$ 20–24

"Historical America"

This pattern was based on the art of Joseph Boggs Beale, and was produced from 1939 to 1958. It is most commonly found in red and white, though blue-and-white examples were also produced. Items in this line feature floral borders. Each piece is marked "Historical America," along with the name of the scene pictured on the piece, and some are marked "Picture Reproduced From Original Painting by Joseph Boggs Beale." Scenes include "Pony Express" (round vegetable bowl), "Ponce de Leon Discovers Florida" (soup bowl), "George Washington Taking Command of the Army" (10-inch dinner plate), "Franklin's Experiment 1752" (cup), and "Arrival of the Mayflower, 1607" (saucer). All prices listed below are for pieces with red-and-white decoration on Homer Laughlin's "Liberty" shape.

Bowl, *individual fruit, 5³/₄-inch diameter*	$ 12–15
Bowl, *soup, 8¹/₂-inch diameter*	$ 30–35
Bowl, *vegetable, oval, 9¹/₂ inches*	$ 45–55
Bowl, *vegetable, round, 8³/₄-inch diameter*	$ 50–60
Cup and saucer	$ 30–35
Creamer	$ 40–50
Gravy boat	$ 80–90
Plate, *dinner, 10-inch diameter*	$ 40–50
Plate, *luncheon, 9¹/₄-inch diameter*	$ 30–40
Plate, *salad, 8¹/₄-inch diameter*	$ 24–30
Platter, *oval, 11³/₄ inches*	$ 45–55
Platter, *oval, 13³/₄ inches*	$ 70–80
Teapot, *5-cup*	$ 200–225

"Jubilee"

This pattern was introduced in 1948 to celebrate the 75th anniversary of the Homer Laughlin Company. It was designed by Don Schreckengost, and initially came in solid colors of Celadon Green, Cream Beige, Mist Gray, and Shell Pink. In 1952, the "Suntone" line was introduced, examples of which featured brown (terra cotta) bodies with white finials and handles, a white foot in the case of the egg cup, and a white underliner in the case of the gravy boat. "Skytone" pieces were also produced; these were the same type of ware as "Suntone," except they were produced in blue and white. Occasionally, "Jubilee" pieces were decorated with decals such as "Flame Flower" and "Stardust." These pieces command prices near the low end of the price ranges listed below. Items in this group are marked both "Jubilee by Homer Laughlin U.S.A." and "Skytone by Homer Laughlin U.S.A."

Bowl, *cereal, 6-inch diameter*	$ 9–12
Bowl, *individual fruit, 5¹/₄-inch diameter*	$ 8–10
Bowl, *soup, 7¹/₂-inch diameter*	$ 12–15
Bowl, *vegetable, round, 7¹/₂-inch diameter*	$ 16–20
Bowl, *vegetable, round, covered*	$ 65–75

Coffeepot, *6-cup*	$ 30–40
Creamer	$ 12–15
Cup and saucer	$ 14–18
Gravy boat with attached underliner	$ 32–42
Plate, *bread and butter, 6¹/₄-inch diameter*	$ 5–7
Plate, *chop, 14-inch diameter*	$ 25–42
Plate, *dinner, 10¹/₂-inch diameter*	$ 12–15
Plate, *luncheon, 9-inch diameter*	$ 10–12
Plate, *salad, 7¹/₂-inch diameter*	$ 6–9
Platter, *oval, 11¹/₂ inches*	$ 23–30
Platter, *oval, 13¹/₂ inches*	$ 28–38
Platter, *oval, 15¹/₂ inches*	$ 42–52
Salt and pepper shakers, *set*	$ 20–25
Sugar bowl	$ 22–25
Teapot, *4-cup*	$ 52–62

"Maxicana," "Mexicana," "Hacienda," and "Conchita"

Over the years, Homer Laughlin used a number of Mexican-themed decals to decorate its various shapes of dinnerware. "Maxicana" depicts pieces of pottery, a cactus, and a man ("Max") resting under his sombrero. "Mexicana" decals are similar to "Maxicana" decals, except there is no "Max" and no cactus; just pottery and plants on the ground. "Hacienda" decals depict a bench in front of an adobe-style house, with pottery on the ground and hanging on the walls; there is also a sombrero on the bench, suggesting that "Max" might live here. "Conchita" decals depict a string of hanging fruit and vegetables, with pottery on the ground—one piece containing a plant, and the other containing flowers. These various decals are often found on Laughlin's "Century" and "Eggshell" shapes.

Bowl, *individual fruit, 5¹/₄-inch diameter*	$ 20–25
Bowl, *soup, 7³/₄-inch diameter*	$ 22–30
Bowl, *vegetable, oval, 9 inches*	$ 70–80
Bowl, *vegetable, round, 8¹/₄-inch diameter*	$ 65–75
Bowl, *vegetable, rectangular, covered*	$ 200–225
Butter dish, *square, 1-pound*	$ 150–200
Creamer	$ 45–55

Cup and saucer	$ 30–40
Jug, *batter*	$ 150–200
Plate, *bread and butter, 6¼-inch diameter*	$ 12–16
Plate, *dinner, 10-inch diameter*	$ 60–70
Plate, *luncheon, 8¾-inch diameter*	$ 28–35
Plate, *salad, 7-inch diameter*	$ 20–26
Platter, *oval, 11½-inch diameter*	$ 70–80
Platter, *oval, 13½-inch diameter*	$ 80–90
Sugar bowl	$ 50–60

"Rhythm"

Designed by Don Schreckengost, "Rhythm" is a clean modern design, produced in solid colors of burgundy, chartreuse, gray, dark green, and Harlequin Yellow, and decorated with decals. One of the line's most popular decals is "American Provincial," which was based on Pennsylvania Dutch (Deutsch) motifs and depicts a farmer and his wife standing in a pose reminiscent of the painting *American Gothic*. "American Provincial" was one of Homer Laughlin's first silk-screened decals and, like the "Rhythm" shape, was also designed by Don Schreckengost. Another common decal decoration is "Golden Wheat," which features a design of brown and yellow wheat.

Solid Colors

Bowl, *individual fruit, 5½-inch diameter*	$ 9–12
Bowl, *soup, 8-inch diameter*	$ 13–18
Bowl, *vegetable, round, 8½-inch diameter*	$ 25–35
Bowl, *round, vegetable, covered*	$ 120–130
Creamer	$ 17–32
Cup and saucer	$ 17–23
Gravy boat	$ 55–65
Plate, *bread and butter, 6-inch diameter*	$ 5–7
Plate, *dinner, 10-inch diameter*	$ 15–22
Plate, *luncheon, 9-inch diameter*	$ 11–14
Plate, *salad, 7¼-inch diameter*	$ 8–12
Platter, *oval, 11½ inches*	$ 40–50
Platter, *oval, 13½ inches*	$ 60–75

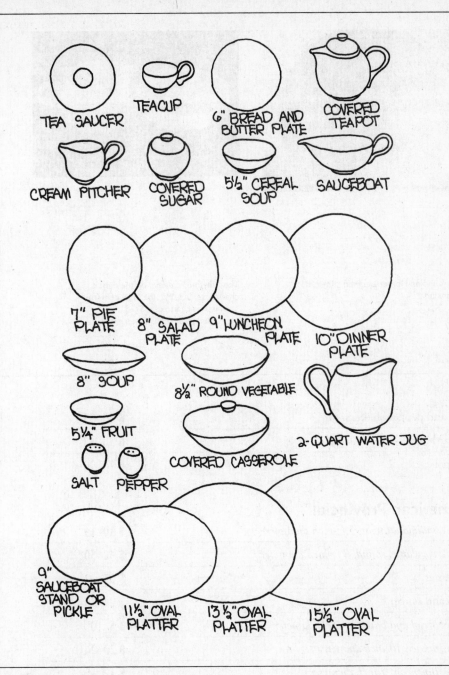

Shapes found in Homer Laughlin's "Rhythm" line.

Mark found on Homer Laughlin "Rhythm" dinnerware.

The "Rhythm" creamer on the right is chartreuse, $17–$32; the individual fruit bowl is also chartreuse, $9–$12.
Items courtesy of Elaine Tomber Tindell.

Salt and pepper shakers, *pair*	$ 25–35
Sugar bowl	$ 30–42
Teapot	$ 75–90

"American Provincial"

Bowl, *individual fruit, 5¹/₂-inch diameter*	$ 10–14
Bowl, *vegetable, round, 8¹/₂-inch diameter*	$ 42–50
Creamer	$ 25–32
Cup and saucer	$ 24–30
Plate, *bread and butter, 6-inch diameter*	$ 8–10
Plate, *dinner, 10-inch diameter*	$ 20–26
Plate, *luncheon, 9-inch diameter*	$ 12–15
Plate, *salad, 8-inch diameter*	$ 10–13
Platter, *oval, 11¹/₂ inches*	$ 40–50

Platter, *oval, 13¹/₂ inches*	$ 50–60
Sugar bowl	$ 40–50

"Golden Wheat"

Bowl, *individual fruit, 5¹/₂-inch diameter*	$ 5–7
Bowl, *vegetable, round, 8¹/₂-inch diameter*	$ 15–20
Bowl, *vegetable, round, covered*	$ 80–90
Creamer	$ 10–14
Cup and saucer	$ 13–16
Gravy boat and underliner	$ 50–60
Plate, *bread and butter, 6-inch diameter*	$ 4–6
Plate, *dinner, 10-inch diameter*	$ 10–15
Plate, *luncheon, 9-inch diameter*	$ 6–8
Plate, *salad, 8-inch diameter*	$ 7–9
Platter, *oval, 11¹/₂ inches*	$ 20–25
Platter, *oval, 13¹/₂ inches*	$ 24–30
Sugar bowl	$ 16–20
Teapot	$ 35–45
Tidbit server, *three-tier*	$ 35–45

"Riviera"

Introduced in 1938 and discontinued in 1950, "Riviera" was yet another Homer Laughlin solid-color dinnerware line, and was manufactured to be sold by the Murphy Company in its five-and-ten-cent stores across the country. Like "Harlequin" pieces, "Riviera" pieces were not marked. "Riviera" shapes are based largely on Laughlin's "Century" shapes, which are generally square or rectangular with square handles (plates, platters, and saucers feature scalloped corners). "Riviera" pieces were produced in blue, light green, red, yellow, and ivory. On rare occasions, cobalt blue or rust-brown pieces will turn up, but these pieces were not part of the regular line and are not included in the price ranges listed below. Of the regular "Riviera" colors, red is the most valuable.

Bowl, *cream soup, and saucer*	$ 75–100
Bowl, *individual fruit, 5¹/₂ inches*	$ 15–22

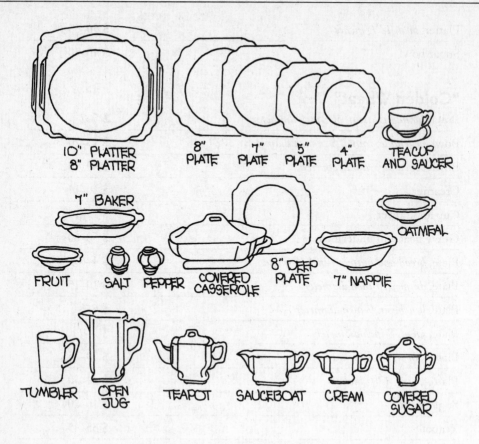

Shapes found in Homer Laughlin's "Century" line.

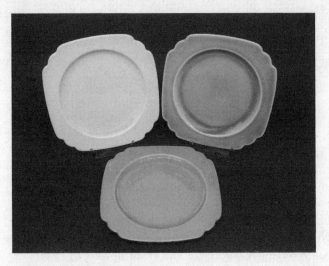

Three 7-inch plates in the "Century" shape from Homer
Laughlin's "Riviera" line, $15 to $20 each.
Items courtesy of Elaine Tomber Tindell.

Bowl, *soup, 8¹/2 inches*	$ 25–35
Bowl, *vegetable, round, 8¹/4-inch diameter*	$ 42–55
Bowl, *vegetable, oval, 9 inches*	$ 50–65
Bowl, *vegetable, rectangular, covered*	$ 150–165
Butter dish, *¹/4-pound, covered*	$ 225–275
Casserole	$ 160–200
Creamer	$ 23–42
Cup and saucer	$ 30–45
Plate, *bread butter, 6 inches*	$ 10–15
Plate, *dinner, 10 inches*	$ 55–70
Plate, *luncheon, 9 inches*	$ 21–30
Platter, *oval, 11¹/2 inches*	$ 55–75
Platter, *oval, 13¹/2 inches*	$ 75–95
Salt and pepper shakers, *set*	$ 25–40
Sauce boat	$ 60–75

Sugar bowl	$ 45–65
Teapot	$ 170–190
Tumbler, *handled*	$ 80–95
Tumbler, *juice*	$ 50–75

"Virginia Rose"

This Homer Laughlin shape was decorated with as many as 450 different decal de-signs. However, many collectors tend to associate the name "Virginia Rose" with two specific patterns, both of which feature wild-rose-type embellishment. The first of these is "JJ59," which was made for J. J. Newberry stores and depicts small pink and white flowers accented with green, gray, and brown leaves. The second is "VR128," which is thought to have been produced in vast quantities for F. W. Wool-worth's. The "VR128" pattern depicts both large and small flowers in shades of pink, white, and purple, accented with leaves that are green with a hint of yellow. "Virginia Rose" was first made in 1933, and was discontinued in the late 1950s. Prices listed below are for "JJ59" and "VR128" pieces; prices for pieces decorated with other decals can be as much as 50 percent lower.

Bowl, *cereal, 6-inch diameter*	$ 23–30
Bowl, *individual fruit, 5¹/₂-inch diameter*	$ 9–12
Bowl, *mixing, "Kitchen Kraft," 6-inch diameter*	$ 65–85
Bowl, *mixing, "Kitchen Kraft," 8-inch diameter*	$ 65–85
Bowl, *mixing, "Kitchen Kraft," 10-inch diameter*	$ 75–95
Bowl, *vegetable, oval, 9 inches*	$ 36–42
Bowl, *vegetable, oval, covered*	$ 135–150
Butter dish, *covered, oblong*	$ 200–225
Casserole	$ 190–220
Cup and saucer	$ 20–25
Egg cup	$ 90–110
Gravy	$ 60–70
Plate, *bread and butter, 6¹/₄ inches*	$ 6–9
Plate, *dinner, 10-inch diameter*	$ 20–25
Plate, *luncheon, 9-inch diameter*	$ 14–18
Plate, *salad, 7-inch diameter*	$ 12–16
Platter, *oval, 11¹/₂ inches*	$ 35–45

Platter, *oval, 13¹/2 inches*	$ 50–65
Sugar bowl	$ 35–45
Tidbit server, *two-tier*	$ 50–60
Tidbit server, *three-tier*	$ 60–70

"Wells"

Like "Fiesta," this line was designed by Frederich Hurten Rhead, and its pieces are distinguished by thin rims and openwork handles. The line originated in 1930, some six years before "Fiesta," and generally has solid-color glazes, although some "Wells" shapes with standard ivory glaze do have decal decoration. These decals include "Flowers of the Dell" (sprays of purple and blue flowers with yellow centers and green leaves), "Hollyhock," "Tulip," "Palm Tree," and "Pink Clover." "Wells," however, is generally associated with mottled or speckled solid-color glazes, called "Wells Art Glazes," and pieces are often marked with this phrase inside a scalloped circle. Pieces are also marked with the word "Wells" under a representation of a peacock with a spread tail. Solid colors include blue, red (rare), Leaf Green, Peach, Rust Brown, Vellum Ivory, and Melon Yellow. Prices listed below are for common colors, with green and pink being the least valuable, and Peach, Rust Brown, and Melon Yellow being the most valuable.

Bowl, *individual fruit, 5¹/4-inch diameter*	$ 12–16
Bowl, *soup, 8-inch diameter*	$ 18–22
Butter dish, *covered*	$ 90–120
Butter pat	$ 16–20
Casserole, *covered, 8-inch diameter*	$ 80–100
Coffeepot, *after-dinner*	$ 125–150
Covered toast	$ 90–110
Creamer	$ 18–22
Cup and saucer	$ 20–28
Gravy boat, *faststand, no spout*	$ 40–50
Jug, *syrup*	$ 120–140
Plate, *bread and butter, 6¹/4-inch diameter*	$ 5–8
Plate, *chop, 11¹/2-inch diameter, handled*	$ 60–75
Plate, *luncheon, 9-inch diameter*	$ 14–18
Plate, *dinner, 10-inch diameter*	$ 18–26

Plate, *salad, 8-inch diameter*	$ 12–16
Platter, *oval, 11¹/2-inch diameter*	$ 40–50
Platter, *oval, 13¹/2 inches*	$ 50–60
Sugar bowl	$ 25–35
Teapot	$ 100–125

"Willow"

This pattern is known to collectors as "Blue Willow," because it was usually made using a blue-and-white color scheme that depicted something resembling a weeping willow tree. This pattern has many, many variations and has been made by dozens of manufacturers around the world since the late 18th century. Typically, the "Willow" pattern features a prominent willow tree, an arched bridge over a body of water, pagoda-like buildings, a pair of birds that are usually called "doves," and Asian figures. These figures may be depicted on the bridge, near the bridge, or on the water in boats. "Willow" was loosely based on Chinese designs associated with the cities of Canton and Nanking, but it is truly the invention of English merchants and Staffordshire potters, who wanted to sell more dinnerware made in England. They invented this pattern for the sole purpose of misleading consumers into thinking the motifs were Chinese, and they told buyers a romantic legend that was supposedly from Chinese mythology. Supposedly, the "Willow" pattern told the story of two lovers fleeing from disapproving parents (the English merchants based this tale on *Romeo and Juliet,* knowing that it would strike a chord with consumers). As the two young lovers crossed the arched bridge in hopeless flight, they prayed to the gods to be united forever, and in response the gods turned them into a pair of doves who flew off above the heads of their parents, who were in pursuit. Despite the fact that this "legend" was a complete fabrication of the English merchants and potters, the pattern was so popular that it is still being made to this day.

Homer Laughlin started making a version of the "Willow" pattern in the 1920s, and initially the company decorated the pieces using a decal. These decals were usually small in size, and when a decal was placed on a piece of flatware, it was located in the center of the piece with a great deal of white space around the image. Around 1936, Laughlin started making its "Willow" pattern dinnerware in the more traditional manner, using transfer prints, which tended to cover most of the surface of the dinnerware items, including the edges, rims, and tops of handles. Homer Laughlin continued to make this pattern until about 1964.

It is important to keep in mind that a large number of companies in England, the United States, and Japan made "Willow"-style patterns, but the pieces made by Homer Laughlin will be marked with the company name and the word "Willow."

Homer Laughlin "Willow" pattern dinner plate, 10-inch diameter, $22–$30.
Item courtesy of Kingston Pike Antique Mall, Knoxville, Tennessee.

It should also be mentioned that Laughlin's "Willow" pieces came in both blue and white and pink and white color schemes, with both color schemes being valued at about the same price. Prices below are for the transfer-decorated pieces, but decaled examples are similarly priced.

Bowl, *cereal, 6-inch diameter*	$ 11–14
Bowl, *individual fruit, 5¹/₄ inches*	$ 5–8
Bowl, *soup, 8¹/₄-inch diameter*	$ 13–16
Bowl, *vegetable, oval, 9 inches*	$ 28–34
Bowl, *vegetable, round, 9-inch diameter*	$ 24–30
Casserole, *round*	$ 70–90
Creamer	$ 20–24
Cup and saucer	$ 16–20
Cup and saucer, *jumbo*	$ 60–75
Gravy boat	$ 50–60
Jug	$ 40–50

Plate, *bread and butter, 6^1/$_4$-inch diameter*	$ 5–8
Plate, *dinner, 10-inch diameter*	$ 22–30
Plate, *luncheon, 9^1/$_4$-inch diameter*	$ 8–11
Plate, *salad, 7^1/$_8$-inch diameter*	$ 6–9
Platter, *oval, 11 inches*	$ 30–35
Platter, *oval, 13 inches*	$ 50–60
Sugar bowl	$ 40–45

A. E. HULL POTTERY COMPANY

Mark commonly found on
pottery made by the *A. E.
Hull Pottery Company*.

Raised mark found on
some *A. E. Hull* pottery.

Addis Emmett Hull began his business life selling stoneware
pottery produced by his brother, J. J., and it did not take him
long to realize that there was a big demand for this product.
In 1901, he established his own pottery, the Globe Stoneware
Company, which quickly began producing a very fine grade
of stoneware. Hull sold his interest in Globe in 1905 and established the A. E. Hull Pottery Company, which was located on China Street in Crooksville, Ohio.

In 1907, Hull expanded by buying the Acme Pottery Company in Crooksville, which was primarily a manufacturer
of dinnerware that had been organized by J. J. Hull
and others in 1903. In the beginning, Hull produced
stoneware, dinnerware, kitchenware, and toilet wares, but
in the late 1930s the company began making the matte-finished, pastel-colored commercial art wares for which Hull
is now famous.

In June of 1950, a devastating flood hit Crooksville, and
water ran through the Hull pottery facility. When it hit the
hot kilns, the kilns exploded, the room ignited, and the old
plant was no more. Hull rebuilt and reopened early in 1952,
but the old glazes used on the art pottery could not be recreated with the new, more modern equipment. New commercial art pottery lines were introduced, many with high-gloss

glazes, but current collectors tend to prefer the matte-finished wares made before the 1950 disaster. Production at Hull finally ceased in 1985.

Art Wares

"Blossom Flite"

This line originated in 1955 and featured embossed flowers and leaves on a basketweave background in high-gloss pink, with blue latticework and metallic-green interior, or with black latticework and a charcoal-gray interior. Handles are textured, and some look like they might be covered in rattan. Just 15 different shapes were produced in this line.

Basket, *6 inches, T2*	$ 80–100
Basket, *low, 8 inches by 9 inches, T8*	$ 175–200
Bowl, *console, with ring handles, $16^{1}/_{2}$ inches by $6^{3}/_{4}$ inches, T10*	$ 150–175
Bowl, *4-sided, handled, 10 inches, T9*	$ 210–245
Candleholder, *with finger ring, T11, each*	$ 60–75
Cornucopia, *$10^{1}/_{2}$ inches, T6*	$ 125–150
Creamer, *T15*	$ 60–75
Honey jug, *6 inches, T1*	$ 80–100
Pitcher, *long spout, $8^{1}/_{2}$ inches, T3*	$ 125–150
Planter/Flower bowl, *handled, $10^{1}/_{2}$ inches, T12*	$ 135–160
Sugar bowl, *T16*	$ 60–75
Teapot, *T14*	$ 175–200
Vase, *basket, ruffled, $8^{1}/_{2}$ inches, T4*	$ 135–160
Vase, *handled, square pedestal, $10^{1}/_{2}$ inches, T7*	$ 125–150
Vase, *ewer-shaped, $13^{1}/_{2}$ inches, T13*	$ 200–225

"Bow-Knot"

This is considered one of Hull's most collectible lines. It was created in 1949, but the explosion of 1950 destroyed the molds. This matte-glazed line featured raised multicolored flowers and bows on a background of either pink and blue, blue, or turquoise and blue. "Bow-Knot" pieces were produced in 29 different shapes.

Basket, *$6^{1}/_{2}$ inches, B25*	$ 375–425
Basket, *$10^{1}/_{2}$ inches, B12*	$ 1,100–1,200

Hull vase, "Bow-Knot," B-9, 8 ½ inches,
$340–$375.
*Item courtesy of Richard Hatch and
Associates, Hendersonville, North Carolina.*

Hull wall pocket, "Bow-Knot" in the shape
of a whisk broom, B-27, 8 inches,
$375–$400.
*Item courtesy of Richard Hatch and
Associates, Hendersonville, North Carolina.*

Basket, *12¹/₂ inches, B29*	$ 2,500–2,750
Bell, *6¹/₂ inches, B7*	$ 325–375
Bell, *loop handle, 6 inches, B8*	$ 400–450
Bowl, *console, 13¹/₂ inches, B16*	$ 175–200
Candleholder, *cornucopia, B17, pair*	$ 325–350
Cornucopia, *7¹/₂ inches, B5*	$ 275–300
Cornucopia, *double, 13 inches, B13*	$ 425–475
Creamer, *B21*	$ 225–260
Ewer, *5¹/₂ inches, B1*	$ 250–300
Ewer, *13¹/₂ inches, B15*	$ 1,750–2,000
Flowerpot, *with attached saucer, B6*	$ 275–300
Jardinière, *with handles, 5³/₄ inches, B18*	$ 265–290
Jardinière, *with handles, 9³/₈ inches, B19*	$ 1,200–1,400
Sugar bowl, *B22*	$ 225–260
Teapot, *B20*	$ 650–750

Vase, *footed, 5 inches, B2*	$ 210–235
Vase, *6¹/₂ inches, B3*	$ 225–250
Vase, *6¹/₂ inches, B4*	$ 270–300
Vase, *8¹/₂ inches, B7*	$ 340–375
Vase, *8¹/₂ inches, B8*	$ 340–375
Vase, *8¹/₂ inches, B9*	$ 340–375
Vase, *10¹/₂ inches, B10*	$ 600–650
Vase, *10¹/₂ inches, B11*	$ 600–650
Vase, *12¹/₂ inches, B14*	$ 1,500–1,750
Wall plaque/plate, *10 inches, B28*	$ 1,500–1,750
Wall pocket, *cup and saucer, 6 inches, B24*	$ 315–340
Wall pocket, *sad iron, no mark*	$ 375–400
Wall pocket, *pitcher, B26*	$ 375–400
Wall pocket, *whisk broom, 8 inches, B27*	$ 375–400

"Butterfly"

Introduced in 1956, this line features embossed, pastel-colored butterflies and flowers, either on white with turquoise interiors or in a combination of matte and gloss white-on-white. "Butterfly" was produced in 25 different shapes. Collectors prefer the matte-glazed pieces to the glossy; for high-gloss examples, subtract 10 to 20 percent from the prices listed below.

Ashtray, *heart-shaped, B3*	$ 45–60
Basket, *8 inches, B13*	$ 175–200
Basket, *three handles, 10¹/₂ inches, B17*	$ 325–350
Bowl, *console, 3 feet, B21*	$ 150–175
Bowl, *fruit, pinched, 10¹/₂ inches by 4³/₄ inches, B16*	$ 125–150
Candleholder, *three feet, pair, B22*	$ 125–150
Candy dish, *bonbon, round, open, B4*	$ 45–60
Candy dish, *urn-shaped, square, open, B6*	$ 65–80
Cornucopia, *6¹/₂ inches, B2*	$ 50–65
Cornucopia, *10¹/₂ inches, B12*	$ 125–150
Creamer, *B19*	$ 95–110

Hull "Butterfly" basket, B17, 10½ inches,
$325–$350.
*Item courtesy of Richard H. Crane, Knoxville,
Tennessee.*

Hull "Butterfly" lavabo, 16 inches, original
hangers, B24/B25, $250–$300.
*Item courtesy of Richard H. Crane, Knoxville,
Tennessee.*

Flower dish, *rectangular, 9³/₄ inches by 6³/₄ inches, B7*	$ 75–95
Jardinière, *6 inches, B5*	$ 75–95
Lavabo, *two pieces, original hanger, B24/B25, 16 inches*	$ 250–300
Sugar bowl, *B20*	$ 90–100
Teapot, *B18*	$ 175–200
Vase, *bud, footed, pitcher-shaped, 6 inches, B1*	$ 65–80
Vase, *3 feet, 7 inches, B10*	$ 75–90
Vase, *3 feet, 9 inches, B9*	$ 75–90
Vase, *3 feet, 10¹/₂ inches, B14*	$ 110–125
Vase/Pitcher, *8³/₄ inches, B11*	$ 190–210
Vase/Pitcher, *13¹/₂ inches, B15*	$ 245–275
Window box, *12³/₄ inches by 4³/₄ inches, B8*	$ 75–95

"Calla Lily" (also known as "Jack-in-the-Pulpit")

Introduced in 1938, these pieces feature embossed flowers with green arrowhead-shaped leaves on various duo-toned, matte-glazed backgrounds. Color combinations include blue/pink, cinnamon/green, cinnamon/turquoise, rose/green, and rose/turquoise. Solid purple pieces are also known to have been produced, and these are the most valuable. For these purple pieces, add 10 percent to the prices listed below.

Bowl, *8 inches, #500-32*	$ 200–225
Bowl, *10 inches, #500-32*	$ 250–275
Bowl, *console, with handles, 13 inches, #590–33*	$ 225–260
Candleholder, *finger ring, #580-39, each*	$ 125–150
Cornucopia, *8 inches, #570-33*	$ 150–175
Ewer, *10 inches, #506*	$ 475–525
Flowerpot with attached saucer	$ 200–225
Jardinière, *7 inches, #591*	$ 375–425
Vase, *5 inches, #530-33*	$ 160–185
Vase, *6 inches, #500-33*	$ 165–185
Vase, *6 inches, #502-33*	$ 165–190
Vase, *6 inches, #503-33*	$ 165–190
Vase, *6 inches, #504-33*	$ 165–190
Vase, *6 inches, #505*	$ 165–190
Vase, *6 inches, #520-33*	$ 165–190
Vase, *6 inches, #540-33*	$ 160–185
Vase, *6¹/₂ inches, #501-33*	$ 175–200
Vase, *7 inches, #510-33*	$ 200–225
Vase, *7 inches, #530-33*	$ 200–225
Vase, *7¹/₂ inches, #550-33*	$ 200–225
Vase, *8 inches, #500-33*	$ 210–245
Vase, *8 inches, #520-33*	$ 225–250
Vase, *13 inches, #550-33*	$ 525–575

"Camellia" (also known as "Open Rose")

First produced around 1943, pieces in this matte-glazed line feature all-white or pink-and-blue backgrounds decorated with raised, hand-colored pink and/or yellow open roses. More than 40 different shapes were made in this line.

Basket, *6¹/₄ inches, #142*	$ 400–450
Basket, *8 inches, #107*	$ 375–425
Basket, *10 inches, #140*	$ 1,250–1,400
Basket, *hanging, 7 inches, #142*	$ 325–360
Bowl, *console, dove head handles, 12 inches, #116*	$ 425–465
Bowl, *low, 7 inches, #117*	$ 175–210
Candleholders, *dove-shaped, pair, 6¹/₂ inches, #117*	$ 450–500
Cornucopia, *8¹/₂ inches, #101*	$ 210–245
Cornucopia, *8¹/₂ inches, #141*	$ 250–300
Creamer, *5 inches, #111*	$ 140–165
Ewer, *4³/₄ inches, #128*	$ 125–145
Ewer, *7 inches, #105*	$ 300–325
Ewer, *8¹/₂ inches, #115*	$ 325–350
Ewer, *13¹/₄ inches*	$ 825–900
Jardinière, *ram's head handles, 8¹/₄ inches, #114*	$ 375–425
Planter, *mermaid with shell, 10¹/₂ inches, #104*	$ 2,500–3,000
Sugar bowl, *open, 5 inches, #112*	$ 140–165
Teapot, *8¹/₂ inches, #110*	$ 400–450
Vase, *4³/₄ inches, #127*	$ 90–110
Vase, *4³/₄ inches, #128*	$ 125–150
Vase, *4³/₄ inches, #130*	$ 110–130
Vase, *4³/₄ inches, #131*	$ 100–125
Vase, *6¹/₄ inches, #120*	$ 150–175
Vase, *6¹/₄ inches, #121*	$ 150–175
Vase, *6¹/₄ inches, #122*	$ 150–175
Vase, *6¹/₄ inches, #133*	$ 150–175
Vase, *6¹/₄ inches, #134*	$ 150–175
Vase, *6¹/₄ inches, #135*	$ 150–175
Vase, *6¹/₄ inches, #136*	$ 150–175
Vase, *6¹/₄ inches, #137*	$ 150–175
Vase, *6¹/₄ inches, #138*	$ 165–185

Vase, $6^1/2$ inches, swan, #118	$ 200–225
Vase, $6^1/2$ inches, #123	$ 165–185
Vase, 7 inches, bud, #129	$ 210–235
Vase, $8^1/2$ inches, #102	$ 250–275
Vase, $8^1/2$ inches, #103	$ 190–220
Vase, $8^1/2$ inches, #108	$ 250–275
Vase, $8^1/2$ inches, #119	$ 190–220
Vase, $8^1/2$ inches, hand, #126	$ 400–450
Vase, $8^1/2$ inches, #141	$ 200–235
Vase, $8^1/2$ inches, #143	$ 250–275
Vase, 12 inches, #124	$ 400–450
Vase, 12 inches, hurricane lamp, #139	$ 450–500
Wall pocket, $8^1/2$ inches, #129	$ 400–450

"Continental"

This line was introduced in 1959. It features sleek modern shapes with high-gloss glaze in shades of Evergreen, Persimmon, and Mountain Blue, decorated with vertical stripes.

Ashtray, 8 inches, A1	$ 50–65
Ashtray, 10 inches, C52	$ 60–75
Ashtray, 12 inches, rectangular, A3	$ 70–85
Ashtray, with pen, free-form, 10 inches, A20	$ 80–95
Basket, $12^3/4$ inches, C55	$ 220–245
Bowl, caladium leaf, 14 inches by $10^1/2$ inches, C63	$ 75–90
Bowl, consolette (bowl with candleholders at each end), $13^1/4$ inches, C70	$ 110–125
Candleholder/planter, footed, square, $4^1/2$ inches, C67	$ 40–50
Candy dish, $8^1/2$ inches, C62C	$ 100–125
Compote, footed/planter, $5^1/2$ inches by $6^3/4$ inches, C62	$ 65–75
Flower bowl, open, footed, square, $9^1/4$ inches, C69	$ 50–65
Flower dish, $15^1/2$ inches by $4^3/4$ inches, C51	$ 45–60
Planter, footed, rectangular, $8^1/2$ inches by $4^1/2$ inches, C51	$ 40–50

Vase, *8¹/₂ inches, C53*	$ 45–55
Vase, *bud, 9¹/₂ inches, C66*	$ 40–50
Vase, *rose, 9³/₄ inches, C28*	$ 45–55
Vase, *two-purpose (vase and candleholder), 10 inches, C61*	$ 75–90
Vase, *rose, 12 inches, C29*	$ 60–75
Vase, *free-form, 12¹/₂ inches, C54*	$ 75–95
Vase, *pitcher form, 12¹/₂ inches, C56*	$ 245–275
Vase, *13³/₄ inches, C58*	$ 90–110
Vase, *open front, 14¹/₂ inches, C57*	$ 110–125
Vase, *slender neck, 15 inches, C59*	$ 80–95
Vase, *pedestal, 15 inches, C60*	$ 80–95

"Dogwood" (also known as "Wild Rose")

This line was introduced in 1942. Pieces came with one of three matte-glaze backgrounds—blue and pink, turquoise and peach, or peach—and were decorated with embossed flower motifs that were hand-colored. Twenty-two different shapes were made.

Basket, *7¹/₂ inches, #501*	$ 400–450
Bowl, *console, cornucopia, 11¹/₂ inches, #511*	$ 395–445
Bowl, *low, 7 inches, #521*	$ 200–225
Candleholders, *cornucopia, 4 inches, #512, pair*	$ 300–350
Cornucopia, *4 inches, #522*	$ 130–145
Ewer, *4³/₄ inches, #520*	$ 165–190
Ewer, *8¹/₂ inches, #505*	$ 375–400
Ewer, *11¹/₂ inches, #506*	$ 650–725
Ewer, *13¹/₂ inches, #519*	$ 950–1,000
Jardinière, *4 inches, #514*	$ 150–175
Teapot, *6¹/₂ inches (beware: this piece without its lid is sometimes sold as a watering can), #507*	$ 600–700
Vase, *4³/₄ inches, #516*	$ 100–120
Vase, *4³/₄ inches, #517*	$ 100–120
Vase, *vessel is suspended between two side supports, 6¹/₂ inches, #502*	$ 350–400

Vase, $6^1/_2$ inches, #513	$ 170–185
Vase, $8^1/_2$ inches, #503	$ 165–190
Vase, $8^1/_2$ inches, #504	$ 165–190
Vase, $8^1/_2$ inches, #515	$ 90–110
Vase, $10^1/_2$ inches, #510	$ 375–425
Window box, rectangular, $10^1/_2$ inches, #508	$ 285–325

"Ebbtide"

First made in 1955, pieces in this line show marine themes of fish, seashells, snails, coral, aquatic plants, and mermaids. Pieces came with one of two glossy-glaze treatments: Shrimp (rose) and turquoise, or Wine and Seaweed (chartreuse). Only 16 shapes were produced.

Ashtray, with mermaid, E8	$ 175–200
Basket, $6^1/_2$ inches by $9^1/_8$ inches, E5	$ 175–200
Basket, $16^1/_2$ inches by $8^3/_4$ inches, E11	$ 250–300
Bowl, console, with snail, $15^3/_4$ inches by 9 inches, E12	$ 200–225
Candleholder, $2^1/_2$ inches, E13, pair	$ 75–100
Cornucopia, $7^1/_2$ inches, with mermaid, E3	$ 175–200
Cornucopia, $11^3/_4$ inches, E9	$ 150–175
Creamer, E15	$ 100–125
Sugar bowl, E16	$ 100–125
Teapot, E14	$ 275–325
Vase, bud, 7 inches, E1	$ 70–90
Vase, twin fish, 7 inches, E2	$ 100–125
Vase, angelfish, $9^1/_4$ inches, E6	$ 175–200
Vase, fish, 11 inches, E7	$ 135–150
Vase/Pitcher, $8^1/_4$ inches, E4	$ 175–200
Vase/Pitcher, 14 inches, E10	$ 270–300

"Iris" (also known as "Narcissus")

There is some disagreement as to when this line was introduced; some references say 1940, others say the mid-1940s. As with many other Hull lines, pieces in this line are decorated with embossed flowers; in this line, the hand-painted blossoms resemble irises. Pieces have matte backgrounds of either solid peach or duo-tones of blue/rose or rose/peach. Prices for all color treatments are comparable, but the solid-peach pieces are slightly less desirable to collectors.

Basket, *7 inches, #408*	$ 370–400
Bowl, *console, 12 inches, #409*	$ 375–400
Bowl, *rose, 4 inches, #412*	$ 125–150
Bowl, *rose, 7 inches, #412*	$ 215–235
Candleholders, *5 inches, #411, pair*	$ 300–325
Ewer, *5 inches, #401*	$ 150–175
Ewer, *8 inches, #401*	$ 350–375
Ewer, *13^1/$_2$ inches, #401*	$ 600–650
Jardinière, *5^1/$_2$ inches, #413*	$ 200–225
Jardinière, *9 inches, #413*	$ 575–600
Vase, *4^3/$_4$ inches, #402*	$ 125–150
Vase, *4^3/$_4$ inches, #403*	$ 125–150
Vase, *4^3/$_4$ inches, #404*	$ 125–150
Vase, *4^3/$_4$ inches, #405*	$ 125–150
Vase, *4^3/$_4$ inches, #406*	$ 125–150
Vase, *4^3/$_4$ inches, #407*	$ 145–170
Vase, *7 inches, #402*	$ 200–225
Vase, *7 inches, #403*	$ 225–250
Vase, *7 inches, #404*	$ 225–250
Vase, *7 inches, #405*	$ 225–250
Vase, *7 inches, #406*	$ 225–250
Vase, *7 inches, #407*	$ 225–250
Vase, *bud, 7^1/$_2$ inches, #410*	$ 200–225
Vase, *8^1/$_2$ inches, #402*	$ 235–265
Vase, *8^1/$_2$ inches, #403*	$ 235–265
Vase, *8^1/$_2$ inches, #404*	$ 235–265
Vase, *8^1/$_2$ inches, #405*	$ 235–265

Vase, 8^1/$_2$ inches, #406	$ 250–275
Vase, 8^1/$_2$ inches, #407	$ 250–275
Vase, 10^1/$_2$ inches, #403	$ 375–400
Vase, 10^1/$_2$ inches, #404	$ 375–400
Vase, 10^1/$_2$ inches, #405	$ 375–400
Vase, 10^1/$_2$ inches, #414	$ 375–400
Vase, 16 inches, #414	$ 650–750

"Magnolia" (Matte-Glazed)

Made only in 1946 and 1947, this pattern features raised magnolia blossoms on matte-glazed backgrounds in pastel colors of pink, blue, dusty rose (which sometimes has a brown tone), and yellow. Twenty-seven different shapes were produced.

Basket, 10^1/$_2$ inches, #10	$ 450–500
Bowl, console, 12^1/$_2$ inches, #26	$ 225–250
Candleholders, 4^1/$_2$ inches, #27, pair	$ 150–175
Cornucopia, 8^1/$_2$ inches, #19	$ 175–200
Cornucopia, double, 12^1/$_2$ inches, #6	$ 235–260
Creamer, #24	$ 80–95
Ewer, 4^3/$_4$ inches	$ 85–100
Ewer, 7 inches, #5	$ 220–235
Ewer, 13^1/$_2$ inches, #18	$ 425–475
Lamp base, 12^1/$_2$ inches	$ 475–525
Sugar bowl, open, #25	$ 80–100
Teapot, #23	$ 275–300
Vase, 4^3/$_4$ inches, #13	$ 70–85
Vase, 6^1/$_4$ inches, #4	$ 90–110
Vase, 6^1/$_4$ inches, #11	$ 90–110
Vase, 6^1/$_4$ inches, #12	$ 90–110
Vase, 6^1/$_4$ inches, #15	$ 90–110
Vase, 8^1/$_2$ inches, #1	$ 200–225
Vase, 8^1/$_2$ inches, #2	$ 200–225

Hull vase, "Magnolia Matte" #9, 10½ inches, $275–$300.
Item courtesy of Francis and Susie Nation, Old School Antique Mall, Sylva, North Carolina.

Vase, *8½ inches, #3*	$ 175–200
Vase, *8½ inches, #7*	$ 200–225
Vase, *10½ inches, #8*	$ 225–250
Vase, *10½ inches, #9*	$ 275–300
Vase, *with winged handles, 12¼ inches, #17*	$ 350–375
Vase, *12½ inches, #22*	$ 350–375
Vase, *with tassel, open handles, 12½ inches, #21*	$ 475–525
Vase, *with tassel, closed handles, 12½ inches, #21*	$ 450–500
Vase, *floor vase, 15 inches, #16*	$ 525–575
Vase, *floor vase, 15 inches, #20*	$ 525–575

"Magnolia" (High-Gloss Glaze)

This line, produced only from 1947 to 1948, is sometimes called "New Magnolia." The shapes in this line are the same as those in the matte-glazed "Magnolia" line, and the pattern depicts pink or blue magnolia blossoms with green leaves against a glossy pink background. Some pieces have gold trim; for this special embellishment, add 10 percent to the prices listed below.

Basket, *10¹/₂ inches, H14*	$ 450–500
Bowl, *console, 13 inches, H23*	$ 175–200
Candleholders, *4 inches, H24, pair*	$ 125–150
Cornucopia, *8¹/₂ inches, H10*	$ 145–165
Cornucopia, *double, 12 inches, H15*	$ 190–225
Creamer, *H21*	$ 65–75
Ewer, *8¹/₂ inches, H11*	$ 175–200
Ewer, *13¹/₂ inches, H19*	$ 500–550
Sugar bowl, *H22*	$ 65–75
Teapot, *H20*	$ 225–250
Vase, *5¹/₂ inches, H1*	$ 65–75
Vase, *5¹/₂ inches, H2*	$ 55–65
Vase, *ewer-shaped, 5¹/₂ inches, H3*	$ 80–90
Vase, *6¹/₂ inches, H4*	$ 65–75
Vase, *6¹/₂ inches, H5*	$ 65–75
Vase, *6¹/₂ inches, H6*	$ 95–105
Vase, *6¹/₂ inches, H7*	$ 65–75
Vase, *8¹/₂ inches, H8*	$ 145–165
Vase, *8¹/₂ inches, H9*	$ 150–175
Vase, *10¹/₂ inches, H12*	$ 185–210
Vase, *10¹/₂ inches, H13*	$ 185–210
Vase, *with winged handles, 12¹/₂ inches, H16*	$ 275–300
Vase, *with tassel, closed handles, 12¹/₂ inches, H17*	$ 300–350
Vase, *12¹/₂ inches, H18*	$ 275–350

"Mardi Gras" (also known as "Granada")

This line's name can be a bit confusing, because it was used twice on very dissimilar sets of wares. The name was first applied to solid-color bowls and vases produced around 1940. Made exclusively for F. W. Woolworth, these items featured either vertical ribs or smooth sides, and were decorated with high-gloss pastel colors. The other "Mardi Gras" line was often referred to as "Granada," and was a commercial art pottery line made both before and after the disastrous flood and fire of 1950. Also made exclusively for F. W. Woolworth, this was a matte-glazed line. Its pieces have either embossed florals or plain shapes molded in an Art Deco style that was not characteristic of the period in which the line was produced. On the pieces with embossed flowers, the flowers are not accented with color. These pieces were produced in pink and blue, peach and rose, or solid colors of white, pink, and yellow. On the commercial art wares, the name "Granada" was used interchangeably with the name "Mardi Gras."

High-Gloss Glaze

Bowl, *mixing, ribbed sides, 5¹/₄ inches*	$ 20–24
Bowl, *mixing, ribbed sides, 6¹/₄ inches*	$ 26–30
Bowl, *mixing, ribbed sides, 7¹/₄ inches*	$ 32–36
Bowl, *mixing, ribbed sides, 8¹/₄ inches*	$ 37–40
Bowl, *mixing, ribbed sides, 9¹/₄ inches*	$ 47–52
Bowl, *mixing, ribbed sides, 10¹/₄ inches*	$ 57–62
Jardinière, *ribbed sides, 6 inches*	$ 37–40
Jardinière, *ribbed sides, 7 inches*	$ 55–65
Jardinière, *ribbed sides, 8 inches*	$ 65–75
Pot, *Italian (ribbed-sided flowerpots), 6³/₄ inches*	$ 32–36
Pot, *Italian, 7¹/₂ inches*	$ 42–45
Pot, *Italian, 8¹/₂ inches*	$ 47–52
Pot, *Spanish (smooth-sided flowerpots with flared rims), 3¹/₄ inches*	$ 18–22
Pot, *Spanish, 4³/₄ inches*	$ 22–26
Pot, *Spanish, 6 inches*	$ 25–30
Pot, *Spanish, 7 inches*	$ 32–36
Pot, *Spanish, 8¹/₄ inches*	$ 40–45
Pot, *Spanish, 9¹/₂ inches*	$ 48–52
Vase, *ribbed sides, 6 inches*	$ 37–42
Vase, *ribbed sides, 8 inches*	$ 37–42
Vase, *ribbed sides, 10 inches*	$ 65–75

Matte Glaze

Basket, *8 inches, #32*	$ 225–250
Basket 8 inches, #65	$ 175–200
Basket, *8 inches, morning glories, #62*	$ 675–725
Ewer, *10 inches, #31*	$ 190–220
Ewer, *11 inches, morning glories, #63*	$ 675–725
Teapot, *#33*	$ 325–350
Vase, *9 inches, #47*	$ 85–90
Vase, *9 inches, #48*	$ 85–90
Vase, *9 inches, #49*	$ 75–85
Vase, *9 inches, #215*	$ 75–85
Vase, *9 inches, #216*	$ 75–85
Vase, *9 inches, #217*	$ 75–85
Vase, *9 inches, #218*	$ 75–85
Vase, *9 inches, #219*	$ 75–85

"Orchid"

First produced in either 1938 or 1939, pieces in this line feature embossed depictions of orchids on a matte-glazed ground of rose pink and ivory, blue and rose pink, or solid blue. There are just 17 shapes in this line, but many come in graduated sizes.

Basket, *7 inches, #305*	$ 900–1,000
Bookends, *7 inches, #316, pair*	$ 1,400–1,500
Bowl, *console, 13 inches, #314*	$ 450–500
Bowl, *low, 7 inches, #312*	$ 220–240
Candleholder, *4 inches, #315, pair*	$ 300–350
Ewer, *13 inches, #311*	$ 800–900
Jardinière, *4³/₄ inches, #317*	$ 175–200
Jardinière, *4³/₄ inches, #310*	$ 200–225
Jardinière, *6 inches, #310*	$ 275–300
Jardinière, *9¹/₂ inches, #310*	$ 535–600
Lamp base, *10 inches, no number*	$ 750–850

Hull candleholders, "Orchid," #315, 4 inches, pair,
$300–$350.
*Item courtesy of Bill Brooker, Old School Antique Mall,
Sylva, North Carolina.*

Vase, *4¹/₂ inches, #308*	$ 150–175
Vase, *4³/₄ inches, #301*	$ 150–175
Vase, *4³/₄ inches, #302*	$ 150–175
Vase, *4³/₄ inches, #303*	$ 150–175
Vase, *4³/₄ inches, #307*	$ 170–185
Vase, *6 inches, #301*	$ 185–210
Vase, *6 inches, #302*	$ 185–210
Vase, *6 inches, #303*	$ 165–180
Vase, *6 inches, #304*	$ 185–210
Vase, *6 inches, #308*	$ 185–210
Vase, *6¹/₂ inches, #307*	$ 190–220
Vase, *bud, 6³/₄ inches, #306*	$ 225–250
Vase, *8 inches, #301*	$ 350–400
Vase, *8 inches, #302*	$ 350–400
Vase, *8 inches, #303*	$ 325–350

Vase, *10 inches, #301*	$ 500–550
Vase, *10¹/₄ inches, #304*	$ 500–550
Vase, *10¹/₂ inches, #308*	$ 500–550

"Parchment and Pine"

Produced from either 1951 or 1952 to 1953, pieces in this line feature raised pinecone sprays on a glossy glaze. Pieces generally have a pearl-gray background with green and brown decoration. Cornucopias were made in both a left-facing version and a right-facing version.

Ashtray, *S14*	$ 200–225
Basket, *6 inches, S3*	$ 125–150
Basket, *16 inches, S8*	$ 250–300
Bowl, *console, 16 inches, S9*	$ 150–175
Candleholder, *2³/₄ inches, S10, pair*	$ 75–85
Coffeepot, *8 inches, S15*	$ 225–250
Cornucopia, *left/right, 8 inches, S2*	$ 75–90
Cornucopia, *left/right, 12 inches, S6*	$ 145–165
Creamer, *S12*	$ 50–60
Ewer, *13¹/₂ inches, S7*	$ 250–275
Planter, *window box, S5*	$ 110–135
Sugar bowl, *S13*	$ 50–60
Teapot, *S11*	$ 140–160
Vase, *6 inches, S1*	$ 75–85
Vase, *10 inches, S4*	$ 120–140

"Poppy"

First produced in 1943, "Poppy" pieces have embossed poppies, usually painted yellow and pink, on a variety of matte-glazed backgrounds, including backgrounds of solid-color cream and duo-tones of pink/blue and pink/cream.

Basket, *9 inches, #601*	$ 1,000–1,200
Basket, *12 inches, #601*	$ 1,800–2,000
Cornucopia, *8 inches, #604*	$ 475–525

Ewer, *4³/₄ inches, #610*	$ 200–225
Ewer, *13¹/₂ inches, #610*	$ 1,250–1,400
Jardinière, *4³/₄ inches, #608*	$ 145–170
Jardinière, *4³/₄ inches, #608*	$ 160–185
Planter/Bowl, *6¹/₂ inches, #602*	$ 275–310
Vase, *4³/₄ inches, #605*	$ 140–165
Vase, *4³/₄ inches, #606*	$ 140–165
Vase, *6¹/₂ inches, #605*	$ 200–240
Vase, *6¹/₂ inches, #606*	$ 200–240
Vase, *6¹/₂ inches, #607*	$ 200–240
Vase, *6¹/₂ inches, # 612*	$ 200–240
Vase, *8¹/₂ inches, #605*	$ 300–350
Vase, *8¹/₂ inches, #606*	$ 300–350
Vase, *8¹/₂ inches, #607*	$ 300–350
Vase, *10¹/₂ inches, #605*	$ 525–575
Vase, *10¹/₂ inches, #606*	$ 525–575
Wall pocket, *9 inches, #609*	$ 450–500

"Rosella"

This is an embossed wild-rose design introduced in 1946. The flowers themselves are generally painted either pink or white, with or without green painted leaves. The "Rosella" background color is high-gloss coral or high-gloss ivory.

Basket, *7 inches*	$ 375–425
Cornucopia, *left- or right-facing, 8¹/₂ inches, R13*	$ 175–200
Creamer, *5¹/₂ inches, R3*	$ 75–90
Ewer, *left- or right-facing, 6¹/₂ inches, R9*	$ 110–125
Ewer, *left- or right-facing, 7 inches, R11*	$ 190–220
Ewer, *9¹/₂ inches, R7*	$ 1,600–1,800
Lamp base, *11 inches, L3*	$ 500–550
Lamp base, *10³/₄ inches, dimpled surface, unmarked*	$ 1,200–1,350
Sugar, *open, 5¹/₂ inches, R4*	$ 75–90

Vase, 5 inches, R1	$ 100–120
Vase, 5 inches, R2	$ 100–120
Vase, 6^1/$_2$ inches, R5	$ 70–85
Vase, 6^1/$_2$ inches, R6	$ 70–85
Vase, 6^1/$_2$ inches, R7	$ 70–85
Vase, heart-shaped, 6^1/$_2$ inches, R8	$ 175–200
Vase, 8^1/$_2$ inches, R14	$ 175–200
Vase, 8^1/$_2$ inches, R15	$ 175–200
Wall pocket, heart-shaped, R10	$ 200–225

"Serenade"

First made in 1957, pieces in this line feature embossed birds on branches and came in three color schemes: Regency Blue with Sunshine Yellow interior, Shell Pink with Pearl Gray interior, or Jonquil Yellow with Willow Green interior. Some pieces have gold trim; for such pieces, add 10 percent to the prices listed below. Other pieces are a solid color with undecorated birds; for these pieces, subtract 25 percent from the prices listed below.

Ashtray, three-sided, 13 inches by 10^1/$_2$ inches, S23	$ 175–200
Basket, bonbon, 6^3/$_4$ inches, S5	$ 175–200
Basket, 12 inches by 11^1/$_2$ inches, S14	$ 550–600
Bowl, footed, fruit (banana boat), 11^1/$_2$ inches, S15	$ 200–225
Candlesticks, 6^1/$_2$ inches, S16, pair	$ 175–200
Candy dish, covered urn, 8^1/$_4$ inches, S3C	$ 200–225
Casserole, covered, 9 inches, S20	$ 175–200
Cornucopia, 11 inches, S10	$ 125–150
Creamer, S18	$ 110–130
Mug, 8-ounce, S22	$ 85–100
Pitcher, beverage, 1^1/$_2$-quart, S21	$ 275–300
Sugar bowl, S19	$ 110–130
Teapot, 6-cup, S17	$ 250–300
Urn, 5^3/$_4$ inches, S3	$ 75–90
Vase, 14 inches, S12	$ 200–225

Hull "Serenade" fruit bowl, S15, 7 inches, $200–$225.
Item courtesy of Richard H. Crane, Knoxville, Tennessee.

Vase, *bud, 6¹/₂ inches, S1*	$ 80–100
Vase, *flared, 8¹/₂ inches, S6*	$ 120–140
Vase, *pedestal, 8¹/₂ inches, S7*	$ 120–140
Vase, *pitcher, 6¹/₂ inches, S2*	$ 130–150
Vase, *pitcher, 8¹/₂ inches, S8*	$ 150–175
Vase, *pitcher, 13¹/₄ inches, S13*	$ 500–575
Vase, *Puritan hat, 5¹/₄ inches, S4*	$ 90–110
Vase, *rectangular, 10¹/₂ inches, S11*	$ 175–200
Window box, *12¹/₂ inches, S9*	$ 100–125

"Sunglow" (also known as "Pansy" or "Pansy and Butterfly")

This pattern consists of embossed flowers, though butterflies and bows are sometimes added to the basic decoration. There is significant disagreement as to when "Sunglow" was introduced; some sources say 1948, others 1952 (just after Hull reopened after the flood and explosion). This was a novelty line that also included vases and kitchenware. Colors are high-gloss, and are either pink on a yellow background or vice versa.

Basket, *6¹/₂ inches, #84*	$ 150–175
Bowl, *mixing, 5¹/₂ inches, #50*	$ 25–30
Bowl, *mixing, 7¹/₂ inches, #50*	$ 35–45
Bowl, *mixing, 9¹/₂ inches, #50*	$ 50–60
Casserole, *covered, 7¹/₂ inches, #51*	$ 90–110
Cornucopia, *7¹/₂ inches, #96*	$ 65–80
Drip jar, *5¹/₄ inches, #53*	$ 75–90
Ewer, *5¹/₂ inches, #90*	$ 50–60
Flowerpot, *5¹/₂ inches, #97*	$ 50–60
Flowerpot, *7¹/₂ inches, #98*	$ 60–70
Pitcher, *24-ounce, #52*	$ 70–85
Pitcher, *ice lip, 7¹/₂ inches, #55*	$ 200–225
Shakers, *2³/₄ inches, #54, pair*	$ 50–60
Vase, *5¹/₂ inches, #88*	$ 50–60
Vase, *5¹/₂ inches, #89*	$ 50–60
Vase, *6¹/₂ inches, #91*	$ 70–80
Vase, *6¹/₂ inches, #92*	$ 70–80
Vase, *6¹/₂ inches, #93*	$ 70–80
Vase, *6¹/₂ inches, #100*	$ 75–85
Vase, *8 inches, #94*	$ 100–110
Vase, *8¹/₂ inches, #95*	$ 100–110
Vase, *embossed flamingo, 8³/₄ inches, #85*	$ 80–95
Wall pocket, *cup and saucer, 6¹/₄ inches, #80*	$ 150–175
Wall pocket, *iron, unmarked, 6 inches, #83*	$ 190–220
Wall pocket, *pitcher, 5¹/₂ inches, #81*	$ 150–175
Wall pocket, *whisk broom, 8¹/₂ inches, #82*	$ 150–175

"Thistle"

This line was made in only four vase shapes. It originated in 1938, and pieces feature raised thistles on a matte-glazed background of blue, pink, or turquoise.

Vase, *6¹/₂ inches, #51*	$ 170–190
Vase, *6¹/₂ inches, #52*	$ 170–190
Vase, *6¹/₂ inches, #53*	$ 170–190
Vase, *6¹/₂ inches, #54*	$ 170–190

"Tokay" and "Tuscany"

Pieces in these two lines have the same embossed decoration of grapes and leaves (with twig-shaped handles on the pieces with handles). The difference between them is their color schemes, and the year in which they were introduced. Tokay originated in 1958, and its pieces feature pink grapes with green leaves on a cream background, with a light-green bottom and a Sweet Pink top, all in high-gloss glazes. "Tuscany" originated two years later, in 1960, and its pieces have either gray-green grapes on a Sweet Pink background, or forest green grapes on a Milk White background, also in glossy colors. Prices are the same for both "Tokay" and "Tuscany" pieces.

Basket, *8 inches, #6*	$ 100–120
Basket, *moon, 10¹/₂ inches, #11*	$ 175–200
Basket, *pedestaled, 12 inches, #15*	$ 325–375
Bowl, *flower, leaf shape, 14 inches by 10¹/₂ inches, #19*	$ 60–70
Candy dish, *covered, 8¹/₂ inches, #9C*	$ 175–200
Consolette, *15³/₄ inches (console bowl with candleholders at either end), #14*	$ 225–260
Cornucopia, *6¹/₂ inches, #1*	$ 70–85
Cornucopia, *11 inches, #10*	$ 90–110
Creamer, *#17*	$ 110–125
Planter, *5¹/₂ inches by 6¹/₂ inches, candy dish bottom, #9*	$ 60–70
Sugar bowl, *#18*	$ 110–125
Teapot, *6-cup, #16*	$ 225–250
Urn, *5¹/₂ inches, #5*	$ 70–80
Vase, *6 inches, #2*	$ 55–65
Vase, *8¹/₄ inches, #4*	$ 110–130
Vase, *10 inches, #8*	$ 130–150
Vase, *12 inches, #12*	$ 160–185
Vase, *ewer, 8 inches, #3*	$ 120–140

Vase, *ewer, 12 inches, #13*	$ 320–350
Vase, *ewer, 14 inches, #14*	$ 375–400

"Tropicana"

This line was made using "Continental" shapes, and was produced in 1959 and 1960. Pieces feature a white background with Tropical Green edges, and are decorated with stylized Caribbean figures. This is a very rare line.

Ashtray, *10 inches by 7^1/$_2$ inches, T52*	$ 450–500
Basket, *12^3/$_4$ inches, T55*	$ 900–1,000
Flower bowl, *15^1/$_3$ by 4^3/$_4$ inches, T51*	$ 450–500
Planter vase, *14^1/$_2$ inches, T57*	$ 850–950
Vase, *flat-sided, 8^1/$_2$ inches, T53*	$ 400–475
Vase, *slender, 12^1/$_2$ inches, T54*	$ 550–600
Vase/pitcher, *12^1/$_2$ inches, T56*	$ 700–800

"Tulip" (also known as "Sueno Tulip")

Pieces in this line have embossed tulips with matte-colored blue bases and pink, cream, or blue tops. "Tulip" was introduced in 1938.

Basket, *6 inches, #102-33*	$ 425–450
Flowerpot with saucer, *4^3/$_4$ inches, #116-33*	$ 175–200
Flowerpot with saucer, *6 inches*	$ 225–250
Jardinière, *5 inches, #117-30*	$ 170–200
Jardinière, *7 inches, #115-33*	$ 375–425
Vase, *suspended, 6 inches, #103-33*	$ 325–350
Vase, *bud, 6 inches, #104-33*	$ 160–185
Vase, *6 inches, #106-33*	$ 165–185
Vase, *6 inches, #107-33*	$ 175–200
Vase, *6 inches, #108-33*	$ 165–185
Vase, *6 inches, #110-33*	$ 170–195
Vase, *6 inches, #111-33*	$ 175–200
Vase, *6^1/$_2$ inches, #100-33*	$ 165–185
Vase, *6^1/$_2$ inches, #101-33*	$ 165–185

Vase, *6¹/₂ inches, #106-33*	$ 165–185
Vase, *8 inches, #100-33*	$ 225–250
Vase, *8 inches, #105-33*	$ 225–250
Vase, *8 inches, #107-33*	$ 225–250
Vase, *ewer, 8 inches, #109-33*	$ 350–425
Vase, *9 inches, #101-33*	$ 350–375
Vase, *10 inches, #100-33*	$ 325–350
Vase, *10 inches, #101-33*	$ 360–400
Vase, *ewer, 13 inches, #109-33*	$ 575–625

"Water Lily"

This matte-glazed line is decorated with embossed images of water lilies and a rippled-water effect. Introduced in 1948, the line was produced in two color schemes: Walnut Brown and Apricot with white flowers, or Turquoise and Sweet Pink with yellow flowers, the latter of which is more popular. For pieces trimmed in gold, add 10 percent to the prices listed below.

Basket, *10¹/₂ inches, L-4*	$ 475–525
Bowl, *console, 13¹/₂ inches, L-21*	$ 280–320
Candleholders, *4¹/₂ inches, L-22, pair*	$ 175–200
Cornucopia, *6¹/₂ inches, L-7*	$ 150–175
Cornucopia, *double, 12 inches, L-27*	$ 285–325
Creamer, *L-19*	$ 110–125
Ewer, *5¹/₂ inches, L-3*	$ 145–165
Ewer, *13¹/₂ inches, L-17*	$ 600–675
Flowerpot with saucer, *5¹/₂ inches, L-25*	$ 225–250
Jardinière, *5¹/₂ inches, L-23*	$ 175–200
Jardinière, *8¹/₂ inches, L-24*	$ 400–450
Lamp base, *7¹/₂ inches, not numbered*	$ 375–425
Sugar bowl, *L-20*	$ 115–130
Teapot, *L-18*	$ 280–320
Vase, *5¹/₂ inches, L-1*	$ 75–90
Vase, *5¹/₂ inches, L-2*	$ 75–90

Hull "Water Lily" vase, L-10, 9½ inches,
$250–$275.
*Item courtesy of Charles Seagrove and Don
Griffith, Old School Antique Mall, Sylva,
North Carolina.*

Vase, 6½ inches, L-4	$ 90–100
Vase, 6½ inches, L-5	$ 90–100
Vase, 6½ inches, L-6	$ 100–120
Vase, 8½ inches, L-A	$ 275–300
Vase, 8½ inches, L-8	$ 200–225
Vase, 8½ inches, L-9	$ 225–250
Vase, 9½ inches, L-10	$ 250–275
Vase, 9½ inches, L-11	$ 250–275
Vase, 10½ inches, L-12	$ 275–300
Vase, 10½ inches, L-13	$ 275–300
Vase, 12½ inches, L-15	$ 550–625
Vase, 12½ inches, L-16	$ 475–525

"Wildflower" (Numbered Series)

Pieces in this line feature embossed, hand-colored wildflower (trillium) sprays on a matte-glazed background of solid cream, or duo-tone shades of blue/pink,

pink/brown, or cream/blue with gold trim. The flowers themselves are painted yellow, pink, and white. This line originated in 1942. Its style numbers do not have a letter prefix, and because of this collectors refer to these early examples as "the numbered series." As a general rule, the later "Wildflower" pieces, which were introduced in 1942, are marked with a "W" plus a number.

Bowl, *console, 12 inches, #70*	$ 500–600
Candleholders, *double, 4 inches, #69, pair*	$ 400–450
Cornucopia, *6$^{1}/_{4}$ inches, #58*	$ 230–250
Creamer, *#73*	$ 300–350
Ewer, *13$^{1}/_{2}$ inches, #55*	$ 1,200–1,350
Jardinière, *4 inches, #64*	$ 175–200
Sugar bowl, *open, #74*	$ 300–350
Teapot, *#72*	$ 1,250–1400
Vase, *4$^{1}/_{2}$ inches, #56*	$ 200–250
Vase, *5$^{1}/_{4}$ inches, #52*	$ 200–250
Vase, *6$^{1}/_{4}$ inches, #54*	$ 235–260
Vase, *6$^{1}/_{4}$ inches, #60*	$ 235–260
Vase, *6$^{1}/_{4}$ inches, #61*	$ 235–260
Vase, *6$^{1}/_{4}$ inches, # 62*	$ 235–260
Vase, *8$^{1}/_{2}$ inches, #51*	$ 350–400
Vase, *8$^{1}/_{2}$ inches, #53*	$ 350–400
Vase, *8$^{1}/_{2}$ inches, #67*	$ 450–500
Vase, *8$^{1}/_{2}$ inches, #75*	$ 450–500
Vase, *8$^{1}/_{2}$ inches, butterfly handles, #76*	$ 450–500
Vase, *8$^{1}/_{2}$ inches, #78*	$ 375–425
Vase, *10$^{1}/_{2}$ inches, #59*	$ 350–400
Vase, *12 inches, #71*	$ 425–475

"Wildflower" (Regular Series)

Pieces in this line have embossed and hand-colored sprays of trillium, mission, and bluebell wildflowers, with matte-glazed backgrounds of either blue and pink or yellow and rose. The line was produced between 1946 and 1947.

Hull "Wildflower" vase, W6, 7½ inches,
$120–$140.
*Item courtesy of Richard Hatch and
Associates, Hendersonville, North Carolina.*

Basket, *10½ inches, W16*	$ 450–500
Bowl, *console, 12 inches, W21*	$ 250–300
Candleholders, *no mark, 2½ inches, pair*	$ 145–175
Cornucopia, *7½ inches, W7*	$ 110–135
Cornucopia, *8½ inches, W11*	$ 200–225
Ewer, *5½ inches, W2*	$ 150–175
Ewer, *8½ inches, W11*	$ 250–275
Ewer, *13½ inches, W19*	$ 550–600
Lamp base, *12½ inches, W17*	$ 325–360
Vase, *5½ inches, W1*	$ 75–95
Vase, *5½ inches, W3*	$ 75–95
Vase, *6½ inches, W4*	$ 95–110
Vase, *6½ inches, W5*	$ 95–110
Vase, *7½ inches, W6*	$ 120–140
Vase, *7½ inches, W8*	$ 110–130

Vase, $8^1/2$ inches, W9	$ 225–250
Vase, $9^1/2$ inches, W12	$ 250–280
Vase, $9^1/2$ inches, W13	$ 235–260
Vase, *fan,* $10^1/2$ inches, W15	$ 280–310
Vase, $12^1/2$ inches, W17	$ 325–360
Vase, $12^1/2$ inches, W18	$ 325–360
Vase, *floor,* 15 inches, W20	$ 525–575

"Woodland"

This line was first made at Hull in 1949 as a matte-glazed grouping, with embossed multicolored floral decoration that includes a pink flower with a yellow center and green leaves. This design appears on both sides of the pieces of pottery. Backgrounds were Harvest Yellow and green or Dawn Rose and peach. Solid-color pieces in glossy colors of white, ivory, or light pink also exist from this time period. "Woodland" was resurrected after the Hull fire of 1950, but the new matte glaze was far inferior to the old, and new pieces featured just one pink flower on one side, and leaves on the reverse. Glossy-glazed, two-toned "Woodland" pieces were introduced in 1953, and can be found in color combinations of pink and peach, chartreuse and rose, or blue and dark green.

Pre-1950 Matte "Woodland"

Basket, *hanging,* $5^1/2$ inches, W31	$ 325–360
Basket, *hanging,* $7^1/2$ inches, W12	$ 800–850
Basket, $8^1/4$ inches, W9	$ 300–325
Basket, $10^1/4$ inches, W22	$ 1,200–1,350
Bowl, *console,* 14 inches, W29	$ 500–575
Candleholders, $3^1/2$ inches, W30, *pair*	$ 350–400
Cornucopia, $5^1/2$ inches, W2	$ 120–140
Cornucopia, $6^1/4$ inches, W5	$ 120–140
Cornucopia, 11 inches, W10	$ 225–260
Cornucopia, *double,* 14 inches, W10	$ 750–800
Creamer, W27	$ 225–250
Ewer, $5^1/2$ inches, W27	$ 175–200
Ewer, $6^1/2$ inches, W6	$ 225–250

Ewer, $13^1/_2$ inches, W24	$ 1,200–1,300
Flowerpot with saucer, $5^3/_4$ inches, W11	$ 280–310
Jardinière, $5^1/_2$ inches, W7	$ 250–275
Jardinière, $9^1/_2$ inches, W21	$ 1,200–1,300
Sugar bowl, W28	$ 235–265
Teapot, W26	$ 575–625
Vase, $5^1/_2$ inches, W1	$ 125–150
Vase, $6^1/_2$ inches, W4	$ 135–165
Vase, $7^1/_2$ inches, W8	$ 180–200
Vase, $7^1/_2$ inches, suspended between two side supports, W17	$ 450–500
Vase, $8^1/_2$ inches, W16	$ 300–350
Vase, $8^1/_2$ inches, double bud vase, W15	$ 265–280
Vase, $10^1/_2$ inches, W18	$ 325–400
Vase, $12^1/_2$ inches, W25	$ 700–775
Wall pocket, shell, $7^1/_2$ inches, W13	$ 300–350
Window box, 10 inches, W14	$ 240–265
Window box, $10^1/_2$ inches, W19	$ 240–265

Post-1950 "Woodland" (Matte and Glossy)

Basket, $8^3/_4$ inches, W9	$ 200–225
Basket, $10^1/_2$ inches, W22	$ 300–330
Bowl, console, 14 inches, W29	$ 180–210
Candleholders, $3^1/_2$ inches, W30, pair	$ 110–125
Cornucopia, $5^1/_2$ inches, W2	$ 65–80
Cornucopia, 11 inches, W10	$ 120–145
Creamer, W27	$ 75–90
Ewer, $5^1/_2$ inches, W3	$ 85–100
Ewer, $6^1/_2$ inches, W6	$ 95–115
Ewer, $13^1/_2$ inches, W24	$ 335–375
Flowerpot with saucer, $5^3/_4$ inches, W11	$ 150–175
Jardinière, $5^1/_2$ inches, W7	$ 110–135

Hull "Woodland" console bowl, post-1950, W29, $180–$210.
Item courtesy of Kingston Pike Antique Mall, Knoxville, Tennessee.

Hull "Woodland" cornucopia, W10, 11 inches, post-1950, $120–$145.
Item courtesy of Kingston Pike Antique Mall, Knoxville, Tennessee.

Sugar bowl, *W28*	$ 75–90
Teapot, *W26*	$ 200–225
Vase, *6¹/₂ inches, W4*	$ 80–100
Vase, *8¹/₂ inches, W16*	$ 150–180
Vase, *double bud, 8¹/₂ inches, W15*	$ 150–175
Vase, *10¹/₂ inches, W18*	$ 180–200
Wall pocket, *shell, 7¹/₂ inches*	$ 185–210
Window box, *10 inches, W14*	$ 100–120

Kitchenware

"Cinderella"

This was a line of kitchenware, introduced in 1940, that came in two similar but distinct patterns. "Blossom" pieces feature a single large pink or yellow flower, while "Bouquet" pieces feature a grouping of three smaller flowers in shades of yellow, blue, and pink. Prices for the two patterns are comparable.

Baker, *7¹/₂ inches, #21*	$ 50–65
Baker, *with lug handles, 8¹/₂ inches, #21*	$ 60–75
Bowl, *mixing, 5¹/₂ inches, #20*	$ 40–55
Bowl, *mixing, 7¹/₂ inches, #20*	$ 60–75
Bowl, *mixing, 9¹/₂ inches, #20*	$ 80–95
Casserole, *baker with lid, 7¹/₂ inches, #21*	$ 70–85
Casserole, *baker with lid, lug handles, 8¹/₂ inches, #21*	$ 80–95
Creamer, *#28*	$ 75–90
Grease jar, *32-ounce, #29*	$ 75–90
Pitcher, *16-ounce, #29*	$ 75–90
Pitcher, *32-ounce, #29*	$ 95–110
Pitcher, *65-ounce, ice lip, #22*	$ 250–275
Shaker, *range top, #25, each*	$ 35–45
Sugar bowl, *#27*	$ 75–90
Teapot, *#26*	$ 225–250

"Crescent"

This line of kitchenware is distinguished by its crescent-shaped finials and by the handles on its pieces that resemble question marks. This is a duo-tone line, with handles and lids of pieces being a different solid color than the bodies. Bowls have one color on the exterior and another on the interior. "Crescent" was made from the mid- to late 1950s.

Bowl, *mixing, 5¹/₂ inches*	$ 18–22
Bowl, *mixing, 7¹/₂ inches*	$ 28–32
Bowl, *mixing, 9¹/₂ inches*	$ 38–42
Casserole, *lug handles, 10 inches*	$ 85–100
Cookie jar	$ 125–150
Creamer	$ 25–30
Mug, *12-ounce*	$ 25–32
Shakers, *pair*	$ 50–65
Sugar bowl	$ 25–30
Teapot, *6-cup*	$ 110–130

"Just Right"

This is a grouping of kitchenware introduced in the 1950s. Pieces in this line featured several patterns, including "Floral" (embossed yellow daisylike flowers with brown centers), "Vegetable" (an embossed pattern on solid colors of coral, green, and yellow), and "Blue Band" (horizontal bands in light and dark blue, used on mixing bowls).

Bowl, *cereal, 6 inches*	$ 65–80
Bowl, *mixing, 5 inches*	$ 20–25
Bowl, *mixing, 6 inches*	$ 30–40
Bowl, *mixing, 7 inches,*	$ 40–50
Bowl, *mixing, 8 inches*	$ 50–60
Bowl, *mixing, 9 inches, lipped*	$ 250–275
Bowl, *salad, serving, 10¹/₂ inches*	$ 85–100
Casserole, *covered, 7¹/₂ inches*	$ 260–280
Casserole, *French, covered, 5 inches*	$ 125–145
Cookie jar, *"Floral,"*	$ 175–225
Cookie jar, *"Vegetable," green*	$ 500–600
Grease jar, *5³/₄ inches*	$ 55–70
Jug, *1-quart*	$ 200–245
Salt and pepper shakers, *pair*	$ 50–65

"Little Red Riding Hood" (or "Red Riding Hood")

There is some controversy about this line. In the past these pieces have been credited to Hull, but many collectors now believe that most of the production was done by Regal China of Antioch, Illinois. It has been suggested that Hull made the ceramic bodies and that Regal added the decaled decoration. In any event, this line was designed by Louise Bauer, was first made in 1943, and was discontinued in 1957. Some pieces are extremely rare and valuable, but care should be taken because reproductions and look-alike pieces do exist.

Advertising plaque, *extremely rare,* *"Little Red Riding Hood Covered by Pat. Des. 135889"*	$ 14,000–18,000
Bank, *standing, 7 inches*	$ 900–1,000
Bank, *wall, slot in basket, 9 inches*	$ 2,750–3,000
Canister, *blank*	$ 750–850

Canister, *"Cereal"*	$ 1,200–1,400
Canister, *"Coffee"*	$ 800–900
Canister, *"Cookies" (unlike the other cookie jars, which feature a full-figured representation of Little Red Riding Hood, this piece resembles the canisters: the figure of Little Red Riding Hood as the lid, and a square base with the word "Cookies" printed neatly in block letters where such designations as "Flour," "Sugar," and "Peanuts" appear on the other canisters of this style)*	$ 6,500–7,500
Canister, *"Flour"*	$ 800–900
Canister, *"Peanuts"*	$ 6,500–7,500
Canister, *"Sugar"*	$ 800–900
Casserole, *11³/₄ inches, embossed figures of Little Red Riding Hood, the Big Bad Wolf, Grandma, and the Woodsman, stick handle, no lid*	$ 2,500–3,000
Cookie jar, *open-end basket (looks something like a taco), any number of floral decals, 13 inches*	$ 500–700
Cookie jar, *closed globular basket, with poinsettia decal*	$ 1,200–1,400
Cookie jar, *closed globular basket, with either gilt accents or floral decal*	$ 600–800
Cookie jar, *with globular "brick base" and Big Bad Wolf lid*	$ 1,200–1,400
Jar, *covered, 8¹/₂ inches*	$ 700–750
Jar, *covered, 9 inches*	$ 750–825
Jar, *spice, six jars to a set: "Allspice," "Cinnamon," "Cloves," "Ginger," "Nutmeg," "Pepper," each*	$ 800–900
Jar, *spice, set of six*	$ 5,250–6,000
Jar, *spice, "Cinnamon"*	$ 800–900
Mustard pot, *with spoon, 5¹/₄ inches*	$ 500–600
Pitcher, *7 inches*	$ 550–625
Pitcher, *8 inches*	$ 500–575
Shaker, *3¹/₄ inches*	$ 100–125
Shaker, *5¹/₄ inches*	$ 125–150
Teapot	$ 500–575

Hull "Little Red Riding Hood" cookie jar, open-ended basket, 13 inches, $500–$700. *Item courtesy of Richard H. Crane, Knoxville, Tennessee.*

"Nuline Bake-Serve"

This line of kitchenware was produced in solid glossy-glaze colors of blue, cream, maroon, pink, turquoise, and yellow. "Nuline Bake-Serve," which first appeared in 1937, was ovenproof and refrigerator safe. Pieces came in three different designs, each marked with a different prefix after the style number: "Diamond Quilt" is "B," "Drape and Panel" is "D," and "Fish Scale" is "C." The value of all three styles is comparable.

Bean pot, *covered, #20*	$ 75–90
Bowl, *mixing, 5-inch diameter, #1*	$ 35–45
Bowl, *mixing, 6-inch diameter, #1*	$ 40–50
Bowl, *mixing, 7-inch diameter, #1*	$ 45–55
Bowl, *mixing, 8-inch diameter, #1*	$ 50–60
Bowl, *mixing, 9-inch diameter, #1*	$ 55–65
Casserole, *covered, $7^{1}/_{2}$ inches, #13*	$ 75–90
Cookie jar, *8 inches, #20*	$ 225–275
Custard, *$2^{3}/_{4}$ inches, #14*	$ 18–22

Jug, *batter, 6 inches, #7*	$ 125–150
Jug, *tilt, ice lip, 7 inches, #29*	$ 125–150
Jug, *8¹/₂ inches, ice lip, 2-quart, #29*	$ 200–225
Mug, *3¹/₂ inches, #25*	$ 75–90
Teapot, *6-cup, #5*	$ 225–275

Novelties

Banks

Dinosaur, *7 inches, made for the Sinclair Oil Company, 1960s*	$ 1,400–1,600
Frog, *3³/₄ inches, 1940s, open mouth, unmarked*	$ 300–350
Owl, *3³/₄ inches, 1940s, unmarked*	$ 225–250
Pig, *bow, 14 inches, may be floral-decorated, circa 1940*	$ 225–260
Pig, *dime bank, 3¹/₂ inches, circa 1958*	$ 250–300
Pig, *"Corky Pig," nose has large cork with ring, 5 inches, pastel colors, circa 1958*	$ 175–195
Pig, *"Corky Pig," brown glaze with color accents, 5 inches, late*	$ 85–100
Pig, *"Corky Pig," jumbo-size, 8 inches, brown glaze with color accents, late*	$ 225–250
Pig, *sitting on haunches, 6 inches, brown*	$ 85–100

Figures

The "Swing Band" series consisted of five figures: "Accordion Player," "Band Leader," "Clarinet Player," "Drummer" (with "Swing Band" printed on his drum), and "Tuba Player." These pieces are matte ivory with hand-painted facial expressions and gold trim. They were produced circa 1940.

Cat with ball, *unmarked, 1¹/₂ inches*	$ 120–140
Cat with bow, *unmarked, 7 inches*	$ 400–450
Cats, *Siamese, two figures, 5³/₄ inches, #63*	$ 150–175
Colt, *5¹/₂ inches, unmarked*	$ 120–140
Dachshund, *6 inches by 14 inches,*	$ 250–275
Girl, *dancing, skirt holder, 7 inches, 1940s, #955*	$ 100–125

Rabbit, *unmarked, 5^1/$_2$ inches*	$ 45–55
Rooster, *7 inches, 1940s, #951*	$ 80–100
"Swing Band" series, *musicians, each*	$ 200–225

Planters

Baby, *5^1/$_2$ inches, #92*	$ 45–55
Baby shoes, *3^1/$_2$ inches, unmarked*	$ 145–170
Clown, *6^1/$_4$ inches, #82*	$ 80–100
Dog with ball of yarn, *5^1/$_2$ inches by 8 inches*	$ 45–55
Duck, *"Bandanna" (actually a kerchief), large, 7 inches by 9 inches, #74*	$ 125–150
Duck, *"Bandanna," 5 inches by 7 inches, medium, #75*	$ 80–100
Duck, *"Bandanna," small, 3^1/$_2$ inches by 3^1/$_2$ inches, #76*	$ 50–65
Duck, *flying, 9 inches by 10 ^{1}/$_2$ inches, #110*	$ 125–150
Geese, *two, 7^1/$_4$ inches, #95*	$ 90–110
Giraffe, *8 inches, #115*	$ 75–95
Girl, *in picture-frame hat standing beside basket, "Basket Girl," 8 inches, #954, matte finish*	$ 90–110
Girl, *in picture-frame hat standing beside basket, "Basket Girl," 8 inches, #954, glossy finish*	$ 50–65
Goose, *12^1/$_4$ inches, #411*	$ 85–110
Kitten, *in a hat, 6^1/$_4$ inches, #37*	$ 200–225
Kitten planter, *7^1/$_2$ inches, #61*	$ 50–65
Knight on horseback, *8 inches, #55*	$ 135–160
Lamb, *8 inches, #965*	$ 50–65
Leaf, *USA, 10^1/$_2$ inches*	$ 60–75
Madonna, *7 inches, F7*	$ 45–60
Parrot, *9^1/$_2$ inches by 6 inches, #60*	$ 75–90
Pheasant, *6 inches by 8 inches, #61*	$ 75–90
Pheasant, *standing behind flower-decorated box, gilt trim, 6 inches, #92*	$ 60–85
Pig, *5 inches, #60*	$ 50–65

Hull planter, figural woman in picture-frame hat, sometimes called "Basket Girl," 8 inches, glossy finish, $50–$65.
Item courtesy of Needful Things, Hendersonville, North Carolina.

Hull planter, figural, pheasant behind block with embossed flower, #92, 6 inches, $60–$85.
Item courtesy of Bill Brooker, Old School Antique Mall, Sylva, North Carolina.

Pig, *standing by wall, 6³/₄ inches by 8 inches, #86*	$ 45–55
Poodle, *8 inches, #114*	$ 75–95
Poodle, *bust, in hat, 6¹/₄ inches, #38*	$ 200–225
Praying hands, *6 inches, F475*	$ 35–45
St. Francis, *11 inches, #89*	$ 80–100
Swan, *8¹/₂ inches, #23*	$ 75–90
Swan, *double, 10¹/₂ inches, #81*	$ 75–90
Teddy bear, *with basket, 7 inches, #811*	$ 55–70

Dinnerware

"Mirror Brown"

This line of dinnerware was made from 1960 to 1985. Pieces feature a Mirror Brown glossy glaze with Ivory Foam edges.

Baker, *oval, 10 inches*	$ 22–28
Baker, *square, 9 inches*	$ 45–55
Bean pot, *2-quart*	$ 22–28
Bean pot, *individual, 12-ounce*	$ 15–20
Bowl, *individual fruit, $5^1/_2$-inch diameter*	$ 5–8
Bowl, *mixing, 6-inch diameter*	$ 15–20
Bowl, *mixing, 7-inch diameter*	$ 20–25
Bowl, *mixing, with pouring spout, 8 inches*	$ 15–20
Bowl, *salad, serving, 10-inch diameter*	$ 45–55
Bowl, *vegetable, oval, divided, $10^3/_4$ inches by $7^1/_4$ inches*	$ 12–15
Bowl, *vegetable, round, $8^1/_2$-inch diameter*	$ 22–28
Butter dish, *$^1/_4$-pound, covered*	$ 15–20
Casserole, *French, covered, 3-pint*	$ 55–65
Casserole, *oval*	$ 35–45
Casserole, *round, covered, 32-ounce*	$ 18–24
Chip and dip, *leaf-shaped*	$ 35–45
Coffeepot, *8-cup*	$ 35–45
Creamer	$ 8–10
Cup and saucer	$ 8–12
Jug, *5-pint*	$ 20–25
Jug, *2-quart*	$ 25–30
Gravy boat, *16-ounce*	$ 20–25
Mug, *coffee*	$ 5–8
Mug, *continental, 10-ounce*	$ 12–15
Mug, *soup, 11-ounce*	$ 8–12
Plate, *bread and butter, $6^3/_4$-inch diameter*	$ 5–8
Plate, *dinner, $10^1/_4$-inch diameter*	$ 14–18
Plate, *luncheon, $9^3/_8$-inch diameter*	$ 14–18
Platter, *oval, $11^3/_4$ inches*	$ 22–28
Platter, *oval, 14 inches, well and tree*	$ 32–40

Salt and pepper shakers, *cork top, set*	$ 10–15
Salt and pepper shakers, *mushroom-shaped, set*	$ 14–18
Sugar bowl	$ 14–18
Teapot, *5-cup*	$ 35–45

IROQUOIS CHINA COMPANY

IROQUOIS
CASUAL
CHINA
by
Russel
Wright

Mark used by the *Iroquois
China Company* on Russel
Wright–designed "Casual
China."

The Iroquois China Company was founded in Syracuse, New York, in 1905. In 1947, the company began manufacturing "Casual China," which was designed by Russel Wright. Prior to that, Iroquois had manufactured mainly commercial and hotel dinnerware. Collectors are also interested in the five lines designed for Iroquois in the 1950s by Ben Seibel. Of these lines, "Impromptu" and "Informal" are the easiest to find, "Inheritance" and "Intaglio" are somewhat more difficult, and "Interplay" is considered rare. Iroquois ceased production in 1969.

"Carrara Modern"

This line was introduced in 1955. Pieces have a modern-looking pattern distinguished by veins of color running through a white or dark-gray background. These pieces (particularly those with white backgrounds) were designed to resemble the famous Italian Carrara marble that was used to make some of the world's finest sculpture. Pieces came in three color schemes: gray with white veining, white with gold veining, and white with black veining. Although the dark-gray-and-white color scheme is very dramatic, white pieces with black veining are slightly more valuable than pieces featuring the other color schemes.

Bowl, *individual fruit, 6¹/₄-inch diameter*	$ 10–13
Bowl, *vegetable, oval, covered, divided*	$ 90–125
Bowl, *vegetable, round, 9¹/₈-inch diameter*	$ 20–35
Bowl, *vegetable, round, 10-inch diameter*	$ 20–35
Coffeepot, *with lock lid*	$ 70–85
Creamer	$ 22–30
Cup and saucer	$ 16–22
Gravy boat	$ 40–50
Gravy boat underliner	$ 12–15
Jug, *covered, 7¹/₂ inches high*	$ 55–65
Plate, *bread and butter, 6¹/₂-inch diameter*	$ 4–7
Plate, *chop, 1¹/₂-inch diameter*	$ 45–60
Plate, *dinner, 10-inch diameter*	$ 16–22
Plate, *luncheon, 9¹/₂-inch diameter*	$ 12–16
Plate, *salad, 7¹/₂-inch diameter*	$ 8–12
Platter, *well and tree*	$ 50–65
Salt and pepper shakers, *pair*	$ 25–32
Sugar bowl	$ 28–35

"Casual China"

"Casual China" was advertised as having the beauty of fine china, without the tendency to chip and craze that had plagued the earlier "American Modern" line (also designed by Russel Wright, but manufactured by Steubenville). Introduced in 1946, the line went through three distinct periods of development before it was discontinued in 1966. The first of these eras was characterized by pieces with heavier bodies than later items, and a very distinct speckled frothy-looking glaze. The line was expanded in 1949, and at this time the name was briefly changed to "Duraline Casual China," with an emphasis placed on the product's toughness and durability. The idea was that the consumer could use this china for baking and storage as well as for setting an elegant table, and if by some misadventure a piece happened to get broken, Iroquois offered to replace it. The third reinvention of "Casual China" began in the 1950s, when Wright tinkered with the designs and made some changes. One of the most noticeable of these changes was the disappearance of lids with pinch grips; these were replaced with knobs because customers were complaining that the pinch grips were hard to use. In the mid-1950s, floral decorations were very popu-

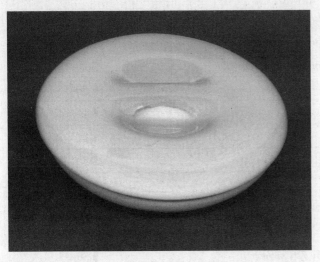

Iroquois China Company's "Casual China," casserole,
note pinch grip on the lid, Ice Blue, $50–$75.
Item courtesy of Jane Roney.

lar with American consumers, and Iroquois pressured Wright to add some decal decorations. He complied, and some pieces with decals were made in limited numbers, though as a general rule these pieces are not as popular with collectors as those with solid-color glazes.

Colors used in this line were Aqua, Avocado Yellow, Brick Red, Cantaloupe, Charcoal Grey, Ice Blue, Lemon Yellow, Lettuce Green, Mustard Gold, Nutmeg Brown, Oyster Gray, Parsley Green, Pink Sherbet, Ripe Apricot, and Sugar White. The rarest and most desirable of these colors are Aqua, Brick Red, and Cantaloupe, in that order.

Avocado Yellow, Ice Blue, Nutmeg Brown, Pink Sherbet, Ripe Apricot, and Sugar White

Sugar White items command prices at the highest end of the price ranges listed below.

Bowl, *cereal, 11^1/$_2$ ounce*	$ 12–28
Bowl, *individual fruit, 5^1/$_2$-inch diameter, old style*	$ 7–11
Bowl, *individual fruit, 5-inch diameter, restyled*	$ 10–17
Bowl, *individual soup, 5 inches, coupe shape*	$ 30–50

Bowl, *individual soup, with lid*	$ 75–110
Bowl, *vegetable, round, 8-inch diameter*	$ 30–40
Bowl, *vegetable, round, covered, pinch handle*	$ 50–75
Bowl, *vegetable, round, covered, knob handle*	$ 50–75
Butter dish, *covered, $^1/_2$-pound*	$ 100–175
Carafe	$ 225–325
Casserole, *2-quart, covered, pinch handle*	$ 50–75
Creamer, *stackable*	$ 15–22
Creamer, *redesigned*	$ 22–30
Cup and saucer	$ 9–15
Dish, *gumbo, $8^1/_4$ inches by $7^3/_4$ inches*	$ 30–43
Mug	$ 100–175
Gravy boat, *lid and underliner*	$ 85–130
Plate, *bread and butter, $6^1/_2$-inch diameter*	$ 4–10
Plate, *chop, 14-inch diameter*	$ 42–55
Plate, *dinner, 10-inch diameter*	$ 12–22
Plate, *luncheon, $9^1/_2$-inch diameter*	$ 11–20
Plate, *salad, $7^3/_8$-inch diameter*	$ 11–20
Platter, *oval, $12^3/_4$ inches*	$ 22–35
Platter, *oval, $14^1/_2$ inches*	$ 35–45
Salt and pepper shakers, *stackable, set*	$ 35–55
Sugar bowl, *stackable*	$ 15–22
Sugar bowl, *redesigned*	$ 24–32
Tidbit server, *two-tier*	$ 42–55
Tidbit server, *three-tier*	$ 50–60
Teapot, *old style*	$ 175–225

Charcoal Gray, Lemon Yellow, Lettuce Green, Oyster Gray, and Parsley Green

Bowl, *cereal, $11^1/_2$-ounce*	$ 20–28
Bowl, *individual fruit, $5^1/_2$-inch diameter, old style*	$ 20–28
Bowl, *individual fruit, 5-inch diameter, restyled*	$ 22–32

Bowl, *individual soup, deep, 5-inch diameter*	$ 45–60
Bowl, *vegetable, round, 8-inch diameter*	$ 40–75
Bowl, *vegetable, round, covered, divided, redesigned with knob*	$ 80–100
Butter dish, *original, $^1/_4$-pound, covered*	$ 200–225
Casserole, *covered, 2-quart, redesigned with knob*	$ 70–95
Creamer, *original*	$ 22–32
Creamer, *redesigned*	$ 35–45
Cup and saucer	$ 15–25
Dish, *gumbo, $8^1/_2$ inches by $7^1/_4$ inches*	$ 90–115
Gravy boat, *with lid, original*	$ 125–185
Gravy boat, *redesigned*	$ 500–650
Mill, *salt and pepper, set*	$ 1,000–1,200
Mug, *old style*	$ 225–250
Mug, *restyled*	$ 95–135
Pitcher, *$1^1/_2$-quart, lidded, original*	$ 165–235
Pitcher, *$1^1/_2$-quart, lidded, redesigned*	$ 550–700
Plate, *bread and butter, $6^1/_2$-inch diameter*	$ 8–14
Plate, *dinner, 10-inch diameter*	$ 24–35
Plate, *luncheon, $9^1/_2$-inch diameter*	$ 26–38
Plate, *salad, $7^1/_2$-inch diameter*	$ 20–27
Platter, *oval, $12^3/_4$ inches*	$ 35–55
Platter, *oval, $14^1/_2$ inches*	$ 70–95
Salt and pepper shakers, *original, stackable, set*	$ 45–60
Sugar bowl, *original, stackable*	$ 22–32
Sugar bowl, *redesigned*	$ 40–55

Aqua, Brick Red, and Cantaloupe

Aqua pieces (colored a rich turquoise) command prices at the top of the price ranges listed below, while Cantaloupe pieces command prices near the bottom. Most shapes with these colors are in the redesigned series.

Bowl, *individual fruit, 5-inch diameter*	$ 40–85
Bowl, *cereal*	$ 40–95

Bowl, *vegetable, round, 8-inch diameter*	$ 150–265
Butter, *covered, ¹/₄-pound*	$ 350–2,200
Creamer	$ 110–275
Cup and saucer	$ 35–100
Gravy boat and attached underliner	$ 275–375
Mug	$ 265–325
Pitcher	$ 1,600–2,750
Plate, *bread and butter, 6¹/₂-inch diameter*	$ 20–50
Plate, *dinner, 10-inch diameter*	$ 45–140
Plate, *salad, 7³/₈-inch diameter*	$ 25–75
Teapot	$ 1,400–2,250

"Impromptu"

Designed by Ben Seibel with clean modern lines, "Impromptu" was introduced in 1956. Pieces were decorated with a large number of different designs, including "Blue Doves" (two doves facing each other among foliage), "Aztec" (triangles around the edge in shades of gold and orange), "Blue Vineyard" (flowers and berries around the rim in blue), "Georgetown" (floral band in green and brown), "Jardinières" (1950s modern look with stylized hanging baskets of flowers in gray, coral, and pink), "Luau" (tropical flowers in red with mustard accents), and "Harvest Time" (three autumn leaves—one orange, one gray, and one yellow). Each "Impromptu" piece is marked with the line name, the name of the designer, and "Iroquois."

Bowl, *individual soup, 7¹/₄-inch diameter*	$ 14–20
Bowl, *vegetable, oval, 10 inches*	$ 14–20
Bowl, *vegetable, oval, divided*	$ 55–70
Bowl, *vegetable, round, covered*	$ 80–95
Butter dish, *¹/₄-pound, covered*	$ 35–45
Casserole, *2-quart*	$ 95–110
Coffeepot, *7-cup*	$ 55–70
Creamer	$ 14–20
Cup and saucer	$ 14–20
Gravy, *faststand*	$ 45–55

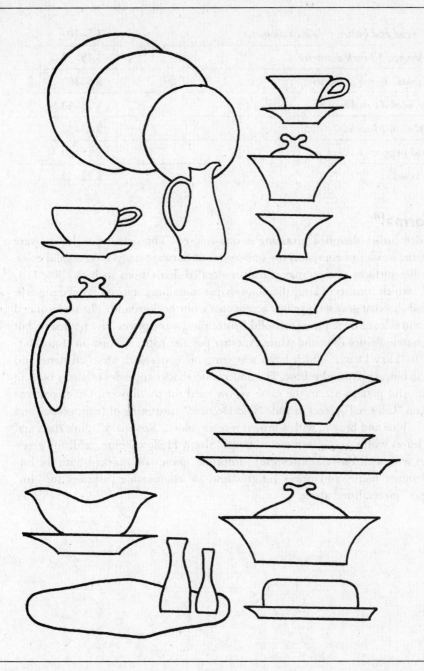

Shapes used in Iroquois China Company's "Impromptu" dinnerware line, designed by Ben Seibel.

Plate, *bread and butter, 6¹/₂-inch diameter*	$ 5–10
Plate, *dinner, 10-inch diameter*	$ 15–22
Plate, *salad, 8-inch diameter*	$ 5–10
Platter, *oval, 11 inches*	$ 33–40
Platter, *oval, 13 inches*	$ 25–32
Salt and pepper shakers, *set*	$ 15–20
Sugar bowl	$ 22–30

"Informal"

This Ben Seibel–designed grouping is duo-colored. The outsides of hollowware pieces, the insides of cups, and the undersides of flatware items have a solid color. The other surfaces of these pieces feature decaled decorations such as "Blue Diamond," which consists of large diamond shapes containing stylized floral designs in blue and charcoal gray with yellow accent on a white background. The undecorated backs and sides of these pieces are solid Bristol Blue; some pieces have no design, but are duo-tone Bristol Blue and white. Another popular pattern found on "Informal" pieces is "Lazy Daisy," which has a scattering of daisies with attached stems and leaves in blue, green, and yellow. The undecorated backs and sides of pieces bearing this cheerful pattern are in the same yellow used for the flowers. Other patterns found on "Informal" pieces include "Old Orchard" (scattering of fruit, grapes, and leaves in blue and brown, with a brown reverse color), "Rosemary" (pink roses and green leaves with a gray-green reverse), and "Sleepy Hollow" (blue, gold, and green flowers with a citron-yellow reverse). "Informal" pieces are marked with the line and designer name, and prices for this line are comparable to prices for "Impromptu" pieces, listed above.

JUGTOWN POTTERY

Typical mark found on *Jugtown* pottery.

"Jugtown" is not a complimentary name. During the Prohibition era, the name referred to a place where country potters made whiskey jugs—primarily for moonshiners. The Jugtown Pottery is located in Moore County, North Carolina, and was organized by Juliana and Jacques Busbee in about 1920 (though their interest in pottery dates to about 1915). The Busbees were fans of traditional North Carolina country pottery, which they felt was an art form in decline, and they wanted to help save it.

The Busbees set up a sales and training agency to encourage North Carolina artisans, and they established a tea room at 60 Washington Square in New York City to showcase and sell the pottery that was made in their home state. During this time, Juliana Busbee ran the tea room, while Jacques supervised the pottery operation back home. Jacques opened a shop at Jugtown in 1921, and in 1923 hired a potter named Ben Owen to help make the pottery's production schedule more dependable.

The products made at Jugtown fall into two basic categories. The first and most common category consists of country pottery: orangey redware with clear glaze, or gray stoneware with blue or white decoration. The second category consists of pieces with fairly simple shapes, covered with Chinese-style glazes in white, black, dark brown, Chi-

Jugtown bowl, red-and-blue Chinese glaze,
4³/₄-inch diameter, $800–$1,000.
*Item courtesy of Richard H. Crane, Knoxville,
Tennessee.*

Jugtown bowl, pushed-in sides, 9³/₄-inch
diameter, orange body with clear glaze,
$150–$200.
*Item courtesy of Needful Things,
Hendersonville, North Carolina.*

nese Blue (turquoise), and Frogskin (green). It is the Chinese-glaze pieces that are
currently most desired by collectors.

Jugtown pottery became very popular, and pieces continued to be made until 1958.
At that time, Ben Owen left to form his own pottery (though some Jugtown pieces
made before his departure are signed with his name). Jugtown was reopened in
1960, and is still in operation today.

Bowl, *3¹/₂ inches by 4³/₄ inches, Chinese-style red and blue glaze,* *exceptional coloration*	$ 800–1,000
Bowl, *9-inch diameter, Korean-style, red over blue glaze*	$ 1,000–1,200
Bowl, *9³/₄-inch diameter, pushed-in sides, orange with* *clear glaze*	$ 150–200
Bowl, *12 inches, Chinese Blue dripping red,* *exceptional coloration*	$ 2,000–2,200
Bowl, *17-inch diameter, two handles, orange with clear glaze*	$ 400–450
Bowl/vase, *8 inches, Chinese-style white glaze, Ben Owen*	$ 400–450
Candlestick, *11³/₄ inches, orange/red clay, flared base,* *candle cup in bowl*	$ 125–150

Jugtown chamberstick, 6½ inches, orange body with clear glaze, $175–$200.
Item courtesy of Tony McCormack, Sarasota, Florida.

Jugtown charger, 15-inch diameter, orange body with clear glaze, $350–$400.
Item courtesy of Needful Things, Hendersonville, North Carolina.

Jugtown jug, 4¾ inches, dark-gray body with green glaze, $150–$200.
Item courtesy of Richard H. Crane.

Jugtown jug, light-gray stoneware, 5 inches, $100–$125.
Item courtesy of Needful Things, Hendersonville, North Carolina.

Candlesticks, *12 inches, Chinese-style white glaze, flared base, candle cup in bowl, pair*	$ 1,000–1,100
Chamberstick, *6¹/₂ inches, orange with clear glaze*	$ 175–200
Charger, *15-inch diameter, orange/red, clear glaze*	$ 350–400
Figure, *chicken, 5 inches, brown glaze*	$ 225–250
Jug, *4³/₄ inches, green glaze over dark-gray body*	$ 150–200
Jug, *5 inches, light-gray stoneware*	$ 100–125
Vase, *4¹/₄ inches, Chinese-style white glaze*	$ 375–425

Jugtown vase, 4¼ inches tall, Chinese White glaze, $375–$425.
Item courtesy of Tony McCormack, Sarasota, Florida.

Vase, *5 inches, globular, blue with red highlights dripping over natural body color*	$ 500–600
Vase, *6 inches, egg-shaped, Chinese Blue glaze*	$ 650–725
Vase, *6¹/₂ inches, egg-shaped, Chinese-style white glaze*	$ 500–550
Vase, *8 inches, Chinese form with four small handles on shoulder, Frogskin glaze*	$ 750–850
Vase, *9 inches, Chinese Blue glaze, bulbous base to flaring neck*	$ 1,500–1,650
Vase, *10 inches, Chinese-style with two handles, globular body rising to wide neck, purple drip over red*	$ 4,500–5,000
Vase, *11 inches, Chinese-style with four handles around shoulder at neck, very unusual yellow-to-orange glaze*	$ 1,800–2,000

KENTON HILLS

TRADE MARK

The most common mark used by *Kenton Hills Porcelains.*

When the famous Rookwood Pottery of Cincinnati, Ohio, encountered financial difficulties in the 1930s, the company's superintendent, Harold Bopp, made some suggestions that he thought might save this beleaguered maker of American art pottery. But Bopp's suggestions were largely ignored, so he decided to start a new pottery with the aim of continuing Rookwood's tradition of artistic excellence.

Kenton Hills Porcelains opened in Erlanger, Kentucky, in 1940. The products made by this company closely resembled those made at Rookwood, and were of a very high quality. Sadly for Kenton Hills' business, World War II intervened, and in 1942 Harold Bopp left the company. A few more kiln loads of pottery were fired thereafter, but soon the factory closed, with the idea that the firm would reopen after the war was over. This never happened.

Bowl, *6 inches, 5-lobed, high-gloss green glaze, artist David Seyler*	$ 75–100
Bowl, *covered, 7 inches, high-gloss green glaze*	$ 250–300
Box, *covered, 6 inches by 3$^1/_2$ inches, high-gloss green glaze, embossed geometric designs*	$ 450–525

Figure, *lamb, 5 inches tall, modern, stylized, turquoise glaze, artist David Seyler*	$ 400–450
Figure, *head of a woman, 6¼ inches, artist David Seyler*	$ 750–800
Figure, *nude holding star, 10 inches, ivory glaze, artist Arthur Conant*	$ 600–700
Paperweight, *4½ inches, woman's head, goldstone glaze*	$ 225–275
Vase, *3½ inches, conical with flared lip, embossed leaves, artist Arthur Conant*	$ 250–300
Vase, *3½ inches, flaring conical form with embossed vertical leaves, green matte glaze, artist Arthur Conant*	$ 200–250
Vase, *6 inches, two small handles on shoulder, flaring neck, high-gloss green glaze, artist Arthur Conant*	$ 250–300
Vase, *6¼ inches, gourd form, painted with stylized florals, artist Charlotte Haupt*	$ 1,200–1,300
Vase, *6¾ inches, flaring conical form, matte pink glaze, embossed floral form, artist William Hentschel*	$ 350–400
Vase, *7 inches, bulbous form, Goldstone (or Late Tiger Eye) glaze*	$ 450–500
Vase, *7 inches, small foot, "U"-shaped bowl with slightly flaring lip, blue matte glaze*	$ 150–300
Vase, *7 inches, globular form, large stylized roses with leaves, artist William Hentschel*	$ 1,100–1,200
Vase, *12 inches, bold stylized florals, artist William Hentschel, drilled to be lamp base*	$ 1,600–1,750
Vase, *12½ inches, cylinder tapering at top to small mouth, painted with stylized tulips, artist William Hentschel, drilled to be lamp base*	$ 1,500–1,650
Vase, *12½ inches, bulbous body to long neck with flaring rim, painted with leaves and berries, artist William Hentschel*	$ 1,200–1,300

EDWIN M. KNOWLES CHINA COMPANY

EDWIN M. KNOWLES
CHINA CO.
MADE IN U.S.A.

One of the marks found on products made by the *Edwin M. Knowles China Company.*

Edwin M. Knowles was the son of Isaac W. Knowles, who founded Knowles, Taylor and Knowles of East Liverpool, Ohio. In 1900, Edwin M. Knowles announced that he was building a pottery plant in Chester, West Virginia, and by 1901 products from this factory were on the market. The company made semiporcelain ware, including toilet ware, dinnerware, and kitchenware. Business was good, and in 1913 a second facility was built in Newell, West Virginia. In 1931, the original plant in Chester was sold to Harker, but the operation in Newell continued until 1963.

"Esquire"

Introduced in 1956, this is another line designed by Russel Wright. However, unlike earlier Wright lines that were based on earth tones, "Esquire" pieces were pastel, and generally were decorated with spare patterns having both modernistic and Asian overtones. The designs themselves were stamped on underglaze, and the gilding (if there was gilding) was applied over glaze. Designs include "Antique White" (a matte-finished white with no decoration), "Fontaine" (tan with no decoration), "Mayfair" (undecorated blue, though one source identifies "Mayfair" as having a rose decal), "Botanica" (a floral design with stems on a wonderfully subtle tan/beige body), "Grass" (lines that suggest stylized blades of grass on blue), "Seeds" (seed pods on yellow), "Snow Flower" (bold stems and small flowers on pink), "Solar" (a sort of atomic symbol with a gilded star on white), and "Queen Anne's Lace" (an artistic representation of the Queen Anne's lace flower on a white background). Major retailers had trouble advertising "Esquire" because its decorations were so subtle that they often did not photograph well. "Esquire" pieces were also rather fragile and subject to damage, and the grouping did not lend itself to an open-stock arrangement, which meant that most of the dinnerware pieces were sold in sets. Due in part to each of these factors, "Esquire" was discontinued in 1962.

Bowl, *individual fruit, 5¹/₂ inches, "Queen Anne's Lace"*	$ 11–15
Bowl, *individual fruit, 5¹/₂ inches, "Seeds"*	$ 10–14
Bowl, *individual soup/cereal, 6¹/₄-inch diameter, "Queen Anne's Lace"*	$ 12–16
Bowl, *individual soup/cereal, 6¹/₄ inches, "Seeds"*	$ 14–18
Bowl, *serving, round, with lid, "Antique White"*	$ 165–200
Bowl, *vegetable, round, 9¹/₄ inches, "Seeds"*	$ 42–52
Bowl, *vegetable, round, 9¹/₄ inches, "Solar"*	$ 70–80
Bowl, *vegetable, oval, divided, 13¹/₄ inches, "Queen Anne's Lace"*	$ 85–100
Creamer, *"Seeds"*	$ 30–40
Cup and saucer, *"Grass"*	$ 22–26
Cup and saucer, *"Queen Anne's Lace"*	$ 16–22
Cup and saucer, *"Seeds"*	$ 20–25
Gravy boat, *6¹/₄ inches by 4¹/₄ inches, "Antique White"*	$ 110–135
Jug, *2-quart, "Antique White"*	$ 185–220
Jug, *2-quart, "Grass"*	$ 175–200
Jug, *2-quart, "Snowflower"*	$ 165–190
Plate, *bread and butter, 6¹/₄-inch diameter, "Grass"*	$ 7–10
Plate, *bread and butter, 6¹/₄-inch diameter, "Queen Anne's Lace"*	$ 4–7
Plate, *bread and butter, 6¹/₄ inches, "Seeds"*	$ 5–8
Plate, *dinner, 10¹/₄-inch diameter, "Queen Anne's Lace"*	$ 13–18
Plate, *dinner, 10¹/₄-inch diameter, "Seeds"*	$ 16–24
Plate, *salad, 8¹/₄-inch diameter, "Grass"*	$ 16–20

Plate, *salad, 8¹/₄-inch diameter,* "Queen Anne's Lace"	$ 10–15
Platter, *oval, 13 inches,* "Queen Anne's Lace"	$ 45–60
Platter, *oval, 13 inches,* "Seeds"	$ 42–52
Platter, *oval, 16 inches,* "Grass"	$ 70–85
Platter, *oval, 16 inches,* "Seeds"	$ 55–65
Salt and pepper shakers, *"Queen Anne's Lace," pair*	$ 80–100
Sugar bowl, *"Seeds"*	$ 40–50
Teapot, *"Antique White"*	$ 285–320
Teapot, *"Botanica"*	$ 325–360
Teapot, *"Seeds"*	$ 210–250
Teapot, *"Solar"*	$ 225–250

"Tia Juana"

This pattern is Edwin M. Knowles's entry into the world of Mexican-themed decals. It depicts a man sitting in the doorway of a hacienda with his back to a room, with colorful pots and hanging fruit on the wall behind him. Some pieces have red trim around the edges and a white background, while others have a cream background and no red rim. This decal is often found on the very popular "Deanna" shape.

Bowl, *cereal, coupe, 6¹/₄-inch diameter*	$ 18–25
Bow, *cereal, lug-handled, 7-inch diameter*	$ 16–22
Cup and saucer	$ 30–40
Cup and saucer, *demitasse*	$ 18–25
Plate, *bread and butter*	$ 9–12
Plate, *dinner, 10-inch diameter*	$ 25–32
Plate, *luncheon, 9-inch diameter*	$ 15–22
Plate, *salad, 7¹/₂-inch diameter*	$ 12–20
Platter, *oval, 15 inches*	$ 90–110

"Yorktown"

Introduced in 1936, the "Yorktown" line has an Art Deco flavor. All its shapes are round—there were no ovals used, even for the serving platters, which are usually oval-shaped in dinnerware sets. "Yorktown" pieces originally came with ivory bodies, but by mid-1936 solid colors had been added, including Cadet Blue, Russet, yellow, burgundy, orange/red, green, pink, and Chinese Red. Decals were added to the "Yorktown" line at about the same time as colors. Some of these decals include "Penthouse" (flowerpots on shelves), "Arbor" (trellis with rose clusters), "Bar Harbor" (sailboats), and "Surrey Village" (an English scene).

Bowl, *individual fruit, 6 inches*	$ 12–18
Bowl, *individual soup, coupe, 8-inch diameter*	$ 15–20
Bowl, *vegetable, round, 8-inch diameter*	$ 20–25
Bowl, *vegetable, round, 9-inch diameter*	$ 25–32
Bowl, *vegetable, round, covered*	$ 115–130
Butter, *open*	$ 30–38
Casserole	$ 35–45
Creamer	$ 25–35
Cup and saucer	$ 20–35
Gravy boat	$ 65–80
Plate, *bread and butter, 6^1/$_2$-inch diameter*	$ 10–14
Plate, *chop, 11^1/$_2$-inch diameter*	$ 55–70
Plate, *dinner, 10-inch diameter*	$ 15–25
Plate, *salad, 8-inch diameter*	$ 12–18
Platter, *13-inch diameter*	$ 30–40
Platter, *15-inch diameter*	$ 35–45
Sugar bowl	$ 42–52

KNOWLES, TAYLOR AND KNOWLES

K.T. & K.
S——V
IVORY.

One of the marks used on
Knowles, Taylor and Knowles
products, other than the
company's Belleek wares.

Mark commonly found on
Knowles, Taylor and Knowles
"Lotus Ware."

There is a rather romantic legend saying that, during the mid-19th century, Isaac Knowles and Isaac Harvey operated a boat up and down the Ohio and Mississippi Rivers selling supplies, including pottery and glass. Pottery sold so well that in 1854 the pair decided to open their own pottery-making facility to cash in on this lucrative trade. Knowles and Harvey established their pottery in East Liverpool, Ohio, where they initially made yellowware, adding Rockingham and other products as time progressed.

Harvey left at some time during the mid- to late 1860s, and in 1870 Isaac Knowles joined forces with his son-in-law, John N. Taylor, and his son, Homer S. Knowles, to form the firm of Knowles, Taylor and Knowles. The company added ironstone, hotel ware, and white graniteware to its lines. Around 1887 (though there is some disagreement about this date), Joshua Poole was brought over from David McBirney and Company, makers of Irish Belleek pottery, to teach the Knowles employees how to make fine Belleek porcelain. It is believed that production of a fine Belleek-like product began in 1888, but the Knowles, Taylor and Knowles Art China Works burned down in 1889.

Porcelain production resumed in either 1890 or 1891 (no one seems to be sure of the exact date), but the products made were not called "Belleek." Instead, Knowles called its

Knowles, Taylor and Knowles whiskey jug, "Meredith's Diamond Club Pure Rye Whiskey," $125–$150.
Item courtesy of Richard H. Crane, Knoxville, Tennessee.

products "Lotus Ware," and they were some of the finest American porcelains ever made. "Lotus Ware" was definitely an art china, meant purely for decoration, and it was exhibited at the Chicago World's Fair in 1893. Unfortunately, "Lotus Ware" production was very expensive, and economic conditions caused production to cease in about 1896 (though some sources say it was 1897).

"Lotus Ware" is generally marked with a circle, with a crown on top and the words "Lotus Ware" underneath. Inside the circle are the initials "K. T. K. Co.," plus a star and a crescent. For a time, Knowles, Taylor and Knowles was one of the largest makers of dinnerware in the United States, but in 1929 it merged with seven other companies to form the American China Corporation, which did not survive the beginning of the Great Depression.

Bowl, *"Lotus Ware," 5-inch diameter, scalloped edge, floral painting in French rococo-style cartouche, probably not factory-decorated*	$ 400–500
Dish, *shell-shaped, 8 inches wide, twig feet, floral decoration, gilt*	$ 500–650
Pitcher, *"Lotus Ware," 5¼ inches, triangular fishnet around base, painted floral decoration above*	$ 700–800

Rose bowl, *"Lotus Ware," 4 inches tall, scalloped beaded edge, raised blossom and branch decoration*	$ 450–550
Tea set, *consisting of teapot, creamer, and covered sugar bowl, fishnet design, white and undecorated*	$ 1,000–1,200

LENOX INC. AND
THE CERAMIC ART COMPANY

The wreath mark found on products made by the *Ceramic Art Company*.

Wreath mark used by *Lenox, Inc.*

Born in Trenton, New Jersey, in 1859, Walter Scott Lenox began his study of the art and science of pottery making at a very early age. While still in his twenties, Lenox became art director of Ott and Brewer, which was the first American company to manufacture Belleek china. In 1889, he and Jonathon Coxon, a fellow employee of Ott and Brewer, founded the Ceramic Art Company, which produced fine Belleek porcelain with very high-quality painted decoration.

It was Walter Lenox's dream to found an American china company that would rival the china companies of Europe, but he faced an uphill battle—American consumers wanted to buy fine European china, and thought any American product inferior. Moreover, production of this type of ware was very expensive, and required a highly skilled labor force. In fact, the company's prospects were so tenuous that Lenox and Coxon's financial backers insisted they build a three-story building that could be converted to tenement apartments if or when the china company failed.

Lenox bought Coxon out of the business in 1894, and continued to make Belleek-style china. Indeed, survival of the company depended almost exclusively on Lenox's tenacity: he was constantly forced to borrow money from friends to make the payroll, and to buy materials for his potters to turn into porcelain. Lenox was also having trouble with the quality of his porcelain; it was too fragile. Over the years, however, Lenox and his ceramists worked hard to produce an ivory-colored product that was as durable as it was beautiful.

The Ceramic Art Company was renamed "Lenox, Inc." in 1906, and the newly named company very quickly received a big break. Shreve and Company had placed a large order for dinnerware to be shipped to its new San Francisco, California, store, and the order arrived just in time for the store to experience the San Francisco earthquake and fire of 1906. When the Lenox china was dug out of the debris, however, the decoration was somewhat the worse for wear, but the dishes themselves were in pristine condition. This incident helped quell the popular notion that American porcelain—and specifically Lenox porcelain—was of inferior quality and not up to European standards.

Congress had long required that all items used in the White House be American-made if possible, but no American president had been able to find suitable American-made dinnerware. That changed in 1917, when President Woodrow Wilson ordered a 1,700-piece state service from Lenox. (It helped that Wilson had previously been the governor of New Jersey, and was thus familiar with the Lenox product.)

Lenox marked some of its wares "Belleek" until 1929, when David McBirney and Company won a lawsuit against the Morgan Belleek China Company. The ruling gave the Irish firm the sole right to use the word "Belleek," which ended use of the name both by Lenox and by all other American companies.

Lenox continued to make fine porcelain dinnerware for the White House, and sets were bought by Franklin Roosevelt, Harry S. Truman, and Ronald Reagan. Lenox also supplied wares to such prestigious companies as Tiffany & Co. and Marshall Field's, and the company maintains its position as America's premier maker of porcelain to this day.

> † *Prices below are retail prices from the secondary market, and do not in any way reflect Lenox factory prices on items that are still in production.*

Dinnerware

"Amethyst"
This pattern is on Lenox's "Cosmopolitan" shape and is platinum-trimmed.

Bowl, *cereal, 6¹/₈-inch diameter*	$ 45–55
Bowl, *individual fruit, 5³/₄-inch diameter*	$ 45–55

Bowl, *soup, 7³/₄-inch diameter*	$ 95–105
Bowl, *vegetable, oval, 9¹/₂ inches*	$ 165–175
Bowl, *vegetable, round, 9-inch diameter*	$ 175–185
Coffeepot, *5-cup*	$ 300–325
Creamer	$ 95–105
Cup and saucer	$ 45–55
Gravy boat and underliner	$ 240–260
Mug	$ 45–55
Plate, *bread and butter, 6¹/₂-inch diameter*	$ 22–30
Plate, *dinner, 10³/₄-inch diameter*	$ 50–60
Plate, *salad, 8¹/₄-inch diameter*	$ 30–40
Platter, *oval, 13 inches*	$ 175–185
Sugar bowl	$ 135–150
Tidbit server, *two-tier*	$ 95–105
Tidbit server, *three-tier*	$ 125–135

"Aristocrat"

This pattern is on Lenox's "Dimension" shape. Pieces feature a tooled gold band around their edges.

Bowl, *cream soup, and under plate*	$ 165–180
Bowl, *individual fruit, 5¹/₂-inch diameter*	$ 60–70
Bowl, *soup/cereal, 5¹/₂-inch diameter*	$ 75–85
Bowl, *vegetable, oval, 8¹/₂ inches*	$ 165–180
Bowl, *vegetable, oval, 10¹/₂ inches*	$ 185–200
Creamer	$ 110–120
Cup and saucer	$ 85–95
Cup and saucer, *demitasse*	$ 75–85
Gravy boat, *faststand*	$ 400–425
Plate, *bread and butter, 6¹/₂-inch diameter*	$ 35–45
Plate, *chop, 12-inch diameter*	$ 225–240
Plate, *dinner, 10³/₄-inch diameter*	$ 95–105

Plate, *salad, 8¹/₄-inch diameter*	$ 50–60
Platter, *oval, 14 inches*	$ 335–350
Platter, *oval, 16¹/₂ inches*	$ 360–375
Platter, *oval, 17¹/₄ inches*	$ 475–500
Sugar bowl	$ 135–145
Tidbit server, *two-tier*	$ 185–200
Tidbit server, *three-tier*	$ 225–240

"Ballad"

This pattern is on Lenox's "Coupe" shape and depicts a single red rose in the center with green leaves and platinum trim.

Bowl, *vegetable, oval, 9¹/₂ inches*	$ 190–210
Cup and saucer	$ 35–45
Gravy boat, *faststand*	$ 275–300
Plate, *bread and butter, 6¹/₂-inch diameter*	$ 25–35
Plate, *dinner, 10¹/₂-inch diameter*	$ 60–70
Plate, *salad, 7³/₄-inch diameter*	$ 35–45
Tidbit server, *two-tier*	$ 125–135
Tidbit server, *three-tier*	$ 160–175

"Belvedere"

This pattern is on Lenox's "Standard" shape. Pieces are decorated with a pink ribbon around the verge, with blue flowers, green leaves, and gold trim.

Bowl, *cream soup, and underliner*	$ 55–65
Bowl, *individual fruit, 5¹/₂-inch diameter*	$ 35–45
Bowl, *individual soup, 8¹/₂-inch diameter*	$ 55–65
Bowl, *vegetable, oval, 9¹/₂ inches*	$ 145–155
Bowl, *vegetable, round, covered*	$ 425–450
Coffeepot	$ 450–475
Creamer, *6-ounce*	$ 105–115
Creamer, *10-ounce*	$ 115–125
Cup and saucer	$ 35–45

Cup and saucer, *demitasse*	$ 55–65
Gravy boat, *faststand*	$ 190–215
Plate, *bread and butter, 6¼-inch diameter*	$ 15–20
Plate, *chop, 12-inch diameter*	$ 215–225
Plate, *dinner, 10½-inch diameter*	$ 35–45
Plate, *salad, 8½-inch diameter*	$ 20–25
Platter, *oval, 13½ inches*	$ 190–210
Platter, *oval, 16¼ inches*	$ 225–250
Sugar bowl	$ 115–125
Tidbit server, *two-tier*	$ 85–100
Tidbit server, *three-tier*	$ 105–120

"Blue Breeze"

This pattern is on Lenox's "Temperware" shape. Flatware pieces feature a profusion of blue flowers, stems, and leaves in their wells, plus a blue band around their rims.

Baker, *round, 6¾-inch diameter*	$ 75–85
Bowl, *cereal, 6⅛-inch diameter*	$ 35–45
Bowl, *individual fruit, 4¾-inch diameter*	$ 35–45
Casserole, *covered, round, 1¼-quart*	$ 95–105
Casserole, *covered, oval, 2½-quart*	$ 175–200
Coffeepot, *7-cup*	$ 115–125
Creamer	$ 22–28
Cup and saucer	$ 10–15
Gravy boat	$ 75–85
Mills, *pepper*	$ 65–75
Plate, *bread and butter, 6½-inch diameter*	$ 10–15
Plate, *dinner, 10½-inch diameter*	$ 30–40
Plate, *salad, 8-inch diameter*	$ 25–35
Pot, *fondue, open, 2-quart, without warmer base*	$ 70–80
Roaster, *oval, 15¼ inches*	$ 60–70
Sugar bowl	$ 35–45

Lenox "Blue Ridge" pattern dinnerware, coffeepot,
$375–$400; 10½-inch dinner plate, $32–$36.
*Item courtesy of Norma King and Kathy Crosby, Old School
Antique Mall, Sylva, North Carolina.*

"Blue Ridge"

This pattern is a blue floral design. Each flatware item has either a solid blue rim or
a rim decorated with a garland of blue laurel leaves and berries.

Bowl, *cereal, 7¹/₂-inch diameter*	$ 42–48
Bowl, *cream soup, with underliner*	$ 38–42
Bowl, *individual fruit, 5¹/₂-inch diameter*	$ 32–36
Bowl, *soup, rim, 8¹/₄-inch diameter*	$ 42–48
Bowl, *vegetable, oval, 9¹/₂ inches*	$ 85–95
Bowl, *vegetable, oval, 10 inches*	$ 135–145
Bowl, *vegetable, round, covered*	$ 315–325
Coffeepot	$ 375–400
Cup and saucer, *bouillon*	$ 52–56
Cup and saucer, *demitasse*	$ 28–32
Cup and saucer, *regular*	$ 32–36
Gravy boat, *faststand*	$ 145–155

Plate, *bread and butter, 6¹/₄-inch diameter*	$ 10–14
Plate, *chop, 12-inch diameter*	$ 155–165
Plate, *dinner, 10¹/₂-inch diameter*	$ 32–36
Plate, *luncheon, 9-inch diameter*	$ 38–45
Plate, *salad, 8¹/₄-inch diameter*	$ 18–22
Platter, *oval, 11 inches*	$ 115–125
Platter, *oval, 13¹/₂ inches*	$ 120–130
Platter, *oval, 15¹/₂ inches*	$ 195–210

"Blue Tree"

This pattern is on Lenox's "Standard" shape and has gold trim.

Bowl, *cereal, 7¹/₄-inch diameter*	$ 50–60
Bowl, *cream soup, and saucer*	$ 115–125
Bowl, *individual fruit, 5¹/₂-inch diameter*	$ 40–50
Bowl, *individual soup, 8¹/₄-inch diameter*	$ 55–65
Bowl, *vegetable, oval, 9¹/₂ inches*	$ 195–210
Bowl, *vegetable, round, covered*	$ 575–625
Cup and saucer	$ 35–45
Cup and saucer, *demitasse*	$ 45–55
Gravy boat, *faststand*	$ 250–265
Plate, *bread and butter, 6¹/₂-inch diameter*	$ 18–24
Plate, *dinner, 10¹/₂-inch diameter*	$ 45–55
Plate, *salad, 8¹/₄-inch diameter*	$ 35–45
Platter, *oval, 13¹/₂ inches*	$ 155–170
Platter, *oval, 16¹/₂ inches*	$ 225–250
Platter, *oval, 17¹/₄ inches*	$ 315–340
Snack set, *plate and cup*	$ 50–60
Sugar bowl	$ 115–125

"Brookdale"

This pattern is on Lenox's "Presidential" shape and has platinum trim.

Bowl, *vegetable, oval, 9³/₄ inches*	$ 190–210
Creamer	$ 95–105
Cup and saucer	$ 45–55
Cup and saucer, *demitasse*	$ 65–75
Plate, *bread and butter, 6¹/₂-inch diameter*	$ 20–30
Plate, *chop, 12-inch diameter*	$ 290–310
Plate, *dinner, 10¹/₂-inch diameter*	$ 50–60
Plate, *salad, 8¹/₂-inch diameter*	$ 35–45
Platter, *oval, 13¹/₂ inches*	$ 240–260
Platter, *oval, 16 inches*	$ 275–290
Sugar bowl	$ 115–125

"Buchanan"

This pattern is on Lenox's "Presidential" shape.

Bowl, *individual fruit, 5¹/₂-inch diameter*	$ 35–45
Bowl, *individual soup, 8¹/₄-inch diameter*	$ 65–75
Bowl, *vegetable, oval, 8¹/₂ inches*	$ 140–150
Bowl, *vegetable, round, 9¹/₂-inch diameter*	$ 155–170
Creamer	$ 95–105
Cup and saucer	$ 55–65
Cup and saucer, *demitasse*	$ 50–60
Gravy boat and underliner	$ 225–250
Plate, *bread and butter, 6¹/₂-inch diameter*	$ 20–28
Plate, *dinner, 10¹/₂-inch diameter*	$ 35–45
Plate, *salad, 8¹/₂-inch diameter*	$ 25–35
Platter, *oval, 13¹/₂ inches*	$ 195–210
Platter, *oval, 16 inches*	$ 275–290
Salt and pepper shakers, *set*	$ 75–85
Sugar bowl	$ 115–125

"Caribbee"

Pieces bearing this pattern feature ink rims, with a simple gold rope around the verge of the flatware items.

Bowl, *cream soup, with underliner*	$ 55–65
Bowl, *individual fruit, 5¹/₂-inch diameter*	$ 50–60
Bowl, *individual soup, 8¹/₂-inch diameter*	$ 95–105
Bowl, *vegetable, oval, 9¹/₂ inches*	$ 155–175
Creamer	$ 85–95
Cup and saucer	$ 30–40
Cup and saucer, *demitasse*	$ 40–50
Gravy boat, *faststand*	$ 195–225
Plate, *bread and butter, 6¹/₂-inch diameter*	$ 15–22
Plate, *chop, 12-inch diameter*	$ 195–220
Plate, *dinner, 10¹/₂-inch diameter*	$ 45–55
Plate, *luncheon, 9¹/₂-inch diameter*	$ 45–55
Plate, *salad, 8¹/₂-inch diameter*	$ 25–35
Platter, *oval, 13¹/₂ inches*	$ 195–225
Platter, *oval, 16 inches*	$ 250–275
Sugar bowl	$ 105–120

"Castle Garden"

This pattern is on Lenox's "Dimension" shape and has gold trim.

Bowl, *cereal/soup, 7¹/₂-inch diameter*	$ 70–80
Bowl, *cream soup, with underliner*	$ 80–90
Bowl, *individual fruit, 5¹/₂-inch diameter*	$ 45–55
Bowl, *vegetable, oval, 8¹/₂ inches*	$ 150–165
Bowl, *vegetable, round, 9¹/₄-inch diameter*	$ 145–155
Bowl, *vegetable, round, covered*	$ 340–360
Creamer	$ 115–125
Cup and saucer	$ 65–75
Gravy boat, *with underliner*	$ 235–250
Plate, *bread and butter, 6¹/₂-inch diameter*	$ 25–35

Plate, *chop, 12-inch diameter*	$ 295–325
Plate, *dinner, 10³/4-inch diameter*	$ 55–65
Plate, *salad, 8-inch diameter*	$ 35–45
Platter, *oval, 16¹/2 inches*	$ 295–325
Platter, *oval, 17¹/4 inches*	$ 345–375
Sugar bowl	$ 115–125
Teapot, *5-cup*	$ 295–325

"Cinderella"

This pattern is on Lenox's "Temple" shape and has gold trim.

Bowl, *cream soup, and underliner*	$ 75–85
Bowl, *individual fruit, 6¹/2-inch diameter*	$ 45–55
Bowl, *individual soup, 8¹/2-inch diameter*	$ 65–75
Bowl, *vegetable, oval, 9³/4 inches*	$ 195–225
Creamer	$ 135–150
Cup and saucer	$ 40–50
Cup and saucer, *demitasse*	$ 50–60
Gravy boat, *faststand*	$ 250–275
Plate, *dinner, 10⁷/8-inch diameter*	$ 45–55
Plate, *luncheon, 9¹/4-inch diameter*	$ 45–55
Plate, *salad, 8¹/2-inch diameter*	$ 30–40
Platter, *oval, 13³/4 inches*	$ 215–230
Platter, *oval, 15¹/2 inches*	$ 260–285
Platter, *oval, 17¹/4 inches*	$ 325–350
Sugar bowl	$ 165–180

"Fair Lady"

This extremely popular pattern is on Lenox's "Dimension" shape and has platinum trim.

Bowl, *individual fruit, 5¹/2-inch diameter*	$ 65–75
Bowl, *vegetable, oval, 8¹/2 inches*	$ 165–180
Bowl, *vegetable, oval, 10¹/4 inches*	$ 175–200

Bowl, *vegetable, round, 9¹/₄-inch diameter*	$ 195–220
Creamer	$ 100–110
Cup and saucer	$ 50–60
Gravy boat, *faststand*	$ 340–375
Plate, *bread and butter, 6¹/₂-inch diameter*	$ 20–30
Plate, *chop, 12-inch diameter*	$ 295–320
Plate, *dinner, 10³/₄-inch diameter*	$ 60–70
Plate, *salad, 8-inch diameter*	$ 40–50
Platter, *oval, 16¹/₂ inches*	$ 275–300
Sugar bowl	$ 115–125

"Golden Wreath"

This pattern features a wreath of gold leaves on a golden-yellow background.

Ashtray	$ 20–30
Bowl, *cream soup, with underliner*	$ 40–50
Bowl, *individual fruit, 5¹/₂-inch diameter*	$ 25–35
Bowl, *individual soup, 8¹/₄-inch diameter*	$ 50–60
Bowl, *vegetable, oval, 9¹/₂ inches*	$ 90–100
Bowl, *vegetable, round, 9¹/₂-inch diameter*	$ 180–200
Bowl, *vegetable, round, covered*	$ 325–350
Coffeepot	$ 265–300
Creamer	$ 75–85
Cup and saucer	$ 25–35
Cup and saucer, *demitasse*	$ 25–35
Cup and saucer, *bouillon*	$ 55–65
Gravy boat, *faststand*	$ 150–165
Plate, *bread and butter, 6¹/₄ inches*	$ 12–16
Plate, *chop, 12-inch diameter*	$ 145–165
Plate, *dinner, 10¹/₂-inch diameter*	$ 30–40
Plate, *luncheon, 9¹/₄-inch diameter*	$ 30–40
Plate, *salad, 8¹/₂-inch diameter*	$ 20–30

Platter, *oval, 13¹/₂ inches*	$ 125–140
Platter, *oval, 16 inches*	$ 165–180
Sugar bowl	$ 95–105
Teapot	$ 290–325

"Harvest"

This pattern is on Lenox's "Standard" shape and has gold trim.

Ashtray, *small*	$ 18–24
Ashtray, *large*	$ 40–50
Bowl, *cream soup, with underliner*	$ 30–40
Bowl, *individual fruit, 5¹/₂-inch diameter*	$ 25–35
Bowl, *individual soup, 8¹/₂-inch diameter*	$ 40–50
Bowl, *vegetable, oval, 9¹/₂ inches*	$ 95–110
Bowl, *vegetable, round, covered*	$ 325–350
Cigarette box	$ 55–65
Creamer	$ 90–100
Cup and saucer	$ 25–35
Gravy boat, *faststand*	$ 165–180
Plate, *bread and butter, 6¹/₄-inch diameter*	$ 10–15
Plate, *dinner, 10¹/₂-inch diameter*	$ 30–40
Plate, *luncheon, 9¹/₈-inch diameter*	$ 25–35
Plate, *salad, 8¹/₂-inch diameter*	$ 14–20
Platter, *oval, 13³/₄ inches*	$ 140–160
Platter, *oval, 16 inches*	$ 195–220
Platter, *oval, 17¹/₂ inches*	$ 225–250
Sugar bowl	$ 95–105
Teapot	$ 250–275

"Imperial"

This pattern is on Lenox's "Standard" shape.

Bowl, *cream soup, and underliner*	$ 45–55
Bowl, *individual fruit, 5¹/₂-inch diameter*	$ 30–40

Bowl, *individual soup, 8¹/₂-inch diameter*	$ 55–65
Bowl, *vegetable, oval, 8¹/₂ inches*	$ 135–150
Bowl, *vegetable, round, 9¹/₂-inch diameter*	$ 195–225
Bowl, *vegetable, round, covered*	$ 350–400
Cup and saucer	$ 30–40
Gravy boat, *faststand*	$ 195–225
Plate, *bread and butter, 6¹/₂-inch diameter*	$ 10–16
Plate, *chop, 12-inch diameter*	$ 150–165
Plate, *dinner, 10¹/₂-inch diameter*	$ 35–45
Plate, *salad, 8¹/₂-inch diameter*	$ 20–30
Platter, *oval, 13³/₄ inches*	$ 160–175
Platter, *oval, 16¹/₂ inches*	$ 195–225
Sugar bowl	$ 95–110

"Kingsley"

This pattern is on Lenox's "Standard" shape and has platinum trim.

Ashtray, *small*	$ 25–35
Ashtray, *large*	$ 35–45
Bowl, *cream soup, and underliner*	$ 65–75
Bowl, *individual fruit, 5¹/₂-inch diameter*	$ 35–45
Bowl, *individual soup, 8¹/₂-inch diameter*	$ 65–75
Bowl, *vegetable, oval, 9¹/₂ inches*	$ 135–150
Bowl, *vegetable, round, covered*	$ 450–475
Coffeepot	$ 395–425
Creamer	$ 85–95
Cup and saucer	$ 35–45
Cup and saucer, *demitasse*	$ 35–45
Gravy boat, *faststand*	$ 195–225
Plate, *bread and butter, 6¹/₂-inch diameter*	$ 20–30
Plate, *chop, 12-inch diameter*	$ 225–250

Plate, *dinner, 10^{1}/$_{2}$ inches*	$ 45–55
Plate, *luncheon, 9^{1}/$_{4}$ inches*	$ 45–55
Plate, *salad, 8^{1}/$_{2}$-inch diameter*	$ 30–45
Platter, *oval, 13^{3}/$_{4}$ inches*	$ 195–225
Platter, *oval, 15^{3}/$_{4}$ inches*	$ 250–280
Platter, *oval, 17^{1}/$_{2}$ inches*	$ 275–310
Shaker, *salt, and pepper mill, set*	$ 75–90
Sugar bowl	$ 115–125

"Lace Point"

This pattern is on Lenox's "Dimension" shape and has platinum trim.

Bowl, *cereal, 6^{1}/$_{4}$-inch diameter*	$ 55–65
Bowl, *individual fruit, 5^{1}/$_{2}$-inch diameter*	$ 55–65
Bowl, *individual soup, 7^{1}/$_{2}$-inch diameter*	$ 80–90
Bowl, *vegetable, oval, 8^{1}/$_{2}$ inches*	$ 115–130
Bowl, *vegetable, oval, 10^{1}/$_{4}$ inches*	$ 145–160
Bowl, *vegetable, round, 9^{1}/$_{4}$-inch diameter*	$ 240–265
Bowl, *vegetable, round, covered*	$ 575–600
Creamer	$ 115–130
Cup and saucer	$ 45–55
Gravy boat, *faststand*	$ 315–330
Mug	$ 45–55
Plate, *bread and butter, 6^{1}/$_{2}$-inch diameter*	$ 20–30
Plate, *dinner, 10^{3}/$_{4}$-inch diameter*	$ 45–55
Plate, *salad, 8^{1}/$_{4}$ inches*	$ 35–45
Platter, *oval, 13^{1}/$_{2}$ inches*	$ 180–210
Platter, *oval, 16^{1}/$_{2}$ inches*	$ 235–250
Sugar bowl	$ 115–130
Teapot	$ 325–350

"Lenox Rose"

This pattern is on Lenox's "Standard" shape and is trimmed in gold.

Ashtray, *4 inches*	$ 12–16
Bowl, *berry, 8³/₄-inch diameter*	$ 195–230
Bowl, *centerpiece, 6¹/₂ inches*	$ 275–300
Bowl, *cream soup, with underliner*	$ 50–60
Bowl, *individual fruit, 5¹/₂ inches*	$ 25–35
Bowl, *individual soup, 9¹/₈-inch diameter*	$ 55–65
Bowl, *vegetable, oval, 9¹/₂ inches*	$ 115–125
Cigarette box	$ 75–85
Coffeepot	$ 395–425
Compote	$ 105–115
Creamer	$ 75–85
Cup and saucer	$ 35–45
Cup and saucer, *bouillon*	$ 35–45
Cup and saucer, *demitasse*	$ 30–40
Gravy boat, *faststand*	$ 195–225
Dish, *ice cream, 6-inch diameter*	$ 45–55
Plate, *bread and butter, 6¹/₂-inch diameter*	$ 10–16
Plate, *chop, 12-inch diameter*	$ 145–165
Plate, *dinner, 10¹/₂-inch diameter*	$ 30–40
Plate, *luncheon, 9¹/₄-inch diameter*	$ 30–40
Plate, *salad, 8¹/₄-inch diameter*	$ 20–30
Plate, *snack, with cup*	$ 55–65
Platter, *oval, 13³/₄ inches*	$ 175–200
Platter, *oval, 15¹/₂ inches*	$ 195–225
Platter, *oval, 16¹/₂ inches*	$ 195–225
Sugar bowl	$ 85–100
Vase, *bud, 7³/₄ inches*	$ 115–125
Vase, *3 inches*	$ 75–85

Vase, *6 inches*	$ 85–95
Vase, *7 inches*	$ 105–120

"Memoir"
This pattern is on Lenox's "Dimension" shape and is trimmed in platinum.

Bowl, *cream soup, with underliner*	$ 100–125
Bowl, *vegetable, oval, 10¹/₄ inches*	$ 160–185
Cup and saucer	$ 45–55
Cup and saucer, *demitasse*	$ 85–95
Plate, *bread and butter, 6¹/₂-inch diameter*	$ 20–30
Plate, *dinner, 10³/₄-inch diameter*	$ 50–60
Plate, *salad, 8¹/₄-inch diameter*	$ 35–45
Platter, *oval, 14 inches*	$ 295–225
Platter, *oval, 16¹/₄ inches*	$ 275–300

"Ming" (also known as "Ming with Birds")
Lenox made several variations of the "Ming" pattern. This is the most elaborate, with a border with images of birds contained in cartouches. This pattern can be found on pieces with both a cream and a white background. Prices listed below are for examples with the more common cream background.

Bowl, *berry, 8¹/₂-inch diameter, handle*	$ 145–165
Bowl, *cereal, 6-inch diameter*	$ 30–40
Bowl, *cream soup, and underliner*	$ 35–45
Bowl, *individual fruit, 5¹/₂-inch diameter*	$ 15–25
Bowl, *individual soup, 8¹/₂-inch diameter*	$ 35–45
Bowl, *individual soup, large, 9-inch diameter*	$ 55–65
Bowl, *salad, serving, 9-inch diameter*	$ 195–225
Bowl, *vegetable, oval, 9¹/₂ inches*	$ 115–125
Bowl, *vegetable, round, covered*	$ 295–325
Butter dish, *covered, round*	$ 195–225
Butter tub	$ 115–125
Coffeepot, *after-dinner*	$ 195–225

Compote	$ 125–140
Creamer	$ 75–85
Cup and saucer	$ 35–45
Cup and saucer, *oversized*	$ 45–55
Cup and saucer, *bouillon*	$ 15–25
Cup and saucer, *chocolate*	$ 55–65
Cup and saucer, *demitasse*	$ 15–25
Dish, *bonbon, with lid*	$ 350–375
Egg cup, *double*	$ 30–40
Gravy boat, *faststand*	$ 145–160
Jar, *jam, covered*	$ 95–110
Jug, *16-ounce*	$ 105–120
Mayonnaise server with underliner	$ 75–90
Plate, *bread and butter, 6¹/₄-inch diameter*	$ 12–18
Plate, *chop, 12-inch diameter*	$ 115–125
Plate, *chop, large, 14-inch diameter*	$ 250–275
Plate, *dinner, 10-inch diameter*	$ 60–70
Plate, *luncheon, 9-inch diameter*	$ 20–30
Plate, *salad, 8¹/₂-inch diameter*	$ 20–30
Plate, *service or "place," 11¹/₄-inch diameter*	$ 65–75
Plate, *snack, with cup*	$ 40–50
Platter, *oval, 11 inches*	$ 115–125
Platter, *oval, 13¹/₂ inches*	$ 135–160
Platter, *oval, 15³/₄ inches*	$ 195–225
Ramekin with underliner	$ 55–65
Sherbet	$ 55–65
Sugar bowl	$ 65–75
Syrup, *lidded*	$ 95–110
Teapot	$ 265–290

"Morning Blossom"

This pattern is on Lenox's "Dimension" shape and has gold trim.

Bowl, *cereal, 6^1/$_8$-inch diameter*	$ 45–55
Bowl, *cream soup, with underliner*	$ 145–165
Bowl, *individual fruit, 5^1/$_4$-inch diameter*	$ 50–60
Bowl, *individual soup, 7^1/$_2$-inch diameter*	$ 75–85
Bowl, *vegetable, oval, 8^1/$_2$ inches*	$ 155–175
Bowl, *vegetable, oval, 10^1/$_4$ inches*	$ 195–225
Bowl, *vegetable, round, 9^1/$_2$-inch diameter*	$ 175–200
Bowl, *vegetable, round, covered*	$ 425–450
Cup and saucer	$ 55–65
Cup and saucer, *demitasse*	$ 95–105
Gravy boat, *faststand*	$ 260–280
Mug	$ 45–55
Plate, *bread and butter, 6^1/$_2$-inch diameter*	$ 25–35
Plate, *dinner, 10^3/$_4$-inch diameter*	$ 50–60
Plate, *luncheon, 9^1/$_2$-inch diameter*	$ 55–65
Plate, *salad, 8^1/$_4$-inch diameter*	$ 35–45
Platter, *oval, 14 inches*	$ 195–225
Platter, *oval, 16^1/$_2$ inches*	$ 295–325
Sugar bowl	$ 145–160
Teapot	$ 295–325

"Noblesse"

This pattern is on Lenox's "Presidential" shape and has gold trim.

Bowl, *cereal, 5^3/$_4$-inch diameter*	$ 65–75
Bowl, *cream soup, with underliner*	$ 150–165
Bowl, *individual fruit, 5^1/$_2$-inch diameter*	$ 65–75
Bowl, *individual soup, 8^1/$_2$-inch diameter*	$ 75–85
Bowl, *vegetable, oval, 9^1/$_2$ inches*	$ 210–230
Bowl, *vegetable, round, 9^1/$_2$-inch diameter*	$ 150–170

Bowl, *vegetable, round, covered*	$ 475–500
Coffeepot	$ 310–330
Cup and saucer	$ 50–60
Cup and saucer, *demitasse*	$ 85–100
Mug	$ 45–55
Plate, *bread and butter, 6¹/₂-inch diameter*	$ 20–30
Plate, *dinner, 10¹/₂-inch diameter*	$ 55–65
Plate, *salad, 8¹/₂-inch diameter*	$ 35–45
Platter, *oval, 13¹/₄ inches*	$ 165–180
Platter, *oval, 15¹/₂ inches*	$ 215–250
Sugar bowl	$ 135–150
Teapot	$ 350–400

"Orleans"

This pattern is on Lenox's "Sculpture" shape and has gold trim.

Ashtray, *small*	$ 25–35
Bowl, *cream soup, with underliner*	$ 115–125
Bowl, *individual fruit, 5¹/₂-inch diameter*	$ 45–55
Bowl, *individual soup, 7¹/₂-inch diameter*	$ 85–95
Bowl, *vegetable, oval, 9¹/₂ inches*	$ 135–150
Creamer	$ 60–70
Cup and saucer	$ 30–40
Cup and saucer, *demitasse*	$ 55–65
Gravy boat, *faststand*	$ 165–180
Plate, *bread and butter, 6¹/₂-inch diameter*	$ 15–22
Plate, *chop, 12-inch diameter*	$ 195–210
Plate, *dinner, 10¹/₂-inch diameter*	$ 45–55
Plate, *salad, 7³/₄ inches*	$ 20–30
Platter, *oval, 13¹/₂ inches*	$ 165–180
Platter, *oval, 16 inches*	$ 235–250
Sugar bowl	$ 50–60

"Pine"

This pattern is on Lenox's "Standard" shape and has gold trim.

Bowl, *cream soup, with underliner*	$ 65–75
Bowl, *individual fruit, 5$^{1}/_{2}$-inch diameter*	$ 30–40
Bowl, *individual soup, 8$^{1}/_{2}$-inch diameter*	$ 65–75
Bowl, *vegetable, oval, 9$^{1}/_{2}$ inches*	$ 145–160
Bowl, *vegetable, round, covered*	$ 425–450
Creamer	$ 95–105
Cup and saucer	$ 30–40
Gravy boat, *faststand*	$ 235–260
Plate, *bread and butter, 6$^{1}/_{2}$-inch diameter*	$ 12–18
Plate, *dinner, 10$^{1}/_{2}$-inch diameter*	$ 45–55
Plate, *luncheon, 9$^{1}/_{4}$-inch diameter*	$ 45–55
Plate, *salad, 8$^{1}/_{2}$-inch diameter*	$ 25–35
Platter, *oval, 13$^{1}/_{2}$ inches*	$ 195–225
Platter, *oval, 16$^{1}/_{4}$ inches*	$ 225–250
Platter, *oval, 17$^{1}/_{2}$ inches*	$ 250–275
Sugar bowl	$ 115–125

"Plum Blossoms"

This pattern is on Lenox's "Standard" shape and has platinum trim.

Bowl, *cream soup, with underliner*	$ 155–175
Bowl, *vegetable, oval, 9$^{1}/_{2}$ inches*	$ 165–180
Bowl, *vegetable, round, 9$^{1}/_{2}$-inch diameter*	$ 225–250
Creamer	$ 115–125
Cup and saucer	$ 30–40
Gravy boat, *faststand*	$ 325–350
Plate, *bread and butter, 6$^{1}/_{2}$-inch diameter*	$ 15–25
Plate, *dinner, 10$^{1}/_{2}$-inch diameter*	$ 35–45
Plate, *salad, 8$^{1}/_{2}$-inch diameter*	$ 30–40
Platter, *oval, 13$^{3}/_{4}$ inches*	$ 250–275

Platter, *oval, 16 inches*	$ 295–325
Sugar bowl	$ 95–110

"Rutledge"

This pattern is on Lenox's "Temple" shape and has gold trim.

Bowl, *cereal, 6-inch diameter*	$ 50–60
Bowl, *cream soup, and underliner*	$ 95–110
Bowl, *individual fruit, 6¹/₂-inch diameter*	$ 45–55
Bowl, *pasta or soup, 9¹/₄-inch diameter*	$ 45–55
Bowl, *vegetable, oval, 9¹/₂-inch diameter*	$ 135–150
Bowl, *vegetable, round, covered*	$ 365–395
Creamer	$ 85–100
Cup and saucer	$ 30–40
Cup and saucer, *demitasse*	$ 55–65
Cup and saucer, *oversized*	$ 55–65
Gravy boat, *faststand*	$ 235–250
Mug	$ 45–55
Plate, *bread and butter, 6¹/₂-inch diameter*	$ 15–25
Plate, *dinner, 10³/₄-inch diameter*	$ 40–50
Plate, *luncheon, 9¹/₄-inch diameter*	$ 35–45
Plate, *salad, 8¹/₂-inch diameter*	$ 25–35
Platter, *oval, 13¹/₂ inches*	$ 195–225
Platter, *oval, 16 inches*	$ 225–250
Platter, *oval, 17 inches*	$ 250–275
Sugar bowl	$ 90–105

"Snow Lily"

This pattern is on Lenox's "Dimension" shape and is trimmed in platinum.

Bowl, *cereal, 6¹/₄-inch diameter*	$ 45–55
Bowl, *individual fruit, 5¹/₂-inch diameter*	$ 45–55
Bowl, *individual salad, 5¹/₂-inch diameter*	$ 55–65
Bowl, *soup, 7¹/₂-inch diameter*	$ 65–75

Bowl, *vegetable, oval, 10¹/₄ inches*	$ 195–225
Bowl, *vegetable, round, 9¹/₄-inch diameter*	$ 145–160
Bowl, *vegetable, round, covered*	$ 375–400
Creamer	$ 45–55
Cup and saucer	$ 55–65
Gravy boat with underliner	$ 275–300
Mug	$ 45–55
Plate, *bread and butter, 6¹/₂ inches*	$ 25–35
Plate, *dinner, 10³/₄ inches*	$ 50–60
Plate, *salad, 8¹/₄-inch diameter*	$ 35–45
Platter, *oval, 14 inches*	$ 195–225
Platter, *oval, 16¹/₂ inches*	$ 275–300
Sugar bowl	$ 135–150
Teapot	$ 325–350

"Temple Blossom"

This pattern is on Lenox's "Temple" shape and has gold trim.

Bowl, *cream soup, with underliner*	$ 195–225
Bowl, *individual fruit, 6¹/₂-inch diameter*	$ 40–50
Bowl, *individual soup, 8¹/₂-inch diameter*	$ 95–110
Bowl, *vegetable, oval, 9³/₄ inches*	$ 125–145
Bowl, *vegetable, round, covered*	$ 325–350
Creamer	$ 75–85
Cup and saucer	$ 30–40
Cup and saucer, *demitasse*	$ 55–65
Gravy boat, *faststand*	$ 240–260
Plate, *bread and butter, 6¹/₂-inch diameter*	$ 12–18
Plate, *dinner, 10³/₄-inch diameter*	$ 45–45
Plate, *salad, 8¹/₂-inch diameter*	$ 30–40
Platter, *oval, 15³/₄ inches*	$ 165–180
Sugar bowl	$ 85–100

"Tuscany"

This pattern is on Lenox's "Dimension" shape and has gold trim.

Bowl, *cereal, 5^{1}/$_{2}$-inch diameter*	$ 95–110
Bowl, *cream soup, with underliner*	$ 135–150
Bowl, *individual fruit, 5^{1}/$_{2}$-inch diameter*	$ 40–50
Bowl, *individual soup, 7^{1}/$_{2}$-inch diameter*	$ 80–90
Bowl, *vegetable, oval, 8^{1}/$_{2}$ inches*	$ 115–125
Bowl, *vegetable, oval, 10^{1}/$_{4}$ inches*	$ 135–150
Bowl, *vegetable, round, covered*	$ 625–675
Creamer	$ 115–125
Cup and saucer	$ 45–55
Gravy boat, *faststand*	$ 275–300
Plate, *bread and butter, 6^{1}/$_{2}$-inch diameter*	$ 20–28
Plate, *chop, 12-inch diameter*	$ 250–275
Plate, *dinner, 10^{3}/$_{4}$-inch diameter*	$ 70–80
Plate, *luncheon, 9^{1}/$_{2}$-inch diameter*	$ 65–75
Plate, *salad, 8^{1}/$_{4}$-inch diameter*	$ 35–45
Platter, *oval, 14 inches*	$ 325–340
Platter, *oval, 16^{1}/$_{2}$ inches*	$ 250–275
Platter, *oval, 17^{1}/$_{2}$ inches*	$ 350–375
Sugar bowl	$ 125–145
Teapot	$ 375–400

"Versailles"

This pattern is on Lenox's "Dimension" shape and has gold trim.

Bowl, *cereal, 5^{1}/$_{2}$-inch diameter*	$ 75–85
Bowl, *cream soup, with underliner*	$ 145–160
Bowl, *individual fruit, 5^{1}/$_{2}$-inch diameter*	$ 60–70
Bowl, *individual soup, 7^{1}/$_{2}$-inch diameter*	$ 75–85
Bowl, *vegetable, oval, 10^{1}/$_{4}$ inches*	$ 195–225
Bowl, *vegetable, round, 9^{1}/$_{2}$-inch diameter*	$ 150–165

Coffeepot	$ 295–325
Creamer	$ 115–125
Cup and saucer	$ 60–70
Gravy boat and underliner	$ 215–235
Mug	$ 45–55
Plate, *bread and butter, 6^1/$_2$-inch diameter*	$ 25–35
Plate, *dinner, 10^3/$_4$-inch diameter*	$ 50–60
Plate, *salad, 8^1/$_4$-inch diameter*	$ 40–50
Platter, *oval, 16^1/$_2$ inches*	$ 210–230
Sugar bowl	$ 125–145

"Washington"

This Lenox pattern has a central rose decoration surrounded by a floral garland. The rims surrounding this central decoration were made in four different colors: pink, yellow, green, and blue. Prices listed below are for items with blue rims; reliable prices for the other colors are not available.

Bowl, *cream soup, with underliner*	$ 115–125
Bowl, *individual fruit, 5^1/$_2$-inch diameter*	$ 55–65
Bowl, *individual soup, 8^1/$_2$-inch diameter*	$ 75–85
Bowl, *salad, serving, 9-inch diameter*	$ 225–250
Creamer	$ 115–130
Cup and saucer	$ 65–75
Cup and saucer, *bouillon*	$ 45–55
Cup and saucer, *demitasse*	$ 55–65
Plate, *bread and butter, 6^1/$_2$-inch diameter*	$ 25–35
Plate, *dinner, 10^1/$_2$-inch diameter*	$ 65–75
Plate, *luncheon, 9-inch diameter*	$ 45–55
Plate, *salad, 8^1/$_2$-inch diameter*	$ 40–50
Plate, *snack, with cup*	$ 65–75
Sugar bowl	$ 135–150
Teapot	$ 340–365

"Westchester"

This pattern is on Lenox's "Presidential" shape and has a heavily encrusted and tooled gold band.

Bowl, *cereal, 5³/₄-inch diameter*	$ 75–85
Bowl, *cream soup, with underliner*	$ 175–200
Bowl, *individual fruit, 5¹/₂-inch diameter*	$ 75–85
Bowl, *individual soup, 8¹/₂-inch diameter*	$ 85–95
Bowl, *individual soup, oversized, 9-inch diameter*	$ 115–125
Bowl, *vegetable, oval, 9¹/₂ inches*	$ 150–165
Bowl, *vegetable, round, 9¹/₂-inch diameter*	$ 250–270
Bowl, *vegetable, round, covered*	$ 340–360
Coffeepot	$ 250–275
Creamer	$ 115–125
Cup and saucer	$ 65–75
Cup and saucer, *bouillon*	$ 95–110
Cup and saucer, *demitasse*	$ 95–110
Gravy boat, *faststand*	$ 295–325
Plate, *bread and butter, 6¹/₂-inch diameter*	$ 35–45
Plate, *dinner, 10¹/₂-inch diameter*	$ 75–85
Plate, *salad, 8¹/₂-inch diameter*	$ 50–60
Plate, *service (place), 12-inch diameter*	$ 115–125
Platter, *oval, 13³/₄ inches*	$ 140–160
Platter, *oval, 16 inches*	$ 275–300
Ramekin and saucer	$ 95–110
Sugar bowl	$ 125–140
Teapot	$ 250–275

"Westchester, Cobalt"

This pattern is the same as the one above, except there is a wide cobalt blue band beside the gold encrusted band.

Bowl, *cream soup, with underliner*	$ 135–150
Bowl, *individual fruit, 6¹/₄-inch diameter*	$ 80–90

Bowl, *individual soup, 9-inch diameter*	$ 115–125
Cup and saucer	$ 85–95
Cup and saucer, *bouillon*	$ 80–90
Cup and saucer, *demitasse*	$ 70–80
Plate, *bread and butter*	$ 45–55
Plate, *dinner, 10^1/$_2$-inch diameter*	$ 75–85
Plate, *luncheon, 8^3/$_4$ inches*	$ 75–85
Ramekin and saucer	$ 85–95

Art and Decorative Wares

Ceramic Art Company

Jug, *6 inches, globular body to short narrow neck, floral design around neck, amateur work, not factory-decorated*	$ 200–225
Mug, *4^1/$_2$ inches tall, gold band at top and bottom, central band of revelers in 18th-century costume, pink luster and enamel, artist-signed but not factory-decorated*	$ 300–375
Mug, *6 inches, amateur-decorated with painted poppies*	$ 175–225
Tea set, *partial, teapot, creamer, and covered sugar bowl, plus five cups and saucers, teapot is 10^1/$_4$ inches tall, lavishly painted with morning glories, artist-signed but not factory-decorated*	$ 1,250–1,400
Vase, *9^1/$_2$ inches tall, egg-shaped body with long neck and two elaborately pierced handles, decorated with gold flowers, leaves, and vines, factory-decorated*	$ 800–1,000
Vase, *10^1/$_4$ inches, twig handles, "stick vase," bulbous base to long slender neck, pink ground with gilt painted flowers*	$ 900–1,200
Vase, *10^1/$_2$ inches transitional mark between "C.A.C." and "Lenox," circa 1905, heavily gilded and enameled ground with reserve of bust of 18th-century woman in elaborately feathered hat, factory-decorated and signed by artist H. Nosek*	$ 3,500–4,000
Vase, *12 inches, ovoid shape to short narrow neck with flared lip, painting of birds on a branch, not factory-decorated*	$ 750–850
Vase, *transition mark between "C.A.C." and "Lenox," 14^1/$_2$ inches tall, lavishly painted roses by factory artist William Morley, some slight damage*	$ 3,000–3,500

Lenox Belleek vase, amateur-decorated with Geisha girl, 5
inches tall, $225–$250.
*Richard Hatch and Associates, Hendersonville, North
Carolina.*

Vase, *18¹/₄ inches, ovoid with long slender neck to flaring mouth,*
scrolled gilt handles, elaborately hand-painted with
chrysanthemums, probably not factory-decorated $ 1,200–1,500

Vase, *18³/₄ inches, bulging cylinder, painted with image of*
Native American chief with headdress $ 2,500–3,000

Lenox Belleek

Starting in 1906, Lenox Belleek pieces were marked with an "L" inside a circle, with
an artist's palette depicted above and to the left. This mark replaced the similar
"C.A.C." (Ceramic Arts Company) palette mark that was used until Lenox officially
changed its name. Lenox continued making wares marked "Belleek" until it was
forced to stop in 1929.

Dish, *11-inch diameter, ruffled raised rim, lily painting* $ 250–325

Mug, *6 inches, winter landscape painted by American artist*
Arthur J. E. Powell, exhibited at Salmagundi Club in
New York City $ 1,500–1,800

Powder jar, *covered, 3¹/₂ inches tall, hand-painted fans, Chinese lanterns, and flowers against a dark band, gold trim, not factory-decorated*	$ 250–300
Powder jar, *covered, 5 inches tall, hand-painted violets, gold trim, not factory-decorated*	$ 325–375
Tea set, *partial, tall teapot with creamer and covered sugar bowl, minimal decoration*	$ 300–400
Tea set, *partial, tall teapot, creamer, and covered sugar bowl, teapot is 10 inches tall, yellow ground with band of Dutch-style windmills around top, not factory-decorated*	$ 900–1,000
Tea set, *partial, globular teapot, creamer, covered sugar bowl, and six cups and saucers, silver overlaid with wreath design on pink ground*	$ 800–1,000
Vase, *cylindrical, 5 inches tall, Geisha decoration, amateur-decorated*	$ 225–250
Vase, *cylinder, 8¹/₄ inches tall, matte black glaze at top and bottom with gold band in center decorated with birds on flowering branch, artist-signed but not factory-decorated*	$ 300–350
Vase, *urn-shaped, 12 inches, two handles on shoulder, painted chrysanthemums by E. Orrison, dated 1912, not factory-decorated*	$ 750–900
Vase, *15 inches, narrow base widening to shoulder, then narrowing to short neck with flared lip, pinecone and pine needles decoration, not factory-decorated*	$ 800–1,000

Other Lenox Decorative Wares

Ashtray, *two cigarette rests, 8¹/₄-inch diameter, gold Shrine symbol in center, made for the 85th Imperial Council Session, Atlantic City, New Jersey, July, 1959*	$ 25–35
Bowl/vase, *"U"-shaped lip, Russian-Green exterior with cream-colored interior*	$ 50–65
Busts, *pair, male and female, 8³/₄ inches tall, cream glaze, green wreath mark*	$ 600–800
Cider set, *composed of tankard pitcher and ten mugs, hand-painted in factory by William Morley, apples and leaves, green wreath mark, circa 1930*	$ 1,500–2,000
Compote, *centerpiece, 12 inches long on dolphin base, bowl is scalloped, cream with gold trim*	$ 150–200

Lenox oversized cup and saucer,
fisherman, green mark, $65–$75.
*Item courtesy of Richard H. Crane, Knoxville,
Tennessee.*

Lenox demitasse cups and saucers,
porcelain liners with sterling silver holders
and saucers, in original box, $350–$400.
*Item courtesy of Richard H. Crane, Knoxville,
Tennessee.*

Cup and saucer, *fisherman, green mark*	$ 65–75
Cups and saucers, *six, demitasse, porcelain cups in sterling silver holders with sterling silver saucers, in original box*	$ 350–400
Dish, *swan-shaped, 5 inches long, pink porcelain, gold trim, green wreath mark*	$ 50–65
Dish, *leaf-shaped, green mark, pink and white, 9 inches*	$ 85–100
Figure, *ballerina, 6 inches, dancer in tutu, hand-painted with roses, green wreath mark*	$ 1,200–1,400
Figure, *"The Reader," 5¹/₂ inches tall, woman in rose-trimmed gown reading a book on lap, green wreath mark*	$ 1,000–1,200
Jug, *Toby, in the shape of William Penn, 6³/₄ inches, undecorated, circa 1930, green wreath mark*	$ 150–200
Jug, *Toby, in the shape of George Washington, 7¹/₂ inches high, enameled*	$ 500–600
Pitcher, *cornucopia-shaped, 6¹/₄ inches, cream-colored, green wreath mark*	$ 85–100

Lenox leaf-shaped dish, pink body with white handle, 9 inches, $85–$100.
Item courtesy of Charles Seagrove and Don Griffin, Old School Antique Mall, Sylva, North Carolina.

Lenox vase, green body with white swan handles, 10 inches tall, green mark, $250–$300.
Item courtesy of Richard H. Crane, Knoxville, Tennessee.

Limited-edition reproduction of the "Walter Scott Lenox" vase, white porcelain, 1989, $500–$600.
Item courtesy of Richard H. Crane, Knoxville, Tennessee.

Mark found on the limited-edition reproduction "Walter Scott Lenox" vase.

Plate, *limited edition, Boehm Birds, 1st edition, "Wood Thrush," circa 1970, 10-inch diameter*	$ 150–175
Plate, *oyster, 10¼ inches, cream-colored, leaf design, green wreath mark*	$ 125–150
Plates, *fish, set of 12, 9-inch diameter, each with a different fish painted in center, cobalt border with gilt enrichment, factory-painted by William Morley, superb work, made to be retailed by Bailey Banks & Biddle*	$ 7,000–8,000

Salt, *gold rim with rose-painted decoration, not factory-painted, green wreath mark*	$ 30–40
Tea set, *partial, consisting of teapot, five cups and saucers, creamer, sugar bowl, and hot water jug, from the "Architects' Tea Set," limited edition, circa 1933, set has sepia decoration of famous American buildings such as Mount Vernon and Faneuil Hall*	$ 650–800
Teapot, *9³/₄ inches, heavy sterling silver overlaid by Reed and Barton, underneath the silver the pot is cobalt blue, there is a reserve for a monogram that has not been used, some wear to silver at top of handle*	$ 850–1,000
Vase, *5¹/₂ inches, green ground with silver overlay in form of flowers and tendrils*	$ 250–300
Vase, *7¹/₄ inches tall, shaped somewhat like a jardinière, black band around rim with platinum trim, green wreath mark*	$ 85–100
Vase, *8¹/₂ inches tall, aorta-shaped, four branches, cream-colored*	$ 65–85
Vase, *10 inches tall, green body with white swan handles, green mark*	$ 250–300
Vase, *14¹/₂ inches tall, with two handles that extend above the rim of the mouth, decorated with pinecones and pine needles, dated 1918*	$ 1,600–1,800

LIMOGES CHINA COMPANY

One of the marks used on products made by the *Limoges China Company of Sebring, Ohio.*

This was the fourth pottery plant owned by the Sebring family of Sebring, Ohio. The company was originally envisioned as a maker of fine china, and was originally called the "Sterling China Company." Construction of the plant began in 1902, and actual production began in late 1902 or early 1903, but by mid-1904 the family had discovered that production of fine porcelain dinnerware was not profitable. In June of 1904, the name of the company was changed to "Limoges China Company," and it produced semiporcelain dinnerware, with kitchenwares added to its repertoire in the 1930s. At that time, the company began using the name "American Limoges" in its advertising, and this became the company's official name after it was sued by the makers of French Limoges china in approximately 1949. The company went out of business in 1955.

"Casino"

Designed by Victor Schreckengost and introduced in 1954, this is a very small line that used playing-card themes for decorations. The cup, creamer, and sugar bowl feature fan and axe designs, which may not seem to be in keeping with this theme, but which are actually the items held by the Queen and King of Hearts as they are traditionally pictured on playing cards. Examples from this line are generally marked "Casino by American Limoges."

Ashtray, *diamond*	$ 40–50
Creamer	$ 30–35
Cup and saucer	$ 30–35
Dish, *heart*	$ 40–50
Plate, *dinner, spade decoration*	$ 20–25
Platter, *diamond*	$ 50–65
Sugar bowl	$ 40–50

"Corinthian/Trojan"

This line uses a fluted shape that was also made by the Sebring Pottery (also located in Sebring, Ohio). Some of the decals used on pieces in this line include "Blue Willow," "Old Dutch," and "Toledo Delight."

Bowl, *individual fruit, 5¹/₂-inch diameter*	$ 8–12
Bowl, *individual soup, 7³/₄-inch diameter*	$ 12–20
Bowl, *vegetable, round, 8³/₄-inch diameter*	$ 35–45
Bowl, *vegetable, round, covered*	$ 120–140
Creamer	$ 30–40
Cup and saucer	$ 25–35
Gravy boat	$ 60–70
Plate, *bread and butter, 6¹/₂-inch diameter*	$ 5–8
Plate, *chop, 12-inch diameter*	$ 65–75
Plate, *dinner, 10-inch diameter*	$ 15–25
Plate, *luncheon, 9¹/₄-inch diameter*	$ 15–22
Plate, *salad, 7¹/₂-inch diameter*	$ 10–18
Platter, *oval, 11¹/₂ inches*	$ 40–50
Platter, *oval, 13¹/₂ inches*	$ 55–65
Sugar bowl	$ 35–45

MARBLEHEAD POTTERY

Marks used by the
Marblehead Pottery of
Marblehead, Massachusetts.

Doctor Herbert Hall thought the patients in his Marblehead, Massachusetts, sanitarium would benefit from doing crafts such as weaving, wood carving, metalwork, and pottery. He began a pottery operation in 1904, but the work became so demanding that the pottery had to be separated from the medical program within a year of beginning its operations.

Marblehead Pottery was a small endeavor; it had only a kick wheel, a turning-lathe, and a six-burner kerosene kiln. At first, the patients were taught pottery by Jessie Luther, but after the pottery was separated from the medical program, Arthur E. Baggs became its director. The pottery's first products were matte-glazed in shades of gray, yellow, green, brown, lavender, and, very rarely, red. Other colors included Marblehead Blue (a deep shade of turquoise), Tobacco Brown, and rose, plus others that were available for special orders.

Marblehead shapes were simple, and the decorations were stylized rather than naturalistic. Decorative themes often revolved around subjects associated with the sea, and floral subjects are not as common on Marblehead pieces as they are on other American art pottery. The designs were sometimes incised on the surface of the pottery, but were sometimes left flat. Most Marblehead pottery is found completely undecorated, and any piece with more than one color and/or some sort of additional decoration commands a premium from collectors.

In 1912, a tin-enameled faience was introduced that had a cream-colored background and could be decorated in a range of colors. The line was not successful, however, and little of this ware can be found today. In 1915, Arthur Baggs became owner of the Marblehead Pottery, and the firm continued production until 1936.

Bowl, *5-inch diameter, high-gloss brown interior, exterior in matte blue, decorated with repeating, raised crescent shapes*	$ 400–450
Bowl, *12-inch widest diameter, 4¹/₂ inches tall, narrow base to wide flaring mouth, interior is matte blue, exterior is green, signed by artist Arthur Baggs*	$ 800–900
Planter, *hanging, 5¹/₂-inch diameter, lavender-gray exterior, purple interior, three small handles for hanging*	$ 500–600
Tile, *4¹/₂ inches square, landscape of trees on hill, small chip to corner*	$ 2,500–2,700
Vase, *3¹/₂ inches, matte granite gray ground with five flying ducks in blue, high-gloss interior*	$ 3,300–3,450
Vase, *4³/₄ inches, cylindrical, sage-green ground with darker-green floral and vine designs around top, high-gloss caramel glaze on interior*	$ 3,800–4,200
Vase, *5¹/₄ inches tall, "V"-shaped, green vase, with blue speckles*	$ 350–400
Vase, *5¹/₂ inches, slightly bulbous vase tapering to top, dark-gray ground decorated with yellow roses around top*	$ 4,400–4,800
Vase, *6¹/₄ inches tall, cobalt-blue matte glaze with matte gray-and-brown highlights, signed by artist Arthur Baggs*	$ 800–900
Vase, *6¹/₄ inches tall, dark matte green glaze*	$ 500–575
Vase/Bowl, *3¹/₂ inches, Marblehead Blue ground with an embossed 1-inch band of leaves, flowers, and berries in shades of green, blue, and rust*	$ 2,900–3,000
Vase/Bowl, *4¹/₂ inches tall, dark-blue glaze, slightly mottled*	$ 350–400

MATT MORGAN POTTERY

One of the marks found on pottery made by *Matt Morgan.*

Matthew Morgan was an English caricaturist and painter who had come to appreciate Spanish pottery. When he moved to Cincinnati, Ohio, in 1878, he called upon George Ligowsky, the inventor of the clay pigeon, to experiment with clays and glazes in order to reproduce the famous Hispano-Moresque pottery, which made extensive use of luster glazes.

Ligowsky succeeded, and the two men founded an art pottery company around 1883 (there is some disagreement as to the exact date), with Ligowsky making the pottery and Morgan doing the decorating, mainly in the Moorish style. Herman C. Mueller, who would later found Mueller Tile Company, joined the company, as did decorators Matthew Daly and N. J. Hirschfield for a brief period before leaving for Rookwood.

Besides Moorish-inspired pottery, Matt Morgan also produced some underglaze slip-decorated wares and low-relief cameo ware. Within the company's first year of operations, however, its investors pressured Matt Morgan to start making commercial pottery instead of just art pottery, and the company went out of business in 1884.

Jardinière, *11¹/₂ inches tall, two handles with collared neck, brown glaze on handles and neck, front of body painted with an elaborate winter scene of a mill, cottages, a man and his dog, and a church spire, reverse is a raised flower, attributed to Matt Morgan but unsigned* $ 2,500–3,000

Vase, *5¹/₂ inches tall, three ball feet on globular form, pumpkin-brown ground with black painting of birds and bamboo in the Japanese style, signed by artist Matt Daly* $ 600–700

METLOX POTTERIES

One of the marks *Metlox Potteries* used on its "Poppytrail" items.

The Metlox Manufacturing Company was founded in 1927 by T. C. Prouty and his son, Willis, with manufacturing facilities in Manhattan Beach, California. The name "Metlox" was derived from the phrase "metallic oxide," which was an important ingredient in the items it produced. Initially, Metlox produced large outdoor advertising signs that could be fitted with neon tubing to make them literally glow in the dark. Its specialty was theater marquees such as the one on the famous Pantages Theater in Hollywood, California, and it prospered in this trade until the beginning of the Great Depression, when demand for this sort of item dwindled. The company also had a factory in Hermosa Beach, California, that specialized in making architectural tiles from talc mined in Death Valley.

T. C. Prouty died in 1931, and his son decided to take Metlox in a different direction: production of dinnerware. The company's first pattern was "California Pottery," introduced in 1932. The "200 Series" debuted in 1934, and this later became known as "Poppytrail," a name that was derived from California's state flower.

World War II curtailed the production of Metlox dinnerware, and the company instead began to manufacture such divergent items as aircraft parts, shell casings, and nuts and bolts. For a time after the war, the company tried to make toys from surplus metal, but in 1946, when this endeavor proved unsuccessful, the Proutys sold the company to Evan K. Shaw.

Shaw owned the American Pottery Company in Los Angeles, and he was party to a highly lucrative contract for the manufacture of Walt Disney ceramic figures. Vernon Kilns had transferred the contract to Shaw in 1942, and all had gone well until the American Pottery Company factory burned down in 1946. With the insurance money from this disaster, Shaw purchased Metlox in order to continue making the Disney figures, and also to begin making dinnerware on a grand scale.

Shaw hired the design team of Bob Allen and Mel Shaw, who had both worked in film animation, and who had designed the famous Howdy Doody puppet. Their first dinnerware line was introduced in 1946, and it was marketed under the old Metlox "Poppytrail" name.

In 1958, the owner of Vernon Kilns decided to leave the business, and he sold the rights to use the Vernon Kilns trade name "Vernonware" to Shaw and Metlox. Along with the trade name came Vernon Kilns' dinnerware patterns and mold shapes. Shaw subsequently set up a "Vernonware" division to match the success of the "Poppytrail" division, and the two prospered until the early 1970s. Increased Japanese competition caused Metlox to struggle, however, and the company finally closed in May of 1989.

Dinnerware

"California Contempora," "California Free Form," and "California Mobile"

These three names refer to a trio of color schemes found on Metlox pieces that share the same distinctive shapes and decorations. The design looks like an abstract form that is said to resemble an Alexander Calder mobile. The pieces are in the company's "Free Form" shape, which has a very 1950s, modern feel: some serving pieces look like boomerangs, and others feature oddly projecting triangular handles. The shape of the flatware is roughly square or rectangular, with the points at the corners rounded to create graceful forms that are almost oval.

"California Free Form" and "California Mobile" were introduced in 1954, and "California Contempora" appeared a year later. "California Free Form" features the abstract design in brown, chartreuse, and yellow against a pale-gray background accented with flecks of color. "Mobile" has the same background, with the decoration in purple, yellow, pink, and turquoise. "Contempora" features the design in shades of pink, black, and gray, with a textured and color-flecked satin background. Of these patterns, "California Mobile" tends to be valued at the top of the price ranges listed below, and "California Free Form" tends to be valued near the bottom, though this relationship is not hard and fast, and does vary from object to object.

a. Seated spaniel figure, Rockingham glaze, attributed to John Knowles, East Liverpool, Ohio, circa 1870, 10¾ inches tall, $6,500–$7,000. *Item courtesy of Olde Hope Antiques, Ed Hild.*

b. T. W. Coleman shouldered jug, North Carolina, late-19th or early-20th century, $195–$225.
Item courtesy of Francis and Susan Nation, Old School Antique Mall, Sylva, North Carolina.

c. Slip-decorated rectangular redware dish, 16½ inches by 11 inches, dated 1788, probably made in southeast Pennsylvania, $6,000–$7,500.
Item courtesy of Old Hope Antiques, Ed Hild.

d. Grouping of American pottery spaniels, large 9-inch-tall yellowware example at rear left, $4,750–$5,000; 8¾-inch-tall brown stoneware at rear right, $675–$750; 6-inch-tall brown stoneware at front left, $625–$675; 6-inch-tall yellowware with Rockingham glaze at front right, $875–$950.
Items courtesy of Roe House Antiques, Illinois.

e. Fine pitcher made by the Eberly Pottery of Strasburg, Virginia; lead, manganese, and copper glaze; 11¼ inches tall; $6,500–$7,000. *Item courtesy of Olde Hope Antiques, Ed Hild.*

1

 *a*

 *b*

 *c*

 *d*

 *e*

a. Stoneware jug, signed "J. N. Hickerson, Strasburg, Va.," 11¾ inches tall, $375–$425. *Item courtesy of Jeff Cupp, Knoxville, Tennessee.*

b. Pitcher, Albany slip-glazed, signed "J. J. Childs," 10½ inches tall, possibly Alabama, $300–$350. *Item courtesy of Jeff Cupp, Knoxville, Tennessee.*

c. Alkaline-glazed pitcher, Georgia, late-19th century, 10 inches tall, $175–$225. *Item courtesy of Jeff Cupp, Knoxville, Tennessee.*

d. Grotesque face jug, horned-devil form, Burlon Craig, second half of 20th century, $1,750–$2,000. *Item courtesy of Richard H. Crane, Knoxville, Tennessee.*

e. Fine storage jar, Middle Tennessee (possibly Putnam County), decorated with applied geometric shapes and garland, mid-19th century, 17 inches tall, $3,500–$4,000. *Item courtesy of Jeff Cupp, Knoxville, Tennessee.*

a   b

c   d

a. **Gray stoneware jug, 2-gallon, 14 inches tall, marked in cobalt, "Hamilton & Jones, Manufacturers, Greensboro, Pa.," $850–$900.** *Item courtesy of Barry and Lisa McAllister.*

e

b. **Stoneware jug, blue-decorated, "John H. Diferth & Co. Wines & Liquors, 27 & 29 Market St., Pittsburgh," 11 inches tall, mid-19th century, $825–$900.** *Item courtesy of Lynn and Fran Morehouse, Old School Antique Mall, Sylva, North Carolina.*

c. **Gray-stoneware covered crock, cobalt-blue tulip decoration, signed "F Stetzenmyer, Rochester, NY," lug handles, $2,750–$3,250.** *Item courtesy of Barry and Lisa McAllister.*

d. **Gray-stoneware water cooler with impressed mark "Satterlee & Mory, Ft. Edward NY," cobalt-blue decoration of bird, $5,250–$5,750.** *Item courtesy of Barry and Lisa McAllister.*

e. **Stoneware jug, signed "W B" for "Washington Beecham," Crawford, Georgia, 10½ inches tall, $650–$750.** *Item courtesy of Jeff Cupp, Knoxville, Tennessee.*

a b

c d

e

a. **Large gray stoneware pitcher, 15 inches tall, cobalt blue decorated with leaves and flowers, mid-19th century, $3,250–$3,750.** *Item courtesy of Steve Still.*

b. **Gray stoneware crock, cobalt blue decorated with leaves, signed "George W. Miller Strasburg," $400–$475.** *Item courtesy of Lynn and Fran Morehouse, Old School Antique Mall, Sylva, North Carolina.*

c. **Covered cake crock, gray stoneware, leaf-and-flower decoration, 10½ inches by 6 inches, $650–$750.** *Item courtesy of Carol and Duane Turnbull, Old School Antique Mall, Sylva, North Carolina.*

d. **Gray stoneware crock, impressed mark "E and LP Norton, Bennington, Vt.," 4-gallon, Albany slip interior, cobalt blue, decorated with bird on branch, $850–$1,000.** *Item courtesy of Phyllis and Dan Morse, Old School Antique Mall, Sylva, North Carolina.*

e. **Gray stoneware crock, lug handles, 11¼ inches tall, cobalt blue decorated with "XXX Butter" and a bird, impressed mark "C M Evans, Grocer, Haverhill" (probably New Hampshire), $9,250–$9,750.** *Item courtesy of Olde Hope Antiques, Ed Hild.*

a. **Yellowware bowl with green accents, garland of leaves and flowers around rim, 4$\frac{1}{2}$ inches tall, \$175–\$225.** *Item courtesy of Munday and Munday Antiques.*

b. **Blue mixing bowl, Ohio, embossed sailing ships and flowers, 9$\frac{1}{4}$-inch diameter, \$275–\$325.** *Item courtesy of Needful Things, Hendersonville, North Carolina.*

c. **Green-glazed mixing bowl, 5$\frac{1}{2}$ inches tall, "wave" design, \$200–\$250.** *Item courtesy of Munday and Munday Antiques.*

d. **Yellowware mixing bowl with blue and pink bands, Acanthus-leaf band around top, 9$\frac{1}{2}$-inch diameter, \$150–\$200.** *Item courtesy of Needful Things, Hendersonville, North Carolina.*

e. **Green-glazed mixing bowl, 4$\frac{1}{2}$ inches tall, "Girl with a Watering Can" design, \$425–\$475.** *Item courtesy of Munday and Munday Antiques.*

a. Milk/cream pitcher with advertisement of rendering company with phone number (1122), late-first quarter of 20th century, sponged glaze, 4½ inches, $125–$150. *Item courtesy of Richard H. Crane, Knoxville, Tennessee.*

b. Gray stoneware crock, impressed mark "E & LP Norton, Bennington, Vt.," 3-gallon, Albany slip interior, cobalt-blue decoration of flower-and-leaf pattern, $350–$450. *Item courtesy of Francis and Susan Nations, Old School Antique Mall, Sylva, North Carolina.*

c. Early Roseville pitcher, embossed ear of corn, 5 inches, unmarked, $175–$225. *Item courtesy of Bill Brooker, Old School Antique Mall, Sylva, North Carolina.*

d. Three-gallon crock with cobalt-blue stencil "Monmouth Pottery Co, Monmouth, Il.," Albany slip interior, $125–$175. *Item courtesy of Betty Winston, Old School Antique Mall, Sylva, North Carolina.*

e. Blue-and-white stoneware pitcher, embossed cattail design, 10 inches tall, $300–$350. *Item courtesy of Charlsie Hine, Old School Antique Mall, Sylva, North Carolina.*

a   b

c   d

a. **Gray stoneware pitcher with embossed flower-and-leaf decoration, painted with cobalt blue, 8 inches tall, $250–$300.** *Item courtesy of Jeff Cupp, Knoxville, Tennessee.*

e

b. **Green-glazed pitcher, "Avenue of Trees" design, Brush-McCoy, 8 inches tall, $225–$275.** *Item courtesy of Munday and Munday Antiques.*

c. **Green-glazed pitcher, attributed to a Nebraska origin, 8 inches tall, embossed flowers and stems, $275–$325.** *Item courtesy of Munday and Munday Antiques.*

d. **Rare American mocha pitcher, made in East Liverpool, Ohio, 4 inches tall, 1870–1880, $575–$625.** *Item courtesy of Barry and Lisa McAllister.*

e. **Pitcher, "Old Sleepy Eye," #3, blue rim, $1,000–$1,200.** *Item courtesy of Douglas L. Solliday.*

a *b*

c *d*

e

a. Yellowware food containers, three pieces: left, 6 inches, $175–$200; center, 6½ inches, $180–$210; right, 8 inches, $275–$325. *Items courtesy of Barry and Lisa McAllister.*

b. Yellowware pot, arch-and-scroll design, 5¼ inches tall, $60–$75. *Item courtesy of Valerie Rogers, The General Store, Loudon, Tennessee.*

c. Blue-and-white stoneware salt crock, wooden lid, 5 inches tall, $350–$400. *Item courtesy of Jeff Cupp, Knoxville, Tennessee.*

d. Yellowware food mold, ear-of-corn design, 7 inches, $200–$250. *Item courtesy of Valerie Rogers, The General Store, Loudon, Tennessee.*

e. Blue-and-white stoneware butter crock, 4½ inches tall, with original bail handle, $350–$400. *Item courtesy of Jeff Cupp, Knoxville, Tennessee.*

Ashtray, *small*	$ 60–70
Ashtray, *large*	$ 75–90
Bowl, *individual fruit, 5³/₄ inches*	$ 15–30
Bowl, *vegetable, oval, divided, 11¹/₂ inches*	$ 100–120
Bowl, *vegetable, round, 9¹/₂-inch diameter*	$ 65–75
Bowl, *vegetable, covered*	$ 425–475
Butter, *¹/₄-pound, covered*	$ 150–175
Coffeepot	$ 325–400
Creamer	$ 25–35
Cup and saucer	$ 20–35
Gravy boat	$ 65–85
Plate, *bread and butter, 6¹/₂ inches*	$ 18–28
Plate, *chop, 12-inch diameter*	$ 95–125
Plate, *dinner, 10 inches*	$ 25–45
Plate, *salad, 7³/₄ inches*	$ 22–32
Platter, *oval, 13 inches*	$ 70–80
Salt and pepper shakers, *set*	$ 55–65
Sugar bowl	$ 50–60
Tumbler, *6¹/₄ inches tall*	$ 70–85

"Aztec"

This line is on the same "Free Form" shape as the items listed above, but is decorated with a design that is quite different: a swirl and squiggly-line decoration in gray and black.

Bowl, *individual fruit, 5³/₄ inches*	$ 6–10
Bowl, *soup, 7 inches*	$ 20–28
Bowl, *soup, chowder, lug handle*	$ 35–45
Bowl, *vegetable, oval, divided, 11 inches*	$ 40–50
Bowl, *vegetable, round, 9¹/₂-inch diameter*	$ 30–40
Bowl, *vegetable, twin*	$ 195–225
Bowl, *vegetable, with lid and triangular handle*	$ 260–285
Butter dish, *¹/₄-pound, covered*	$ 100–120

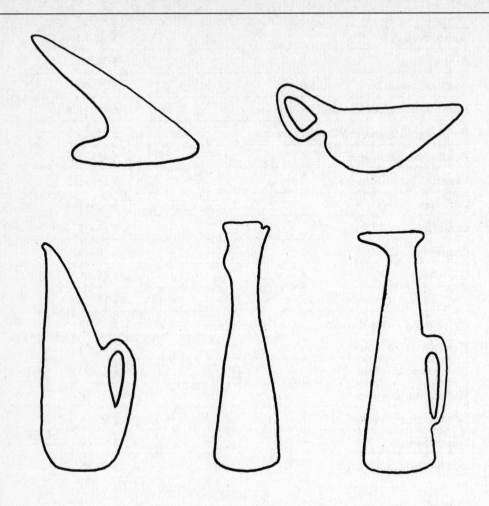

Drawing of the some of the shapes featured in Metlox's "Aztec" line.

Coffeepot	$ 225–250
Creamer	$ 15–22
Cup and saucer	$ 10–15
Gravy boat	$ 30–40
Plate, *bread and butter, 6¹/₂ inches*	$ 8–14
Plate, *dinner, 10 inches*	$ 15–25
Plate, *salad*	$ 25–35
Platter, *oval, 9 inches*	$ 35–45
Platter, *oval, 11 inches*	$ 55–65
Salt and pepper shakers, *set*	$ 30–40
Sugar bowl	$ 35–45

"California Ivy"

This was the first design created for Metlox by the design team of Bob Allen and Mel Shaw. It was innovative and modern-feeling, with plates and bowls in coupe shapes, with gently rolled-up edges, and without pronounced or flattened rims. The pattern was introduced in 1946, and remained in production until 1984. It was an unqualified success, and comedian Gracie Allen was pictured on the company's brochure at home with her "California Ivy" dinnerware. For this pattern, the design was stamped on the item and then the color was applied by hand. The background was pure white, and the handles and finials were attractively formed to suggest vines.

Bowl, *individual fruit, 5¹/₄-inch diameter*	$ 10–16
Bowl, *individual soup, with stick handle, 5 inches*	$ 25–35
Bowl, *salad, serving, 11-inch diameter*	$ 65–75
Bowl, *vegetable, oval, divided, 11 inches*	$ 30–40
Bowl, *vegetable, round, 9-inch diameter*	$ 20–30
Bowl, *vegetable, round, covered*	$ 75–90
Butter dish, *¹/₄-pound, covered*	$ 35–45
Coaster	$ 20–30
Coffeepot, *7-cup*	$ 125–150
Creamer	$ 12–18
Cup and saucer	$ 12–18
Dish, *relish, divided*	$ 22–28

Dish, *celery, 12 inches*	$ 45–55
Gravy boat with underliner	$ 35–45
Jug, *2¹/₂-quart*	$ 85–100
Plate, *bread and butter, 6¹/₂-inch diameter*	$ 5–9
Plate, *chop, buffet server, 13-inch diameter*	$ 45–55
Plate, *dinner, 10¹/₈-inch diameter*	$ 15–25
Plate, *luncheon, 9-inch diameter*	$ 12–19
Plate, *salad, 8-inch diameter*	$ 15–25
Platter, *oval, 11 inches*	$ 30–40
Platter, *oval, 13 inches*	$ 35–45
Salt and pepper shakers, *set*	$ 25–35
Sugar bowl	$ 20–30
Teapot, *6-cup*	$ 145–160
Tumbler, *13-ounce*	$ 20–28

"California Peach Blossom"

This line was created in 1952 by Allen and Shaw, and was the first of Metlox's sculptured patterns. "California Peach Blossom" is similar to the embossed patterns made by other companies, and the raised pattern was made by carving the design into the mold. This pattern reveals a decidedly Asian influence, with pink blossoms and brown twigs arranged artistically around part of the rim on flatware pieces, with the rest of the rim left bare. Another variety of this pattern, "California Golden Blossom," featured the same embossed design with yellow flowers and brown twigs. The flatware pieces in this grouping are primarily square and rectangular, with rounded corners.

Bowl, *individual fruit*	$ 15–20
Bowl, *individual soup*	$ 20–28
Bowl, *salad, serving*	$ 115–125
Bowl, *soup, lug handle*	$ 30–35
Bowl, *vegetable, covered*	$ 115–125
Butter dish, *¹/₄-pound, covered*	$ 80–95
Coffeepot	$ 150–175
Creamer	$ 40–50
Cup and saucer	$ 20–25

Metlox "Peach Blossom" creamer and lidded sugar bowl
on a tray that probably also served as a pickle or relish
server, set $120–$145.
Item courtesy of Richard H. Crane, Knoxville, Tennessee.

Gravy boat	$ 55–65
Plate, *bread and butter, 6^1/$_2$ inches*	$ 10–15
Plate, *dinner, 10^1/$_2$ inches*	$ 20–25
Plate, *luncheon, 9^5/$_8$ inches*	$ 35–42
Plate, *salad*	$ 15–20
Platter, *oval, 13 inches*	$ 65–75
Salt and pepper shakers, *set*	$ 35–45
Sugar bowl	$ 40–50
Teapot	$ 140–160
Tumbler	$ 60–70

"Camellia"

This pattern originated in 1946, just a few months before Willis Prouty sold Metlox
to Evan Shaw. It was a hand-decorated line, and its pieces featured embossed designs around their rims that were very reminiscent of such Gladding, McBean patterns as "Apple" and "Desert Rose." The Metlox pattern, as the name suggests, has
pink camellia blossoms with stems and leaves encircling the rims of flatware items.

Pieces featured cream-colored backgrounds, and the hollowware pieces with lids had camellia-shaped finials. This pattern came in two color schemes, one with brown trim and the other with green trim.

Bowl, *individual fruit, 6¹/₄ inches*	$ 7–11
Bowl, *soup, 8¹/₂-inch diameter*	$ 14–22
Bowl, *vegetable, round, 9³/₄-inch diameter*	$ 30–45
Creamer	$ 25–32
Cup and saucer	$ 17–25
Plate, *bread and butter*	$ 7–11
Plate, *chop, 13-inch diameter*	$ 35–50
Plate, *dinner, 10-inch diameter*	$ 18–28
Plate, *luncheon, 9-inch diameter*	$ 14–20
Plate, *salad, 7¹/₂-inch diameter*	$ 10–18
Sugar bowl	$ 30–38

"Delphinium"

This is a confusing pattern because it goes by two names: "Delphinium" and "Autumn Bloom." "Delphinium" was first made in 1942. It was Metlox's first effort to make dinnerware like that of certain highly successful Gladding, McBean lines that featured embossed, naturalistic, hand-colored designs. The "Delphinium" pieces had raised blossoms that were painted underglaze in shades of blue and pink against a background in one of three colors: blue, pink, or cream. World War II curtailed production of the "Delphinium" line and, when dinnerware production was resumed in 1946, the same design was used on a cream ground with orange flowers and was given the name "Autumn Bloom." Collectors generally consider both variations to be the same pattern, and pieces in both lines are thus generally referred to as "Delphinium."

Bowl, *individual fruit, 6¹/₄-inch diameter*	$ 10–15
Bowl, *vegetable, 10 inches*	$ 45–55
Coffeepot	$ 85–100
Creamer	$ 28–35
Cup and saucer	$ 25–30
Plate, *bread and butter, 6¹/₂-inch diameter*	$ 8–12
Plate, *chop, 13-inch diameter*	$ 55–65

Plate, *dinner, 10-inch diameter*	$ 25–30
Plate, *luncheon, 9-inch diameter*	$ 12–18
Plate, *salad, 7^1/$_2$-inch diameter*	$ 10–15
Salt and pepper shakers, *set*	$ 30–40
Sugar bowl	$ 30–38
Teapot	$ 85–100

"Homestead Provincial"

This is one of nine patterns Metlox made using its "Provincial" shapes, which were inspired by American 19th-century objects crafted from pewter, wood, tin, and rattan. The coffeepot, for example, was made to resemble a tin coffeepot with rivets down the side, and there was a covered dish shaped like a Victorian hen-on-the-nest with a basketweave base. "Homestead" pieces are decorated with farm scenes executed in the American folk art tradition, with a stylized tulip border reminiscent of Pennsylvania Dutch (Deutsch) design. "Homestead Provincial" used a dark-green and burgundy color scheme. A similar pattern, "Colonial Heritage," used shades of red and brown. Pieces in the "Provincial Blue" line feature the same scenic decorations in blue. "Homestead Provincial" and "Provincial Blue" were introduced in 1950, while "Colonial Heritage" was not introduced until 1956.

Ashtray, *square, 4^1/$_2$ inches*	$ 15–20
Ashtray, *square, 6^3/$_8$ inches*	$ 30–40
Ashtray, *square, 8^1/$_4$ inches*	$ 35–45
Bowl, *individual fruit, 6-inch diameter*	$ 10–16
Bowl, *individual soup, 8^1/$_2$-inch diameter*	$ 20–30
Bowl, *salad, serving, 11^1/$_8$-inch diameter*	$ 70–80
Bowl, *vegetable, rectangular, divided, 12 inches*	$ 25–32
Bowl, *vegetable, round, 9-inch diameter*	$ 20–28
Bowl, *vegetable, round, 10-inch diameter*	$ 22–30
Bowl, *vegetable, round, covered*	$ 55–65
Box, *cigarette*	$ 145–165
Box, *dower chest*	$ 150–170
Bread server, *rectangular, 9^1/$_2$ inches*	$ 35–45
Butter dish, *^{1}/$_4$-pound, covered*	$ 45–55
Canister, *coffee*	$ 50–60

Metlox "Provincial Blue" coffeepot showing the distinctive "riveted" early American-style shape, $100–$125.
Item courtesy of Kingston Pike Antique Mall, Knoxville, Tennessee.

Metlox "Provincial Blue" salt box, $145–$165.
Item courtesy of Kingston Pike Antique Mall, Knoxville, Tennessee.

Canister, *flour*	$ 65–75
Canister, *sugar*	$ 60–70
Canister, *tea*	$ 45–55
Casserole, *hen-on-the-nest, 1¹/₂-quart*	$ 85–100
Casserole, *kettle, 2¹/₂-quart, with warmer stand*	$ 195–225
Coaster	$ 12–18
Coffeepot	$ 55–65
Cookie jar	$ 175–200
Creamer	$ 15–22
Cruet set, *2 pieces, oil and vinegar with wooden stand*	$ 135–155
Cup and saucer	$ 10–18
Egg cup, *double*	$ 45–55
Gravy boat	$ 40–48
Jar, *mustard*	$ 55–65
Jug, *1-pint*	$ 55–65

Metlox "Poppytrail" "Homestead Provincial" 12½-inch
chop plate or buffet server, $75–$100.
Item courtesy of Larry and Terri Waters.

Jug, *1-quart*	$ 75–90
Matchbox holder	$ 95–110
Mug, *8-ounce*	$ 50–60
Mug, *tankard, 1-pint*	$ 55–65
Plate, *bread and butter, 6¹/₂-inch diameter*	$ 5–9
Plate, *chop, 12¹/₂-inch diameter*	$ 75–100
Plate, *dinner, 10-inch diameter*	$ 15–25
Plate, *luncheon, 9-inch diameter*	$ 30–40
Plate, *salad, 7¹/₂-inch diameter*	$ 15–25
Platter, *oval, 11 inches*	$ 30–38
Platter, *oval, 13¹/₂ inches*	$ 35–45
Platter, *oval, 16 inches*	$ 175–200
Salt and pepper shakers, *set, regular*	$ 20–35
Salt and pepper shakers, *set, rooster and hen*	$ 75–90
Sugar bowl	$ 25–35

Teapot	$ 125–145
Tureen with hen-shaped lid and ladle	$ 750–825

"La Mancha"

This pattern is found on Metlox's "American Traditional" shapes, which are based on forms associated with 19th-century ironstone. The flatware pieces feature a scalloped edge, with a rim that is divided by raised lines. "La Mancha" was introduced in 1968 and came in shades of gold, green, or white, accented by two lines of dark charcoal around the edge, with a thick line on the inside edge and a thinner line just inside that one. An unusual feature of this design is that the salad plate has a bold, dark-charcoal, flower-shaped medallion decal in its center, intended to evoke the literary legend of "Don Quixote." In general, white pieces command prices at the lower end of the price ranges listed below, while green pieces command prices near the higher end.

Bowl, *cereal, 6¹/₂-inch diameter*	$ 9–14
Bowl, *individual fruit, 5¹/₂-inch diameter*	$ 7–12
Bowl, *individual soup, 8¹/₄-inch diameter*	$ 8–14
Bowl, *vegetable, rectangular, divided*	$ 40–50
Bowl, *vegetable, round, 8-inch diameter*	$ 24–35
Bowl, *vegetable, round, divided, 8-inch diameter*	$ 35–55
Butter dish, *¹/₄-pound, covered*	$ 20–40
Canister, *coffee*	$ 28–40
Canister, *sugar*	$ 30–50
Coffeepot	$ 60–70
Creamer	$ 10–20
Cup and saucer	$ 10–18
Gravy boat	$ 30–45
Plate, *bread and butter, 6¹/₂-inch diameter*	$ 5–8
Plate, *dinner, 10³/₄-inch diameter*	$ 14–22
Plate, *salad, 8¹/₂-inch diameter*	$ 7–12
Platter, *oval, 10 inches*	$ 25–35
Platter, *oval, 11³/₄ inches*	$ 27–37
Platter, *oval, 14¹/₄ inches*	$ 25–38
Salt and pepper shakers, *set*	$ 18–28

Sugar bowl	$ 10–24
Teapot	$ 50–65

"Pintoria"

Produced by Metlox for only a short period of time between 1937 and 1939, "Pintoria" is a very distinctive line of single-color dinnerware. There are only nine different shapes in this abbreviated grouping, and it is believed to have been designed as a luncheon set. The flatware pieces are rectangular with sleek, circular, dished-out center wells, and the cups have very straight sides. "Pintoria" pieces feature a glossy glaze in shades of blue, yellow, orange, turquoise, cream, rust, or rose. Some pieces also feature pastel colors with a matte glaze.

Bowl, *vegetable, 11 inches by 9 inches*	$ 200–225
Creamer	$ 130–145
Cup and saucer	$ 90–110
Dish, *cereal, soup or fruit, 7 inches by 5³/₄ inches*	$ 80–100
Plate, *7¹/₂ inches by 6 inches*	$ 65–80
Plate, *10¹/₂ inches by 8¹/₂ inches*	$ 90–110
Plate, *12¹/₂ inches by 10³/₄ inches*	$ 160–185
Sugar bowl, *open*	$ 130–145

"Rooster"

This is the name collectors apply to several Metlox patterns that were made using the same "Provincial" shapes as the "Homestead" line. The first "Rooster" pattern is "California Provincial," which was introduced in 1950 and features a strutting rooster in shades of maroon, Leaf Green, and Straw Yellow against a maple-colored background. The border on this grouping is an undulating line with interspersed dots in green and Coffee Brown. The next pattern is "Red Rooster—Decorated," which has the same strutting barnyard bird in shades of red, yellow, charcoal, brown, and Leaf Green on a textured white background with a smoky-colored edge. The third grouping is "Red Rooster—Red," which appears on the same shapes as the other two "Rooster" patterns, but is a solid red color with no other decoration. The final pattern is "Bleu Rooster," which was introduced in 1966. This pattern features the same bird rendered in shades of blue, yellow, green, and orange, with a flower-and-vine edge. Of the four patterns, "Red Rooster—Red" is generally the least valuable, and its pieces were often used as accent items for items in the "California Provincial" and "Red Rooster—Decorated" lines.

"California Provincial"

Ashtray, *4¹/₂ inches*	$ 40–48
Ashtray, *8¹/₄ inches*	$ 45–55
Bowl, *individual fruit, 6-inch diameter*	$ 8–16
Bowl, *cereal, 7¹/₄-inch diameter*	$ 45–55
Bowl, *individual soup, 8¹/₂ inches*	$ 30–40
Bowl, *salad, serving, 11¹/₈-inch diameter*	$ 100–115
Bowl, *vegetable, round, 10-inch diameter*	$ 30–40
Bowl, *vegetable, round, covered*	$ 70–80
Box, *cigarette*	$ 195–225
Bread server	$ 55–65
Butter, *¹/₄-pound, covered*	$ 125–140
Canister, *coffee*	$ 95–105
Canister, *flour*	$ 105–115
Canister, *sugar*	$ 115–125
Canister, *tea*	$ 115–125
Casserole, *individual, hen-on-the-nest*	$ 115–125
Casserole, *1¹/₄ quart, hen-on-the-nest, lid*	$ 210–235
Coaster	$ 22–28
Coffee carafe with warmer stand	$ 195–225
Coffeepot	$ 110–135
Cookie jar	$ 340–365
Creamer	$ 15–25
Cruet, *vinegar*	$ 70–80
Cup and saucer	$ 15–22
Egg cup, *double*	$ 100–110
Gravy boat	$ 45–55
Jug, *1¹/₂-pint*	$ 115–125
Marmalade	$ 75–85
Mug, *8-ounce*	$ 55–65
Mug, *tankard, 1-pint*	$ 45–55

Mustard, *cruet set*	$ 80–90
Plate, *bread and butter, 6¹/₂-inch diameter*	$ 8–16
Plate, *chop, 12-inch diameter*	$ 45–55
Plate, *dinner, 10¹/₂-inch diameter*	$ 15–25
Plate, *luncheon, 9-inch diameter*	$ 45–55
Plate, *salad, 7¹/₂-inch diameter*	$ 20–30
Platter, *oval, 11 inches*	$ 55–65
Platter, *oval, 13¹/₂ inches*	$ 60–70
Salt and pepper shakers, *regular, set*	$ 25–35
Salt and pepper shakers, *rooster and hen, set*	$ 100–125
Salt box with wooden lid	$ 225–250
Sugar bowl	$ 22–32
Teapot	$ 200–225
Tumbler, *11-ounce*	$ 125–150
Tureen with ladle	$ 1,200–1,300

"Red Rooster—Decorated"

Ashtray, *6³/₈ inches*	$ 25–35
Bowl, *cereal, 7¹/₄-inch diameter*	$ 12–18
Bowl, *individual fruit, 6-inch diameter*	$ 5–8
Bowl, *soup, 8¹/₂-inch diameter*	$ 12–18
Bowl, *vegetable, rectangular, divided*	$ 40–50
Bowl, *vegetable, round, 10-inch diameter*	$ 20–30
Canister, *coffee*	$ 65–75
Canister, *flour*	$ 75–85
Canister, *sugar*	$ 65–75
Canister, *tea*	$ 55–65
Casserole, *individual, hen-on-the-nest*	$ 100–110
Casserole, *1¹/₄-quart, hen-on-the-nest*	$ 145–160
Casserole, *2¹/₂-quart, kettle*	$ 150–175
Cup and saucer	$ 15–22
Plate, *bread and butter, 6¹/₂-inch diameter*	$ 6–9

Metlox "Red Rooster—Decorated" salad plate, $10–$16.
*Item courtesy of Kingston Pike Antique Mall, Knoxville,
Tennessee.*

Plate, *chop, 12-inch diameter*	$ 30–40
Plate, *dinner, 10¹/₂-inch diameter*	$ 15–22
Plate, *salad, 7¹/₂-inch diameter*	$ 10–16
Platter, *oval, 13¹/₂ inches*	$ 25–35

"Bleu Rooster"

Bowl, *vegetable, round, 10-inch diameter*	$ 45–55
Coffeepot	$ 135–150
Creamer	$ 25–35
Cup and saucer	$ 15–22
Plate, *bread and butter, 6¹/₂-inch diameter*	$ 10–15
Plate, *dinner, 10¹/₂-inch diameter*	$ 30–40
Plate, *salad, 7¹/₂-inch diameter*	$ 12–18
Platter, *oval, 13¹/₂ inches*	$ 55–65
Sugar bowl	$ 30–40

"Red Rooster—Red"

Ashtray, *4¹/₂ inches*	$ 15–20
Bowl, *salad, serving, 11-inch diameter*	$ 75–85
Bowl, *vegetable, rectangular, divided*	$ 25–35
Bread server	$ 25–35
Butter dish, *¹/₄-pound, covered*	$ 35–45
Canister, *coffee*	$ 65–75
Canister, *flour*	$ 75–85
Canister, *sugar*	$ 65–75
Canister, *tea*	$ 55–65
Coaster	$ 12–18
Coffee carafe	$ 115–125
Coffeepot	$ 75–85
Creamer	$ 12–20
Cup and saucer	$ 8–15
Egg cup, *double*	$ 25–35
Gravy boat	$ 30–40
Mug, *8-ounce*	$ 25–35
Mug, *tankard*	$ 35–45
Mustard, *cruet set*	$ 30–40
Salt and pepper shakers, *regular, set*	$ 12–18
Sugar bowl	$ 20–30
Teapot	$ 100–115
Tumbler, *11-ounce*	$ 30–40

"Sculptured Grape"

This design appears on Metlox's "Traditional" shapes, and was first produced in 1963. An embossed pattern with raised grapes, leaves, and vines, "Sculptured Grape" is hand-painted in shades of green, blue, and brown. The handles and the finials of its pieces are formed in the shape of grapevines. There are several variations of this pattern, including "Antique Grape" (the same raised pattern decorated in beige against an off-white background), "Vintage Pink" (the same representation of grapes, painted in shades of cranberry and chartreuse with soft brown vines), and

"Grape Arbor" (the same pattern painted in various shades of green to simulate the type of grapes used to make white wine).

Bowl, *cereal, 7¹/₂-inch diameter*	$ 14–20
Bowl, *individual fruit, 6¹/₄ inches*	$ 10–16
Bowl, *salad, serving, 12-inch diameter*	$ 75–85
Bowl, *soup, 8-inch diameter*	$ 25–35
Bowl, *vegetable, round, 8¹/₂-inch diameter*	$ 15–25
Bowl, *vegetable, round, 9¹/₂-inch diameter*	$ 15–25
Bowl, *vegetable, round, divided, 8¹/₂-inch diameter*	$ 25–35
Bowl, *vegetable, round, divided, 9¹/₂-inch diameter*	$ 30–40
Butter dish, *¹/₄-pound, covered*	$ 50–60
Canister, *coffee*	$ 110–125
Canister, *flour*	$ 150–165
Canister, *sugar*	$ 135–150
Canister, *tea*	$ 95–110
Coffeepot	$ 80–95
Compote, *footed, 8¹/₂ inches*	$ 70–80
Creamer	$ 16–22
Cup and saucer	$ 12–18
Gravy boat, *faststand*	$ 25–35
Jug, *1¹/₂-pint*	$ 35–45
Jug, *1¹/₄-quart*	$ 65–75
Jug, *2¹/₄-quart*	$ 95–110
Mug, *8-ounce*	$ 40–48
Plate, *bread and butter, 6¹/₂-inch diameter*	$ 8–12
Plate, *chop, 12-inch diameter*	$ 45–55
Plate, *dinner, 10¹/₂-inch diameter*	$ 20–30
Plate, *luncheon, 9¹/₂-inch diameter*	$ 40–50
Plate, *salad, 7¹/₂-inch diameter*	$ 10–15
Platter, *oval, 9³/₄ inches*	$ 30–40
Platter, *oval, 12¹/₂ inches*	$ 30–40

Salt and pepper shakers, *set*	$ 25–35
Sauce boat, *1-pint*	$ 40–50
Sugar bowl	$ 30–40
Teapot	$ 130–145
Tumbler, *10-ounce*	$ 35–45
Utility fork	$ 50–60
Utility spoon	$ 40–50

"200 Series" (also known as "Poppy Trail" and "Plain")

This grouping originated in 1934, and its pieces were marked with the phrase "Poppy Trail" (two words rather than one, as was used in later spellings). The name was derived from Evelyn White's book *California Poppy Trails,* which was about wildflowers found in the state of California. It is said that Willis Prouty wanted to recreate the vivid colors of the state's wildflowers on this line of dinnerware, which was manufactured for approximately nine years. Initially, the "200 Series" came in seven glossy-glaze colors: Sea Green, Delphinium Blue, Old Rose, Canary Yellow, Poppy Orange, Ivory White, and Turquoise Blue. In 1935 and 1936, the coffee mug and coffee jug were offered in glossy red, and these are the only items that were ever made in this shade. Glossy cream and rust were added in 1937, but the original Ivory White was discontinued. In 1938, several matte (or satin) colors were added to this grouping: Opaline Green, Powder Blue, Petal Pink, Pastel Yellow, Satin Turquoise, and Peach. The final color, Satin Ivory, was added in 1940. The flatware in the "200 Series" actually came in two different profiles: flatware for table settings had rims, while the flatware for buffet service was made in a coupe shape that did not have rims.

Bowl, *cereal, 6-inch diameter*	$ 20–28
Bowl, *chili, 4^1/$_2$-inch diameter*	$ 26–32
Bowl, *cream soup, with cover and saucer*	$ 50–60
Bowl, *individual fruit, 5^1/$_2$-inch diameter*	$ 15–20
Bowl, *individual salad, 6-inch diameter*	$ 20–28
Bowl, *punch, 14-inch diameter*	$ 180–200
Bowl, *salad, serving, 17-inch diameter*	$ 160–175
Bowl, *individual soup, 8^1/$_4$-inch diameter*	$ 30–38
Bowl, *vegetable, oval, 9^1/$_2$ inches*	$ 45–55
Bowl, *vegetable, oval, 10^1/$_2$ inches*	$ 50–60

Butter dish, *¹/₄-pound, covered*	$ 60–70
Casserole, *1¹/₂-quart*	$ 85–100
Casserole, *2-quart*	$ 120–135
Coffee jug with cover, *1¹/₂-quart*	$ 70–85
Creamer	$ 30–40
Cup and saucer	$ 15–25
Cup and saucer, *bouillon*	$ 40–48
Cup and saucer, *demitasse*	$ 35–45
Cup and saucer, *jumbo*	$ 35–45
Jar, *jam, covered*	$ 55–65
Jar, *mustard, covered*	$ 55–65
Jug, *wine, with stopper, 1-quart*	$ 100–120
Plate, *bread and butter, 6¹/₂-inch diameter*	$ 10–15
Plate, *buffet, salad, 6-inch diameter*	$ 14–18
Plate, *buffet, service, 8¹/₂-inch diameter*	$ 16–22
Plate, *buffet, service, 10-inch diameter*	$ 20–28
Plate, *chop, 12-inch diameter*	$ 40–50
Plate, *chop, 14-inch diameter*	$ 45–55
Plate, *grill, 10¹/₂ inches*	$ 25–35
Plate, *dinner, 10-inch diameter*	$ 18–28
Plate, *luncheon, 9-inch diameter*	$ 15–22
Plate, *salad, 7¹/₄-inch diameter*	$ 12–18
Platter, *oval, 11¹/₂ inches*	$ 40–50
Platter, *oval, 13³/₄ inches*	$ 45–55
Sauce boat	$ 30–40
Sugar bowl	$ 30–40
Teapot, *6-cup*	$ 75–90

"Vernon Della Robbia"

This is the name given to a shape introduced by the Vernonware Division of Metlox in 1965. The embossed decoration was composed of a garland of fruit, flowers, and foliage that was meant to evoke the work of the Florentine Della Robbia family, who worked during the Italian Renaissance. There were three variations on this dinnerware: "Vernon Della Robbia," (hand-painted in brown, orange, green, and yellow against an antique-white background), "Vernon Florence" (in which the design was painted in blue, chartreuse, yellow, green, and Almond against a tinted white background), and "Vernon Antiqua" (the most subtle of the lot, with a beige-accented garland against an antique-white background). "Vernon Della Robbia" pieces generally command prices near the bottom of the price ranges listed below, while "Vernon Florence" pieces command prices near the top.

Bowl, *cereal, 7-inch diameter*	$ 11–20
Bowl, *individual fruit, 6-inch diameter*	$ 11–20
Bowl, *individual soup, 8¹/₂-inch diameter*	$ 25–45
Bowl, *vegetable, oval, divided, 11¹/₄ inches*	$ 30–60
Bowl, *vegetable, round, 9³/₄-inch diameter*	$ 20–38
Butter dish, *¹/₄-pound, covered*	$ 40–50
Coffeepot	$ 60–135
Creamer	$ 14–25
Cup and saucer	$ 12–20
Gravy boat, *faststand*	$ 25–50
Plate, *bread and butter, 6¹/₂-inch diameter*	$ 10–18
Plate, *dinner, 10¹/₂-inch diameter*	$ 20–45
Plate, *salad, 8-inch diameter*	$ 12–24
Platter, *oval, 12 inches*	$ 22–50
Salt and pepper shakers, *set*	$ 25–50
Sugar bowl	$ 22–35
Teapot	$ 85–175

"Yorkshire"

This pattern followed the "200 Series" ("Poppytrail") in either 1936 or 1937, and became a very good seller. Ostensibly the swirled pattern was based on an 18th-century English pattern, but it closely resembles Gladding, McBean's "Colorado" pattern. It is a solid-color line that came in vivid gloss shades of Canary Yellow, Delphinium Blue, Old Rose, Poppy Orange, Rust, and Turquoise Blue. The matte glaze colors were Opaline Green, Peach, Pastel Yellow, Petal Pink, Powder Blue, Satin Ivory, and Satin Turquoise. All the glossy colors were discontinued in 1941, and collectors thus tend to associate "Yorkshire" more with its pastel matte glazes.

Bowl, *cream soup, with underliner*	$ 50–60
Bowl, *individual fruit, 6-inch diameter*	$ 11–18
Bowl, *salad, serving, 12-inch diameter*	$ 70–80
Bowl, *vegetable, round, 9-inch diameter*	$ 50–60
Butter dish, *¼-pound, covered*	$ 60–70
Carafe, *covered*	$ 60–70
Creamer	$ 30–38
Cup and saucer	$ 15–25
Cup and saucer, *after-dinner*	$ 32–42
Gravy boat, *faststand*	$ 40–50
Jug, *2-quart*	$ 70–80
Plate, *bread and butter, 6½ inches*	$ 6–12
Plate, *chop, 14-inch diameter*	$ 45–55
Plate, *dinner, 10-inch diameter*	$ 16–24
Plate, *luncheon, 9-inch diameter*	$ 12–18
Platter, *oval, 11 inches*	$ 50–60
Salt and pepper shakers, *set*	$ 30–38
Sugar bowl, *open*	$ 30–38
Teapot, *4-cup*	$ 80–95
Teapot, *6-cup*	$ 85–100

Cookie Jars

Acorn with woodpecker finial	$ 675–750
Apple, *red*	$ 175–225
Apple, *yellow*	$ 200–275
Automobile with mouse family, *luggage finial*	$ 300–350
Barn with rooster finial	$ 575–625
Barrel of apples	$ 110–135
Barrel of cookies	$ 275–325
Barrel of nuts, *chipmunk finial*	$ 175–225
Barrel of pretzels	$ 275–325

Bear, *Beau, with large bow at neck*	$ 120–145
Bear, *dressed as a clown*	$ 950–1,100
Bear, *in sweater holding a cookie, red or blue sweater*	$ 160–200
Bear, *in sweater holding a cookie, stoneware finish, blue sweater*	$ 165–210
Bear, *in sweater holding a heart, blue sweater*	$ 325–375
Bear, *in tutu*	$ 200–250
Bear, *Koala, holding light-green leaf*	$ 325–350
Bear, *Koala, holding dark-green leaf*	$ 425–450
Bear, *Panda, with lollipop*	$ 600–650
Bear, *Panda, without lollipop*	$ 275–310
Bear, *roller skating*	$ 225–265
Bear, *sombrero*	$ 200–235
Bear, *Uncle Sam*	$ 1,000–1,100
Beaver, *with bouquet of flowers*	$ 200–250
Box with strawberries (or tangerines)	$ 400–450
Boy, *Cub Scout, head*	$ 1,450–1,600
Cabbage with rabbit finial, *light-green*	$ 325–375
Cabbage with rabbit finial, *dark-green*	$ 425–475
Calf, *head ("Calf-Says-Moo")*	$ 350–400
Cat, *Alley*	$ 375–425
Cat, *head, hat lid*	$ 275–325
Cat, *stylized, calico*	$ 500–550
Chef, *head*	$ 600–650
Chicken (mother hen)	$ 425–500
Clown, *full figure, two buttons, blue and white or black and white*	$ 275–325
Clown, *full figure, two buttons, yellow*	$ 175–200
Clown, *head*	$ 750–850
Corncobs, *all color schemes*	$ 225–275
Cow, *with flowers and bell around neck, butterfly finial, purple*	$ 400–450
Cow, *with flowers and bell around neck, butterfly finial, yellow*	$ 425–475

Debutante, *arms akimbo*	$ 675–725
Dinosaur, *Monoclonius*	$ 350–400
Dinosaur, *Stegosaurus*	$ 350–400
Dinosaur, *Stegosaurus, lavender*	$ 500–550
Dinosaur, *Tyrannosaurus Rex*	$ 350–400
Dinosaur, *Tyrannosaurus Rex, black-and-white "cow" paint*	$ 850–950
Dog, *Basset Hound*	$ 750–800
Dog, *Fido*	$ 325–375
Dog, *Scottie, white*	$ 400–450
Dog, *Scottie, black*	$ 200–250
Dog, *stylized*	$ 275–325
Doll, *boy, "Raggedy Andy"*	$ 400–450
Doll, *girl, "Raggedy Ann"*	$ 400–450
Doll, *girl, "Pretty Anne"*	$ 425–475
Doll, *rag, bisque or cold paint*	$ 275–325
Doll, *rag, painted underglaze*	$ 425–475
Drum, *children playing embossed on sides*	$ 300–350
Drum major, *head*	$ 550–600
Duck, *in hat, "Francine"*	$ 200–250
Duck, *in rain gear, "Puddles"*	$ 175–225
Duck, *"Sir Francis Drake"*	$ 175–225
Dutch boy	$ 450–500
Dutch girl	$ 450–500
Eggplant	$ 250–300
Fish ("Pescado")	$ 450–500
Frog, *in tie and collar*	$ 325–375
Girl, *black, sitting ("Topsy"), red and white polka dots*	$ 700–750
Girl, *black, sitting ("Topsy"), yellow and white polka dots*	$ 500–550
Girl, *black, sitting ("Topsy"), no polka dots, blue apron*	$ 650–700
Girl, *head with cap ("Brownie")*	$ 1,250–1,400
Girl with doll in pocket, *underglaze decorated*	$ 450–550

Goose with hat and shawl, *"Mother Goose"*	$ 600–650
Goose with mobcap and shawl, *"Lucy"*	$ 250–300
Grapefruit	$ 375–425
Grapes	$ 175–225
Hen, *blue, closed beak*	$ 400–450
Hippo, *"Bubbles"*	$ 500–550
House, *"Mushroom Cottage"*	$ 325–375
Humpty-Dumpty, *full figure, on wall, eyes open*	$ 450–500
Humpty-Dumpty, *no wall, eyes closed, common colors*	$ 1,200–1,400
Lamb, *head, hat lid ("Lamb-says-Baa")*	$ 400–450
Lamb, *sitting, with collar*	$ 650–700
Lamb, *sitting, with flower wreath around neck*	$ 500–550
Lion	$ 250–300
Little Red Riding Hood	$ 1,500–1,700
Mammy, *yellow and white polka dots*	$ 500–550
Mammy, *blue and white polka dots*	$ 600–650
Mouse chef, *"Pierre"*	$ 200–250
Noah's Ark	$ 400–450
Nun	$ 1,000–1,200
Owl, *stylized, painted details*	$ 225–275
Owl, *stylized, largely white*	$ 125–150
Parrot	$ 450–500
Pear	$ 225–250
Pelican in sailor's hat ("Salty")	$ 225–250
Penguin in hat and scarf	$ 225–250
Pig, *"Little," sitting, piggy bank form*	$ 250–300
Pig, *with scarf, standing*	$ 250–300
Pig, *in dress on scale*	$ 250–300
Pineapple	$ 150–175
Pinecone with bluebird finial	$ 275–325
Pinecone with squirrel finial	$ 200–250

Pinocchio	$ 550–600
Pumpkin	$ 425–475
Rabbit, *"Mrs. Bunny"*	$ 325–375
Rabbit, *lying down, clover finial*	$ 350–375
Raccoon with three apples, *bisque finish*	$ 275–325
Raccoon with three apples, *painted underglaze*	$ 325–375
Rooster with beak open	$ 425–475
Rose	$ 500–550
Santa Claus, *head*	$ 600–650
Santa Claus, *standing, white*	$ 550–600
Santa Claus, *standing, black*	$ 650–725
Seal	$ 1,200–1,400
Squash	$ 275–325
Stagecoach	$ 1,400–1,500
Strawberry	$ 125–150
Stump, *owl finial*	$ 225–275
Walrus	$ 400–450
Watermelon	$ 550–625
Wheat shock	$ 225–250

Figures

Metlox made a large grouping of miniature animal and human figures—some realistic, some whimsical. These figures came in a variety of glaze colors, and some were even painted underglaze. The most desirable color is solid black; pieces in this color command prices that are double the highest prices listed below.

Aardvark	$ 200–225
Alligator/crocodile, *9 inches*	$ 225–275
Armadillo, *nine-banded, 1³/₄ inches*	$ 200–225
Bear, *5 inches*	$ 250–300
Bird, *Dodo, 6 inches*	$ 150–175
Bumblebee	$ 150–175

Camel, *Bactrian, 5 inches*	$ 185–220
Camel, *reclining*	$ 500–600
Caterpillar	$ 150–175
Dinosaur, *4¹/₂ inches*	$ 500–600
Dog, *cubistic, 5 inches*	$ 225–275
Dog, *Scottie, 6¹/₂ inches*	$ 100–125
Dog, *Wirehaired Terrier, 12¹/₂ inches*	$ 650–750
Donkey, *3 inches*	$ 100–125
Elephant, *on ball, 6¹/₂ inches*	$ 400–450
Elephant, *sitting, trunk down, 3³/₄ inches*	$ 200–225
Fish, *3 inches*	$ 75–100
Fish, *5¹/₂ inches*	$ 200–225
Giraffe, *5³/₄ inches*	$ 150–175
Hippo	$ 200–225
Horse, *cubistic, prancing*	$ 400–450
Horse, *small, 3 inches*	$ 200–225
Horse, *circus, front left leg up, 6 inches*	$ 350–400
Lizard, *9¹/₂ inches*	$ 250–275
Lizard, *plated*	$ 500–525
Monkey, *on all fours, 4¹/₂ inches*	$ 325–375
Monkey, *sitting, 3¹/₂ inches*	$ 150–175
Otter	$ 200–225
Penguin, *2¹/₂ inches*	$ 75–100
Rhinoceros, *Indian*	$ 200–225
Sea horse, *4¹/₂ inches*	$ 150–175
Turtle, *standing*	$ 250–275

Miscellaneous Art Wares and Giftwares

"Beau"

First produced in 1937, pieces in this line featured embossed designs that were a modern adaptation of 18th-century French rococo designs, generally with floral and exotic bird motifs. The line also included a hard-to-find vase decorated with an embossed French-style Art Deco woman. Colors include pastel shades of Opaline Green, Peach, and yellow, as well as Satin Turquoise, Matte Ivory, and cream.

Ashtray, *6 inches, Opaline Green*	$ 45–60
Jardinière, *8 inches tall, Peach*	$ 175–200
Plate, *cake, 12-inch diameter, #170, yellow*	$ 150–175
Vase, *Art Deco Woman, 8¹/₂ inches*	$ 350–425
Vase, *13¹/₂ inches tall, Satin Turquoise*	$ 300–350

"Celadon"

This line, along with the "Beau" line, represented Metlox's first attempt to produce a line of art ware. It was introduced in 1937, and consisted of vases, bowls, and ashtrays done in Chinese-inspired shapes and glazes. Colors include pastel shades of Opaline Green, Peach, and yellow, as well as Satin Turquoise, Matte Ivory, and cream.

Bowl, *5-inch diameter, #137, with separate base*	$ 110–140
Covered ginger or incense jar, *5¹/₄ inches tall, Satin Turquoise*	$ 100–125
Vase, *#132, 5¹/₂ inches high, Peach*	$ 65–80

Other Art Wares

Bottle, *wine, Art Deco style, 12¹/₄ inches*	$ 75–95
Box, *cigarette, covered, 4³/₄ inches by 3³/₄ inches*	$ 65–80
Cactus container, *baby shoe, 4³/₄ inches*	$ 45–60
Cactus container, *cat*	$ 150–175
Cactus container, *elephant, 3¹/₂ inches*	$ 125–150
Cactus container, *hippopotamus, 3 inches*	$ 125–150
Candleholders, *shell, 4¹/₂ inches by 2 inches, pair*	$ 75–100
Candleholders, *spiral, 7¹/₂ inches high, pair*	$ 125–150
Console bowl, *with ram's heads on either end,* "Mission Bell" line	$ 85–110
Console bowl, *in the shape of a shell, 12 inches by 8¹/₂ inches by 3³/₄ inches*	$ 60–75
Flower frog, *6 inches*	$ 35–50

Vase, *bud, form of a boot, 5¹/₄ inches*	$ 45–60
Vase, *bud, form of a Toby jug, 3¹/₂ inches*	$ 75–90
Vase, *fan-shaped, 12¹/₄ inches wide*	$ 60–75
Vase, *"V"-shaped, "V" for Victory," #121, 6 inches*	$ 60–75

Disney Figures and Accessories

Vernon Kiln started manufacturing Disney-based figures and dinnerware in 1940, but found it unprofitable and eventually returned the contract to Evan K. Shaw's American Pottery Company. After Shaw acquired Metlox in 1946, he continued to make the Disney items, but when his contract expired in 1955, it was not renewed. Examples of Disney-themed items made by Shaw and Metlox are marked either "American Pottery" or "Evan K. Shaw Company"—never "Metlox" or "Poppytrail." Most of these items were marked only with paper labels, which were easily lost.

Bambi

Bowl, *child's*	$ 110–135
Cup, *child's*	$ 85–100
Figure, *Bambi, jumbo size*	$ 1,600–1,750
Figure, *Bambi, miniature, butterfly on back, 2¹/₂ inches*	$ 310–340
Figure, *Bambi, miniature, no butterfly, 2¹/₂ inches*	$ 295–320
Figure, *Bambi, miniature, prone, 1¹/₂ inches*	$ 295–320
Figure, *Flower, large*	$ 85–110
Figure, *Flower, medium*	$ 120–145
Figure, *Flower, miniature, 1¹/₂ inches*	$ 200–225
Figure, *stag (Bambi's father)*	$ 1,600–1,750
Figure, *Thumper, miniature, 1³/₄ inches*	$ 200–225
Plate, *child's*	$ 100–125

Cinderella

Cookie jar	$ 6,000–7,500
Figure, *Cinderella in rags*	$ 575–625
Figure, *Cinderella in ball gown*	$ 625–700
Figure, *Gus*	$ 300–350

Figure, *Jaq*	$ 300–350
Figure, *Prince Charming*	$ 400–450

Pinocchio

Figure, *Figaro, all sizes and configurations*	$ 250–300
Figure, *Jiminy Cricket, large size*	$ 500–600
Figure, *Jiminy Cricket, miniature, 1¹/₄ inches*	$ 250–300
Figure, *Pinocchio, large size*	$ 500–600
Figure, *Pinocchio, miniature, 2 inches*	$ 300–350

Snow White

Figure, *Seven Dwarfs, large size, each*	$ 300–350
Figure, *Seven Dwarfs, miniature, 2 inches, each*	$ 300–350
Figure, *Snow White, large size*	$ 600–700
Figure, *Snow White, miniature, 3 inches*	$ 700–800

Miscellaneous

Figure, Alice in Wonderland, *Alice*	$ 450–525
Figure, Alice in Wonderland, *Mad Hatter*	$ 325–375
Figure, Alice in Wonderland, *Tweedle Dee, Tweedle Dum, each*	$ 300–350
Figure, Alice in Wonderland, *White Rabbit*	$ 325–375
Figure, *Donald Duck with guitar*	$ 325–375
Figure, Lady and the Tramp, *Lady, sitting or standing, 1³/₄ inches*	$ 150–175
Figure, Lady and the Tramp, *Tramp, 2¹/₂ inches*	$ 300–350
Figure, *Mickey Mouse, miniature, waving, 2¹/₂ inches*	$ 450–525
Figure, *Minnie Mouse*	$ 350–400
Figure, *Peter Pan*	$ 500–575
Figure, Peter Pan, *Tinker Bell*	$ 600–700
Figure, Peter Pan, *Wendy*	$ 450–525
Figure, *Pluto, sniffing*	$ 300–350
Planter, *Brer Rabbit,* Song of the South	$ 4,500–5,250

Planter, *Donald Duck, beehive*	$ 3,000–3,500
Planter, *Pluto, doghouse*	$ 700–800
Teapot, Alice in Wonderland, *"Tea for 3"*	$ 450–525
Wall pocket, *Mickey Mouse*	$ 400–450

"Nostalgia"

Produced from the late 1940s to early 1960s, this line of giftware was designed to recall items associated with life in late 19th- and early 20th-century America. Many of the pieces were practical—planters and the like—but other items were purely decorative.

"Americana Figures"

Boy, *"Hitching Post,"* #650	$ 100–120
Coachman, *#651*	$ 80–95
Doctor	$ 75–95
Family, *either "Mama" #652, "Papa" #653, or "Mary Jane" #654, each*	$ 75–95
Reindeer, *either "Donder" #656 or "Blitzen" #657, each*	$ 150–175
Santa, *#655*	$ 110–135
Sulky Driver	$ 75–90
Wagon Master, *Budweiser*	$ 200–250

"American Royal Horses"

Arabian, *$7^3/_4$ inches by $8^1/_4$ inches, #646*	$ 185–210
Circus Horse, *large, 11 inches by 8 inches, #643*	$ 225–250
Circus Horse, *medium, 6 inches by 6 inches, #684*	$ 190–210
Clydesdale, *9 inches by 9 inches, #645*	$ 325–375
Currier and Ives (high-stepping trotter), *11 inches by $7^3/_4$ inches, #640*	$ 200–225
Dobbin, *workhorse with blinders and harness, 9 inches by 11 inches, #641*	$ 175–200
Gaited, *Palomino, large, 9 inches by 11 inches*	$ 200–225
Gaited, *Palomino, medium, 4 inches by 3 inches, #667*	$ 150–175
Hackney, *large, #644, $8^3/_4$ inches*	$ 200–225

Metlox, "Nostalgia" line large hackney horse, #644,
$200–$225.
Item courtesy of Richard H. Crane, Knoxville, Tennessee.

Hackney, *medium, #679, 6¹/₄ inches by 6¹/₂ inches*	$ 150–175
Morgan, *7³/₄ inches by 8¹/₂ inches, #648*	$ 185–210
Mustang, *large, 10 inches by 8 inches*	$ 200–225
Mustang, *medium, 7 inches by 5¹/₂ inches*	$ 150–175
Pinto Pony, *6 inches by 7¹/₂ inches, #642*	$ 150–200
Thoroughbred, *large, 8³/₄ inches by 8¹/₂ inches, #649*	$ 200–225
Thoroughbred, *medium, 6³/₄ inches by 6¹/₄ inches, #666*	$ 175–200

"Antique Automobiles"

Cadillac, *#612*	$ 100–120
Chevrolet, *#619*	$ 100–120
Merrie Oldsmobile, *#618*	$ 100–120
Old Ford, *#602*	$ 100–120

Metlox, "Nostalgia" line Victorian carriage, #625, $110–$130.
Item courtesy of Richard H. Crane, Knoxville, Tennessee.

Metlox, "Nostalgia" line doctor's buggy, #640, $75–$90.
Item courtesy of Richard H. Crane, Knoxville, Tennessee.

"Carriage Collection"

Buggy, *#691*	$ 75–85
Cab, *Hansom, # 628*	$ 90–110
Carriage, *Victorian, 11 inches, #625*	$ 110–130
Carriage, *Victoria, 10¹/₂ inches, #650*	$ 100–120
Cart, *Pony, #629*	$ 70–80
Cutter Sleigh, *#627*	$ 95–110
Doctor's Buggy, *#640*	$ 75–90
Sleigh, *Bob, #626*	$ 120–140
Stagecoach, *#617*	$ 120–140
Sulky, *Racing, #658*	$ 65–75
Surrey with fabric fringe, *#660*	$ 100–120
Surrey with metal fringe, *#624*	$ 100–120
Wagon, *Beer, Budweiser, 12¹/₂ inches*	$ 550–650

Metlox, "Nostalgia" line surrey with a fabric fringe, #660,
$100–$120.
Item courtesy of Richard H. Crane, Knoxville, Tennessee.

Wagon, *Fire, #659*	$ 110–125
Wagon, *Ice, #632*	$ 90–110
Wagon, *Mail, #630*	$ 90–110
Wagon, *Package, #610*	$ 100–120
Wagon, *R. F. D. Mail Delivery, #620*	$ 100–120

MORTON POTTERY COMPANY

One of the marks found on products made by the *Morton Pottery Company.*

The history of the Morton Pottery Company of Morton, Illinois, is rather confusing, but it began in 1877 when the six Rapp Brothers founded the Rapp Brothers Brick and Tile Company. Initially, bricks and tiles were the company's only products, but in 1878 the brothers also founded the Morton Pottery Works, which made utilitarian wares to meet the needs of the local population. The name of the company was changed to the Morton Earthenware Company in 1915, but it closed in 1917 due to American involvement in World War I. (Ironically, the six Rapp brothers had fled Germany in 1877 to avoid mandatory service in the German army.)

The company reopened in 1920 as Cliftwood Art Potteries, which made commercial art wares until about 1940. In 1922, the son of one of the original founders of Rapp Brothers Brick and Tile established a new factory that was named the Morton Pottery Company. This company is best known for its utilitarian pottery, including its "Pilgrim" line, its "Amish Pantry Ware," and its novelties. The Morton Pottery Company went into bankruptcy in 1971, and was eventually sold.

The various Morton, Illinois, potteries used local clay for their products until 1940, when the deposits became depleted. This clay is very distinctive, because it turned to a yellow/beige color when fired. The new clay used by the Morton companies fired white, and this provided collectors with a way to distinguish pre-1940 pieces from post-1940 items.

Banks

Acorn	$ 40–50
Bulldog, *3³/₄ inches by 3 inches*	$ 35–45
Cat, *reclining, 4 inches by 6 inches*	$ 35–45
Hen, *4 inches by 3 inches*	$ 40–50
Pig, *5¹/₂ inches by 3 inches*	$ 60–70
Pig, *"Skedaddle," legs out*	$ 35–45
Pig, *"Skedoodle," legs crossed*	$ 35–45
Scottie Dog, *7 inches*	$ 60–70
Shoe House, *9 inches*	$ 35–45
Uncle Sam, *4 inches by 2 inches*	$ 30–40

Cookie Jars

Basket of fruit	$ 60–75
Bluebird, *9 inches*	$ 75–90
Coffeepot, *"Cookies"*	$ 50–60
Cylinder, *circus animal decals and tent-top lid*	$ 50–60
French Poodle, *head, white, with cold-painted bow at neck*	$ 85–100
Hen, *with chick finial*	$ 175–200
Hillbilly head, *with straw hat*	$ 65–90
Milk Can, *"Cookies"*	$ 35–45
Owl, *chartreuse and dark green with cold-painted eyes*	$ 40–50
Panda	$ 55–65
Pineapple, *14 inches*	$ 35–45
Turkey with chick as finial, *brown with red wattle*	$ 200–225
Turkey with chick as finial, *white*	$ 225–250

Lamps and Television Lamps

Black panther television lamp, *28 inches*	$ 75–100
Buffalo on rocky cliff, *television lamp, natural colors, 11 inches*	$ 135–150
Cat staring at fishbowl, *television lamp, with glass fishbowl*	$ 60–75
Davy Crockett table lamp, *with original shade showing Davy walking through the forest carrying his rifle, pottery portion of lamp is a tall tree stump with Davy and a bear*	$ 250–300
Dog with pheasant in mouth, *table lamp, base doubles as a planter, no shade*	$ 100–125
Horse head, *television lamp, 18 inches*	$ 60–75
Leopard, *natural colors, television lamp, 14 inches*	$ 60–75
Lioness on log, *black and brown, 10 inches*	$ 60–75

Christmas Novelties

Cigarette container, *head of Santa, hat becomes ashtray*	$ 60–75
Planter, *Mrs. Claus, 9¹/₂ inches*	$ 50–65
Planter, *Santa Claus, 9¹/₂ inches*	$ 60–70
Planter, *snowman, white with black hat and red-and-green scarf, 9³/₄ inches*	$ 35–45
Plate, *Santa face, 8 inches*	$ 55–65
Plate, *Santa face, 12 inches*	$ 100–125
Punch set, *Santa face, bowl and eight punch cups, green stone eyes*	$ 250–300
Sleigh, *Victorian, red with holly and berries, small*	$ 50–60
Sleigh, *Victorian, white, small*	$ 40–50
Sleigh, *large, red*	$ 60–75

MOUNT CLEMENS POTTERY COMPANY

Mark of the *Mt. Clemens Pottery Company.*

Located in Mount Clemens, Michigan, this company was formed in 1914 and began production of semiporcelain dinnerware in January of 1915. It became a wholly owned subsidiary of the S. S. Kresge Company in 1920, and produced large amounts of dinnerware for that firm. The company changed hands in 1965, and by 1974 had changed its name to Jamestown China, though the name changed back to Mount Clemens Pottery in 1980. The company closed its facility in 1987.

"Mildred"

Flatware pieces bearing this pattern have notched edges and a floral garland interspersed with floral cartouches around their rims. Some "Mildred" pieces also came with a small central floral decoration.

Bowl, *cereal*	$ 18–22
Bowl, *individual fruit, 5-inch diameter*	$ 8–12
Bowl, *individual soup, 7³/₄-inch diameter*	$ 18–22
Bowl, *vegetable, round, 7¹/₂-inch diameter*	$ 28–35

Creamer	$ 28–35
Cup and saucer	$ 15–22
Plate, *bread and butter*	$ 6–9
Plate, *dinner, 10-inch diameter*	$ 28–35
Plate, *luncheon, $9^1/_4$-inch diameter*	$ 14–18
Plate, *salad, $7^1/_4$-inch diameter*	$ 9–12
Platter, *oval, $9^3/_4$ inches*	$ 28–35
Platter, *oval, $11^1/_4$ inches*	$ 30–37
Sugar bowl	$ 28–35

"Petal"

This shape, with its petal-like rim, was produced in burgundy, pink, white, dark blue, medium green, light green, and yellow. It may have been designed to compete with Homer Laughlin's "Fiesta" but, unlike the "Fiesta" line, was most commonly produced in medium green. Some pieces in this line were also decorated with decals.

Bowl, *cereal, 6-inch diameter*	$ 12–18
Bowl, *individual fruit, $5^1/_4$-inch diameter*	$ 12–18
Bowl, *individual soup, 8-inch diameter*	$ 16–22
Bowl, *vegetable, round, $7^1/_2$-inch diameter*	$ 32–40
Bowl, *vegetable, round, $8^1/_2$-inch diameter*	$ 35–45
Bowl, *vegetable, round, covered*	$ 115–125
Creamer	$ 12–18
Cup and saucer	$ 22–30
Gravy boat	$ 60–70
Plate, *bread and butter, 6-inch diameter*	$ 6–10
Plate, *luncheon, $9^1/_4$-inch diameter*	$ 12–18
Plate, *salad, $7^1/_2$-inch diameter*	$ 8–12
Platter, *oval, $11^1/_4$ inches*	$ 45–55
Platter, *oval, $13^1/_2$ inches*	$ 55–65
Platter, *lug, 15 inches*	$ 65–75
Sugar bowl	$ 22–30

"Vogue"

Pieces in this line feature attractive embossed decoration of birds, flowers, and urns. They were produced both in solid colors and with decal decorations.

Bowl, *individual fruit, 5¹/₈-inch diameter*	$ 8–12
Bowl, *vegetable, round, 8¹/₂-inch diameter*	$ 25–32
Cup and saucer	$ 12–18
Plate, *bread and butter, 6¹/₄-inch diameter*	$ 4–6
Plate, *dinner, 10¹/₄-inch diameter*	$ 12–18
Platter, *oval, 11¹/₄ inches*	$ 23–30
Sugar bowl	$ 18–22

MUNCIE CLAY PRODUCTS AND MUNCIE POTTERIES

Paper label used on products made by *Muncie Potteries*.

An example of the letter and number designations found on *Muncie* pottery. These designations also appear without the word "Muncie."

The history of this company begins with that of James S. Gill and Sons, a company that began making pots in Bellaire, Ohio, in 1882. These pots were unlike other wares that have been discussed in this book; rather, they were large industrial pots used primarily by glass makers to hold ingredients as they were heated to their melting points. In 1892, after the death of James Gill, the company's offices were moved to Muncie, Indiana, where a huge supply of natural gas—the so-called "Trenton Field"—had been discovered, and was beginning to attract an industry centered around the usefulness of this gas as fuel.

The company changed its name to "Gill Brothers," and began to supply the industrial pottery that was needed by the many new manufacturers in the Muncie area. Ownership of the company changed in 1908, and it became known as the Gill Clay Pot Company. During World War I, when German clay was no longer available to American potteries, the company began to mine, prepare, and ship high-grade clay. After the war was over, it also imported clay from Germany for sale to American potters.

In 1918, anticipating an upturn in business, the company decided to add a line of clay items for consumers, and Muncie Clay Products was founded and incorporated in

1919. The company still produced industrial clay products, but it had also experimented with art pottery from 1920 to 1921, and a new plant was constructed in 1923 to produce this high-end product for the consumer market. Molds were made and glazes were perfected, and production seemed to be proceeding smoothly by 1925. The company name was changed to Muncie Potteries in 1931. Sadly, however, the firm closed in 1939, a victim of the Great Depression.

Some of the Muncie pieces most desired by collectors are those designed by Reuben Haley, who had designed similar pieces to be produced in glass by the Consolidated Glass Company of Coraopolis, Pennsylvania. Several of these designs were based on pieces created by Rene Lalique. They were highly sculptural forms, and included raised images of archers, seagulls, lovebirds (parakeets), katydids (grasshoppers), and a fish. Haley also designed a line, similar to the "Ruba Rombic" line he had created for Consolidated, that consisted of cubistic forms. Today, all of these pieces are difficult to find.

Muncie pottery is seldom found marked, but occasionally a piece marked "Muncie" will turn up. After about 1925, pieces were often marked with workmen's identification numbers, often coupled with a letter of the alphabet—for example, "2A" or "E4." The letters "A," "B," "D," "E," "K," and "M" were all used in these marks. Other pieces were marked with paper labels.

Ashtrays, *bridge-themed set of four, one each in the shape of a heart, spade, diamond, and club, various glazes, shape #270, set*	$ 275–300
Bookends, *three-lobed, 5 inches, gloss peach skin, embossed decoration, unmarked, shape #254, pair*	$ 400–450
Candlesticks, *bottle-shaped, 9 inches tall, blue drip over white, shape #150, pair*	$ 350–400
Chamberstick, *Arts and Crafts–style, 4 inches, green drip over pumpkin, 4 inches*	$ 235–265
Compote, *square bowl and base, 11 inches, light-brown and peach skin, shape #183*	$ 350–400
Compote, *12$^{1}/_{2}$ inches, embossed design of lovebirds by Reuben Haley, matte light green, shape #434*	$ 850–1,000
Ewer, *12 inches tall, matte bittersweet orange, marked "3B," shape # 136*	$ 150–200
Jar, *covered, 7$^{1}/_{2}$ inches tall, ginger jar form, matte green drip over rose, marked, shape #190*	$ 275–325
Planter, *canoe-shaped, 11$^{1}/_{2}$ inches, gloss green over white, unmarked, shape #253*	$ 250–300

Planter, *Dutch shoe, 5 inches, blue drip over rose, shape #U20* $ 300–350

Planter, *strawberry, 6¹/₂ inches, matte white drip over blue, shape #G2* $ 200–235

Pot, *flower, large, with saucer, horizontal ribs, 7 inches, matte white drip over rose, shape #G5* $ 250–300

Tumblers, *juice, 4 inches, six cups, bittersweet orange, marked, shape #494* $ 225–265

Vase, *6¹/₂ inches, embossed Reuben Haley design of katydids, orange peel, marked, shape #194* $ 400–500

Vase, *7 inches, Ruba Rombic line designed by Reuben Haley, four stacked cubes, matte green drip over rose, shape number #307* $ 1,200–1,400

Vase, *9 inches, embossed Reuben Haley design of lovebirds, gloss light green, shape #193* $ 650–750

Vase, *9 inches, embossed Reuben Haley design of fish, matte white drip over blue, shape #189* $ 600–700

Vase, *11 inches, bottle-shaped with embossed decoration, drip gloss green over white, marked, shape #137* $ 375–425

Vase, *11 inches, drip matte green over rose, melon-ribbed, handled, unmarked, shape #423* $ 325–375

Vase, *12 inches, drip matte glaze, white over blue, marked, shape #144* $ 250–325

Wall pocket, *salamander shape, 9 inches, blue drip over rose, unmarked, rare, shape #251* $ 1,200–1,400

Wall pocket, *10 inches, conical with a flared top and zigzag design around middle, matte green over rose, shape #252* $ 300–350

NEWCOMB COLLEGE POTTERY

Incised mark found on *Newcomb College* pottery. This should be one of several designations found on the bottom of *Newcomb College* products.

Organized in 1886, H. Sophie Newcomb Memorial College is the women's college associated with Tulane University in New Orleans, Louisiana. Newcomb College opened in 1887, but pottery production was not added to its curriculum until 1894 (or, according to some sources, 1895).

Ellsworth Woodward believed that vocational training in the arts was good for women, because those who did not get married could use what they had learned to support themselves, and those who did get married could use their training to enrich their local arts communities. The pottery Woodward established at Sophie Newcomb was to serve as a means for practical application of what was learned in other art and design courses taught at the college, though an experienced potter was hired to actually throw the pieces of pottery. The first of these potters was Frenchman Jules Gabry, but the most famous was Joseph Fortune Meyer, whose "J. M." mark is found on a large percentage of the Newcomb College pottery encountered by most collectors.

Initially, a young undergraduate woman would select the shape of the piece she wanted to decorate, and the piece would be thrown by the potter. The young woman could then either add her decoration at the college or take the piece home to work on it. Mary Given Sheerer was hired to supervise the students who decorated the pottery after

Meyer had thrown it. The idea was to give the young women practical experience in design, and to raise money at the same time, since each piece of pottery would be sold when it was finished. Half the money would go to the student decorator, and the other half to the college.

If a student showed promise, she was given two years of free education, and after graduation she was given a studio in which to work. After a time, much of the decoration of Newcomb College pottery was done by the young women who had shown promise, graduated, and then been given their own studios at the college. In 1918, the pottery moved to the basement of the Art Building on the new Newcomb College campus, and the production process changed: the pottery became a laboratory, though the decorators were once again undergraduate women studying art and design. Under this new arrangement, the women sometimes threw their own pots, and could make entire pieces of pottery from start to finish. Due to failing eyesight, Joseph Meyer, the potter most associated with Newcomb, retired in the mid-1920s. He died in 1931.

In the pottery's early years, the nature of the design on each piece was left up to the decorator, with the stipulation that each piece had to be an original with no duplicates, and the finished products had to be approved by Mary Sheerer before they could be offered for sale. Decorative motifs tended to reflect the flora and landscape found around New Orleans and southern Louisiana. These motifs included depictions of such things as irises, water lilies, pine trees, tree-lined roads, crocuses, pinecones, lotus blossoms, jasmine, wild roses, and, of course, the famous depiction of moonlight shining through the Spanish moss hanging from oak trees.

Early pieces of Newcomb pottery feature either red or buff-colored bodies, but, by the turn of the 20th century, the most common bodies were white. Early pieces sometimes were covered by glossy transparent glaze over their decorations, and collectors are particularly anxious to find these pieces because they are much rarer than matte-glazed pieces.

Pottery was produced at Sophie Newcomb for many years, but although some highly regarded sources suggest that the pottery continued into the 1950s, sources from the college itself report that production stopped in 1940.

Bowl, 5¹/₂-inch diameter, blue matte glaze with a band of nasturtiums around the shoulder to the neck, signed by artist Sadie Irvine	$ 2,400–2,600
Bowl, 5³/₄-inch diameter, blue matte ground with a band of ivory and yellow jonquils on the shoulder to the neck, signed by artist Anna Francis Simpson	$ 2,500–2,800
Bowl, 7 inches, shallow, cabbage rose decoration, Anna Francis Simpson	$ 2,800–3,200

Bowl, *10-inch diameter, incised decoration of leaves and buds or seed pods, gray ground with blue banding, rare high-gloss glaze, artist Mary Williamson Summey, circa 1905* $ 6,500–7,500

Pitcher, *5¹/₂ inches, tall cylinder with band of carved florals around top, blue-and-green matte glaze, signed by artist Alma Munsen, slight damage to foot* $ 1,600–1,800

Vase, *3¹/₄-inch diameter, ovoid with design of Spanish moss in oak trees, signed by artist Anna Francis Simpson* $ 3,500–4,000

Vase, *3¹/₂ inches, band of green leaves and pink flowers with yellow centers around the neck, matte glaze, signed by artist Sadie Irvine* $ 2,500–2,800

Vase, *3¹/₂ inches high, three oak trees with Spanish moss, artist Henrietta Bailey* $ 3,800–4,200

Vase, *5 inches tall, oak trees and Spanish moss, not a night scene, artist Anna Francis Simpson* $ 3,500–4,000

Vase, *6 inches, moon through the Spanish moss, oak trees, globular form, artist Sadie Irvine* $ 5,000–6,000

Vase, *8 inches, carved pinecone design in purple and green against a blue ground, signed by artist Henrietta Bailey* $ 8,000–8,500

Vase, *10 inches, cylinder, morning glories, blue matte ground, artist Sadie Irvine* $ 9,500–11,000

Vase, *11 inches, moon through Spanish moss, very strongly done, artist Sadie Irvine* $ 14,000–16,000

Vase, *12 inches, tall cylinder bulging at the shoulder to narrow collared neck, strong floral and leaves, artist Henrietta Bailey* $ 16,000–20,000

NILOAK POTTERY COMPANY

One of the marks found on *Niloak* pottery.

The Hytens had been making pottery in Benton, Arkansas, since the late 19th century, but it was Charles "Bullet" Hyten who began making pottery using different clays in 1909 (or 1910, depending on the source). The area around Benton was full of clay deposits with different hues: blue, beige, red, white, gray, and brown. Hyten would place these different-colored clays on a potter's wheel, and form them into vessels characterized by spiraling streaks of different colors. In addition to naturally colored clays, he also occasionally used pigments to create colors: ferric oxide to create red, cobalt oxide to create blue, and chromic oxide to create gray.

The process was a difficult one, because each type of clay shrank in the kiln at a different rate, which could cause problems. Hyten developed his own process to deal with this problem, and received a patent for this process in 1928. Part of his secret was to bake the pottery for anywhere from a day and a half to a little over two days, with temperatures that rose gradually over time.

Hyten began marketing his swirled art pottery in 1910. He called it "Niloak," which is "kaolin" (one of the two most important ingredients used in making porcelain) spelled backwards. This type of pottery is also known as "Missionware." At first the pottery was glazed both inside and outside, but soon only the inside was glazed to hold water, and the outside was left unglazed and was sanded to impart a satin finish. Early pieces are often a swirled combination of brown, cream, and blue, but the most common pieces are dark brown and blue. "Niloak" pieces with a predominately white or light-colored background are rare, and examples with pink, green, and blue combinations are also desirable to collectors.

Other types of wares were also produced by Hyten, including a floral line called "Hywood" (produced only in the early 1930s), which consisted of molded wares often in the shape of animals. Some pieces of "Hywood" are hand-thrown, and feature unusual glazes. Collectors consider these pieces art pottery, and they are often marked "Hywood Art Pottery." Marbleized "Niloak" was discontinued in 1942, and Charles Hyten died in 1944.

"Missionware" (or "Marbleized Niloak")

Ashtray, *4³/₄-inch diameter, blue, brown, cream, and gray*	$ 135–160
Bean pot, *covered, 7¹/₄ inches, brown, blue, tan, and gray swirl, circa 1925*	$ 1,100–1,250
Bottle, *9¹/₄ inches tall, blue, gray, rust, and cream swirl*	$ 950–1,100
Candlestick, *9³/₄ inches, two colors, each*	$ 450–550
Chamberstick, *4³/₄ inches high, handle, very dark swirl*	$ 275–325
Compote, *8¹/₄ inches by 6 inches, light gray, cream, and brown*	$ 750–850
Cracker jar, *7-inch diameter, caramel and brown swirl, exterior glaze, early "Benton, Arkansas," mark*	$ 1,800–2,250
Ewer, *10¹/₂ inches, circa 1920, blue, cream, light brown, dark brown*	$ 950–1,100
Flower frog, *4-inch diameter, brown, tan, and blue swirl*	$ 145–165
Humidor, *Rust Red with gray-and-tan swirl, circa 1920*	$ 550–600
Inkwell, *2¹/₂ inches, typical swirl pattern, brown, gray, and tan*	$ 375–425
Jar, *covered, 8 inches tall, Chocolate Brown, blue, tan, Rust Red*	$ 1,000–1,100
Jardinière, *5³/₄ inches, dark brown, Chocolate Brown, cream, and blue*	$ 450–525
Mug, *4 inches, gray, blue, rust, and cream swirl, circa 1925*	$ 375–425
Mug, *5¹/₂ inches, three colors, gray, brown, and tan, circa 1920*	$ 425–475
Paperweight, *elephant-shaped, 2 inches, brown, cream, and blue swirl, unmarked*	$ 1,000–1,100

Niloak vase, "Missionware," 6 inches tall, typical Rust Red, cream, and brown swirl, $275–$325.
Item courtesy of Kingston Pike Antique Mall, Knoxville, Tennessee.

Niloak vase, "Missionware," 8¼ inches, swirled green, blue, cream, and Rust Red with a bold green stripe, $375–$425.
Item courtesy of Patty Tower, Old School Antique Mall, Sylva, North Carolina.

Pedestal for jardinière, *7³/4 inches, dark brown, Chocolate Brown, cream, and blue*	$ 550–650
Pitcher, *6¹/2 inches tall, squatty, gray and cream swirl with some tan, circa 1915*	$ 850–1,000
Pitcher, *10¹/2 inches, three colors, Rust Red, tan, and gray, circa 1920*	$ 1,250–1,400
Pitcher, *tankard, 10¹/2 inches, blue, gray, brown, cream*	$ 1,100–1,250
Tumble-up, *bottle-shaped water bottle covered with tumbler, blue, cream, Chocolate Brown, and dark brown*	$ 900–1,000
Vase, *6 inches, Rust Red, cream, blue, and brown*	$ 275–325
Vase, *fan, 7¹/2 inches, Rust Red, brown, gray, and cream*	$ 425–475
Vase, *7¹/2 inches, cylinder, fine swirled pattern, circa 1920*	$ 350–400
Vase, *8 inches, bulbous body to short neck, unusual swirl pattern, three colors of tan and brown*	$ 350–400
Vase, *8 inches, baluster form, almost totally gray with white-and-gray swirls at base, circa 1915*	$ 350–400

Vase, 8¹/₄ inches, green, blue, cream, and Rust Red, bold stripe of green	$ 375–425
Vase, 9 inches, brown, tan, and rust swirl, exterior glaze, early "Benton, Arkansas," mark	$ 1,400–1,650
Vase, 10¹/₂ inches, baluster form, very unusual swirl pattern of red and white/cream	$ 550–650
Vase, 11¹/₂ inches tall, large cylinder with gray, cream, and brown swirl	$ 700–750
Wall pocket, 6¹/₄ inches, blue, cream, brown swirl, marked with a paper label	$ 375–425

"Hywood" Art Pottery

Pitcher, creamer-size, 4¹/₄ inches, Ozark Dawn II glaze, rose to blue	$ 60–75
Vase, 8 inches, two applied handles, Peacock Blue mottled glaze	$ 525–600
Vase, 9 inches, beautiful Sea Green mottled glaze	$ 600–650
Vase, 9 inches, Ozark Dawn II glaze, rose to blue, three handles, shoulder to lip	$ 325–375
Vase, 9¹/₂ inches, dark Pearlized Green glaze, two handles from shoulder to just below lip, brownish cream-colored lip	$ 650–700

"Hywood" Commercial Art Wares

Basket, 5¹/₂ inches, blue over tan matte glazes	$ 110–125
Bowl, with three-dimensional figure of Peter Pan sitting on edge, dark green	$ 35–50
Candlestick, 3¹/₂ inches, cup shaped like flower, Ozark Dawn II glaze, rose to blue, each	$ 60–70
Coffeepot, 9 inches tall, Ozark Dawn II glaze, rose to blue	$ 125–150
Cookie jar, 9¹/₂ inches, Ozark Blue glaze	$ 175–225
Cornucopia, 7 inches, Ozark Blue glaze	$ 85–100
Cup and saucer, Ozark Blue glaze	$ 85–100
Cup and saucer, "Bouquet" dinnerware, embossed flowers	$ 35–45
Dish, relish, 9³/₄ inches, triangular, three-part, Fox Red glaze	$ 85–100

Ewer, $10^3/_4$ inches, embossed flower and leaves, Ozark Blue glaze	$ 110–125
Figure, *Cannon*, 3 inches, Canary Yellow Bright	$ 85–100
Figure, *Donkey*, on base, $2^3/_4$ inches, brown glaze, hand-detailed face	$ 140–160
Figure, *Pigeon*, $4^3/_4$ inches, Ozark Dawn II glaze	$ 175–200
Figure, *Scottie Dog*, $3^3/_4$ inches, unmarked, Mirror Black	$ 85–100
Figure, *Tank*, $2^1/_4$ inches, Ozark Blue	$ 85–100
Figure, *Trojan Horse*, $8^3/_4$ inches, ivory glaze	$ 200–250
Jug, $4^1/_2$ inches, with cork, Canary Yellow Bright glaze	$ 50–60
Pitcher, $9^1/_4$ inches, ball-shaped with raised concentric rings on body, Ozark Blue glaze	$ 110–125
Planter, *Australian Kangaroo*, with boxing gloves, tan glaze	$ 50–60
Planter, *Camel*, $3^3/_4$ inches, Ozark Blue	$ 85–100
Planter, canoe-shaped, 11 inches long, Ozark Dawn II glaze	$ 65–75
Planter, *Clown and Donkey*, 7 inches, ivory glaze	$ 55–65
Planter, *Clown Drummer*, $7^1/_2$ inches, light-blue glaze	$ 45–60
Planter, *Cradle*, 6 inches long, Ozark Dawn II glaze	$ 85–100
Planter, *Deer*, in grass, $3^1/_2$ inches, ivory glaze	$ 30–40
Planter, *Deer*, freestanding, 10 inches, Ozark Blue glaze	$ 225–250
Planter, *Dutch Shoe*, 5 inches long, Ozark II glaze	$ 15–20
Planter, *Elephant*, trunk raised, $4^1/_4$ inches, Ozark Dawn II glaze	$ 75–90
Planter, *Fish*, 9 inches long, Fox Red glaze	$ 55–65
Planter, *Poodle*, $3^1/_2$ inches, Ozark Dawn II glaze	$ 175–200
Planter, *Rabbits*, two, 5 inches, Ozark Dawn II glaze	$ 85–100
Planter, *Rocking Horse*, $6^1/_4$ inches, Ozark Blue	$ 110–125
Planter, *Rooster*, $6^1/_4$ inches, Fox Red glaze	$ 30–40
Planter, *Scottie Dog*, $3^1/_2$ inches, Ozark Blue	$ 50–65
Planter, *Squirrel*, 6 inches, blue-and-tan matte glaze	$ 50–65
Planter, *Swan*, $6^1/_2$ inches, Ozark Blue	$ 30–40
Planter, *Teddy Bear*, $3^3/_4$ inches, Ozark Blue glaze	$ 85–100

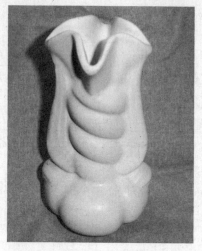

Niloak pitcher, cast ware, floral decoration, $50–$65.
Item courtesy of Elaine and Del Delcuze, Old School Antique Mall, Sylva, North Carolina.

Niloak vase, designed by Joe Allen, "Winged Victory," 6¾ inches tall, light-green glaze, $25–$35.
Item courtesy of Richard H. Crane, Knoxville, Tennessee.

Planter, *Turtle, 8¹/₂ inches long, Fox Red glaze*	$ 75–90
Planter, *Wishing Well, covered, 8 inches, Ozark Dawn II glaze, rose to blue*	$ 60–70
Planter, *Wishing Well, open, 8¹/₂ inches, Ozark Blue glaze*	$ 110–125
Plate, *dinner, 10-inch diameter, Ozark Blue glaze, embossed leaf border*	$ 100–110
Plate, *salad, 8-inch diameter, Ozark Dawn II glaze, rose to blue, embossed leaf border*	$ 85–100
Refrigerator water bottle with lid, *6 inches tall, streamlined triangular design, Ozark Blue glaze*	$ 225–250
Refrigerator water bottle with stopper, *7³/₄ inches, Ozark Blue glaze*	$ 140–160
Salt and pepper shakers, *bird figural, maroon glaze, unmarked, set*	$ 55–65
Salt and pepper shakers, *in the shape of bullets, Ozark Dawn II glaze, paper label, set*	$ 175–200
Strawberry jar, *5 inches tall, Ozark Blue glaze*	$ 30–40

Teapot, *6½ inches, Ozark Dawn II glaze, rose to blue*	$ 140–160
Teapot, *Aladdin-style, 6½ inches, horizontal ribs, Fox Red glaze*	$ 110–125
Tumbler, *4 inches, Ozark Dawn II glaze*	$ 30–40
Tumbler, *5½ inches, Ozark Blue, embossed gazelle decoration*	$ 50–60
Vase, *6¼ inches, ring handles, Pearlized Green glaze*	$ 110–125
Vase, *6½ inches, two handles, loving cup-shaped, maroon glaze*	$ 50–60
Vase, *7½ inches, two handles, embossed flamingo design, Ozark Dawn II glaze, rose to blue*	$ 85–100
Wall pocket, *cup-shaped with embossed flowers, "Bouquet" pattern dinnerware, Canary Yellow Bright glaze*	$ 50–65

NORTH DAKOTA SCHOOL OF MINES

North Dakota School of Mines mark.

Mark commonly found on pottery made at the University of North Dakota School of Mines.

Few people associate North Dakota with deposits of clay suitable for making pottery, but in the late 19th century, Dean E. J. Babcock made a survey of the state's mineral resources and discovered some deposits that looked promising. The North Dakota School of Mines, which was part of the University of North Dakota at Grand Forks, hired a potter and began experimenting with making pottery from this native clay. In 1904, a selection of this ware was shown at the St. Louis World's Fair. Margaret Cable was hired to teach pottery making at the school in 1910, and she remained there until her retirement in 1949. Other pottery teachers followed.

The pottery made at the North Dakota School of Mines tends to feature matte glaze in shades such as brown, blue, green, pink, or lavender. Some of the best decorations were hand-carved, and featured North Dakota themes such as native animals, flowers, covered wagons, and the like. Pieces were marked with the University's name until 1963, when the names of the student potters were substituted. Pieces signed by Margaret Cable are prized by collectors.

North Dakota School of Mines bowl, 2¼ inches by 3 inches, impressed leaf/vine border, $250–$300.
Item courtesy of Richard H. Crane, Knoxville, Tennessee.

North Dakota School of Mines vase, signed by artist "Jackson," 6 inches tall, $500–$600.
Item courtesy of Tony McCormack, Sarasota, Florida.

Bowl, *3 inches by 2¹/₂ inches, simple impressed leaf-and-vine border*	$ 250–300
Bowl, *4-inch diameter, painted shoulder with dots and triangles, high-gloss cobalt-blue ground, light-blue-and-white decoration*	$ 400–450
Bowl, *6¹/₂-inch diameter, iridescent green glaze, signed by artist Wavra, dated 1955*	$ 225–275
Trivet/Tile, *round, 5 inches, covered wagon pulled by oxen, blue, tan, and brown*	$ 625–675
Trivet/Tile, *round, 5³/₄-inch diameter, carved floral, lavender/gray ground with dark-blue and light-blue accents*	$ 850–900
Vase, *3 inches, carved acorn band on shoulder and center of globular body, signed by artist Julia Mattson, green-and-brown matte glaze*	$ 1,100–1,200
Vase, *3¹/₂ inches tall, Native American-style rectangular carving between shoulder and neck, green interior, blue-and-white exterior, artist-initialed*	$ 450–500

Mark found on the North Dakota School of Mines vase,
signed by artist "Jackson."

Vase, 5$^1/_2$ inches, bulbous base to long neck, horizontal ribbing around base, high-gloss blue glaze	$ 300–350
Vase, 6 inches tall, pierced border, signed by artist "Jackson"	$ 500–600
Vase, globular form, 6 inches tall, painted band of mushrooms around top in turquoise and blue, cream background, dated 1949, signed by artist June Mayhs	$ 3,250–3,400

OHR POTTERY

**G. E. OHR
Biloxi Miss.**

Incised mark used by
George Ohr.

George Ohr was called the "Mad Potter of Biloxi," and there is no doubt that he earned this name and was proud of it. Ohr thought himself the greatest potter of all time, but he sold very little of his work during his lifetime, reportedly because he wanted to sell all of his work at once, as opposed to selling odd pieces here and there. Though he gave some pieces to the Smithsonian Institution, most of his work was stored in a shed as a legacy for his children, with the expectation that someday the United States government would wish to buy it all. Self-esteem was not a problem for George Ohr, though self-delusion may have been.

Ohr was born in Biloxi, Mississippi, in 1857. As a young man, he ran away to New Orleans to work as a ship's chandler. He held a number of jobs until Joseph Meyers, later the potter at Newcomb College, invited him to learn pottery making. After only a few years, Ohr had singlehandedly built his own pottery in Biloxi (he claimed to have chopped pine trees for lumber, made the mortar for his kiln, and done all requisite iron work entirely by himself). His pottery burned down in 1893, but it was rebuilt in 1894. Ohr stopped making pottery in 1906, and joined his son selling Cadillac automobiles. He died in 1918, believing himself to be the greatest potter who had ever lived.

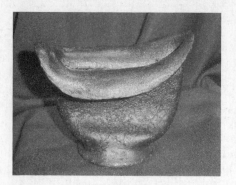

George Ohr "Vagina" bank, 3³/₄ inches tall,
4⅝ inches wide, gunmetal gray glaze,
$1,800–$2,000.
*Item courtesy of Tony McCormack, Sarasota,
Florida.*

George Ohr candlestick, 4¹/₂ inches tall,
mottled green glaze with white spots,
$2,300–$2,500.
*Item courtesy of Tony McCormack, Sarasota,
Florida.*

George Ohr inkwell, 1¹/₂ inches tall, flower-
form top, brown glaze, $1,200–$1,400.
*Item courtesy of Tony McCormack, Sarasota,
Florida.*

During his career as a potter, Ohr made everything from molded souvenir wares to outrageous avant-garde items that he modeled himself. He made inkwells in such forms as a donkey's head, a log cabin, an artist's palette, a printer's tray, and a cannon, as well as a statue depicting a common spud. His work displayed tremendous variety, and he crafted miniature pieces as well as items that were almost the size of a standing person. Some of his best pieces have extremely thin walls that have been deliberately crushed and twisted until they look like they may have melted in the kiln.

Ohr glazes were also very varied, and ranged from a variety of metallic and luster glazes to a vivid pink glaze with drip enhancement. Brown glazes are rather typical, and many pieces are speckled and mottled.

Bank, *"Vagina" form, 3³/₄ inches tall by 4⁵/₈ inches wide,* gunmetal gray glaze	$ 1,800–2,000
Candlestick, *4¹/₂ inches, two handles, mottled green glaze with white spots*	$ 2,300–2,500
Inkwell, *in form of Beauvoir, the home of Jefferson Davis, incised "Home of Jefferson Davis 1887," some areas of roughness, including a chip to the front staircase*	$ 4,000–4,500
Inkwell, *flower-form top, brown glaze, 1¹/₂ inches tall*	$ 1,200–1,400
Pitcher, *3 inches, cutout handle, pinched sides, high-gloss cobalt-and-green glaze*	$ 4,000–4,500
Pitcher, *3¹/₄ inches, twisted form, squat body, olive-green glaze*	$ 3,500–4,000
Vase, *2³/₄ inches, globular form with low collar neck, swirl design with emerald green, black, tan, and deep brown, some damage to rim*	$ 1,500–1,800
Vase, *3 inches high, six-color glaze, irregular globular form*	$ 8,000–8,500
Vase, *3¹/₂ inches, bulbous with lobed and dimpled shoulder, amber-and-green speckled glaze, restoration to glaze flaw*	$ 4,000–4,500
Vase, *3³/₄ inches, bulbous footed vase to flaring lip, black mottled glaze*	$ 1,500–1,800
Vase, *4¹/₄ inches, two loop handles on shoulder that do not touch the tall neck, unglazed bisque*	$ 2,500–2,800
Vase, *5¹/₂ inches, bulbous base to flared neck, high-gloss blue, green, and white glaze*	$ 2,800–3,200

OTT AND BREWER

The mark used by *Ott and Brewer* on its Belleek wares.

In 1863, during the middle of the American Civil War, Joseph Ott, William Bloor, and Thomas Booth formed a partnership to make ceramics in Trenton, New Jersey. The early production of white graniteware and cream-colored wares was based on the talents of William Bloor, who had been trained in the English Staffordshire district, which was the heart of Britain's pottery and porcelain industry.

Over the years, the partnership changed, and both William Bloor and Thomas Booth dropped out of the business. By around 1871, the firm was known as Ott and Brewer (the "Brewer" was for John Hart Brewer, who became a partner in 1865). During the early 1870s, the company began making parian porcelain, which is a type of white porcelain that is said to resemble fine Parian marble, and ivory porcelain. Sculptor Isaac Broom was hired in 1875 to model figures, and in 1876, Ott and Brewer won a medal for its statuary ware at the Philadelphia Centennial Exposition. It was also at this exposition that Irish Belleek made by David McBirney & Company was introduced to the American public.

Belleek porcelain wares were much finer than the products being made by American companies, and Ott and Brewer set out to produce a product that was just as fine. To do this, they hired both William Bromley Jr. and William Bromley Sr., who had worked for William Henry Goss, who is said to have actually invented Belleek china. Sometime around the end of 1893 or the beginning of 1894, Ott and Brewer succeeded in making a fine Belleek-style ware, which is considered by many to be the finest American Belleek ever made.

Unfortunately, Ott and Brewer fell on hard times in the 1890s, and the company went out of business in 1893.

Basket, $3^1/2$ inches tall, twig handle, incised diamond background, gilt decoration of leaves	$ 800–950
Bowl, *square, 10 inches, applied gilded leaves and a bud, gilt thistle decoration*	$ 1,000–1,200
Cup and saucer, *embossed beading in "V" shapes with gilt floral decoration*	$ 325–375
Egg server, *7-inch diameter, dolphin center handle, bamboo decoration*	$ 650–800
Ewer, *$10^1/2$ inches, twig handle, gold daisies on a white ground*	$ 1,200–1,500
Finger bowl and underliner, *embossed bamboo-style decoration, no hand-painted designs, ruffled top, pink interior, ivory exterior, bowl is 5 inches in diameter, made for Tiffany & Co.*	$ 500–600
Mustard or condiment pot, *$3^1/4$ inches tall, silver-plated lid with opening for spoon, floral-decorated*	$ 425–475
Pin tray shaped like a woman reclining on a shell, *11 inches long, shell feet, mainly white with some gilt accents*	$ 2,400–2,500
Pitcher, *ribbed with thorned twig handle terminating in a three-dimensional flower bud, three-dimensional lotus blossom on shoulder, gilt and floral painting in panels alternating with unpainted panels*	$ 1,800–2,000
Pitcher, *$5^1/2$ inches tall, flattened disk, embossed florals on body, gilt thistles under spout*	$ 600–700
Plate, *bread and butter, $6^1/2$-inch diameter, gold thistle decoration, embossed shell pattern on surface*	$ 275–325
Plate, *luncheon, $8^3/4$-inch diameter, elaborate marsh scene with water lily and cattails, gilt and color*	$ 1,000–1,150
Tea set, *consisting of teapot, creamer, and open sugar bowl, embossed shell background, twig-style ring handles, minimal gilt decoration of butterfly and flowers, 3 pieces*	$ 1,750–2,000
Tray, *$8^1/4$ inches square, delicate ruffled edge, floral-decorated with flowers and leaves outlined in gold and then colored*	$ 1,000–1,200

Urn, 8^{1}/$_{2}$ inches tall at handles, in the Etruscan style with two tall reticulated handles, footed, heavily decorated with flowers and gilt	$ 2,000–2,400
Vase, 10 inches, four-sided, gilt tones of flying birds among Asian-style foliage	$ 3,000–3,500
Vase, 10 inches, bottle-shaped, olive-green ground painted with the image of a long-tailed bird of paradise on a flowering branch, rare decoration and ground color	$ 6,000–6,500

OVERBECK POTTERY

One of the marks used at
Overbeck Pottery.

Born Margaret, Hannah, Elizabeth, and Mary Overpeck,
the sisters who ran this pottery changed their name to
"Overbeck" after their parents' deaths. All four sisters had
been trained in the arts and pottery making, with Margaret
even serving on the art faculty at DePauw University. Margaret was the sister who pushed the sisters to establish a pottery in their hometown of Cambridge, Indiana, which they
did in 1911. Unfortunately, Margaret died shortly thereafter.

The kiln used to fire the Overbeck Pottery was literally in
the backyard of the sisters' house, the workshop was in their
basement, the studio was on the first floor of their house,
and sometimes the sisters used red clay found in their orchard to actually make the pottery. Hannah was a decorator, but she died in 1931, leaving Elizabeth and Mary to
continue the family business. Elizabeth died in 1937, but
Mary, the sole surviving sister, continued to make pottery
on a much reduced scale until 1955, when she too passed on.

The wares made by the Overbeck sisters were very artistic
(for the most part), with an emphasis on carving and various intricate glaze treatments such as inlays. The sisters did
some work with molds, but the majority of the Overbeck
production was entirely hand-done. After Elizabeth's
death, things changed drastically at Overbeck, and Mary

began making various small sculptural pieces such as people in vintage or antique clothing, animals, birds, and grotesque depictions of the human form. She also did some sculptural portraiture of family friends and their pets. Collectors are most interested in the Overbeck pieces produced before 1937.

Bowl, *6 inches high, footed conical shape, textured aqua-colored glaze, artist-signed*	$ 1,000–1,200
Bowl, *3 inches tall, blue high glaze, decorated with a village scene*	$ 3,800–4,200
Bowl, *3¹/₂ inches, high-gloss mauve glaze*	$ 500–600
Bowl, *3¹/₂ inches high, stylized florals in brown, mauve, and green matte glaze, artist-signed*	$ 5,500–6,200
Candlestick, *9¹/₂ inches, blue matte glaze with stylized design, artist-signed*	$ 3,500–4,000
Chamberstick, *5 inches, curved shield back, handle, blue matte glaze*	$ 1,200–1,400
Figure, *2 inches, bluebird*	$ 525–550
Figure, *2 inches, rabbit*	$ 700–800
Figure, *2¹/₂ inches, squirrel*	$ 375–425
Figure, *2¹/₂ inches, dog*	$ 600–700
Figure, *2¹/₂ inches, turtle*	$ 750–800
Figure, *3 inches, dachshund*	$ 475–525
Figure, *3 inches, bird eating corn*	$ 425–475
Figure, *3¹/₂ inches, elderly lady in bonnet*	$ 375–425
Figure, *4 inches, boy playing cello*	$ 600–650
Figure, *4 inches, goose wearing tutu*	$ 700–750
Figure, *4¹/₄ inches, choir boy*	$ 550–600
Figure, *4¹/₄ inches, donkey wearing saddle*	$ 525–575
Figure, *4¹/₂ inches, cowboy*	$ 550–600
Figure, *4¹/₂ inches, African-American with cane and pipe*	$ 750–800
Figure, *4¹/₂ inches, lady holding basket*	$ 400–450
Figure, *4¹/₂ inches, Southern belle with shawl*	$ 425–475
Figure, *5 inches, bearded man in hat eating watermelon*	$ 700–800
Figure, *5 inches, rooster*	$ 500–550

Figure, *5 inches, southern belle*	$ 400–450
Mug, *2¹/2 inches, floral design at zigzag handle, high-gloss yellow exterior*	$ 850–950
Vase, *4 inches, high-gloss green/blue glaze*	$ 450–500
Vase, *4¹/2 inches tall, red matte glaze with carved figures in medallions, artist-signed, excellent example*	$ 7,000–8,000
Vase, *5¹/2 inches, bulbous base tapering to long neck, painted with stylized tulips, artist-signed*	$ 3,200–3,600

J. B. OWENS POTTERY COMPANY

OWENS
UTOPIAN

Mark often found on J. B.
Owens Pottery Company's
brown, slip-decorated
"Utopian" pottery.

Born in 1859, John B. Owens began his career as a traveling salesman for a line of stoneware. Owens began making his own pottery in Roseville, Ohio, in 1885, but he mainly produced common flowerpots rather than art pottery. Despite the nature of its product, the Owens pottery was very successful, and in 1892 a new plant was opened in Zanesville, Ohio. In 1895, the company branched out and began manufacturing Rockingham-glazed items, and in 1897 it began making slip-decorated art pottery (though some say the date was actually 1896).

Owens hired the best available talent available to create glazes and design lines of art pottery, including such artists as William A. Long (who brought his line of "Lonhuda" ware, which later became Owens's "Utopian" line), Frank Ferrel (the future art director at Roseville), and John Herald (who would later develop some important lines at Roseville). Unfortunately the factory burned down in 1902, but the facility was quickly rebuilt, and production continued until 1907, when art pottery was abandoned in favor of making floor and wall tiles.

The J. B. Owens Pottery Company is considered one of the "big three" manufacturers of American Art Pottery in Zanesville, Ohio (the other two are Weller and Roseville). Owens's "Utopian" line, which was first produced in 1897, is the line most commonly found by collectors on today's market. In most cases, its pieces feature a high-gloss brown glaze with underglaze slip painting, usually depicting flowers or fruit, but sometimes depicting such other subjects as animals and portraits of Native Americans (these pieces are particularly prized by collectors). Examples from the "Utopian" line can also be found with blue backgrounds, though these pieces are rare and can be pricey.

Other Owens lines include:

- **"Aborigine."** Loosely based on Native American designs, this line consisted of rather crude, matte-glazed pieces, which were first produced in 1907.

- **"Alpine."** Introduced in 1905, the name of this line derives from the white tops of its pieces, which are reminiscent of snow-capped mountain peaks. Below the white tops, pieces are shaded brown, gray, green, or blue, and are slip-decorated with painted designs that usually depict either fruit or flowers.

- **"Aqua Verdi."** Pieces in this line feature embossed figures or designs (usually neoclassical) with a slightly iridescent green glaze and uneven surfaces.

- **"Art Vellum."** Introduced in 1905, this line is characterized by underglaze decoration against a velvety background in brown "Utopian" colors or autumn shades of orange and other earth tones.

- **"Corona Animals."** This line features figures of animals that range in size from $4^1/2$ to 43 inches tall. Pieces are unglazed and in natural colors; the larger sizes were designed for garden use.

- **"Cyrano."** Pieces have raised graffito designs against a high-gloss background in shades of either blue, red, black, or dark brown. The decoration usually has a lacelike or filigree quality similar to that of designs found on "Turada" pieces made by Weller. This line was first produced by Owens in 1898.

- **"Delft."** Pieces in this line feature blue Dutch scenes against a white background in the style of Dutch delft wares.

- **"Feroza."** Introduced in 1901, this line has an iridescent glaze similar to that featured in Weller's "Sicard" line.

- **"Henry Deux."** First produced in 1900, this line features Art Nouveau-style designs cut into the bodies of pieces, which are inlaid with color.

- **"Lotus."** Pieces in this line have light-colored shaded backgrounds with underglaze slip-painted decorations and high-gloss glaze. The line was

Owens tile, butterfly/moth design, 5½ inches by 6 inches, $400–$475.
Item courtesy of Richard Hatch and Associates, Hendersonville, North Carolina.

Owens pitcher/vase, 10 inches tall, $575–$650.
Item courtesy of B and D Antiques and Art Pottery.

introduced in 1906. Pieces usually feature background colors in several shades of gray, white, or cream.

- **"Matt Utopian."** This line has slip-painted designs against soft, light-colored matte-finished backgrounds. Background colors are typically buff, dark brown, or blue. Decorations are generally floral. The line was first produced in 1902.

- **"Mission."** Pieces in this line are characterized by designs of Mission churches and Western landscapes with a matte glaze, and each came with an oak stand. Lesser pieces in this grouping may feature a drip or swirl glaze, with no pictorial content. This line was first produced in 1903.

- **"Navarre."** This line has white painted Art Nouveau-style figures against dark backgrounds.

- **"Opalescent Inlaid"** (also called "Opalescent Utopian"). Pieces feature light-colored backgrounds in solid colors, with wavy lines in gold, silver, or bronze, and with inlaid floral decorations outlined in black.

- **"Poster."** Pieces have Utopian Brown backgrounds decorated with images of ancient Greek actors and musicians.

- **"Red Flame."** Pieces have red backgrounds with embossed floral decorations.

- **"Soudanese."** Pieces feature black backgrounds inlaid with decorations such as animals, flowers, and birds, all in pastel colors. The line was first produced in 1907.

- **"Venetian."** In this line, iridescent metallic glaze was applied to pottery surfaces with both raised and depressed areas that accented the nature of the glaze.

- **"Wedgwood Jasper."** This line was an imitation of Josiah Wedgwood's "Jasperware" line.

"Aborigine"

Bowl, *with small sun sign decoration in red on buff band, the sun sign resembles a swastika, 2³/₄ inches*	$ 100–150
Pitcher with tubelike spout, *bands of red and buff, 7³/₄ inches*	$ 350–450
Vase, *Native American-style with red geometric designs on buff ground with black rim, 8³/₄ inches*	$ 650–750

"Alpine"

Vase, *long neck, slip-painted flowers, very pale, 8 inches tall*	$ 600–675

"Art Vellum"

Jardinière, *ruffled top, 6¹/₂ inches, floral decoration*	$ 500–600
Vase, *rectangular form, 5³/₄ inches, floral decoration*	$ 400–475

"Cyrano"

Jardinière, *rectangular, 7 inches by 8 inches, decorated with band around body*	$ 700–800
Jardinière, *cylindrical with pinched-in waist, 8¹/₄ inches, beading at rim, band of decoration around waist in diamonds and teardrop shapes*	$ 450–525

"Feroza"

Pitcher, *tankard, 11^1/$_2$ inches*	$ 925–1,000
Vase, *bulbous, 6 inches*	$ 525–600

"Henry Deux"

Umbrella stand, *"Art Nouveau" woman, 22^1/$_2$ inches*	$ 1,000–1,400
Vase, *10^1/$_2$ inches, multicolored floral decoration on a brown ground*	$ 550–650

"Lotus"

Pitcher, *tankard, bluish-gray background, 12^1/$_4$ inches*	$ 1,000–1,200
Teapot, *flattened shape, floral decoration, gray background, artist-signed*	$ 550–650
Vase, *6 inches, cylindrical, mushrooms on a gray background, artist-signed*	$ 500–575
Vase, *14^1/$_2$ inches, flying birds, artist-signed, blue shading to gray*	$ 3,800–4,500

"Majolica"

Dish, *fern, leaf motifs, 3^1/$_2$ inches*	$ 225–275
Jardinière and pedestal, *dolphins and putti, 17^1/$_2$ inches*	$ 575–675
Paperweight, *rectangular with rounded corners, embossed stag's head with "Edmiston Horney Co. Zanesville, Ohio" below, blue or green or brown*	$ 110–145

"Matt Utopian"

Jug, *6^1/$_2$ inches, floral decoration*	$ 325–400
Pitcher, *13 inches, tankard, leaf decoration*	$ 700–850
Vase, *7 inches tall, three-handled loving cup form, floral decoration, artist-signed*	$ 425–500
Vase, *13 inches tall, floral decoration, artist-signed*	$ 375–450
Vase, *13^1/$_2$ inches tall, floral decoration, artist-signed*	$ 400–475

Owens "Utopian Opalescent" vase, 14 inches tall, $1,200–$1,400. *Item courtesy of Tony McCormack, Sarasota, Florida.*

Owens "Utopian" vase, twist form, decorated with leaves, 4 inches tall, $200–$250. *Item courtesy of Francis and Suzie Nation, Old School Antique Mall, Sylva, North Carolina.*

"Mission"

Ball-shaped vase in its original wooden holder, *12 inches tall, elaborate painting of a California mission* $ 3,250–3,500

"Soudanese"

Vase, *4 inches tall, pansies*	$ 500–600
Vase, *12 inches, Japanese-style chrysanthemum decoration*	$ 1,000–1,200

"Utopian"

Ewer, *10 inches, floral decoration*	$ 475–550
Humidor, *7¹/₄ inches, cigar and matches*	$ 750–825
Jug, *6³/₄ inches, floral decoration*	$ 300–350
Mug, *5 inches, floral decoration*	$ 175–250
Mug, *5 inches, floral decoration, artist-signed*	$ 700–800
Planter, *crescent moon-shaped, 4¹/₂ inches, floral decoration*	$ 225–275

Stein, *7 inches, floral decoration*	$ 275–325
Umbrella stand, *24 inches, portrait of Native American, artist-signed, high-quality artistry*	$ 12,000–14,000
Vase, *3¹/₂ inches, twisted form, floral decoration*	$ 175–225
Vase, *4 inches tall, twisted form, leaf decoration*	$ 200–250
Vase, *5¹/₄ inches, footed, floral decoration*	$ 200–250
Vase, *7¹/₂ inches, long neck, floral, artist-signed*	$ 225–275
Vase, *8¹/₂ inches, floral decoration*	$ 375–450
Vase, *10¹/₂ inches, floral decoration*	$ 400–475
Vase, *pillow-shaped, portrait of a kitten, artist-signed*	$ 3,000–3,250
Vase, *pillow-shaped with portrait of a man in Renaissance-style dress, 13 inches, artist-signed*	$ 3,000–3,250
Vase, *pillow-shaped with horse head, 13 inches, artist-signed*	$ 3,750–4,000
Vase, *15 inches, floral decoration*	$ 500–600
Vase, *20 inches, portrait of Native American chief, artist-signed, high artistry*	$ 12,000–14,000

PADEN CITY POTTERY COMPANY

Mark used by *Paden City Pottery Company* on its Russel Wright-designed "Highlight" pieces.

There is some disagreement as to the exact year in which the Paden City Pottery Company of Paden City, West Virginia, was founded—some sources say 1907, others 1914. Whichever date is correct, the company remained in business until 1963. Paden City is often credited with being the first pottery to use decal decorations under its glaze. This method of application helped protect the decals from later damage that might be incurred during normal, everyday household use. Unfortunately, this method also limited the range of colors that could be used in the manufacturing process, because most hues were destroyed by the intense heat of the firing process. (It should be pointed out that Paden City also applied decals over the glaze on some of its wares, which was the standard practice of the time).

The Paden City decals that were applied under the glaze are said to look like they were hand-painted, and beginning collectors have been known to mistake wares featuring such decals for genuine hand-painted wares.

"Caliente"

This is yet another line of solid-color dinnerware cast in the "El Patio," "Ring," and "Fiesta" tradition. "Caliente," which was referred to in its advertisements as "Colorful Gay Caliente Ware," was introduced in 1936—the same year that

Homer Laughlin began making "Fiesta." The line initially used Paden City's "Elite" shapes, but in 1938 the company began to use the new "Shell-Krest" shape, which is often distinguished by the vestigial lug handles that appear on flatware items. "Caliente" (which takes its name from the Spanish word for "hot") can also be found on Paden City's "Regina" and "New Virginia" shapes. Pieces in this line feature such colors as Tangerine Red, Turquoise Green, Sapphire Blue, and Lemon Yellow.

Bowl, *cream soup, with saucer*	$ 35–45
Bowl, *individual fruit, 5¹/₄ inches*	$ 7–11
Bowl, *individual soup*	$ 22–28
Creamer	$ 15–20
Cup and saucer	$ 12–16
Gravy boat	$ 36–45
Plate, *bread and butter, 6¹/₂ inches*	$ 5–8
Plate, *dinner, 10¹/₂ inches*	$ 15–20
Plate, *luncheon, 9¹/₂ inches*	$ 10–15
Plate, *salad, 7¹/₂ inches*	$ 7–11
Platter, *oval, 14¹/₂ inches*	$ 55–65
Salt and pepper shakers, *set*	$ 20–28
Sugar bowl	$ 20–25

"Highlight"

This pattern was designed by Russel Wright and was produced for only a short time between 1951 and 1953. It was manufactured in both a matte and a glossy finish in Citron, Pepper, Nutmeg, Blueberry, white, and green. White and green were added to the line later than the other colors, and are the two most difficult shades to find. "Highlight" pieces damage easily, and are often chipped. Pieces are marked with the designer's name and the name of the distributor, "Justin Tharaud & Son," as well as the Paden City name, and, on occasion, its logo.

Bowl, *cereal, white and green*	$ 40–50
Bowl, *cereal, other colors*	$ 30–40
Bowl, *individual fruit, white and green*	$ 30–40
Bowl, *individual fruit, other colors*	$ 18–22
Bowl, *vegetable, covered, white and green*	$ 300–375
Bowl, *vegetable, covered, other colors*	$ 150–175

Creamer, *white and green*	$ 70–90
Creamer, *other colors*	$ 25–45
Cup and saucer, *white and green*	$ 45–60
Cup and saucer, *other colors*	$ 25–35
Plate, *bread and butter, 6-inch diameter, white and green*	$ 15–22
Plate, *bread and butter, 6-inch diameter, other colors*	$ 7–12
Plate, *dinner, white and green*	$ 45–55
Plate, *dinner, common colors*	$ 25–35
Platter, *oval, white and green*	$ 150–200
Platter, *oval, other colors*	$ 70–85
Sugar bowl, *covered, white and green*	$ 75–95
Sugar bowl, *covered, other colors*	$ 75–95

"Shenandoah"

First produced in 1944, this is one of the Paden City groupings that often has underglaze prints, which are sometimes mistaken for hand-painting. However, overglaze decals were also used on some pieces in this line. Pieces generally appear on "New Virginia" flatware shapes. Most of the decorations are based on floral or botanical themes with pattern names such as "Poppy," "Cosmos," "Strawberry," "Morning Glory," "Jonquil," and "Minerva Rose." Of these decaled patterns, "Morning Glory" is the most valuable, and commands prices at the top of the ranges listed below. "Shenandoah" pieces also came in a solid-color line often referred to as "Shenandoah Pastels," which is listed below. Common colors include green, blue, gray, pink, and yellow. "Shenandoah" pieces are generally marked either with the words "Shenandoah Ware," or with a Paden City logo and the word "underglaze" below.

Bowl, *cereal, 7^1/$_4$-inch diameter*	$ 12–20
Bowl, *individual fruit, 5^1/$_4$-inch diameter*	$ 10–17
Bowl, *vegetable, round, 8^3/$_4$-inch diameter*	$ 40–52
Bowl, *vegetable, round, covered*	$ 90–125
Cup and saucer	$ 18–30
Plate, *bread and butter, 6^1/$_2$-inch diameter*	$ 6–11
Plate, *dinner, 10^1/$_2$-inch diameter*	$ 16–25
Plate, *luncheon, 9^1/$_2$-inch diameter*	$ 13–17
Plate, *salad, 7^1/$_2$-inch diameter*	$ 10–15

Platter, *oval, 13³/₄ inches*	$ 50–68
Sugar bowl	$ 35–47

"Shenandoah Pastels"

Pink pieces are the most valuable, commanding prices at the top of the ranges listed below.

Bowl, *individual fruit, 5¹/₄-inch diameter*	$ 10–15
Bowl, *individual soup, 8-inch diameter*	$ 14–20
Creamer	$ 22–30
Cup and saucer	$ 16–25
Plate, *bread and butter, 6¹/₂-inch diameter*	$ 5–9
Plate, *chop, 12-inch diameter*	$ 45–75
Plate, *dinner or luncheon, 9¹/₂-inch diameter*	$ 14–22
Sugar bowl	$ 25–35

"Willow"

As has been mentioned earlier in this book, the "Willow" pattern was produced by a number of companies, primarily in England, the United States, and Japan. The typical version of this very popular pattern features a blue transfer print or decal of an Asian scene, with willow trees, houses, a bridge, and birds on a white background. Paden City, however, put a new spin on this traditional design. This involved etching a photographic image of a typical "Willow" design into the surface of a piece of dinnerware, and then covering its entire surface with a dark-blue glaze so the pattern showed through as shallow indentions. Paden City's "Willow" came in only seven shapes: a 9-inch plate, a 7-inch plate, a cup, a saucer, a 10-inch platter, a cereal bowl with lug handles, and a 9-inch salad bowl. These pieces were intended to comprise either a breakfast or luncheon set, and were sold in boxed sets, with each set containing six of each piece, except the platter and the salad bowl, of which there was only one per set.

Bowl, *cereal*	$ 12–18
Bowl, *salad, 9-inch diameter*	$ 40–60
Cup and saucer	$ 18–25
Plate, *luncheon, 9-inch diameter*	$ 25–35
Plate, *salad, 7-inch diameter*	$ 14–20
Platter, *10 inches*	$ 35–50

PAUL REVERE POTTERY

Mark used by *Paul Revere Pottery*, "Saturday Evening Girls."

Marks used at the *Paul Revere Pottery*. The "S.E.G." in the top mark stands for "Saturday Evening Girls," which is the name by which many collectors know this pottery.

In turn-of-the-century Boston, a group of young immigrant women met every Saturday night to perfect their reading skills and to work with crafts. These meetings were designed not only to keep the women busy and out of trouble, but also to teach them skills that would make them more employable and better able to support themselves with dignity. They were known as the "Saturday Evening Girls," or "S.E.G.," and eventually their program was expanded to include the making of ceramics.

In 1906, a kiln was purchased, and the young women began to make and decorate pottery under the direction of an English ceramist. In either 1908 or 1912 (there is some disagreement as to the exact date), the program was moved to the Library Club House, which was located very close to the Old North Church that had played such an important role in American history. Because of its proximity to this landmark, the pottery was named the "Paul Revere Pottery," though it was also known as the "Bowl Shop."

Immigrant women at the Paul Revere Pottery were trained in the pottery trade in congenial surroundings. The young ladies were read to as they worked, and the work rooms were decorated with flowers. They worked eight-hour days, which was unusual in the early 20th century, and they worked only a half-day on Saturdays. The art pottery produced by these women was very popular, and sold so well that eventually the operation had to be expanded and moved to new quarters in Brighton, Massachusetts. The women's guiding spirit was Edith Brown, who was the principal designer until her death in 1932. The Paul Revere Pottery ceased operations in 1942.

While in existence, the company specialized in making children's dishes (which were often decorated with charming designs such as chickens, roosters, rabbits, ducks, boats, cats, trees, flowers, and nursery rhymes), as well as dinnerware and tiles decorated with various scenes of Boston. The pottery also produced all sorts of bowls, ranging in size from large salad bowls to small salt dishes. Vases were generally decorated either with large flowers or with smaller, stylized floral bands around their tops or on their shoulders. A few pieces with scenic decorations were also made, but these are relatively rare.

Bowl, *4¹/₂-inch diameter, band of ducks in grass around top*	$ 800–1,000
Bowl, *6-inch diameter, Mustard Gold ground with incised border around inside rim featuring landscape with trees, initialed "J. J. S." for "James Jackson Storrow," who reportedly ordered the piece*	$ 1,500–1,750
Calendar holder, *rectangular, 3 inches by 3¹/₄ inches, yellow ground with rectangular reserve at top of cottage scene, artist-signed, some edge roughness*	$ 1,800–2,000
Candle sconce, *8 inches, shield back, elaborate landscape with trees, mountains, and water*	$ 5,000–6,000
Cream soup cup with underliner, *yellow and white, saucer is 5¹/₂ inches in diameter*	$ 350–400
Creamer, *3¹/₂ inches, matte ivory ground, band with chirping chick and haystack around rim, dated 1913 and artist-signed*	$ 325–375
Creamer, *3¹/₂ inches, matte ivory ground, band with geese around neck*	$ 400–450
Cup and saucer, *blue ground with darker-blue band, circular reserve with landscape, monogrammed*	$ 800–1,000
Cup and saucer, *ivory ground with band of pinecone decoration, dated October, 1917, artist-signed*	$ 600–750
Cup and saucer, *ivory ground with band of lotus blossoms, dated 1910*	$ 1,100–1,250
Mug, *6 inches, decoration of three boats with sails, green base*	$ 3,000–3,500

Paul Revere cream soup cup and underliner, yellow and
white, saucer is 5½ inches in diameter, $350–$400.
Item courtesy of Tony McCormack, Sarasota, Florida.

Mug and plate, *set, probably intended for a child, white with blue band and circular reserve with image of a bunny rabbit in a landscape, artist-signed, plate is 7¹/₂-inch diameter*	$ 2,000–2,200
Pitcher, *4¹/₂ inches tall, three white swans swim in band around top, green ground*	$ 1,500–1,750
Plate, *6¹/₄-inch diameter, blue rim with dark-blue inner rim and circular incised landscape in center, dated 1926, artist-signed*	$ 1,200–1,400
Plate, *6¹/₂-inch diameter, blue-and-ivory band around rim, center features a circular reserve with three rabbits, dated 1921, artist-signed*	$ 1,400–1,600
Tile, *circular, 4¹/₄-inch diameter, painted view of Paul Revere's ride, white horse, dated 1926, artist-signed, slight damage to lower edge*	$ 1,000–1,200
Tile, *square, 5¹/₄ inches, glossy blue ground with black outlined drawing of stylized whaling ship and whale*	$ 550–600
Vase, *4 inches, green ground with blue band at top featuring running rabbits, dated 1914, artist-signed*	$ 3,750–4,000
Vase, *8¹/₄ inches tall, ovoid, solid Lavender Pink glaze, artist-signed, dated 1917*	$ 400–450

PENNSBURY POTTERY

Pennsbury
Pottery

Mark commonly found
incised on pieces made by
Pennsbury Pottery.

In 1950, Henry Below (formerly the general manager of the Stangl Pottery Company) opened Pennsbury Pottery in Morrisville, Pennsylvania. The company produced hand-decorated and hand-cast pieces, often in the Pennsylvania Dutch (Deutsch) tradition with birds, hearts, hex signs, and representations of Amish people. Much of the dinnerware is hand-incised, which is somewhat reminiscent of the work done at Stangl. Below died in 1959, and the business was carried on by his wife until her death in 1968. Ernst Below, the Belows' eldest son, continued with Pennsbury until the company went bankrupt in 1970. The factory burned down in 1971.

Dinnerware

"Black Rooster"
Pieces in this line feature a black-and-brown rooster with foliage scrolls.

Butter dish, *square, covered*	$ 40–50
Canister, *flour*	$ 210–250
Creamer	$ 18–25
Cup and saucer	$ 30–40
Dish, *pie, serving, 9-inch diameter*	$ 75–85

Plate, *bread and butter, 6¹/₂-inch diameter*	$ 20–30
Plate, *dinner, 10-inch diameter*	$ 30–40
Plate, *snack with cup*	$ 20–30
Salt and pepper shakers, *set*	$ 35–45
Sugar bowl	$ 20–30
Tray, *relish, five-section, 14¹/₂ inches*	$ 250–275

"Red Rooster"

Pieces in this line are the same as those in the "Black Rooster" line, except that red is included in their color scheme, and pieces are accented with brown-and-green bands.

Bowl, *cereal*	$ 35–45
Bowl, *individual soup*	$ 40–50
Bowl, *vegetable, divided*	$ 85–100
Creamer	$ 35–45
Cup and saucer	$ 25–35
Jug, *¹/₂-pint*	$ 35–45
Jug, *1-pint*	$ 40–50
Jug, *1-quart*	$ 100–130
Plate, *dinner, 10-inch diameter*	$ 40–50
Plate, *salad, 8-inch diameter*	$ 35–45
Plate, *snack with cup*	$ 30–40
Platter, *oval, 11 inches*	$ 60–75
Platter, *oval, 14 inches*	$ 75–95
Sugar bowl	$ 40–50
Teapot, *4-cup*	$ 100–125
Tumbler, *3³/₄ inches*	$ 60–70
Tureen with ladle and metal stand	$ 300–350

Birds

The bird figures made early in Pennsbury's history have hand-painted marks; later versions and birds of lesser quality have an incised mark. Solid-white or solid-ivory examples are considered rare.

Audubon's Warbler, *4 inches*	$ 300–350
Barn Swallow, *6¹/₄ inches*	$ 350–400
Blue Jay, *with leaf, 10¹/₂ inches*	$ 550–650
Blue Jay, *without leaf, 10¹/₂ inches*	$ 600–700
Bluebird, *pink chest, white crest, 4 inches*	$ 165–190
Cardinal, *6¹/₂ inches*	$ 300–350
Chickadee, *3¹/₂ inches*	$ 165–190
Created Chickadee, *4 inches*	$ 165–190
Hen, *all color schemes except multicolored, 10¹/₂ inches*	$ 310–350
Hen, *multicolored*	$ 350–400
Rooster, *all color schemes except multicolored, 11¹/₂ inches*	$ 310–350
Rooster, *multicolored*	$ 350–400
Scarlet Tanager, *5¹/₂ inches*	$ 350–400

PEWABIC POTTERY

One of the marks used by
*Pewabic Pottery of Detroit,
Michigan.*

Mary Chase Perry was a china painter who studied art in
both Cincinnati and New York. In 1903, while living in Detroit, Michigan, she decided to start a pottery with her next-
door neighbor, Horace James Caulkins, who was a maker
of kilns. The pair gave their enterprise the unusual name
"Pewabic Pottery." "Pewabic" was the Native American
name for a local river, but was also a word that meant
"copper-colored clay."

Among the pottery's first products were jars, bowls, and
vases covered with a dark-green matte glaze. The company
also made small architectural tiles, and some square blue-
glazed covered jars that were sold in South America with
cosmetics inside. In 1904, Pewabic exhibited more sophisti-
cated wares at the Louisiana Purchase Exhibition in St.
Louis, Missouri. Thrown by a potter that Perry and
Caulkins had hired, these wares were made from simple
shapes and were covered with flowing matte glazes that
Perry had formulated in shades of yellow, buff, and brown.

In 1906, the company opened a new pottery structure—
more a laboratory and studio than a manufacturing facility—at 10125 East Jefferson Street in Detroit, and the new
facility went into operation the next year. The number of
glazes the company used was greatly expanded, and Pewabic became famous for its Persian Blue glaze, as well as

for its flowing glazes in a variety of hues such as blue, purple, yellow, and white. The making of tiles for public and private buildings had also become something of a specialty for Pewabic; its great success in this field had begun when it was granted a contract to supply tiles for the floor of the new St. Paul's Cathedral in Detroit. Soon it was supplying tiles for a number of important building projects in the Eastern and Midwestern United States, including the Cathedral of St. John the Divine in New York City and the Detroit Institute of Art.

Mary Perry married William Stratton in 1918, and continued to run Pewabic Pottery even after the death of Horace Caulkins in 1923. The Great Depression slowed down Pewabic's business considerably, but the company nonetheless continued to function under Mrs. Stratton until her death in 1961. At that time, the pottery became part of Michigan State University, and was reopened in 1968 under its old name as a ceramics school and studio.

Ashtray, *triangular, 4 inches, gray over red*	$ 125–150
Bookends, *squirrel-like animal motif, 5 inches, blue-green glaze*	$ 600–700
Bowl, *3 inches, turquoise-blue glaze to bare foot (unglazed)*	$ 500–600
Candleholder attached to ruffled-edge drip tray, *4 inches, crystalline-blue glaze*	$ 400–500
Candlestick, *tall, 12 inches, flowing blue-and-black glaze*	$ 1,600–1,800
Plate, *11-inch diameter, decorated using squeeze-bag technique, rabbit-and-tree design*	$ 3,500–4,000
Tile, *4 inches square, impressed home building tool in impressed circle, iridescent plum glaze*	$ 175–200
Tile, *11 inches, scene from Arabian Nights*	$ 600–675
Vase, *3 inches, gray ground with black drip glaze*	$ 800–900
Vase, *4 inches, bulbous bottom to short cylindrical neck, matte yellow and brown flambé glaze*	$ 800–900
Vase, *4 inches, olive-green ground with metallic brown drip from shoulder*	$ 2,000–2,250
Vase, *5 inches, stylized painting of flowers and foliage*	$ 600–700
Vase, *5 inches, iridescent volcanic glaze*	$ 800–1,000
Vase, *5¹/₂ inches tall, bulbous form, orange matte glaze*	$ 650–700
Vase, *7 inches, variegated blue iridescent glaze*	$ 1,600–1,750
Vase, *7 inches, cylinder tapering to shoulder at top, high-gloss glaze with painting of red flowers on long curving stems*	$ 1,800–2,200

Vase, 7 inches, bulbous base to long neck with embossed flower heads on long stems, matte green glaze	$ 6,000–6,500
Vase, 8 inches, lavender, beige, and brown glaze, tall cylinder tapering to collar neck	$ 1,100–1,250
Vase, 8 inches tall, prominent ridges from hand-throwing, glaze is lavender and green with large areas of gold, exceptional work	$ 3,900–4,000

PFALTZGRAFF POTTERY COMPANY

The castle mark used by *Pfaltzgraff Pottery Company,* reportedly based on the outline of the family castle in Germany.

Pfaltzgraff is reportedly the oldest continuously operating family-owned pottery in America. It is located in York, Pennsylvania, and is believed to have been founded in 1811 (though there is some debate as to the exact year, and some believe it might have been founded as early as 1805). Originally the Pfaltzgraff family was from the Pfaltz area of the Rhineland in Germany, and an outlined representation of the family castle (which is still in existence) appears in one of the company's marks.

Initially, there were several Pfaltzgraff potteries scattered around the area making redware and stoneware for local consumption. There are stories of the Pfaltzgraffs allowing parties to be held in their building in the winter, because the heat from the kilns kept the rooms warm and comfortable. It is also said that they allowed local housewives to bake beans in their kilns as they were being heated to the high temperature necessary for firing pottery. Pfaltzgraff adopted the name "Pfaltzgraff Pottery Company" in 1896, and remains in business to this day. Over the years, the company has produced a wide range of items—from animal feeders and redware flowerpots to some commercial art wares and dinnerware, which is the product most associated with Pfaltzgraff today.

"Country Time"

Advertised as "American's complete line of serving accessories . . . complete with place settings," this dinnerware grouping was designed by Ben Seibel and introduced in 1952—the same year that Roseville began making Seibel's "Raymor" line. (The "Country-Time" cup with closed handle has the same shape as the "Raymor" cup.) "Country-Time" was an extensive line with some unusual features, such as platters that could hang from the wall, and metal stands for accessory items with either copper, nickel, or brass plating. "Country-Time" was manufactured in solid colors of Aztec Blue or Teal Blue, but pieces can also be found decorated with underglaze designs featuring either a sunburst or fruit-and-leaf motif. These designs were done in blue with Saffron Yellow or Smoke Grey glaze, or in brown with a white glaze.

Bowl, *individual salad, 6-inch diameter*	$ 15–20
Bowl, *salad, serving, 10¹/2-inch diameter*	$ 35–45
Casserole, *individual, 12-ounce*	$ 38–48
Casserole, *2-quart*	$ 50–65
Casserole, *three-part, three separated lids*	$ 110–125
Coffee samovar, *28-cup*	$ 120–145
Coffeepot, *10-cup*	$ 85–100
Creamer	$ 18–24
Cup and saucer	$ 15–22
Gravy, *stick handle*	$ 45–55
Plate, *barbecue, divided, 11¹/4-inch diameter*	$ 25–35
Plate, *dinner, 10-inch diameter*	$ 22–28
Plate, *luncheon, 8¹/2-inch diameter*	$ 15–22
Platter, *11 inches*	$ 25–35
Platter, *12 inches*	$ 35–45
Platter, *13 inches*	$ 45–55
Salt and pepper shakers, *set*	$ 35–45
Sugar bowl	$ 22–30
Tureen, *6-quart*	$ 85–110

"Gourmet"

First introduced in 1940 as a line of kitchenware, this line was reintroduced in 1950 as the "Gourmet Royale" line, which included dinnerware with a rich brown "Albany slip" glaze and accents of white drip. "Albany slip" glaze got its name from the rich brown clay, discovered in Albany, that was widely used after the mid-19th century. Today the line is known simply as "Gourmet."

Baker, *oval, 7¹/₂ inches*	$ 18–24
Baker, *oval, 9¹/₂ inches*	$ 18–24
Bean pot, *2-quart, New England*	$ 35–45
Bean pot, *3-quart, New England*	$ 38–48
Bowl, *cereal, 5¹/₂-inch diameter*	$ 5–8
Bowl, *chip-and-dip, one-piece*	$ 18–22
Bowl, *individual fruit, 5-inch diameter*	$ 7–10
Bowl, *individual soup, 8¹/₂-inch diameter*	$ 20–28
Bowl, *individual soup, coupe shape*	$ 20–28
Bowls, *mixing, 6-inch diameter*	$ 18–22
Bowl, *salad, serving, 9-inch diameter*	$ 22–28
Bowl, *vegetable, oval, 10 inches*	$ 32–40
Bowl, *vegetable, divided, oval, 12 inches*	$ 22–28
Bowl, *vegetable, round, 8¹/₂-inch diameter*	$ 20–26
Bowl, *vegetable, round, 10-inch diameter*	$ 36–42
Bowl and pitcher set	$ 75–85
Butter dish, *¹/₄-pound, covered*	$ 18–24
Canister, *coffee*	$ 28–35
Canister, *flour*	$ 32–38
Canister, *tea*	$ 18–24
Casserole, *covered, individual, both styles*	$ 8–12
Casserole, *covered, 1 quart, stick handle*	$ 15–22
Casserole, *covered, 2-quart, stick handle*	$ 25–32
Casserole, *covered, 3-quart, stick handle*	$ 35–45
Casserole, *hen-on-the-nest, 2-quart*	$ 80–90
Coffee set, *sugar, creamer, and tray, 3 pieces*	$ 40–50
Coffeepot, *10-cup*	$ 18–24
Creamer	$ 8–12

Cup, *custard*	$ 3–5
Cup and saucer	$ 10–14
Gravy boat	$ 10–14
Jar, *jelly, metal stand*	$ 22–27
Jug, *32-ounce*	$ 18–22
Jug, *60-ounce, ice lip*	$ 22–28
Lazy Susan, *five-piece*	$ 45–55
Mug, *12-ounce*	$ 12–16
Pie baker, *9$^1/_2$ inches*	$ 28–35
Plate, *dinner, 10-inch diameter*	$ 20–26
Plate, *salad, 7-inch diameter*	$ 7–10
Plate, *snack with cup*	$ 18–22
Platter, *oval, 12 inches*	$ 18–22
Platter, *oval, 14 inches*	$ 25–35
Platter, *oval, 16 inches*	$ 35–45
Relish, *three-part*	$ 10–14
Relish, *four-part*	$ 20–26
Salt and pepper shakers, *set*	$ 10–14
Sugar bowl	$ 15–20
Tray, *two-tier*	$ 20–28
Tureen, *no ladle, 5-quart*	$ 65–75
Tureen and ladle, *2$^1/_2$-quart*	$ 75–85

"Yorktowne"

At last report, this pattern is still in production. Based on Pfaltzgraff's 19th-century blue decorated stoneware, it was designed by Maury Mountain and was introduced in 1967. Flatware items usually feature a blue band around the edge of the well, and a blue flower against a gray-blue matte glazed background in the center. The earlier and most desirable pieces feature a Pennsylvania Dutch (Deutsch)-style tulip, but later examples have two blossoms arching out of several leaves (or, in some cases, only one blossom or no blossoms at all).

Au gratin, *8 inches*	$ 15–22
Au gratin, *9 inches*	$ 15–20

Baker, *oval, 7 inches*	$ 18–24
Baker, *oval, 1-quart, 9^1/$_2$ inches*	$ 20–26
Baker, *square, 10 inches*	$ 23–30
Baker, *rectangular, 13 inches*	$ 28–35
Baker, *rectangular, 14 inches*	$ 38–48
Bean pot, *2^1/$_2$-quart*	$ 45–55
Bowl, *batter, 2^1/$_2$-quart, handle and spout*	$ 65–75
Bowl, *cereal, 6^1/$_4$-inch diameter*	$ 7–10
Bowl, *dough or punch, 8-quart*	$ 95–110
Bowl, *individual fruit, 5-inch diameter*	$ 7–10
Bowl, *individual soup, 6^1/$_2$-inch diameter*	$ 7–10
Bowl, *individual soup, 8^1/$_2$-inch diameter*	$ 8–12
Bowl, *mixing, 6-inch diameter, 1-pint*	$ 12–18
Bowl, *mixing, 8-inch diameter, 1^1/$_2$-quart*	$ 22–28
Bowl, *mixing, 10 inches, 3-quart*	$ 23–30
Bowl, *vegetable, oval, divided, 12 inches*	$ 23–30
Bowl, *vegetable, round, 7^1/$_2$-inch diameter*	$ 11–15
Bowl, *vegetable, round, 8^1/$_2$-inch diameter*	$ 12–16
Bread tray	$ 12–18
Butter dish, *^{1}/$_4$-pound, covered*	$ 18–24
Butter tub	$ 15–22
Cake stand, *pedestal*	$ 32–40
Canister, *coffee*	$ 18–24
Canister, *flour*	$ 28–35
Canister, *tea*	$ 18–24
Casserole, *individual, 12-ounce, covered*	$ 15–20
Casserole, *2-quart, covered*	$ 25–32
Chip-and-dip bowl, *12 inches*	$ 38–45
Clock	$ 28–35
Coaster	$ 5–8
Coffeepot, *8-cup*	$ 38–45

Cookie jar	$ 28–35
Corn dish	$ 9–12
Creamer	$ 8–12
Crock, *cheese*	$ 5–9
Crock, *onion soup, stick handle, open*	$ 10–14
Crock, *utensils*	$ 14–18
Cup and saucer	$ 5–8
Cup and saucer, *demitasse*	$ 8–12
Custard cup, *heart-shaped or regular*	$ 5–8
Egg cup, *chicken-shaped, single*	$ 10–15
Gravy boat	$ 12–16
Jam server with lid	$ 16–22
Loaf pan	$ 28–35
Mug, *14-ounce*	$ 8–12
Napkin holder	$ 26–32
Napkin holder, *figural*	$ 28–35
Napkin ring	$ 2–3
Pitcher, *1-quart*	$ 35–45
Pitcher, *2¹/₂-quart*	$ 45–55
Pitcher and bowl set	$ 130–145
Plate, *bread and butter, 6¹/₂-inch diameter*	$ 4–7
Plate, *dinner, 10-inch diameter*	$ 9–12
Plate, *luncheon, 8¹/₂-inch diameter*	$ 11–15
Plate, *salad, 7-inch diameter*	$ 4–6
Plate, *snack with cup*	$ 12–18
Plate, *steak, oval, 12 inches*	$ 14–18
Platter, *oval, 14 inches*	$ 22–28
Platter, *oval, 16 inches*	$ 38–45
Platter, *oval, 18 inches, turkey*	$ 45–55
Porringer	$ 18–24
Quiche, *9 inches*	$ 20–28

Relish, *three-part*	$ 22–28
Relish, *four-part, with metal holder*	$ 52–60
Salt box, *lidded*	$ 45–55
Shaker, *cinnamon or spice*	$ 18–24
Shaker, *sugar*	$ 18–24
Shakers, *salt and pepper, set*	$ 12–16
Shakers, *salt and pepper, range set*	$ 28–35
Soufflé, *6 inches*	$ 17–23
Soufflé, *8 inches*	$ 20–26
Sugar bowl	$ 10–14
Tankard, *19-ounce, eagle decoration*	$ 12–16
Teapot, *19-ounce*	$ 28–32
Teapot, *42-ounce*	$ 42–50
Tidbit server, *two-tier*	$ 32–40
Trivet, *square*	$ 14–18
Tureen	$ 55–65
Tureen with ladle and underliner	$ 95–110
Vase, *5 inches*	$ 14–18

Cookie Jars

Clown, *with drum*	$ 400–450
Cookie Bag	$ 300–350
Cookie Clock	$ 275–325
Cookie Cop	$ 750–850
Cookie House	$ 375–425
Derby Dan, *"Muggsy"*	$ 500–575
Engine (Cookie Flyer)	$ 325–400
French Chef	$ 825–925
Handy Harry, *"Muggsy"*	$ 500–550
Old Lady in Shoe	$ 350–425
Stagecoach	$ 650–750

PICKARD CHINA COMPANY

Mark first used by the
Pickard China Company in
1898.

This company was founded by Wilder Pickard in Edgerton, Wisconsin, in 1893, but soon moved to Chicago, Illinois. At first, the company did not make china—it merely decorated blanks bought from other manufacturers in France, Germany, Japan, and, to a lesser extent, the United States. The company hired superb artists who did first-rate work, however, and modern collectors look for pieces signed "Challinor," "Marker," "Weiss," "Yeschek," "Kubasch," "Aldrich," and others.

Pickard began manufacturing its own china in the 1930s, and in 1937 it leased the old Corona fountain pen factory in Antioch, Illinois, to begin manufacturing in earnest. In later years, Pickard produced dinnerware for such notable clients as Queen Elizabeth II, Camp David, Blair House, and United States embassies around the world.

Artwares

Bowl, *two-handled, signed by artist Edward Mentges, Limoges blank, poppies and lavish gold*	$ 1,100–1,200
Celery dish, *floral decoration, not artist-signed, circa 1915*	$ 325–375

Pickard two-handled bowl, artist-signed: "Edward Mentges," Limoges blank, $1,100–$1,200.
Item courtesy of Charles Seagrove and Don Griffin, Old School Antique Mall, Sylva, North Carolina.

Pickard celery dish, not artist-signed, $325–$375.
Item courtesy of Charles Seagrove and Don Griffin, Old School Antique Mall, Sylva, North Carolina.

Pickard pitcher, large, artist-signed: "H. Tolley," "Poinsettia and Lustre" pattern, Limoges blank, $500–$600.
Item courtesy of Charles Seagrove and Don Griffin, Old School Antique Mall, Sylva, North Carolina.

Pickard scenic plate, 7¼-inch diameter, artist-signed: "Marker," $150–$200.
Item courtesy of Richard Crane, Knoxville, Tennessee.

Console bowl, *two handles, gold interior and handles with marbleized exterior, Japanese blank, no artist signature, mid-1930s*	$ 200–225
Creamer and sugar set, *etched gold, circa 1910*	$ 70–80
Ewer, *10 inches, unusual dark background with image of an ear of corn, gold top and handle, artist-signed, Austrian blank, circa 1910*	$ 1,250–1,400
Pitcher, *circa 1910, 3¼ inches tall, gold at top and bottom, rose decoration, artist-signed*	$ 90–110

Pickard scenic plate, 8³/₄-inch diameter, artist-signed: "Challinor," $300–$375. *Item courtesy of Richard Crane, Knoxville, Tennessee.*

Pickard scenic plate, 8³/₄-inch diameter, artist-signed: "W. Rawlings," $225–$275. *Item courtesy of Charles Seagrove and Don Griffin, Old School Antique Mall, Sylva, North Carolina.*

Pickard scenic plate, 8³/₄-inch diameter, artist-signed, $250–$300. *Item courtesy of Charles Seagrove and Don Griffin, Old School Antique Mall, Sylva, North Carolina.*

Pickard tea set consisting of teapot, creamer, and sugar bowl, "Butterfly" pattern, not artist-signed, $1,100–$1,200. *Item courtesy of Wade and Brenda Ford, Old School Antique Mall, Sylva, North Carolina.*

Pitcher, *large, signed by artist H. Tolley, Limoges blank, "Poinsettia and Lustre" decoration, wear to gilding*	$ 500–600
Plate, *bread and butter, 6¹/₂-inch diameter, gold band with violets, not artist-signed*	$ 40–50
Plate, *bread and butter, 6³/₄-inch diameter, signed by artist "Marker," buttercup decoration, circa 1920*	$ 60–75
Plate, *7¹/₄-inch diameter, scenic decoration, signed "Marker"*	$ 150–200
Plate, *8³/₄-inch diameter, scenic design, signed "Challinor," circa 1915*	$ 300–375

Plate, *8³/₄-inch diameter, scenic decoration, signed by artist* "W. Rawlings"	$ 225–275
Plate, *8³/₄-inch diameter, scenic decoration, artist-signed*	$ 250–300
Sugar bowl, *lidded, 3 inches tall, gold at top, on lid, and on handles, painted with "Dahlia Rubra" pattern, signed by artist A. Richter, circa 1912*	$ 185–200
Tea set consisting of a teapot, sugar bowl, and cream pitcher, *"Butterfly" design, not artist-signed*	$ 1,100–1,200
Vase, *15 inches tall, lavishly decorated on the front with wisteria, and on the back with a sprig of wisteria, artist-signed, on Austrian blank, circa 1910*	$ 1,600–1,750

Dinnerware

"April"

This pattern features a large bouquet of flowers in yellow, purple, and pink. The pattern is positioned off-center on the flatware items, with scattered single blossoms on their edges.

Bowl, *cream soup, with underliner*	$ 70–80
Bowl, *soup, 8-inch diameter*	$ 30–36
Bowl, *vegetable, oval, 9 inches*	$ 80–90
Coffeepot	$ 185–195
Cup and saucer	$ 40–50
Gravy boat, *with underliner*	$ 135–145
Plate, *bread and butter, 6¹/₄-inch diameter*	$ 12–16
Plate, *dinner, 10¹/₄-inch diameter*	$ 35–45
Plate, *salad, 8-inch diameter*	$ 20–26

"Athenian"

This pattern is distinguished by a heavily tooled and encrusted gold band around the edges of flatware and hollowware.

Bowl, *cream soup, with underliner*	$ 75–85
Bowl, *individual fruit, 5-inch diameter*	$ 35–45
Bowl, *soup, 8-inch diameter*	$ 85–95
Bowl, *vegetable, oval, 9¹/₂ inches*	$ 155–165

Bowl, *vegetable, round, 9¹/₄-inch diameter*	$ 185–195
Bowl, *vegetable, round, covered*	$ 600–625
Creamer	$ 145–155
Cup and saucer	$ 65–75
Cup and saucer, *demitasse*	$ 55–65
Gravy boat, *faststand*	$ 245–255
Plate, *bread and butter, 6¹/₂-inch diameter*	$ 30–40
Plate, *dinner, 10¹/₂-inch diameter*	$ 75–85
Plate, *luncheon, 9¹/₄-inch diameter*	$ 65–75
Plate, *salad, 8-inch diameter*	$ 55–65
Platter, *oval, 12¹/₂ inches*	$ 200–220
Platter, *oval, 15¹/₄ inches*	$ 250–260

"Blue Skies"

This pattern won the Altman award for American design in 1955. It features a blue ground with a scattering of white tree-like designs that terminate in silver teardrops.

Coffeepot	$ 195–210
Creamer	$ 40–50
Cup and saucer	$ 45–55
Gravy boat, *faststand*	$ 155–165
Plate, *bread and butter, 6¹/₄ inches*	$ 20–25
Plate, *dinner, 10¹/₄-inch diameter*	$ 40–50
Plate, *salad, 8-inch diameter*	$ 25–32
Platter, *oval, 12¹/₂ inches*	$ 135–145
Platter, *oval, 15¹/₂ inches*	$ 185–200
Sugar bowl, *lidded*	$ 85–95

"Brocade"

This is Pickard's best-selling pattern. The design is white on a white floral-and-leaf brocade.

| Bowl, *individual fruit, 5¹/₄-inch diameter* | $ 35–45 |
| Bowl, *soup, 8¹/₄-inch diameter* | $ 55–65 |

Bowl, *vegetable, oval, 9¹/₂ inches*	$ 145–155
Bowl, *vegetable, round, 9¹/₂-inch diameter*	$ 135–145
Creamer	$ 70–80
Cup and saucer	$ 32–40
Gravy boat, *faststand*	$ 195–210
Plate, *bread and butter, 6¹/₂-inch diameter*	$ 18–22
Plate, *dinner, 10¹/₂-inch diameter*	$ 45–55
Plate, *salad, 8¹/₄-inch diameter*	$ 25–35
Platter, *oval, 12¹/₂ inches*	$ 165–175
Sugar bowl, *lidded*	$ 90–100

"Cattails"

On flatware, this pattern consists of a grouping of cattails and foliage in the center, with scattered cattails around the rim.

Bowl, *cereal, 5-inch diameter*	$ 25–32
Bowl, *cream soup, with underliner*	$ 75–85
Bowl, *soup, 8-inch diameter*	$ 30–38
Bowl, *vegetable, oval, 9¹/₂ inches*	$ 85–95
Bowl, *vegetable, round, covered*	$ 265–275
Coffeepot	$ 145–155
Creamer	$ 42–48
Cup and saucer	$ 45–55
Cup and saucer, *demitasse*	$ 35–45
Gravy boat, *faststand*	$ 125–135
Plate, *bread and butter, 6¹/₂-inch diameter*	$ 28–34
Plate, *chop, 12-inch diameter*	$ 125–135
Plate, *dinner, 10¹/₂-inch diameter*	$ 30–38
Plate, *salad, 8¹/₄-inch diameter*	$ 18–22
Platter, *oval, 12¹/₂ inches*	$ 85–95
Platter, *oval, 15¹/₄ inches*	$ 135–150
Sugar bowl, *lidded*	$ 70–80

"Washington"

This pattern is distinguished by a cobalt blue band around the outer rims of flatware pieces, with a gold decoration around the inner edge of the band and a plain gold band around the verge.

Bowl, *individual fruit, 5-inch diameter*	$ 45–55
Bowl, *soup, 8¹/₄-inch diameter*	$ 70–80
Bowl, *vegetable, oval, 9¹/₂ inches*	$ 165–175
Bowl, *vegetable, round, 9¹/₂-inch diameter*	$ 175–185
Creamer	$ 115–125
Cup and saucer	$ 75–85
Gravy boat, *faststand*	$ 235–245
Plate, *bread and butter, 6¹/₂-inch diameter*	$ 30–36
Plate, *dinner, 10³/₄-inch diameter*	$ 60–70
Plate, *salad, 8¹/₄-inch diameter*	$ 40–50
Platter, *oval, 12¹/₄ inches*	$ 175–185
Platter, *oval, 15¹/₄ inches*	$ 215–225
Sugar bowl, *lidded*	$ 135–145
Teapot, *three-cup*	$ 295–310

PISGAH FOREST POTTERY

Potter's wheel mark used by *Pisgah Forest Pottery*.

Walter B. Stephen was a stonemason working in West Tennessee when he discovered clay while digging a well with his father. Stephen's mother was artistic, and she and her son began making pottery from the clay they had discovered. Mrs. Stephen decorated the pots with raised designs that featured such things as covered wagons and other scenes from American frontier life. The pottery was christened the "Nonconnah Pottery," and operated until 1910 when Walter Stephen's parents died.

Stephen relocated to western North Carolina, near Asheville, in 1913. He settled near the foot of Mt. Pisgah, and began to make pottery with C. P. Ryman. This partnership dissolved in 1916, but Stephen began to make pottery again around 1920, and he continued to do so until his death in 1961. The Pisgah Forest Pottery continued for many years after his death.

The most desired Pisgah Forest products are pieces with crystalline glazes and pieces decorated with raised cameo-like designs similar to the ones originated by Stephen's mother at the Nonconnah Pottery.

Pisgah Forest bean pot, cameo ware, brown and white, $1,200–$1,400. *Item courtesy of Richard Hatch and Associates, Hendersonville, North Carolina.*

Pisgah Forest batter jug, cameo ware, matte green, wagon train design, $800–$900. *Item courtesy of Richard Hatch and Associates, Hendersonville, North Carolina.*

Pisgah Forest pitcher, typical turquoise-and-purple glaze, 5 inches, $75–$100. *Item courtesy of Richard Hatch and Associates, Hendersonville, North Carolina.*

Pisgah Forest vase, cameo, 4½ inches, mottled blue/green glaze below, green above with pink interior, wagon train design, $600–$675. *Item courtesy of Richard Hatch and Associates, Hendersonville, North Carolina.*

Batter jug, 7½ inches, green, cameo decoration, wagon train	$ 800–900
Bean pot, 6 inches, cameo, brown and white, "They Ate Beans Instead of King's Meat, Dan. 1–15"	$ 1,200–1,400
Pitcher, 5 inches, turquoise-and-purple glaze	$ 75–100
Vase, 4½ inches tall, cameo, wagon train, mottled blue and green below, green above with pink interior, dated 1933	$ 600–675
Vase, 4½ inches tall, typical turquoise glaze	$ 75–100
Vase, 5 inches, bulbous, yellow-and-green crystalline glaze	$ 450–525

Pisgah Forest vase, yellow-and-green crystalline glaze, 5 inches, $450–$525.
Item courtesy of Richard H. Crane, Knoxville, Tennessee.

Pisgah Forest vase, cameo, 5¼ inches, 32nd degree Knight Kidosh, Masonic, 1960, $800–$900.
Item courtesy of Richard Hatch and Associates, Hendersonville, North Carolina.

Pisgah Forest vase, turquoise glaze, 7½ inches, $150–$200.
Item courtesy of Richard Hatch and Associates, Hendersonville, North Carolina.

Vase, 5¼ inches, cameo, "32nd degree Knight Kidosh, Masonic," dated 1960	$ 800–900
Vase, 5½ inches, white-and-yellow crystalline glaze	$ 550–650
Vase, 5½ inches, bulbous with flared lip, brown flowing into white glaze	$ 375–425
Vase, 7 inches, green-and-yellow crystalline glaze, bulbous form	$ 700–800
Vase, 7½ inches, turquoise glaze	$ 150–200

Vase, *cameo, 9 inches, covered wagon with oxen, blue below, dark green above*	$ 750–900
Vase, *9¹/₂ inches, striking crystalline glaze, yellow ground with blue crystals*	$ 1,600–1,750
Vase, *cameo, 11 inches, bulbous shape with black ground on the base and matte blue above, a white line separates the two with a scene of a covered wagon pulled by oxen, horsemen, dog, cabin, and mountains, fine quality, signed "W. B. Stephen"*	$ 1,000–1,200

POPE-GOSSER CHINA COMPANY

Wreath mark used by the
*Pope Gosser China
Company* (the company
name often appears with a
hyphen: "Pope-Gosser").

Charles F. Gosser and Bentley Pope founded the Pope-Gosser China Company in Coshocton, Ohio, in 1902. The firm's early wares were very fine, highly vitrified pieces that were somewhat translucent. These wares proved to be unprofitable, however, and the company switched to making semiporcelain dinnerware that was somewhat harder than most of the semiporcelain products produced by other companies at the time. In 1904 and 1907, Pope-Gosser won medals at world's fairs for their china and semiporcelain.

In 1929, in an attempt to cope with the Great Depression, Pope-Gosser joined the ill-fated American China Corporation, which was bankrupt by 1931. The company was reorganized in 1932, and continued to produce dinnerware until 1958.

"Briar Rose"

This lovely pattern features a grouping of embossed roses on a diamond-hatched trellis background. Flatware items are basically square with elaborately shaped edges. Pope-Gosser acquired this pattern from the Salem China Company.

Bowl, *cereal, coupe shape, 6³/₄ inches*	$ 20–25
Bowl, *individual fruit, 5¹/₂ inches*	$ 15–20
Bowl, *vegetable, round, covered*	$ 125–140

Cup and saucer	$ 30–35
Dish, *celery, 12 inches*	$ 40–50
Plate, *bread and butter, 6^1/$_2$-inch diameter*	$ 8–12
Plate, *dinner, 10^1/$_2$ inches*	$ 20–28
Plate, *luncheon, 9^1/$_2$ inches*	$ 18–25
Plate, *salad, 7^1/$_2$ inches*	$ 12–16
Platter, *oval, 13^1/$_2$ inches*	$ 70–85
Relish, *7^1/$_2$ inches*	$ 25–35

"Rosepoint"

This is perhaps Pope-Gosser's most popular pattern, and is in fact one of the most popular patterns in the history of American dinnerware. It was first produced in 1934 in plain white, with decal decorations added in 1935. The design features embossed trailing roses, and the covered pieces have rose finials. The handles of some pieces also feature a raised rose.

Bowl, *cereal, rim or lugged*	$ 17–22
Bowl, *cream soup, with underliner*	$ 25–35
Bowl, *individual fruit, 5^3/$_4$-inch diameter*	$ 8–12
Bowl, *individual soup, 8-inch diameter*	$ 18–24
Bowl, *vegetable, oval, 9^1/$_2$ inches*	$ 25–35
Bowl, *vegetable, round, 8^3/$_4$-inch diameter*	$ 30–38
Bowl, *vegetable, covered*	$ 85–100
Coffeepot	$ 115–130
Creamer	$ 16–22
Cup and saucer	$ 11–17
Gravy boat, *faststand*	$ 45–52
Plate, *bread and butter, 6^1/$_2$-inch diameter*	$ 4–7
Plate, *dinner, 10-inch diameter*	$ 22–30
Plate, *luncheon, 9-inch diameter*	$ 17–22
Plate, *salad, 7^1/$_2$-inch diameter*	$ 15–20
Platter, *oval, 11 inches*	$ 38–45
Sugar bowl	$ 30–40
Teapot, *4-cup*	$ 135–150

POTTERY GUILD

"Pottery Guild" was a name used by Block China, which was a distribution company located in New York City. The cookie jars listed below were made by the Cronin China Company of Minerva, Ohio.

Balloon Lady, *rose-colored skirt, decorated top*	$ 225–275
Chef, *with tray of cookies, decorated*	$ 450–550
Dutch Boy, *blue or pink*	$ 225–275
Dutch Boy, *brown bottom, decorated lid*	$ 250–325
Dutch Girl, *blue or pink*	$ 225–275
Dutch Girl, *blue bottom, decorated lid*	$ 250–325
Elsie the Cow, *in barrel, "Elsie, Handle with Care"*	$ 1,000–1,200
Little Girl, *blue bottom, decorated lid*	$ 450–500
Little Red Riding Hood	$ 225–275
Ole King Cole	$ 850–950

PURINTON POTTERY

In 1936, Bernard Purinton purchased the East Liverpool Potteries Company in Wellsville, Ohio, and founded Purinton Pottery. When the Wellsville facility proved inadequate for the company's needs, a new plant was constructed in Shippenville, Pennsylvania, and the new facility began operations in 1941. The company did not use decal or transfer-printed decoration on its dinnerware; it used only hand-painting underglaze. In the late 1950s, the company ran into financial trouble. After a failed attempt to allow Taylor, Smith & Taylor to take over management of the company's operations, Purinton closed in 1959.

"Apple"

This is said to be Purinton's first and most successful pattern. The design consists of a large apple with a thick red band surrounding an ivory-and-brown center, and is accented with green leaves and brown twigs.

Baker, *7 inches*	$ 32–40
Bowl, *cereal, 5$^{1}/_{2}$-inch diameter*	$ 14–22
Bowl, *individual fruit, 4-inch diameter*	$ 12–16
Bowl, *salad, serving, 11-inch diameter*	$ 75–85
Bowl, *vegetable, oval, 8 inches*	$28–36

Purinton "Autumn Leaf" pattern creamer, $50–$60.
Item courtesy of Kingston Pike Antique Mall, Knoxville, Tennessee.

Purinton "Fruit" pattern creamer, $25–$35.
Item courtesy of Kingston Pike Antique Mall, Knoxville, Tennessee.

Purinton "Fruit" pattern teapot, $35–$45.
Item courtesy of Bill Brooker, Old School Antique Mall, Sylva, North Carolina.

Purinton "Red Blossom Ivy" jug, $30–$40.
Item courtesy of Bill Brooker, Old School Antique Mall, Sylva, North Carolina.

Bowl, *vegetable, oval, covered*	$ 70–80
Canister, *flour*	$ 60–70
Cookie jar, *ceramic top, square*	$ 250–300
Creamer	$ 22–32
Cup and saucer	$ 20–28
Jug, *Kent, 1-pint*	$ 32–40
Marmalade jar	$ 58–65

Purinton "Yellow Blossom Ivy" creamer,
$25–$30.
*Item courtesy of Bill Brooker, Old School
Antique Mall, Sylva, North Carolina.*

Purinton "Apple" creamer, $22–$32.
*Item courtesy of Bill Brooker, Old School
Antique Mall, Sylva, North Carolina.*

Pickle dish, *6 inches*	$ 130–150
Plate, *dinner, 9³/₄-inch diameter*	$ 38–48
Plate, *luncheon, 8¹/₂-inch diameter*	$ 20–28
Plate, *salad, 6³/₄-inch diameter*	$ 24–32
Plate, *snack with cup*	$ 190–210
Platter, *oblong, 12 inches*	$ 45–55
Relish, *three-part*	$ 38–46
Sugar bowl	$ 30–38
Teapot	$ 95–110
Tumbler, *juice, 6-ounce*	$ 14–18
Tumbler, *12-ounce*	$ 28–35

"Heather Plaid" and "Normandy Plaid"

The "Heather Plaid" pattern consists of two crisscrossing bands of turquoise accented with thinner lines of burgundy and yellow. "Normandy Plaid" is the same pattern, but with crisscrossing bands of burgundy accented with thinner bands of chartreuse and forest green. "Heather Plaid" pieces command prices at the top of the ranges listed below, while "Normandy Plaid" pieces command prices near the bottom.

Baker, *7 inches*	$ 22–30
Bowl, *fruit, footed, 12-inch diameter*	$ 70–90
Bowl, *individual fruit, 4-inch diameter*	$ 11–20
Bowl, *vegetable, oval, 8 inches*	$ 30–40
Butter dish, *$^1/_4$-pound, open*	$ 80–100
Cruet, *oil and vinegar, jug-shaped, square*	$ 80–110
Cup and saucer	$ 18–26
Plate, *bread and butter, 6$^3/_4$-inch diameter*	$ 12–18
Plate, *dinner, 9$^3/_4$-inch diameter*	$ 22–30
Plate, *luncheon, 8$^1/_2$-inch diameter*	$ 18–25
Salt and pepper shakers, *set*	$ 30–40

"Intaglio"

This unusual pattern has narrow serpentine bands of lighter color undulating across a darker, solid-color background. The design is accented with an etched image of a flower with leaves. Some pieces feature a different etched decoration, such as a palm tree. "Intaglio" pieces are most often brown, though turquoise, baby blue, caramel, coral, and sapphire blue pieces were made as well. Prices quoted below are for brown pieces; add 20 percent for turquoise pieces, and 50 percent for all other pieces.

Bean pot, *individual*	$ 30–40
Bowl, *cereal, 5$^1/_2$-inch diameter*	$ 8–14
Bowl, *individual fruit, 4-inch diameter*	$ 8–14
Bowl, *vegetable, oval, 8 inches*	$ 30–40
Bowl, *vegetable, oval, covered*	$ 115–125
Butter, *$^1/_4$-pound, open*	$ 70–85
Creamer	$ 16–24
Cruet, *oil*	$ 38–45
Cruet, *vinegar*	$ 38–45
Cup and saucer	$ 20–30
Dish, *jam*	$ 25–32

Jug, *Kent, 1-pint*	$ 38–45
Mug, *beer, 5 inches*	$ 25–35
Mug, *beer, palm tree decoration, 5 inches*	$ 165–225
Pickle dish	$ 25–35
Plate, *bread and butter, 6³/₄-inch diameter*	$ 5–10
Plate, *chop, 12 inches*	$ 65–75
Plate, *dinner, 9³/₄-inch diameter*	$ 17–25
Plate, *luncheon, 8¹/₂ inches*	$ 14–20
Plate, *luncheon, 8¹/₂ inches, with palm tree*	$ 150–210
Plate, *snack, with cup*	$ 20–28
Platter, *oblong, 12 inches*	$ 45–55
Relish, *three-part*	$ 22–30
Salt and pepper shakers, *set*	$ 20–28
Tray, *roll, 11 inches*	$ 42–50

RED WING POTTERIES

One of the marks used by *Red Wing Potteries.*

One of the marks used by *Red Wing Potteries.*

In 1861, deposits of clay were discovered near Red Wing, Minnesota, by German immigrant Joseph Paul. Paul made some utilitarian stoneware pots from the clay, but he soon left the area. In 1868, David Hallem began using this local clay to make stoneware pottery at his home in Red Wing, but this venture failed after only a few years.

In 1878, a group of local investors organized the Red Wing Stoneware Company and made Hallem its manager. The firm became one of the leading makers of stoneware in the United States, but by the late 19th century it faced serious competition from the Minnesota Stoneware Company (organized in 1883) and the Northstar Company (founded in 1892).

Northstar went out of business, however, and in 1900 both Red Wing's and Minnesota Stoneware's facilities burned to the ground. Both companies rebuilt, and in 1908 merged to become the Red Wing Union Stoneware Company. Besides crocks, churns, jugs, and other utilitarian stoneware items, the company made other types of pottery and began making decorative art pottery around 1920.

In 1933, Red Wing began making commercial art ware designed by George Rumrill, who owned Arkansas Products of Little Rock, Arkansas. Arkansas Products was a distribution firm, and its wares are marked "Rumrill" rather

Red Wing Potteries "Capistrano" pattern dinnerware on the company's "Anniversary" shape. First introduced in 1953, this pattern consists of wonderful swooping swallows hand-painted on each piece. Sugar bowl, $20–$25 (creamer, not pictured, is the same price); rectangular bread tray, $35–$50; and buffet bowl, $35–$50.
Items courtesy of Kingston Pike Antique Mall, Knoxville, Tennessee.

Red Wing Potteries, "Plain" pattern pitcher, 6½ inches, green glaze, $80–$100.
Item courtesy of Elaine Delcuze, Old School Antique Mall, Sylva, North Carolina.

than "Red Wing." Rumrill's relationship with Red Wing ended in 1938, but "Rumrill" pottery was made by other companies (particularly Gonder) until Rumrill died in 1942.

Red Wing began making dinnerware in 1935, and changed its name to "Red Wing Potteries" in 1936. Its first dinnerware lines consisted of solid-color wares similar to Homer Laughlin's "Fiesta" pieces, but Red Wing is best known for its hand-painted designs that were made until the company closed in 1967.

Dinnerware

"Bob White"

First produced in 1956, "Bob White" pieces were hand-painted in shades of brown and turquoise on a beige speckled ground. Some pieces were also made with all-white backgrounds. "Bob White" was the most widely made Red Wing dinnerware pattern, and pieces are easily found today. "Bob White" items were made using Red Wing's "Casual" shapes.

Beverage server, *with stopper*	$ 105–115
Bowl, *cereal, 6½-inch diameter*	$ 25–30

Red Wing Potteries hors d'oeuvre server in the "Bob White" pattern.
This piece is in the form of a bobwhite quail and has holes in the back
to hold toothpicks. $75–$95.
Item courtesy of Kingston Pike Antique Mall, Knoxville, Tennessee.

Bowl, *individual fruit, 5³/₄-inch diameter*	$ 24–30
Bowl, *salad, serving, 12-inch diameter*	$ 60–70
Bowl, *vegetable, oval, divided, 14 inches*	$ 35–42
Bowl, *vegetable, round, 9¹/₂-inch diameter*	$ 32–40
Casserole, *1-quart, with metal holder*	$ 95–105
Casserole, *1-quart, no metal holder*	$ 75–85
Casserole, *2-quart, with metal holder*	$ 105–115
Casserole, *4-quart, with metal holder*	$ 135–145
Cookie jar	$ 145–160
Creamer	$ 24–30
Cup and saucer	$ 15–20
Gravy boat, *stick handle, with lid*	$ 55–65
Hors d'oeuvre holder, *bird*	$ 75–95
Jug, *water, small, 60-ounce*	$ 42–52
Mug	$ 75–85

Plate, *bread and butter, 6¹/₂-inch diameter*	$ 10–14
Plate, *dinner, 10-inch diameter*	$ 18–24
Plate, *dinner, 10-inch diameter, white background*	$ 150–200
Plate, *salad, 8-inch diameter*	$ 22–28
Platter, *oval, 13 inches*	$ 35–45
Platter, *oval, 20 inches*	$ 125–135
Relish dish, *three sections*	$ 45–55
Shakers, *salt and pepper, bird form, set*	$ 35–45
Shakers, *tall, salt and pepper, set*	$ 30–40
Sugar bowl	$ 28–35
Tray, *bread, rectangular, 24 inches*	$ 115–125

"Flight"

A precise date for this rare Red Wing line of dinnerware is difficult to establish, but it probably originated in the early 1960s. This particular pattern is composed of black, brown, and beige ducks in flight over a stylized marsh background.

Bowl, *divided vegetable*	$ 85–100
Cup and saucer	$ 65–85
Gravy boat, *covered*	$ 100–125
Jug, *1¹/₂-quart*	$ 125–150
Plate, *dinner*	$ 110–140

"Lexington" (or "Lexington Rose")

Introduced in 1941, the "Lexington" (or "Lexington Rose") pattern features bold pink roses in full bloom with green leaves against a white background. Pieces were made using Red Wing's "Casual" shapes.

Bowl, *individual fruit, 5¹/₄-inch diameter*	$ 8–12
Casserole, *round, 1¹/₄-quart*	$ 90–100
Creamer	$ 22–35
Cup and saucer	$ 18–22
Plate, *bread and butter, 6¹/₂-inch diameter*	$ 5–8
Plate, *dinner, 10¹/₂-inch diameter*	$ 16–22
Plate, *salad, 7¹/₄-inch diameter*	$ 10–14

Platter, *oval, 13 inches*	$ 45–60
Shakers, *salt and pepper, set*	$ 25–30
Tray, *supper, three compartments with a cup holder*	$ 28–35

"Plum Blossom"

This pattern is the only one found on Red Wing's "Dynasty" shapes. It is painted with either pink or yellow Asian-inspired flowers with brown stems and twigs. The pattern first appeared in 1949, and the flatware pieces are hexagonal with 6 deep notches around their edges.

Bowl, *individual fruit, 6 inches*	$ 13–17
Bowl, *individual soup, 7¹/₂ inches*	$ 17–22
Bowl, *vegetable, round, 9 inches*	$ 45–55
Creamer	$ 34–42
Cup and saucer	$ 25–32
Cup and saucer, *demitasse*	$ 22–30
Gravy boat, *faststand*	$ 70–80
Plate, *bread and butter, 6¹/₂ inches*	$ 7–10
Plate, *dinner, 10¹/₂ inches*	$ 18–26
Plate, *salad, 8 inches*	$ 12–16
Platter, *oval, 13 inches*	$ 60–70
Platter, *oval, 15 inches*	$ 85–95
Shakers, *salt and pepper, set*	$ 35–45
Sugar bowl	$ 42–50

"Provincial"

"Provincial" is actually the name of a Red Wing shape that was introduced in 1941, and on which Red Wing produced its first hand-decorated dinnerware. There were four patterns produced: "Brittany" (distinguished by a large full-blown yellow rose in the lower center of the flatware, and surrounded by other flowers, leaves, and buds in yellow, blue, and green), "Orleans" (similar to "Brittany" but with a red rose), "Normandy" (a red apple, green leaves, and white apple blossoms; also available with a striped edge and plain center), and "Ardennes" (a wreath of green leaves around the outer edge; early examples feature the leaves against a white background, while a later version features a light-green background). "Brittany" and

"Orleans" pieces command prices near the top of the price ranges listed below, "Normandy" pieces command prices in the middle, and "Ardennes" pieces command prices near the bottom.

Bowl, *individual fruit, 5¹/₂ inches*	$ 12–22
Bowl, *vegetable, round, 9-inch diameter*	$ 50–62
Casserole, *1-quart*	$ 100–125
Creamer	$ 25–38
Cup and saucer	$ 20–30
Gravy boat, *faststand*	$ 70–85
Plate, *bread and butter, 6¹/₂-inch diameter*	$ 6–12
Plate, *chop, 12-inch diameter*	$ 50–65
Plate, *dinner, 10¹/₄-inch diameter*	$ 20–32
Plate, *salad, 7-inch diameter*	$ 10–18
Shakers, *salt and pepper, set*	$ 30–42

"Reed"

This is the name of the solid-color dinnerware introduced by Red Wing in 1935. The pattern is very simple, with a reeded band around the edge of flatware items and around the body of cups and other hollowware items. "Reed" was made in shades of ivory, orange, royal blue, turquoise, and yellow. Royal blue is the most sought-after color, and royal blue pieces command prices at the top of the price ranges listed below.

Bowl, *cereal*	$ 18–25
Bowl, *mixing, 5-inch diameter*	$ 30–45
Bowl, *mixing, 6-inch diameter*	$ 35–50
Bowl, *mixing, 7-inch diameter*	$ 40–60
Bowl, *mixing, 8-inch diameter*	$ 40–60
Bowl, *mixing, 9-inch diameter*	$ 40–60
Bowl, *mixing, 10-inch diameter*	$ 45–65
Casserole, *7¹/₂ inches*	$ 35–50
Casserole, *8¹/₂ inches*	$ 50–65
Creamer	$ 18–25

Cup and saucer, *coffee (low and squatty)*	$ 12–25
Cup and saucer, *demitasse*	$ 25–40
Cup and saucer, *tea (taller, fancier handle)*	$ 20–35
Dish, *covered toast*	$ 50–75
Gravy boat, *faststand*	$ 45–60
Jug, *ball-shaped, 8-ounce*	$ 20–30
Jug, *ball-shaped, 11-ounce*	$ 25–35
Jug, *ball-shaped, 16-ounce*	$ 30–40
Jug, *ball-shaped, 24-ounce*	$ 35–45
Jug, *batter, 56-ounce*	$ 75–100
Plate, *artichoke, three-compartment*	$ 30–45
Plate, *bread and butter, 6-inch diameter*	$ 7–12
Plate, *dinner, 9¹/₂-inch diameter*	$ 12–20
Plate, *luncheon, 8¹/₂-inch diameter*	$ 8–14
Platter, *oval, 12 inches*	$ 22–32
Platter, *oval, 14 inches*	$ 25–37
Sugar bowl, *covered*	$ 20–32
Sugar bowl, *open*	$ 15–25
Teapot, *6-cup*	$ 60–75
Teapot, *8-cup*	$ 75–100

"Round-Up"

This pattern is difficult to find. It was produced on Red Wing's "Casual" shapes, and has designs that feature images of cowboys roping and branding. "Round-Up" was introduced in 1958.

Bowl, *individual fruit, 5³/₄-inch diameter*	$ 50–65
Bowl, *vegetable, oval, divided*	$ 160–175
Bowl, *vegetable, round, 9¹/₂-inch diameter*	$ 165–180
Butter dish, *¹/₄-pound, covered*	$ 200–225
Creamer	$ 100–120
Cup and saucer	$ 70–85
Gravy boat and lid	$ 215–230

Gravy boat and lid with metal stand	$ 300–350
Plate, *bread and butter, 6^1/$_2$-inch diameter*	$ 35–50
Plate, *dinner, image of chuck wagon, 10^1/$_2$-inch diameter*	$ 150–175
Plate, *dinner, image of cowboys around fire, 10^1/$_2$ inches*	$ 225–275
Platter, *oval, 13 inches*	$ 200–225
Shakers, *salt and pepper, set*	$ 200–225
Sugar bowl	$ 120–135
Tray, *bread, 24 inches*	$ 200–250

"Smart Set"

Made on Red Wing's "Casual" shapes, "Smart Set" is distinguished by its squares and trapezoids in black and yellow. It was introduced in 1955, and many of the items—such as the cruet set, the teapot, the beverage server, and the various sizes of casseroles—had metal holders. When these pieces are found with their original metal accessories, their prices will be about 30 percent higher than the prices listed below.

Beverage server, *with stopper*	$ 250–300
Casserole, *1-quart*	$ 90–110
Cruets, *two, with stoppers and stand*	$ 250–300
Cup and saucer	$ 35–45
Lazy Susan, *five dishes, with carrier and tray*	$ 200–250
Plate, *bread and butter, 6^1/$_2$-inch diameter*	$ 12–18
Plate, *dinner, 10^1/$_2$-inch diameter*	$ 20–25
Plate, *salad, 7^1/$_2$-inch diameter*	$ 15–20
Platter, *20 inches, with metal stand*	$ 175–200

"Tampico"

Introduced in 1954, "Tampico" is a hand-painted design with an exotic look: it features hanging melons, scattered leaves, and a wicker-wrapped wine bottle. The background is lightly flecked with brown, and the design is executed in shades of brown, green, and pinkish red. "Tampico" appears on Red Wing's "Futura" shapes.

Bowl, *cereal, 6^1/$_2$-inch diameter*	$ 25–30
Bowl, *individual fruit, 5^1/$_2$-inch diameter*	$ 12–17
Bowl, *individual soup, 7^3/$_4$ inches*	$ 28–35

Bowl, *vegetable, oval, divided, 10 inches*	$ 58–65
Bowl, *vegetable, round, 8-inch diameter*	$ 40–48
Casserole, *1¹/₂-quart*	$ 80–90
Creamer	$ 22–28
Cup and saucer	$ 14–18
Gravy boat, *faststand*	$ 48–55
Plate, *bread and butter, 6¹/₂-inch diameter*	$ 6–10
Plate, *dinner, 10¹/₂-inch diameter*	$ 19–25
Plate, *salad, 8¹/₂-inch diameter*	$ 18–24
Platter, *oval, 15 inches*	$ 60–70
Sugar bowl	$ 30–38

"Town and Country"

This line was produced only in 1947. Designed by Eva Zeisel, "Town and Country" pieces are solid-color wares with very modern, irregular shapes. Handles are often off-center or are extensions of rims, and pitchers and jugs are ergonomically shaped to comfortably fit the human hand. Plates are coupe-shaped, but with one side slightly higher than the other. This line is typically unmarked, but can be recognized by its unusual shapes and distinctive glossy or half-matte colors of bronze (metallic brown or gunmetal), gray, rust, Chalk White, chartreuse, coral, Dusk Blue, forest green, sand, peach, jade, Ming Green, Lime Green, light blue, or plum (Mulberry). In the late 1990s, Eva Zeisel gave permission for World of Ceramics to reissue some of the "Town and Country" shapes in colors other than the originals. A syrup pitcher, mixing bowl, and salt and pepper shakers were made, and were marked with the initials "EZ" and a number indicating the year of production—for example, "EZ97."

Baker, *oval, 10 inches*	$ 95–120
Bean pot	$ 250–350
Bowl, *cereal, 5³/₄-inch diameter*	$ 40–60
Bowl, *individual fruit, 6 inches*	$ 18–32
Bowl, *vegetable, round, 8-inch diameter*	$ 65–85
Creamer	$ 50–65
Cup and saucer	$ 35–50
Marmite	$ 70–85

Mug	$ 75–90
Plate, *bread and butter, 6^1/$_2$-inch diameter*	$ 20–32
Plate, *dinner, 10^1/$_2$-inch diameter*	$ 50–65
Plate, *luncheon, 8-inch diameter*	$ 35–50
Relish, *7 inches by 5 inches*	$ 30–50
Relish, *9 inches by 6 inches*	$ 42–57
Sugar bowl	$ 70–85

"Village Green" and "Village Brown"

This line was introduced in 1953, and is characterized by its flatware and hollowware, which is green on the interior and brown on the exterior. All of the lids on "Village Green" pieces are green. In 1955, Red Wing introduced "Village Brown," and all the pieces in this grouping were solid brown.

Baker, *6 inches*	$ 38–42
Bean pot, *lidded*	$ 85–95
Bowl, *cereal, 6-inch diameter*	$ 24–32
Bowl, *individual fruit, 5^3/$_4$-inch diameter*	$ 8–12
Bowl, *individual soup, 8^1/$_2$-inch diameter*	$ 22–30
Bowl, *vegetable, oval, divided*	$ 25–32
Bowl, *vegetable, round, 9-inch diameter*	$ 28–35
Casserole, *individual*	$ 18–25
Casserole, *1-quart*	$ 46–56
Casserole, *2-quart*	$ 75–85
Coffeepot	$ 68–75
Creamer	$ 15–23
Cup and saucer	$ 17–22
Gravy boat, *faststand*	$ 60–68
Marmite, *handled, lidded*	$ 22–26
Mug, *beverage*	$ 16–24
Plate, *bread and butter, 6-inch diameter*	$ 8–12
Plate, *chop, 14-inch diameter*	$ 48–55
Plate, *dinner, 10-inch diameter*	$ 28–35

Plate, *salad, 8 inches*	$ 30–38
Platter, *oval, well-and-tree, 13 inches*	$ 38–45
Platter, *oval, well-and-tree, 15 inches*	$ 68–75
Shakers, *salt and pepper, set*	$ 20–25
Sugar bowl	$ 22–30
Teapot, *6-cup*	$ 68–75

Cookie Jars

Apple, *yellow and turquoise*	$ 225–275
Apple, *orange and pink*	$ 300–350
Apple, *cobalt blue*	$ 350–400
Bananas, *yellow and pink*	$ 350–400
Bananas, *orange, green, and turquoise*	$ 375–425
Bananas, *cobalt blue*	$ 450–500
Carousel	$ 1,100–1,250
Chef, *Pierre, black*	$ 400–475
Chef, *Pierre, blue*	$ 450–550
Chef, *Pierre, brown*	$ 225–300
Chef, *Pierre, green*	$ 325–375
Chef, *Pierre, pink, speckled*	$ 450–550
Chef, *Pierre, yellow*	$ 325–375
Chef, *Pierre, white and cold-paint red*	$ 450–550
Drummer Boy, *toy soldier sitting on drum*	$ 1,400–1,600
Dutch Girl, *Katrina, blue*	$ 175–225
Dutch Girl, *Katrina, brown*	$ 225–300
Dutch Girl, *Katrina, green*	$ 375–425
Dutch Girl, *Katrina, yellow*	$ 175–225
Dutch Girl, *Katrina, white*	$ 350–425
Friar Tuck, *"Thou Shalt Not Steal," blue*	$ 275–325
Friar Tuck, *"Thou Shalt Not Steal," brown*	$ 250–300
Friar Tuck, *"Thou Shalt Not Steal," green*	$ 325–375

Friar Tuck, *"Thou Shalt Not Steal," yellow*	$ 175–225
Grapes, *cluster, light turquoise*	$ 250–300
Grapes, *cluster, blue*	$ 325–375
Grapes, *cluster, green, orange, pink, or yellow*	$ 375–425
Jack Frost, *on pumpkin, short*	$ 850–1,000
Jack Frost, *on pumpkin, tall*	$ 1,000–1,200
King of Tarts, *blue, speckled cream, light green, and yellow*	$ 1,250–1,400
King of Tarts, *blue speckled, pink speckled*	$ 1,650–1,800
King of Tarts, *cinnamon*	$ 3,250–3,500
Pear, *pink, turquoise, green, or yellow*	$ 250–325
Pear, *cobalt blue*	$ 400–450
Peasants, *dancing*	$ 100–165
Pineapple, *green, yellow, pink, turquoise*	$ 250–350
Pineapple, *cobalt blue*	$ 450–550

Figures

Asian god, *fully decorated*	$ 150–200
Asian god, *solid color*	$ 75–100
Asian goddess, *fully decorated*	$ 150–200
Asian goddess, *solid color*	$ 75–100
Asian man with jug, *solid color*	$ 95–120
Asian woman, *solid color*	$ 95–120
Boy with apple, *fully decorated, 8¹/₂ inches high*	$ 175–225
Cowboy, *fully decorated, 11 inches high*	$ 200–250
Cowboy, *solid color, 11 inches*	$ 100–125
Cowgirl, *fully decorated, 11 inches high*	$ 200–250
Cowgirl, *solid color, 11 inches high*	$ 100–125
Girl with flower, *fully decorated, 8¹/₂ inches*	$ 175–225
Maiden with lyre and deer, *"The Muse," solid color*	$ 110–150
Maidens, *two, "The Nymphs," solid color, 16¹/₂ inches*	$ 110–150
Man with accordion, *fully decorated*	$ 175–225

Red Wing Potteries ewer, 5¾ inches, blue glaze,
$100–$125.
Item courtesy of Richard H. Crane, Knoxville, Tennessee.

Man with accordion, *solid color*	$ 85–110
Man with bouquet, *next to hydrant, solid color, 10¼ inches*	$ 90–115
Satyr, *solid color*	$ 85–110
Woman with tambourine, *fully decorated*	$ 175–225
Woman with tambourine, *solid color*	$ 85–110

REGAL CHINA COMPANY

Founded in 1938, the Regal China Company of Antioch, Illinois, was purchased by the Royal China and Novelty Company, a distributing company, in the 1940s. Regal China became the manufacturer for Royal China and Novelty's contract and premium business, producing such items as milk pitchers for the Ovaltine Company, cookie jars for Quaker Oats, and ship's decanters for the Shulton Corporation's Old Spice brand.

Regal China is perhaps best known for its figural bottles or decanters made for Jim Beam Distilleries. Regal reportedly became a wholly owned subsidiary of Jim Beam Distilleries, and went out of business in 1992 after interest in these decanters declined sharply.

Alice in Wonderland
These pieces were made under license from the Walt Disney Company, and are based on Walt Disney cartoons.

Cookie jar, *Alice*	$ 3,400–3,600
Creamer, *White Rabbit, with watch*	$ 800–900
Jug, *milk, King of Hearts*	$ 1,500–1,650
Shaker, *Alice, fully decorated, pair*	$ 850–950
Shaker, *Alice, decorated head and feet with gold, pair*	$ 700–800

Shaker, *Alice, with gold, pair*	$ 700–800
Sugar bowl, *White Rabbit, with rabbit head finial*	$ 850–950
Teapot, *Mad Hatter*	$ 3,200–3,400

Cookie Jars and Related Items

See also "Red Riding Hood" in the Hull section of this book.

Asian Lady, *with basket*	$ 800–875
Baby Pig, *in pinned diaper*	$ 600–700
Barn (from "Old McDonald" series)	$ 500–575
Boy with Butter Churn	$ 450–500
Cat, *wearing hat*	$ 500–600
Clown, *full figure*	$ 900–1,000
Davy Crockett, *head*	$ 600–675
Dutch Girl	$ 950–1,100
Dutch Girl, *shakers, salt and pepper, set*	$ 450–525
French Chef	$ 500–575
French Chef, *shakers, salt and pepper, set*	$ 400–450
Goldilocks, *with baby bear*	$ 1,500–1,650
Goldilocks, *salt and pepper, set*	$ 375–425
Humpty-Dumpty	$ 425–475
Lion, *Hubert*	$ 950–1,100
Majorette	$ 500–550
Miss Muffett	$ 450–525
Peek-a-Boo, *bear in pajamas*	$ 1,650–1,750
Peek-a-Boo, *salt and pepper shakers, small, set*	$ 350–425
Peek-a-Boo, *salt and pepper shakers, large, set*	$ 725–800
Poodle, *Fifi*	$ 875–925
Poodle, *Fifi, shakers, salt and pepper, set*	$ 525–600
Three bears	$ 500–575
Toby	$ 1,000–1,000
Uncle Mistletoe	$ 3,250–3,500

ROBINSON-RANSBOTTOM POTTERY COMPANY

R.R.P. Co.
Roseville Ohio
1500—
U.S.A.

This is one of the *Robinson-Ransbottom* marks that often confuses collectors. It is not a mark used by the more famous Roseville Pottery Company.

Sometime before the turn of the 20th century, Alfred Ransbottom operated a small pottery near Roseville, Ohio. Sometime between 1900 and 1902, Ransbottom's four sons purchased the Oval Ware and Brick Company in Beem City, Ohio (one mile north of Roseville), and founded the Ransbottom Brothers Pottery. They made stoneware products and redware flowerpots, and soon became the world's leading manufacturer of stoneware jars. In 1908, the company incorporated as the Ransbottom Brothers Pottery Company, and when demand for utilitarian stoneware jars declined in the early 1920s, Ransbottom merged with Robinson Clay Products of Akron, Ohio, to become Robinson-Ransbottom Pottery Company. The company is still in business, and its pieces are often marked with "RRPCo" and "Roseville, Ohio." (This mark is often mistaken for a mark of the much more famous Roseville Pottery Company.)

Cookie Jars

Chef, *no gold trim*	$ 200–250
Chef, *gold trim*	$ 325–400
Cow over the Moon (Hey Diddle Diddle), *no gold trim*	$ 400–450

Cow over the Moon (Hey Diddle Diddle), *gold trim*	$ 475–525
Dutch Boy, *no gold trim*	$ 400–450
Dutch Boy, *gold trim*	$ 500–575
Dutch Girl, *no gold trim*	$ 400–450
Dutch Girl, *gold trim*	$ 500–575
Monkey, *"Jocko"*	$ 525–600
Oscar, *smiley face with hat*	$ 225–260
Owl, *with glasses and book, "Cookie Stories," no gold trim*	$ 225–250
Owl, *with glasses and book, "Cookie Stories," gold trim*	$ 300–325
Peter, Peter Pumpkin Eater, *no gold*	$ 450–500
Peter, Peter Pumpkin Eater, *gold trim*	$ 550–600
Sheriff Pig, *no gold trim*	$ 175–200
Sheriff Pig, *gold trim*	$ 225–250
Snowman, *"Frosty"*	$ 925–1,000
Whale, *with hat*	$ 900–975
World War II Sailor, *"Jack"*	$ 425–500
World War II Soldier, *"Bud," dark-brown uniform*	$ 425–500
World War II Soldier, *"Bud," head is a bank with coin slot*	$ 600–650

Miscellany

Crock, *with lid, 5¼ inches tall, blue sponge decoration*	$ 45–55
Pitcher, *with drip brown glaze, 7 inches tall*	$ 15–20

ROOKWOOD POTTERY

Rookwood first used the initials "R" and "P," as seen in this mark, in 1886. Each year thereafter, a flame was added—so in 1887 there was one flame above the mark, and in 1900 there were 14 flames above the mark. After that, a roman-numeral date was added below the initials. Thus, the pictured mark signifies that the piece it appears on was made in 1901.

Many serious collectors consider Cincinnati, Ohio's Rookwood Pottery to be the most important of all the American art potteries. Rookwood was founded in 1880 by Maria Longworth Nichols, who had become an avid decorator of china in 1873. After seeing the pottery exhibition at the Philadelphia Centennial Exposition in 1875, she decided to found an American company that could make wares of the quality she had seen on display—particularly in the Japanese and French exhibits.

Initially, Mrs. Nichols wanted to import Japanese ceramists and open up her own Japanese pottery in Ohio, but that project was abandoned. In the meantime, Mrs. Nichols was experimenting with underglaze decorations like those used on wares made by Haviland and Company in France. She is said to have been the first person in the United States to successfully create this type of decoration. Mrs. Nichols conducted her experiments together with a group of other women at the Frederick Dallas Pottery, but the company's kiln was deemed unsuitable (too hot) for her work, and she subsequently sent pieces to New York City and Long Island to be fired.

In 1880, Mrs. Nichols's father gave her an old schoolhouse that he had purchased at a sheriff's sale in which to make her pottery. The name chosen for the venture was "Rookwood Pottery"—"Rook" as a tribute to the birds that inhabited the woods behind her father's estate, and "Wood" because the name reminded Mrs. Nichols of the famous Wedgwood Pottery in England.

Rookwood got off to a slow start, making dinnerware with white granite or cream-colored bodies. However, Mrs. Nichols also continued to work on a much more ambitious project: perfecting her art pottery. In 1881, the Rookwood School for Pottery Decoration was opened at the pottery, in the hopes of bringing in revenue from students and finding talented artists and decorators to work there. In that same year, Laura A. Fry (who would become so important to Rookwood's future success) joined the firm, as did a number of other talented artists. Together, they formed the company's first decorating department.

Slowly, the pottery assembled a professional staff. Joseph Bailey Sr. came to Rookwood from the now-defunct Frederick Dallas Pottery to supervise production, and William Watts Taylor (Mrs. Nichol's business partner) came to handle the business and marketing side of the growing enterprise. One of Taylor's first business decisions was to close the Rookwood School for Pottery and Decoration, and he also discontinued products that were not selling well.

In 1883, Laura Fry developed a method of spraying on background color using an atomizer. This led to a more even application of glaze, and allowed for more subtle and artistic shading of the pottery's wares. This process formed the basis for Rookwood's standard glaze, which consisted of underglaze decoration on grounds of brown, yellow, red, and green, with brown usually the predominant color. This ware was to be Rookwood's "bread and butter" until the turn of the 20th century, and in 1889 Fry patented the process used to make it.

Around 1884, a happy kiln accident produced a glaze called "Tiger Eye" that was characterized by golden streaks below colored glaze. This mishap led Rookwood to the conclusion that a chemist was needed, and Karl Langenbeck was hired early in 1885. Modern collectors are very interested in "Tiger Eye" pieces, as well as "Gold-stone" pieces, the glaze on which is similar to that of "Tiger Eye" pieces, but less pronounced and with golden flecks rather than actual streaks.

The Rookwood Pottery gained international prominence in 1889 when it won gold metals for excellence at both the Exposition Universelle in Paris and the Exhibition of American Art Industry in Philadelphia. Mrs. Nichols's husband had died in 1885, and in 1886 she married Bellamy Storer. After her remarriage, Nichols's interest in the pottery seemed to wane, and she retired in 1890 with William Taylor acquiring her interests.

Once again, sales of Rookwood pottery were enhanced by success at international exhibitions, and the facilities had to be expanded on several occasions. Eventually, Rookwood moved to new quarters on Mt. Adams, one of the numerous hills in

Cincinnati. The company continued to expand its artistic lines, and began making architectural tiles in 1902. Rookwood's artistic pieces were both signed by the artists who decorated them and marked with the company's logo, but starting in the early 20th century commercial art wares were also produced that were not signed by artists. These non-artist-signed wares were molded, unpainted, and produced in relatively large numbers. They were Rookwood's attempt to compete with other companies that were making similar commercial art wares, though today these Rookwood items are much less valuable than the examples that are signed by their decorators.

In 1886, Rookwood adopted its famous mark, which consists of an "R" and a "P" placed back to back. Each year after 1886, a single flame was placed above or beside this monogram—which means that in 1887 there was one flame directly above the mark, in 1888 there were two flames, and in 1900 there were 14 flames encircling the "R" and "P." In 1901, the Roman numeral "I" was placed below the "RP" and flames to indicate the year of manufacture, in 1902 the numeral "II" was used, and so forth. This Roman numeral system continued until the factory finally closed in 1967 (the company had been bought by the Herschede Hall Clock Company in 1959, and had moved from Cincinnati to Starkville, Mississippi).

In the late 1920s, Rookwood fell upon hard times both artistically and financially. During the Great Depression, few people could afford the luxury of expensive art pottery, and artistically decorated Rookwood wares reportedly ceased being made in 1937. Modern collectors are generally less interested in examples of later Rookwood pottery, and prefer pieces that were made before about 1928. Examples from the 1940s, 1950s, and 1960s are often scorned by very serious collectors.

Some of the more important Rookwood lines include:

- **"Butterfat."** Produced primarily in the 1930s, pieces in this line feature a matte glaze that appears to be soft and creamy like butter. Pieces were primarily made in yellow with underglaze decoration.

- **"Iris."** The glaze effect featured on pieces in this line is similar to that of the standard glaze, except the predominant color is gray with soft blended shades of blue, pink, green, yellow, and creamy white.

- **"Jewel Porcelain."** This line is characterized by semiporcelain bodies with incised lines and embossed decorations covered in rich glazes. These pieces were made from the 1920s to the 1960s.

- **"Porcelain."** Marked with an impressed "P," these pieces are made from semiporcelain and are covered with a glossy glaze. Initially the glaze was over embossed designs; later pieces (produced after about 1923) were often decorated with underglaze slip-painting.

- **"Sea Green."** Generally marked with an impressed "G," these pieces are characterized by a glossy, opalescent green glaze that can be rather dark. Some pieces were also produced with blue, yellow, or red glaze.

- **"Vellum."** Marked with an impressed "V," pieces featuring this glaze are considered some of Rookwood's best, and are highly desirable to collectors. "Vellum" is a transparent matte glaze that produces a surface resembling old parchment. It was used quite successfully for painted decoration. Scenic pieces are rare, and plaques are highly sought after.

- **"Wax Matte."** Pieces in this line feature a matte glaze with a waxy appearance, and backgrounds that are bi-colored. Decorations appear to be fuzzy.

Art Wares

"Iris"
Vase, *dated 1911, 7 inches tall, waisted cylindrical shape, painted star flower decoration, gray blending to pink at top, signed by artist Elizabeth Neave Lingenfelter Lincoln, marked with an "X" denoting it as a second (no visible problem)* $ 1,200–1,400

Vase, *dated 1907, 9 inches tall, grape decoration, signed by artist Sallie E. Coyne* $ 3,500–3,600

Vase, *dated 1909, 11¹/₂ inches tall, brown panels at top and bottom with a wide band of painted dogwood blossoms on shaded green, signed by Fred Rothenbusch, marked with a "W" for "Iris" glaze and an "X" to denote it as a second (reason is not apparent)* $ 2,600–2,800

"Jewel Porcelain"
Vase, *dated 1922, 7³/₄ inches, square section with four feet, floral decoration in shades of blue, teal, and red on a swirled background of dark green and crimson, signed by artist Edward Timothy Hurley* $ 4,250–4,500

"Porcelain"
Flower frog, *dated 1917, three-dimensional dolphin, green glaze, marked with a "P" for "porcelain"* $ 600–650

Vase, *dated 1919, 3³/₄ inches tall, high-gloss ground shaded blue to pink, floral decoration, signed by artist Patti M. Conant* $ 3,300–3,400

Vase, *dated 1916, 8 inches high, globular shape with high-gloss turquoise-blue ground with cobalt blue top, decorated with Art Nouveau-style flowing floral, exquisite and unusual work, signed by artist Charles Jasper McLaughlin* $ 4,000–4,200

Vase, *dated 1921, 9³/₄ inches tall, elaborate floral decoration in arches, signed by artist William Hentschel* $ 3,200–3,350

"Standard Glaze"

Basket, *dated 1882, 20¹/₂ inches wide, bird and landscape on one side with spiderweb and spiders on other, signed by artist Albert Humphreys* $ 6,500–7,000

Bowl, *dated 1887, 4 inches by 2¹/₂ inches, leaf decoration, average-quality artwork, artist's signature unidentified* $ 450–500

Creamer, *dated 1901, 3¹/₂ inches tall, good floral decoration, signed by artist Howard Altman* $ 600–700

Ewer, *dated 1900, 5¹/₂ inches, painted with orange poppies, average-quality artwork, signed by artist Howard Altman* $ 450–500

Ewer, *dated 1889, 6³/₄ inches, painted with nasturtiums, above-average artwork, signed by artist Amelia Sprague* $ 1,250–1,400

Jar, *covered, spike finial, dated 1898, clover decoration, average quality, signed by artist Rose Fechheimer* $ 1,300–1,500

Jug, *honey, dated 1882, 4¹/₂ inches tall, decorated with dragonfly, signed by artist N. J. Hirschfield (Note: collectors should be careful when buying this type of standard-glaze honey jug, as a number of them with early dates were reproduced and are very convincing. Most of these were decorated with flying birds and signed by artist Matthew Daly.)* $ 850–900

Jug with stopper, *dated 1896, 8 inches, portrait of a gentleman drinking from a wine glass, signed by artist Grace Young* $ 3,000–3,200

Mug, *dated 1904, 5¹/₈ inches tall, painted with portrait of a stag's head, signed by artist E. T. Hurley* $ 1,800–1,900

Mug, *dated 1899, 6 inches, mug has offset handle, grape cluster decoration, signed by artist Fred Rothenbusch* $ 1,200–1,300

Vase, *dated 1889, 5 inches tall, three handles and pierced shoulder, flower-decorated, unusual form, signed by artist Harriet Wilcox* $ 1,900–2,000

Vase, *dated 1906, 6 inches, lily-of-the-valley decoration, average-quality artwork* $ 550–650

Rookwood "Standard Glaze" vase, dated 1905, chrysanthemum decoration, 6 inches, $600–$700.
Item courtesy of Richard Hatch and Associates, Hendersonville, North Carolina.

Rookwood "Standard Glaze" vase, dated 1904, peony decoration, 8½ inches, $825–$875.
Item courtesy of Richard Hatch and Associates, Hendersonville, North Carolina.

Vase, *dated 1900, 6 inches, bottle form, clusters of grapes and leaves, average-quality artwork, signed by artist Fred Rothenbusch*	$ 550–650
Vase, *dated 1905, decorated with chrysanthemums*	$ 600–700
Vase, *dated 1897, 6½ inches, green clove around shoulder, average-quality artwork, signed by artist Josephine Zettel*	$ 600–675
Vase, *dated 1900, 7 inches tall, superb poppy decoration, signed by artist Constance Baker*	$ 1,150–1,250
Vase, *dated 1902, 7 inches tall, decorated around the circumference with realistic and well-painted daisies, signed by artist Jeanette Swing*	$ 1,000–1,100
Vase, *dated 1908, 7½ inches, fine floral decoration, signed by artist Charles Schmidt*	$ 1,200–1,300
Vase, *dated 1904, 7½ inches, painted with narcissus flowers, signed by artist Charles Schmidt*	$ 750–800
Vase, *dated 1904, 8½ inches, peony decoration*	$ 825–875

Vase, *dated 1906, 9 inches, apple tree branches with blossoms, fine work signed by artist Clara C. Linderman*	$ 1,000–1,100
Vase, *dated 1887, 11³/₄ inches, high-quality painting of daisies, signed by artist Albert Valentien*	$ 4,000–4,250
Vase, *dated 1890, 12 inches tall, small bulbous bottom with long leg terminating in flared rim, painted with nasturtium flowers, superb quality, signed by artist Anna Marie Bookprinter Valentien*	$ 2,650–2,800
Vase, *dated 1900, decorated with lotus blossoms and signed by Kataro Shirayamadani, exceptional quality*	$ 8,500–9,000
Vase, *dated 1902, 14 inches tall, superb painting of parrot tulips, signed by artist John D. Wareham*	$ 6,750–7,000
Vase, *dated 1894, 15¹/₂ inches tall, superb painting of peonies, signed by artist Matt Daly*	$ 3,500–3,750

"Vellum" and "Scenic Vellum"

Bowl, *dated 1920, 6 inches high by 9¹/₄-inch diameter, blue ground, dandelion-and-leaf decoration, signed by artist Lenore Asbury*	$ 3, 250–3,500
Plaque, *5 inches tall, entitled "Woodland Stream," large tree on bank of a stream, signed by artist Elizabeth McDermott*	$ 7,500–8,000
Vase, *dated 1931, 4¹/₂ inches high, blue matte glaze with exquisite flowers on shoulder and to the middle of the ovoid body, signed with "V" for "Vellum," signed by artist Elizabeth Neave Lingenfelter Lincoln*	$ 2,500–2,800
Vase, *dated 1930, 5¹/₂ inches high, background shaded grayish blue to pink at top with painting of bird in branches, signed by artist Edward Hurley*	$ 3,500–3,750
Vase, *dated 1937, 6¹/₄ inches, marked with an "S" to label it as a special demonstration piece, pale creamy-yellow ground shading to pale rose with exceptional flower-and-leaf painting, signed by artist Kataro Shirayamadani*	$ 8,000–8,200
Vase, *dated 1913, 7 inches, cylindrical vase with pastel colors with painted wild roses, marked on base with "V" for "Vellum," signed by artist Caroline Frances Steinle, average-quality artwork*	$ 800–900
Vase, *dated 1915, 7 inches tall, "Scenic Vellum" rolling hills and trees, with pink glow as at sunrise, signed by artist Sallie Coyne*	$ 3,400–3,500

Vase, *dated 1920, 7¹/₄ inches, matte blue on exterior, pink interior, narrow band of flowers on the shoulder around the lip, marked with "V" for "Vellum" and signed by artist Lorinda Epply* $ 1,100–1,250

Vase, *dated 1910, 7¹/₂ inches, peacock feather painted around base, signed by artist Caroline Steinle* $ 2,400–2,600

Vase, *dated 1917, 9¹/₂ inches tall, dark matte blue ground with wide band of flowers and berries around shoulder, marked with a "V," signed by artist Fred Rothenbusch* $ 1,250–1,400

Vase, *dated 1915, 10 inches tall, "Scenic Vellum," landscape, trees in a meadow, signed by artist Sara Elizabeth Coyne* $ 4,000–4,200

Vase, *dated 1909, 10 inches tall, blue florals, signed by artist Fred Rothenbusch* $ 1,300–1,450

Vase, *dated 1914, 11¹/₂ inches tall, "Scenic Vellum," nicely painted landscape, signed by artist Lenore Asbury* $ 3,500–4,000

Vase, *dated 1909, 12 inches tall, "Scenic Vellum" landscape with water and trees, signed by artist Arthur T. Hurley* $ 4,200–4,500

"Wax Matte"

Vase, *dated 1926, 5¹/₂ inches, red flowers on a purple ground, signed by artist Margaret McDonald* $ 1,250–1,400

Vase, *dated 1930, 5³/₄ inches tall, "stick" vase form with bulbous bottom and long cylindrical neck, mottled pink and blue/gray with rose flowers and green leaves, signed by artist Katherine Jones* $ 850–1,000

Vase, *dated 1928, 5³/₄ inches, soft sea-green ground with bold painting of flowers in mauve and mottled colors, signed by artist Sarah Elizabeth Coyne* $ 1,700–1,900

Vase, *dated 1930, 6 inches, signed by artist Jens Jensen* $ 1,000–1,100

Vase, *dated 1928, 6 inches, rectangular section with two handles near top, pinecone and pine needle painting, signed by artist Elizabeth Lincoln* $ 1,600–1,750

Vase, *dated 1929, 10¹/₂ inches, beautiful blue background with floral decoration, signed by artist John Wesley Pullman* $ 3,000–3,200

Vase, *dated 1926, 11 inches, band of fruit and leaves around top, signed by artist Sallie Coyne* $ 2,600–2,750

Rookwood bookends (photograph of one), bears,
7 inches by 4½ inches, mottled green-and-white glaze,
$850–$1,000, pair.
Item courtesy of Richard Hatch and Associates,
Hendersonville, North Carolina.

Miscellaneous

Bookends, *dated 1946, 6 inches tall, figure of Dutch Boy on one, Dutch Girl on other, mottled blue, green, and pink matte glaze, signed by artist*	$ 600–700
Bookends, *dated 1927, 4½ inches by 7 inches, mottled green-and-white glaze, bears*	$ 850–1,000
Bowl, *dated 1922, 8-inch diameter, yellow exterior painted with leaves, brown interior accented with high-gloss drip of blue, green, and brown, signed by artist William Hentschel*	$ 700–800
Font, *holy water, dated 1947, figure of St. Francis holding small bowl, artist-signed*	$ 250–325
Tankard, *dated 1906, 7¼ inches, raised floral decoration, signed by artist Orville Hicks*	$ 950–1,100
Vase, *dated 1945, 6 inches tall, painted floral on light blue ground, signed by artist*	$ 450–525
Vase, *dated 1945, 6½ inches, stylized floral and leaves, signed by artist Jens Jensen*	$ 1,900–2,000

Vase, *dated 1921, ovoid vase with later "Tiger Eye" or "Goldstone" glaze in chartreuse and Empire Green, painted and incised with a flower-and-foliage design, signed by Charles S. Todd; this piece may actually be "Jewel Porcelain"*	$ 3,900–4,100
Vase, *dated 1926, 7³/₄ inches, bulbous body with long neck and flaring mouth, floral painting on blue ground, artist-signed*	$ 800–900
Vase, *dated 1951, 7³/₄ inches tall, "Vista Blue," thick runny glaze over gray ground, signed by artist Rubin Menzel, marked with an "X" to denote it as a second*	$ 650–700
Vase, *dated 1913, 8¹/₂ inches, cylinder vase with carved peacock feathers, matte blue ground, signed by artist Charles Todd*	$ 1,200–1,400
Vase, *dated 1949, 8¹/₂ inches tall, flared roll-over rim, dark high-gloss green body decorated with embossed morning glories, interior is vibrant high-gloss canary yellow, signed by artist Kataro Shirayamadani*	$ 850–900
Vase, *dated 1923, 8³/₄ inches, panels with red and blue florals, caramel ground, signed by artist Vera Tischler*	$ 1,000–1,200
Vase, *dated 1917, 10 inches tall, blue/green ground with white band of painted flowers, signed by artist Ed Diers*	$ 1,200–1,400
Vase, *dated 1912, 10 inches tall, incised fruit-and-leaf design, signed by artist Charles Todd*	$ 1,800–2,000
Vase, *dated 1921, 10 inches, matte-colored rose ground with underglaze slip-painting of hanging vines with red and yellow flowers, signed by artist Elizabeth Lincoln*	$ 2,300–2,400

Production Line (or Commercial Art Wares)

Ashtray, *dated 1949, glossy green glaze on round body with three projecting cigarette rests*	$ 80–90
Bookends, *dated 1927, 6 inches tall, basket-of-flowers shape, green glaze, pair*	$ 575–625
Bowl, *dated 1930, 4³/₄ inches by 2³/₄ inches, embossed rooks in flight around shoulder, dark-green glaze*	$ 350–400
Bowl, *dated 1937, 5¹/₄-inch diameter, buff exterior, green interior, embossed gazelles*	$ 400–450
Bowl, *dated 1918, footed, stylized leaf band around top, glaze is matte dusty rose shading to dusty green*	$ 325–375

Rookwood footed bowl, dated 1918, leaf band around top, matte dusty rose shading to dusty green, $325–$375.
Item courtesy of Kingston Pike Antique Mall, Knoxville, Tennessee.

Rookwood bowl and flower frog, bowl is dated 1925 and is 14 inches in diameter, flower frog is dated 1926. The bowl is golden yellow with a green exterior and the flower frog is golden yellow, $700–$750.
Item courtesy of Richard Hatch and Associates, Hendersonville, North Carolina.

Rookwood candlesticks, dated 1921, 11¾ inches tall, dolphin base, twist columns, gloss blue glaze, $600–$650.
Item courtesy of Richard Hatch and Associates, Hendersonville, North Carolina.

Rookwood figure of a collie, dated 1928, 6 inches by 5½ inches, $400–$450.
Item courtesy of Richard Hatch and Associates, Hendersonville, North Carolina.

Bowl/Vase, *dated 1930, 3½ inches, squatty body with flaring lip, two small handles on shoulder, green glaze*	$ 250–300
Bowl with flower frog, *14-inch diameter bowl is dated 1925 and is golden yellow on the interior and green on the exterior; flower frog is dated 1926 and is golden yellow*	$ 700–750
Box, *covered, dated 1923, 7¼-inch by 3-inch rectangle, molded design on cover and sides, orange exterior, gloss black interior*	$ 375–425
Candlesticks, *dated 1921, 11¾ inches, dolphin base with twist shafts, gloss blue glaze, pair*	$ 600–650

Cocktail shaker, *dated 1951, 12 inches high, matte green glaze*	$ 700–750
Creamer, *dated 1959, $3^1/4$ inches tall, matte brown exterior, cream interior accented with glossy blue*	$ 75–90
Figure, *dated 1928, collie, $5^1/2$ inches by 6 inches, light brown with golden highlights*	$ 400–450
Flower frog, *dated 1915, $3^1/4$-inch diameter, matte green glaze*	$ 85–100
Jar, *covered, dated 1927, 11 inches, has four pieces: lid, inner lid, body, and wooden base, reticulation around the neck below the lid, beautiful blue glaze*	$ 550–650
Letter holder, *dated 1955, $3^1/4$ inches tall, blue glaze with embossed image of first U. S. postage stamp*	$ 275–325
Mug, *advertising, dated 1948, $5^1/2$ inches tall, Weideman Brewery*	$ 400–450
Pin dish, *dated 1951, $5^1/2$ inches at widest diameter, raised figure of a rose on edge, creamy yellow glaze*	$ 145–175
Smoker's set, *dated 1922, set consists of covered cigarette box and two ashtrays, box has embossed decoration of a bird dog, glossy jade-green glaze*	$ 400–450
Teapot, *dated 1910, $4^3/4$ inches high, rose-and-green matte glaze*	$ 475–525
Tile, *dated 1915, 6 inches square, decorated with Glasgow Rose, matte glaze in red and green*	$ 375–425
Tile or trivet, *dated 1924, $5^3/4$ inches square, decorated with image of purple-and-blue bird, with original box*	$ 475–525
Tray, *dated 1949, $4^1/2$ inches high by $6^3/4$ inches, three-dimensional figure of a rook*	$ 675–725
Vase, *dated 1931, $4^1/2$ inches tall, globular with large embossed flowers around the circumference, pink/mauve matte glaze*	$ 200–250
Vase, *dated 1935, 5 inches, matte green glaze, raised butterflies*	$ 250–300
Vase, *dated 1930, 5 inches, bulbous with embossed floral decoration on shoulder below rim, pink matte glaze*	$ 250–300
Vase, *dated 1933, $5^1/2$ inches, later "Tiger Eye" or "Goldstone" glaze, high-gloss mahogany color, some glaze problems associated with manufacturing process*	$ 450–500
Vase, *pillow (rectangular Chinese form), dated 1934, $5^1/2$ inches tall, panels of embossed flowers, leaves, and berries; because of a glaze flaw, this piece is marked as a second with an "X" on the bottom, green glaze*	$ 225–275

Rookwood three-piece smoker's set, embossed dog decoration, gloss jade-green glaze, $400–$450.
Item courtesy of Richard Hatch and Associates, Hendersonville, North Carolina.

Rookwood vase, dated 1913, 6 inches, American Arts and Crafts-style, matte yellow glaze, $375–$425.
Item courtesy of Richard H. Crane, Knoxville, Tennessee.

Vase, *dated 1919, 5³/4 inches, embossed sea horses*	$ 350–400
Vase, *dated 1926, 5³/4 inches, tapered cylinder with butterflies at base, aqua with red overglaze*	$ 350–400
Vase, *dated 1913, 6 inches tall, in the American Arts and Crafts style, matte yellow glaze*	$ 375–425
Vase, *dated 1925, 6 inches tall, narrow base to wide shoulder, embossed band of decoration around top of shoulder, matte mauve glaze*	$ 500–550
Vase, *dated 1912, 6¹/2 inches, leaf decoration in narrow panels, brown matte glaze*	$ 350–400
Vase, *dated 1922, 6¹/2 inches tall, decorated with panels, matte caramel-colored glaze*	$ 250–300
Vase, *dated 1933, 7¹/2 inches, speckled blue/green matte glaze, decorated with panels of embossed flowers*	$ 650–700
Vase, *dated 1924, 7 inches, dragonfly decoration, attractive shape with narrow base, wide shoulder and small mouth, mottled blue glaze*	$ 450–500

Rookwood vase, dated 1965, Starkville, Mississippi,
embossed leaf-and-floral decoration, yellow glaze,
$375–$425.
Item courtesy of Tony McCormack, Sarasota, Florida.

Vase, *dated 1923, 7 inches tall, embossed flower buds all over body, two small handles at waist*	$ 400–450
Vase, *dated 1922, $7^1/2$ inches, band of rooks in panels on shoulder, matte lavender or purple, "X" to denote it as a second (because of glaze problems)*	$ 450–525
Vase, *dated 1916, $7^1/2$ inches tall, embossed owls, matte lavender glaze*	$ 375–425
Vase, *dated 1937, $7^3/4$ inches tall, golden yellow glaze with red/brown specking, embossed deer in forest*	$ 350–400
Vase, *dated 1920, $7^3/4$ inches tall, embossed florals around small bulbous base, brown glaze*	$ 350–400
Vase, *fan, dated 1944, $7^3/4$ inches, turquoise crackle glaze fading to white on edges, embossed woman's face on one side*	$ 400–475
Vase, *dated 1935, $9^1/4$ inches tall, two handles near base, flared foot with flared conical body, molded neoclassical figures, gray semimatte glaze*	$ 325–375
Vase, *dated 1924, 10 inches tall, six-sided form in the Chinese style with blue glaze*	$ 400–450

Vase, *tall, slender, bottle-shaped, dated 1921, 10^1/$_2$ inches, mahogany-brown high-gloss glaze*	$ 550–600
Vase, *dated 1949, 10^1/$_2$ inches tall, dolphin handles, high-gloss emerald-green glaze*	$ 300–350
Vase, *dated 1923, 11 inches tall, green with blue mottling, ribbed*	$ 425–475
Vase, *dated 1927, 13^3/$_4$ inches, strong leaf-and-floral embossing, mottled blue glaze*	$ 1,200–1,400
Vase, *dated 1965, Starkville, Mississippi, production, 14 inches, embossed floral-and-leaf design, yellow glaze*	$ 375–425

ROSEVILLE POTTERY

Roseville script mark commonly found on its commercial art wares.

The Roseville Pottery Company was founded in 1892 by George Young, who previously had held a wide variety of jobs—from Singer sewing-machine salesman to schoolteacher—without much success. Roseville's first plant was the old J. B. Owens pottery, and in this facility the company began producing such items as flowerpots and stoneware storage jugs. Roseville enjoyed a great deal of early success, and began to expand by buying other pottery companies in the area. In 1892, Roseville bought its first plant in nearby Zanesville, which was the Linden Avenue facility originally built for the Clark Stoneware Company. In 1902 it bought another Zanesville facility, which had previously been built for the Muskingum Stoneware Company. By 1910, Roseville had left the town of Roseville entirely and moved all of its operations to Zanesville.

Roseville mark used on its "Raymor" dinnerware.

Roseville seal mark used on "Rozane Mara" items. Similar marks were used on other early "Rozane" wares.

Roseville started making art wares around 1900, and the trade name chosen for these wares was "Rozane"—an amalgam of "Roseville" and "Zanesville." The first "Rozane" wares belonged to a line called "Rozane Royal, Dark," which consisted of pieces with shaded brown backgrounds and underglaze slip decorations, similar to pieces in Rookwood's "Standard Glaze" line. A little later, "Rozane Royal, Light" was introduced. This line was similar to its "Dark" counterpart, but its pieces featured slip-painted decorations on light-colored shaded backgrounds that were reminiscent of pieces in Rookwood's "Iris" line.

Other "Rozane" lines include:

- **"Crystalis."** This line is characterized by flowing crystalline glazes in various colors.

- **"Egypto."** Some of the easiest-to-find "Rozane" wares, "Egypto" pieces feature soft matte green glaze on vessels that are supposed to be reminiscent of ancient Egypt.

- **"Fugi" or "Fugiyama."** Pieces in this desirable grouping feature matte-finished backgrounds with sgraffito (incised) decorations enhanced with glossy enamels. Created by Gazo Fudji about 1905, this line is very similar to "Rozane Woodland." Backgrounds were often pitted or dotted with pin pricks, and the decoration usually depicted stylized flowers, insects, or geometric designs consisting of wavy and zigzag lines.

- **"Mara."** Pieces in this line are very rare, and are distinguished by an iridescent metallic glaze that is similar to the one used on Weller's "Sicard" or "Sicardo" pottery.

- **"Mongol."** Pieces in this line are glazed with a dark-red color often referred to as "Chinese Red" or "Rouge Flame." The glaze generally has a crystalline component, and some pieces were made with a silver overlay, though others simply feature the red glaze.

- **"Olympic."** This pottery is very similar to wares made in England during the mid-19th century. Pieces have a red ground with transfer-printed decorations (white with black outlining) of ancient Greek figures. These scenes are titled at the bottom of each piece. This is an extremely rare line, and is seldom marked.

There are two important points to keep in mind when attempting to identify "Rozane" pieces. First, Roseville had special marks for its early "Rozane" ware, but many pieces were completely unmarked, and these somewhat rare and valuable pieces can thus be easily overlooked by novice collectors. Second, Roseville introduced a separate "Rozane Ware" line in 1917. Pieces in this line feature raised flowers that look like roses surrounded by green leaves on a cream-colored background. This is really a line of molded commercial art ware, and most collectors would not include these pieces in the same category as pieces from the earlier "Rozane" art lines.

Pieces from the "Della Robbia" collection—another important Roseville line—may also feature a "Rozane Ware" mark. Created by Frederick Rhead, "Della Robbia" pieces were produced in 75 different patterns with backgrounds that were literally carved away to produce raised designs with a high-gloss glaze. Some later pieces also featured designs created using the sgraffito technique.

Another rare and valuable line often associated with "Rozane" ware is the "Pauleo" line. "Pauleo" pieces came in two varieties. The first featured a red metallic glaze, while the second featured a veined marbleized finish in one of several colors. Few of these pieces were produced, but those that exist are generally marked either "Pauleo Pottery" or "Pauleo Rozane."

Around the time of World War I, Roseville began abandoning its art lines in favor of less expensive commercial art lines that were made using a molding process. One of the first of these lines, and one of the most successful, was called "Donatello." Pieces in this line feature reeded tops and bottoms, with a band in between that was decorated with raised cherubs among trees. This design was developed in 1915 by Harry Rhead, who copied it from a jardinière made in Czechoslovakia. Roseville also made vast quantities of other commercial art wares in dozens of patterns that are very popular with modern collectors. Patterns such as "Blackberry," "Pinecone," "Futura," and "Ferrella" are highly desired, and the best pieces can fetch high prices.

Roseville prospered through the 1940s, but by the 1950s had run into financial troubles and was slowly slipping into bankruptcy. In an attempt to save the company, Roseville commissioned Ben Seibel to design a line of solid-color dinnerware known as "Raymor." This line was introduced in 1952, and was produced for only a short time because the company went out of business in 1954. "Raymor" pieces came in a variety of colors in both matte and glossy finishes. Glossy "Raymor" pieces have a mottled look to their glazes that the matte pieces do not have. The glossy pieces were made in the same color as the matte-glazed items, but the mottled effect of the glaze makes some of the hues look different. The matte-finished colors include Autumn Brown (which many collectors call "Chocolate"), Terra Cotta, Beach Gray, and Avocado Green (which came in two versions: a light version that looks as its name suggests, and a darker variety that collectors call "Frogskin"). Other available "Raymor" colors include Contemporary White, Robin's Egg Blue, and chartreuse. Of these colors, Autumn Brown is the most readily available today, and Frogskin is the color most sought after by collectors.

Roseville "Raymor" bean pot with trivet, #187 and #188,
Beach Gray, $275–$325.
*Item courtesy of Bill Brooker, Old School Antique Mall,
Sylva, North Carolina.*

Dinnerware

"Raymor"

AUTUMN GREEN (GLOSSY)

Bread and butter plate, *7³/4 inches*	$ 14–20
Casserole with lid, *individual, round*	$ 70–80
Cup and saucer	$ 40–50
Dinner plate, *12 inches*	$ 33–40
Sugar bowl, *with lid*	$ 70–80
Oval serving platter, *14 inches*	$ 100–110

BEACH GRAY (GLOSSY)

Bean pot with stand	$ 275–325
Bread and butter plate, *7³/4 inches*	$ 15–22
Casserole with lid, *individual, round*	$ 70–80
Chop plate, *round, 16 inches*	$ 60–70

Cup and saucer	$ 48–55
Dinner plate, *12 inches*	$ 34–42
Oval, *vegetable, 9¹/₄ inches*	$ 75–85
Pepper shaker	$ 30–38

BEACH GRAY (MATTE)

Bread and butter plate, *7³/₄ inches*	$ 15–22
Cup and saucer	$ 50–60
Soup bowl, *lug handles*	$ 33–40

CONTEMPORARY WHITE (MATTE)

Casserole with lid, *individual, round*	$ 50–60
Cup and saucer	$ 38–45

Art Lines

"Aztec"

Produced with solid-color backgrounds of blue, green, gray, beige, brown, teal, or olive, "Aztec" pieces are distinguished by their simple, slip-trailed, geometric decorations done in contrasting colors. First made in 1916, pieces in this line are generally unmarked, except for occasional artist signatures.

Lamp base, *11 inches, electrified, gray ground with swag decoration in white around the font, three-color slip trailing*	$ 400–450
Pitcher, *gray, three-color slip trailing, 5 inches*	$ 450–500
Vase, *6¹/₂ inches, cylindrical, gray background with white, orange, and blue ribbons of slip, artist-initialed*	$ 300–350
Vase, *10 inches, flared foot, two-color slip trailing against a blue ground, decoration only on shoulder near flared lip*	$ 450–500
Vase, *11 inches, blue background with five-color slip trailing*	$ 650–700

"Della Robbia"

Introduced in 1906, this line is considered by many collectors to be the finest made by Roseville. Designs are hand-carved and naturalistic, with many having a strong Art Nouveau feel. Examples from this line are extremely rare and valuable, and collectors will sometimes excuse a little damage if it does not render the piece unsightly. Though they are often unmarked, pieces in this line can also carry a "Rozane Ware" seal mark.

Tankard pitcher, *triangular stylized trees, 10¹/₂ inches*	$ 4,500–5,000
Teapot, *large leaves and small flower heads around body, 6 inches, marked*	$ 2,800–3,000
Vase, *9¹/₂ inches tall, #46, bulbous body with stylized flower heads contained within teardrop forms*	$ 7,000–7,500

"Egypto"

Introduced in 1905, this line is composed of shapes that are supposed to suggest the pottery of ancient Egypt (hence its name). Pieces are covered with a green matte glaze, and are often marked with a seal mark that reads "Rozane Ware, Egypto."

Lamp, *oil, double spout, 5 inches*	$ 850–925
Lamp base, *three-dimensional elephants with riders, 10 inches, unmarked*	$ 2,250–2,500
Vase, *chalice form in the shape of a tree, 11 inches*	$ 2,400–2,600
Vase, *bronze form, two small handles near rim, 6¹/₂ inches*	$ 900–1,000

"Rozane Royal" and "Rozane Royal, Light"

In 1900, Roseville began making a line of underglaze slip-decorated art pottery similar to the pottery made by Rookwood and other manufacturers. These dark-background pieces were originally called "Rozane," but the name was changed to "Rozane Royal" in 1904. The pieces had shaded brown backgrounds. "Rozane Royal, Light" is a line of very similar wares with lighter-colored backgrounds in shades of gray, blue, green, ivory, and pink. These lines are often unsigned, but may be marked "Rozane, RPCo." or be marked with the "Rozane Royal" seal mark.

Jardinière, *with pedestal, "Rozane Royal," dark-brown background, floral-decorated, artist-signed, 12-inch jardinière, 32-inch pedestal*	$ 2,600–2,750
Lamp base, *waisted vase-shaped, drilled base, "Rozane Royal," dark-brown background, floral decoration, 11 inches, #974*	$ 325–375
Pitcher, *tankard, "Rozane Royal," dark-brown background, floral-decorated, not artist-signed, 11 inches, #921*	$ 550–600
Stein, *"Rozane Royal," dark-brown background, fruit-decorated, artist-signed, 6 inches, #965*	$ 300–350
Vase, *"Rozane Royal, Light," pink shaded to gray with floral decoration, artist-signed, 7¹/₄ inches*	$ 700–775
Vase, *"Rozane Royal, Light," 8³/₄ inches, with underglaze slip painting of flowers and leaves, background is gray, marked*	$ 800–900

Vase, *pillow-shaped with ruffled top, "Rozane Royal," dark-brown background, 9 inches, slip painting of bird dog with bird in mouth, artist-signed*	$ 2,500–3,000
Vase, *"Rozane Royal," dark-brown background, unusual shape with vessel held within pierced circle, floral-decorated, not artist-signed, 5 inches, #872*	$ 350–400
Vase, *"Rozane Royal," dark background, 14 inches, portrait of Native American, artist-signed*	$ 4,500–5,000

Commercial Art Lines

"Baneda"

First produced around 1933, "Baneda" pieces are distinguished by an embossed band of leaves, flowers, and pods against a rose/red, green, or (rarely) blue background. The pods resemble small pumpkins. Pieces were generally either unmarked or marked with paper labels.

Bowl, *12-inch diameter, #237, rose*	$ 800–900
Bowl, *12-inch diameter, #237, green*	$ 900–1,000
Bowl, *hexagonal, 10-inch diameter, #234, rose*	$ 700–775
Bowl, *hexagonal, 10-inch diameter, #234 green*	$ 800–875
Bowl, *round, 6-inch diameter, #232, rose*	$ 375–450
Bowl, *round, 6-inch diameter, #232, green*	$ 450–525
Candlestick, *4 inches, #1088, rose, each*	$ 300–350
Candlestick, *4 inches, #1088, green, each*	$ 325–375
Candlestick, *5 inches tall, #1087, rose, each*	$ 400–475
Candlestick, *5 inches tall, #1087, green, each*	$ 475–535
Jardinière, *4 inches, #626, rose*	$ 375–425
Jardinière, *4 inches, #626, green*	$ 475–525
Jardinière, *5 inches, #626, rose*	$ 475–525
Jardinière, *5 inches, #626, green*	$ 575–650
Jardinière, *6 inches, #626, rose*	$ 525–575
Jardinière, *6 inches, #626, green*	$ 600–700
Jardinière, *7 inches, #626, rose*	$ 675–725
Jardinière, *7 inches, #626, green*	$ 750–825

Jardinière, *8 inches, #626, rose*	$ 875–975
Jardinière, *8 inches, #626, green*	$ 950–1,000
Jardinière, *9 inches, #626, rose*	$ 1,400–1,600
Jardinière, *9 inches, #626, green*	$ 1,750–1,900
Jardinière, *10 inches, #626, rose*	$ 1,800–2,000
Jardinière, *10 inches, #626, green*	$ 2,200–2,400
Vase, *4 inches, #587, rose*	$ 300–350
Vase, *4 inches, #587, green*	$ 350–400
Vase, *4 inches, #603, rose*	$ 350–400
Vase, *4 inches, #603, green*	$ 400–450
Vase, *5 inches, #235, rose*	$ 575–625
Vase, *5 inches, #235, green*	$ 625–675
Vase, *5 inches, #601, rose*	$ 400–450
Vase, *5 inches, #601, green*	$ 475–525
Vase, *6 inches, #588, rose*	$ 525–575
Vase, *6 inches, #588, green*	$ 625–675
Vase, *6 inches, #589, rose*	$ 575–625
Vase, *6 inches, #589, green*	$ 675–725
Vase, *6 inches, #591, rose*	$ 625–675
Vase, *6 inches, #591, green*	$ 725–775
Vase, *6 inches, #602, rose*	$ 525–575
Vase, *6 inches, #602, green*	$ 625–675
Vase, *6 inches, #605, rose*	$ 725–775
Vase, *6 inches, #605, green*	$ 825–875
Vase, *7 inches, #590, rose*	$ 575–625
Vase, *7 inches, #590, green*	$ 700–750
Vase, *7 inches, #592, rose*	$ 600–650
Vase, *7 inches, #592, green*	$ 675–725
Vase, *7 inches, #604, rose*	$ 800–850
Vase, *7 inches, #604, green*	$ 950–1,000
Vase, *7 inches, #606, rose*	$ 800–850

Vase, *7 inches, #606, green*	$ 950–1,000
Vase, *7 inches, #610, rose*	$ 800–850
Vase, *7 inches, #610, green*	$ 950–1,000
Vase, *8 inches, #593, rose*	$ 775–825
Vase, *8 inches, #593, green*	$ 875–950
Vase, *8 inches, #595, rose*	$ 1,000–1,100
Vase, *8 inches, #595, green*	$ 1,250–1,350
Vase, *9 inches, #594, rose*	$ 750–850
Vase, *9 inches, #594, green*	$ 850–950
Vase, *9 inches, #596, rose*	$ 1,000–1,100
Vase, *9 inches, #596, green*	$ 1,100–1,250
Vase, *10 inches, #597, rose*	$ 1,400–1,600
Vase, *10 inches, #597, green*	$ 1,750–1,900
Vase, *12 inches, #598, rose*	$ 1,850–2,200
Vase, *12 inches, #598, green*	$ 2,250–2,500
Vase, *15 inches, #600, rose*	$ 3,000–3,500
Vase, *15 inches, #600, green*	$ 3,600–3,759
Wall box, *8 inches, #233, rose*	$ 600–650
Wall box, *8 inches, #233, green*	$ 675–725
Wall pocket, *8 inches, #1269, rose*	$ 3,800–4,200
Wall pocket, *8 inches, #1269, green*	$ 4,600–4,850

"Blackberry"

First produced in 1933, pieces in this line have a green textured background with a band of leaves and berries. This is a difficult-to-find, highly desirable line, and its pieces are typically marked only with paper labels.

Basket, *6¹/₂ inches, #334*	$ 1,250–1,400
Basket, *7 inches, #335*	$ 1,250–1,400
Basket, *8 inches, #336*	$ 1,200–1,500
Bowl, *6 inches, #226*	$ 600–650
Bowl, *8 inches, #227*	$ 700–750
Bowl, *10 inches, #228*	$ 750–800

Candlestick, *4¹/₂ inches, #1086, pair*	$ 1,000–1,200
Jardinière, *4 inches, #623*	$ 500–550
Jardinière, *5 inches, #623*	$ 600–650
Jardinière, *6 inches, #623*	$ 700–750
Jardinière, *7 inches, #623*	$ 950–1,000
Jardinière, *8 inches, #623*	$ 1,250–1,400
Jardinière, *9 inches, #623*	$ 1,600–1,800
Vase, *4 inches, #567*	$ 600–650
Vase, *5 inches, #569*	$ 700–750
Vase, *6 inches, #571*	$ 750–800
Vase, *6 inches, #573*	$ 850–900
Vase, *8 inches, #575*	$ 1,100–1,250
Vase, *10 inches, #577*	$ 1,750–1,850
Vase, *12 inches, #578*	$ 2,250–2,400
Wall pocket, *8 inches, #1267*	$ 2,250–2,400

"Carnelian II"

This line was introduced in 1915, and is distinguished by its multicolored mottled or drip glaze. The best pieces have a thick glaze with four, five, or more strong colors. Lesser examples generally feature fewer colors, and the glaze is not so strong or well done. These pieces are generally unmarked, or have either the "Rv" signature or a black paper label.

Vase, *7 inches, no number*	$ 425–475
Vase, *8 inches, #440*	$ 1,600–1,750
Vase, *8 inches, #441*	$ 1,600–1,750
Vase, *9 inches, #439*	$ 850–1,000
Vase, *12 inches, #442*	$ 1,600–1,750
Vase, *12 inches, #443*	$ 1,800–2,250
Vase, *12 inches, #444*	$ 1,800–2,250
Vase, *12 inches, #445*	$ 1,800–2,250
Vase, *12 inches, #446*	$ 3,800–4,500
Vase, *14 inches, #450*	$ 3,200–3,750
Vase, *20 inches, #456*	$ 4,000–4,500

Roseville "Carnelian II" vase, 7 inches,
$425–$475.
*Item courtesy of Richard Hatch and
Associates, Hendersonville, North Carolina.*

"Cherry Blossom"

Pieces in this line are distinguished by a fencelike latticework around their bases, with cherry blossoms, leaves, and twigs around their tops. "Cherry Blossom" was introduced in 1933 and was produced in two color schemes: blue with pink lattice, and yellow with brown lattice. Examples in this grouping are marked with paper labels.

Bowl, *5 inches, brown, #239*	$ 500–550
Bowl, *5 inches, pink, #239*	$ 600–650
Bowl, *8 inches, brown, #240*	$ 550–600
Bowl, *8 inches, pink, #240*	$ 650–700
Candlesticks, *brown, #1090, pair*	$ 700–750
Candlesticks, *pink, #1090, pair*	$ 850–900
Jardinière, *4 inches, brown, #627*	$ 450–500
Jardinière, *4 inches, pink, #627*	$ 550–600
Jardinière, *5 inches, brown, #627*	$ 500–550
Jardinière, *5 inches, pink, #627*	$ 650–700
Jardinière, *6 inches, brown, #627*	$ 550–600

Jardinière, *6 inches, pink, #627*	$ 750–800
Jardinière, *7 inches, brown, #627*	$ 650–700
Jardinière, *7 inches, pink, #627*	$ 850–900
Jardinière, *9 inches, brown, #627*	$ 1,100–1,200
Jardinière, *9 inches, pink, #627*	$ 1,600–1,750
Jardinière, *10 inches, brown, #627*	$ 2,000–2,200
Jardinière, *10 inches, pink, #627*	$ 2,400–2,600
Vase, *3¹/₂ inches, brown, #617*	$ 400–450
Vase, *3¹/₂ inches, pink, #617*	$ 550–600
Vase, *5 inches, brown, #618*	$ 550–600
Vase, *5 inches, pink, #618*	$ 650–700
Vase, *7 inches, brown, #620*	$ 600–650
Vase, *7 inches, pink, #620*	$ 750–800
Vase, *8 inches, brown, #624*	$ 750–800
Vase, *8 inches, pink, #624*	$ 850–900
Vase, *10 inches, brown, #626*	$ 1,250–1,400
Vase, *10 inches, pink, #626*	$ 1,500–1,600
Vase, *12 inches, brown, #627*	$ 1,600–1,750
Vase, *12 inches, pink, #627*	$ 2,400–2,600
Vase, *15 inches, brown, #628*	$ 3,250–3,500
Vase, *15 inches, pink, #628*	$ 4,250–4,500
Wall pocket, *8 inches, brown, #1270*	$ 1,250–1,400
Wall pocket, *8 inches, pink, #1270*	$ 2,000–2,250

"Columbine"

First produced in 1940, pieces in this line feature arrangements of flowers and leaves against a pink, blue, or tan background. Each piece is marked with the "Roseville" script signature.

Basket, *7 inches, #365*	$ 300–350
Basket, *8 inches, #366*	$ 350–400
Basket, *10 inches, #367*	$ 400–450
Basket, *12 inches, #368*	$ 575–625

Roseville "Columbine" bowl, 12 inches,
with flower frog, $600–$650.
*Item courtesy of Elaine Delcuze, Old School
Antique Mall, Sylva, North Carolina.*

Roseville "Columbine" ewer, #18, 7 inches
tall, $300–$350.
*Item courtesy of Richard Hatch and
Associates, Hendersonville, North Carolina.*

Bookends, *planters, #8, pair*	$ 450–500
Bowl, *6 inches, #401*	$ 200–250
Bowl, *8 inches, #402*	$ 225–275
Bowl, *10 inches, #403*	$ 250–300
Bowl, *12 inches, #405*	$ 275–325
Bowl, *14 inches, #406*	$ 275–325
Bowl, *rose, 4 inches, #399*	$ 175–225
Bowl, *rose, 6 inches, #400*	$ 225–275
Bowl and flower frog, *bowl is 12 inches*	$ 600–650
Candlesticks, *2¹/₂ inches, pair*	$ 200–250
Candlesticks, *4¹/₂ inches, pair*	$ 275–325
Cornucopia, *6 inches, #149*	$ 200–250
Ewer, *7 inches, #18*	$ 300–350
Flower frog, *#42*	$ 225–275
Flowerpot with saucer, *5 inches, #656*	$ 275–300

Jardinière, *3 inches, #655*	$ 175–200
Jardinière, *4 inches, #655*	$ 200–225
Jardinière, *5 inches, #655*	$ 225–250
Jardinière, *6 inches, #655*	$ 300–325
Jardinière, *8 inches, with pedestal, #655*	$ 2,000–2,200
Vase, *4 inches, #12*	$ 150–175
Vase, *6 inches, #13*	$ 175–200
Vase, *7 inches, #16*	$ 200–225
Vase, *8 inches, #19*	$ 250–275
Vase, *9 inches, #21*	$ 275–300
Vase, *10 inches, #23*	$ 350–375
Vase, *12 inches, #25*	$ 475–500
Vase, *14 inches, #26*	$ 750–800
Vase, *16 inches, #27*	$ 1,250–1,400
Wall pocket, *8 inches, #1290*	$ 850–900

"Corinthian"

Similar to pieces in Roseville's "Normandy" series and the more famous "Donatello" line, "Corinthian" pieces feature vertical fluting in ivory and green, with embossed bands of blue grapes, green leaves, and flowers. "Corinthian" pieces were first produced in 1923, and are either unmarked or marked with the "Rv" signature.

Basket, *hanging, 6 inches, #336*	$ 200–265
Basket, *hanging, 8 inches, #336*	$ 225–285
Bowl, *5 inches, #121*	$ 90–110
Bowl, *6 inches, #121*	$ 90–110
Bowl, *7 inches, #121*	$ 90–110
Bowl, *8 inches, #121*	$ 100–120
Bowl, *ferner, 5 inches, #255*	$ 125–145
Bowl, *ferner, 6 inches, #255*	$ 135–160
Bowl, *ferner, 5 inches, #256*	$ 140–160
Bowl, *ferner, 6 inches, #256*	$ 175–210
Jardinière, *6 inches, #601*	$ 135–165

Jardinière, *8 inches, #601*	$ 260–290
Jardinière, *9 inches, #601*	$ 425–475
Vase, *6 inches, #212*	$ 120–145
Vase, *6 inches, #213*	$ 145–180
Vase, *8 inches, #217*	$ 120–145
Vase, *10 inches, #219*	$ 200–250
Wall pocket, *12 inches, #1229*	$ 275–325

"Cosmos"

Pieces in this line are distinguished by representations of flowers in a scattered band against a background of blue, green, or tan. "Cosmos" pieces were first produced in 1940, and are signed "Roseville," either impressed or in relief.

Basket, *10 inches, #357*	$ 450–500
Basket, *12 inches, #358*	$ 525–575
Bowl, *6 inches, #369*	$ 200–250
Bowl, *8 inches, #370*	$ 200–250
Bowl, *10 inches, #371*	$ 275–325
Bowl, *12 inches, #373*	$ 325–375
Bowl, *14 inches, #374*	$ 375–425
Bowl, *rose, 4 inches, #375*	$ 225–275
Bowl, *rose, 6 inches, #376*	$ 275–325
Candlestick, *2 inches, #1137, pair*	$ 325–375
Candlestick, *4¹/₂ inches, #1137, pair*	$ 325–375
Cornucopia, *6 inches, #136*	$ 200–250
Cornucopia, *8 inches, #137*	$ 225–275
Ewer, *10 inches, #955*	$ 400–450
Ewer, *15 inches, #957*	$ 1,100–1,250
Flower frog, *#39*	$ 175–225
Flowerpot with saucer, *5 inches, #650*	$ 400–450
Jardinière, *3 inches, #649*	$ 150–200
Jardinière, *4 inches, #649*	$ 200–250

Roseville "Cosmos" pattern flower frog, 4 inches, $175–$225.
Item courtesy of Bill Brooker, Old School Antique Mall, Sylva, North Carolina.

Roseville "Cosmos" jardinière and pedestal, 8-inch jardinière, $2,200–$2,400.
Item courtesy of Richard H. Crane, Knoxville, Tennessee.

Jardinière, *5 inches, #649*	$ 250–300
Jardinière, *6 inches, #649*	$ 275–325
Jardinière, *8 inches, with pedestal, #649*	$ 2,200–2,400
Vase, *4 inches, #944*	$ 135–160
Vase, *5 inches, #945*	$ 175–200
Vase, *6 inches, #946*	$ 200–225
Vase, *7 inches, #948*	$ 300–325
Vase, *8 inches, #950*	$ 325–350
Vase, *9 inches, #952*	$ 325–350
Vase, *10 inches, #954*	$ 400–450
Vase, *12 inches, #956*	$ 475–525
Vase, *18 inches, #958*	$ 1,500–1,650
Wall pocket, *6 inches, #1285*	$ 550–600
Wall pocket, *8 inches, #1286*	$ 650–700

"Donatello"

Designed by Frederick Hurten Rhead, the "Donatello" line was based on a Czecho-slovakian piece of pottery that Rhead brought back to Zanesville after a trip to Europe. Pieces are decorated with an embossed band of cherubs (or "putti") and trees, ostensibly in the style of the Italian Renaissance sculptor Donatello. Pieces also feature vertical fluting above and below the band of putti, and most pieces are found in shades of ivory and green. Rare examples of pieces with lavender-gray fluting and ivory and brown bands do exist, but are fairly uncommon. "Donatello" pieces are usually unmarked, but occasionally are found with the "Rv" insignia.

Ashtray, *three-sided, #15*	$ 100–120
Ashtray, *round, #16*	$ 120–140
Ashtray, *round, flared top, #17*	$ 100–120
Basket, *#233*	$ 140–165
Basket, *9 inches, #301*	$ 250–290
Basket, *10¹/₂ inches, #302*	$ 350–375
Basket, *11 inches, #303*	$ 475–525
Basket, *12 inches, #304*	$ 475–525
Basket, *14 inches, #305*	$ 550–625
Basket, *14 inches, #306*	$ 550–625
Basket, *hanging, 6 inches, #327*	$ 250–300
Basket, *hanging, 8 inches, #327*	$ 275–325
Bowl, *#88*	$ 150–185
Bowl, *#89*	$ 110–130
Bowl, *#90*	$ 120–145
Bowl, *#91*	$ 120–145
Bowl, *#92*	$ 145–175
Bowl, *4 inches, #227*	$ 75–100
Bowl, *5 inches, #227*	$ 110–135
Bowl, *5 inches, #238*	$ 110–135
Bowl, *6 inches, #53*	$ 110–135
Bowl, *6 inches, #60*	$ 110–135
Bowl, *6 inches, #227*	$ 120–145
Bowl, *6 inches, #238*	$ 120–145

Bowl, *7 inches, #53*	$ 120–145
Bowl, *7 inches, #238*	$ 145–165
Bowl, *8 inches, #54*	$ 145–165
Bowl, *8 inches, #60*	$ 120–145
Bowl, *10 inches, #55*	$ 175–210
Bowl, *10 inches, #60*	$ 145–165
Bowl, *12 inches, #60*	$ 175–210
Bowl, *footed, 4 inches, #231*	$ 110–135
Bowl, *footed, 5 inches, #231*	$ 120–145
Bowl, *footed, 6 inches, #231*	$ 145–165
Candleholder, *finger ring, #1011*	$ 110–135
Candlestick, *finger ring, #10091*	$ 110–135
Candlestick, *7¹/₂ inches, #1008*	$ 135–165
Candlestick, *10 inches, #36*	$ 145–165
Candlestick, *10 inches, #1022*	$ 175–210
Compote, *#232*	$ 175–210
Flower frog, *2¹/₂ inches, #14*	$ 30–45
Flower frog, *3¹/₂ inches, #14*	$ 40–55
Flowerpot with saucer, *4 inches, #580*	$ 175–210
Flowerpot with saucer, *5 inches, #580*	$ 200–225
Flowerpot with saucer, *6 inches, #580*	$ 225–250
Incense burner	$ 285–325
Jardinière, *4 inches, #575*	$ 85–110
Jardinière, *5 inches, #575*	$ 120–145
Jardinière, *6 inches, #579*	$ 175–210
Jardinière, *8 inches, #579*	$ 250–300
Jardinière, *10 inches, #579*	$ 350–400
Jardinière, *12 inches, #579*	$ 425–475
Pitcher, *#1307*	$ 425–475
Plate, *6 inches, #61*	$ 200–225
Plate, *8 inches, #61*	$ 225–250

Roseville "Donatello" wall pocket, 10 inches, $300–$350.
Item courtesy of Elaine Delcuze, Old School Antique Mall, Sylva, North Carolina.

Powder jar, *#1*	$ 350–400
Powder jar, *#2*	$ 400–450
Vase, *bud, 6 inches, #116*	$ 125–150
Vase, *6 inches, #118*	$ 100–125
Vase, *7 inches, #113*	$ 150–170
Vase, *8 inches, #101*	$ 175–210
Vase, *8 inches, #102*	$ 175–210
Vase, *8 inches, #103*	$ 175–210
Vase, *8 inches, #104*	$ 175–210
Vase, *8 inches, #113*	$ 150–175
Vase, *8 inches, #118*	$ 125–150
Vase, *8 inches, #184*	$ 175–210
Vase, *10 inches, #105*	$ 200–245
Vase, *10 inches, #106*	$ 200–245
Vase, *10 inches, #107*	$ 200–245

Vase, *10 inches, #108*	$ 200–245
Vase, *10 inches, #113*	$ 200–245
Vase, *bud, 10 inches, #115*	$ 150–175
Vase, *10 inches, #184*	$ 175–210
Vase, *12 inches, #109*	$ 245–285
Vase, *12 inches, #110*	$ 245–285
Vase, *12 inches, #111*	$ 250–300
Vase, *12 inches, #112*	$ 300–350
Vase, *12 inches, #113*	$ 300–350
Vase, *12 inches, #184*	$ 275–325
Vase, *15 inches, #113*	$ 600–675
Wall pocket, *10 inches, #1202*	$ 300–350
Wall pocket, *12 inches, #1212*	$ 375–425

"Falline"

Introduced in 1933, this line features pieces with tan backgrounds that shade to green and royal blue or Chocolate Brown. The bodies have raised panels with designs that are generally said to resemble peapods. Pieces are either unmarked or have paper labels.

Bowl, *8 inches, tan/green/royal blue, #244*	$ 750–850
Bowl, *8 inches, tan/chocolate brown, #244*	$ 550–650
Candlestick, *3¹/₂ inches, tan/green/royal blue, #1092*	$ 400–500
Candlestick, *3¹/₂ inches, tan/chocolate brown, #1092*	$ 300–400
Vase, *6 inches, tan/green/royal blue, #642*	$ 850–1,000
Vase, *6 inches, tan/chocolate brown, #642*	$ 600–700
Vase, *6 inches, tan/green/chocolate brown, #643*	$ 800–950
Vase, *6 inches, tan/chocolate brown, #643*	$ 550–650
Vase, *6 inches, tan/green/royal blue, #644*	$ 1,250–1,400
Vase, *6 inches, tan/chocolate brown, #644*	$ 650–750
Vase, *6 inches, tan/green/royal blue, #650*	$ 1,250–1,400
Vase, *6 inches, tan/chocolate brown, #650*	$ 750–850
Vase, *6¹/₂ inches, tan/green/royal blue, #645*	$ 1,250–1,400

Vase, 6^1/2 inches, tan/chocolate brown, #645	$ 650–750
Vase, 7 inches, tan/green/royal blue, #647	$ 1,250–1,400
Vase, 7 inches, tan/chocolate brown, #647	$ 750–850
Vase, 7 inches, tan/green/royal blue, #648	$ 1,250–1,400
Vase, 7 inches, tan/chocolate brown, #648	$ 750–850
Vase, 8 inches, tan/green/royal blue, #646	$ 1,600–1,750
Vase, 8 inches, tan/chocolate brown, #646	$ 950–1,100
Vase, 8 inches, tan/green/royal blue, #649	$ 1,600–1,750
Vase, 8 inches, tan/chocolate brown, #649	$ 1,000–1,250
Vase, 8 inches, tan/green/royal blue, #651	$ 1,800–2,200
Vase, 8 inches, tan/chocolate brown, #651	$ 1,600–1,750
Vase, 9 inches, tan/green/royal blue, #652	$ 1,800–2,200
Vase, 9 inches, tan/chocolate brown, #652	$ 1,600–1,750
Vase, 12 inches, tan/green/royal blue, #653	$ 2,800–3,250
Vase, 12 inches, tan/chocolate brown, #653	$ 2,000–2,400
Vase, 13^1/2 inches, tan/green/royal blue, #654	$ 3,250–3,750
Vase, 13^1/2 inches, tan/chocolate brown, #654	$ 2,800–3,200
Vase, 15 inches, tan/green/royal blue, #655	$ 3,600–3,800
Vase, 15 inches, tan/chocolate brown, #655	$ 2,800–3,200

"Ferella"

First produced in 1930, pieces in this line are predominantly either rose or brown, and have a mottled glaze. They are decorated with yellow/green shells around their tops and bases, with cutout areas between each shell.

Bowl, 8 inches, rose, #211	$ 800–900
Bowl, 8 inches, brown, #211	$ 700–800
Bowl, footed, 4 inches, rose, #210	$ 500–600
Bowl, footed, 4 inches, brown, #210	$ 400–500
Bowl, footed, 12 inches by 7 inches, rose, #212	$ 900–1,000
Bowl, footed, 12 inches by 7 inches, brown, #212	$ 800–900
Bowl with flower frog, 8 inches, rose, #87	$ 900–1,000
Bowl with flower frog, 8 inches, brown, #87	$ 800–1,000

Candlestick, *4 inches, rose, #1078*	$ 400–450
Candlestick, *4 inches, brown, #1078*	$ 375–425
Flower frog, *2¹/₂ inches, rose, #15*	$ 110–125
Flower frog, *2¹/₂ inches, brown, #15*	$ 100–110
Flower frog, *3¹/₂ inches, rose, #15*	$ 120–140
Flower frog, *3¹/₂ inches, brown, #15*	$ 110–125
Flowerpot, *5 inches, rose, #620*	$ 1,250–1,400
Flowerpot, *5 inches, brown, #620*	$ 1,100–1,200
Vase, *4 inches, rose, #497*	$ 450–550
Vase, *4 inches, brown, #497*	$ 400–450
Vase, *4 inches, rose, #498*	$ 450–550
Vase, *4 inches, brown, #498*	$ 400–550
Vase, *5 inches, rose, #500*	$ 675–725
Vase, *5 inches, brown, #500*	$ 575–625
Vase, *5 inches, rose, #503*	$ 675–725
Vase, *5 inches, brown, #503*	$ 575–625
Vase, *5¹/₂ inches, rose, #504*	$ 675–725
Vase, *5¹/₂ inches, brown, #505*	$ 575–625
Vase, *6 inches, rose, #499*	$ 550–650
Vase, *6 inches, brown, #499*	$ 500–550
Vase, *6 inches, rose, #501*	$ 850–950
Vase, *6 inches, brown, #501*	$ 675–725
Vase, *6 inches, rose, #502*	$ 850–950
Vase, *6 inches, brown, #502*	$ 675–725
Vase, *6 inches, rose, #505*	$ 775–825
Vase, *6 inches, brown, #505*	$ 675–725
Vase, *8 inches, rose, #508*	$ 1,250–1,400
Vase, *8 inches, brown, #508*	$ 850–950
Vase, *8 inches, rose, #509*	$ 1,250–1,400
Vase, *8 inches, brown, #509*	$ 850–950
Vase, *9 inches, rose, #507*	$ 1,250–1,400

Vase, *9 inches, brown, #507*	$ 850–950
Vase, *10 inches, rose, #511*	$ 1,650–1,750
Vase, *10 inches, brown, #511*	$ 1,250–1,400
Wall pocket, *red, 6¹/₂ inches, #1266*	$ 1,750–2,000
Wall pocket, *brown, 6¹/₂ inches, #1266*	$ 1,450–1,650

"Florentine"

Made between 1924 and 1928, pieces in this line feature panels with textured interiors alternating with vertical garlands of leaves and berries. Most pieces were made in shades of brown, though some ivory and green pieces also exist. "Florentine" pieces are generally marked with the "Rv" backstamp.

Ashtray, *3 inches, #17*	$ 110–135
Basket, *6 inches, #320*	$ 210–235
Basket, *7 inches, #321*	$ 250–300
Basket, *8 inches, #322*	$ 325–375
Basket, *hanging, 6 inches, #337*	$ 210–235
Basket, *hanging, 7 inches, #337*	$ 310–335
Bowl, *4 inches, #125*	$ 80–110
Bowl, *5 inches, #125*	$ 110–135
Bowl, *6 inches, #125*	$ 120–145
Bowl, *7 inches, #125*	$ 140–165
Bowl, *4 inches, #130*	$ 110–135
Candlestick, *8 inches, #1049*	$ 140–165
Candlestick, *10 inches, #1050*	$ 165–185
Flower frog, *2¹/₂ inches, #15*	$ 45–60
Flower frog, *3¹/₂ inches, #15*	$ 60–75
Jardinière, *5 inches, #602*	$ 140–165
Jardinière, *6 inches, #602*	$ 165–185
Jardinière, *7 inches, #602*	$ 235–265
Jardinière, *8 inches, #602*	$ 335–365
Jardinière, *9 inches, #602*	$ 435–465
Jardinière and pedestal, *9-inch jardinière, #602*	$ 1,100–1,250

Roseville "Florentine" jardinière and pedestal, 9-inch jardinière, $1,100–$1,250. *Item courtesy of Roberta Bull, Old School Antique Mall, Sylva, North Carolina.*

Vase, *6 inches, #229*	$ 140–160
Vase, *8 inches, #230*	$ 210–240
Vase, *10 inches, #232*	$ 310–340
Vase, *12 inches, #234*	$ 350–400
Wall pocket, *7 inches, #1238*	$ 275–325
Wall pocket, *8 inches, #1238*	$ 350–400
Wall pocket, *10 inches, #1230*	$ 425–475
Wall pocket, *12 inches, #1231*	$ 475–525

"Freesia"

First produced in 1945, "Freesia" pieces have a grouping of flowers and leaves on either a Tropical Green, Delft Blue, or Tangerine shaded background. Examples of "Freesia" are signed with the "Roseville" script signature.

Basket, *7 inches, #390*	$ 250–275
Basket, *8 inches, #391*	$ 300–325
Basket, *10 inches, #392*	$ 375–400

Bookends, *#15, pair*	$ 375–425
Bowl, *6 inches, #464*	$ 135–160
Bowl, *8 inches, #465*	$ 225–250
Bowl, *10 inches, #466*	$ 250–275
Bowl, *12 inches, #468*	$ 275–300
Bowl, *14 inches, #469*	$ 300–325
Candlesticks, *2 inches, #1160, pair*	$ 150–175
Candlesticks, *4¹/₂ inches, #1161*	$ 225–250
Cookie jar, *#4*	$ 550–600
Cornucopia, *6 inches, #197*	$ 150–175
Cornucopia, *8 inches, #198*	$ 175–200
Creamer, *#6-C*	$ 110–135
Ewer, *6 inches, #19*	$ 250–275
Ewer, *10 inches, #20*	$ 375–425
Ewer, *15 inches, #21*	$ 1,100–1,250
Flowerpot with saucer, *5 inches, #670*	$ 250–275
Jardinière, *4 inches, #669*	$ 175–200
Jardinière, *6 inches, #669*	$ 175–200
Vase, *6 inches, #117*	$ 200–225
Vase, *7 inches, #119*	$ 200–225
Vase, *8 inches, #121*	$ 250–275
Vase, *9 inches, #123*	$ 300–325
Vase, *10 inches, #125*	$ 300–325
Vase, *12 inches, #127*	$ 375–425
Vase, *15 inches, #128*	$ 950–1,000
Vase, *18 inches, #129*	$ 1,250–1,400
Wall pocket, *8 inches, #1296*	$ 450–500
Window box, *8 inches, #1392*	$ 225–250

"Futura"

The "Futura" line is very difficult to categorize. Some of its pieces have an Art Deco look, others have an almost futuristic flair, and others feature floral decorations that suggest later Roseville lines such as "Pinecone" and "Teasel." Examples are generally unmarked, except for a paper label.

Bowl, *"Aztec," 8 inches, rose, #188*	$ 2,000–2,250
Bowl, *"Aztec," 8 inches, brown, #188*	$ 750–850
Bowl, *10 inches, #195*	$ 1,250–1,400
Bowl, *flower, rectangular, 12 inches by 5 inches, #196*	$ 750–850
Candlestick, *4 inches, pair, #1075*	$ 1,250–1,400
Candlestick, *4 inches, pair, #1072*	$ 1,100–1,200
Candlestick, *4 inches, pair, #1073*	$ 700–800
Jardinière, *7 inches, brown, #616*	$ 525–575
Planter, *5 inches, square, footed, #198*	$ 1,250–1,400
Planter, *6 inches, #189-4*	$ 700–800
Planter, *6 inches, #190-3¹/₂*	$ 500–575
Vase, *pillow, 4 inches, #85*	$ 475–525
Vase, *rectangular, 5 inches by 1 inch by 5 inches, #81*	$ 650–700
Vase, *5 inches, #421*	$ 475–525
Vase, *6 inches, #82*	$ 525–575
Vase, *6 inches, #380*	$ 650–700
Vase, *6 inches, #381*	$ 450–550
Vase, *6 inches, #397*	$ 525–575
Vase, *6 inches, #422*	$ 525–575
Vase, *6 inches, #423*	$ 600–650
Vase, *7 inches, #382*	$ 600–675
Vase, *7 inches, #387*	$ 1,250–1,400
Vase, *7 inches, #399*	$ 750–825
Vase, *7 inches, #403*	$ 950–1,100
Vase, *7 inches, #424*	$ 800–900
Vase, *7¹/₂ inches, #405*	$ 900–1,000
Vase, *8 inches, #383*	$ 700–750
Vase, *8 inches, #384*	$ 700–750
Vase, *8 inches, #385*	$ 650–700

Roseville "Futura" jardinière, brown, $525–$575.
Item courtesy of Richard Hatch and Associates, Sylva, North Carolina.

Vase, *8 inches, brown, #386*	$ 1,600–1,750
Vase, *8 inches, pink and green*	$ 900–1,000
Vase, *8 inches, #401*	$ 850–925
Vase, *8 inches, #402*	$ 750–800
Vase, *8 inches, blue, #404*	$ 1,750–2,200
Vase, *8 inches, green, #404*	$ 1,600–1,750
Vase, *8 inches, #425*	$ 800–875
Vase, *8 inches, #427*	$ 1,100–1,250
Vase, *8 inches, #428*	$ 850–925
Vase, *9 inches, #388*	$ 850–925
Vase, *9 inches, #389*	$ 1,250–1,400
Vase, *9 inches, #407*	$ 2,000–2,200
Vase, *9 inches, #409*	$ 1,250–1,400
Vase, *9 inches, #429*	$ 1,250–1,400
Vase, *9 inches, #430*	$ 1,250–1,400

Vase, *10 inches, blue, #390*	$ 1,100–1,250
Vase, *10 inches, brown, #390*	$ 900–975
Vase, *10 inches, #391*	$ 1,250–1,400
Vase, *10 inches, #392*	$ 1,100–1,250
Vase, *10 inches, #395*	$ 1,250–1,400
Vase, *10 inches, #408*	$ 1,250–1,400
Vase, *10 inches, #431*	$ 1,100–1,250
Vase, *10 inches, #432*	$ 1,250–1,400
Vase, *10 inches, #433*	$ 1,250–1,400
Vase, *10 inches, #434*	$ 4,500–5,500
Vase, *10 inches, #435*	$ 2,000–2,200
Vase, *12 inches, #393*	$ 1,500–1,750
Vase, *12 inches, #410*	$ 2,000–2,200
Vase, *12 inches, #436*	$ 5,500–6,500
Vase, *12 inches, #437*	$ 2,000–2,200
Vase, *14 inches, #411*	$ 3,400–3,600
Vase, *15 inches, #438*	$ 3,200–3,400
Window box, *15 inches by 4 inches by 6 inches, #375*	$ 2,250–2,400

"Magnolia"

Pieces from this 1940s line feature raised white magnolia blossoms against a textured background of green, blue, or tan. "Magnolia" is a common pattern, and pieces are generally marked with the script "Roseville" signature.

Ashtray, *#28*	$ 175–200
Basket, *7 inches, #383*	$ 250–275
Basket, *8 inches, #384*	$ 275–300
Basket, *10 inches, #385*	$ 375–400
Basket, *12 inches, #386*	$ 475–500
Bookends, *#13, pair*	$ 325–375
Bowl, *rose, 4 inches, #446*	$ 200–225
Bowl, *rose, 6 inches, #446*	$ 225–250
Bowl, *6 inches, #447*	$ 175–200

Bowl, *8 inches, #448*	$ 225–250
Bowl, *10 inches, #449*	$ 250–275
Bowl, *12 inches, #451*	$ 300–325
Bowl, *14 inches, #452*	$ 350–375
Candlestick, *2$^{1}/_{2}$ inches, pair*	$ 175–200
Candlestick, *4$^{1}/_{2}$ inches, pair*	$ 250–275
Compote, *10 inches, #5*	$ 225–250
Conch shell, *6 inches, #452*	$ 250–300
Conch shell, *8 inches, #454*	$ 300–325
Cookie jar, *#2*	$ 550–600
Creamer, *#4-C*	$ 110–125
Ewer, *6 inches, #13*	$ 225–250
Ewer, *10 inches, #14*	$ 350–400
Ewer, *15 inches, #15*	$ 850–900
Flower frog, *#49*	$ 150–175
Flowerpot with saucer, *5 inches, #666*	$ 275–300
Jardinière, *3 inches, #665*	$ 110–125
Jardinière, *4 inches, #665*	$ 150–175
Jardinière, *5 inches, #665*	$ 225–250
Jardinière, *8 inches, with pedestal, #665*	$ 1,250–1,400
Pitcher, *7 inches, ball-shaped, #132*	$ 600–650
Sugar bowl, *lidded, #4-S*	$ 110–125
Teapot, *#4*	$ 450–500
Vase, *4 inches, #86*	$ 150–175
Vase, *4$^{1}/_{2}$ inches, double bud, gate-shaped*	$ 225–250
Vase, *6 inches, #87*	$ 200–225
Vase, *7 inches, #89*	$ 225–250
Vase, *bud, 7 inches, #179*	$ 200–225
Vase, *8 inches, #91*	$ 250–275
Vase, *9 inches, #93*	$ 300–325
Vase, *10 inches, #95*	$ 375–400

Vase, *12 inches, #96*	$ 550–600
Vase, *14 inches, #97*	$ 650–700
Vase, *15 inches, #98*	$ 850–900
Vase, *16 inches, #99*	$ 1,100–1,250
Vase, *18 inches, #100*	$ 1,250–1,400
Wall pocket, *8 inches, #1294*	$ 450–500
Window box, *6 inches, #388*	$ 225–250
Window box, *8 inches, #389*	$ 250–275

"Mostique"

The "Mostique" line represents a transition between Roseville's early art pottery and its later commercial art lines. First produced in 1915, "Mostique" pieces feature Native American–inspired designs of stylized, colored, slip-decorated flowers and arrowhead leaves against a textured bisque background. Typically, interiors have a glossy, solid-color glaze. "Mostique" pieces are usually unmarked, but occasional examples are marked "Rv."

Basket, *hanging, 6 inches, #334*	$ 275–350
Basket, *hanging, 8 inches, #334*	$ 325–400
Bowl, *4 inches, #131*	$ 110–135
Bowl, *5 inches, #73*	$ 110–135
Bowl, *5 inches, #131*	$ 135–160
Bowl, *6 inches, #72*	$ 110–135
Bowl, *6 inches, #131*	$ 135–160
Bowl, *6 inches, #221*	$ 300–375
Bowl, *7 inches, #73*	$ 135–160
Bowl, *7 inches, #131*	$ 165–190
Bowl, *8 inches, #72*	$ 165–190
Bowl, *8 inches, #222*	$ 375–425
Candlestick, *4 inches, each, #1083*	$ 375–425
Flower frog, *2¹/₂ inches*	$ 15–25
Flower frog, *3¹/₂ inches*	$ 25–40
Jardinière, *low, 5 inches, #253*	$ 185–210
Jardinière, *low, 6 inches, #253*	$ 235–260

Jardinière, *6 inches, #592*	$ 210–235
Jardinière, *6 inches, #606*	$ 210–235
Jardinière, *7 inches, #593*	$ 210–235
Jardinière, *7 inches, #606*	$ 265–290
Jardinière, *7 inches, #622*	$ 365–390
Jardinière, *8 inches, #593*	$ 265–290
Jardinière, *8 inches, #606*	$ 365–390
Jardinière, *8 inches, #622*	$ 550–650
Jardinière, *9 inches, #593*	$ 385–410
Jardinière, *9 inches, #606*	$ 465–490
Jardinière, *9 inches, #622*	$ 385–410
Jardinière, *10 inches, #592*	$ 485–525
Jardinière, *10 inches, with pedestal, #606*	$ 1,500–1,600
Jardinière, *10 inches, with pedestal, #622*	$ 1,750–1,900
Jardinière, *12 inches, #593*	$ 600–675
Spittoon, *#631*	$ 450–550
Strawberry jar, *10 inches, #99*	$ 1,100–1,200
Strawberry jar, *10 inches, #100*	$ 1,250–1,400
Vase, *6 inches, #1*	$ 165–190
Vase, *6 inches, #2*	$ 165–190
Vase, *6 inches, #3*	$ 165–190
Vase, *6 inches, #4*	$ 165–190
Vase, *6 inches, #5*	$ 165–190
Vase, *6 inches, #6*	$ 165–190
Vase, *6 inches, #164*	$ 165–190
Vase, *6 inches, #532*	$ 265–310
Vase, *8 inches, #7*	$ 240–295
Vase, *8 inches, #8*	$ 240–295
Vase, *8 inches, #9*	$ 240–295
Vase, *8 inches, #10*	$ 240–295
Vase, *8 inches, #11*	$ 240–295

Vase, *8 inches, #12*	$ 240–295
Vase, *8 inches, #13*	$ 240–295
Vase, *8 inches, #14*	$ 240–295
Vase, *8 inches, #164*	$ 210–235
Vase, *8 inches, #532*	$ 340–395
Vase, *8 inches, #533*	$ 425–475
Vase, *8 inches, #534*	$ 525–575
Vase, *8 inches, #535*	$ 425–475
Vase, *9 inches, #536*	$ 525–575
Vase, *10 inches, #15*	$ 325–400
Vase, *10 inches, #16*	$ 325–400
Vase, *10 inches, #17*	$ 325–400
Vase, *10 inches, #18*	$ 325–400
Vase, *10 inches, #19*	$ 325–400
Vase, *10 inches, #20*	$ 325–400
Vase, *10 inches, #21*	$ 325–400
Vase, *10 inches, #22*	$ 325–400
Vase, *10 inches, #23*	$ 325–400
Vase, *10 inches, #24*	$ 325–400
Vase, *10 inches, #164*	$ 300–375
Vase, *10 inches, #532*	$ 475–525
Vase, *10 inches, #537*	$ 600–675
Vase, *12 inches, #25*	$ 400–475
Vase, *12 inches, #26*	$ 400–475
Vase, *12 inches, #27*	$ 400–475
Vase, *12 inches, #28*	$ 400–475
Vase, *12 inches, #29*	$ 400–475
Vase, *12 inches, #30*	$ 400–475
Vase, *12 inches, #164*	$ 375–425
Vase, *12 inches, #532*	$ 650–750
Vase, *15 inches, #164*	$ 750–850

Roseville "Panel" covered vase, $475–$525. *Item courtesy of Barbara and Karl Mueller, Old School Antique Mall, Sylva, North Carolina.*

Wall pocket, *10 inches, #1224*	$ 575–625
Wall pocket, *12 inches, #1224*	$ 675–725

"Panel"

First produced in 1920, pieces in this line have backgrounds of either dark green or dark brown, with panels of naturalistic or stylized flora or depictions of nudes. Items with nudes command much higher prices than items with flowers or leaves. Examples of "Panel" are typically marked with the "Rv" stamp.

Bowl, *4 inches, urn-shaped*	$ 175–200
Candlesticks, *8 inches, #1067, pair*	$ 475–525
Vase, *6 inches, #285*	$ 175–200
Vase, *8 inches, #292*	$ 300–350
Vase, *10 inches, #297*	$ 375–425
Vase, *10 inches, nude, #296*	$ 1,500–1,750
Vase, *covered, 9 inches, #295*	$ 475–525
Wall pocket, *9 inches, #1244*	$ 350–400

"Peony"

Pieces in this line are usually dominated by depictions of either one or two large blossoms. The blossoms have prominent centers and green leaves, and appear on textured backgrounds in shades of yellow and brown, pink and blue, or green. "Peony" was first made in 1930, and pieces are marked with the script "Roseville" signature.

Ashtray, #27	$ 150–175
Basket, 7 inches, #376	$ 225–250
Basket, 8 inches, #377	$ 275–300
Basket, 10 inches, #378	$ 325–350
Basket, 12 inches, #379	$ 425–475
Bookends, #11, pair	$ 300–350
Bowl, 6 inches, #428	$ 150–175
Bowl, 8 inches, #429	$ 175–200
Bowl, 10 inches, #430	$ 200–225
Bowl, 12 inches, #432	$ 275–300
Bowl, 14 inches, #433	$ 325–375
Candelabra, two-cup, #1153	$ 150–175
Candlesticks, 2 inches, #1151	$ 150–175
Candlesticks, 4^1/$_2$ inches, #1152	$ 200–225
Compote, 10 inches, #4	$ 225–250
Conch shell, #436	$ 225–250
Cornucopia, 6 inches, #170	$ 150–175
Cornucopia, 8 inches, #171	$ 175–200
Creamer, #3-C	$ 110–135
Ewer, 6 inches, #7	$ 200–225
Ewer, 10 inches, #8	$ 325–375
Ewer, 15 inches, #15	$ 650–700
Flowerpot and saucer, 5 inches, #662	$ 250–275
Jardinière, 3 inches, #661	$ 150–175
Jardinière, 4 inches, #661	$ 175–200

Roseville "Peony" cider set consisting of a pitcher and four mugs, $850–$950.
Item courtesy of Kingston Pike Antique Mall, Knoxville, Tennessee.

Roseville, "Peony" bowl, 12 inches, $275–$300.
Item courtesy of Kingston Pike Antique Mall, Knoxville, Tennessee.

Jardinière, *5 inches, #661*	$ 200–225
Jardinière, *6 inches, #661*	$ 250–275
Jardinière, *10 inches, with pedestal, #661*	$ 1,250–1,400
Mug, *#2*	$ 100–120
Pitcher, *#1326*	$ 300–350
Sugar bowl, *#3-S*	$ 110–135
Teapot, *#3*	$ 375–425
Vase, *4 inches, #57*	$ 150–175
Vase, *6 inches, #58*	$ 175–200
Vase, *7 inches, #60*	$ 175–200
Vase, *8 inches, #62*	$ 200–225
Vase, *9 inches, #64*	$ 250–275
Vase, *10 inches, #66*	$ 300–350
Vase, *12 inches, #67*	$ 375–425
Vase, *14 inches, #68*	$ 600–650

Vase, *15 inches, #69*	$ 750–800
Vase, *18 inches, #70*	$ 1,000–1,200
Wall pocket, *8 inches, #1293*	$ 375–425

"Pinecone"

This line was created by Frank Ferrell and went into production in 1931. It is very popular with current collectors, and the design features images of pinecones with long pine needles. Pieces were produced in brown, green, blue, and (very rarely) pink, and are generally marked "Roseville" or have a black paper label.

Ashtray, *3 rests, #25, green*	$ 210–235
Ashtray, *3 rests, #25, brown*	$ 290–325
Ashtray, *3 rests, #25, blue*	$ 325–375
Basket, *8 inches, #352, green*	$ 425–475
Basket, *8 inches, #352, brown*	$ 575–625
Basket, *8 inches, #352, blue*	$ 725–800
Bowl, *5 inches, #320, green*	$ 235–260
Bowl, *5 inches, #320, brown*	$ 300–350
Bowl, *5 inches, #320, blue*	$ 375–425
Bowl, *6 inches, #354, green*	$ 200–235
Bowl, *6 inches, #354, brown*	$ 245–275
Bowl, *6 inches, #354, blue*	$ 325–375
Bowl, *8 inches, #355, green*	$ 265–300
Bowl, *8 inches, #355, brown*	$ 325–365
Bowl, *8 inches, #355, blue*	$ 400–450
Bowl, *9 inches, #321, green*	$ 310–350
Bowl, *9 inches, #321, brown*	$ 375–425
Bowl, *9 inches, #321, blue*	$ 525–575
Bowl, *12 inches, #322, green*	$ 425–475
Bowl, *12 inches, #322, brown*	$ 500–550
Bowl, *12 inches, #322, blue*	$ 700–750
Bowl, *15 inches, #323, green*	$ 475–525
Bowl, *15 inches, #323, brown*	$ 600–650

Bowl, *15 inches, #323, blue*	$ 800–850
Bowl, *rose, 4 inches, #278, green*	$ 300–350
Bowl, *rose, 4 inches, #278, brown*	$ 375–425
Bowl, *rose, 4 inches, #278, blue*	$ 475–525
Bowl, *rose, 6 inches, #261, green*	$ 350–400
Bowl, *rose, 6 inches, #261, brown*	$ 400–450
Bowl, *rose, 6 inches, #261, blue*	$ 550–600
Candlestick, *single, #1123, green, pair*	$ 300–350
Candlestick, *single, #1123, brown, pair*	$ 350–400
Candlestick, *single, #1123, blue, pair*	$ 400–450
Candlestick, *double, #1124, green, each*	$ 275–300
Candlestick, *double, #1124, brown, each*	$ 325–350
Candlestick, *double, #1124, blue, each*	$ 375–425
Candlestick, *triple, #1106, green, each*	$ 325–375
Candlestick, *triple, #1106, brown, each*	$ 400–450
Candlestick, *triple, #1106, blue, each*	$ 550–600
Cornucopia, *6 inches, #126, green*	$ 225–275
Cornucopia, *6 inches, #126, brown*	$ 250–300
Cornucopia, *6 inches, #126, blue*	$ 300–350
Cornucopia, *8 inches, #128, green*	$ 250–300
Cornucopia, *8 inches, #128, brown*	$ 300–350
Cornucopia, *8 inches, #128, blue*	$ 375–425
Ewer, *10 inches, #909, green*	$ 600–650
Ewer, *10 inches, #909, brown*	$ 650–700
Ewer, *10 inches, #909, blue*	$ 750–800
Ewer, *15 inches, #851, green*	$ 1,600–1,750
Ewer, *15 inches, #852, brown*	$ 1,900–2,000
Ewer, *15 inches, #852, blue*	$ 2,250–2,400
Flower frog, *#32, green*	$ 200–225
Flower frog, *#32, brown*	$ 275–300
Flower frog, *#32, blue*	$ 325–350

Flower frog, *#33, green*	$ 200–225
Flower frog, *#33, brown*	$ 275–300
Flower frog, *#33, blue*	$ 325–350
Flower frog, *4 inches, #20, green*	$ 250–300
Flower frog, *4 inches, #20, brown*	$ 300–350
Flower frog, *4 inches, #20, blue*	$ 375–425
Flower frog, *5 inches, #21, green*	$ 250–300
Flower frog, *5 inches, #21, brown*	$ 300–350
Flower frog, *5 inches, #21, blue*	$ 375–425
Flowerpot, *with saucer, 5 inches, #633, green*	$ 350–400
Flowerpot, *with saucer, 5 inches, #633, brown*	$ 400–450
Flowerpot, *with saucer, 5 inches, #633, blue*	$ 550–600
Jardinière, *3 inches, #632, green*	$ 160–185
Jardinière, *3 inches, #632, brown*	$ 185–210
Jardinière, *3 inches, #632, blue*	$ 250–300
Jardinière, *4 inches, #632, green*	$ 200–250
Jardinière, *4 inches, #632, brown*	$ 250–300
Jardinière, *4 inches, #632, blue*	$ 325–375
Jardinière, *5 inches, #632, green*	$ 250–300
Jardinière, *5 inches, #632, brown*	$ 325–375
Jardinière, *5 inches, #632, blue*	$ 425–475
Jardinière, *6 inches, #632, green*	$ 375–425
Jardinière, *6 inches, #632, brown*	$ 425–475
Jardinière, *6 inches, #632, blue*	$ 525–575
Jardinière, *7 inches, #632, green*	$ 425–475
Jardinière, *7 inches, #632, brown*	$ 525–575
Jardinière, *7 inches, #632, blue*	$ 675–725
Jardinière, *8 inches, with pedestal, #632, green*	$ 1,900–2,000
Jardinière, *8 inches, with pedestal, #632, brown*	$ 2,250–2,400
Jardinière, *8 inches, with pedestal, #632, blue*	$ 2,600–2,750
Jardinière, *9 inches, #632, green*	$ 800–850

Roseville "Pinecone" mug-shaped vase, green, 4 inches,
$225–$285.
Item courtesy of Kingston Pike Antique Mall.

Jardinière, *9 inches, #632, brown*	$ 950–1,000
Jardinière, *9 inches, #632, blue*	$ 1,250–1,400
Jardinière, *10 inches, with pedestal, #632, green*	$ 2,250–2,400
Jardinière, *10 inches, with pedestal, #632, brown*	$ 2,600–2,750
Jardinière, *10 inches, with pedestal, #632, blue*	$ 4,200–4,400
Planter, *5 inches, #124, green*	$ 300–350
Planter, *5 inches, #124, brown*	$ 375–425
Planter, *5 inches, #124, blue*	$ 475–525
Umbrella stand, *20 inches, #777, green*	$ 2,250–2,400
Umbrella stand, *20 inches, #777, brown*	$ 3,200–3,400
Umbrella stand, *20 inches, #777, blue*	$ 3,600–3,750
Vase, *4 inches, mug-shaped, #960, green*	$ 225–285
Vase, *4 inches, mug-shaped, #960, brown*	$ 200–250
Vase, *4 inches, mug-shaped, #960, blue*	$ 225–275
Vase, *6 inches, #748, green*	$ 235–265

Vase, 6 inches, #748, brown	$ 300–350
Vase, 6 inches, #748, blue	$ 400–450
Vase, 6 inches, #838, green	$ 225–275
Vase, 6 inches, #838, brown	$ 275–325
Vase, 6 inches, #838, blue	$ 375–425
Vase, 6 inches, #839, green	$ 225–275
Vase, 6 inches, #839, brown	$ 275–325
Vase, 6 inches, #839, blue	$ 375–425
Vase, 7 inches, #841, green	$ 350–375
Vase, 7 inches, #841, brown	$ 400–450
Vase, 7 inches, #841, blue	$ 475–525
Vase, urn, 7 inches, #121, green	$ 250–300
Vase, urn, 7 inches, #121, brown	$ 325–375
Vase, urn, 7 inches, #121, blue	$ 400–450
Vase, 8 inches, #842, green	$ 425–475
Vase, 8 inches, #842, brown	$ 500–550
Vase, 8 inches, #842, blue	$ 600–650
Vase, 8 inches, #843, green	$ 425–475
Vase, 8 inches, #843, brown	$ 500–550
Vase, 8 inches, #843, blue	$ 600–650
Vase, 8 inches, #844, green	$ 375–425
Vase, 8 inches, #844, brown	$ 425–475
Vase, 8 inches, #844, blue	$ 500–550
Vase, 8 inches, #845, green	$ 500–550
Vase, 8 inches, #845, brown	$ 550–600
Vase, 8 inches, #845, blue	$ 650–700
Vase, bud, 8 inches, #113, green	$ 350–400
Vase, bud, 8 inches, #113, brown	$ 400–450
Vase, bud, 8 inches, #113, blue	$ 500–550
Vase, urn, 8 inches, #908, green	$ 400–450
Vase, urn, 8 inches, #908, brown	$ 500–550

Vase, *urn, 8 inches, #908, blue*	$ 600–650
Vase, *9 inches, #848, green*	$ 650–700
Vase, *9 inches, #848, brown*	$ 700–750
Vase, *9 inches, #848, blue*	$ 850–900
Vase, *10 inches, #747, green*	$ 550–600
Vase, *10 inches, #747, brown*	$ 650–700
Vase, *10 inches, #747, blue*	$ 800–850
Vase, *10 inches, #804, green*	$ 550–600
Vase, *10 inches, #804, brown*	$ 650–700
Vase, *10 inches, #804, blue*	$ 800–850
Vase, *10 inches, #848, green*	$ 650–700
Vase, *10 inches, #848, brown*	$ 700–750
Vase, *10 inches, #848, blue*	$ 850–900
Vase, *10 inches, #849, green*	$ 600–650
Vase, *10 inches, #849, brown*	$ 650–700
Vase, *10 inches, #849, blue*	$ 750–800
Vase, *urn, 10 inches, #910, green*	$ 650–700
Vase, *urn, 10 inches, #910, brown*	$ 700–750
Vase, *urn, 10 inches, #910, blue*	$ 850–900
Vase, *12 inches, #805, green*	$ 750–800
Vase, *12 inches, #805, brown*	$ 850–900
Vase, *12 inches, #805, blue*	$ 950–1,000
Vase, *12 inches, #806, green*	$ 800–850
Vase, *12 inches, #806, brown*	$ 900–950
Vase, *12 inches, #806, blue*	$ 1,100–1,200
Vase, *urn, 12 inches, #911, green*	$ 750–800
Vase, *urn, 12 inches, #911, brown*	$ 850–900
Vase, *urn, 12 inches, #911, blue*	$ 950–1,000
Vase, *14 inches, #850, green*	$ 1,250–1,400
Vase, *14 inches #850, brown*	$ 1,600–1,750
Vase, *14 inches, #850, blue*	$ 1,900–2,000

Vase, *15 inches, #807, green*	$ 1,750–1,850
Vase, *15 inches, #807, brown*	$ 2,250–2,400
Vase, *15 inches, #807, blue*	$ 3,200–3,400
Vase, *urn, 15 inches, #912, green*	$ 1,600–1,750
Vase, *urn, 15 inches, #912, brown*	$ 2,250–2,400
Vase, *urn, 15 inches, #912, blue*	$ 3,200–3,400
Vase, *urn, 18 inches, #913, green*	$ 2,000–2,200
Vase, *urn, 18 inches, #913, brown*	$ 2,600–2,750
Vase, *urn, 18 inches, #913, blue*	$ 3,400–3,500
Wall bracket, *5 inches by 8 inches, #1, green*	$ 550–600
Wall bracket, *5 inches by 8 inches, #1, brown*	$ 650–700
Wall bracket, *5 inches by 8 inches, #1, blue*	$ 750–800
Wall flowerpot, *4 inches, #1283, green*	$ 750–800
Wall flowerpot, *4 inches, #1283, brown*	$ 1,000–1,200
Wall flowerpot, *4 inches, #1283, blue*	$ 1,400–1,500
Wall pocket, *double, 8 inches, #1273, green*	$ 550–600
Wall pocket, *double, 8 inches, #1273, brown*	$ 650–700
Wall pocket, *double, 8 inches, #1273, blue*	$ 800–850
Window box, *10 inches by 5^1/$_2$ inches, #380, green*	$ 1,250–1,400
Window box, *10 inches by 5^1/$_2$ inches, #380, brown*	$ 1,600–1,750
Window box, *10 inches by 5^1/$_2$ inches, #380, blue*	$ 2,200–2,400

"Poppy"

First made in 1930, pieces in this line (as its name suggests) were decorated with poppy flowers and green leaves against a shaded background of either blue or pink. Pieces are marked with an impressed "Roseville."

Basket, *10 inches, #347*	$ 375–425
Basket, *12 inches, #348*	$ 575–625
Bowl, *5 inches, #336*	$ 225–250
Bowl, *8 inches, #337*	$ 250–275
Bowl, *10 inches, #338*	$ 300–350
Bowl, *12 inches, #339*	$ 350–375

Roseville "Poppy" vase, #871, 8 inches, $375–$425.
Item courtesy of Richard Hatch and Associates, Hendersonville, North Carolina.

Bowl, *14 inches, #340*	$ 400–450
Candlesticks, *5 inches, #1130*	$ 150–175
Ewer, *10 inches, #876*	$ 525–600
Ewer, *18 inches, #880*	$ 1,100–1,200
Flowerpot with saucer, *5 inches, #643*	$ 325–350
Jardinière, *4 inches, #642*	$ 200–225
Jardinière, *5 inches, #642*	$ 250–275
Jardinière, *6 inches, #642*	$ 375–425
Jardinière, *7 inches, #642*	$ 475–525
Jardinière, *8 inches, #642*	$ 550–600
Jardinière, *10 inches, with pedestal, #642*	$ 1,600–1,750
Vase, *6 inches, #886*	$ 200–225
Vase, *7 inches, #868*	$ 275–325
Vase, *8 inches, #871*	$ 375–425

Vase, *9 inches, #872*	$ 425–475
Vase, *10 inches, #874*	$ 475–525
Vase, *12 inches, #877*	$ 650–700
Vase, *15 inches, #878*	$ 1,000–1,100
Vase, *18 inches, #879*	$ 1,250–1,400
Wall pocket, *8 inches, #1281*	$ 850–900

"Rosecraft Hexagon"

Introduced in 1924, this line is distinguished by its six-sided shapes. Pieces are generally dark green or dark brown (though some blue pieces were also made), and feature a medallion with a long stylized leaf shape dripping down from one side. Prices listed below are for green and brown examples; blue pieces command prices that are up to 50 percent higher. Pieces are generally marked with the "Rv" backstamp.

Bowl, *4 inches, #124*	$ 275–325
Bowl, *4 inches, #135*	$ 300–350
Bowl, *5 inches, #136*	$ 275–325
Bowl, *6 inches, #137*	$ 300–350
Jardinière, *4 inches, #138*	$ 325–375
Vase, *4 inches, #266*	$ 300–350
Vase, *5 inches, #267*	$ 350–400
Vase, *6 inches, #268*	$ 425–475
Vase, *6 inches, #269*	$ 375–425
Vase, *7 inches, #8*	$ 475–525
Vase, *8 inches, # 270*	$ 600–650
Vase, *8 inches, #271*	$ 525–575
Vase, *10 inches, #272*	$ 800–850
Vase, *bud, double, 5 inches, #47*	$ 300–350
Wall pocket, *8 inches, #1240*	$ 750–800

"Rosecraft Vintage"

Pieces in this grouping feature dark-colored backgrounds that range from brown through dark purple, and are distinguished by a band of sensuously curving vines with leaves and berries on the shoulder of each item. Pieces with charcoal-black or green backgrounds were also produced, though such pieces are rare. Like "Rosecraft Hexagon," this line originated in 1924, and pieces were typically marked with the "Rv" stamp. Prices listed below are for typical colorations; green pieces command prices up to 50 percent higher.

Bowl, *3 inches, #143*	$ 250–300
Bowl, *footed, 3 inches, #139*	$ 150–175
Bowl, *footed, 4 inches, #140*	$ 200–225
Bowl, *footed, 5 inches, #141*	$ 175–200
Bowl, *footed, 6 inches, #142*	$ 200–225
Jardinière, *5 inches, #607*	$ 275–300
Jardinière, *6 inches, #607*	$ 325–350
Jardinière, *6 inches, #144*	$ 250–275
Jardinière, *7 inches, #607*	$ 400–450
Jardinière, *8 inches, #607*	$ 475–525
Jardinière, *9 inches, #607*	$ 575–625
Jardinière, *10 inches, with pedestal, #607*	$ 1,600–1,750
Vase, *3 inches, #9*	$ 200–225
Vase, *4 inches, #273*	$ 250–300
Vase, *bud, double, 4¹/₂ inches, #48*	$ 275–325
Vase, *5 inches, #274*	$ 275–325
Vase, *6 inches, #275*	$ 300–350
Vase, *6 inches, #276*	$ 325–375
Vase, *8 inches, #277*	$ 400–450
Vase, *8 inches, #278*	$ 475–525
Vase, *10 inches, #279*	$ 600–650
Vase, *12 inches, #280*	$ 675–725
Wall pocket, *8 inches, #1241*	$ 550–600
Window box, *10 inches, #372*	$ 450–500

"Rozane"

Although this line shares its name with the earlier Roseville art line, it is quite different from its namesake. Collectors sometimes call this line "Rozane, 1917" or

Roseville "Rozane 1917" vase, 8 inches,
$165–$190.
*Item courtesy of Kingston Pike Antique Mall,
Knoxville, Tennessee.*

"Rozane Pattern" or "Late Rozane" to distinguish it from the earlier line of artistically decorated pieces, which were first made at the turn of the 20th century. First
produced in 1917, pieces in this line feature textured backgrounds that are often said
to resemble honeycombs (though some have also described this background as
"pockmarked," or like the surface of a golf ball). Pieces were produced in ivory,
green, pink, yellow, and blue, and feature clusters of raised roses and leaves. Pieces
are marked "Roseville Pottery, Rozane" in black, brown, or blue ink.

Bowl, *6 inches, #407*	$ 150–175
Bowl, *9 inches, #395*	$ 175–200
Bowl, *10 inches, #396*	$ 200–225
Bowl, *14 inches, #397*	$ 225–250
Candlesticks, *3 inches, #1144*	$ 175–200
Conch shell, *#410*	$ 200–225
Cornucopia	$ 175–200
Flower frog	$ 175–200
Vase, *6 inches*	$ 110–130

Vase, *8 inches*	$ 165–190
Vase, *9 inches*	$ 225–250
Vase, *10 inches*	$ 250–275
Vase, *12 inches*	$ 275–300
Vase, *15 inches*	$ 550–600

"Tuscany"

Generally unmarked, pieces in this line were first produced in 1927 and feature mottled glazes in shades of pink, gray, or (much more rarely) turquoise green. The only decorations found on "Tuscany" pieces are raised leaves and grapes at the bases of handles. Prices listed below are for pink and gray items; green items generally command prices about 20 percent higher.

Bowl, *4 inches, #67*	$ 150–175
Bowl, *4 inches, #68*	$ 175–200
Bowl, *6 inches, #171*	$ 175–200
Bowl, *9 inches, #172*	$ 225–250
Bowl, *10 inches, #173*	$ 250–275
Bowl, *12 inches, #174*	$ 275–300
Bowl, *15 inches, #112*	$ 400–450
Candlestick, *3¹/₂ inches, #1066, pair*	$ 200–225
Candlestick, *4 inches, #1067, pair*	$ 225–250
Flowerpot with saucer, *6 inches, #615*	$ 300–325
Vase, *5 inches, #70*	$ 225–250
Vase, *5 inches, #341*	$ 250–275
Vase, *6 inches, #71*	$ 225–250
Vase, *6 inches, #342*	$ 250–275
Vase, *7 inches, #343*	$ 275–300
Vase, *8 inches, #80*	$ 300–325
Vase, *8 inches, #344*	$ 325–350
Vase, *8 inches, #345*	$ 325–350
Vase, *9 inches, #346*	$ 400–450
Vase, *10 inches, #347*	$ 550–600

Vase, *10 inches, #348*	$ 600–650
Vase, *12 inches, #349*	$ 750–800
Vase/Flower arranger, *5 inches, #69*	$ 175–200
Vase/Flower arranger, *5 inches, #66*	$ 175–200
Wall pocket, *7 inches, #1254*	$ 450–500
Wall pocket, *8 inches, #1255*	$ 475–525

"Water Lily"

First produced in the 1940s, "Water Lily" pieces feature raised yellow, white, or pink lilies with their pads against tan-to-brown, blue, or pink-to-green backgrounds. Pieces are marked with "Roseville" in script.

Basket, *8 inches, #380*	$ 275–300
Basket, *10 inches, #381*	$ 325–350
Basket, *12 inches, #382*	$ 375–400
Bookends, *#12, pair*	$ 350–400
Bowl, *6 inches, #439*	$ 150–175
Bowl, *8 inches, #440*	$ 200–225
Bowl, *10 inches, #441*	$ 225–250
Bowl, *12 inches, #443*	$ 275–300
Bowl, *14 inches, #444*	$ 325–375
Bowl, *rose, 4 inches, #437*	$ 175–200
Bowl, *rose, 6 inches, #437*	$ 225–250
Candlestick, *2 inches, #1154, pair*	$ 200–225
Candlestick, *4$^{1}/_{2}$ inches, #1155, pair*	$ 225–250
Conch shell, *6 inches, #445*	$ 225–250
Conch shell, *8 inches, #438*	$ 275–300
Cookie jar, *#1*	$ 650–750
Cornucopia, *6 inches, #177*	$ 175–200
Cornucopia, *8 inches, #178*	$ 225–250
Ewer, *6 inches, #10*	$ 225–250
Ewer, *10 inches, #11*	$ 300–350
Ewer, *15 inches, #15*	$ 600–650

Roseville "Water Lily" cookie jar, $650–$750.
Item courtesy of B and D Antiques and Art Pottery.

Flowerpot and saucer, *5 inches, #664*	$ 300–350
Jardinière, *3 inches, #663*	$ 135–150
Jardinière, *4 inches, #663*	$ 175–200
Jardinière, *5 inches, #663*	$ 200–225
Jardinière, *8 inches, with pedestal, #663*	$ 1,250–1,400
Vase, *4 inches, #71*	$ 135–150
Vase, *6 inches, #72*	$ 175–200
Vase, *7 inches, #74*	$ 200–225
Vase, *8 inches, #76*	$ 250–275
Vase, *9 inches, #78*	$ 300–325
Vase, *10 inches, #80*	$ 300–325
Vase, *12 inches, #81*	$ 375–425
Vase, *14 inches, #82*	$ 475–525
Vase, *15 inches, #83*	$ 550–600

Vase, *16 inches, #84*	$ 700–750
Vase, *18 inches, #85*	$ 1,100–1,250

"White Rose"

This is a line that was made during the 1940s. It featured depictions of white roses with yellow centers and green leaves against backgrounds of blue, brown shading to green, and pink shading to green. Examples are marked with the raised "Roseville" script mark.

Basket, *8 inches, #362*	$ 250–300
Basket, *10 inches, #363*	$ 300–350
Basket, *12 inches, #364*	$ 350–400
Bowl, *6 inches, #389*	$ 175–225
Bowl, *8 inches, #390*	$ 200–250
Bowl, *10 inches, #391*	$ 225–275
Bowl, *12 inches, #393*	$ 275–325
Bowl, *14 inches, #394*	$ 325–375
Candelabra, *two-cup, #1142*	$ 200–250
Candlesticks, *4$^{1}/_{2}$ inches, #1142, pair*	$ 200–250
Cornucopia, *6 inches, #143*	$ 200–250
Cornucopia, *8 inches, #144*	$ 225–275
Creamer, *#1-C*	$ 110–135
Ewer, *10 inches, #990*	$ 350–400
Ewer, *15 inches, #993*	$ 650–700
Flower frog, *#41*	$ 175–200
Jardinière, *3 inches, #653*	$ 110–135
Jardinière, *4 inches, #653*	$ 160–185
Jardinière, *5 inches, #653*	$ 200–225
Jardinière, *6 inches, #653*	$ 250–275
Jardinière, *7 inches, #653*	$ 325–350
Jardinière, *10 inches, with pedestal, #653*	$ 1,600–1,750
Pitcher, *#1324*	$ 375–425

Roseville "White Rose" flower frog,
$175–$200.
*Item courtesy of Bill Brooker, Old School
Antique Mall, Sylva, North Carolina.*

Roseville "White Rose" teapot, #1-T,
$425–$475.
*Item courtesy of Richard Hatch and
Associates, Hendersonville, North Carolina.*

Sugar bowl, *lidded, #1-S*	$ 110–135
Teapot, *#1-T*	$ 425–475
Vase, *4 inches, #978*	$ 110–135
Vase, *6 inches, #979*	$ 135–165
Vase, *7 inches, #982*	$ 225–250
Vase, *8 inches, #985*	$ 275–300
Vase, *9 inches, #986*	$ 325–350
Vase, *10 inches, #988*	$ 350–400
Vase, *12 inches, #991*	$ 475–525
Vase, *15 inches, #992*	$ 650–700
Vase, *18 inches, #994*	$ 1,100–1,250
Wall pocket, *6 inches, #1288*	$ 375–425
Wall pocket, *8 inches, #1289*	$ 425–475

"Zephyr Lily"

First made in the 1940s, "Zephyr Lily" is decorated with raised long-stemmed lilies in white and yellow against a swirled background in shades of either "Bermuda Blue," "Evergreen," or "Sierra Tan." Of these, the blue is the most valuable and at the high end of the scale listed below, and "Evergreen" is at the low end of the scale listed below. "Zephyr Lily" is marked with the raised "Roseville" mark.

Basket, *7 inches, #393*	$ 250–275
Basket, *8 inches, #394*	$ 300–325
Basket, *10 inches, #395*	$ 350–375
Bookends, *#16, pair*	$ 350–375
Bowl, *5 inches, #470*	$ 200–225
Bowl, *6 inches, #472*	$ 175–200
Bowl, *8 inches, #474*	$ 225–250
Bowl, *10 inches, #476*	$ 250–300
Bowl, *12 inches, #478*	$ 300–350
Bowl, *oval, 14 inches, #479*	$ 325–375
Bowl, *footed, 6 inches, #473*	$ 150–175
Bowl, *footed, 10 inches, #8*	$ 225–250
Candleholder, *2 inches, #1162, pair*	$ 200–225
Candlestick, *4¹/₂ inches, #1163, pair*	$ 225–250
Cookie jar, *#5*	$ 700–850
Creamer, *#7-C*	$ 100–115
Ewer, *6 inches, #22*	$ 200–225
Ewer, *10 inches, #23*	$ 325–350
Ewer, *15 inches, #24*	$ 850–900
Flowerpot with saucer, *5 inches, #672*	$ 250–275
Jardinière, *4 inches, #671*	$ 175–200
Jardinière, *6 inches, #671*	$ 250–275
Jardinière, *6 inches, #671*	$ 225–250
Jardinière and pedestal, *8-inch jardinière*	$ 1,600–1,800
Sugar bowl, *#7-S*	$ 100–115
Teapot, *#7-T*	$ 375–425

Roseville "Zephyr Lily" cookie jar, #5,
$700–$850.
*Item courtesy of B and D Antiques and Art
Pottery.*

Roseville "Zephyr Lily" jardinière and
pedestal, 8-inch jardinière, $1,600–$1,800.
*Item courtesy of Betty and Randolph
Winston, Old School Antique Mall, Sylva,
North Carolina.*

Roseville "Zephyr Lily" teapot, #7–T,
$375–$425.
*Item courtesy of Richard Hatch and
Associates, Hendersonville, North Carolina.*

Roseville ashtray, creamware, advertising,
3½ inches, $175–$225.
*Item courtesy of Tony McCormack, Sarasota,
Florida.*

Tray, *console boat, 10 inches, #475*	$ 250–275
Tray, *leaf-shaped, 12 inches, #447*	$ 250–275
Vase, *6 inches, #130*	$ 175–200
Vase, *cornucopia, 6 inches, #203*	$ 175–200
Vase, *6 inches, #205*	$ 225–250
Vase, *7 inches, #131*	$ 225–250
Vase, *7 inches, #132*	$ 225–250

Roseville pitcher, cow decoration, pre-1916, 7½ inches, $275–$325.
Item courtesy of Carol and Duane Turnbill, Old School Antique Mall, Sylva, North Carolina.

Roseville "Cremona" vase, 10 inches, $450–$525.
Item courtesy of Richard Hatch and Associates, Hendersonville, North Carolina.

Roseville "Orian" vase, 8 inches, two handles, $550–$625.
Item courtesy of Tony McCormack, Sarasota, Florida.

Vase, *bud, 7 inches, #201*	$ 200–225
Vase, *7 inches, #206*	$ 250–275
Vase, *8 inches, #133*	$ 225–250
Vase, *8 inches, #134*	$ 250–275
Vase, *8 inches, #203*	$ 175–200
Vase, *8 inches, #204*	$ 200–225
Vase, *9 inches, #136*	$ 275–325

Vase, *10 inches, #137*	$ 275–325
Vase, *10 inches, #138*	$ 300–350
Vase, *12 inches, #139*	$ 350–400
Vase, *12 inches, #140*	$ 375–425
Vase, *15 inches, #141*	$ 950–1,100
Vase, *floor, 18 inches, #142*	$ 1,250–1,400
Wall pocket, *8 inches, #1297*	$ 375–425
Window box, *8 inches, #1393*	$ 250–300

ROYAL CHINA COMPANY

Crown marks used by the *Royal China Company*.

The Royal China Company moved from Omaha, Nebraska, to Sebring, Ohio, in 1933, and began operations in the old E. H. Sebring Pottery Company facility in 1934. Royal China produced a wide variety of semiporcelain dinnerware, as well as kitchenware and items that were designed to be given away as premiums at grocery stores and gas stations. Royal was bought by the Jeanette Glass Company in 1969 (Jeanette also bought Harker Pottery that same year), and ceased operations in 1986. As a general rule, it is Royal's later pieces (from the 1950s and 1960s) that most interest current collectors.

Mark used by the *Royal China Company* on its "Currier and Ives" dinnerware.

"Bucks County"

Produced only in shades of brown and yellow, pieces bearing this pattern have a stylized tulip border reminiscent of the folk art associated with the Pennsylvania Dutch (Deutsch) of Bucks County, Pennsylvania. The image in the center of flatware items depicts two houses with trees and a boy flying a kite. "Bucks Country" was first produced in the 1950s, and pieces are marked with the words "Bucks County" crudely lettered on a two-board sign with a stylized bird perched on top.

Mark used by *Royal China* on its "Colonial Homestead" pattern dinnerware.

Mark used by *Royal China* on its "Old Curiosity Shop" dinnerware.

Bowl, *cereal, 6^1/$_4$-inch diameter*	$ 9–14
Bowl, *individual fruit, 5^1/$_2$-inch diameter*	$ 5–9
Bowl, *individual soup, 8^1/$_2$-inch diameter*	$ 12–17
Bowl, *vegetable, round, 9-inch diameter*	$ 22–28
Bowl, *vegetable, covered*	$ 75–85
Creamer	$ 18–24
Cup and saucer	$ 12–17
Gravy boat with underliner	$ 42–48
Mug	$ 16–22
Plate, *bread and butter, 6^1/$_2$-inch diameter*	$ 3–5
Plate, *chop, 12-inch diameter*	$ 35–42
Plate, *dinner, 10-inch diameter*	$ 10–15
Plate, *luncheon, 9-inch diameter*	$ 8–12
Plate, *salad, 7^1/$_4$-inch diameter*	$ 12–17
Platter, *oval, serving, 13 inches*	$ 32–38
Sugar bowl	$ 25–32

"Colonial Homestead"

Pieces bearing this Royal China pattern came in both green and gray, with gray examples being far rarer and more valuable than green pieces. "Colonial Homestead" pieces feature a wood-grain border resembling boards with nails driven in where the boards intersect. In the center of each piece is the image of a room with a beamed ceiling, with a large stone fireplace as the focal point. A hooked rug lies on the floor and a kettle crane rests in the fireplace, with a long rifle hung above the mantel.

Green

Bowl, *cereal, 6^1/$_2$-inch diameter*	$ 14–20
Bowl, *individual fruit, 5^1/$_2$-inch diameter*	$ 4–6
Bowl, *individual soup, 8^1/$_2$-inch diameter*	$ 9–14
Bowl, *vegetable, round, 9-inch diameter*	$ 12–16
Bowl, *vegetable, round, 10-inch diameter*	$ 20–28
Bowl, *vegetable, round, covered*	$ 65–75

Royal China charger, "Colonial Homestead," 13¼ inches,
$65–$75.
*Item courtesy of Needful Things, Hendersonville, North
Carolina.*

Charger, *13¹/₄-inch diameter*	$ 65–75
Creamer	$ 10–15
Cup and saucer	$ 8–12
Gravy boat and underliner	$ 45–55
Plate, *bread and butter, 6¹/₂-inch diameter*	$ 3–5
Plate, *chop, 12-inch diameter*	$ 12–16
Plate, *dinner, 10-inch diameter*	$ 8–12
Plate, *luncheon, 9-inch diameter*	$ 12–16
Plate, *pie, serving, 10-inch diameter*	$ 38–45
Plate, *salad, 7¹/₂-inch diameter*	$ 11–15
Platter, *oval, 13 inches*	$ 35–45
Shakers, *salt and pepper, set*	$ 22–30
Sugar bowl	$ 22–28
Teapot	$ 105–115

Gray

Bowl, *individual fruit, 5¹/₂-inch diameter*	$ 12–16
Bowl, *vegetable, round, 10-inch diameter*	$ 50–60
Creamer	$ 30–35
Cup and saucer	$ 20–26
Plate, *bread and butter, 6¹/₂-inch diameter*	$ 5–8
Plate, *chop, 12-inch diameter*	$ 65–75
Plate, *dinner, 10-inch diameter*	$ 18–24

"Currier and Ives"

This is the pattern most often associated with Royal China. It was produced as a premium for the Atlantic and Pacific Tea Company (A&P) grocery stores, and was designed by Gordon Parker in 1949 and 1950. Pieces were reportedly made as late as 1983. "Currier and Ives" pieces feature a wide variety of nostalgic American scenes in blue and white, pink and white, and green and white (pie plates were also produced in black and white and brown and white). Scenes include a house and ice skaters, a couple in a horse-drawn sleigh, a train, a boy at a well, a lady driving a buggy, an old grist mill, and a rare Rocky Mountain view.

Blue and White

Ashtray	$ 6–9
Baker, *oval, 9 inches*	$ 25–35
Baker, *rectangular, 13 inches*	$ 50–60
Bowl, *cereal, 5-inch diameter*	$ 14–18
Bowl, *cereal, 6³/₄-inch diameter*	$ 12–16
Bowl, *individual fruit, 5¹/₂-inch diameter*	$ 5–8
Bowl, *individual soup, 8¹/₂-inch diameter*	$ 8–12
Bowl, *vegetable, round, 9-inch diameter*	$ 22–27
Bowl, *vegetable, round, 10-inch diameter*	$ 32–37
Butter, *¹/₄-pound, covered*	$ 75–85
Creamer	$ 9–14
Cup and saucer	$ 8–12
Gravy boat and underliner	$ 55–65

Royal China 10-inch diameter dinner plate, "Currier and Ives," $8–$12.

Mug, *3³/₄ inches*	$ 22–27
Plate, *calendar, 1977*	$ 18–24
Plate, *bread and butter*	$ 4–7
Plate, *chop, 12-inch diameter*	$ 22–30
Plate, *dinner, 10-inch diameter*	$ 8–12
Plate, *luncheon, 9-inch diameter*	$ 20–25
Plate, *pie, serving, 10-inch diameter*	$ 20–28
Plate, *salad, 7¹/₂-inch diameter*	$ 15–20
Platter, *oval, 13 inches*	$ 35–40
Shakers, *salt and pepper, set*	$ 35–45
Sugar bowl	$ 24–30
Teapot	$ 165–180
Tidbit server, *two-tier*	$ 42–50
Tidbit server, *three-tier*	$ 52–60

Pink and White

Bowl, *cereal, 6¹/₄-inch diameter*	$ 18–24
Bowl, *soup, 8¹/₂-inch diameter*	$ 15–20
Bowl, *vegetable, round, 9-inch diameter*	$ 32–42
Cup and saucer	$ 12–18
Plate, *bread and butter, 6¹/₂-inch diameter*	$ 5–8
Plate, *dinner, 10-inch diameter*	$ 18–24
Plate, *salad, 7¹/₂-inch diameter*	$ 15–20
Tidbit server, *two-tier*	$ 55–65
Tidbit server, *three-tier*	$ 60–70

Black and White, Brown and White, Green and White

Plate, *pie, serving, black and white, 10 inches*	$ 45–55
Plate, *pie, serving, brown and white, 10 inches*	$ 55–65
Plate, *pie, serving, green and white, 10 inches*	$ 65–75

"Fair Oaks"

This 1950s pattern is a brown-on-white transfer print with accents of green, red, and yellow, all applied underglaze. The design of the print is very reminiscent of 19th-century English pastoral examples: it depicts cows, a drover, and a dog, with a stream and saltbox-style house surrounded by trees. The border is floral.

Bowl, *cereal, lugged, 7¹/₄-inch diameter*	$ 12–16
Bowl, *individual fruit, 5¹/₂-inch diameter*	$ 7–10
Bowl, *individual soup, 8¹/₄-inch diameter*	$ 7–10
Bowl, *vegetable, round, 9-inch diameter*	$ 20–26
Bowl, *vegetable, round, 10-inch diameter*	$ 22–28
Creamer	$ 12–16
Cup and saucer	$ 7–10
Plate, *bread and butter, 6¹/₂-inch diameter*	$ 3–5
Plate, *dinner, 10-inch diameter*	$ 10–15
Platter, *oval, 13 inches*	$ 25–32
Sugar bowl	$ 18–25

"Memory Lane"

Pieces in this line feature the pastoral transfer print used to decorate the centers of flatware pieces in the "Fair Oaks" line, though the overall color scheme of "Memory Lane" items is pink and white, and the borders are composed of acorns rather than flowers.

Ashtray, *5$^1/_2$ inches*	$ 8–12
Bowl, *cereal, 6$^1/_2$-inch diameter*	$ 15–22
Bowl, *individual fruit, 5$^1/_2$-inch diameter*	$ 5–8
Bowl, *individual soup, 8$^1/_2$-inch diameter*	$ 10–15
Bowl, *vegetable, round, 9-inch diameter*	$ 22–28
Bowl, *vegetable, round, covered*	$ 75–85
Butter, *covered, $^1/_4$-pound*	$ 55–65
Casserole, *round, 1$^1/_4$-quart*	$ 75–85
Creamer	$ 12–16
Cup and saucer	$ 8–12
Gravy boat	$ 25–35
Plate, *bread and butter, 6$^1/_2$-inch diameter*	$ 5–8
Plate, *chop, 12-inch diameter*	$ 28–34
Plate, *dinner, 10-inch diameter*	$ 10–15
Plate, *pie, serving, 10-inch diameter*	$ 25–35
Plate, *salad, 7$^1/_2$-inch diameter*	$ 18–24
Platter, *oval, 13 inches*	$ 32–38
Shakers, *salt and pepper, set*	$ 35–45
Sugar bowl	$ 22–28
Teapot	$ 135–150
Tidbit server, *two-tier*	$ 45–55
Tidbit server, *three-tier*	$ 52–58

"Old Curiosity Shop"

Another Royal China pattern with a "days of yesteryear" theme is "Old Curiosity Shop," which features a wood-grain border decorated with curved strap hinges. In the center of the flatware is the image of a gabled building. This pattern was pro-

Royal China 10-inch diameter dinner plate, "Old Curiosity Shop," $8–$12.
Item courtesy of Needful Things, Hendersonville, North Carolina.

duced only in green, though a different pattern was reportedly produced in pink. The scene featured on these pink-patterned pieces depicts a bay window overlooking a quaint New England-esque street scene, with trinkets (or "old curiosities") scattered on the walls and in the window. Prices are not available for this rare pink variant; all the prices below are for the much more common green items.

Ashtray	$ 8–12
Bowl, *cereal, 6^1/$_2$-inch diameter*	$ 22–28
Bowl, *individual fruit, 5^1/$_2$-inch diameter*	$ 4–7
Bowl, *individual soup, 8^1/$_2$-inch diameter*	$ 8–12
Bowl, *vegetable, round, 9-inch diameter*	$ 18–24
Butter dish, *covered, ^{1}/$_4$-pound*	$ 115–125
Casserole, *1^1/$_2$-quart, round*	$ 135–150
Creamer	$ 12–16
Cup and saucer	$ 8–12
Gravy boat and under plate	$ 40–50
Plate, *bread and butter, 6^1/$_2$-inch diameter*	$ 3–6

Plate, *chop, 12-inch diameter*	$ 28–35
Plate, *dinner, 10-inch diameter*	$ 8–12
Plate, *luncheon, 9-inch diameter*	$ 22–32
Plate, *pie, serving, 10-inch diameter*	$ 55–65
Plate, *salad, 7^1/$_2$-inch diameter*	$ 20–30
Platter, *oval, 13 inches*	$ 32–40
Shakers, *salt and pepper, set*	$ 35–45
Sugar bowl	$ 20–25
Teapot	$ 190–210
Tidbit server, *two-tier*	$ 52–60
Tidbit server, *three-tier*	$ 54–62

"Willow"

Royal began producing a standard "Willow" pattern in the 1930s, and the design was applied using a rubber stamp. It was made with at least three border variations, and was available in the standard blue and white, plus red and white and gold and white. The second version of this pattern originated in the 1940s, and was transfer-printed rather than rubber-stamped. Manufactured until the company closed in 1986, this version came in blue and white, pink and white, green and white, and brown and white. The brown-and-white pieces are by far the rarest. Prices for the stamped Royal China Company "Willow" pieces from the 1930s are about 20 percent less than prices for the transfer-printed examples.

Blue and White

Ashtray	$ 7–10
Bowl, *cereal, 6^1/$_2$-inch diameter*	$ 8–12
Bowl, *individual fruit, 5^1/$_2$-inch diameter*	$ 3–5
Bowl, *vegetable, round, 9-inch diameter*	$ 18–24
Bowl, *vegetable, round, 10-inch diameter*	$ 24–30
Bowl, *vegetable, round, covered*	$ 85–95
Creamer	$ 10–15
Cup and saucer	$ 6–10
Gravy boat	$ 28–35
Plate, *bread and butter, 6^1/$_2$-inch diameter*	$ 3–5

Plate, *chop, 12-inch diameter*	$ 20–28
Plate, *dinner, 10-inch diameter*	$ 8–12
Plate, *grill, 10^1/$_2$ inches*	$ 14–18
Plate, *luncheon, 9-inch diameter*	$ 7–11
Plate, *pie, serving, 10-inch diameter*	$ 32–40
Plate, *salad, 7^1/$_2$-inch diameter*	$ 7–11
Plate, *snack, with cup*	$ 14–18
Shakers, *salt and pepper, pair*	$ 28–35
Sugar bowl	$ 22–28
Teapot	$ 115–125
Tidbit server, *two-tier*	$ 38–45
Tidbit server, *three-tier*	$ 40–48

Pink and White

Bowl, *cereal, 7-inch diameter*	$ 12–16
Bowl, *individual fruit, 5^1/$_2$-inch diameter*	$ 7–11
Bowl, *individual soup, 8^1/$_2$-inch diameter*	$ 12–16
Bowl, *vegetable, round, 9-inch diameter*	$ 28–35
Cup and saucer	$ 15–22
Plate, *bread and butter*	$ 5–8
Plate, *chop, 12-inch diameter*	$ 28–35
Plate, *dinner, 10-inch diameter*	$ 14–22
Plate, *luncheon, 9-inch diameter*	$ 12–15
Plate, *salad, 7^1/$_2$-inch diameter*	$ 8–12
Platter, *oval, 13 inches*	$ 38–45

Green and White

Bowl, *individual fruit, 5^1/$_2$-inch diameter*	$ 9–12
Bowl, *individual soup, 8^1/$_2$-inch diameter*	$ 15–20
Bowl, *vegetable, 9-inch diameter*	$ 35–42
Creamer	$ 25–32

Cup and saucer	$ 22–30
Plate, *bread and butter, 6$^1/_2$-inch diameter*	$ 5–9
Plate, *chop, 12-inch diameter*	$ 42–50
Plate, *dinner, 10-inch diameter*	$ 28–35
Plate, *salad, 7$^1/_2$-inch diameter*	$ 15–20
Shakers, *salt and pepper, set*	$ 38–45

RUMRILL POTTERY COMPANY

RUMRILL MADE IN USA

One of the marks used on pottery made by the *RumRill Pottery Company.*

In the early 1930s, George Rumrill founded the Arkansas Products Company as a distribution firm. Initially the company marked wares for Camark, but in 1933 Rumrill contracted with Red Wing Potteries to make a line of commercial art ware he named "RumRill." At first the line was made using Red Wing shapes, but soon Rumrill was designing his own shapes for the line that carried his name. He severed his relationship with Red Wing in 1938, at which point the company's history becomes somewhat unclear.

Some sources say that Rumrill contracted with the Florence Pottery of Mt. Gilead, Ohio, while others say he entered into an arrangement with the Shawnee Pottery Company of Zanesville, Ohio. Whichever version of events is correct, it is certain that RumRill pottery was also made for a time by Gonder. One timeline suggests that RumRill pottery was made at Shawnee during the company's transition between the Red Wing and Florence potteries, and was then made at Gonder after Florence burned down in 1941. The business closed in late 1942, and George Rumrill died just a few months later.

Glazes on items produced after the company's relationship with Red Wing ended are almost always solid colors. Pieces made by Red Wing featured exteriors of solid colors,

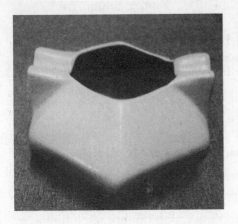

RumRill ashtray, 2½ inches, signed with a paper label, $50–$60.
Item courtesy of Elaine Delcuze, Old School Antique Mall, Sylva, North Carolina.

RumRill vase, #310, 4½ inches, black interior, white exterior, from the "Mandarin" group, $65–$80.
Item courtesy of Bill Brooker, Old School Antique Mall, Sylva, North Carolina.

blended colors, or stippled colors, and their interiors sometimes featured contrasting shades. The most common hues are Dutch Blue (stippled blue and white), Eggshell (matte white), Pompeiian (antique ivory), Ripe Wheat (darker brown blending into tan), Robin's Egg Blue, matte pink, and matte turquoise. Harder-to-find colors include Marigold (a rich yellow) and Jade (matte green). Rare colors include Crocus (gray-green exterior with pink interior), Mermaid (brown stippling on green), Gypsy Orange, Lotus (yellow interior with ivory exterior), matte black, Snowdrop (green and ivory), and Stippled Lavender. The hardest-to-find color, and the most highly desired by collectors, is Nokomis—an olive gray that is considered at its best when it features a bit of green and copper in its color mix. Prices listed below are for pieces with standard glazes.

RumRill items made by Red Wing are often (though not always) marked "Rumrill" in block letters, with a three-digit style or shape number going up to "731." Pieces made by companies other than Red Wing are generally marked with an embossed "RumRill" in large letters, with a two-digit style number preceded by a letter of the alphabet—for example, "H-15."

"Athenian Group"

This group of RumRill items incorporated representations of the female nude, and is one of the most sought-after of the various RumRill lines.

Bowl, *8¹/2 inches, #567*	$ 1,000–1,250

"Classic Group"

This grouping of RumRill pottery is characterized by widespread grooves.

Basket, *footed, 8 inches, #285*	$ 120–140
Bowl, *6 inches, #276*	$ 35–45
Vase, *5¹/2 inches, #500*	$ 80–100

"Grecian Group"

Consisting mainly of vase shapes, this grouping is characterized by smooth surfaces and either circular or comma-shaped handles.

Vase, *handled, 7¹/2 inches, #506*	$ 70–90
Vase, *two handles, 10-inch diameter, #200*	$ 185–225

"Indian Group"

Pieces in this line feature smooth flowing shapes with no decoration except the glaze. This is one of the RumRill lines on which a Nokomis glaze might be found.

Bowl, *4¹/2 inches, #315*	$ 65–80
Jug with stopper, *#50*	$ 75–100
Vase, *5¹/2 inches, #291*	$ 60–75

"Neo-Classical Group"

Pieces in this grouping are decorated with columns of spheres.

Bowl, *10 inches, #672*	$ 100–125
Candlesticks, *pair, 4 inches*	$ 75–95
Vase, *footed, fan, 10 inches, #668*	$ 200–250
Vase, *footed, 12 inches, #666*	$ 175–225
Vase, *15 inches, #674*	$ 260–300

"Renaissance Group"

This line is distinguished by raised vertical feathers in all items except the figural deer insert.

Bowl, *10¹/₂ inches, #530*	$ 75–90
Bowl, *low, 12 inches, #526*	$ 40–55
Candleholder, *#529, each*	$ 35–45
Figure, *deer, 10 inches, #531*	$ 80–100
Vase, *6 inches, #522*	$ 70–85
Vase, *footed, #496*	$ 75–90
Vase, *footed, #528*	$ 75–90

"Shell Group"

Items in this line are characterized by elaborate designs based on shell motifs, particularly the scallop shell.

Candlesticks, *3³/₄ inches, pair, #417*	$ 85–100
Creamer, *small, 4¹/₂ inches, #460*	$ 30–40
Sugar bowl, *small, #459*	$ 30–40
Sugar bowl, *large, #429*	$ 40–55
Vase, *7³/₄ inches, #432*	$ 75–95
Vase, *double cornucopia, 9¹/₂ inches*	$ 125–150

"Sylvan Group"

Large, symmetrically arranged leaves circle each piece in this line.

Bowl, *ruffled top, 8 inches, #445*	$ 75–90
Candlestick, *pair, 3¹/₂ inches, #433*	$ 45–60
Vase, *fan, footed, 7 inches, #439*	$ 75–90
Vase, *8 inches, #447*	$ 85–100

Miscellaneous

Every Red Wing and RumRill catalog featured a grouping of art wares that were labeled "Miscellaneous," and did not belong to any particular line.

Bowl, *7 inches, #341*	$ 65–80
Centerpiece, *eagle, 15¹/₂ inches, #548*	$ 200–250
Cornucopia, *double, 3 inches, #650*	$ 40–50
Vase, *7¹/₂ inches, #505*	$ 65–80
Vase, *ball, three holes, 6 inches, #600*	$ 90–110
Vase, *ball, three holes, 8 inches, #600*	$ 100–125
Vase, *two handles, 6¹/₂ inches high, #636*	$ 75–90
Vase, *two handles, 7 inches, #641*	$ 75–90
Vase, *7 inches, #644*	$ 70–85

SALEM CHINA COMPANY

TRICORNE
By
Salem
U. S. PATENT
D. 94245

Mark used by *Salem* on its
"Tricorn" dinnerware

As is the case with many other pottery companies discussed in this book, the exact dates of many events in the history of Salem China Company are not known. However, it is known that the company was founded in Salem, Ohio, in 1898, and that production of pottery began in 1899. The company was founded by Pat and John McNichol, Dan Cronin, and William Smith of East Liverpool, who reportedly were not optimistic about the future of the pottery business in their hometown.

Initially, Salem China was not terribly successful, and the company was in financial trouble when it was purchased by the Sebring family in 1918. The Sebrings—an important force in American ceramics who had opened their first pottery in East Liverpool in 1887—purchased the company because they wanted a place for their son, Frank Sebring Jr., when he returned from fighting in World War I.

The Salem China Company went into business making white graniteware, but later branched out into production of earthenware, kitchen items, and semiporcelain dinnerware. Most sources say that Salem is still in business as a distributor, though it stopped being a manufacturer in either 1960 or 1967. Much of the Salem dinnerware introduced in the 1930s and 1940s was designed by the company's art di-

Salem China fish-shaped platter, 10 inches, $130–$145.
Item courtesy of Needful Things, Hendersonville, North Carolina.

rector, Victor Schreckengost, who was one of the most important ceramics designers of the 20th century.

Salem China is known for the quality of its decaled designs. Decals were used on a variety of shapes, though the decal names changed based on the shapes on which they were used. (Thus, the same decal might have been named "Petitpoint Basket" when it appeared on the "Victory" shape, "Sampler" when it appeared on another shape, and "Flower Basket" when it appeared on a third shape).

Salem China used a dating system to mark each piece with its date of manufacture, right down to the quarter of the year in which the piece was made. The system used numbers, stars, and letters: the numbers indicate the year of manufacture, and the number of stars indicates the quarter of the year in which the item was manufactured. (Thus, "57 **" would indicate that an item was made in the second quarter of 1957, and the number "57" with no stars would mean that an item was produced in the last quarter of 1957.) The letters indicate the piece's decorator, though this fact is of little importance to most collectors.

"Colonial Fireside"

This charming Salem China decal pattern features "authentic" Colonial American scenes designed by Victor Schreckengost. The line was first made in 1939, and its pieces feature four different views of interiors, all of which centered around a fireplace. All pieces were executed in shades of brown, tan, and green.

Bowl, *cereal, 6¹/₄-inch diameter*	$ 15–20
Bowl, *individual fruit*	$ 12–16
Bowl, *individual soup, 8¹/₂-inch diameter*	$ 15–22
Bowl, *vegetable, round, 8-inch diameter*	$ 40–48
Cup and saucer	$ 25–32
Plate, *bread and butter, 6-inch diameter*	$ 6–10
Plate, *dinner, 10-inch diameter*	$ 22–30
Plate, *luncheon, 9¹/₄-inch diameter*	$ 15–20
Plate, *salad, 7-inch diameter*	$ 12–16
Platter, *oval, 11 inches*	$ 55–65
Platter, *oval, 13 inches*	$ 65–75

"Freeform"

"Freeform" is the name for a very modern Salem China Company shape that was designed by Victor Schreckengost in the 1940s. The flatware items in this line are simple, round coupe shapes, but the cups have unusual ball feet, and the teapot looks like a long-nosed cartoon animal with a "comma" or crescent moon-shaped finial, tripod feet, and a "U"-shaped open-ended handle that looks like a tail. Three very distinctive decorations appear on "Freeform" shapes. The first, and perhaps most interesting, is called "Primitive," and is reminiscent of cave drawings that depict stylized human beings chasing deer. The deer with antlers are rather fully drawn, but the humans look like stick figures doing ballet. The second design is called "Hopscotch," and consists of lines that converge to make abstract star designs. The last design is "Southwind," and depicts windswept branches in charcoal with leaves of turquoise, burnt orange, and green/gold.

Bowl, *cereal, 6-inch diameter*	$ 15–20
Bowl, *individual fruit, 5¹/₂-inch diameter*	$ 12–16
Bowl, *vegetable, round, 10¹/₂-inch diameter*	$ 60–70
Coffee server	$ 50–70
Creamer	$ 32–40
Cup and saucer	$ 25–32
Plate, *bread and butter, 6-inch diameter*	$ 6–10

Plate, *dinner, 10-inch diameter*	$ 18–25
Platter, *oval, 14¹/₂ inches*	$ 65–75
Teapot	$ 60–75

"Godey Prints" (or "Godey Fashions")

This pattern consists of several prints based on images appearing in *Godey's Lady's Book,* a magazine published by Louis Antoine Godey (1804–1878). *Lady's Book* was the first successful American magazine for women, and was very influential in the world of fashion during the mid-19th century. Salem China used these decals on a number of its shapes, including "Briar Rose" and "Victory." Prices listed below are for "Godey Prints" designs on the "Victory" shape, which was designed by Victor Schreckengost and was first produced in 1938. This shape is characterized by thin ribs surrounding the rims of the flatware items, and vertical ribs around the bottoms of the hollowware pieces. Prices for "Godey Prints" on other Salem shapes are comparable to those listed below.

Ashtray	$ 15–20
Bowl, *cereal, lug-handled, 6³/₄-inch diameter*	$ 15–22
Bowl, *individual fruit, 5¹/₂-inch diameter*	$ 7–12
Bowl, *individual soup, 8¹/₂-inch diameter*	$ 15–20
Bowl, *vegetable, oval, 9¹/₄ inches*	$ 30–38
Bowl, *vegetable, round, 9-inch diameter*	$ 30–38
Coffeepot	$ 135–150
Creamer	$ 25–32
Cup and saucer	$ 25–32
Cup and saucer, *demitasse*	$ 15–20
Plate, *bread and butter, 6¹/₂-inch diameter*	$ 7–12
Plate, *dinner, 10-inch diameter*	$ 24–30
Plate, *luncheon, 9¹/₂-inch diameter*	$ 15–20
Plate, *salad, 8¹/₄-inch diameter*	$ 15–20
Platter, *oval, 13 inches*	$ 40–48
Sugar bowl, *open*	$ 50–60

The "Godey Prints" pattern was also available on 11-inch diameter service plates, with filigree-decorated rims done in varying colors. These service plates feature a variety of prints showing the *Godey's* ladies in various outfits and configurations.

Plates, *service, 11-inch diameter, all variations* $ 28–35

"Tricorn"

The "Tricorn" line is very distinctive, because its flatware items are triangular in shape with outcurving sides, and the hollowware items have very angular handles. This pattern originated in 1934 with a shockingly bright solid-color glaze called "Mandarin Red." In this grouping, the outside of the hollowware pieces were solid Mandarin Red, and the flatware pieces had wide red bands around the rims. Later, "Tricorn" pieces were decorated with concentric bands of color on the verge in shades such as Coral Red, Royal Blue, and Artiste (platinum). Decals were also used, but prices listed below are specifically for "Tricorn" pieces in Mandarin Red; prices for pieces with other decorations are comparable.

Bowl, *individual fruit, 5¹/₄ inches*	$ 10–15
Coffeepot	$ 100–125
Creamer	$ 18–25
Cup and saucer	$ 20–26
Cup and saucer, *demitasse*	$ 40–50
Nut dish, *3³/₄ inches*	$ 28–35
Plate, *dinner or party, 9 inches*	$ 20–26
Plate, *6¹/₂ inches*	$ 10–15
Plate, *5¹/₂ inches*	$ 8–12
Sugar bowl	$ 35–45

SCIO POTTERY

In the late 1920s, Scio, Ohio, was already a small town of only 1,200 people. But when the pottery production facility owned by the Carrollton China Company of Carrollton, Ohio, closed down in 1927, the town's population plummeted even further, to just 400 souls. The pottery facility remained closed until 1932, when Lew Reese happened to come across it while hunting for rabbits. Reese worked at a pottery in New Cumberland, West Virginia, and decided the facility would make a perfect place to open a dinnerware company to mass-produce dinnerware that could compete with the Japanese. Production began in 1933 and continued until 1985. Until 1950, the company produced only white dinnerware, but it later added underglaze decoration to its pieces. It did not mark its wares with the company name. Scio Pottery is reportedly still in business as a distributor.

"Blue Willow"

Scio's version of this ubiquitous pattern is found unmarked on simple coupe shapes with straight sides.

Bowl, *cereal, 6³/4-inch diameter*	$ 6–10
Bowl, *individual fruit, 5¹/2-inch diameter*	$ 6–10
Bowl, *vegetable, round, 8¹/2-inch diameter*	$ 10–15

Bowl, *vegetable, round, covered*	$ 65–75
Creamer	$ 8–12
Cup and saucer	$ 8–12
Mug	$ 6–10
Plate, *chop, 12-inch diameter*	$ 32–40
Plate, *dinner, 10-inch diameter*	$ 8–12
Plate, *luncheon, 9^1/$_4$-inch diameter*	$ 7–10
Plate, *salad, 7^1/$_2$-inch diameter*	$ 5–8
Platter, *oval, 11^1/$_2$ inches*	$ 14–18
Platter, *oval, 13 inches*	$ 16–20
Sugar bowl	$ 18–22

"Currier and Ives"

This pattern is very similar to Royal's "Currier and Ives" pattern. The major difference is that, on Scio's pieces, the borders have plows and ox harnesses around their rims. This pattern was produced in green. Pieces are unmarked.

Bowl, *cereal, 6^3/$_4$-inch diameter*	$ 9–12
Bowl, *individual fruit, 5^1/$_2$-inch diameter*	$ 7–10
Bowl, *individual soup, 7^1/$_2$-inch diameter*	$ 12–16
Bowl, *vegetable, 8^1/$_2$-inch diameter*	$ 25–32
Creamer	$ 15–20
Cup and saucer	$ 12–16
Plate, *bread and butter, 6-inch diameter*	$ 3–6
Plate, *dinner, 9^1/$_4$-inch diameter*	$ 11–15
Platter, *oval, 11^1/$_2$ inches*	$ 28–35
Sugar bowl	$ 20–25

"Orleans"

This pattern has a green, almost wood-grain border with an octagonal reserve decorated with a weathervane or signpostlike design. The design is composed of a flat shield featuring the image of a building and a carriage pulled by four horses. This pattern was typically produced in green.

Bowl, *cereal, 6³/₄-inch diameter*	$ 12–16
Bowl, *individual fruit, 5¹/₂-inch diameter*	$ 10–15
Cup and saucer	$ 18–22
Plate, *bread and butter, 6-inch diameter*	$ 5–8
Plate, *dinner, 10-inch diameter*	$ 15–20
Plate, *luncheon, 9¹/₄ inches*	$ 12–15

SEBRING POTTERY COMPANY

ASBURY

Mark used by *Sebring Pottery Company* on "Pegasus"-shaped dinnerware featuring its "Asbury" pattern.

One of the marks used by the *Sebring Pottery Company.*

The Sebring family established its first pottery in East Liverpool, Ohio, in 1887. The patriarch of the family was George A. Sebring, and he had five sons: Oliver, George, Ellsworth, Frank, and Joseph. Over the years, the family established several potteries in East Liverpool and East Palestine, and in 1899 they purchased land in Mahoning County, Ohio, where they established a town that bore the family name. Much of the Sebring family moved to this new town, and the second pottery factory built there was named the "Sebring Pottery Company." The various Sebring family potteries—such as the Limoges China Company and the French-Saxon China Company—are often a source of confusion for collectors, because these potteries often shared shapes, decals, and even marks from time to time.

In 1923, the Sebring Pottery Company began a revolution in dinnerware when it introduced "Ivory Porcelain." Before this time, dinnerware was customarily produced on white bodies, but Sebring's ivory-colored bodies took the industry by storm, and many other companies adopted this color for their wares—a trend that caused white-bodied dinnerware to go out of vogue until the 1940s. Sebring is also known for its patterns, which incorporate fancy filigree borders. Sebring was bought by National Unit Distributors in 1943, and the company name went out of use.

Sebring bowl-and-pitcher set, bowl is 12 inches in diameter, $175–$225.
Item courtesy of Richard Crane, Knoxville, Tennessee.

Sebring Pottery Company tankard set consisting of a 12½-inch tall tankard pitcher and six matching mugs, drinking monk decal decoration, $400–$450.
Item courtesy of Tom and Fay Crosby, Old School Antique Mall, Sylva, North Carolina.

Sebring Pottery Company pitcher, golden ground, 6½ inches, $45–$55.
Item courtesy of Needful Things, Hendersonville, North Carolina.

"Chantilly"

This pattern has a filigree border that was available in several types. The decal decoration depicts a dancing couple in 18th-century apparel; a musician is visible in the background. This pattern can be found on several Sebring Pottery Company shapes. Examples with maroon or burgundy-colored borders under the filigree command prices at the top of the ranges listed below, while pieces with plain filigree command prices near the bottom.

Bowl, *individual fruit, 5 -inch diameter*	$ 5–11
Bowl, *individual soup, 8-inch diameter*	$ 10–18

Bowl, *vegetable, round, 8¹/₂-inch diameter*	$ 24–35
Creamer	$ 20–29
Cup and saucer	$ 18–25
Plate, *bread and butter, 6¹/₂-inch diameter*	$ 4–8
Plate, *dinner, 9³/₄-inch diameter*	$ 13–20
Platter, *oval, 13³/₄ inches*	$ 45–60
Platter, *oval, 15 inches*	$ 48–65
Sugar bowl	$ 22–35

"China Bouquet"

This lovely pattern features a typical Sebring Pottery Company filigree border. A cluster of pink roses and green leaves decorates the center of flatware pieces.

Bowl, *cereal, 6¹/₄-inch diameter*	$ 8–12
Bowl, *individual fruit, 5¹/₂-inch diameter*	$ 7–10
Bowl, *individual soup, 8-inch diameter*	$ 12–16
Bowl, *vegetable, round, 9-inch diameter*	$ 32–38
Bowl, *vegetable, round, covered*	$ 75–85
Creamer	$ 22–28
Cup and saucer	$ 18–25
Gravy boat and underliner	$ 45–60
Plate, *bread and butter, 6¹/₂-inch diameter*	$ 4–7
Plate, *dinner, 9³/₄-inch diameter*	$ 15–20
Plate, *salad, 7¹/₄-inch diameter*	$ 7–10
Platter, *oval, 11³/₄ inches*	$ 20–26
Platter, *oval, 13³/₄ inches*	$ 40–48
Shakers, *salt and pepper, set*	$ 22–28

"Fortune"

"Fortune" is another Sebring Pottery Company pattern with a filigree border. It has a decal of roses in the center, surrounded by an arched flower garland.

Bowl, *cereal, 6¹/₂-inch diameter*	$ 10–14
Bowl, *individual fruit, 5¹/₂-inch diameter*	$ 7–10

Bowl, *individual soup, 8-inch diameter*	$ 15–20
Bowl, *vegetable, round, 9-inch diameter*	$ 45–50
Bowl, *vegetable, round, covered*	$ 115–125
Creamer	$ 28–34
Cup and saucer	$ 20–28
Plate, *bread and butter, 6^1/$_2$-inch diameter*	$ 5–8
Plate, *dinner, 9^3/$_4$-inch diameter*	$ 16–22
Plate, *salad, 7^1/$_4$-inch diameter*	$ 7–10
Platter, *oval, 11^3/$_4$ inches*	$ 42–52
Shakers, *salt and pepper, set*	$ 28–35
Sugar bowl	$ 38–45

"Poppy"

This pattern of scattered orange and yellow flowers is found on a number of Sebring Pottery Company shapes. Prices listed below are for examples found on the company's "Golden Maize" bodies.

Bowl, *cereal, 6^1/$_2$-inch diameter*	$ 17–22
Bowl, *individual fruit, 5^1/$_2$-inch diameter*	$ 15–20
Bowl, *individual soup, 8-inch diameter*	$ 20–27
Bowl, *vegetable, oval, 9^1/$_4$ inches*	$ 55–65
Bowl, *vegetable, round, 8^1/$_2$-inch diameter*	$ 55–65
Creamer	$ 35–45
Cup and saucer	$ 35–45
Gravy boat and underliner	$ 110–125
Plate, *bread and butter, 6^1/$_2$-inch diameter*	$ 10–15
Plate, *dinner, 9^3/$_4$-inch diameter*	$ 32–40
Plate, *luncheon, 9-inch diameter*	$ 18–25
Plate, *salad, 7-inch diameter*	$ 15–20
Platter, *oval, 15^3/$_4$ inches*	$ 120–145

Sebring Pottery Company 9³/₄-inch diameter dinner plate, "Serenade" pattern, burgundy border, $17–$22. *Item courtesy of Needful Things, Hendersonville, North Carolina.*

"Serenade"

This rococo-inspired decal features a garden setting with a man playing a lute while two women in 18th-century costume listen. It can be found on various Sebring shapes, and with several border styles. One very distinctive version came with a bold burgundy border overlaid with a filigree design, but other variations came with less colorful floral filigree borders.

Bowl, *cereal, 6-inch diameter*	$ 7–10
Bowl, *individual fruit, 5¹/₂-inch diameter*	$ 5–8
Bowl, *individual soup, 8-inch diameter*	$ 17–22
Bowl, *vegetable, round, 8³/₄-inch diameter*	$ 25–32
Creamer	$ 25–32
Cup and saucer	$ 16–24
Plate, *bread and butter, 6¹/₂-inch diameter*	$ 3–5
Plate, *dinner, 9³/₄-inch diameter*	$ 17–22
Plate, *salad, 7¹/₄-inch diameter*	$ 7–10

Sebring Pottery Company cake plate, "Vermilion Rose" pattern, $30–$35.
Item courtesy of Needful Things, Hendersonville, North Carolina.

Platter, *oval, 11³/₄ inches*	$ 25–32
Sugar bowl	$ 40–48

"Vermilion Rose"

As its name suggests, this pattern is distinguished by a decal decoration featuring a large vermilion-colored rose and a bud with leaves and stems.

Bowl, *cereal, 6-inch diameter*	$ 8–12
Bowl, *individual fruit, 5¹/₂-inch diameter*	$ 7–10
Bowl, *soup, 8¹/₄-inch diameter*	$ 12–15
Bowl, *vegetable, round, 8¹/₂-inch diameter*	$ 30–36
Bowl, *vegetable, round, covered*	$ 85–95
Creamer	$ 20–24
Cup and saucer	$ 15–19
Dish, *relish*	$ 12–16
Gravy boat	$ 45–55

Plate, *bread and butter, 6¹/₂-inch diameter*	$ 3–5
Plate, *cake, lug handles, 11 inches*	$ 30–35
Plate, *dinner, 10-inch diameter*	$ 13–16
Plate, *salad, 7¹/₄-inch diameter*	$ 5–8
Platter, *oval, 12 inches*	$ 30–35
Shakers, *salt and pepper, set*	$ 25–30

SHAWNEE POTTERY COMPANY

Shawnee
U.S.A.

One of the marks used by
the *Shawnee Pottery
Company.*

Paper label used by the
Shawnee Pottery Company
on its "Kenwood" line.

The Shawnee Pottery Company was founded in 1937 in the old American Encaustic Tiling Company plant in Zanesville, Ohio. It is said that the name for the company (and its logo) were inspired by an arrowhead found on the site before the new company opened. The arrowhead evoked the Shawnees, a Native American tribe believed to have had a village on the factory site at one time.

Shawnee opened for business at a time when American consumers displayed great resistance toward products made in Germany and Japan, both of which supplied a great deal of pottery and porcelain to the American market. As a result, Shawnee's business was brisk. Initially, such retailers as S. S. Kresge, S. H. Kress, F. W. Woolworth, and McCrory supplied the designs for products they wanted made, and Shawnee modeled the pieces and made the molds. In addition, Sears, Roebuck and Company sent personnel to provide Shawnee with input for a line of dinnerware that would become "Valencia."

During World War II, the Army Air Force took over Shawnee's pottery for use as a supply depot and parts-manufacturing facility. The plant was returned to Shawnee in 1946, and production resumed until the company closed in 1961.

The most famous and highly desired of Shawnee's products are its figural cookie jars—particularly "Smiley Pig" and "Winnie Pig"—and pieces from the "Corn King" and "Corn Queen" lines of dinnerware.

Cookie Jars

Shawnee made its first cookie jars in 1937 as part of the "Valencia" line, but its figural cookie jars did not appear until 1942. It is said that Rudy Ganz, who was the chief designer at Shawnee, happened to see a picture of a pig in overalls, and this inspired him to create "Smiley Pig."

Clown, *"JoJo," seal finial, no gold trim*	$ 600–675
Clown, *"JoJo," seal finial, gold trim*	$ 1,200–1,400
Corn King	$ 300–350
Corn Queen	$ 300–350
Cottage	$ 1,650–1,750
Dog, *"Muggsy," blue bow around head*	$ 650–725
Dog, *"Muggsy," gold trim and floral decals*	$ 1,200–1,230
Dog, *"Muggsy," green bow around head, gold trim and floral decals*	$ 2,500–2,750
Drum Major, *no gold trim*	$ 650–750
Drum Major, *gold trim*	$ 1,200–1,300
Dutch Boy, *"Jack," hands in pocket, plain, yellow, or blue pants*	$ 150–175
Dutch Boy, *"Jack," striped pants (diamond shape)*	$ 325–350
Dutch Boy, *"Jack," double-striped pants (diamond shape)*	$ 700–775
Dutch Boy, *"Jack," gold trim, blond hair, patches on pants*	$ 600–650
Dutch Girl, *"Jill," plain, blue, or yellow skirt*	$ 150–175
Dutch Girl, *"Jill," gold trim and decals*	$ 500–600
Elephant, *"Lucky," cold-painted, paint in average condition*	$ 300–375
Elephant, *"Lucky," hand-painted floral decoration*	$ 1,250–1,500
Elephant, *"Lucky," gold-trimmed with floral decals*	$ 1,200–1,400
Fernware, *octagon, solid color*	$ 100–125
Fernware, *octagon, decal decoration*	$ 225–250
Great Northern Dutch Boy (similar to "Jack" but marked "Great Northern")	$ 600–675

Shawnee Dutch Girl "Jill" cookie jar, tulip decal, $500–$600.
Item courtesy of Needful Things, Hendersonville, North Carolina

Great Northern Dutch Girl (similar to "Jill" but marked "Great Northern"), *blond hair, green dress*	$ 600–675
Great Northern Dutch Girl (similar to "Jill" but marked "Great Northern"), *brown hair, white dress*	$ 500–575
Hexagon, *basketweave, solid color*	$ 100–125
Hexagon, *basketweave, decorated, gold trim*	$ 200–250
Jug, *Pennsylvania Dutch (Deutsch) painted design*	$ 325–400
Jug, *blue, green, or yellow, plain*	$ 225–275
Little Chef, *octagon, solid color, green, caramel, or yellow*	$ 275–325
Little Chef, *octagon, cream with hand-painted decoration*	$ 225–275
Little Chef, *octagon, white with gold trim*	$ 375–425
Owl, *winking, white, no gold trim*	$ 200–250
Owl, *brown, gold trim*	$ 475–525
Pig, *"Smiley," red bandanna, plain, some cold painting*	$ 175–225
Pig, *"Smiley," blue bandanna, plain, no gold, brown hooves*	$ 575–625

Pig, "Smiley," green bandanna, shamrock painting, no gold	$ 500–575
Pig, "Smiley," red bandanna, chrysanthemums, no gold trim	$ 500–575
Pig, "Smiley," red bandanna, chrysanthemums, gold trim	$ 850–925
Pig, "Smiley," yellow bandanna, "Smiley" written in gold, hair decal on head	$ 1,250–1,400
Pig, "Smiley," blue bandanna, hand-painted black hair, floral decals, gold trim	$ 1,500–1,750
Pig, "Smiley," shamrock decoration, butterfly painted on head	$ 1,500–1,750
Pig, "Smiley," yellow bandanna, hand-painted black hair, bug painted on face, gold trim, floral decals	$ 1,650–1,850
Pig, "Smiley," green bandanna, hand-painted red hair, chrysanthemum decoration	$ 2,000–2,200
Pig, "Winnie," blue, green, or peach, no gold trim	$ 475–525
Pig, "Winnie," caramel-colored coat	$ 675–725
Pig, "Winnie," blueberries on hat, gold trim, green collar	$ 1,250–1,400
Pig, "Winnie," clover blossom on hat, no gold trim	$ 850–950
Pig, "Winnie," clover on hat and coat, green collar, gold trim	$ 1,750–1,900
Pig, "Winnie," dark-green coat, gold trim	$ 2,000–2,250
Puss 'n Boots, maroon ribbon, plain, both short tail and tail over boot	$ 250–300
Puss 'n Boots, floral decals, maroon bow, no gold trim	$ 700–750
Puss 'n Boots, floral decals, white bowl, gold-trimmed	$ 875–925
Sailor Boy, cold-painted, blue or black kerchief, plain	$ 225–265
Sailor Boy, black hair, gold trim, "USN" and star on hat	$ 1,250–1,400
Sailor Boy, blonde hair, gold trim, floral decals	$ 1,500–1,750

Dinnerware

"Corn King"

The "Corn King" line was first produced in 1946. Its pieces are somewhat larger than those in the original line, which was called "White Corn." First produced in 1941 to be used as premiums by Proctor and Gamble, "White Corn" pieces feature white corn kernels and green leaves. "Corn King" pieces have bright-yellow kernels and light-green husks. Prices for "White Corn" pieces are generally about 20 percent higher than those listed below.

Shawnee "Corn King" covered casserole, $85–$110.
Item courtesy of Needful Things, Hendersonville, North Carolina.

Bowl, *individual fruit, 6-inch diameter*	$ 85–95
Bowl, *multipurpose, soup, cereal*	$ 60–70
Bowl, *mixing, 5-inch diameter*	$ 55–65
Bowl, *mixing, $6^1/_2$-inch diameter*	$ 65–75
Bowl, *vegetable, 9 inches*	$ 65–75
Butter dish, *$^1/_4$-pound*	$ 70–80
Casserole, *$1^1/_2$-quart*	$ 85–110
Creamer	$ 30–40
Cup and saucer	$ 55–65
Mug, *8-ounce*	$ 70–80
Jug, *10-ounce*	$ 85–95
Plate, *dinner, 10-inch diameter*	$ 50–60
Plate, *salad, 8 inches*	$ 45–55
Platter, *12 inches*	$ 65–75
Range set, *three pieces*	$ 85–95

Relish tray	$ 45–55
Shakers, *3¹/₂ inches, salt and pepper, set*	$ 45–55
Shakers, *5¹/₂ inches, salt and pepper, set*	$ 55–65
Sugar bowl	$ 45–55
Teapot, *10-ounce*	$ 225–250
Teapot, *30-ounce*	$ 200–225

"Corn Queen"

This line is exactly like "Corn King," except for the color scheme, which has darker-green husks and lighter-yellow corn kernels. This line was in production from 1954 until the plant's closing in 1961.

Bowl, *individual fruit, 6-inch diameter*	$ 55–65
Bowl, *mixing, 6¹/₂-inch diameter*	$ 45–55
Bowl, *multipurpose, soup, cereal*	$ 65–75
Bowl, *vegetable, 9 inches*	$ 65–75
Butter dish, *covered, ¹/₄-pound*	$ 70–80
Creamer	$ 35–45
Cup and saucer	$ 65–75
Mug, *8-ounce*	$ 55–65
Plate, *dinner, 10-inch diameter*	$ 45–55
Plate, *salad, 8-inch diameter*	$ 40–50
Platter, *oval, 12 inches*	$ 65–75
Range set, *three pieces*	$ 125–145
Relish tray	$ 35–45
Shakers, *3¹/₄ inches, salt and pepper, set*	$ 45–55
Shakers, *5¹/₄ inches, salt and pepper, set*	$ 55–65
Sugar bowl	$ 40–50
Teapot, *10-ounce*	$ 225–250
Teapot, *30-ounce*	$ 150–160

"Lobster"

Introduced in 1954, this line was part of Shawnee's "Kenwood Ceramics" line, which featured higher-end products designed to be sold in department stores and gift shops. Initially these pieces were made in Van Dyke Brown or Charcoal Gray, but Charcoal Gray was later discontinued, and Mirror Black was substituted. The lids on covered pieces were white with red lobster-shaped handles or finials. Some pieces were all red, such as the lobster-shaped souvenir pin, the hors d'oeuvre holders, the double spoon holder, and the lobster-shaped salt and pepper shakers. The claw-shaped salt and pepper shakers were red with a white base. This line did not sell well, and was discontinued in 1956.

Bean pot, *40-ounce*	$ 825–875
Bowl, *batter, handled*	$ 65–75
Bowl, *mixing, 5-inch diameter*	$ 45–55
Bowl, *mixing, 7-inch diameter*	$ 50–60
Bowl, *salad, serving or spaghetti*	$ 45–55
Butter dish, *covered, ¹/₄-pound*	$ 120–135
Casserole, *French, individual, 10-ounce*	$ 80–100
Casserole, *French, 16-ounce*	$ 35–45
Creamer	$ 60–70
Hors d'oeuvre holder	$ 300–350
Mug, *8-ounce*	$ 90–100
Shakers, *claw-shaped, salt and pepper, set*	$ 45–55
Shakers, *full-bodied lobsters, salt and pepper, set*	$ 250–275
Spoon holder, *double*	$ 275–325

"Valencia"

In 1937, Shawnee's designer, Louise Bauer, created the "Valencia" line in conjunction with the Housewares division of Sears, Roebuck and Company. This was a solid-color line with swirled flutes that originally came in shades of cobalt blue, Spruce Green, tangerine, and yellow. Burgundy and maroon were added a year later, and pieces in ivory and light yellow are also known to exist. "Valencia" pieces were designed to be inexpensive (a 20-piece starter set was given away with each refrigerator sold by Sears), and pieces were prone to damage. "Valencia" was discontinued in 1940. Pieces are seldom marked, though some were impressed with "Valencia" or "USA."

Ashtray	$ 15–18
Bowl, *individual fruit, 6-inch diameter*	$ 22–26
Bowl, *onion soup, covered*	$ 40–50

Candleholder, *bulb-type, pair*	$ 50–60
Carafe, *lidded*	$ 60–70
Casserole, *7¹/₂ inches*	$ 60–70
Casserole, *8¹/₂ inches*	$ 75–85
Coaster	$ 16–22
Coffeepot, *regular*	$ 45–55
Coffeepot, *demitasse*	$ 40–50
Creamer	$ 16–22
Cup and saucer	$ 25–30
Cup and saucer, *demitasse*	$ 25–30
Egg cup	$ 18–22
Jug, *ball, ice lip, 64-ounce*	$ 50–60
Plate, *bread and butter, 6¹/₂-inch diameter*	$ 10–14
Plate, *chop, 13-inch diameter*	$ 30–35
Plate, *dinner, 10³/₄-inch diameter*	$ 15–20
Plate, *grill, compartmented*	$ 28–32
Plate, *luncheon, 9³/₄-inch diameter*	$ 14–18
Plate, *salad, 7³/₄-inch diameter*	$ 12–16
Relish tray, *five dishes in holder, similar to "Fiesta" relish tray*	$ 150–175
Shakers, *ball-type, salt and pepper, set*	$ 35–40
Sugar bowl	$ 30–35
Teapot	$ 70–80
Vase, *bud*	$ 20–25

Figures

The majority of these figures are not marked, or are marked simply with the initials "USA."

Dog, *"Muggsy," gold trim, 5¹/₂ inches*	$ 90–100
Dog, *Poodle, 6¹/₂ inches, no gold trim*	$ 35–45
Dog, *Terrier, or Scottie, 7¹/₂ inches, no gold trim*	$ 35–45
Dog, *with leg in sling, cold-painted, 5¹/₄ inches, no gold trim*	$ 35–45

Donkey, *6¹/₂ inches, no gold trim*	$ 15–20
Gazelle, *10¹/₂ inches long*	$ 90–100
Lamb, *6 inches*	$ 35–45
Rabbit, *plain*	$ 65–75
Rabbit, *gold trim with decal decoration*	$ 120–140
Raccoon, *plain*	$ 65–75
Raccoon, *gold trim with decal decoration*	$ 120–140

Miniature Figures

Like their larger cousins, these small figures are generally either unmarked or bear the initials of their country of origin: "USA." These figures were first produced in the late 1930s, and were glazed in shades of blue, white, Old Ivory, turquoise, and Dusty Rose. Most were discontinued circa 1942.

Bear Cub, *2³/₈ inches*	$ 20–24
Bird, *baby, sitting*	$ 20–24
Bird, *flying*	$ 20–24
Circus Horse, *2⁵/₈ inches*	$ 20–24
Deer, *4¹/₂ inches*	$ 20–24
Doe, *4¹/₂ inches*	$ 20–24
Fawn, *4¹/₂ inches*	$ 20–24
Southern Girl, *in bonnet and hoop skirt, 4¹/₂ inches*	$ 25–30

Flowerpots with Saucers

African violet pot with flared rim, *mottled glaze, 5 inches, #534*	$ 17–19
Burlap or textured surface, *4 inches*	$ 14–16
Diamond-quilted, *4 inches*	$ 14–16
Diamond-quilted, *6 inches, #486*	$ 16–18
Diamond-quilted, *with four petal flowers on each point,* 3 inches	$ 14–16
Diamond-quilted, *with four petal flowers on each point,* 6 inches	$ 15–17
Leaf-embossed and ribbed, *5 inches, #465*	$ 18–21
Square, *with scalloped rim, #410*	$ 14–16

Shawnee "Smiley Pig" creamer, no gold, $40–$50.
Item courtesy of Bill Brooker, Old School Antique Mall,
Sylva, North Carolina.

Kitchenwares (Figural)

This category includes a wide variety of kitchenware in the shapes of animals, people, and other objects.

Creamers

Elephant, *white, red ears, no decoration or gold trim*	$ 25–30
Elephant, *white, decal decoration, red ears, gold trim*	$ 375–425
Elephant, *allover gold or platinum*	$ 425–475
Puss 'n Boots, *white with red bow, no decoration or gold trim*	$ 27–32
Puss 'n Boots, *gold trim*	$ 150–175
Puss 'n Boots, *allover gold or platinum*	$ 200–250
Smiley Pig, *embossed flower, no gold trim*	$ 40–50
Smiley Pig, *embossed flower, gold trim*	$ 200–225
Smiley Pig, *embossed flower, allover gold or platinum*	$ 425–450

Sugar Bowls (covered utility bowls)

Basket, *red handle and rim, decal-decorated, lid resembles cloth cover*	$ 125–150
Basket, *fruit-filled, #81*	$ 50–60
Bucket, *wood grain, decal-decorated with gold*	$ 100–125

Jugs/Pitchers

Chanticleer, *rooster, red and blue, no gold trim*	$ 75–90
Chanticleer, *rooster, decal-decorated with gold trim*	$ 425–475
Chanticleer, *rooster, allover gold or platinum*	$ 475–525
Little Bo Peep, *small, 30-ounce, no gold*	$ 125–150
Little Bo Peep, *large, 40-ounce, painted details*	$ 100–125
Little Bo Peep, *small, 30-ounce, gold trim*	$ 200–250
Little Bo Peep, *large, 40-ounce, gold trim and decals*	$ 250–300
Little Boy Blue, *red and blue, no gold trim*	$ 110–125
Little Boy Blue, *gold trim*	$ 225–250
Smiley Pig, *embossed clover blossom*	$ 225–250
Smiley Pig, *embossed flowers on chest, with gold trim*	$ 225–250
Smiley Pig, *apple*	$ 275–325
Smiley Pig, *allover gold or platinum*	$ 650–750

Salt and Pepper Shakers

LARGE SIZE (APPROXIMATELY 5 INCHES TALL)

Chanticleer, *cold-painted, no gold trim, set*	$ 60–70
Chanticleer, *gold trim, set*	$ 200–225
Dutch Boy and Dutch Girl, *blue, set*	$ 35–45
Dutch Boy and Dutch Girl, *brown, set*	$ 40–50
Dutch Boy and Dutch Girl, *gold trim, set*	$ 80–90
Fruit	$ 45–55
Jack and Jill, *cold-painted, plain, set*	$ 60–70
Jack and Jill, *decals and gold trim, set*	$ 250–300
Muggsy, *plain, set*	$ 200–225

Shawnee "Chanticleer" pitcher, $75–$90.
Item courtesy of Bill Brooker, Old School Antique Mall, Sylva, North Carolina.

Shawnee "Little Bo Peep" pitcher, $125–$150.
Item courtesy of Richard H. Crane, Knoxville, Tennessee.

Shawnee "Little Boy Blue" pitcher, $110–$125.
Item courtesy of Richard H. Crane, Knoxville, Tennessee.

Muggsy, *decals and gold trim, set*	$ 425–450
Smiley Pig, *blue, green, peach, or red neckerchief, set*	$ 150–175
Smiley Pig, *decals and gold trim, set*	$ 200–225
Smiley Pig and Winnie Pig, *heart, set*	$ 200–225
Smiley Pig and Winnie Pig, *clover, set*	$ 250–300
Swiss Boy and Swiss Girl, *no gold trim, set*	$ 50–60
Swiss Boy and Swiss Girl, *gold trim, set*	$ 75–85

Shawnee "Farmer Pig" salt and pepper shakers, 3½ inches, $85–$95.
Item courtesy of Bill Brooker, Old School Antique Mall, Sylva, North Carolina.

SMALL SIZE (APPROXIMATELY 3¼ INCHES TALL)

Bo Peep and Blue Boy, *no gold trim, set*	$ 35–45
Bo Peep and Blue Boy, *gold trim, set*	$ 60–70
Chanticleer, *no gold trim, set*	$ 40–50
Chanticleer, *gold trim, set*	$ 175–185
Chef, *one marked "S," other marked "P," no gold trim, set*	$ 30–40
Chef, *one marked "S," other marked "P," gold trim, set*	$ 50–60
Cottage, *set*	$ 400–450
Duck, *set*	$ 35–45
Farmer pig with hat and shovel, *no gold trim, set*	$ 85–95
Farmer pig with hat and shovel, *gold trim, set*	$ 125–135
Flower cluster, *no gold trim, set*	$ 30–40
Flower cluster, *gold trim, set*	$ 65–75
Flower in pot, *no gold trim, set*	$ 30–40
Flower in pot, *all-white, set*	$ 60–70

Flower in pot, *gold trim, set*	$ 60–70
Flower in pot, *gold center to flower, set*	$ 65–75
Fruit, *set*	$ 35–45
Milk can, *no gold trim*	$ 40–50
Milk can, *gold trim and decals*	$ 135–145
Muggsy, *no gold trim*	$ 70–80
Muggsy, *gold trim*	$ 225–250
Owl, *gray eyes, no gold, set*	$ 35–45
Owl, *green eyes, no gold, set*	$ 40–54
Owl, *gold trim, set*	$ 85–100
Puss 'n Boots, *no gold, set*	$ 40–50
Puss 'n Boots, *gold trim*	$ 175–200
Smiley Pig, *blue, green, or red neckerchief, no gold trim, set*	$ 40–50
Smiley Pig, *pointed neckerchief, no gold trim, set*	$ 85–100
Smiley Pig, *pointed gold neckerchief, set*	$ 110–125
Smiley and Winnie Pig, *clover, no gold trim, set*	$ 90–100
Smiley and Winnie Pig, *heart, no gold trim, set*	$ 65–75
Smiley and Winnie Pig, *gold trim, set*	$ 90–100
Watering can, *no gold, set*	$ 30–40
Wheelbarrow, *no gold trim, set*	$ 30–40
Wheelbarrow, *gold trim, set*	$ 125–140

Teapots

Cottage, *5-cup*	$ 700–750
Elephant, *5-cup, red ears, no gold trim*	$ 150–165
Elephant, *5-cup, gold trim*	$ 300–350
Granny Ann, *7-cup, no gold trim*	$ 200–250
Granny Ann, *7-cup, gold trim*	$ 250–300
Tom Tom the Piper's Son, *5-cup, white pants, gold trim*	$ 175–200
Tom Tom the Piper's Son, *5-cup, white pants, no gold trim*	$ 110–135
Tom Tom the Piper's Son, *5-cup, blue pants, no gold trim*	$ 110–135
Tom Tom the Piper's Son, *5-cup, blue pants, gold trim*	$ 175–200

Shawnee "Granny Ann" teapot, 7-cup, no gold trim, $200–$250. *Item courtesy of Needful Things, Hendersonville, North Carolina.*

Shawnee "Tom Tom the Piper's Son" teapot, white pants, no gold trim, $110–$135. *Item courtesy of Needful Things, Hendersonville, North Carolina.*

Kitchenware (Nonfigural)

"Fernware"

Produced before World War II, this line is also called "Wheat" because its pieces feature a vertical fernlike sprig that also looks like a wheat stalk. The shapes are octagonal, and pieces came in solid colors of turquoise, powder blue (Flax Blue), yellow, and peach. The mixing bowls were also produced in Dusty Rose and Old Ivory. Items with gold trim command prices that are double those listed below.

Bowl, *mixing, 5-inch diameter*	$ 20–25
Bowl, *mixing, 6-inch diameter*	$ 20–25
Bowl, *mixing, 7-inch diameter*	$ 20–25
Bowl, *mixing, 8-inch diameter*	$ 25–30
Bowl, *mixing, 9-inch diameter*	$ 25–30
Canister, *2$^1/_2$-quart, 7$^1/_4$ inches*	$ 75–85
Coffeemaker, *with pottery drip*	$ 100–125
Cookie jar, *4-quart, 8$^1/_2$ inches*	$ 100–125

Creamer	$ 50–60
Jug, *1¹/₂-pint*	$ 75–85
Jug, *ball-shaped, 2-quart*	$ 60–70
Matchbox holder	$ 125–150
Salt box	$ 140–160
Shakers, *salt and pepper, set*	$ 50–60
Sugar bowl/Grease jar, *covered*	$ 65–76
Teapot, *2-cup*	$ 100–120
Teapot, *6-cup*	$ 90–100

"Flower and Fern"

These pieces are marked "USA" and are decorated with an embossed five-petal flower on a stem that is glanced by fern fronds. This line can be found in powder blue, yellow, turquoise, dark blue, burgundy, dark green, and Old Ivory. "Flower and Fern" was produced before the beginning of World War II. Pieces with gold trim command prices that are double those listed below.

Coffeemaker, *pottery drip, 5-cup*	$ 100–120
Creamer	$ 28–32
Creamer, *"Aladdin" or shell-shaped*	$ 25–30
Creamer, *ball-shaped*	$ 28–32
Grease jar	$ 50–60
Jardinière, *2¹/₄ inches*	$ 10–14
Jardinière, *4 inches*	$ 12–16
Jardinière, *7 inches*	$ 22–26
Jug, *ball-shaped, 4-cup*	$ 28–32
Matchbox holder	$ 115–125
Salt box, *covered*	$ 100–110
Shakers, *salt and pepper, 3 inches, set*	$ 25–30
Shakers, *salt and pepper, 4 inches, set*	$ 25–30
Shakers, *salt and pepper, 5 inches, set*	$ 20–24
Sugar bowl, *open*	$ 28–32
Sugar bowl, *"Aladdin" or shell-shaped, open*	$ 25–30

Teapot, *2-cup*	$ 45–55
Teapot, *6-cup*	$ 50–60

"Snowflake"

Pieces in this line are decorated with parallel horizontal lines and incised snowflakes, and are marked "USA." The line was introduced before the beginning of World War II, and in 1942 all items except the bowls were discontinued. Colors include powder blue, dark blue, burgundy, dark green, Old Ivory, turquoise, white, and yellow. Smaller "Snowflake" pieces were given away as premiums by Proctor and Gamble. Pieces with gold trim command prices that are double those listed below.

Bowl, *batter*	$ 28–32
Bowl, *mixing, 5-inch diameter*	$ 14–18
Bowl, *mixing, 6-inch diameter*	$ 14–18
Bowl, *mixing, 7-inch diameter*	$ 14–18
Bowl, *mixing, 8-inch diameter*	$ 16–20
Bowl, *mixing, 9-inch diameter*	$ 16–20
Canister, *2-quart, lug handles*	$ 65–75
Coffeepot, *with aluminum drip*	$ 100–120
Creamer	$ 20–25
Grease jar	$ 50–60
Jug, *ball-shaped, 2-quart*	$ 50–60
Jug, *utility, 1¹/₂-pint*	$ 50–60
Shakers, *salt and pepper, set*	$ 30–35
Sugar bowl, *open*	$ 20–25
Teapot, *2-cup*	$ 60–70
Teapot, *5-cup*	$ 65–75
Teapot, *8-cup*	$ 70–80

"Sunflower"

This line is also called "Daisy," and was introduced circa 1947. Pieces are deco-rated with an embossed image of a sunflower that is decorated underglaze with yel-low petals and a brown center, plus green leaves and a brown stem, all against a white background. Pieces with gold trim command prices that are double those listed below.

Coffeepot/Covered jug	$ 130–140
Creamer, *ball-shaped*	$ 45–55
Jug, *ball-shaped*	$ 80–90
Shaker, *range, set, 5 inches*	$ 35–42
Shaker, *small, set, 3¹/₂ inches*	$ 30–35
Sugar	$ 40–45
Teapot, *7-cup*	$ 50–60

Lamps

Shawnee lamps were typically made for other companies, and are unmarked. Lamp bases feature glazed interiors and undersides, and generally have an inner ring called a "strength ring."

Asian Man, *with musical instrument, low base*	$ 45–55
Asian Woman, *with musical instrument, low base*	$ 45–55
Asian Man, *with musical instrument, high base*	$ 50–60
Asian Woman, *with musical instrument, high base*	$ 50–60
Clown, *with umbrella, cold-painted*	$ 70–80
Deer	$ 55–65
Duck, *with drum*	$ 70–80
Elephant, *one foot on ball, cold-painted*	$ 75–85
Heads, *Moors, turbaned, one male and one female, pair*	$ 135–150
Mother Goose	$ 100–125
Polynesian Man, *kneeling with drum, and Polynesian Woman with hand on head, pair*	$ 125–150
Ribbed, *with bows, blue and pink*	$ 60–70
Spanish Dancers	$ 50–60
Victorian Man	$ 45–55
Victorian Woman	$ 45–55
Victorian Man and Woman	$ 65–75

Miscellany

Ashtray, *"Flight," boomerang, 8½ inches*	$ 15–18
Ashtray, *"Flight," boomerang, 11 inches*	$ 18–22
Ashtray, *"Flight," boomerang, 13 inches*	$ 20–24
Ashtray, *Arrowhead with Native American, Shawnee logo*	$ 275–325
Ashtray, *Panther Paw*	$ 30–35
Ashtray, *triangular, flying geese*	$ 20–24
Ashtray, *with figural squirrel*	$ 32–36
Bank, *Bulldog*	$ 250–275
Bank, *Howdy Doody, riding a pig*	$ 600–700
Bank, *Tumbling Bear*	$ 250–275
Basket, *hanging, square, 8 inches*	$ 75–85
Bookends, *dog heads*	$ 85–100
Bookends, *flying geese, planter, pair*	$ 85–100
Candleholder, *Aladdin's lamp shape, single*	$ 14–17
Candleholder, *cornucopia, pair*	$ 20–25
Candleholder, *magnolia blossom, gold trim, pair*	$ 40–50
Cigarette Box, *rectangular with raised Shawnee logo of arrowhead and Native American*	$ 650–750
Clock, *trellis, with ivy leaves, square*	$ 125–150
Clock, *triangular*	$ 200–225
Flower Frog, *Bouquet*	$ 50–60
Flower Frog, *Dolphin, either low or high base*	$ 50–60
Flower Frog, *Sea Horse*	$ 50–60
Flower Frog, *Snail*	$ 55–65
Flower Frog, *Swan*	$ 50–60
Flower Frog, *Turtle*	$ 50–60
Wall Pocket, *Chef*	$ 50–60
Wall Pocket, *Girl, holding doll*	$ 50–60
Wall Pocket, *Little Bo Peep, square*	$ 45–55
Wall Pocket, *Little Jack Horner, square*	$ 45–55

Shawnee bookends/planters, flying geese, $85–$100.
*Item courtesy of Bill Brooker, Old School Antique Mall,
Sylva, North Carolina.*

Wall Pocket, *mantel clock*	$ 50–60
Wall Pocket, *Scottie Dog*	$ 80–90
Wall Pocket, *Tall Case Clock*	$ 60–70
Wall Pocket, *Wall Telephone*	$ 70–80

Planters

Asian Boy and Girl, *with musical instrument, no gold trim, #573*	$ 13–17
Asian Boy and Girl, *with musical instrument, gold trim, #573*	$ 18–24
Asian Lady, *with umbrella and bowl, no gold trim, #701*	$ 13–17
Asian Lady, *with umbrella and bowl, gold trim, #701*	$ 18–24
Asian Man, *with basket and umbrella, no gold trim, #617*	$ 13–17
Asian Man, *with basket and umbrella, gold trim, #617*	$ 18–24
Asian Man, *with basket and umbrella, no gold trim, #574*	$ 13–17
Asian Man, *with book, gold trim, #574*	$ 18–24

Asian Man, *with rickshaw, no gold trim, #539*	$ 13–17
Asian Man, *with rickshaw, gold trim, #539*	$ 18–24
Asian Men, *carrying basket, no gold trim, #537*	$ 13–17
Asian Men, *carrying basket, gold trim, #537*	$ 18–24
Automobile, *convertible, either four or eight spokes on wheels, #506*	$ 30–35
Basket, *#640*	$ 40–45
Bear and Wagon, *7¹/₄ inches long, #731*	$ 60–70
Bicycle Built for Two, *9³/₄ inches, #735*	$ 75–85
Bird, *Cockatiel, #523*	$ 16–20
Bird, *head up, tail up, #523*	$ 12–16
Bird, *head down, tail up*	$ 12–16
Bird, *Lovebirds*	$ 14–18
Bird, *on rim of planter, #767*	$ 35–42
Boy, *with chicken, #645*	$ 25–30
Boy, *with hat at high stump, #532*	$ 16–20
Boy, *with hat at low stump, #532*	$ 28–32
Boy, *with stump, leaning, #533*	$ 15–18
Boy, *with wheelbarrow, #750*	$ 22–26
Boy and Dog, *#582*	$ 15–18
Boy at Gate, *no gold trim*	$ 14–18
Boy at Gate, *gold trim*	$ 22–30
Bridge, *#765*	$ 24–28
Buddha, *#524*	$ 28–32
Bull, *#668*	$ 25–30
Bull and Leaf	$ 70–80
Butterfly, *gold trim, #524*	$ 30–35
Canopy Bed, *#734*	$ 85–100
Cat, *playing horn (saxophone) # 729*	$ 40–50
Cat, *reclining*	$ 18–22
Chick and Egg, *#730*	$ 45–52

Children and Shoe, #525	$ 22–26
Circus Wagon	$ 55–65
Clock, *alarm*, #1262	$ 18–22
Clown, *no gold trim*, #607	$ 22–28
Clown, *with gold trim*, #607	$ 32–38
Coal Scuttle, *embossed flower*	$ 35–40
Colonial Lady, #616	$ 40–50
Covered Wagon, *large, no gold trim*, #733	$ 45–55
Covered Wagon, *large, gold trim*, #733	$ 80–100
Covered Wagon, *small, no gold trim*, #514	$ 12–16
Cradle, *embossed flower*, #J542P	$ 35–40
Cradle, *embossed lambs*, #625, *gold trim*	$ 24–28
Deer and Fawn, *no gold trim*, #669	$ 20–25
Deer and Fawn, *gold trim*, #669	$ 30–35
Dog, *in a boat*, #736	$ 45–55
Dog, *Chihuahua, in front of doghouse*, #738	$ 30–40
Dog, *hound with jug*, #610	$ 12–16
Dog, *Irish Setter, sitting*	$ 14–18
Dog, *Poodle on Bicycle*, #712	$ 40–50
Dog, *Poodle, with carriage*, #704	$ 40–50
Dog, *Puppy, on shoe, two- or three-button styles*	$ 15–18
Dog, *Puppy, with fly on rear*	$ 18–22
Dog, *sitting*	$ 18–22
Dog, *Spaniel, in front of doghouse*, #739	$ 30–40
Dog, *Terrier, in front of doghouse*, #740	$ 30–40
Dogs, *Hound and Pekingese*, #611	$ 25–35
Donkey and Cart, *small*, #538	$ 14–18
Donkey and Cart, *small*, #538, *gold trim*	$ 20–28
Donkey with Basket, *head down*, #671	$ 40–48
Donkey with Basket, *head up*, #722	$ 35–42
Donkey with Basket, *head up*, #722	$ 35–42

Dove, *and planting dish, #2025*	$ 50–60
Duck, *pulling cart, #752*	$ 35–40
Duckling, *#720*	$ 30–35
Elephant and Howdah (basket)	$ 25–30
Elephant and Leaf base	$ 70–80
Elf, *with shoe, no gold trim, #765*	$ 16–20
Elf, *with shoe, gold trim, #765*	$ 25–32
Fawn, *with fern, #737*	$ 25–30
Fawn, *with log, #766*	$ 45–52
Fawn, *with stump, no gold trim, #624*	$ 20–25
Fawn, *with stump, gold trim, #624*	$ 30–35
Fish, *10¹/₂ inches long, #717*	$ 65–75
Fish, *on waves, small, #845*	$ 20–25
Fish, *mouth open, tail up, Dolphin*	$ 15–20
Fox and Bag, *#2029*	$ 75–85
Frog on Lily Pad, *#726*	$ 40–48
Gazelle, *with baby, heads, #840*	$ 80–90
Gazelle, *pink and white, scalloped on mirror, black base, #522*	$ 110–125
Giraffe, *lying down, #521*	$ 35–40
Girl, *playing musical instrument, #576*	$ 28–32
Girl and Basket, *#534*	$ 16–20
Girl at Gate, *#581*	$ 22–26
Girl with Parasol, *#560*	$ 32–38
Goose, *small*	$ 14–18
Goose, *flying, #707*	$ 30–35
Goose, *flying in relief, #820*	$ 22–28
High Chair, *with kitten, #727*	$ 75–85
Hobby Horse, *#660*	$ 24–28
House, *#J543P*	$ 40–45
Kitten, *full figure, #723*	$ 40–50
Kitten and Basket, *#2026*	$ 35–45

Lamb, *with bow, black with gold, #724*	$ 40–50
Lamb, *upright at trough*	$ 28–35
Man with Pushcart, *"Tony the Peddler," #621*	$ 40–48
Man with Pushcart, *"Tony the Peddler," "Rum Carioca," #621*	$ 75–85
Mill, *Dutch, gold trim, #715*	$ 40–45
Mill, *"Old Mill," #769*	$ 40–45
Mouse, *leaning on a piece of cheese, #705*	$ 42–50
Panda and Cradle, *#2031*	$ 35–40
Piano, *#528*	$ 35–40
Pig, *#760*	$ 18–22
Pig and Wheelbarrow, *both styles*	$ 18–22
Pixie, *no gold trim, #536*	$ 12–15
Pixie, *gold trim, #536*	$ 24–30
Pixie, *with leaf and flower, wheelbarrow*	$ 20–25
Polynesian Girl, *#896*	$ 50–60
Pony, *#506*	$ 45–55
Pushcart, *#J544P*	$ 40–50
Rabbit and Stump, *#606*	$ 18–22
Rabbit with Basket	$ 20–28
Rabbit with Turnip, *#703*	$ 38–42
Rabbit with Wheelbarrow, *#728*	$ 40–50
Ram, *#515*	$ 30–35
Rocking Horse, *solid color, #526*	$ 28–35
Rooster, *#503*	$ 40–48
Shell, *conch, gold trim, #665*	$ 20–24
Shoe, *baby, right or left, each*	$ 14–18
Shoe, *elf, no gold trim, #765*	$ 14–18
Shoe, *elf, gold trim, #765*	$ 22–28
Shoe, *high-heeled*	$ 15–18
Shoes, *baby, on base*	$ 14–18
Skunk, *#512*	$ 40–50

Shawnee "Standing Horse" planter, pink glaze, $18–$22.
Item courtesy of Kingston Pike Antique Mall, Knoxville, Tennessee.

Squirrel, *#664*	$ 14–18
Squirrel, *gold trim, #664*	$ 25–32
Squirrel and Nut, *#713*	$ 40–50
Squirrel and Nut, *gold trim, #713*	$ 80–100
Stagecoach, *#J545P*	$ 40–45
Standing Horse	$ 18–22
Stove, *potbellied*	$ 35–40
Swan and Elf, *"Kenwood," #2030*	$ 60–70
Three Pigs	$ 16–20
Tractor and Trailer, *#680 and #681*	$ 40–45
Train, *Boxcar, #552*	$ 60–70
Train, *Caboose, #553*	$ 60–70
Train, *Coal Car, #551*	$ 60–70
Train Engine, *fully detailed*	$ 70–80
Train Engine, *#550*	$ 60–70

Trellis, *with three pots, #517*	$ 30–35
Water Trough, *with pump, #716*	$ 28–32
Watering Can, *basketweave, embossed iris*	$ 20–25
Watering Can, *smooth, embossed flower*	$ 35–40
Wheelbarrow, *wood-grained, #775*	$ 12–15
Wishing Well with Dutch Boy and Girl, *#710*	$ 32–38
World Globe, *#635*	$ 60–70

Vases

Basketweave, *#842*	$ 15–18
Bow Knot, *with gold trim, #819*	$ 30–35
Bud, *# 705*	$ 16–19
Bud, *with gold trim, #735*	$ 16–19
Bud, *Swan, #725*	$ 14–17
Bud, *#1125*	$ 18–22
Bud, *#1135*	$ 16–19
Bud, *leaf, 7$^1/2$ inches, with gold trim, #821*	$ 26–30
Burlap surface, *5 inches, #885*	$ 14–17
Cornucopia, *no gold trim,#835*	$ 12–15
Cornucopia, *gold trim, #835*	$ 18–22
Cornucopia, *#865*	$ 18–22
Dolphin, *pitcher shape, with gold trim, #828*	$ 50–60
Flowered, *with gold trim, #1225*	$ 30–35
Girl with Cornucopia or Boy with Cornucopia, *each*	$ 15–18
Hand, *8 inches*	$ 20–25
Leaves, *gold, #823*	$ 50–60
Leaves, *Philodendron, embossed, gold trim, #805*	$ 45–55
Moor's Head, *female, turban*	$ 65–75
Moor's Head, *male, turban*	$ 65–75
Pineapple, *no gold trim, #839*	$ 18–22
Pineapple, *gold trim, #839*	$ 26–30

Pouter Pigeons, *no gold trim, #829*	$ 20–25
Pouter Pigeons, *gold trim, #829*	$ 28–32
Swan, *no gold trim, #806*	$ 22–28
Swan, *with gold trim, #806*	$ 30–35
Tulip, *no gold trim, #1115*	$ 15–18
Tulip, *with gold trim, #1115*	$ 18–22

SHENANGO CHINA COMPANY/ SHENANGO POTTERY COMPANY

SHENANGO CHINA
NEW CASTLE, PA.

One of the many marks used by the *Shenango China Company.*

The Shenango China Company was founded in New Castle, Pennsylvania, in 1901. The first decade of the company's existence was very difficult, and it seemed doubtful that Shenango would survive past its infancy. A receiver was appointed, however, and the firm was reorganized and renamed the Shenango Pottery Company; its name was not changed back to the "Shenango China Company" until 1954.

The company began to prosper under new management in 1909, but it fell victim to a devastating flood in 1913. In spite of these trials, Shenango stayed in business making semi-porcelain dinnerware, toilet sets, and odd dishes. The company learned how to make true porcelain dinnerware in 1928, but the onset of the Great Depression curtailed its production until the mid-1930s.

In 1936, Shenango was approached to make fine china for the Theodore Haviland Company of Limoges, France. Reportedly, Shenango made porcelain marked "Haviland, New York" from 1936 to 1958, using the French company's porcelain formula, molds, and decals. (See the "Castleton China" section of this book for a discussion of how this division of Shenango made fine porcelain dinnerware under the auspices of the German Rosenthal Company.)

In 1979, Shenango became part of the Anchor Hocking Corporation.

"Blue Willow"

This is a standard willow pattern similar to those made by a number of different companies around the world. Shenango's version appears on semiporcelain bodies. Prices listed below are for the blue-and-white version, though Shenango also produced teal-and-white and pink-and-white willow patterns. The teal version is slightly less expensive than is indicated by the prices listed below, while the pink is slightly more expensive.

Bowl, *cereal, 6-inch diameter*	$ 20–25
Bowl, *individual fruit, 5-inch diameter*	$ 15–20
Bowl, *soup, 8-inch diameter*	$ 22–28
Creamer	$ 26–32
Cup and saucer	$ 32–40
Dish, *relish*	$ 38–44
Plate, *bread and butter*	$ 8–14
Plate, *dinner, 10-inch diameter*	$ 28–35
Plate, *grill, 10¹/₂ inches*	$ 32–38
Plate, *luncheon, 9-inch diameter*	$ 18–24
Plate, *salad, 7-inch diameter*	$ 15–20
Plate, *service, 11¹/₂-inch diameter*	$ 45–55
Platter, *oval, 11³/₄ inches*	$ 75–85
Sugar bowl, *open*	$ 42–50

"Centenary"

This pattern often confuses collectors, because it is a reissue of the "Centenary" pattern, first produced in 1938, that was used by the B&O Railroad. The rims of flatware pieces bearing this pattern feature representations of historic railroad engines, and the centers feature an image of the Thomas Viaduct.

Bowl, *individual fruit, oval, 5³/₄ inches*	$ 35–42
Bowl, *soup, 9-inch diameter*	$ 52–60
Butter pat	$ 25–30
Cup and saucer	$ 70–80
Plate, *bread and butter, 6¹/₂-inch diameter*	$ 25–32
Plate, *dinner, 10¹/₂-inch diameter*	$ 60–70

SOUTHERN POTTERIES

One of the marks used by *Southern Potteries* on its "Blue Ridge" dinnerware line.

Erwin, Tennessee, was the perfect location to build a pottery. The hills of upper East Tennessee and Western North Carolina held the natural resources needed to make both pottery and porcelain, and there was a local labor force eager for employment and a chance to better its standard of living. During World War I, the Carolina, Clinchfield and Ohio Railroad sold land to E. J. Owens and his son, Ted, to build a pottery. The railroad needed industry along its route so it could transport the freight associated with manufacturing, and a pottery could fulfill this need.

The pottery, which was originally named the "Clinchfield Pottery," opened in 1918 and produced fairly typical transfer-printed dinnerware. In 1920, the business was incorporated as "Southern Potteries." Unfortunately, the products the company produced were not a resounding success, and in 1922 the Owens family sold the business to Charles Foreman, who promptly revitalized its product line.

Foreman utilized the large pool of unemployed mountain women in the vicinity of Erwin to hand-paint designs on the company's dinnerware, instead of using the standard transfer prints favored by Clinchfield. These vibrantly colored, sometimes primitive designs offered an attractive alternative to the dinnerware that was available at the time, and Southern Potteries prospered.

"Blue Ridge" dinner plate in the "Waffle"
(or "Monticello") shape.

Southern Potteries "Blue Ridge"
dinnerware plate in "Autumn Apple"
pattern, $25–$35.
*Item courtesy of Kingston Pike Antique Mall,
Knoxville, Tennessee.*

Southern Potteries "Blue Ridge"
dinnerware plate in "Weathervane"
pattern, $45–$65.
*Item courtesy of Kingston Pike Antique Mall,
Knoxville, Tennessee.*

Southern Potteries "Blue Ridge" china
cake tray on "Maple Leaf" shape,
$85–$100.
*Item courtesy of Richard H. Crane, Knoxville,
Tennessee.*

The company's "hand-painted under the glaze" ware was sold under the trade name "Blue Ridge," and was most popular from the 1930s until the early 1950s. Much of this ware was sold by mass merchandisers such as Sears, Roebuck and Montgomery Ward, but the company also sold dinnerware (mainly "seconds") to small rural customers from the back of a pickup truck.

Though this number is a bit hard to comprehend, Southern Potteries hand-painted more than 300,000 items per week to keep up with demand during the peak of its production. World War II contributed to the company's success, because dinnerware imports from Japan and Germany were curtailed, and "Blue Ridge" dinnerware helped fill the gap left by the unavailability of imported products.

Southern Potteries "Blue Ridge" snack tray on "Martha" shape, "Rose of Sharon" pattern, $200–$225.
Item courtesy of Bill Brooker, Old School Antique Mall, Sylva, North Carolina.

Southern Potteries "Blue Ridge" 12½-inch platter, "Skyline" shape, "Nesting Birds" pattern, $50–$65.
Item courtesy of Bill Brooker, Old School Antique Mall, Sylva, North Carolina.

Southern Potteries "Blue Ridge" gravy boat, "Orchard Glory" pattern, $45–$60.
Item courtesy of Lillian Barber, Old School Antique Mall, Sylva, North Carolina.

Southern Potteries "Blue Ridge" dinnerware plate, 8¼ inches, "Candlewick" shape, "Ham N' Eggs" pattern, $90–$110.
Item courtesy of Needful Things, Hendersonville, North Carolina.

"Blue Ridge" dinnerware came in 12 basic shapes: "Astor," "Candlewick," "Clinchfield," "Colonial," "Palisades," "Piecrust," "Skyline," "Skyline Studioware," "Trailway," "Trellis," "Waffle," and "Woodcrest." Of these, the "Waffle" (also called "Monticello") and "Trellis" shapes are the rarest and most highly desired by collectors. Current collectors are somewhat less interested in "Palisades," "Piecrust," "Skyline," "Trailway," and "Woodcrest," because these shapes originated after 1948 and their painting is often not as attractive or as well done as that appearing on earlier shapes.

Toward the end of its operation, Southern Potteries modified the way it hand-painted its dinnerware. In the new method, stamps were used to apply a design outline onto the china body, and painters then simply colored the design the way a child would color the pictures in a coloring book with crayons. By the mid-1950s, Japanese and European pottery companies were once again operating at full strength, and this competition forced Southern Potteries to close its doors in January of 1957.

Dinnerware

"Chintz"

This is an elaborate floral pattern consisting of a profusion of posies and their stems strewn across the surface of the dinnerware pieces. The brown stems and green leaves seem to form a network that is dotted with blossoms in colors of red, pink, blue, and yellow (though all of these colors may not appear on all pieces). The centers of these flowers are often dark, but a yellow flower may be painted with a rich golden center that is almost red. This pattern appears largely on "Colonial" shapes.

Bowl, *vegetable, oval, 9¹/₂ inches*	$ 125–140
Bowl, *vegetable, round, 9¹/₂-inch diameter*	$ 115–125
Cup and saucer	$ 55–65
Dish, *leaf-shaped, celery, 10 inches*	$ 95–110
Gravy boat	$ 195–210
Pitcher, *"Milady," 40-ounce*	$ 195–210
Plate, *bread and butter, 6¹/₂-inch diameter*	$ 25–32
Plate, *chop, 11-inch diameter*	$ 185–200
Plate, *dinner, 10¹/₂-inch diameter*	$ 60–70
Plate, *luncheon, 9¹/₂-inch diameter*	$ 40–50
Plate, *salad, 7¹/₄-inch diameter*	$ 30–40
Platter, *oval, 13¹/₂ inches*	$ 135–150
Platter, *oval, 15¹/₂ inches*	$ 235–250
Sugar bowl, *open*	$ 95–110

"French Peasant"

This pattern is based on the famous French "Quimper" pieces, with the flatware items featuring the portrait of either a man or a woman dressed in Breton-style peasant attire, surrounded by a border of leaves and flowers. On "French Peasant" pieces, the male figure is holding a whip that is shaped somewhat like a capital "R," while the female figure wears a white cap and holds a flower. Large pieces of "French Peasant" may have both the man and the woman.

Southern Potteries "Blue Ridge" "Milady" pitcher,
"Chintz" pattern, $195–$210.
*Item courtesy of Bill Brooker, Old School Antique Mall,
Sylva, North Carolina.*

Different "Blue Ridge" lines feature many variations on this theme, including "Brittany" (which features similar male and female portraits with a border of stylized red leaves), "Lyonaise" (which has similar figures and a bright-yellow rim accented with black concentric rings), "Picardy" (decorated with a wide pink border around the rim and a European-looking couple in the center—he in a cloak with a feather in his cap, and she in a pink dress with a blue apron), and "Orleans" (which has the couple in the center with simple branches and leaves, and a wide multicolored border around the rim). Prices quoted below are for "French Peasant" pieces.

Bowl, *cereal, 7-inch diameter*	$ 50–60
Bowl, *individual fruit, 5^1/2-inch diameter*	$ 40–50
Bowl, *individual soup, 8-inch diameter*	$ 65–75
Bowl, *vegetable, oval, 9^1/2 inches*	$ 145–160
Chocolate pot	$ 500–550
Creamer	$ 95–110
Cup and saucer	$ 100–115
Gravy boat	$ 145–160

Southern Potteries "Blue Ridge" "French Peasant"
pattern plate, 9½-inch diameter, $60–$70.
*Item courtesy of Bill Brooker, Old School Antique Mall,
Sylva, North Carolina.*

Plate, *bread and butter, 6½-inch diameter*	$ 35–45
Plate, *chop, 11-inch diameter*	$ 225–250
Plate, *dinner, 10½-inch diameter*	$ 85–95
Plate, *luncheon, 9½-inch diameter*	$ 60–70
Platter, *oval, 15½ inches*	$ 300–325
Sugar, *open*	$ 135–150

"Chrysanthemum"

As its name suggests, this pattern usually features two large, stylized, full-blown chrysanthemum blossoms—one in red and the other in dark blue—with smaller, red-and-blue budlike flowers, and green leaves radiating from the entire arrangement.

Bowl, *individual fruit, 5½-inch diameter*	$ 15–22
Bowl, *vegetable, oval, 9½ inches*	$ 55–65
Bowl, *vegetable, round, covered*	$ 125–145

Southern Potteries "Blue Ridge" teapot, "Fruit Fantasy" pattern, $175–$225.
Item courtesy of Lillian Barber, Old School Antique Mall, Sylva, North Carolina.

Cup and saucer	$ 35–42
Plate, *bread and butter, 6¹/₂-inch diameter*	$ 10–15
Plate, *dinner, 10¹/₂-inch diameter*	$ 35–45
Plate, *luncheon, 9¹/₂-inch diameter*	$ 18–25
Plate, *salad, 8¹/₂-inch diameter*	$ 15–22
Platter, *oval, 11³/₄ inches*	$ 55–65
Platter, *oval, 14 inches*	$ 95–110
Sugar bowl, *with lid*	$ 50–60

"Fruit Fantasy"

This pattern features an arrangement of three different types of fruit: a bunch of grapes, a pear, and cherries. There is also an irregular green border around the edge of the flatware pieces, and around the rim or edges of the hollowware items.

Bowl, *cereal, 6-inch diameter*	$ 22–30
Bowl, *individual fruit, 5¹/₂-inch diameter*	$ 15–25

Bowl, *vegetable, round, 9¹/₂-inch diameter*	$ 75–85
Creamer	$ 50–60
Cup and saucer	$ 40–50
Plate, *bread and butter, 6¹/₂-inch diameter*	$ 12–18
Plate, *dinner, 10¹/₂-inch diameter*	$ 40–50
Plate, *luncheon, 9¹/₂-inch diameter*	$ 20–28
Plate, *salad, 8¹/₂-inch diameter*	$ 18–25
Plate, *snack, with cup, set*	$ 40–50
Platter, *oval, 11³/₄ inches*	$ 85–95
Teapot	$ 175–225

"Whirligig"

The major flower in this pattern looks something like a bow made for a package, or a child's pinwheel (or "whirligig"). It is bicolored—red and grayish blue—and the pattern is completed with red buds, green leaves, and usually an irregular green border.

Bowl, *cereal, 7¹/₄-inch diameter*	$ 12–18
Bowl, *individual fruit, 5¹/₂-inch diameter*	$ 12–18
Creamer	$ 30–40
Cup and saucer	$ 25–32
Plate, *dinner, 10¹/₂-inch diameter*	$ 22–30
Plate, *luncheon, 9¹/₂-inch diameter*	$ 18–25
Plate, *salad, 7¹/₂-inch diameter*	$ 12–18
Platter, *oval, 14 inches*	$ 80–90
Sugar bowl, *oversized, open*	$ 40–50

"Wild Cherry #3"

There are a number of variants on the "Wild Cherry" pattern, and this is one of the most interesting. The major elements of this design are large, bicolored leaves arranged either in twos or in threes. Typically these leaves are brown and green, with red cherries scattered either between them or above and below them. This pattern often appears on the "Piecrust" shape, and the edges of the flatware are accented with large splotches of color—usually dark green.

Bowl, *cereal, 7-inch diameter*	$ 15–22
Bowl, *individual fruit, 5^1/$_2$-inch diameter*	$ 12–18
Bowl, *individual soup, 8-inch diameter*	$ 15–25
Bowl, *vegetable, round, 9^1/$_2$-inch diameter*	$ 55–65
Creamer	$ 35–45
Cup and saucer	$ 25–32
Gravy boat	$ 65–75
Plate, *bread and butter, 6^1/$_2$-inch diameter*	$ 8–14
Plate, *dinner, 10^1/$_2$-inch diameter*	$ 22–30
Plate, *luncheon, 9^1/$_2$-inch diameter*	$ 15–22
Plate, *salad, square, 8 inches*	$ 15–22
Platter, *oval, 11^3/$_4$ inches*	$ 60–70
Sugar bowl, *with lid*	$ 45–55

"Wild Strawberry"

This pattern is very simple, but also very charming. Most pieces are painted with a single red strawberry surrounded by a triple-pointed leaf that is as large as, or larger than, the strawberry itself. Sometimes the surrounding design appears to be just one leaf, other times it appears to be three leaves. Larger flatware items may feature two strawberries.

Bowl, *cereal, 7-inch diameter*	$ 25–35
Bowl, *individual fruit, 5^1/$_2$-inch diameter*	$ 15–22
Bowl, *vegetable, oval, 9^1/$_2$ inches*	$ 50–60
Bowl, *vegetable, round, 9^1/$_2$-inch diameter*	$ 55–65
Creamer	$ 35–45
Cup and saucer	$ 30–40
Gravy boat	$ 75–85
Plate, *bread and butter, 6^1/$_2$-inch diameter*	$ 10–15
Plate, *chop, 11-inch diameter*	$ 75–85
Plate, *dinner, 10^1/$_2$-inch diameter*	$ 30–40
Plate, *luncheon, 9^1/$_2$-inch diameter*	$ 20–28
Plate, *salad, 8^1/$_2$-inch diameter*	$ 20–28
Platter, *oval, 13^1/$_2$ inches*	$ 75–85

Artist-Signed Plates and Character Jugs

Character Jugs

In the 1950s, Southern Potteries introduced four different character jugs in the style that is often associated with England's Royal Doulton. The four jugs were "Daniel Boone" (6 inches tall), "Paul Revere" (6^1/$_2$ inches tall), "Indian" (6^3/$_4$ inches tall), and "Pioneer Woman" (6^1/$_2$ inches tall). A miniature "Pioneer Woman" (4 inches tall) was also made, but these jugs are thought to have been made experimentally, and never went into larger-scale production. Pieces are often marked with the "Blue Ridge" pine tree mark, but not always. Many, but not all, pieces (except the "Indian" jug) were also incised with their names.

Copies of these jugs have been made, and it is important to remember that the originals were made from porcelain, while the copies are generally earthenware. In addition, the original character jugs had applied handles, while the copies have handles that were created in the mold. This means that the copies have holes on the interiors of the jugs where the handles join the bodies, while the originals are smooth.

Daniel Boone	$ 700–800
Indian	$ 675–750
Paul Revere	$ 625–675
Pioneer Woman, *large size*	$ 600–700

Artist-Signed Plates

The images of turkeys and quail found on these pieces are based on the work of John James Audubon.

Plate, *"Flower Cabin," 10^1/$_2$-inch diameter*	$ 450–550
Plate, *"Gold Cabin," 10^1/$_2$-inch diameter*	$ 450–550
Plate, *"Green Mill," 10^1/$_2$-inch diameter*	$ 450–550
Plate, *"Quail," 11^3/$_4$ inches*	$ 450–525
Plate, *"Tom Turkey"* (or *"Turkey Gobbler"*), *10^1/$_2$-inch diameter*	$ 750–850
Plate, *"White Mill," 10^1/$_2$-inch diameter*	$ 450–550
Platter, *"Tom Turkey," 17^1/$_2$ inches*	$ 1,500–1,650
Platter, *"Wild Turkey"* (or *"Turkey Hen"*), *17^1/$_2$ inches*	$ 1,700–1,850

Southern Potteries "Blue Ridge"
Christmas tree plate, 10¼-inch diameter,
$100–$125.
*Item courtesy of Kingston Pike Antique Mall,
Knoxville, Tennessee.*

Southern Potteries "Blue Ridge"
Thanksgiving turkey plate, $100–$125.
*Item courtesy of Bill Brooker, Old School
Antique Mall, Sylva, North Carolina.*

Southern Potteries "Blue Ridge" "Turkey
with Acorns" plate, $120–$140.
*Item courtesy of Bill Brooker, Old School
Antique Mall, Sylva, North Carolina.*

Southern Potteries "Blue Ridge" "Betsey"
pitcher, earthenware, $200–$225.
*Item courtesy of Bill Brooker, Old School
Antique Mall, Sylva, North Carolina.*

Children's Items

Southern Potteries' children's pieces are charming, and include such characters as "Lady Mouse" (a mouse in a big dress carrying a flower), "Playful Puppy," "Fruit Children" (pears, peaches, and cherries dressed up as children), "Duck in a Hat," and "Humpty-Dumpty." The company also produced some Disney-inspired pieces, particularly the "Three Little Pigs" pieces (which are typically marked "Three Little Pigs Walt E. Disney") and a "Mickey Mouse" set.

Child's cereal bowl, *6¼-inch diameter*	$ 150–200
Child's feeding dish, *divided, 6¾-inch diameter*	$ 200–250

Southern Potteries "Blue Ridge" boot-shaped vase, 5½ inches, $110–$125.
Item courtesy of Lillian Barber, Old School Antique Mall, Sylva, North Carolina.

Southern Potteries "Blue Ridge" two-handled vase, 8 inches, $135–$175.
Item courtesy of Lillian Barber, Old School Antique Mall, Sylva, North Carolina.

Southern Potteries "Blue Ridge" bookends, $250–$300.
Item courtesy of Bill Brooker, Old School Antique Mall, Sylva, North Carolina.

Child's mug, 2³/4 *inches*	$ 200–235
Child's plate	$ 165–200
Child's tea set, *complete*	$ 400–475

Holiday Items

These items are non-artist-signed, and feature both Christmas and Thanksgiving scenes.

Plate, *Christmas, "Christmas Tree"*	$ 100–125
Plate, *Christmas, "Christmas Doorway"*	$ 90–100
Plate, *"Thanksgiving Turkey"*	$ 100–125
Plate, *"Turkey with Acorns"*	$ 120–140
Platter, *oval, "Turkey,"* 15 inches	$ 300–350

STANFORD POTTERY

George Stanford had been the manager at Spaulding China in Sebring, Ohio, before he founded Stanford Pottery in the same city in 1945. The company made semiporcelain gift-wares for both National Silver and China and Glass Distributors. Its most collectible line is "Corn," which is very similar to the corn-shaped lines made by Shawnee. Pieces are generally marked "Stanford" or "Stanfordware." In 1961, a fire caused the company to close its doors.

"Corn"

Casserole, *individual, lidded*	$ 45–55
Cookie jar	$ 150–200
Creamer	$ 35–45
Dish, *relish, 9¹/₂ inches by 3¹/₄ inches*	$ 45–55
Drip jar	$ 65–80
Jug, *7¹/₂ inches*	$ 55–65
Plate, *party, oval, 9 inches*	$ 45–55
Shakers, *salt and pepper, set*	$ 65–75
Sugar bowl, *lidded*	$ 45–55
Teapot	$ 95–110
Tumbler, *4¹/₂ inches*	$ 55–65

STERLING CHINA COMPANY

One of the marks used by the *Sterling China Company* on its Russel Wright–designed dinnerware.

Organized in Wellsville, Ohio, in 1917, the Sterling China Company mainly produced dinnerware for institutional purposes. It began making vitreous hotel china such as bowls, mugs, and cups, and during World War I the company also produced a great deal of dinnerware for the United States military. It is still in business today, and might be relatively unknown to today's collectors if not for its brief association with Russel Wright in 1948 or 1949, which resulted in production of the well-known "Russel Wright" line.

"Russel Wright"

With this appealing line, Sterling may have been attempting to bridge the gap between dinnerware made for home use and dinnerware made for restaurants. Wright's main role in the production of this line was to design its shapes and select its colors. He did a brilliant job creating shapes that would be advantageous for restaurateurs, with innovations such as rolled rims for plates, which made the plates easy to grasp so they would not slip out of servers' hands. He also designed lids with recessed finger grips that allowed them to be easily—and securely—removed. In addition, the pieces were sturdy and practical, and were often designed to be used for more than one purpose.

The colors Wright chose for his designs were ones that he felt would look good with food: Ivy Green, Straw Yellow, Suede Gray, and Cedar Brown. Sterling expanded this color palette by producing Wright's shapes in standard white for the restaurant trade, and Shell Pink for the homeowner.

Wright's association with Sterling ended after just one year, but Sterling continued manufacturing the designs long after the great industrial designer had departed. Wright designed some decal decorations for this line, notably a pattern called "Polynesian," which featured images of palm trees and Hawaiian and Asian themes. These pieces were created for use in the Shun Lee Dynasty Restaurant in New York City, and are difficult to find. It was Sterling's art department, however, that created most of the decorations found on the "Russel Wright" shapes. These were produced to meet the needs of Sterling's commercial customers, and a wide variety of logos and other designs exist today. The Carnation Milk Company, for example, had pieces made for its restaurants that were emblazoned with—of course—carnations. Enthusiasts interested in collecting Sterling's "Russel Wright" dinnerware should be aware that not all pieces are marked, and large quantities do not bear the Sterling "Russel Wright" mark shown above, but instead feature a more generic "Sterling" backstamp. The rarest color in this line is Shell Pink, followed by Ivy Green, with "Polynesian" pieces also commanding high prices.

In general, decal-decorated pieces of Sterling's "Russel Wright" dinnerware are 20 to 25 percent less valuable than pieces that are undecorated. Advertising examples, however, may be more expensive, especially if they feature Western themes such as cowboys and covered wagons.

Ashtray, *common colors*	$ 75–85
Ashtray, *Ivy Green*	$ 100–120
Ashtray, *white*	$ 130–145
Bowl, *bouillon, common colors*	$ 22–26
Bowl, *individual fruit, 5 inches, common colors*	$ 12–15
Bowl, *individual soup, 6¹/₂ inches, common colors*	$ 20–25
Bowl, *rice, "Polynesian" pattern*	$ 65–80
Coffee bottle, *common colors*	$ 125–175
Coffee bottle, *Ivy Green*	$ 165–200
Coffeepot, *"Polynesian" pattern*	$ 265–285
Creamer, *individual, 1-ounce, common colors*	$ 10–15
Creamer, *individual, 1-ounce, Ivy Green*	$ 16–22
Creamer, *individual, 3-ounce, common colors*	$ 12–18

Creamer, *individual, 3-ounce, Ivy Green*	$ 20–25
Cup and saucer, *coffee or tea, common colors*	$ 20–25
Cup and saucer, *coffee or tea, Shell Pink*	$ 28–32
Cup and saucer, *demitasse, common colors*	$ 80–90
Cup and saucer, *demitasse, Ivy Green*	$ 110–125
Gravy/Sauce boat, *open handle, common colors*	$ 35–42
Jug, *ball-shaped, Straw Yellow, Suede Grey, or Cedar Brown*	$ 200–225
Jug, *ball-shaped, Ivy Green*	$ 275–300
Jug, *ball-shaped, Shell Pink*	$ 350–400
Jug, *water, original shape, 2-quart, common colors*	$ 160–180
Jug, *water, original shape, 2-quart, Ivy Green*	$ 175–200
Plate, *bread and butter, 6^1/$_4$-inch diameter, common colors*	$ 6–10
Plate, *bread and butter, 6^1/$_4$-inch diameter, Shell Pink*	$ 12–16
Plate, *dinner, 10^1/$_4$-inch diameter, common colors*	$ 18–22
Plate, *luncheon, 9-inch diameter, common colors*	$ 15–20
Plate, *salad, 7^1/$_2$-inch diameter, common colors*	$ 12–16
Plate, *salad, 7^1/$_2$-inch diameter, Ivy Green*	$ 14–18
Plate, *service, 11^1/$_2$-inch diameter, common colors*	$ 25–30
Platter, *oval, 7 inches, common colors*	$ 18–22
Platter, *oval, 7 inches, Ivy Green*	$ 24–28
Platter, *oval, 10^1/$_2$ inches, common colors*	$ 25–30
Platter, *oval, 11^3/$_4$ inches, common colors*	$ 25–30
Platter, *oval, 13^1/$_2$ inches, common colors*	$ 28–35
Platter, *oval, 13^1/$_2$ inches, Shell Pink*	$ 45–55
Relish, *four sections, oval, 16^1/$_2$ inches, common colors*	$ 100–125
Relish, *four sections, oval, 16^1/$_2$ inches, Ivy Green*	$ 140–160
Teapot, *10-ounce, common colors*	$ 130–145
Teapot, *10-ounce, Ivy Green*	$ 165–185
Teapot, *10-ounce, Shell Pink*	$ 120–240
Teapot, *10-ounce, white*	$ 175–200

STETSON CHINA COMPANY

One of the marks used by
the *Stetson China Company.*

Louis Stetson was an ambitious Polish immigrant. While working in his uncle's clothing store in Chicago, Illinois, Stetson learned that he could make money by buying undecorated china "blanks" (or "white ware"), decorating them with decals or hand-painting, and then reselling them. He made an arrangement with the Mt. Clemens Pottery Company of Mt. Clemens, Michigan, to produce these blanks for him. This venture proved successful, and Stetson brought in his nephew from Poland, who eventually took over the company after his uncle's death. Stetson also bought blanks from the Illinois China Company in Lincoln, Illinois, and in 1946 he purchased the company to assure himself a steady supply of china.

Stetson bought odd lots of decals to use on his dinnerware, and these decorations sometimes make Stetson's products look very much like wares made by other companies. For a time, Stetson discontinued the use of decals and began hand-painting designs in the style of "Blue Ridge" and Red Wing pieces. Many of Stetson's later wares were sold to jobbers, who in turn sold them to furniture stores, gas stations, and grocery stores to be used as premiums. Stetson closed in 1965 or 1966.

Stetson China Company hand-painted plate with cattail design, 9½-inch diameter, $20–$30.
Item courtesy of Needful Things, Hendersonville, North Carolina.

"Golden Empress"

This pattern was a favorite for use on store premiums, and is distinguished by its wide gold border with filigree accents. Various decals were used to decorate these pieces, but one of the most commonly found has the image of a lady and gentleman in 18th-century dress (the gentleman is holding a tricorn hat) dancing with a musician in the background. This decal can also be found on pieces made by several other companies.

Bowl, *individual fruit, 5¼-inch diameter*	$ 10–15
Bowl, *soup, 8-inch diameter*	$ 15–22
Creamer	$ 35–45
Cup and saucer	$ 20–28
Plate, *bread and butter, 6½-inch diameter*	$ 7–12
Plate, *dinner, 10-inch diameter*	$ 25–32
Plate, *luncheon, 9-inch diameter*	$ 15–22
Platter, *oval, 13½ inches*	$ 60–70

"Lady Evette"

This elegant pattern is distinguished by a brown border with gold filigree. The center of the flatware pieces may be either plain or decorated with a decal decoration of a grouping of flowers dominated by a large tulip.

Bowl, *cereal, 6-inch diameter*	$ 10–14
Bowl, *individual fruit, 5¼-inch diameter*	$ 8–12
Bowl, *soup, 8-inch diameter*	$ 12–17
Bowl, *vegetable, round, 8½-inch diameter*	$ 32–38
Creamer	$ 22–28
Cup and saucer	$ 17–22
Plate, *bread and butter, 6¼-inch diameter*	$ 4–7
Plate, *dinner, 10-inch diameter*	$ 15–20
Plate, *luncheon, 9-inch diameter*	$ 10–15
Platter, *oval, 9½ inches*	$ 30–36
Sugar bowl, *lidded*	$ 28–34

"Lady Marlowe" and "Duchess of Greencastle"

The decals found on the pieces in these two lines are very similar, as are the border treatments. "Lady Marlowe" pieces have wide burgundy borders, with a red rose in the center of the flatware items. "Duchess of Greencastle" pieces feature wide green borders surrounding floral centers that have been described as laurel blossoms, but which actually look more like white roses (on account of their leaves). Both patterns have black "V"-shaped accents between the border and the well. In general, "Lady Marlowe" pieces are a bit more expensive than "Duchess of Greencastle" pieces.

Bowl, *cereal, 6-inch diameter, "Lady Marlowe"*	$ 15–20
Bowl, *cereal, 6-inch diameter, "Duchess of Greencastle"*	$ 11–15
Bowl, *individual fruit, 5¼-inch diameter, "Lady Marlowe"*	$ 12–18
Bowl, *individual fruit, 5¼-inch diameter, "Duchess of Greencastle"*	$ 8–12
Bowl, *soup, 8-inch diameter, "Lady Marlowe"*	$ 15–20
Bowl, *soup, 8-inch diameter, "Duchess of Greencastle"*	$ 12–18
Bowl, *vegetable, round, 8¾-inch diameter, "Lady Marlowe"*	$ 45–55
Bowl, *vegetable, round, 8¾-inch diameter, "Duchess of Greencastle"*	$ 40–50

Creamer, *"Lady Marlowe"*	$ 30–38
Creamer, *"Duchess of Greencastle"*	$ 25–32
Cup and saucer, *"Lady Marlowe"*	$ 25–32
Cup and saucer, *"Duchess of Greencastle"*	$ 18–24
Plate, *bread and butter, 6¼-inch diameter, "Lady Marlowe"*	$ 7–10
Plate, *bread and butter, 6¼-inch diameter,* *"Duchess of Greencastle"*	$ 5–8
Plate, *dinner, 10-inch diameter, "Lady Marlowe"*	$ 25–32
Plate, *dinner, 10-inch diameter, "Duchess of Greencastle"*	$ 18–24
Platter, *oval, 13½ inches, "Lady Marlowe"*	$ 65–75
Platter, *oval, 13½ inches, "Duchess of Greencastle"*	$ 60–70
Sugar bowl, *lidded, "Lady Marlowe"*	$ 35–42
Sugar bowl, *lidded, "Duchess of Greencastle"*	$ 32–40

"Madam Du Barry"

This pattern consists of a wide, royal-blue band around the rims of the flatware items, accented with a floral filigree design. The center decoration is composed of one of two different decal designs: the tulip-dominated floral decal found in the center of Stetson's "Lady Evette" pieces, or a circular floral garland surrounding a central floral bouquet. "Madam Du Barry" pieces featuring the latter decal are priced at the top of the ranges listed below, while examples featuring the former design are priced at the lower end.

Bowl, *cereal, 5¾-inch diameter*	$ 11–20
Bowl, *individual fruit, 5-inch diameter*	$ 11–18
Bowl, *soup, 7¾-inch diameter*	$ 15–22
Creamer	$ 30–40
Cup and saucer	$ 22–32
Gravy boat	$ 45–60
Plate, *bread and butter, 6-inch diameter*	$ 6–10
Plate, *dinner, 10-inch diameter*	$ 19–30
Platter, *oval, 13½ inches*	$ 60–80
Shakers, *salt and pepper, set*	$ 30–40

STEUBENVILLE POTTERY COMPANY

MFG. BY STEUBENVILLE

One of the marks found on "American Modern" dinnerware, which was designed by Russel Wright.

Organized in Steubenville, Ohio, in 1879, Steubenville Pottery Company was immediately successful, and had seven firing and six glost kilns working by 1889. By the early 20th century, the company was producing dinnerware and sanitary wares in granite, semiporcelain, and true porcelain. Financial trouble struck Steubenville in the 1950s, however, and pieces bearing the ominous mark "Final Kiln" were produced in 1959.

This, however, is not where the story ends. The Steubenville name, equipment, and molds were purchased by the Barium Chemical Company and moved to Cannonsburg, Pennsylvania. The Steubenville items were then sold to the Cannonsburg Pottery Company, which had been founded by W. S. George in 1900. Cannonsburg began producing wares from the original molds, and marked them with the Steubenville name or with "The Steubenville Division Cannonsburg Pottery Co." Modern collectors are most interested in the Steubenville products made before 1959, the year in which the Steubenville Pottery Company closed.

"American Modern"

This extensive solid-color line was designed by Russel Wright and was made between 1939 and 1959. It is said that during this 20-year time period, Steubenville produced between 70 and 125 million pieces of dinnerware. "American Modern" is said to be the first mass-produced dinnerware created by an industrial designer, and in 1941 it was named the best ceramic design of the year by the American Designers' Institute.

Initially, pieces came in six colors: Seafoam Blue, Granite Gray, Chartreuse Curry, coral, Bean Brown, and white. Bean Brown was dropped during World War II. In 1950 or 1951, Black Chutney and Cedar Green were added to the lineup and Seafoam Blue was dropped. Other colors in this line include Steubenville Blue, Cantaloupe, and Glacier Blue, which is a powder blue flecked with a darker blue. The most sought-after colors are Bean Brown, Cantaloupe, Glacier Blue, Steubenville Blue, and white; the least desired colors are Granite Gray and coral.

"American Modern" dinnerware is subject to crazing, and pieces that have suffered this glaze degradation are greatly devalued. Decorated examples of "American Modern" do turn up, but they do not command premium prices.

Bean Brown

Bowl, *individual fruit, 6-inch diameter*	$ 16–22
Bowl, *soup, lug-handled, 6³/₄ inches*	$ 26–32
Bowl, *vegetable, oval, 10 inches*	$ 55–65
Casserole, *2-quart, lidded*	$ 85–95
Creamer	$ 24–30
Cup and saucer	$ 24–30
Cup and saucer, *demitasse*	$ 55–65
Dish, *celery*	$ 50–60
Gravy boat and underliner	$ 100–120
Plate, *bread and butter, 6-inch diameter*	$ 10–16
Plate, *chop, square, 12 inches*	$ 95–110
Plate, *dinner, 10-inch diameter*	$ 24–30
Plate, *salad, 8-inch diameter*	$ 32–40
Platter, *oval, 13¹/₂ inches*	$ 75–85
Sugar bowl, *lidded*	$ 48–55

Black Chutney

Bowl, *individual fruit, 6-inch diameter*	$ 18–24
Bowl, *vegetable, oval, 10 inches*	$ 32–38
Bowl, *vegetable, oval, divided, 13¹/₃ inches*	$ 115–125

Bowl, *soup, lug-handled, 6³/₄ inches*	$ 16–22
Casserole, *2-quart, covered*	$ 65–75
Creamer	$ 16–22
Cup and saucer	$ 12–16
Gravy boat and underliner	$ 55–65
Plate, *bread and butter, 6-inch diameter*	$ 6–10
Plate, *chop, square, 12 inches*	$ 60–70
Plate, *dinner, 10-inch diameter*	$ 18–24
Plate, *salad, 8-inch diameter*	$ 22–28
Platter, *oval, 13¹/₂ inches*	$ 45–55
Shakers, *salt and pepper, set*	$ 25–32
Sugar bowl, *lidded*	$ 32–40

Cantaloupe

Bowl, *individual fruit, 6-inch diameter*	$ 60–70
Creamer	$ 60–70
Cup and saucer	$ 32–40
Plate, *bread and butter, 6-inch diameter*	$ 14–20
Plate, *chop, square, 12 inches*	$ 225–250
Plate, *dinner, 10-inch diameter*	$ 42–50
Plate, *salad, 8-inch diameter*	$ 75–85
Sugar bowl, *lidded*	$ 70–80
Teapot	$ 550–625

Cedar Green

Bowl, *individual fruit, 6-inch diameter*	$ 20–28
Bowl, *vegetable, oval, 10 inches*	$ 36–44
Butter dish, *¹/₄-pound, covered*	$ 400–425
Creamer	$ 22–30
Cup, *coffee, covered*	$ 195–210
Cup and saucer	$ 16–20
Dish, *relish (or gravy boat underliner)*	$ 27–32

Gravy boat	$ 35–45
Plate, *bread and butter, 6-inch diameter*	$ 8–12
Plate, *dinner, 10-inch diameter*	$ 20–28
Plate, *salad, 8-inch diameter*	$ 28–34
Platter, *oval, 13^1/$_2$ inches*	$ 55–65
Sugar bowl, *lidded*	$ 32–40
Tumbler/Mug	$ 120–130

Chartreuse Curry

Bowl, *soup, lug-handled, 6^3/$_4$ inches*	$ 18–24
Bowl, *vegetable, oval, 10 inches*	$ 24–30
Bowl, *vegetable, round, covered*	$ 55–65
Casserole, *2-quart, covered*	$ 45–55
Coffeepot, *demitasse*	$ 95–110
Creamer	$ 18–24
Cup, *coffee, covered*	$ 145–155
Cup and saucer	$ 14–20
Cup and saucer, *demitasse*	$ 28–34
Dish, *celery*	$ 25–32
Gravy boat and underliner	$ 45–52
Plate, *bread and butter, 6-inch diameter*	$ 6–10
Plate, *chop, square, 12 inches*	$ 42–50
Plate, *dinner, 10-inch diameter*	$ 14–20
Plate, *salad, 8-inch diameter*	$ 18–24
Platter, *oval, 13^1/$_2$ inches*	$ 28–34
Shakers, *salt and pepper, set*	$ 22–28
Sugar bowl, *lidded*	$ 26–32
Tumbler/Mug	$ 85–95

Coral and Granite Gray

Baker, *round, 9-inch diameter*	$ 42–52
Bowl, *individual fruit, 6-inch diameter*	$ 13–18

Steubenville Pottery Company "American Modern" teapot, granite gray, $140–$160. *Item courtesy of Cindy and William Hall, Old School Antique Mall, Sylva, North Carolina.*

Steubenville Pottery Company "American Modern" gravy boat and underliner, coral, $45–$55. *Item courtesy of Cindy and William Hall, Old School Antique Mall, North Carolina.*

Steubenville Pottery Company "American Modern" pitcher, coral with decal decoration, $95–$110. *Item courtesy of Needful Things, Hendersonville, North Carolina.*

Bowl, *salad, serving, 11-inch diameter*	$ 22–30
Bowl, *vegetable, oval, 10 inches*	$ 20–26
Bowl, *vegetable, oval, divided, 13 inches*	$ 110–125
Bowl, *vegetable, round, covered*	$ 62–72
Casserole, *2-quart, covered*	$ 45–55
Coaster	$ 20–26
Coffeepot, *demitasse*	$ 135–155

Creamer	$ 11–16
Cup, *coffee, covered*	$ 195–210
Cup and saucer	$ 10–15
Cup and saucer, *demitasse*	$ 28–34
Dish, *celery*	$ 22–32
Gravy boat, *with underliner*	$ 45–55
Jug, *water, tall*	$ 95–110
Plate, *bread and butter, 6-inch diameter*	$ 5–9
Plate, *chop, square, 12 inches*	$ 40–52
Plate, *dinner, 10-inch diameter*	$ 11–17
Plate, *salad, 8-inch diameter*	$ 15–20
Platter, *oval, 13 inches*	$ 22–20
Shakers, *salt and pepper, set*	$ 20–28
Sugar bowl, *lidded*	$ 22–28
Teapot	$ 140–160
Tumbler/Mug	$ 95–110

Glacier Blue

Bowl, *individual fruit, lug-handled*	$ 35–45
Casserole, *2-quart, covered*	$ 145–155
Coffeepot, *demitasse*	$ 210–225
Creamer	$ 20–25
Cup and saucer	$ 30–38
Butter dish, *$^1/_4$-pound, covered*	$ 1,100–1,200
Jug, *tall, water*	$ 700–800
Plate, *bread and butter, 6-inch diameter*	$ 15–20
Plate, *chop, square, 12 inches*	$ 140–150
Plate, *dinner, 10-inch diameter*	$ 60–70
Plate, *salad, 8-inch diameter*	$ 55–65
Sugar bowl, *covered*	$ 55–65

Seafoam Blue

Bowl, *individual fruit, 6 inches, lug-handled*	$ 14–18
Bowl, *soup, lug-handled, 6³/₄ inches*	$ 18–22
Bowl, *vegetable, oval, 9³/₄ inches*	$ 32–40
Bowl, *vegetable, round, covered*	$ 100–110
Casserole, *round, covered, 2-quart*	$ 75–85
Creamer	$ 18–22
Cup and saucer	$ 15–19
Cup and saucer, *demitasse*	$ 32–38
Dish, *relish, rosette*	$ 235–245
Gravy boat and underliner	$ 55–65
Jug, *tall, water*	$ 120–130
Plate, *bread and butter, 6-inch diameter*	$ 8–12
Plate, *chop, square, 12 inches*	$ 55–65
Plate, *dinner, 10-inch diameter*	$ 18–22
Plate, *salad, 8-inch diameter*	$ 25–30
Platter, *oval, 13¹/₂ inches*	$ 45–52
Shakers, *salt and pepper, set*	$ 30–36
Sugar bowl, *covered*	$ 32–40
Teapot	$ 155–165

White

Bowl, *individual fruit, 6 inches*	$ 30–38
Bowl, *soup, lug-handled*	$ 38–45
Bowl, *vegetable, round, covered*	$ 145–155
Butter dish, *¹/₄-pound, covered*	$ 700–800
Coffeepot, *demitasse*	$ 225–235
Cup and saucer	$ 25–30
Dish, *celery*	$ 45–55
Gravy boat, *with underliner*	$ 95–110
Plate, *bread and butter, 6-inch diameter*	$ 12–15
Plate, *chop, square, 12 inches*	$ 75–85

Steubenville Pottery Company "Antique Adam" pattern chop plate, $40–$50.
Item courtesy of Richard H. Crane, Knoxville, Tennessee.

Plate, *dinner, 10-inch diameter*	$ 28–34
Plate, *salad, 8-inch diameter*	$ 32–40
Platter, *oval, 13¹/₂ inches*	$ 70–80
Sugar bowl, *covered*	$ 48–54

"Antique Adam"

This pattern is inspired by the work of English architect and designer James Adam (1728–1792), who is best known for his work in the neoclassical style. Pieces in this dinnerware line are distinguished by their embossed borders consisting of covered urns interlaced with garlands and leaves. The rims of the flatware pieces are also gadrooned. This pattern was introduced in 1932, and the creamy-white examples with no decoration look very much like an English pattern that might have been made by a company such as Wedgwood. Steubenville did make decorated "Antique Adam" pieces with a number of different floral decals, but the prices listed below are for the creamy-white examples.

Bowl, *cream soup, with underliner*	$ 14–18
Bowl, *individual fruit, 5¹/₂-inch diameter*	$ 10–14

Bowl, *soup, 8¹/₂-inch diameter*	$ 10–14
Bowl, *vegetable, oval, 9 inches*	$ 25–32
Bowl, *vegetable, oval, 10 inches*	$ 35–45
Bowl, *vegetable, round, 8³/₄-inch diameter*	$ 22–28
Bowl, *vegetable, round, covered*	$ 65–75
Coffeepot	$ 75–85
Creamer	$ 15–20
Cup and saucer, *regular coffee or tea*	$ 12–15
Cup and saucer, *bouillon*	$ 14–18
Cup and saucer, *demitasse*	$ 7–10
Gravy boat, *faststand*	$ 50–60
Plate, *chop, 14-inch diameter*	$ 35–45
Plate, *dinner, 10¹/₂-inch diameter*	$ 18–24
Plate, *luncheon, 9-inch diameter*	$ 9–13
Plate, *salad, square, 7³/₄ inches*	$ 10–14
Platter, *oval, 11 inches*	$ 25–32
Platter, *oval, 12³/₄ inches*	$ 35–45
Platter, *oval, 14¹/₂ inches*	$ 42–50
Sugar bowl, *lidded*	$ 28–34

"Betty Pepper"

Introduced in 1939, this line was made for the member department stores of the Associated Merchandising Corporation, which included Bloomingdale's in New York City and Hudson's in Detroit, Michigan. These were plain shapes decorated with a variety of decals that were mainly floral in nature. These pieces were marked with the signature "Betty Pepper" and the "A.M.C." logo.

Bowl, *vegetable, oval*	$ 25–35
Casserole	$ 50–65
Creamer	$ 12–16
Cup and saucer	$ 12–16
Gravy boat, *faststand*	$ 30–40
Plate, *bread and butter, 6¹/₄ inches*	$ 5–9

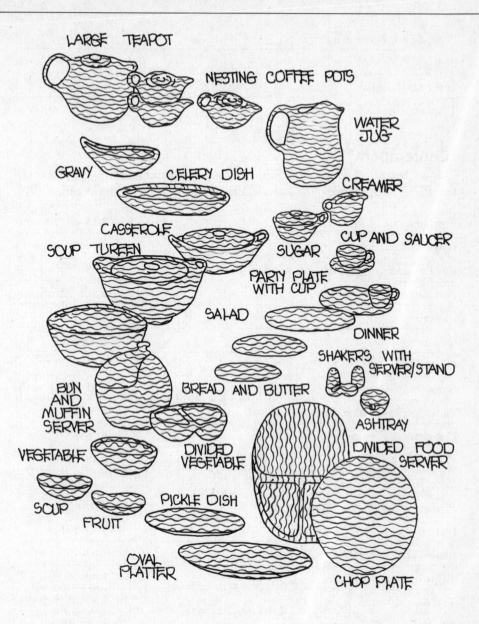

Shapes associated with Steubenville's "Contempora" dinnerware line.

Plate, *dinner, 9-inch diameter*	$ 15–20
Platter, *13¹/₂ inches*	$ 35–45
Sugar bowl, *lidded*	$ 22–30
Teapot, *2-cup*	$ 50–65

"Contempora"

This is a Ben Seibel design distinguished by modern shapes and a rippling glaze effect. Pieces were produced in Charcoal, Fawn, Mist Gray, and Sand White.

Bowl, *cereal, 6 inches*	$ 15–20
Bowl, *soup*	$ 7–10
Bowl, *vegetable, round, divided, 9 inches*	$ 65–75
Bun and muffin server	$ 275–325
Casserole	$ 90–100
Creamer	$ 30–38
Cup and saucer	$ 24–30
Gravy boat	$ 55–65
Plate, *bread and butter, 7 inches*	$ 8–12
Plate, *chop, 14¹/₄ inches*	$ 75–85
Plate, *dinner, 10¹/₂ inches*	$ 18–24
Plate, *party, 10¹/₂ inches*	$ 12–16
Platter, *divided, three-section, food server*	$ 90–100
Platter, *oval, 10¹/₂ inches*	$ 45–55
Platter, *oval, 14¹/₂ inches*	$ 60–70
Sugar bowl, *lidded*	$ 40–48
Teapot	$ 125–135
Tureen, *soup, covered*	$ 450–550

"Rosepoint"

This is the same "Rosepoint" pattern that was produced by Pope-Gosser. Steubenville bought the molds when Pope-Gosser went out of business in 1958, but closed just one year later in 1959, and thus did not actually produce many "Rosepoint" pieces of its own. Despite this fact, the prices for Steubenville's "Rosepoint" pieces are, in many cases, currently slightly lower than those for Pope-Gosser "Rose-point" pieces.

Bowl, *cereal, rim, 6¹/₂-inch diameter*	$ 14–18
Bowl, *individual fruit, 5³/₄-inch diameter*	$ 8–12
Bowl, *soup, 8-inch diameter*	$ 18–24
Bowl, *vegetable, oval, 9¹/₂ inches*	$ 25–32
Bowl, *vegetable, round, 8³/₄-inch diameter*	$ 32–38
Bowl, *vegetable, round, covered*	$ 95–105
Coffeepot	$ 125–135
Creamer	$ 18–24
Cup and saucer	$ 8–12
Plate, *bread and butter, 6¹/₂-inch diameter*	$ 4–7
Plate, *dinner, 10-inch diameter*	$ 15–20
Plate, *salad, 7¹/₂ inches*	$ 12–16
Plate, *snack with cup*	$ 18–22
Platter, *oval, 11 inches*	$ 35–42
Platter, *oval, 13¹/₄ inches*	$ 45–52
Sugar bowl, *lidded*	$ 30–38

"Shalimar"

This dinnerware is subtly decorated with a lightly embossed pattern of flowers, tendrils, and leaves against a solid-color background. Introduced in 1938, the design shows an Islamic influence, and was produced in colors of beige/ivory, blue/gray, and pink. Pieces are marked "Shalimar by Steubenville."

Bowl, *cereal, lug-handled, 7-inch diameter*	$ 15–20
Bowl, *individual fruit, 5¹/₂-inch diameter*	$ 11–15
Bowl, *vegetable, round, 10¹/₄-inch diameter*	$ 42–50
Creamer	$ 20–28
Coffeepot	$ 85–95
Cup and saucer	$ 28–35
Cup and saucer, *demitasse*	$ 15–20

Plate, *chop, 12-inch diameter*	$ 45–52
Plate, *salad, 8^1/$_2$-inch diameter*	$ 11–15
Sugar bowl, *lidded*	$ 40–50

"Woodfield"

This line is distinguished by its leaf-shaped plates and by the leaf pattern found on its hollowware items. "Woodfield" first appeared in 1941, and used many of the same glazes found on "American Modern" pieces, though the glazes were renamed. The first colors were Dove Gray, Golden Fawn (chartreuse), Jungle Green, and Salmon Pink. In 1951, Rust and Tropic Green were added to the palette. Rust is probably the most desired color in the line, followed by Jungle Green and Tropic Green. This line is known for its snack (or "party plate") sets. These cup-and-plate pairs came in two sizes; Steubenville called the smaller "Tea and Toast," and the larger "Video Set."

Ashtray, *4^1/$_2$ inches*	$ 8–14
Bowl, *vegetable, oval, 10^1/$_2$ inches*	$ 35–45
Bowl, *salad, serving, round, 11-inch diameter*	$ 45–55
Creamer	$ 25–35
Cup and saucer	$ 18–28
Dish, *relish, two-part*	$ 22–30
Gravy boat and underliner	$ 75–85
Plate, *bread and butter, 6^3/$_4$ inches*	$ 7–12
Plate, *chop, 13^1/$_2$ inches*	$ 55–65
Plate, *dinner, 10^1/$_2$ inches*	$ 22–32
Plate, *salad, 9 inches*	$ 10–15
Plate, *party, with cup, "Tea and Toast," 9 inches*	$ 17–26
Plate, *party, with cup, "Video Set," 11^1/$_2$ inches*	$ 20–30
Platter, *oval, 13^1/$_2$ inches*	$ 50–60
Shakers, *salt and pepper, set*	$ 27–35
Sugar bowl, *lidded*	$ 35–45
Teapot	$ 95–105

SYRACUSE CHINA COMPANY

One of the marks used by the *Syracuse China Company.*

The Syracuse China Company traces its origins to 1841, when W. H. Farrah opened a small pottery to make utilitarian Rockingham-glazed pottery and some animal figures. This operation became the Empire Pottery in 1855, and the Onondaga Pottery in 1871. "Syracuse China" was first used as a trade name in 1879, but did not become the official name of the company until 1966.

Initially, the dinnerware made by Onondaga was white graniteware marked with a representation of the coat of arms of the state of New York. The company introduced a semivitreous ware in 1885, and in 1888 began making true porcelain dinnerware called "Imperial Geddo."

In 1970, Syracuse ceased production of china for home use, and began focusing on production of fine china for institutional use by hotels, airlines, and restaurants.

"Bracelet"

Introduced in 1941, this pattern features an elaborate gold-encrusted border. Pieces were made in Old Ivory using Syracuse's "Virginia" shape. The line was discontinued in 1970.

Syracuse "Old Ivory" bread and butter plate decorated
with blue berries, 6½ inches, $15–$20.
Item courtesy of Richard H. Crane, Knoxville, Tennessee.

Bowl, *cereal, 6¹/₄-inch diameter*	$ 30–40
Bowl, *cream soup, with underliner*	$ 30–38
Bowl, *individual fruit, 5-inch diameter*	$ 14–18
Bowl, *soup, 8³/₄-inch diameter*	$ 45–55
Bowl, *vegetable, oval, 10¹/₂ inches*	$ 85–95
Bowl, *vegetable, round, 9-inch diameter*	$ 105–120
Bowl, *vegetable, round, covered*	$ 195–210
Creamer	$ 42–50
Cup and saucer, *bouillon*	$ 26–34
Cup and saucer, *demitasse*	$ 22–28
Cup and saucer, *regular*	$ 32–36
Gravy boat, *faststand*	$ 120–135
Plate, *bread and butter, 6¹/₄-inch diameter*	$ 12–16
Plate, *chop, 12-inch diameter*	$ 135–150
Plate, *dinner, 9³/₄ inches*	$ 35–42

Plate, *dinner or service, 10¹/₂ inches*	$ 55–65
Plate, *luncheon, 9-inch diameter*	$ 20–27
Plate, *salad, 8-inch diameter*	$ 22–28
Platter, *oval, 12¹/₄ inches*	$ 75–85
Platter, *oval, 14 inches*	$ 100–110
Platter, *oval, 16 inches*	$ 175–190
Sugar bowl, *lidded*	$ 55–65

"Briarcliff"

This pattern was introduced in 1938 and discontinued in 1969. It is distinguished by a scattering of floral sprays surrounding a slender, circular floral wreath. Pieces were created using Syracuse's "Federal" shape.

Bowl, *cereal, 5¹/₂-inch diameter*	$ 28–34
Bowl, *cream soup, with saucer*	$ 32–40
Bowl, *individual fruit, 5-inch diameter*	$ 14–18
Bowl, *soup, 8-inch diameter*	$ 23–30
Bowl, *vegetable, oval, 9¹/₄ inches*	$ 45–55
Bowl, *vegetable, oval, 10-inch diameter*	$ 55–65
Bowl, *vegetable, round, 9-inch diameter*	$ 75–85
Bowl, *vegetable, round, covered*	$ 115–125
Coffeepot	$ 275–300
Creamer	$ 30–36
Cup and saucer	$ 30–35
Gravy boat, *faststand*	$ 75–85
Plate, *bread and butter, 6¹/₂-inch diameter*	$ 8–12
Plate, *chop, 13-inch diameter*	$ 95–110
Plate, *dinner, both 10-inch and 10¹/₂-inch diameter sizes*	$ 28–34
Plate, *luncheon, 9-inch diameter*	$ 20–26
Plate, *salad, 8-inch diameter*	$ 17–22
Platter, *oval, 12 inches*	$ 45–55
Platter, *oval, 14 inches*	$ 50–60

Platter, *oval, 16 inches*	$ 85–95
Sugar bowl, *lidded*	$ 46–54

"Celeste"

This pattern, which features blue leaves scattered around the rims of the flatware pieces, was made between 1954 and 1969.

Bowl, *individual fruit, 5-inch diameter*	$ 15–22
Bowl, *vegetable, oval, 10 inches*	$ 85–95
Bowl, *vegetable, round, 8¹/₂-inch diameter*	$ 85–95
Creamer	$ 32–40
Cup and saucer	$ 25–35
Gravy boat, *faststand*	$ 115–125
Plate, *bread and butter, 6¹/₂-inch diameter*	$ 8–12
Plate, *dinner, 10¹/₄-inch diameter*	$ 22–30
Plate, *salad, 8-inch diameter*	$ 10–15
Platter, *oval, 12 inches*	$ 55–65
Platter, *oval, 14 inches*	$ 65–75
Platter, *oval, 16 inches*	$ 155–170
Sugar bowl, *lidded*	$ 42–50

"Meadow Breeze"

Pieces bearing this pattern were made from 1955 to 1970 using Syracuse's "Carolina" shape. The rims of flatware items are blue/green, and the centers feature stylized arrangements of flowers and tendrils.

Bowl, *cereal, lug-handled, 6-inch diameter*	$ 35–45
Bowl, *individual fruit, 5-inch diameter*	$ 30–36
Bowl, *soup, 8³/₄-inch diameter*	$ 55–65
Bowl, *vegetable, oval, 10 inches*	$ 95–110
Bowl, *vegetable, round, 8¹/₂-inch diameter*	$ 115–125
Creamer	$ 55–65
Cup and saucer	$ 28–34
Plate, *bread and butter, 6¹/₂-inch diameter*	$ 8–12

Plate, *dinner, 10³/₄-inch diameter*	$ 22–30
Plate, *salad, 8-inch diameter*	$ 10–15
Platter, *oval, 12-inch diameter*	$ 115–125
Platter, *oval, 14 inches*	$ 120–135
Platter, *oval, 16 inches*	$ 185–200
Sugar bowl, *lidded*	$ 65–75

"Minuet"

This pattern was made between 1955 and 1970. The rims of the flatware pieces feature garlands of white leaves and dark stems on a blue background. "Minuet" pieces were made using Syracuse's "Carolina" shape.

Bowl, *individual fruit, 5-inch diameter*	$ 32–40
Bowl, *soup, 7¹/₂-inch or 8³/₄-inch diameter*	$ 65–75
Bowl, *vegetable, oval, 10 inches*	$ 95–110
Bowl, *vegetable, round, 8¹/₂-inch diameter*	$ 115–125
Creamer	$ 35–45
Cup and saucer	$ 28–34
Gravy boat, *faststand*	$ 135–150
Plate, *bread and butter, 6¹/₂-inch diameter*	$ 12–16
Plate, *dinner, 10¹/₄-inch or 10³/₄-inch diameter*	$ 38–45
Plate, *salad, 8-inch diameter*	$ 22–28
Platter, *oval, 12 inches*	$ 95–105
Platter, *oval, 14 inches*	$ 100–110
Platter, *oval, 16 inches*	$ 155–170
Sugar bowl, *lidded*	$ 55–65

"Monticello"

This simple pattern has a wide gold rim around the edges of flatware pieces, with a narrower band just inside, and another narrow gold band around the verge. It is part of Syracuse's "Old Ivory" line.

Bowl, *cereal, 6¹/₄-inch diameter*	$ 20–25
Bowl, *cream soup, with saucer*	$ 25–35

Bowl, *individual fruit, 5-inch diameter*	$ 18–22
Bowl, *soup, 7¹/₂-inch diameter*	$ 22–28
Bowl, *vegetable, oval, 10 inches*	$ 75–85
Bowl, *vegetable, round, covered*	$ 135–150
Creamer	$ 32–40
Cup and saucer	$ 34–40
Cup and saucer, *bouillon*	$ 45–52
Cup and saucer, *demitasse*	$ 30–36
Gravy boat, *faststand*	$ 115–125
Plate, *bread and butter, 6¹/₂-inch diameter*	$ 8–12
Plate, *dinner, 9³/₄-inch diameter*	$ 26–32
Plate, *dinner, large, 10¹/₂-inch diameter*	$ 28–34
Plate, *salad, 8-inch diameter*	$ 18–22
Platter, *oval, 12 inches*	$ 65–75
Platter, *oval, 14 inches*	$ 75–85
Sugar bowl, *lidded*	$ 45–55

"Old Cathay"

This line was Syracuse's version of the numerous "Blue Willow" wares produced by other companies. Pieces were made using the company's "Carefree" shapes. Flatware pieces feature a willow pattern in the center, with blue bands around the rim.

Bowl, *vegetable, round, 8-inch diameter*	$ 35–45
Creamer	$ 23–30
Cup and saucer	$ 14–20
Gravy boat, *faststand*	$ 60–70
Plate, *bread and butter, 6¹/₂-inch diameter*	$ 16–22
Plate, *dinner, 10-inch diameter*	$ 22–28
Plate, *salad, 8-inch diameter*	$ 18–24
Sugar bowl, *lidded*	$ 28–35

"Sherwood"

Flatware pieces bearing this pattern feature a ring of leaves and berries on their rims, with a gold band on the rim and verge. Pieces were made using Syracuse's "Virginia" shape, and were manufactured between 1940 and 1970.

Bowl, *cereal, 6¹/₄ inches*	$ 27–35
Bowl, *cream soup, with saucer*	$ 28–34
Bowl, *individual fruit, 5-inch diameter*	$ 12–16
Bowl, *soup, 8³/₄-inch diameter*	$ 20–25
Bowl, *vegetable, oval, 10¹/₂ inches*	$ 65–75
Bowl, *vegetable, round, 9-inch diameter*	$ 75–85
Bowl, *vegetable, round, covered*	$ 115–125
Coffeepot	$ 200–220
Creamer	$ 28–35
Cup and saucer	$ 32–40
Cup and saucer, *bouillon*	$ 28–34
Cup and saucer, *demitasse*	$ 23–28
Dish, *relish*	$ 42–50
Gravy boat, *faststand*	$ 65–75
Plate, *bread and butter, 6¹/₂-inch diameter*	$ 10–15
Plate, *chop, 12-inch diameter*	$ 135–150
Plate, *dinner, 9³/₄-inch diameter*	$ 18–25
Plate, *salad, 8-inch diameter*	$ 16–22
Platter, *oval, 12 inches*	$ 40–50
Platter, *oval, 14 inches*	$ 65–75
Platter, *oval, 16 inches*	$ 115–125
Sugar bowl, *lidded*	$ 32–40

"Stansbury"

Pieces bearing this pattern were made between 1938 and 1969 using Syracuse's "Federal" shape. This is said to be an old Haviland design, and it features lavish scatterings of flowers and leaves in shades of pink, green, and gray.

Bowl, *individual fruit, 5-inch diameter*	$ 10–15
Bowl, *vegetable, oval, 9^1/$_4$ inches*	$ 55–65
Bowl, *vegetable, oval, 10^1/$_2$ inches*	$ 55–65
Bowl, *vegetable, round, 9-inch diameter*	$ 85–95
Creamer	$ 32–40
Cup and saucer	$ 27–32
Cup and saucer, *demitasse*	$ 35–45
Gravy boat, *faststand*	$ 85–95
Plate, *bread and butter, 6^1/$_2$-inch diameter*	$ 10–15
Plate, *chop, 13-inch diameter*	$ 125–140
Plate, *dinner, 10-inch diameter*	$ 25–30
Plate, *dinner, large, 10^1/$_2$-inch diameter*	$ 27–32
Plate, *luncheon, 9-inch diameter*	$ 22–28
Plate, *salad, 8-inch diameter*	$ 14–20
Platter, *oval, 12 inches*	$ 42–48
Platter, *oval, 14 inches*	$ 65–75
Platter, *oval, 16 inches*	$ 115–125
Sugar bowl, *lidded*	$ 35–45
Teapot	$ 300–320

"Suzanne"

Found on pieces made using Syracuse's "Federal" shape, this pattern consists of small pink, blue, and yellow flowers scattered around the rims of flatware pieces, with a gold line around the verge and a plain center. This pattern was in production between 1938 and 1970.

Bowl, *cereal, 5^1/$_2$-inch diameter*	$ 28–34
Bowl, *cream soup, with saucer*	$ 35–42
Bowl, *individual fruit, 5-inch diameter*	$ 12–16

Bowl, *soup, 8-inch diameter*	$ 28–34
Bowl, *vegetable, oval, 10¹/₂ inches*	$ 45–55
Bowl, *vegetable, round, 9-inch diameter*	$ 85–95
Bowl, *vegetable, round, covered*	$ 150–170
Creamer	$ 38–44
Cup and saucer	$ 32–40
Cup and saucer, *demitasse*	$ 32–40
Gravy boat, *faststand*	$ 75–85
Plate, *bread and butter, 6¹/₂-inch diameter*	$ 10–14
Plate, *dinner, 10-inch diameter*	$ 32–40
Plate, *luncheon, 9-inch diameter*	$ 22–30
Plate, *salad, 8-inch diameter*	$ 20–28
Platter, *oval, 12 inches*	$ 40–50
Platter, *oval, 14 inches*	$ 55–65
Platter, *oval, 16 inches*	$ 95–110
Sugar bowl, *lidded*	$ 48–55

"Sweetheart"

This Syracuse pattern is found on "Silhouette" shapes that feature fluting around the rims of the flatware pieces. The pattern itself is a simple ring around the verge of small roses with leaves and tendrils. "Sweetheart" was introduced in 1960 and discontinued in 1970.

Bowl, *vegetable, oval, 10 inches*	$ 95–110
Creamer	$ 42–50
Cup and saucer	$ 38–45
Gravy boat, *faststand*	$ 185–200
Plate, *bread and butter, 6¹/₂-inch diameter*	$ 12–16
Plate, *dinner, 10¹/₂-inch diameter*	$ 38–45
Plate, *salad, 8-inch diameter*	$ 15–22
Platter, *oval, 14 inches*	$ 115–125
Platter, *oval, 16 inches*	$ 190–210
Sugar bowl, *lidded*	$ 50–60

"Victorian"

This pattern is distinguished by the large rose and leaves located in the center of the flatware pieces. There are also smaller depictions of roses spaced regularly around the rim of each piece, and a narrow gold band around the verge. Pieces were made between 1939 and 1970 on Syracuse's "Old Ivory" shapes.

Bowl, *cream soup, with saucer*	$ 45–55
Bowl, *individual fruit, 5-inch diameter*	$ 12–16
Bowl, *soup, 8-inch diameter*	$ 28–35
Bowl, *vegetable, oval, 9 inches*	$ 70–80
Bowl, *vegetable, oval, 10½ inches*	$ 60–70
Bowl, *vegetable, round, covered*	$ 140–160
Coffeepot	$ 275–300
Creamer	$ 38–45
Cup and saucer	$ 32–38
Cup and saucer, *demitasse*	$ 35–45
Gravy boat, *faststand*	$ 115–125
Plate, *bread and butter, 6½-inch diameter*	$ 10–15
Plate, *dinner, 10-inch diameter*	$ 28–34
Plate, *dinner, large, 10½-inch diameter*	$ 32–40
Plate, *luncheon, 9-inch diameter*	$ 23–28
Plate, *salad, 8-inch diameter*	$ 17–22
Platter, *oval, 12 inches*	$ 55–65
Platter, *oval, 14 inches*	$ 70–80
Platter, *oval, 16 inches*	$ 115–125
Sugar bowl, *lidded*	$ 48–55

"Wayside"

This charming and unusual line was in production for a relatively short time, between 1962 and 1970. Pieces were made using Syracuse's "Carefree" shape, and are decorated with a bold pattern of fruit (apple, pear, grapes) and leaves.

Bowl, *soup, 6¾-inch diameter*	$ 40–50
Bowl, *vegetable, oval, divided, 10 inches*	$ 45–55

Bowl, *vegetable, round, 8-inch diameter*	$ 45–55
Bowl, *vegetable, round, 9¹/₂-inch diameter*	$ 55–65
Butter dish, *¹/₄-pound, covered*	$ 50–60
Coffeepot	$ 85–95
Creamer	$ 30–38
Cup and saucer	$ 15–20
Dish, *celery*	$ 40–48
Gravy boat, *faststand*	$ 55–65
Mug	$ 45–55
Pitcher, *32-ounce*	$ 65–75
Plate, *bread and butter, 6¹/₂-inch diameter*	$ 15–20
Plate, *dinner, 10-inch diameter*	$ 18–22
Plate, *salad, 8-inch diameter*	$ 18–22
Platter, *oval, 11¹/₂ inches*	$ 25–35
Platter, *oval, 12¹/₂ inches*	$ 45–55
Shakers, *salt and pepper, set*	$ 35–45
Sugar bowl, *lidded*	$ 38–45

TAMAC POTTERY

This pottery was founded in 1946 in Perry, Oklahoma, by Leonard and Marjorie Tate and Allen and Betty Macauley. The name of the company was derived from the first two letters of the Tates' last name ("TA") and the first three letters of the Macauleys' last name ("MAC"). Initially the pottery was located behind Leonard Macauley's father's garage, but in 1949 a new factory was built, which became something of a tourist attraction. The Macauleys sold their interest in the business to the Tates, but the Tates went bankrupt in 1952. The company then changed hands twice before going out of business in 1972.

Tamac's most collectible products are pieces from a free-form dinnerware line that featured unusual glazes, including "Butterscotch" (yellow with brown trim around the edges), "Avocado" (yellow-green with darker green around the edges), "Frosty Pine" (pine green with a foamy white trim), "Frosty Fudge" (soft brown with a foamy white trim), and "Raspberry" (pink with a foamy white trim). Of these, "Raspberry" is by far the rarest. Prices listed below are for colors other than "Raspberry."

Dinnerware

Ashtray	$ 8–12
Bowl, *cereal or soup*	$ 12–17
Bowl, *individual fruit, 5¹/₄ inches*	$ 10–15
Bowl, *salad, serving, 13 inches*	$ 65–75
Bowl, *vegetable, oval, 8 inches*	$ 35–42
Candlestick	$ 18–25
Creamer	$ 25–35
Cup, *barbeque, 10-ounce*	$ 14–20
Cup and saucer	$ 15–27
Decanter with stopper	$ 110–125
Goblet, *6-ounce*	$ 18–24
Gravy boat, *faststand*	$ 35–45
Plate, *barbecue, 15 inches*	$ 25–35
Plate, *bread and butter, 7 inches*	$ 7–12
Plate, *chop, 18 inches*	$ 50–60
Plate, *dinner, 10 inches*	$ 18–24
Plate, *luncheon, 9 inches*	$ 14–20
Plate, *salad, 8¹/₄ inches*	$ 10–14
Platter, *oval, 12 inches*	$ 45–55
Shakers, *salt and pepper, set*	$ 25–35
Sugar bowl, *lidded*	$ 38–45

TAYLOR, SMITH AND TAYLOR

One of the marks used by *Taylor, Smith and Taylor* on its "Lu-Ray Pastels" dinnerware line.

There is some disagreement about the origins of this company, which had manufacturing facilities in Chester, West Virginia, and offices across the Ohio River in East Liverpool, Ohio. However, the most reliable sources maintain that William Smith, Charles Smith, John Taylor, W. L. Taylor, Homer Taylor, and Joseph Lee founded this enterprise in 1899 as Taylor, Lee and Smith. Shortly thereafter, the Taylors bought out Joseph Lee, and the company became Taylor, Smith and Taylor. Sometime between 1903 and 1906 (depending on the source consulted), the Smiths bought out the Taylors. The Smiths ran Taylor, Smith and Taylor until 1972, when the company was sold to Anchor Hocking. Anchor Hocking operated the company until it closed in 1981.

The Taylor, Smith and Taylor factory went into operation in 1900 making white graniteware and semiporcelain dinnerware, kitchenware, toilet wares, and specialty items. Some Taylor, Smith and Taylor items are dated, but the company stopped dating its items in the 1950s. Under the various company marks, pieces often feature a grouping of three numbers. The first two numbers in these groupings indicate the piece's date of manufacture; thus, in the example "11 39 2," the date of manufacture would be November of 1939. The third number in the series indicates the work team that was responsible for making the piece.

Taylor, Smith and Taylor's "Lu-Ray Pastels," Persian
Cream 10-inch diameter dinner plate, $38–$48; Windsor
Blue individual fruit bowl, $5–$9; and Sharon Pink bread
and butter plate, $3–$6.
Items courtesy of Jane Roney, Knoxville, Tennessee.

"Lu-Ray Pastels"

This line was named for Virginia's famous Luray Caverns, and was introduced in 1938. It can be found on two Taylor, Smith and Taylor shapes: "Empire," which is a simple round shape with budlike finials on lidded pieces, and "Laurel," which is a thin-edged shape. Initially, "Lu-Ray Pastels" came in shades called Windsor Blue, Persian Cream (yellow), Surf Green, and Sharon Pink. Chatham Gray was added in 1948, and today is the hardest-to-find and most valuable color. Most examples of "Lu-Ray Pastels" are solid-colored, but pieces decorated with decals were also produced. Collectors might also find pieces marked "Coral-Craft," which are "Lu-Ray Pastels" pieces with simple white decorations in patterns called "Maple Leaf," "Tulip," "Floral Border," "Laurel Wreath," and "Chinese Temple." Prices for "Coral-Craft" pieces are comparable to those for "Lu-Ray Pastels" pieces.

Chatham Gray

Bowl, *individual fruit, 5-inch diameter*	$ 27–35
Bowl, *soup, lug-handled, 7-inch diameter*	$ 60–68
Bowl, *vegetable, oval, 10½ inches*	$ 85–95
Creamer	$ 75–85

Cup and saucer	$ 48–55
Plate, *bread and butter, 6¼-inch diameter*	$ 20–28
Plate, *dessert, 7½-inch diameter*	$ 22–30
Plate, *dinner, 10-inch diameter*	$ 75–85
Plate, *luncheon, 9¼-inch diameter*	$ 35–45
Plate, *salad, 8½-inch diameter*	$ 45–55
Platter, *oval, 11½ inches*	$ 65–75
Platter, *oval, 13½ inches*	$ 75–85
Shakers, *salt and pepper, set*	$ 100–120

Other Colors

Bowl, *cream soup, with saucer*	$ 125–160
Bowl, *individual fruit, 5-inch diameter*	$ 5–9
Bowl, *mixing, 5½-inch diameter*	$ 200–250
Bowl, *mixing, 10-inch diameter*	$ 295–320
Bowl, *salad, serving, 10-inch diameter*	$ 75–85
Bowl, *soup, lug-handled*	$ 25–32
Bowl, *36s, 4¾-inch diameter*	$ 55–70
Bowl, *vegetable, oval, 10 inches*	$ 22–28
Bowl, *vegetable, round, 9-inch diameter*	$ 28–35
Butter dish, *¼-pound, covered*	$ 135–150
Casserole, *8 inches*	$ 125–145
Cup and saucer	$ 10–15
Cup and saucer, *demitasse*	$ 40–50
Egg cup	$ 45–55
Epergne	$ 325–360
Gravy boat, *faststand*	$ 35–45
Jug, *juice, 38-ounce*	$ 215–240
Jug, *water, 76-ounce, flat*	$ 250–265
Jug, *water, 76-ounce, footed*	$ 115–125
Plate, *bread and butter, 6¼-inch diameter*	$ 3–6

Plate, *chop, 14-inch diameter*	$ 35–45
Plate, *dessert, 7¹/₂-inch diameter*	$ 11–17
Plate, *dinner, 10-inch diameter*	$ 38–48
Plate, *grill, 10-inch diameter*	$ 35–45
Plate, *luncheon, 9¹/₄-inch diameter*	$ 11–17
Plate, *salad, 8¹/₂-inch diameter*	$ 25–32
Platter, *oval, 11¹/₂ inches*	$ 15–20
Platter, *oval, 13¹/₂ inches*	$ 18–25
Relish, *four-section*	$ 125–145
Sugar bowl, *lidded*	$ 28–35
Shakers, *salt and pepper, set*	$ 25–35
Teapot	$ 225–240
Tumbler, *juice, 5-ounce*	$ 115–125
Tumbler, *water, 9-ounce*	$ 125–145

"Pebbleford"

This line was designed by John Giles, and consists of solid-color dinnerware with a twist. The background of these pieces was a solid color such as Honey Beige, Mint Green, pink, sand, teal, turquoise, Sunburst Yellow, granite, Celery Green, burnt orange, or Marble White. A fleck of color—usually brown—was then added, which gave the surfaces of the pieces a slight speckled effect. "Pebbleford" pieces are generally marked "Pebbleford by Giles," coupled with a Taylor, Smith and Taylor backstamp.

Bowl, *cereal, lug-handled, 7¹/₄-inch diameter*	$ 6–10
Bowl, *individual fruit, 5¹/₂-inch diameter*	$ 5–9
Bowl, *soup, coupe-shaped, 6¹/₂-inch diameter*	$ 9–12
Bowl, *soup, with lid, 7³/₄ inches*	$ 20–26
Bowl, *vegetable, oval, 8¹/₂ inches*	$ 20–25
Bowl, *vegetable, oval, divided, 12 inches*	$ 25–30
Bowl, *vegetable, round, 8¹/₂-inch diameter*	$ 25–30
Bowl, *vegetable, round, covered*	$ 60–70
Butter, *¹/₄-pound, covered*	$ 25–35

Casserole	$ 60–70
Casserole, 1³/₄-quart	$ 100–120
Coffeepot	$ 55–75
Creamer	$ 8–12
Cup and saucer	$ 14–20
Gravy boat	$ 40–50
Plate, *bread and butter*	$ 3–6
Plate, *chop, 12-inch diameter*	$ 35–42
Plate, *dinner, 10-inch diameter*	$ 10–15
Plate, *salad, 8-inch diameter*	$ 5–9
Platter, *oval, 11 inches*	$ 14–24
Platter, *oval, 13 inches*	$ 22–32
Sauce boat, *lidded*	$ 35–42
Shakers, *salt and pepper, set*	$ 16–22
Sugar bowl, *lidded*	$ 11–16

"Silhouette"

This line's decal decoration, which depicts two men dressed in Colonial garb sitting across a tavern table from one another, is exactly the same decoration Hall used to make its "Taverne" pattern. Both lines were made for Hellick's Coffee, and occasionally a Taylor, Smith and Taylor "Silhouette" cup will crop up with the words "You are Drinking Hellick's Triple City Blend" emblazoned on its back.

Bowl, *cereal, 6¹/₂-inch diameter*	$ 12–16
Bowl, *individual fruit, 5¹/₂-inch diameter*	$ 8–12
Bowl, *soup, 7¹/₂ inches*	$ 17–22
Bowl, *vegetable, oval, 9¹/₂ inches*	$ 28–35
Bowl, *vegetable, round, 9-inch diameter*	$ 45–55
Butter dish, *covered, round*	$ 65–75
Creamer	$ 28–34
Cup and saucer	$ 20–25
Plate, *bread and butter, 6¹/₂ inches*	$ 6–9
Plate, *dinner/luncheon, 9¹/₄-inch diameter*	$ 18–25

Platter, *oval, 11¹/₂ inches*	$ 45–55
Platter, *oval, 13¹/₂ inches*	$ 55–65
Sugar bowl	$ 35–45

"Vistosa"

First produced in 1938, the "Vistosa" line is thought to represent Taylor, Smith and Taylor's attempt to acquire a share of Homer Laughlin's lucrative "Fiesta" market. "Vistosa" was made for only a few years, and pieces were produced in colors of Mango Red, cobalt blue, light green, and deep yellow. Ivory-colored "Vistosa" has also been found, along with decal-decorated items. The shape of "Vistosa" pieces is very distinctive, with flatware items having a kind of crimped piecrust rim.

Bowl, *individual fruit, 5-inch diameter*	$ 13–18
Creamer	$ 38–45
Cup and saucer	$ 18–25
Plate, *bread and butter, 6-inch diameter*	$ 6–10
Plate, *dinner, 10-inch diameter*	$ 24–30
Plate, *luncheon, 9-inch diameter*	$ 17–22
Sugar bowl, *lidded*	$ 45–55

TECO GATES

American Terra Cotta mark.

Mark often found on *"Teco"*
wares.

William Day Gates was an Illinois lawyer who founded the
American Terra Cotta and Ceramic Company in Terra
Cotta, Illinois, in 1886. This company produced top-quality
sewer tile, brick, and terra cotta items for architectural applications. Using this operation as a base, Gates began experimenting with making art pottery, and sometime
between 1901 and 1903 he introduced a line called "Teco"—
a name derived from the first two letters of the words
"terra" ("TE") and "cotta" ("CO").

"Teco" pieces were meticulously made by both molding
and throwing, but were never embellished with painted
decoration. The wares were covered in a variety of glazes,
including a high-gloss green, plus beautiful crystalline and
metallic glazes. Gates also used matte glazes and colors of
gray, brown, platinum, blue, red, purple, and yellow. The
shapes of the pots were often quite extravagant, and collectors tend to like pieces that feature buttresses and exuberant
naturalistic designs (which were often based on the aquatic
plant life found in a pond behind the plant, or on other
plant forms found in the surrounding woods).

The year in which the company stopped producing "Teco"
pieces is open to debate: some sources say 1915, others 1922
or 1923, though the later dates seem more likely.

American Terra Cotta doorstop in the form
of a flower basket, 4¼ inches by 5½ inches,
$475–$525.
*Item courtesy of Tony McCormack, Sarasota,
Florida.*

Teco Gates vase, 7¼ inches, matte green
glaze, $2,500–$2,800.
*Item courtesy of Richard H. Crane, Knoxville,
Tennessee.*

Bowl, *footed, 7 inches wide by 4 inches tall, matte brown glaze, American Arts and Crafts design in panels, small chip to underside of foot*	$ 700–800
Box, *rectangular, 3½ inches wide, matte green glaze, designed by N. L. Clark*	$ 900–1,200
Chamberstick, *10½ inches tall, handle, matte green glaze*	$ 1,400–1,600
Dish, *pin tray, 7½ inches long with unusual grotesque face design, marked with full company name ("American Terra-Cotta")*	$ 575–625
Vase, *3 inches tall, bulbous body with flared mouth, matte green glaze*	$ 500–575
Vase, *4-inch diameter, ball-shaped, pink glaze*	$ 850–950
Vase, *4½ inches tall, green matte glaze with charcoal specking, simple shouldered-vase form*	$ 975–1,100
Vase, *7 inches tall, conical body with reverse conical top, matte green glaze*	$ 950–1,100

Vase, 7¹/₄ inches tall, bulbous body, low collar neck, matte green glaze	$ 900–1,000
Vase, 7¹/₄ inches tall, cylinder to more bulbous top with carved openings, matte green glaze	$ 2,500–2,800
Vase, 8³/₄ inches tall, organic form with four-lobed top, base is carved to suggest petal edges, matte green glaze	$ 3,250–3,500
Vase, 10³/₄ inches, architectural look with curved "V"-shaped buttresses at base, matte green glaze	$ 6,500–7,000
Wall pocket, 7 inches, circular base surmounted by rectangular top, base is decorated with a raised sun sign (fylfot)	$ 1,600–1,850

TIFFANY POTTERY

"LCT" monogram mark used at *Tiffany Pottery*.

According to legend, Tiffany Studios began making art pottery in order to produce pottery lamp bases it had previously been buying from Grueby Pottery for use with its leaded-glass shades. However, modern research indicates that this legend is false.

As early as 1898, Tiffany began experimenting with making art pottery at its Corona facility in Long Island, New York. It first exhibited its pottery at the Louisiana Purchase Exposition in St. Louis, Missouri, in 1904. The wares had white semiporcelain bodies, and were both wheel-thrown and molded (though more were molded than wheel-thrown). Both glazed and unglazed pieces were produced, and the early glazed pieces were primarily ivory-colored, with yellow-green hues shading to brown. A green glaze was later introduced, and examples of Tiffany Pottery can also be found with crystalline and iridescent glazes and blue, red, and bronze finishes.

Though glazed examples of Tiffany pottery were offered at Tiffany and Company, they did not sell well, and the pottery lamp bases were seldom used with Tiffany lampshades. It is thought that Louis Comfort Tiffany began losing interest in pottery about 1914, and production ceased sometime around 1920 (with some sources indicating that it stopped as early as 1917). Pieces of Tiffany Pottery are rare, and are marked with an "LCT" monogram.

Lamp base, *7 inches tall, collar rim, flambé glaze in brown and gunmetal*	$ 3,500–4,000
Vase, *7 inches, embossed tulips, rich ivory glaze*	$ 8,000–8,500
Vase, *11 inches high, floral shape arising from base that resembles artichoke leaves, ivory-and-brown glaze*	$ 7,000–7,500
Vase, *17 inches, footed cylinder flaring slightly to shoulder, matte cobalt blue over turquoise, small hairline in base, some glaze nicks*	$ 4,000–4,500

TREASURE CRAFT

Just after the end of World War II, Alfred A. Levin began working as a jobber buying pottery from its makers and selling it to retail outlets. In 1948, the Levin family began manufacturing its own pottery in Compton, California, making such things as wall planters and mugs. Today, the company is best known for its cookie jars, which were added to the line in the early 1950s. Much of the design work was done by Al Levin, but Don Winton of Twin Winton also did some of the designs, and Treasure Craft reportedly bought some of its cookie jar molds from Twin Winton after that company went out of business in 1975. In 1972, Treasure Craft also started a company called "Pottery Craft" to make stoneware items. Treasure Craft was acquired by Pfaltzgraff in 1993.

Cookie Jars

Adobe House	$ 110–125
Angel	$ 175–200
Ball, *Baseball*	$ 110–125
Ball, *Basketball*	$ 110–125
Ball, *Bowling*	$ 110–125
Ball, *Eight Ball*	$ 200–225
Ball, *Football*	$ 110–125

Ball, *Golf*	$ 110–125
Ball, *Soccer*	$ 110–125
Ball, *Tennis*	$ 110–125
Balloon, *Hot Air, "Cookie Balloon"*	$ 450–500
Bandito	$ 175–200
Barn, *with owl finial, "Cookie Barn"*	$ 110–125
Baseball Boy	$ 85–100
Bear, *Panda, with baby*	$ 125–150
Bear, *Circus Bear, standing on hands*	$ 125–150
Bear, *Police Chief*	$ 125–150
Bear, *visored cap and bow tie*	$ 70–85
Bear, *carrying honey barrels*	$ 150–175
Bear, *with railroad cap and neckerchief*	$ 175–200
Boot, *Cowboy, with gun finial*	$ 150–175
Cactus	$ 75–90
Canister, *"Cookies"*	$ 45–60
Cat, *in a floppy hat*	$ 225–275
Cat, *on pillow, "Cookies"*	$ 75–90
Cat, *with checked neckerchief*	$ 200–225
Cat, *with a cookie jar*	$ 100–125
Cat, *with mouse finial*	$ 110–135
Caterpillar Coach, *"Rose Petal Place"*	$ 1,500–1,650
Chef, *in toque with spoon, "Cookie Chef," dark coloration*	$ 85–110
Chef, *in toque with spoon, "Cookie Chef," light coloration*	$ 110–135
Clown, *sitting, dark coloration*	$ 110–135
Clown, *sitting, light coloration*	$ 175–225
Coffeepot, *"Cookies"*	$ 85–110
Cookbooks	$ 125–250
Cop, *in old-fashioned uniform*	$ 250–300
Covered Wagon	$ 75–95
Cow	$ 75–95

Cowboy Pig, *with rabbit*	$ 90–110
Cowboy, *with lasso*	$ 90–125
Dalmatian, *lying on back with glass bowl on tummy*	$ 85–110
Dinosaur	$ 100–125
Dog, *with barrel around neck, "Cookies"*	$ 85–110
Dog, *in a floppy hat*	$ 225–260
Dog, *in a barrel*	$ 110–135
Dog, *with checkered neckerchief*	$ 200–250
Dog, *on sled*	$ 175–200
Duck	$ 65–85
Elephant, *in sailor's clothes, "U.S.N."*	$ 125–150
Fish	$ 100–125
Football, *with coach, "Rose Petal Place"*	$ 525–575
Fox, *in hat*	$ 200–225
Girl, *with bunny in apron pocket, "Sugar"*	$ 175–225
Girl, *with bunny in apron pocket, "Spice"*	$ 110–135
Goose, *with bow around neck*	$ 125–135
Goose, *with flowing ribbon and bow around neck*	$ 70–85
Grandma, *with bowl of cookies, yellow dress*	$ 150–200
Grandma, *with bowl of cookies, blue dress*	$ 90–110
Gumball Machine	$ 125–150
Hedgehog, *"Tumbles," "Rose Petal Place"*	$ 1,000–1,200
Hen, *either black, white, and red, or blue and white*	$ 90–110
Hobo, *with cigar stub*	$ 125–150
House, *Gingerbread*	$ 110–135
House, *Victorian*	$ 90–120
Ice Wagon, *with "Home" finial*	$ 175–225
Jukebox, *Wurlitzer*	$ 200–250
Katrina	$ 1,000–1,200
Kermit the Frog	$ 90–120
Lamb	$ 80–100

Leopard	$ 150–175
Log Cabin	$ 80–100
Miss Piggy	$ 90–120
Monkey	$ 80–100
Mushroom House, *"Cookie Club"*	$ 125–150
Noah's Ark, *with two owl finials*	$ 165–185
Owl, *with apron*	$ 60–75
Pig, *with hat and rabbit in pocket*	$ 95–110
Rabbit, *with baseball bat*	$ 80–100
Radio	$ 175–225
Sheepdog, *with butterfly finial*	$ 110–135
Slot Machine	$ 175–225
Snail, *Seymour, "Rose Petal Place"*	$ 1,000–1,200
Stove, *potbellied, dark colors*	$ 110–125
Stove, *potbellied, light colors*	$ 75–95
Teepee	$ 80–100
Toucan	$ 100–125
Train, *B & R Railroad, dark-colored*	$ 90–110
Train, *B & R Railroad, light-colored*	$ 150–175
Treasure Chest	$ 150–175
Tree, *with book, bird finial, "Rose Petal Place"*	$ 1,500–1,600
Trolley, *with kids, "Cookie Trolley"*	$ 200–250
Truck, *Pickup, brown*	$ 110–125
Truck, *Pickup, red, limited edition*	$ 600–700
Van, *"Cookie Van"*	$ 175–225
Water Can, *"Rose Petal Place"*	$ 850–950

TWIN WINTON

At the tender age of sixteen, in either 1935 or 1936, twin brothers Don and Ross Winton went into the pottery business with Helen Burke. The twins went out on their own in 1939, and then closed shop in 1943 to join the military. They reopened the company in 1946, at which time their brother, Bruce, also joined the business. In 1952, the twins sold their interest in the business to Bruce, and began freelancing for him and for other manufacturers such as Treasure Craft.

TWIN WINTON
Pasadena, Calif.

One of the marks used by *Twin Winton.*

The company's original facilities were in Pasadena, California, but moved to El Monte in 1953 and to San Juan Capistrano in 1964. The company closed in 1975.

Cookie Jars and Related Items

Apple, *house with worm at doorway*	$ 225–275
Barn, *"Cookie Barn," Collector Series*	$ 350–400
Barn, *"Cookie Barn," gold seal*	$ 200–250
Barn, *"Cookie Barn," wood tone*	$ 175–225
Barn, *canister, "Coffee Coop"*	$ 70–85
Barn, *canister, "Flour Stable"*	$ 75–90
Barn, *canister, "Sugar Dairy"*	$ 75–90
Barn, *canister, "Tea Sty"*	$ 55–70

Barn, *shakers, salt and pepper, set*	$ 65–85
Barrel, *with sacks, "Grandma's Cookies"*	$ 175–200
Barrel, *shakers, with sacks, salt and pepper, set*	$ 90–110
Bear, *with forest ranger's hat, Collector Series*	$ 350–425
Bear, *with forest ranger's hat, gold seal*	$ 110–135
Bear, *with forest ranger's hat, wood tone*	$ 75–90
Bear, *with forest ranger's hat, wall pocket*	$ 110–135
Bear, *with forest ranger's hat, standing by tree trunk, lamp base*	$ 600–700
Bear, *in sheriff's outfit, Collector Series*	$ 350–400
Bear, *in sheriff's outfit, brown*	$ 100–125
Bucket, *"Ye Olde Cookie Bucket," green or wood tone*	$ 100–120
Bucket, *canister, "Ye Olde Coffee Bucket"*	$ 75–95
Bucket, *canister, "Ye Olde Flour Bucket"*	$ 135–160
Bucket, *canister, "Ye Olde Sugar Bucket"*	$ 110–135
Bucket, *canister, "Ye Olde Salt Bucket"*	$ 50–65
Bucket, *canister, "Ye Olde Tea Bucket"*	$ 65–85
Buddha (Hotei)	$ 250–300
Buddha (Hotei), *shakers, salt and pepper, set*	$ 75–95
Bull, *sitting, smiling*	$ 150–200
Bull, *shakers, sitting and smiling*	$ 80–100
Butler	$ 350–400
Butler, *napkin holder*	$ 225–250
Cable Car	$ 110–125
Castle, *with turrets*	$ 1,200–1,400
Cat, *in a basket*	$ 100–125
Cat, *Persian kitten*	$ 250–300
Cat, *Persian kitten, shakers, salt and pepper, set*	$ 80–100
Chef, *with bowl of cookies*	$ 350–400
Child in Shoe	$ 80–100
Child in Shoe, *green*	$ 125–150
Chipmunk, *with sack of acorns*	$ 150–200

Churn, *with cat*	$ 200–250
Clock, *mouse finial, "Cookie Time"*	$ 80–100
Coach, *pumpkin, Cinderella and mouse*	$ 250–300
Coffee Grinder	$ 225–275
Cop, *Keystone-style, saluting, brown*	$ 125–150
Cop, *Keystone-style, saluting, Collector Series*	$ 350–400
Cop, *Keystone-style, saluting, shakers, salt and pepper*	$ 75–95
Cow, *with white spots*	$ 120–150
Deer, *with tree trunk, squirrel finial*	$ 225–250
Dinosaur	$ 225–275
Dog Catcher, *"Cookie Catcher," brown*	$ 200–250
Dog in Basket	$ 100–125
Dog on Drum	$ 400–450
Donkey, *with boater hat and jacket, ears sticking out, Collector Series*	$ 225–250
Donkey, *with boater hat and jacket, ears sticking out, brown*	$ 175–200
Donkey and Cart	$ 150–200
Duck (Rubber Ducky)	$ 250–300
Dutch Girl, *Collector Series*	$ 300–350
Dutch Girl, *brown dress, yellow tulips*	$ 225–275
Dutch Girl, *shakers, salt and pepper, set*	$ 75–90
Elephant, *with sailor hat, Collector Series*	$ 250–300
Elephant, *with sailor hat, brown with red jumper*	$ 185–220
Elephant, *with sailor hat, shakers, salt and pepper*	$ 75–95
Elf Bakery Tree Stump	$ 175–225
Elf on Stump, *with cookies, brown*	$ 125–150
Elf on Stump, *with cookies, dark green*	$ 200–250
Elf on Stump, *shakers, salt and pepper, set*	$ 120–250
Fire Engine, *brown*	$ 110–135
Fire Engine, *red*	$ 180–210
Fox, *in pirate outfit, Collector Series*	$ 400–450

Frog, *licking lips*	$ 250–300
Grandma, *with bowl of cookies*	$ 180–220
Grandma, *with spoon*	$ 150–175
Guard, *in shelter, "Cookie Guard"*	$ 575–625
Hen on Nest	$ 200–250
Hen on Nest, *shakers, salt and pepper, set*	$ 75–100
Horse, *sitting, wearing straw hat, brown*	$ 200–250
Horse, *sitting, wearing straw hat, gray*	$ 250–300
Horse, *sitting, wearing straw hat, shakers, salt and pepper, pair*	$ 125–150
House, *"Candy House"*	$ 70–90
House, *two stories, "Cookies"*	$ 275–325
House, *two stories, shakers, salt and pepper, set*	$ 150–175
Howard Johnson's Restaurant	$ 2,800–3,200
Kangaroo	$ 400–450
Kangaroo, *shakers, salt and pepper, set*	$ 175–200
King, *"Ole King Cole"*	$ 600–700
Lamb, *"For Good Little Lambs Only," Collector Series*	$ 350–400
Lion, *wearing crown*	$ 250–300
Lion, *wearing crown, shakers, salt and pepper, set*	$ 120–145
Monk, *"Thou Shalt Not Steal," Friar Tuck*	$ 110–135
Monk, *bank, Friar Tuck*	$ 175–225
Mother Goose, *Collector Series*	$ 400–450
Mother Goose, *wood tone or gray*	$ 225–250
Mother Goose, *salt and pepper shakers, set*	$ 110–125
Mouse, *wearing sailor hat, Collector Series*	$ 375–425
Mouse, *wearing sailor hat, gold seal*	$ 275–325
Mouse, *wearing sailor hat, wood tone*	$ 110–135
Noah's Ark, *blue, orange, brown, or mustard*	$ 250–300
Noah's Ark, *white and brown, high gloss*	$ 425–475
Nut, *with squirrel finial*	$ 110–135
Owl, *with glasses and mortarboard, Collector Series*	$ 125–150

Owl, *with glasses and mortarboard, brown, white, or gray*	$ 100–125
Pig, *standing, "Porky"*	$ 250–300
Poodle, *behind "Cookie Counter"*	$ 200–250
Pot, *with cookies, "Pot O' Cookies"*	$ 200–225
Rabbit, *in cowboy outfit with gun belt, Collector Series*	$ 375–425
Rabbit, *in cowboy outfit with gun belt, shakers, salt and pepper, set*	$ 90–110
Raccoon, *wearing sweater (also called "Pirate Fox")*	$ 175–225
Raggedy Andy, *on drum*	$ 375–425
Raggedy Ann	$ 375–425
Rocking Horse	$ 350–425
Rooster, *Collector Series*	$ 200–250
Rooster, *wood tone*	$ 150–175
Safe, *"Cookie Safe"*	$ 110–135
Shack, *"Cookie Shack," green or orange*	$ 175–225
Shack, *"Cookie Shack," gray*	$ 200–250
Squirrel, *with cookie*	$ 80–120
Squirrel, *with cookie, shakers, salt and pepper, set*	$ 75–100
Stove, *old-fashioned wood-burning*	$ 125–150
Stove, *old-fashioned wood-burning, red*	$ 175–225
Teddy Bear, *with ribbon tie, brown*	$ 110–135
Teddy Bear, *with ribbon tie, gray*	$ 150–200
Tortoise, *with hare finial*	$ 200–250
Train, *with face, "97"*	$ 110–135
Tugboat	$ 450–500
Walrus, *with clown hat*	$ 350–400
Wheelbarrow	$ 325–375

Hillbilly

These items were based on the Paul Webb comic strip *Blue Ridge Mountain Boys*.

Ashtray, *Clem*	$ 65–85
Bank, *hillbilly in barrel, "Mountain Dew 100 Proof"*	$ 100–125

Two Twin Winton "Hillbilly" mugs, 4½ inches, $55–$75.
Items courtesy of Bill Brooker, Old School Antique Mall,
Sylva, North Carolina.

Bowl, *pretzel, half-barrel*	$ 50–65
Ice Bucket, *"Bottoms Up"*	$ 500–575
Ice Bucket, *hillbilly bathing in a barrel*	$ 400–450
Ice Bucket, *hillbilly with jug*	$ 400–450
Ice Bucket, *hillbilly with suspenders*	$ 400–450
Jar, *hillbilly in outhouse*	$ 450–525
Mug, *with hillbilly handle, clutching barrel body*	$ 55–75

UHL POTTERY

892

One of the marks used by the *Uhl Pottery Company*.

August Uhl came to this country in 1846 and settled in Evansville, Indiana. He was joined by his brother, Louis, in 1849, and together they founded the A. and L. Uhl Pottery. The Uhls initially used clay they found near Evansville, but its quality was not satisfactory, and they began importing clay from deposits near Huntingburg, Indiana. In 1879, Louis Uhl bought out his brother's interest in the company, and changed its name to "Louis Uhl and Sons." One year later, after yet another ownership change, the firm's name was changed to "Uhl Potteries."

Louis Uhl died in 1908, and the company's manufacturing facilities were moved closer to the raw material necessary to make the pottery. Labor troubles arose in 1940, which contributed to the closing of the plant in 1944. Vogue Pottery took over the Uhl factory in 1945, and produced some items using the Uhl molds until it closed in 1947. Louisville Pottery then took over in 1948, and also made pottery using the Uhl molds until it went out of business in late 1950.

Uhl made a wide variety of stoneware items, but much of its work was not marked. Pieces marked "Uhl Pottery Company, Huntingburg, Ind." are much more common than those marked "Evansville."

Ashtrays

Acorn, *brown*	$ 325–400
Advertising, *Cannelton Sewer Pipe*	$ 125–145
Advertising, *Meier Winery, round, 4³/₄-inch diameter*	$ 300–350
Advertising, *Shell Gas, square*	$ 225–250
Dog, *raising right leg to fire hydrant*	$ 600–650
Donkey, *figural*	$ 2,000–2,200
Elephant, *figural, #173*	$ 1,000–1,200
Pig, *2 inches, various colors*	$ 350–375
Round, *#140, 4¹/₂-inch diameter*	$ 95–135

Beverage Items

Jug, *shoulder, brown and white, marked with Uhl acorn mark and a "3" for "3 gallons"*	$ 100–125
Mug, *barrel-shaped, blue-and-white stoneware stenciled "Home Sweet Home," 16-ounce*	$ 450–525
Mug, *barrel-shaped, advertising, brown or yellow glaze, 16-ounce*	$ 100–125
Mug, *white background with blue sponge decoration, 4 inches*	$ 125–160
Pitcher, *ball-shaped, solid-color glaze, 5-pint*	$ 150–175
Pitcher, *blue-and-white stoneware, embossed image of Abraham Lincoln, 3-quart*	$ 850–950
Pitcher, *blue-and-white stoneware, embossed image of Abraham Lincoln, 2-quart*	$ 750–850
Pitcher, *blue-and-white stoneware, 1-quart, embossed image of Abraham Lincoln*	$ 550–650
Pitcher, *blue-and-white stoneware, 1-pint, embossed image of Abraham Lincoln*	$ 450–550
Pitcher, *blue-and-white stoneware, ¹/₂-pint, embossed image of Abraham Lincoln*	$ 350–450
Pitcher, *barrel-shaped, blue-and-white stoneware, 3-quart, stenciled "Home Sweet Home"*	$ 1,200–1,400
Pitcher, *tall, blue-and-white stoneware, embossed with grapes, 3-quart*	$ 225–250

Pitcher, *tall, blue-and-white stoneware, embossed with grapes, 2-quart*	$ 250–300
Pitcher, *tall, blue-and-white stoneware, embossed with grapes, 1-quart*	$ 275–325
Pitcher, *squatty, blue stoneware, embossed with grapes, covered, solid blue glaze*	$ 275–325
Pitcher, *11 inches tall, white background with blue sponge decoration*	$ 650–750
Pitcher, *$1/4$-gallon, bulbous body, cylindrical neck, white background, blue sponge decoration*	$ 600–700
Ring jug, *circular with open center, white background, blue sponge decoration, $7^3/4$-inch diameter*	$ 850–950
Water cooler, *blue-and-white stoneware, lidded, "Polar Bear" pattern, 6-gallon*	$ 1,300–1,450
Water cooler, *blue and white, banding, "Ice Water 5" stenciled on side, 5-gallon, covered*	$ 600–700
Water jug with stopper, *circular disk shape, "Cattail" design, 10 inches high, various colors*	$ 350–400
Water jug with stopper, *circular disk shape, "Polar Bear" design, 10 inches high, various designs*	$ 375–425

Figures

Bear, *miniature, $1^1/2$ inches*	$ 175–225
Cat, *miniature, $1^3/4$ inches*	$ 150–200
Dog, *miniature, $1^1/2$ inches*	$ 150–200
Dog, *right leg raised, figure*	$ 110–135
Frog, *$3^1/2$ inches*	$ 300–350
Frog, *6 inches*	$ 450–500
Frog, *9 inches*	$ 650–700
Frog, *13 inches*	$ 1,600–1,750
Rabbit, *$5^1/2$ inches*	$ 165–200
Turtle, *$3^1/2$ inches*	$ 400–450
Turtle, *6 inches*	$ 450–500

Turtle, *9 inches*	$ 750–850
Turtle, *13 inches*	$ 1,600–1,750

Figural Planters

Donkey	$ 325–350
Elephant, *smooth*	$ 110–135
Elephant, *wrinkled*	$ 250–300
Lamb, *7 inches*	$ 165–200
Pig	$ 600–675
Rabbit	$ 165–200
Rabbit with basket	$ 165–200
Scottie	$ 450–550
Swan	$ 375–425

Hand-Thrown Pieces

Basket, *tall, 11³/₄ inches*	$ 450–500
Candleholder, *shield back, 6¹/₂ inches*	$ 250–300
Coffeepot with bail handle, *8¹/₂ inches*	$ 800–900
Pitcher, *tall, 14 inches*	$ 450–500
Teapot, *Japanese-style with stick handle, 5³/₄ inches*	$ 1,200–1,400
Vase, *double gourd shape, 5 inches*	$ 150–175

Kitchenware

Bean pot, *lidded, 5 inches high, single handle with lug or "ear" on opposite side, various colors*	$ 275–325
Bean pot, *lidded, ¹/₄-gallon, brown and white, "Boston Baked Beans" stenciled on side in blue*	$ 65–80
Bean pot, *lidded, ¹/₂-gallon, white background with blue sponge decoration, one handle*	$ 375–425
Bean pot, *lidded, two handles, 6 inches high, various colors*	$ 250–275
Bowl, *batter, 8¹/₂ inches, assorted solid colors*	$ 75–100
Bowl, *mixing, 10-inch diameter, "Arches"*	$ 125–150

Uhl Pottery blue-glazed pitcher, 8¼ inches, $145–$175.
Item courtesy of Needful Things, Hendersonville, North Carolina.

Butter crock, *with lid and bail handle, white with Uhl acorn mark on the side and "#4" for "4 gallons"*	$ 275–325
Butter crock, *with bail handle and lid, blue sponge decoration*	$ 250–275
Coffeemaker, *drip, various colors*	$ 800–950
Cookie jar, *covered, crock-style, blue stenciling, "Cookies"*	$ 325–375
Creamer, *individual, 1-ounce, various colors, straight-sided dairy container shape*	$ 225–350
Grease jar, *lidded, plain, various colors, lug or "ear" handles*	$ 60–75
Jar, *barrel-shaped, covered, 4 inches high, various colors*	$ 325–375
Jar with lid, *clamp on bail to secure top, various colors*	$ 75–95
Pitcher, *gravy, three-spout, 1¼ inches*	$ 175–200
Pitcher, *blue glaze, 8¼ inches*	$ 145–175
Salt crock, *blue-and-white stoneware, original pottery lid, grape pattern*	$ 250–325
Shakers, *salt and pepper, pair, assorted solid colors*	$ 65–80
Syrup pitchers, *lidded, 6 inches tall, solid colors*	$ 150–175

Teapot, *2-cup, various colors*	$ 210–235
Teapot, *8-cup, various colors*	$ 145–175

Miniatures

Bud vase, *#22*	$ 100–125
Bud vase, *#23*	$ 100–125
Bud vase, *#24*	$ 200–225
Bud vase, *#30*	$ 150–175
Churn, *top, and dasher with bail handle*	$ 1,000–1,200
Cookie jar, *#522*	$ 175–200
Cookie jar, *globe, blue*	$ 300–325
Cookie jar, *globe, brown*	$ 135–160
Flowerpot with saucer, *solid color, horizontal ribs, 2 inches*	$ 300–325
Flowerpot with saucer, *solid color, horizontal ribs, 3 inches*	$ 250–300
Jug, *acorn, 4-ounce*	$ 90–110
Jug, *acorn, 10-ounce*	$ 65–85
Jug, *baseball, white, $2^5/8$ inches*	$ 50–65
Jug, *canteen, small, 2-ounce*	$ 70–85
Jug, *canteen, large, 4-ounce*	$ 75–95
Jug, *chicken, body is vessel, head is stopper, $4^1/4$ inches*	$ 1,600–1,750
Jug, *$5/8$-inch, demijohn*	$ 650–750
Jug, *dog, right leg raised, 2 inches*	$ 400–450
Jug, *elephant, 3 inches*	$ 90–110
Jug, *football, $3^3/8$ inches*	$ 275–325
Jug, *football, small, $2^1/2$ inches*	$ 45–60
Jug, *ring, solid color, 1-ounce*	$ 135–165
Jug, *softball, white, $3^1/4$ inches*	$ 300–350
Jug, *tank, facing backward*	$ 600–675
Shoe, *Cowboy Boots, 3 inches, pair*	$ 300–325
Shoe, *Cowboy Boots, $3^3/4$ inches, pair, painted*	$ 425–475
Shoe, *Dutch, #2, 3 inches*	$ 75–90

Uhl Pottery butter churn, 4-gallon, original top,
$275–$300.
*Item courtesy of Needful Things, Hendersonville, North
Carolina.*

Shoe, *Dutch, #3, 4 inches long*	$ 110–125
Shoe, *Dutch, #6, 6³/₄ inches long*	$ 145–165
Shoe, *Military Boots, 2³/₄ inches, solid color, pair*	$ 130–150
Shoe, *slipper, 2¹/₂ inches*	$ 60–75
Spittoon, *2 inches, blue sponge decoration*	$ 175–200

Miscellaneous

Bank, *acorn, 3 inches*	$ 185–220
Bank, *jug form, 5 inches*	$ 200–225
Bank, *pig, 5¹/₂ inches*	$ 500–575
Bank, *pig, 7 inches*	$ 550–625
Bank, *pig, 9¹/₂ inches*	$ 700–750
Bird House, *Wren, #525, circular with conical roof*	$ 425–450
Bowl, *Dog, Scotties, embossed, 7-inch diameter*	$ 85–110
Churn, *butter, 14¹/₂ inches tall, 4-gallon, original lid*	$ 275–300

Lamp, *Cat, 11^1/$_2$ inches*	$ 2,200–2,400
Lamp, *oil-type, with flaring base and font on stem, various colors*	$ 225–300
Lamp, *Scottie*	$ 550–650
Wall plaque, *bust of Abraham Lincoln, brown*	$ 700–800

Vases and Gardenware

Birdbath, *embossed leaves, two pieces, 26 inches, #U10*	$ 250–300
Bud vase, *#107, 4^1/$_2$ inches*	$ 65–85
Bud vase, *#112, 5 inches*	$ 85–95
Bud vase, *#106, 7 inches*	$ 85–100
Bud vase, *#516, 8 inches*	$ 125–150
Cut-flower vase, *#116, 5 inches*	$ 95–120
Cut-flower vase, *#113, 8 inches*	$ 65–85
Cut-flower vase, *#123, 8 inches*	$ 85–95
Cut-flower vase, *#114, 10 inches*	$ 85–100
Cut-flower vase, *#117, 10 inches*	$ 90–110
Cut-flower vase, *#115, 10 inches*	$ 120–140
Cut-flower vase, *#526, Greek key top, 15 inches*	$ 425–475
Flowerpot, *Doric, embossed flowers and leaves, 10^1/$_2$ inches*	$ 90–110
Jardinière and pedestal, *Athenian, #515*	$ 250–300
Orange blossom vase, *4 inches*	$ 65–80
Strawberry jar, *hanging, #518*	$ 110–135
Strawberry jar, *large, 30 inches*	$ 425–450
Sundial and pedestal, *24 inches*	$ 350–400
Thieves jar, *3 inches*	$ 275–325
Thieves jar, *5 inches*	$ 325–350
Thieves jar, *7 inches*	$ 275–325
Thieves jar, *9 inches*	$ 225–275
Vase, *#134, ruffled top, bulbous bottom*	$ 95–110

UNIVERSAL POTTERIES, INC.

Mark used by *Universal Potteries, Inc.* on its "Ballerina" dinnerware.

The history of this company is a very convoluted one that involves a number of mergers and ownership changes. Most sources agree that this history begins with the Bradshaw China Company of Niles, Ohio, which was organized in 1901. The company made semiporcelain dinnerware, toilet sets, and novelties. It was sold to the Sebring family sometime between 1912 and 1916, and then sold again in 1921. For a brief period, it was called the "Crescent China Company," but this name was quickly changed to the "Atlas China Company." The firm then merged with the Globe Pottery of Cambridge, Ohio, to become the Atlas-Globe China Company.

The owner of Atlas-Globe also owned the Oxford Pottery in Cambridge, which manufactured brown kitchenware such as bean pots, custard cups, and teapots made from the red clay that was mined on land surrounding the factory. In 1934 (though some sources say 1932), the company was reorganized to merge Atlas-Globe and Oxford into one pottery, and its name was changed to "Universal Potteries, Incorporated." Universal made dinnerware until 1956, when it shifted its emphasis to production of floor and wall tiles and became the Oxford Tile Division of Universal Potteries. The company went out of business in 1960.

Universal Potteries, Inc. 11½-inch "Ballerina" platter in chartreuse with lug handles, $18–$25.
Item courtesy of Elaine Tomber Tindell, Knoxville, Tennessee.

"Ballerina"

The most important shape made by Universal was "Ballerina," which can be identified easily by a mark featuring the company name and the image of a dancer in toe shoes and a tutu. This line originated in the late 1940s, and the original solid colors were Jade Green, Jonquil Yellow, Periwinkle Blue, and Dove Gray. Chartreuse and forest green were added to the palette in 1949, and pink, burgundy, and charcoal were added in 1955. Pieces were also produced in Sierra Rust, though there is no information as to when this color entered the lineup. A wide variety of decals were also used on "Ballerina" dinnerware, and these are generally found on pieces with ivory-colored backgrounds. Pink, Sierra Rust, and charcoal pieces are priced at the top of the ranges listed below, while Dove Gray, forest green, and chartreuse pieces are priced near the bottom.

Bowl, *individual fruit, 5½-inch diameter*	$ 8–14
Bowl, *individual salad, 7-inch diameter*	$ 14–22
Bowl, *soup, 7¾-inch diameter*	$ 14–22
Bowl, *vegetable, round, 7¾-inch diameter*	$ 18–28
Bowl, *vegetable, round, 9-inch diameter*	$ 35–45
Bowl, *vegetable, round, covered*	$ 95–110

Creamer	$ 15–32
Cup and saucer	$ 14–22
Gravy boat and underliner	$ 55–75
Plate, *bread and butter, 6^1/$_4$-inch diameter*	$ 3–8
Plate, *chop, 13-inch diameter*	$ 38–60
Plate, *dinner, 10-inch diameter*	$ 14–22
Plate, *luncheon, 9^1/$_8$-inch diameter*	$ 8–14
Plate, *salad, 7^1/$_2$-inch diameter*	$ 8–14
Platter, *11^1/$_2$ inches, lug handles*	$ 18–25
Shakers, *salt and pepper, set*	$ 21–31
Sugar bowl, *lidded*	$ 22–40

"Thistle"

One of the more common decal patterns found on "Ballerina" shapes is "Thistle," which is decorated with pink and yellow thistle blooms and grayish-green leaves.

Bowl, *individual fruit, 5^1/$_2$-inch diameter*	$ 10–14
Bowl, *soup, coupe, 7^3/$_4$-inch diameter*	$ 16–20
Bowl, *vegetable, round, 7^3/$_4$-inch diameter*	$ 35–40
Creamer	$ 28–32
Cup and saucer	$ 22–26
Gravy boat	$ 65–75
Plate, *bread and butter, 6^1/$_4$-inch diameter*	$ 6–8
Plate, *dinner, 10-inch diameter*	$ 20–24
Plate, *luncheon, 9^1/$_8$-inch diameter*	$ 12–15
Plate, *salad, 7^1/$_2$-inch diameter*	$ 9–12
Sugar bowl, *lidded*	$ 35–42
Teapot	$ 90–110

"Bittersweet"

This pattern was introduced in 1949, and pieces were produced exclusively for the Jewel Tea Company to use as premiums. The pattern consists of bright scarlet bittersweet berries with vines.

Bowl, *individual fruit, 6-inch diameter*	$ 12–20
Bowl, *salad, serving, 9¹/₂-inch diameter*	$ 65–75
Casserole, *round, 1¹/₄-quart*	$ 95–105
Casserole, *round, 2¹/₄-quart*	$ 135–145
Creamer	$ 20–25
Cup and saucer	$ 26–35
Plate, *dinner, 9-inch diameter*	$ 22–32
Plate, *salad, 7¹/₈-inch diameter*	$ 14–20
Platter, *oval, 13¹/₂ inches*	$ 35–45
Shakers, *salt and pepper, set*	$ 25–35
Shakers, *salt and pepper, range, set*	$ 60–75
Sugar bowl	$ 30–40

"Calico Fruit"

The center design of this charming decal pattern consists of a straight-sided blue bowl containing a pile of fruit shapes that appear to have been made from pieces of colorful fabric. The fruit appears to spill over the edges and onto the surface surrounding the bowl, and most of the pieces featuring this decal are accented with a red line that runs around the rims and edges. "Calico Fruit" was sold in department stores such as Montgomery Ward. The line also includes matching metalware and glassware. The decals tend to fade rather badly, and the prices below are for examples in good condition.

Bowl, *cereal, 5³/₄-inch diameter*	$ 25–35
Bowl, *individual fruit, 5¹/₄-inch diameter*	$ 15–22
Bowl, *mixing, 6-inch diameter*	$ 40–48
Bowl, *mixing, 7-inch diameter*	$ 45–55
Bowl, *salad, serving, 9-inch diameter*	$ 75–85
Bowl, *soup, 7³/₄-inch diameter*	$ 40–48
Bowl, *vegetable, oval, 9 inches*	$ 40–48
Bowl, *vegetable, round, 8³/₄-inch diameter*	$ 45–55
Creamer	$ 45–55
Cup and saucer	$ 45–55
Jar, *refrigerator, large, 4³/₄ inches*	$ 75–85

Universal Potteries mixing bowls and covers, "Calico
Fruit," $150–$175.
*Items courtesy of Needful Things, Hendersonville, North
Carolina.*

Jar, *refrigerator, medium, 3¹/₂ inches*	$ 55–65
Plate, *bread and butter, 6¹/₂-inch diameter*	$ 12–20
Plate, *dinner, 10-inch diameter*	$ 75–85
Plate, *luncheon, 9¹/₄-inch diameter*	$ 35–45
Plate, *pie, serving, 10-inch diameter*	$ 55–65
Plate, *salad, 7¹/₂-inch diameter*	$ 32–42
Platter, *oval, 13¹/₂ inches*	$ 80–92
Platter, *oval, 14¹/₂ inches*	$ 85–95

"Cattail"

This is perhaps the most popular pattern found on Universal Potteries dinnerware.
It is often found on the "Ballerina" shape, but was also used on a variety of other
shapes, including "Camwood," "Laurella," "Old Holland," and "Mt. Vernon." The
"Cattail" decal was introduced in the 1930s, and was in use into the 1940s and be-
yond. It featured a grouping of red cattails with green leaves and stems. However,
the pattern was not exclusive to Universal Potteries; other manufacturers also used
the design, and in the 1940s, Sears, Roebuck offered a kitchen table, four chairs, a
nine-piece luncheon tablecloth-and-napkin set, plus a 32-piece dinnerware group-

Universal Potteries "Cattail" water jug, stoppered,
6½ inches, $100–$125.
*Item courtesy of Roberta Bull, Old School Antique Mall,
Sylva, North Carolina.*

ing, all with the "Cattail" decoration, for just $23.89. Prices below are for "Cattail" pieces on shapes other than "Old Holland"; prices for "Old Holland" pieces are listed separately below.

Bowl, *cereal, 6-inch diameter*	$ 12–16
Bowl, *individual fruit, 5^1/$_2$-inch diameter*	$ 8–12
Bowl, *mixing, 6-inch diameter*	$ 35–40
Bowl, *mixing, 7-inch diameter*	$ 38–44
Bowl, *mixing, 8-inch diameter*	$ 50–55
Bowl, *soup, 7^3/$_4$-inch diameter*	$ 15–20
Bowl, *vegetable, oval, 9 inches*	$ 32–40
Bowl, *vegetable, round, 8^3/$_4$-inch diameter*	$ 28–34
Creamer	$ 22–28
Cup and saucer	$ 25–30
Jug, *2-quart, 5^7/$_8$ inches*	$ 50–60
Leftover, *5-inch diameter*	$ 68–75

Plate, *bread and butter, 6^1/$_4$-inch diameter*	$ 5–8
Plate, *grill, 9^3/$_4$-inch diameter*	$ 38–44
Plate, *dinner, 9^3/$_4$-inch diameter*	$ 35–45
Plate, *luncheon, 9-inch diameter*	$ 12–18
Plate, *salad, 7-inch diameter*	$ 12–16
Platter, *oval, 11^1/$_2$ inches*	$ 28–34
Platter, *oval, 13^1/$_2$ inches*	$ 45–55
Water jug, *stoppered, 6^1/$_2$ inches*	$ 100–125

"Cattail" pieces on "Old Holland" (or "Netherlands") shapes

Flatware pieces in this shape have very elaborate and distinctive embossed decorations of Dutch-style scenes.

Bowl, *individual fruit, 5^1/$_2$-inch diameter*	$ 12–16
Bowl, *soup, 7^3/$_4$-inch diameter*	$ 22–30
Cup and saucer	$ 32–36
Plate, *bread and butter, 6^1/$_2$-inch diameter*	$ 8–12
Plate, *dinner, 10-inch diameter*	$ 45–52
Plate, *luncheon, 9-inch diameter*	$ 18–24

"Laurella"

This solid-color line was introduced in 1948, and is distinguished by an embossed band of laurel leaves around the edges of the flatware. Pieces were produced in four pastel colors: "Cocotan" (cocoa/tan), Jade Green, Jonquil Yellow, and Periwinkle Blue. Examples are generally marked with the name "Laurella" and a Universal Potteries mark.

Bowl, *cereal, lug-handled*	$ 12–16
Bowl, *individual fruit, 5^1/$_2$-inch diameter*	$ 7–12
Bowl, *soup, 8-inch diameter*	$ 14–20
Bowl, *vegetable, round, 9-inch diameter*	$ 30–38
Creamer	$ 22–28
Cup and saucer	$ 14–22
Gravy boat, *faststand*	$ 52–60

Plate, *bread and butter, 6¹/₂-inch diameter*	$ 5–8
Plate, *chop, 13-inch diameter*	$ 25–32
Plate, *dinner, 10-inch diameter*	$ 16–22
Plate, *luncheon, 9¹/₂-inch diameter*	$ 12–16

"Woodvine"

Universal marketed "Woodvine" as a "booster" line, meaning that it was sold to grocery stores and other merchants for use as a premium to "boost" sales. This is an attractive pattern with red star-shaped flowers among two-toned green leaves. "Woodvine" was reportedly Universal's most popular "booster" line of the 1930s and 1940s.

Bowl, *individual fruit, 5¹/₂-inch diameter*	$ 6–10
Bowl, *mixing, 6-inch diameter*	$ 30–35
Bowl, *mixing, 8-inch diameter*	$ 42–48
Bowl, *salad, serving, 9-inch diameter*	$ 55–62
Bowl, *vegetable, oval, 9 inches*	$ 35–42
Bowl, *vegetable, round, 9-inch diameter*	$ 45–50
Cup and saucer	$ 15–18
Gravy boat	$ 60–70
Plate, *dinner, 10-inch diameter*	$ 20–26
Plate, *luncheon, 9¹/₂-inch diameter*	$ 8–12
Plate, *salad, 7¹/₂-inch diameter*	$ 8–12

UNION PORCELAIN WORKS

One of the marks used by
the *Union Porcelain Works.*

Charles Cartlidge is thought to have founded this important American porcelain company in 1854, though he may have founded it as early as 1848. Located in Greenpoint on Long Island, New York, the company made true hard-paste porcelain, and was known for its exceptionally fine artistic products. It is also said to have produced bone china. Union Porcelain Works closed sometime in the early 20th century—again, the exact date is unknown, though one source indicates it closed after 1912.

Cup and saucer, *figure of "Liberty" on handle, cup features relief decoration of "Justice" and "Hermes," saucer has a band of animals, very fine mold*	$ 1,200–1,400
Dish, *covered, 6³/₄ inches by 4 inches, oblong with rounded corners, handles, floral-painted*	$ 750–850
Gravy boat, *7¹/₂ inches tall, figures of Uncle Sam and John Bull in a boat, all white, some damage (chip and repaired crack)*	$ 800–1,000
Oyster plate, *9¹/₄-inch diameter, elaborately decorated with sea creatures and seaweed, six indentions for oysters*	$ 1,500–2,000

Oyster plate, *10¹/₄ inches long, shaped like a clam shell with six indentions for oysters, scallop shell-shaped indention for sauce, scattered sea life*	$ 1,200–1,400
Paperweight, *advertising, Union Porcelain Works "Fine China Works," figure of bulldog on conical base, worn gilding on dog's collar and base*	$ 1,000–1,250
Pitcher, *9³/₄ inches, designed by Karl L. H. Muller, spout is the head of a walrus with three-dimensional tusks, handle features a figure of a bear, body has relief decoration of King Gambrinus, his brother Jonathan, Bill Nye, and Ah Sin, some enameling and gilt with wear to the gilding*	$ 15,000–18,000
Vase, *8¹/₂ inches, figural turtle grasping the stem of what looks like a pitcher plant, all-white*	$ 1,250–1,500

VAN BRIGGLE POTTERY

Mark used by the *Van Briggle Pottery*. The "1902" at the bottom is a date, and not a style number.

Artus Van Briggle was a rising star at the Rookwood Pottery in Cincinnati. Born in Felicity, Ohio, in 1869, he began working for Rookwood in 1887 at the tender age of eighteen. By the early 1890s he was a senior decorator, and the company sent him to Europe in 1893 to study with Jean-Paul Laurens and Benjamin Constant.

While studying in Paris, Van Briggle became fascinated with the matte glazes he saw on Chinese ceramics—which, because of their complete lack of reflectivity, are called "dead glazes." In Europe, Van Briggle was introduced to the Art Nouveau style, and adopted it for his own work. He also met a talented artist, Anne Louise Gregory, who became his wife in 1902.

Van Briggle returned to Rookwood in 1896, and began experimenting with dead glazes. He was successful by 1898, and Rookwood exhibited his work in Paris in 1900, where it won great approval. Unfortunately, Van Briggle had been suffering from tuberculosis since childhood, and decided to move to Colorado Springs for the sake of his health. After the move, he worked at Colorado College attempting to perfect his matte glaze.

The first kiln of Van Briggle pottery was fired in 1901, and the new wares won international recognition and awards almost immediately. The best designs were those modeled by Van Briggle himself, and the Louvre Museum in Paris paid $3,000 for a vase he produced that was known as "Despondency." This piece features the three-dimensional figure of a grieving (or "despondent") man draped around its mouth. Other important Artus Van Briggle designs include the "Toast Cup" (a large cuplike vessel with a carved representation of an Art Nouveau-style woman), "Lorelei" (a vase with a woman draped around the top and sides, similar to "Despondency"), and "Lady of the Lily" (a nude woman propped against a lily).

Pieces of Van Briggle pottery made between 1901 and 1920 are generally dated, and these examples are the most desirable to collectors, with early examples demanding a premium. In the 1920s, Van Briggle Pottery shifted its emphasis from art pottery to production of more commercial wares and novelties, though its trademark pieces (such as "Lorelei" and "Despondency") were produced in very recent times, and may still be in production today.

Artus Van Briggle died from tuberculosis in 1904, and his widow carried on the business. It went bankrupt in 1913, however, and was taken over by other owners. The pottery burned down in 1919, but was rebuilt and continues to operate to this day.

Bookends, *5 inches, figural owls, brown-and-green glaze, circa 1920*	$ 400–450
Bowl, *5¹/₂ inches, Mountain Craig Brown, with green overspray, ribbed sides, 1920s*	$ 600–650
Bowl, *8 inches, raised dragonfly decoration, dark-brown shaded glaze, circa 1920*	$ 350–400
Bowl with attached flower frog, *6-inch diameter, Mulberry-colored glaze, dated 1915*	$ 425–500
Chalice, *"Mermaid," 10¹/₂ inches, green-and-blue glaze, embossed figure of mermaid around bowl of chalice, early 20th century*	$ 6,750–7,250
Paperweight in the form of a bunny, *3 inches, dark-brown glaze, dated 1920*	$ 175–225
Planter, *9¹/₂ inches, swan design, green-and-blue glaze, four-footed, 1930s*	$ 150–175
Plaques, *5¹/₂ inches, oval with raised head of Native American, turquoise glaze, 1960s, pair*	$ 150–175
Vase, *3¹/₂ inches tall, with embossed moth or butterfly decoration, Mulberry with blue accents, 1920s*	$ 145–165

Van Briggle rabbit paperweight, dated
1920, $175–$225.
*Item courtesy of Richard Crane, Knoxville,
Tennessee.*

Van Briggle matte-glazed vase, embossed
butterfly design, $145–$165.
*Item courtesy of Tony McCormack, Sarasota,
Florida.*

Van Briggle vase, 4 inches by 6 inches,
globular, mottled gray over light-brown
glaze, circa 1915, $875–$925.
*Item courtesy of Tony McCormack, Sarasota,
Florida.*

Vase, *4 inches, bulbous body, long neck, green glaze with brown overtones, marks obscured by glaze, circa 1910*	$ 450–525
Vase, *4 inches by 6 inches, globular, mottled gray over light-brown glaze, circa 1915*	$ 875–925
Vase, *5 inches tall, raised leaf design, green with brown undertones, dated 1915*	$ 600–650
Vase, *6³/4 inches tall, brown with green overspray, two handles on shoulder, 1920s*	$ 300–350

Vase, 7 inches, matte blue glaze, panel-sided, dated 1916	$ 600–650
Vase, 7 inches, raised dragonfly decoration, shaded blue glaze, second quarter of the 20th century	$ 350–400
Vase, 7¼ inches, stylized mistletoe decoration, mottled blue/green glaze with yellow overspray, marks obscured, 1906	$ 1,250–1,400
Vase, 8 inches, ovoid-shaped, two handles on shoulder, purple matte glaze, dated 1904	$ 2,000–2,250
Vase, 8 inches, green-over-brown glaze, ribbed bulbous base with tapered cylindrical top, second quarter of the 20th century	$ 250–300
Vase, 11½ inches, "Lady of the Lily," Persian Rose matte glaze, no flowers on base, early second quarter of the 20th century	$ 2,000–2,250

VERNON POTTERIES, LTD./ VERNON KILNS

SALAMINA
Designed by

Rockwell Kent

VERNON KILNS
Made in USA.

One of the marks used by *Vernon Kilns* on its "Salamina" dinnerware line, designed by famed American artist Rockwell Kent.

In 1912, the Poxon China Company was founded in Vernon, California, by George Poxon, who owned the ranch on which the pottery was located. At first, the company specialized in making tiles to be used on bathroom floors, though it also produced some art pottery. At the beginning of World War I, Vernon Potteries switched to making dinnerware, largely for commercial use in hotels and restaurants.

In 1931, Faye Bennison bought the pottery from Poxon, and he renamed the company "Vernon Kilns." These were the years of the Great Depression, and times were rough for the majority of the pottery companies in the United States and around the world. The situation got worse for Vernon Kilns in 1933, when an earthquake damaged the firm's kilns and destroyed much of its stock.

The disaster prompted Vernon Kilns to redesign its products, and in the mid- to late 1930s the company repositioned itself to make art wares, which in turn influenced its dinnerware production. The company hired a number of new designers, including Gale Turnbill, Don Blandings, and the important American illustrator and artist, Rockwell Kent. Dinnerware inspired by Walt Disney's animated feature film *Fantasia* was also produced, and is among the most desired of all the Vernon Kilns wares.

Blanding's designs are very recognizable because they often feature Hawaiian themes, two of which feature images of tropical flowers, and two others of which are emblazoned with representations of colorful fish. Rockwell Kent designed for Vernon Kilns between 1938 and 1940, and during this period he was responsible for three innovative dinnerware lines that are highly sought after by modern collectors: "Salamina," "Moby Dick," and "Our American."

Bennison sold Vernon Kilns to Metlox in 1958, and Metlox later created a Vernonware division to produce lines that it hoped would match the success of its "Poppytrail" line.

Dinnerware

"Brown-Eyed Susan"

This cheerful pattern features depictions of brown-eyed Susans in yellow and brown. It was first introduced around 1940. The first pieces were made using "Ultra" shapes, though most examples use the simpler "Montecito" shapes.

Bowl, *individual fruit, 5¹/₂-inch diameter*	$ 12–17
Bowl, *cereal, lug-handled, 7¹/₂-inch diameter*	$ 14–20
Bowl, *soup, 8-inch diameter*	$ 15–20
Bowl, *vegetable, oval, 9³/₄ inches*	$ 32–38
Bowl, *vegetable, oval, divided, 11 inches*	$ 45–50
Bowl, *vegetable, round, 9-inch diameter*	$ 32–38
Coffee server, *10-cup*	$ 35–45
Creamer	$ 18–22
Cup and saucer	$ 12–16
Gravy boat	$ 28–34
Plate, *bread and butter, 6¹/₂-inch diameter*	$ 5–8
Plate, *chop, 12-inch diameter*	$ 22–26
Plate, *dinner, 10-inch diameter*	$ 25–30
Plate, *luncheon, 9¹/₂-inch diameter*	$ 10–14
Plate, *salad, 7¹/₂-inch diameter*	$ 8–12
Platter, *oval, 10 inches*	$ 32–38

Vernon Kilns "Brown-Eyed Susan" chop plate, 12-inch diameter, $22–$26.
Item courtesy of Richard H. Crane, Knoxville, Tennessee.

Platter, *oval, 12 inches*	$ 38–42
Shakers, *salt and pepper, set*	$ 18–25
Sugar bowl, *lidded*	$ 22–28
Tidbit server, *two-tier*	$ 50–60
Tidbit server, *three-tier*	$ 55–65
Tumbler, *14-ounce*	$ 28–34

"Chatelaine"

This very unusual dinnerware line was designed by Sharon Merrill and was first marketed in 1953. Flatware items in this grouping are squares and rectangles, with a cluster of raised leaves placed at one or more of their corners. This line did not sell well because it was too avant-garde for most consumers, and was considered impractical. Pieces came in four colors: bronze (a rich chocolate brown), topaz (warm beige), jade (soft green with lighter-green and beige accents), and platinum (ivory with yellow and reddish-brown accents on the leaves). Jade and platinum items command prices at the top of the ranges listed below, while bronze and topaz items command prices near the bottom.

Topaz and Bronze

Cup and saucer, *coffee, flat*	$ 17–25
Cup and saucer, *pedestaled teacup*	$ 20–28
Plate, *bread and butter, 6^1/$_2$ inches*	$ 8–12
Plate, *chop, 14 inches*	$ 50–60
Plate, *dinner, leaf in one corner, 10^1/$_2$ inches*	$ 16–24
Plate, *dinner, leaf in four corners, 10^1/$_2$ inches*	$ 18–26
Plate, *salad, 7^1/$_2$-inch diameter*	$ 22–30
Platter, *16 inches*	$ 70–80
Shakers, *salt and pepper, set*	$ 25–35
Sugar bowl, *lidded*	$ 28–35
Teapot	$ 175–225

Platinum and Jade

Cup and saucer, *coffee, flat*	$ 20–28
Cup and saucer, *pedestaled teacup*	$ 24–30
Plate, *bread and butter, 6^1/$_2$ inches*	$ 12–18
Plate, *chop, 14 inches*	$ 60–70
Plate, *dinner, leaf in one corner, 10^1/$_2$ inches*	$ 24–30
Plate, *dinner, leaf in four corners, 10^1/$_2$ inches*	$ 30–40
Plate, *salad, 7^1/$_2$ inches*	$ 35–45
Platter, *16 inches*	$ 85–100
Shakers, *salt and pepper, set*	$ 30–40
Sugar bowl, *lidded*	$ 45–55
Teapot	$ 300–375

"Coronado"

This is a variation on the "Montecito" shape. Pieces were produced in solid colors of blue, brown, green, light blue, light green, orange, pale blue-gray, peach, pink, turquoise, and yellow. The line was first produced around 1936, and pieces were largely available as premiums from gas stations and supermarkets. Much of this ware is unmarked, but is easily identified by what is generally described as a "Cubist" band around the rims of flatware items and the shoulders of hollowware. "Coronado" was produced in a very limited number of pieces.

Bowl, *individual fruit, 5¹/₂-inch diameter*	$ 10–15
Bowl, *soup, 7¹/₂-inch diameter*	$ 18–25
Bowl, *vegetable, 9-inch diameter*	$ 22–30
Carafe, *wooden handle, stopper*	$ 65–85
Creamer	$ 18–25
Cup and saucer	$ 20–30
Plate, *bread and butter, 6¹/₂-inch diameter*	$ 8–12
Plate, *dinner, 10¹/₂-inch diameter*	$ 20–30
Platter, *oval, 12¹/₂ inches*	$ 28–35
Sugar bowl, *lidded*	$ 20–28
Sugar bowl, *open*	$ 16–24
Tumbler, *7¹/₂ inches*	$ 22–30

"Early California" and "Modern California"

These solid-color lines were produced by Vernon Kilns from around 1937 until about 1950. "Early California" pieces were initially made in bright shades of yellow, turquoise, green, brown, dark blue, light blue, orange, and pink, with peach added to the lineup around 1946. Pieces in ivory and maroon were also produced. "Modern California" pieces, on the other hand, came in satin-finish pastel colors of azure, Pistachio, yellow, Orchid (this color came in two shades: lavender and light pink), Mist (gray), and beige. Both lines were made using Vernon Kilns' "Montecito" shapes. "Modern California" pieces in Orchid (the light-pink variety) and Pistachio are priced at the top of the ranges listed below; "Early California" pieces in turquoise and light blue are priced at the bottom of these ranges.

Bowl, *cereal, lug-handled, 7¹/₂-inch diameter*	$ 11–16
Bowl, *chowder, lug handles, 6 inches (see note below)*	$ 17–70†
Bowl, *individual fruit, 5¹/₂-inch diameter*	$ 8–12
Bowl, *vegetable, oval, 10 inches*	$ 35–45
Bowl, *vegetable, round, 9-inch diameter*	$ 40–50
Creamer	$ 22–28
Cup and saucer	$ 13–20
Cup and saucer, *demitasse*	$ 22–30
Gravy boat, *faststand*	$ 48–58

Vernon Kilns "Early California" 14-inch oval platter,
orange, $55–$65.
Item courtesy of Elaine Tomber Tindell, Knoxville, Tennessee.

Plate, *bread and butter, 6¹/₂-inch diameter*	$ 5–10
Plate, *chop, 12-inch diameter*	$ 42–52
Plate, *chop, 14-inch diameter*	$ 55–65
Plate, *dinner, 10¹/₂-inch diameter*	$ 20–30
Plate, *luncheon, 9¹/₂-inch diameter*	$ 20–27
Plate, *salad, 7¹/₂-inch diameter*	$ 16–22
Platter, *oval, 9 inches*	$ 25–35
Platter, *oval, 12 inches*	$ 42–52
Platter, *oval, 14 inches*	$ 55–65
Platter, *oval, 16 inches*	$ 65–75
Shakers, *salt and pepper, set*	$ 25–35
Sugar bowl, *lidded*	$ 32–40
Tumbler, *juice*	$ 25–35

† *Most chowder bowls sell in the $17 to $34 range; yellow "Early California" items command higher prices.*

"Fantasia" (or "Walt Disney")

Reportedly made from 1940 to 1941, the Disney-inspired "Fantasia" pattern is probably the rarest of all the Vernon Kilns dinnerware patterns. There were a number of different designs in this grouping, including "Nutcracker," "Flower Ballet," "Dewdrop Fairies," "Fairyland," and "Milkweed Dance." These are transfer prints in colors of blue, brown, or maroon, in some cases with hand-tinting. Some pieces have allover prints; other items, such as those in the "Milkweed Dance" grouping, feature border designs surrounding white centers. Generally these pieces were made using Vernon Kilns' "Ultra" shapes, though some hollowware items use the "Montecito" shapes.

Chop plate, *17-inch diameter*	$ 800–900
Creamer	$ 150–200
Cup and saucer	$ 175–225
Muffin cover	$ 900–1,000
Plate, *bread and butter, 6^1/$_2$-inch diameter*	$ 75–110
Plate, *dinner, 10^1/$_2$-inch diameter*	$ 175–225
Plate, *luncheon, 9^1/$_2$-inch diameter*	$ 150–200
Plate, *salad, 8^1/$_2$-inch diameter*	$ 150–200
Plate, *dessert, 7^1/$_2$-inch diameter*	$ 85–125
Shakers, *salt and pepper, set*	$ 200–275
Sugar bowl, *lidded*	$ 225–275
Teapot	$ 700–850

"Frontier Days" (or "Winchester '73")

Pieces with this print-and-paint dinnerware pattern were initially used as promotional items for the 1950 feature film *Winchester '73,* which starred Jimmy Stewart and Shelley Winters. Pieces were made using Vernon Kilns' "Montecito" shapes, and featured western-themed images created by Paul Davidson. Such images included a cowboy on a fence, a buffalo hunt, a prospector and his burro, and a cavalry charge, among many others. In 1953, a dispute with the Winchester Arms Company over the continued use of the "Winchester" name caused Vernon Kilns to change the name of its pattern to "Frontier Days." Earlier pieces have either ivory- or soft green-colored backgrounds, but later items feature only green backgrounds. This is a relatively expensive pattern, and examples are difficult to find.

Bowl, *soup, rimmed, 8^1/$_2$ inches, stagecoach holdup*	$ 105–115
Bowl, *vegetable, oval, 10 inches*	$ 155–165

Bowl, *vegetable, oval, divided, prospector and burro*	$ 195–210
Cup and saucer, *buffalo hunt*	$ 85–95
Cup and saucer, *demitasse*	$ 95–110
Plate, *chop, 12-inch diameter, bucking bronco*	$ 195–210
Plate, *luncheon, 9¹/₂-inch diameter, wagon train*	$ 85–95
Platter, *oval, 16 inches*	$ 290–310
Tidbit server, *two-tier*	$ 235–250

"Fruitdale," "May Flower," and "Monterey"

All of these patterns appear on Vernon Kilns' "Melinda" shapes, which were designed by the important industrial designer Royal Hickman, and were introduced in 1942. "Melinda" shapes are distinguished by a rope of embossed leaves around the outer edges of the flatware and the bases of the hollowware items. Objects with handles have embossed leaves on the tops of the handles, and the finials on lids are shaped to resemble flowers. "Monterey" pattern pieces have embossed leaves colored red and blue. "Fruitdale" pieces feature embossed leaves that are unembellished, but a large image of fruit and flowers covers the entire center well of the flatware items. "May Flower" pieces are much the same as "Fruitdale" pieces, but are decorated only with flowers. Prices for pieces bearing each of these patterns are comparable, but "Monterey" pieces are generally the least valuable. (Pieces in the "Carmel" and "Philodendron" lines are also similar to "Monterey" pieces, except "Carmel" pieces have embossed leaves painted brown and yellow, and "Philodendron" pieces feature embossed leaves painted in shades of green and yellow.)

Bowl, *cereal, lug-handled, 7¹/₂-inch diameter*	$ 15–20
Bowl, *individual fruit, 5³/₄-inch diameter*	$ 8–12
Bowl, *salad, serving, footed, 12-inch diameter*	$ 60–80
Bowl, *soup, 8¹/₂-inch diameter*	$ 14–19
Bowl, *vegetable, oval, 9¹/₂ inches*	$ 32–40
Bowl, *vegetable, round, 9-inch diameter*	$ 40–50
Butter dish, *¹/₄-pound, covered*	$ 55–75
Creamer	$ 22–28
Cup and saucer	$ 15–20
Egg cup	$ 20–30
Gravy boat	$ 45–55
Plate, *bread and butter, 6¹/₂-inch diameter*	$ 5–10

Plate, *chop, 12-inch diameter*	$ 35–45
Plate, *chop, 14-inch diameter*	$ 40–50
Plate, *dinner, 10¹/₂-inch diameter*	$ 18–25
Plate, *luncheon, 9¹/₂-inch diameter*	$ 18–25
Plate, *salad, 7¹/₂-inch diameter*	$ 10–15
Platter, *oval, 12¹/₂ inches*	$ 45–55
Platter, *oval, 13³/₄ inches*	$ 48–58
Shakers, *salt and pepper, set*	$ 24–28
Sugar bowl, *lidded*	$ 32–40
Tidbit server, *two-tier*	$ 50–60
Tidbit server, *three-tier*	$ 55–65

"Hawaiian Flowers," "Honolulu," "Hilo," "Lei Lani," and "Hawaii"

These are the names given to a transfer-printed pattern designed by Don Blanding. The pattern consists of a lotus blossom floral motif in a variety of color schemes on two different Vernon Kilns shapes. The "Hawaiian Flowers" version of this pattern was made in shades of blue, maroon, pink, or orange (yellow). "Honolulu" is the exact same print, with hand-tinted yellow flowers on a blue background. "Hilo" is the same pattern in brown with hand-tinted flowers, and "Lei Lani" is maroon with hand-tinted flowers. All four patterns appear on Vernon Kilns' "Ultra" shapes, which can often be identified by their upside-down handles. The "Hawaii" pattern is the same as "Lei Lani," but was made using Vernon Kilns' "Melinda" shapes. These designs first appeared in 1939, and were mainly produced in the 1940s.

Bowl, *individual fruit, 5¹/₂-inch diameter*	$ 45–55
Bowl, *vegetable, round, 9-inch diameter*	$ 95–110
Creamer	$ 55–65
Cup and saucer	$ 35–45
Cup and saucer, *demitasse*	$ 55–65
Plate, *bread and butter, 6¹/₂-inch diameter*	$ 14–24
Plate, *dinner, 10¹/₂-inch diameter*	$ 45–55
Plate, *luncheon, 8¹/₂-inch diameter*	$ 35–45
Plate, *salad, 7¹/₂-inch diameter*	$ 35–45
Shakers, *salt and pepper, set*	$ 55–65
Sugar bowl, *lidded*	$ 80–100

"Heavenly Days" and "Tickled Pink"

First produced in 1955, these two patterns both appear on the "San Clemente" (or "Anytime") shape. Both patterns feature the same design of small squares and crosses, but with different color schemes. "Heavenly Days" pieces are primarily aqua, pink, and Mocha-Charcoal, with solid-turquoise cups and serving pieces (casseroles have patterned lids). "Tickled Pink" pieces are pink and charcoal, with solid-pink cups and serving pieces (again, the casseroles have patterned lids). Lids on the coffeepots and sugar bowls are solid-colored to match the colors of their particular pattern.

Bowl, *cereal, 6-inch diameter*	$ 14–18
Bowl, *individual fruit, 5^1/$_2$-inch diameter*	$ 10–15
Bowl, *vegetable, oval, 9^1/$_4$ inches*	$ 22–30
Bowl, *vegetable, oval, divided*	$ 25–35
Bowl, *vegetable, round, 7^1/$_2$-inch diameter*	$ 18–22
Bowl, *vegetable, round, 9-inch diameter*	$ 22–26
Bowl, *vegetable, round, covered*	$ 65–75
Butter, *^{1}/$_4$-pound, covered*	$ 35–45
Coffeepot	$ 55–65
Creamer	$ 15–20
Cup and saucer	$ 10–15
Gravy boat	$ 22–30
Jug, *1-pint*	$ 30–36
Jug, *2-quart, 9^1/$_2$ inches*	$ 45–55
Mug	$ 35–45
Plate, *bread and butter, 6^1/$_4$-inch diameter*	$ 6–10
Plate, *chop, 13-inch diameter*	$ 25–35
Plate, *dinner, 10-inch diameter*	$ 14–18
Plate, *salad, 7^1/$_2$-inch diameter*	$ 8–12
Platter, *oval, 9^1/$_2$ inches*	$ 20–27
Platter, *oval, 13^1/$_2$ inches*	$ 25–32
Shakers, *salt and pepper, set*	$ 20–30
Teapot	$ 85–95
Tidbit server, *two-tier*	$ 40–50

Tidbit server, *three-tier*	$ 45–55
Tumbler, *14-ounce*	$ 22–28

"Moby Dick"

First produced in 1938, "Moby Dick" became the most popular of all the Rockwell Kent designs, even though some consider it a strange design for a dinnerware pattern. The design was taken from Kent's illustrations for Herman Melville's book *Moby Dick,* and consists of stirring images of fully rigged sailing ships, leaping porpoises, and soaring sea birds in shades of blue, maroon, brown, or, very rarely, orange (yellow). "Moby Dick" is found on "Ultra" shapes, and prices below are for the more common colors of blue, maroon, and brown. For pieces in yellow, add at least 25 percent to the prices listed below.

Bowl, *individual fruit, 5³/₄-inch diameter*	$ 45–55
Bowl, *chowder, lug-handled*	$ 95–110
Cup and saucer	$ 75–85
Cup and saucer, *demitasse*	$ 85–100
Plate, *bread and butter, 6¹/₂-inch diameter*	$ 42–50
Plate, *chop, 12-inch diameter*	$ 175–200
Plate, *chop, 14-inch diameter*	$ 350–400
Plate, *dinner, 10¹/₂-inch diameter*	$ 100–115
Plate, *luncheon, 9¹/₂-inch diameter*	$ 72–82
Plate, *salad, 7¹/₂-inch diameter*	$ 60–70
Shakers, *salt and pepper, pair*	$ 100–125

"Organdie"

This grouping of patterns, which collectors tend collectively to refer to as "Plaid," is among Vernon Kilns' best sellers. "Organdie" originated in the late 1930s, and the original patterns were designed by Gale Turnbull, whose signature appears on the back of each piece as part of the Vernon Kilns mark. Each piece was hand-painted under the glaze. What follows is a list of the various "Plaid" patterns and their color schemes, along with their style numbers, if they are known.

"Calico," *pink and blue*
"Coronation Organdie," *T-508, gray and rose*
"Gingham," *green and yellow with a green border*
"Homespun," *green, rust, and yellow with a rust-colored border*

"Organdie," *brown and yellow*

"Organdie," *T-511, brown and yellow, but with more detailed painting than regular*

"Organdie"

"Organdie," *T-512, deep rose and green*

"Organdie," *T-513, yellow and green*

"Plaid," *T-515, gray and forest green*

"Plaid," *T-604, rust brown and medium blue with a medium-blue border*

"Tam O'Shanter," *rust, chartreuse, and green with a green-colored border*

"Tweed," *gray and forest green*

Of these patterns, "Calico" and "Homespun" tend to be the most valuable.

"Calico"

Bowl, *cereal, lug-handled*	$ 25–32
Bowl, *vegetable, oval, divided*	$ 55–65
Bowl, *vegetable, round, 9-inch diameter*	$ 45–55
Cup and saucer	$ 30–40
Cup and saucer, *demitasse*	$ 50–60
Gravy boat	$ 55–65
Plate, *bread and butter, 6¹/₂-inch diameter*	$ 12–16
Plate, *chop, 12-inch diameter*	$ 45–55
Plate, *dinner, 10¹/₂-inch diameter*	$ 37–45
Plate, *luncheon, 9¹/₂-inch diameter*	$ 17–24
Plate, *salad, 7¹/₂-inch diameter*	$ 25–35
Platter, *oval, 12¹/₂ inches*	$ 45–55

"Gingham"

Ashtray, *medium, 4¹/₂ inches square*	$ 25–32
Bowl, *individual fruit, 5¹/₂-inch diameter*	$ 10–14
Bowl, *mixing, 5-inch diameter*	$ 35–45
Bowl, *mixing, 6-inch diameter*	$ 40–50
Bowl, *mixing, 7-inch diameter*	$ 45–55

Bowl, *mixing, 8-inch diameter*	$ 50–60
Bowl, *vegetable, oval, divided*	$ 30–38
Bowl, *vegetable, round, 8^1/$_2$-inch diameter*	$ 22–28
Butter dish, *^{1}/$_4$-pound, covered*	$ 45–55
Butter pat	$ 25–32
Casserole, *chicken pie, lidded, stick handle*	$ 35–45
Casserole, *individual, lidded*	$ 38–44
Casserole, *round, covered, 1^1/$_2$-quart*	$ 42–50
Creamer	$ 18–22
Cup and saucer	$ 10–14
Cup and saucer, *demitasse*	$ 40–50
Cup and saucer, *colossal, 4-quart*	$ 290–310
Plate, *bread and butter, 6^1/$_2$-inch diameter*	$ 3–5
Plate, *chop, 12-inch diameter*	$ 25–32
Plate, *chop, 14-inch diameter*	$ 28–34
Plate, *dinner, 10^1/$_2$-inch diameter*	$ 20–30
Plate, *luncheon, 9^1/$_2$-inch diameter*	$ 10–15
Platter, *oval, 10^1/$_2$ inches*	$ 22–28
Platter, *oval, 12 inches*	$ 28–34
Platter, *oval, 14 inches*	$ 45–52
Sauce boat	$ 25–32
Shakers, *salt and pepper, set*	$ 17–25
Sugar bowl, *lidded*	$ 25–32

"Homespun"

Bowl, *individual fruit, 5^1/$_2$-inch diameter*	$ 10–15
Bowl, *mixing, 5-inch diameter*	$ 45–55
Bowl, *mixing, 6-inch diameter*	$ 47–57
Bowl, *mixing, 7-inch diameter*	$ 55–65
Bowl, *mixing, 8-inch diameter*	$ 65–75
Bowl, *vegetable, oval, divided*	$ 25–32
Bowl, *vegetable, round, 9-inch diameter*	$ 22–28

Casserole, *round, covered, 1¹/₂-quart*	$ 55–65
Coffee carafe, *with stopper*	$ 45–55
Creamer	$ 12–16
Cup and saucer	$ 12–16
Cup and saucer, *demitasse*	$ 45–55
Gravy boat	$ 32–40
Jug, *1-pint, bulb bottom*	$ 25–35
Jug, *1-quart, bulb bottom*	$ 45–55
Plate, *bread and butter, 6¹/₂-inch diameter*	$ 4–7
Plate, *chop, 12-inch diameter*	$ 22–28
Plate, *dinner, 10¹/₂ inches*	$ 22–32
Plate, *luncheon, 9¹/₂-inch diameter*	$ 8–12
Plate, *salad, 7¹/₂-inch diameter*	$ 10–14
Platter, *oval, 10¹/₂ inches*	$ 25–35
Platter, *oval, 12 inches*	$ 27–37
Platter, *oval, 14 inches*	$ 32–42
Platter, *oval, 12 inches*	$ 55–65
Sauce boat	$ 32–40
Shakers, *salt and pepper, set*	$ 18–25
Sugar bowl, *lidded*	$ 18–24
Teapot	$ 100–120

"Organdie" (T-511)

Ashtray, *small, 3 inches square*	$ 22–28
Bowl, *individual fruit, 5¹/₂-inch diameter*	$ 8–12
Bowl, *vegetable, oval, divided*	$ 25–35
Bowl, *vegetable, round, 9-inch diameter*	$ 15–22
Butter dish, *¹/₄-pound, covered*	$ 45–55
Casserole, *chicken pie, lidded, stick handle*	$ 35–45
Coffee carafe, *with stopper*	$ 65–75
Creamer	$ 15–20

Creamer, *lidded*	$ 22–28
Cup and saucer	$ 12–16
Cup and saucer, *demitasse*	$ 45–55
Egg cup	$ 45–55
Gravy boat	$ 25–35
Jug, *1-pint, bulb bottom*	$ 22–28
Jug, *1-quart, bulb bottom*	$ 35–45
Jug, *2-quart, streamlined*	$ 75–85
Mug	$ 38–45
Plate, *bread and butter, 6^1/$_2$-inch diameter*	$ 4–7
Plate, *chop, 12-inch diameter*	$ 22–30
Plate, *dinner, 10^1/$_2$-inch diameter*	$ 20–28
Plate, *luncheon, 9^1/$_2$-inch diameter*	$ 6–10
Plate, *salad, 7^1/$_2$-inch diameter*	$ 10–15
Platter, *oval, 10^1/$_2$ inches*	$ 25–35
Platter, *oval, 12 inches*	$ 32–38
Platter, *oval, 14 inches*	$ 45–52
Sauce boat	$ 25–35
Shakers, *salt and pepper, set*	$ 18–24
Sugar bowl, *lidded*	$ 20–26
Teapot	$ 75–85
Tidbit server, *two-tier*	$ 75–82
Tumbler, *14-ounce*	$ 25–35

"Tam O'Shanter"

Bowl, *individual fruit, 5^1/$_2$-inch diameter*	$ 10–15
Bowl, *vegetable, oval, divided*	$ 25–35
Bowl, *vegetable, round, 9-inch diameter*	$ 22–28
Casserole, *chicken pie server, covered, stick handle*	$ 25–32
Creamer	$ 15–20
Cup and saucer	$ 16–20

Cup and saucer, *colossal, 4-quart*	$ 290–310
Cup and saucer, *demitasse*	$ 40–48
Gravy boat	$ 32–38
Jug, *2-quart, streamlined*	$ 55–65
Plate, *bread and butter, 6^1/$_2$-inch diameter*	$ 4–7
Plate, *chop, 12-inch diameter*	$ 25–35
Plate, *dinner, 10^1/$_2$-inch diameter*	$ 45–55
Plate, *luncheon, 9^1/$_2$-inch diameter*	$ 12–16
Plate, *salad, 7^1/$_2$-inch diameter*	$ 12–16
Platter, *oval, 10^1/$_2$ inches*	$ 16–22
Platter, *oval, 12 inches*	$ 25–32
Platter, *oval, 14 inches*	$ 35–42
Sauce boat	$ 35–42
Shakers, *salt and pepper, set*	$ 18–25
Sugar bowl, *lidded*	$ 22–26
Teapot	$ 85–95
Tumbler, *14-ounce*	$ 25–32

"Tweed"

Bowl, *vegetable, round, 9-inch diameter*	$ 45–52
Casserole, *chicken pie server, lidded, stick handle*	$ 45–50
Creamer	$ 25–35
Cup and saucer	$ 20–25
Plate, *bread and butter, 6^1/$_2$-inch diameter*	$ 4–7
Plate, *chop, 12-inch diameter*	$ 45–55
Plate, *dinner, 10^1/$_2$-inch diameter*	$ 40–50
Plate, *luncheon, 9^1/$_2$-inch diameter*	$ 15–20
Plate, *salad, 7^1/$_2$-inch diameter*	$ 12–16
Platter, *oval, 12 inches*	$ 55–62
Platter, *oval, 14 inches*	$ 57–65
Sauce boat	$ 65–75
Shakers, *salt and pepper, set*	$ 35–45

"Our America"

Pieces in this ambitious Rockwell Kent series featured emblematic scenes from eight different regions of the United States: New England, the Middle Atlantic region, the Southern Colonial region, the Mississippi River, the Great Lakes, the Plains and Mountains region, the Gulf region, and the Pacific region. The series included more than 30 different designs in shades of brown, blue, maroon, and green on cream-colored backgrounds. Of these colors, brown is the most common and green is the rarest. This series was produced on Vernon Kilns' "Ultra" shapes, and was first made in 1940. As a general rule, prices for "Our America" pieces are comparable to those for Kent's "Moby Dick" pieces, which are listed above.

"Salamina"

As was the case with the "Moby Dick" line, pieces in this grouping have an unusual Rockwell Kent pattern based on illustrations done for a book. In this case, the book was Kent's *Salamina*, which is a chronicle of Kent's life in Greenland. Salamina was Kent's housekeeper during this adventure, and he thought her a woman of great nobility and beauty who represented the better qualities of the women of Greenland. Most of the pieces in this line, which was made in 1939, feature depictions of Salamina in a very Art Moderne manner among glaciers and the northern lights. The most famous of these images depicts Salamina with a bird flying above one shoulder. A Vernon Kilns sales brochure proclaimed that "Salamina" dinnerware was "beautiful enough for the wall of an art museum." Examples are hand-tinted on "Ultra" shapes, and this pattern is considered one of the two most valuable of Vernon Kilns' designs. Collectors should beware, however, since reproductions of "Salamina" pieces have been reported.

Bowl, *soup, 8¹/₄-inch diameter*	$ 140–160
Plate, *chop, 12-inch diameter*	$ 575–625
Plate, *chop, 14-inch diameter*	$ 700–775
Plate, *dinner, 10¹/₂-inch diameter*	$ 225–250
Plate, *luncheon, 9¹/₂-inch diameter*	$ 185–210
Shakers, *salt and pepper, set*	$ 185–210

Disney Figures

Vernon Kilns manufactured figures for the Walt Disney Company for about a year and a half before its contract was reassigned to Evan K. Shaw's American Pottery. Both companies produced these Disney figures, but Vernon Kilns' are usually marked with an incised number, while the pieces made by American Pottery are not. Regardless of which company produced them, all of these figures are difficult to find.

#1 Satyr, *4¹/₂ inches*	$ 275–325
#2 Satyr, *4¹/₂ inches*	$ 275–325
#3 Satyr, *4¹/₂ inches*	$ 275–325
#4 Satyr, *4¹/₂ inches*	$ 275–325
#5 Satyr, *4¹/₂ inches*	$ 275–325
#6 Satyr, *4¹/₂ inches*	$ 275–325
#7 Sprite, *4¹/₂ inches*	$ 325–375
#8 Sprite, *reclining, 3 inches*	$ 425–475
#9 Sprite, *4¹/₂ inches*	$ 325–475
#10 Sprite, *winged, 4¹/₂ inches*	$ 325–475
#11 Sprite, *arms folded, 4¹/₂ inches*	$ 325–475
#12 Sprite, *4¹/₂ inches*	$ 325–475
#13 Unicorn, *black with yellow horn*	$ 425–475
#14 Unicorn, *sitting, 5 inches*	$ 525–575
#15 Unicorn, *rearing, 6 inches*	$ 525–575
#16 Donkey Unicorn, *reclining, 5¹/₂ inches*	$ 750–825
#17 Centaurette, *sitting, 5¹/₂ inches*	$ 850–950
#18 Centaurette, *posing, 7¹/₂ inches*	$ 1,100–1,200
#19 Pegasus, *baby, black, 4¹/₂ inches*	$ 325–375
#20 Pegasus, *white, head turned, 5 inches*	$ 850–950
#21 Pegasus, *white, 5¹/₂ inches*	$ 350–400
#22 Centaurette, *arms around head*	$ 1,200–1,400
#23 Centaurette, *Nubian, 8 inches*	$ 1,200–1,400
#24 Centaurette, *Nubian, left hand at throat, 7¹/₂ inches*	$ 1,000–1,100
#25 Elephant, *5 inches*	$ 425–475
#26 Elephant, *trunk raised*	$ 425–475
#27 Elephant, *dancing, trunk up*	$ 425–475
#28 Ostrich Ballerina, *on pointe, 6 inches*	$ 1,600–1,750
#29 Ostrich Ballerina, *bowing, 8 inches*	$ 1,250–1,350
#30 Ostrich, *9 inches*	$ 1,600–1,750
#31 Centaur, *bunch of grapes in each arm, 10 inches*	$ 1,100–1,200

#32 Hippo in Tutu, *arms out, 5¹/₂ inches*	$ 400–450
#33 Hippo, *holding tutu*	$ 375–450
#34 Hippo, *hands on hips*	$ 375–450
#35 / #36 Hop Low, *shakers, mushroom-shaped, 3¹/₂ inches, pair*	$ 145–175
#37 Baby Weems, *sitting, 6 inches*	$ 375–425
#38 Timothy Mouse, *6 inches*	$ 525–575
#39 Mr. Crow	$ 1,600–1,750
#40 Dumbo, *falling on his ear, 5 inches*	$ 175–200
#41 Dumbo, *sitting, 5 inches*	$ 175–200
#42 Mr. Stork, *pointing left wing, 8³/₄ inches*	$ 2,200–2,400

Disney Vases and Bowls

These items were produced in solid colors of pink, blue, turquoise, or white, or were hand-painted.

#120 Bowl, *Mushroom, rectangular*	$ 225–250
#121 Bowl, *Goldfish, hand-painted*	$ 650–750
#121 Bowl, *Goldfish, solid color*	$ 425–475
#122 Bowl, *Winged Nymph, solid color*	$ 325–375
#122 Bowl, *Winged Nymph, hand-painted*	$ 650–700
#123 Vase, *Winged Nymph, hand-painted*	$ 525–600
#124 Bowl, *Satyr, solid color*	$ 325–375
#124 Bowl, *Satyr, hand-painted*	$ 650–700
#125 Bowl, *Sprite, hand-painted*	$ 525–600
#126 Vase, *Goddess, solid color, 10¹/₂ inches*	$ 1,250–1,400
#126 Vase, *Goddess, cameo effect, 10¹/₂ inches*	$ 2,200–2,400
#127 Vase, *Pegasus, solid color*	$ 750–800
#127 Vase, *Pegasus, hand-painted*	$ 1,500–1,600

Souvenir and Specialty Plates

These are the Vernon Kilns items most commonly encountered by collectors. They were made using "Montecito," "Melinda," "San Fernando," and "Ultra" shapes, and can be found in 8½-inch, 10½-inch, and 12½-inch sizes, with the 10½-inch size being the most common. Initially these items were manufactured using blue, brown, or maroon transfer prints, but starting in 1953, items featured either "print-and-paint" designs or transfer prints with a little hand-coloring. Examples of Vernon Kilns souvenir plates can also be found in shades of purple or green, but generally these items do not command premium prices. Many of these pieces were stock items, but others were special orders that are somewhat more rare. A great number of these plates were made, and the lists below provide only a small sampling of what is available.

Presidents and Famous Personages

Chopin, *portrait of the composer in center*	$ 20–30
Davis, Jefferson	$ 30–40
Eisenhower, Dwight, and Nixon, Richard	$ 85–100
Lincoln, Abraham, *16th President, "Melinda" shape, 10½-inch diameter*	$ 30–40
Marti, José, *hand-colored, 10½-inch diameter*	$ 50–60
Pope Pius XII	$ 50–60
Rogers, Will, *"1879–1935," 10½ inches*	$ 30–40
Roosevelt, Franklin, *"Commander of the Armed Forces"*	$ 60–70
Twain, Mark, *center portrait, 10½-inch diameter*	$ 30–40
Washington, George, *"The Father of His Country"*	$ 25–35

Transportation

"Chicago Railroad Fair," *Marshall Field's and Company or Consolidated Concessions, seven reserves of trains, 10½-inch diameter*	$ 65–75
"Durango, Colorado, The Narrow Gauge Capital of the World," *train on trestle, blue, 10½-inch diameter, special order*	$ 65–75
The "Emma Sweeney," *10½-inch diameter*	$ 60–70
"In My Merry Oldsmobile," *music around edge, 10½-inch diameter*	$ 70–80
Virginia & Truckee Railroad, *red band around edge, 8½-inch diameter*	$ 45–55

Vernon Kilns souvenir plate, 8½ inches, "Picture Map of Washington," $25–$35.
Item courtesy of Kingston Pike Antique Mall, Knoxville, Tennessee.

Vernon Kilns plate, 8½ inches "Bits of the Old South," "House Boat on the River," $35–$45.
Item courtesy of Needful Things, Hendersonville, North Carolina.

Vernon Kilns plate, 8½ inches, "Bits of the Old South," "Down on the Levee," $35–$45.
Item courtesy of Needful Things, Hendersonville, North Carolina.

World War II

Airborne Division, *"Montecito" shape, 8½-inch diameter*	$ 65–75
Army Air Corps Song	$ 60–70
Convair, *center design of five World War II vintage airplanes, special order, 10½-inch diameter*	$ 75–85
Douglas, *"First Around the World"*	$ 75–85
Marine Corps Hymn	$ 60–75

"Martin," *center design of six World War II vintage airplanes, special order, 10¹/₂-inch diameter*	$ 75–85
US Naval Air Gunner's School, *Purcell, Oklahoma*	$ 35–45
US Naval Air Station, *Pensacola, Florida*	$ 35–45

Miscellaneous

Christmas, *Christmas tree with gifts, chop plate, 12-inch diameter, hand-painted*	$ 65–75
Christmas, *Santa Claus head, surrounded by children's toys, a Christmas tree, and a fireplace, 10¹/₂-inch diameter*	$ 55–65
Cocktail Hour, *provocative woman in center, rim with various kinds of cocktail glasses, "Singapore Sling," "Bacardi," "Pink Lady," etc., brown print, 8¹/₂-inch diameter, each*	$ 60–75
"Easter Fires of Fredericksburg, Texas," *1949, three egg-shaped reserves with Easter bunnies, hand-colored, 10¹/₂-inch diameter*	$ 85–100
French Opera, *reproductions of 19th-century examples, all marked by Vernon Kilns, "Barbiere de Seville," "Guillaume Tell," "Faust," etc., hand-colored, 8¹/₂-inch diameter, each*	$ 25–30
Horse, *"Citation," 10¹/₂-inch diameter*	$ 85–100

WAHPETON POTTERY COMPANY (ROSEMEADE)

Rosemeade

One of the "Rosemeade" marks used by *Wahpeton Pottery*.

This pottery is best known to collectors by its trade name: Rosemeade. The pottery was located in Wahpeton, North Dakota, and was founded in 1940 by Robert Hughes and Laura Taylor, who were married in 1943.

Taylor had been a schoolteacher by trade when, wanting to provide better art projects for her students, she enrolled in a teachers' college in order to develop skills in drawing and modeling. When Taylor returned to her students, they so enjoyed making items from clay that she furthered her education in this field by taking classes from Glen Lukens, an accomplished studio potter. Starting in 1932, Taylor attended the University of North Dakota to study art and ceramics, and during her time there she began making pottery that was sold to the public. In 1939, Taylor demonstrated the art of pottery making at the New York World's Fair.

Back in North Dakota, Robert Hughes wanted to promote industry in North Dakota, and he also wanted to explore the possibilities of native clay. Hughes saw Taylor's pottery demonstration at the World's Fair, and proposed that they join forces to open a pottery in North Dakota. The company was founded in 1940. Taylor did the modeling, which was very strongly naturalistic, with an emphasis on animals and birds.

Howard Lewis, who had previously worked at Niloak, joined the firm in 1944 as a ceramics engineer, and was responsible for creating the glazes. While at Rosemeade, he introduced a rare type of swirled ware.

Unfortunately, Laura Taylor Hughes died in 1959, and production at Wahpeton ceased in 1961, though its salesroom remained open until 1964.

Ashtrays

Wahpeton produced state-shaped ashtrays representing 28 of the 50 states.

Advertising ashtray, *figure of winged ear of corn, Dekalb, cigarette rest in center, 5 inches*	$ 275–325
Advertising ashtray, *figure of Black Angus bull, rectangular, 7³/₄ inches*	$ 450–500
Advertising ashtray, *Red Wing Shoes, round with three-dimensional boot, cigarette rests on side*	$ 1,250–1,400
Alabama shape	$ 65–85
Cow on ashtray with cigarette rests in center, *5 inches, three-dimensional Holstein or Guernsey*	$ 425–450
Cowboy hat, *advertising*	$ 95–120
Fish, *6¹/₄ inches*	$ 135–160
Florida shape	$ 145–175
Fort Abercrombie, *three-dimensional block house, octagonal ashtray, 5 inches*	$ 375–435
Georgia shape	$ 90–110
Great Smoky Mountains, *three-dimensional bear, cigarette rests in center, 5 inches*	$ 275–300
Indiana shape	$ 110–140
Iowa shape	$ 225–275
Minnesota, *three-dimensional gopher, cigarette rest in center, 5 inches*	$ 250–300
Minnesota, *in shape of state*	$ 145–165
Oval ashtray with embossed image of Native American in headdress, *5¹/₂ inches*	$ 200–225
Pony on oval ashtrays, *7 inches*	$ 320–340

Tennessee shape	$ 45–65
Viking ship, *three-dimensional ship, elliptical ashtray, with cigarette rests in center, 5 inches*	$ 325–375
Wildcat on ashtray with cigarette rests in center, *5 inches*	$ 500–550
Wisconsin, *three-dimensional badger, cigarette rest in center, 5 inches*	$ 550–600
Wyoming shape	$ 65–85

Figures

Animals

Bear, *walking, 6$^{1}/_{2}$ inches by 3$^{1}/_{2}$ inches*	$ 325–375
Bluegill fish, *1$^{1}/_{2}$ inches by 1$^{1}/_{4}$ inches*	$ 225–250
Buffalo, *standing, 3$^{1}/_{2}$ inches by 2$^{1}/_{2}$ inches*	$ 125–175
Cat, *sitting, 8 inches, white or blue*	$ 950–1,200
Cocker Spaniels, *paws up, one lying down, set*	$ 550–600
Coyote, *howling, 4$^{1}/_{2}$ inches by 3$^{3}/_{4}$ inches*	$ 250–350
Deer, *standing among foliage, 7$^{3}/_{4}$ inches by 7$^{3}/_{4}$ inches*	$ 100–150
Dove, *2$^{3}/_{4}$ inches by 1$^{3}/_{4}$ inches*	$ 275–325
Duck, *both drakes and hens, 1$^{3}/_{4}$ inches by 1 inch*	$ 200–225
Flamingo, *head up on nest, 3$^{3}/_{4}$ inches by 2 inches, head curved down in nest, 3 inches by 2 inches, pair*	$ 300–325
Foxes, *two, with tails curled around them, 3$^{1}/_{4}$ inches by 2$^{1}/_{4}$ inches*	$ 575–650
Frog, *2$^{3}/_{4}$ inches by 1$^{3}/_{4}$ inches*	$ 200–250
Gopher, *holding nut, 2 inches by 1$^{1}/_{2}$ inches*	$ 65–90
Hippopotamus, *3$^{1}/_{2}$ inches by 3$^{1}/_{2}$ inches*	$ 325–375
Horse, *circus, 4$^{1}/_{4}$ inches by 4$^{1}/_{4}$ inches*	$ 350–450
Jackrabbit, *running, on base, 3$^{1}/_{4}$ inches by 1$^{3}/_{4}$ inches*	$ 250–350
Kitten, *tail up, 2 inches by 2 inches*	$ 45–60
Koala bear on tree trunk, *8$^{1}/_{2}$ inches by 3$^{1}/_{2}$ inches*	$ 275–350
Panda, *walking, 5 inches by 3$^{1}/_{2}$ inches*	$ 750–850
Parakeet, *on tall vaselike base, 7 inches tall*	$ 225–250

Pelican, *3¹/₄ inches by 3 inches*	$ 110–130
Pheasant, *cock, 13 inches by 7 inches, head up*	$ 325–375
Pheasant, *hen, 11¹/₂ inches by 4 inches, head down*	$ 425–475
Pointer, *4³/₄ inches by 2³/₄ inches*	$ 650–750
Pony, *lying down, 6 inches by 3³/₄ inches*	$ 250–350
Pouter Pigeon, *with chest puffed out, 3 inches by 2³/₄ inches*	$ 350–400
Prairie dog, *1¹/₄ inches by 1 inch*	$ 65–85
Puppy, *begging, 3 inches by 2³/₄ inches*	$ 100–120
Rainbow trout, *2³/₄ inches by 1³/₄ inches*	$ 375–425
Rooster, *strutting, 3³/₄ inches*	$ 175–225
Roosters, *fighting, 4 inches by 3 inches, beaks open, dark colors, pair*	$ 275–325
Seahorse, *8 inches by 3¹/₄ inches*	$ 275–325
Turkey, *6¹/₂ inches by 6 inches*	$ 175–200
Walrus, *6¹/₂ inches by 4¹/₄ inches*	$ 575–625
Zebra, *stylized, 4 inches by 1¹/₂ inches*	$ 475–550

Other

Blockhouse, *Fort Lincoln State Park, 1 inch*	$ 225–275
Brussels Sprout, *1³/₄ inches by 1¹/₄ inches*	$ 85–100
Mount Rushmore, *5 inches by 3³/₄ inches*	$ 525–575
Potato, *2¹/₂ inches by 1¹/₂ inches*	$ 140–160

Salt and Pepper Shakers

Badgers, *set*	$ 575–675
"Bambi," *set*	$ 135–165
Bear Cubs, *set*	$ 65–85
Black Angus, *pair*	$ 375–425
Bloodhound head, *set*	$ 75–100
Bluegills, *4 inches, set*	$ 475–550
Boston Terriers, *set*	$ 275–350

Brussels Sprouts, *set*	$ 45–60
Buffalo, *set*	$ 145–175
Cactus, *"Devil's Finger," set*	$ 145–175
Canopic jars, *set of four*	$ 650–750
Cats, *sitting, 3¹/₂ inches, set*	$ 90–110
Chihuahuas, *set*	$ 425–500
Corn ears, *2¹/₄ inches, set*	$ 45–60
Cucumbers, *set*	$ 45–60
Ducks, *miniature, Mallard, 1³/₄ inches by 1 inch, set*	$ 150–200
Horses' heads, *Palomino, set*	$ 65–85
Jackrabbits, *running, set*	$ 145–175
Kangaroo	$ 375–425
Native American "God of Peace," *4 inches, set*	$ 225–275
Native American "God of Peace," *6³/₄ inches, set*	$ 525–600
Oxen, *set*	$ 95–110
Parrots, *2¹/₂ inches, set*	$ 165–210
Paul Bunyan and Babe the Blue Ox, *set*	$ 145–175
Pigs, *sitting, 3³/₄ inches*	$ 145–175
Potatoes on tray, *set*	$ 375–475
Pouter Pigeons, *"S" and "P" on chests, set*	$ 275–350
Prairie dogs, *2¹/₂ inches, set*	$ 65–85
Quail, *with real feather topknots, set*	$ 110–135
Quail, *no feathers, set*	$ 70–85
Roadrunners, *set*	$ 175–225
Roosters, *strutting, 3³/₄ inches, set*	$ 85–120
Sailboat, *3¹/₂ inches, set*	$ 375–450
Swans, *2 inches, set*	$ 85–120
Trout, *5 inches, set*	$ 475–550
Turkeys, *Tom and Hen, miniature, set*	$ 200–250
Viking ships, *3¹/₂ inches, set*	$ 425–500
Windmill, *3¹/₂ inches*	$ 185–225

Plaques and Wall Pockets

Plaque, *Chinese ring-necked pheasants, pair*	$ 1,000–1,200
Plaque, *dove, 6¼ inches*	$ 145–185
Plaque, *fish, salmon, crappie, muskie, northern pike, bluegill, brook trout, walleye, or small-mouthed bass, oval mounting, 6 inches by 3½ inches, each*	$ 250–325
Plaque, *pigeon, flying, 8 inches by 5¾ inches*	$ 275–350
Plaque, *horse head, 4 inches*	$ 375–450
Plaque, *lovebirds in crescent moon, 6¼ inches by 6¼ inches*	$ 475–550
Wall Pocket, *crescent moon, small size, 4¼ inches*	$ 70–90
Wall Pocket, *deer, 5 inches*	$ 65–85
Wall Pocket, *Egyptian theme, with original liner*	$ 325–375
Wall Pocket, *Egyptian theme, without original liner*	$ 225–275
Wall Pocket, *kitten in stocking*	$ 800–925
Wall Pocket, *leaves, 4½ inches*	$ 65–90

Planters

Bird on log, *6 inches by 3 inches*	$ 60–75
Cornucopia, *grapes, 8 inches*	$ 95–115
Deer with stump and flowers, *3¾ inches*	$ 65–80
Dove, *6¼ inches*	$ 145–185
Dutch wooden shoe	$ 60–75
Dutch wooden shoe, *decorated*	$ 90–110
Elephant, *planter, 5½ inches*	$ 95–115
Goat, *baby, 5¼ inches*	$ 95–115
Grapes, *square, 4½ inches*	$ 95–115
Horse, *circus*	$ 95–115
Kangaroo	$ 120–145
Lamb, *6½ inches,*	$ 175–225
Mermaid	$ 225–275
Mule, *6 inches*	$ 275–325
Pheasant, *9¼ inches*	$ 525–575

Rooster, *flat, 7^1/$_2$ inches by 5 inches*	$ 250–375
Sleigh, *Dutch*	$ 95–120
Swan, *5 inches by 4^3/$_4$ inches*	$ 60–80
Wolfhound, *11^1/$_4$ inches*	$ 475–550
Viking ship, *10 inches*	$ 225–275
Viking ship, *12 inches*	$ 250–325
Watering can, *with raised rabbit design on side, 4^1/$_2$ inches*	$ 90–115

Spoon Holders

Bat, *5^3/$_4$ inches*	$ 550–650
Cocker Spaniel	$ 375–450
Elephant, *5^3/$_4$ inches*	$ 145–175
Horse	$ 150–200
Pansy, *4 inches*	$ 90–115
Pig	$ 165–200
Prairie rose, *4^1/$_4$ inches*	$ 90–110
Roosevelt (Teddy) Centennial, *8^3/$_4$ inches*	$ 145–175
Rooster, *8^3/$_4$ inches*	$ 125–115
Sunflower, *5 inches*	$ 125–175
Tulip, *5 inches*	$ 90–115
Turkey, *Tom, 5^1/$_2$ inches*	$ 450–550
Water lily	$ 90–110

Jewelry

Pin, *duck head, Mallard*	$ 1,000–1,200
Pin, *duck, full figure, flying, Mallard*	$ 1,000–1,200
Pin, *heart-shaped, with bluebird in apple tree, 2 inches*	$ 575–650
Pin, *heart-shaped, with squirrel*	$ 575–650
Pin, *horse's head, several variations*	$ 1,000–1,200
Pin, *red-winged blackbird, 2^1/$_4$ inches*	$ 1,000–1,200
Pin, *squirrel with acorn, 2^3/$_4$ inches*	$ 1,000–1,200

Television Lamps

Elk, *Wapiti, 11¹/₄ inches*	$ 625–700
Deer, *jumping, pine bows*	$ 550–625
Horse, *in foliage*	$ 475–600
Panther, *13 inches*	$ 550–625
Pheasant, *11³/₄ inches*	$ 550–625
Rooster, *14¹/₂ inches*	$ 1,700–1,850
Wolfhound	$ 450–575

Miscellaneous

Bank, *bear, 5³/₄ inches*	$ 425–475
Basket with twist handle, *5¹/₄ inches*	$ 120–140
Bell, *elephant, 4¹/₄ inches*	$ 175–225
Bell, *tulip, 3³/₄ inches*	$ 145–175
Bell, *peacock*	$ 275–325
Butter dish, *¹/₄-pound, covered, rooster*	$ 200–250
Candleholders, *prairie rose, 4¹/₂ inches, pair*	$ 190–220
Cup and saucer, *hand-thrown, 4¹/₂ inches*	$ 275–325
Dish, *relish, oval, divided, 9 inches*	$ 65–80
Flower frog, *in form of stump, 3¹/₂ inches*	$ 120–140
Hen on a nest, *covered dish or casserole*	$ 425–475
Hors d'oeuvre server, *3³/₄ inches, rooster*	$ 120–140
Jam jar, *apple finial on cover*	$ 145–175
Jar, *honey, with bee finial on lid, 3¹/₂ inches*	$ 175–225
Mug, *Chief Sitting Bull*	$ 325–375
Mug, *with decal decoration of ring-necked pheasant, Les Kouba*	$ 145–175
Mug, *in shape of Teddy Roosevelt's head*	$ 200–250
Pitcher, *modified ball-shaped, 3¹/₄ inches*	$ 65–85
Pitcher, *swirled clay in style of Niloak, two colors, 3 inches*	$ 220–250
Strawberry pot, *hanging*	$ 210–240
Sugar and creamer set, *Mallard*	$ 165–185

Sugar and creamer set, *twist handles, 2 inches*	$ 210–235
Toothpick holder, *barrel-shaped*	$ 90–110
Vase, *Native American "God of Peace," 8 inches*	$ 525–575
Vase, *Egyptian theme, 8 inches*	$ 265–290
Vase, *peacock, 7³/₄ inches*	$ 320–350
Vase, *swirled clay in style of Niloak, three colors, 5¹/₄ inches*	$ 225–275

WATT POTTERY COMPANY

One of the marks used by
the *Watt Pottery Company*.

W. J. Watt was born in Ohio in 1857, and established the
Brilliant Stoneware Company on his farm in Rose Hill
Farm, Ohio, while he was in his late twenties. The venture
was a success, and grew from a "bluebird" operation (an
outdoor pottery that could operate only in the sunshine—
during the warm weather that came after the bluebirds returned from their winter migration) to a manufacturing
facility. Unfortunately, the plant burned down in 1897, and
W. J. Watt left the pottery business for a while.

Watt had married into the Ransbottom family of Robinson-
Ransbottom fame, and had a large family that included
three sons: Harry, Thomas, and Marion. In 1921, Watt and
his three sons purchased the old Globe Stoneware Company in Crooksville, Ohio, and on July 5, 1922, Watt Pottery
was incorporated. W. J. Watt had a stroke in 1923, and died
in 1926. That same year, the Watt family lost control of
Watt Pottery when Brush Pottery acquired controlling interest in the company, but Brush sold its stock back to the
Watt family in 1931.

The first Watt Pottery products were stoneware jugs, jars,
and mixing bowls, but reportedly these were not marked,
and modern collectors cannot identify these items.

Oven-safe kitchenwares were added in 1935, but the most
collectible Watt products—the hand-painted dinnerware

and kitchenware—were not made until the late 1940s and early 1950s. In 1965, the Watt Pottery facility was destroyed by fire, and was not rebuilt.

"American Red Bud" (or "Teardrop" or "Bleeding Heart")

This pattern originated around 1957, and features hand-painted pendant red buds with green leaves and brown stems.

Dinnerware

Bean cups, *individual, no lid, #75*	$ 45–60
Bowl, *salad, 9$^{1}/_{2}$-inch diameter, #73*	$ 110–145
Casserole, *individual, French handle, 8 inches, #18*	$ 140–160
Casserole, *oval, 1$^{1}/_{2}$-quart, 10 inches, #86*	$ 850–1,000
Creamer, *#62*	$ 275–325
Dish, *cereal/salad, 5$^{1}/_{2}$ inches, #74*	$ 25–40
Jug, *1-pint, #15*	$ 70–85
Jug, *2-pint, #16*	$ 210–235
Jug, *square, 5-pint, #69*	$ 450–525
Shaker, *barrel, salt and pepper, #45 or #46, each*	$ 125–160
Shaker, *hourglass, salt and pepper, #117 or #118, each*	$ 110–135

Kitchenware

Baker, *square, lidded, #84*	$ 650–750
Baker, *rectangular, #85*	$ 450–550
Bean pot, *2 handles, 6$^{1}/_{2}$ inches, #76*	$ 85–100
Bowl, *deep, 2-pint, #63*	$ 75–100
Bowl, *deep, 4-pint, #64*	$ 75–100
Bowl, *deep, 6-pint, #65*	$ 75–100
Bowl, *mixing, lipped, 5-inch diameter, #5*	$ 50–70
Bowl, *mixing, lipped, 6-inch diameter, #6*	$ 50–70
Bowl, *mixing, lipped, 7-inch diameter, #7*	$ 50–70
Bowl, *mixing, lipped, 8-inch diameter, #8*	$ 50–70
Bowl, *mixing, lipped, 9-inch diameter, #9*	$ 50–70
Bowl, *mixing, ribbed, 4-inch diameter, #04*	$ 40–50

Bowl, *mixing, ribbed, 5-inch diameter, #05*	$ 40–50
Bowl, *mixing, ribbed, 6-inch diameter, #06*	$ 40–50
Bowl, *mixing, ribbed, 7-inch diameter, #07*	$ 40–50
Bowl, *spaghetti, #39*	$ 275–350
Canister, *coffee, #82*	$ 275–350

"Apple" (or "Red Apple")

First made in 1952, this pattern was produced in a number of variations. Prices listed below are for pieces decorated with a single red apple, with two or three green leaves and a twig. There is generally a price differential between the two-leaf examples and the three-leaf examples, with the two-leaf pieces being more valuable. There are at least three variants on the apple pattern, and all command a premium price: "Double Apple" (which features two apples instead of one), "Open Apple" (which has a red outline with the core and seed showing on the interior), and "Reduced Apple" (which has a simplified heart-shaped apple with leaves but no twigs).

Dinnerware

Baker, *1¹/₂-quart, 8 inches, two-leaf, lidded, #67*	$ 175–225
Baker, *1¹/₂-quart, 8 inches, three-leaf, lidded, #67*	$ 145–175
Baker, *1¹/₂-quart, 8 inches, three-leaf, no lid, #67*	$ 110–130
Baker, *lidded, 8¹/₂ inches, three-leaf, #96*	$ 125–175
Bean cup, *individual, no lid, three-leaf, #75*	$ 275–350
Bowl, *flat soup; individual spaghetti, 8 inches, inside banded, #44*	$ 375–425
Bowl, *flat soup, individual spaghetti, 8 inches, outside banded, #44*	$ 135–165
Bowl, *salad, 9¹/₂ inches, two-leaf, #73*	$ 100–125
Bowl salad, *9¹/₂ inches, three-leaf, #73*	$ 60–75
Bowl, *salad, footed, 11 inches, #106*	$ 350–425
Bowl, *spaghetti, 13 inches, two-leaf, #39*	$ 150–200
Casserole, *individual, tab-handled, 5 inches, three-leaf, #18*	$ 200–250
Casserole, *individual, French handle (finger grips on the underside of the handle), 8 inches, #18*	$ 225–275
Casserole, *individual, stick handle (no finger grips), 7¹/₂ inches, #18*	$ 210–250

Watt Pottery jug, #17, "Apple" pattern, three leaves,
$240–$280.
*Item courtesy of Kingston Pike Antique Mall, Knoxville,
Tennessee.*

Casserole, *8$^{1}/_{2}$ inches, #3/19*	$ 275–350
Casserole/Covered salad, *9$^{1}/_{2}$ inches, #73*	$ 225–275
Cheese crock, *8 inches, three-leaf, #80*	$ 1,600–1,750
Chip 'n dip, *two bowls, metal holder*	$ 250–300
Coffeepot, *9$^{3}/_{4}$ inches, #115*	$ 2,500–3,000
Creamer, *three-leaf, #62*	$ 100–125
Creamer, *two-leaf, #62*	$ 125–150
Cruet, *china-tipped cork, embossed "O" or "V," set, #126*	$ 1,700–1,800
Dish, *cereal, salad, 5$^{1}/_{2}$-inch diameter, #74*	$ 85–100
Dish, *cereal, 6 inches, #94*	$ 85–100
Drip jar, *5$^{1}/_{2}$ inches, #01*	$ 350–425
Ice bucket, *flat lid, 7$^{1}/_{4}$ inches, #59*	$ 225–275
Jug, *1-pint, three-leaf, #15*	$ 75–95
Jug, *2-pint, three-leaf, #16*	$ 100–125
Jug, *5-pint, plain lip, three-leaf, #17*	$ 240–280

Jug, *5-pint, ice lip, three-leaf, #17*	$ 200–240
Jug, *square, 5-pint, two- or three-leaf, #69*	$ 450–550
Mug, *barrel, #501*	$ 375–450
Mug, *coffee, #121*	$ 200–225
Mug, *cutout finger hole, #701*	$ 375–450
Pie baker, *9 inches, #33*	$ 145–175
Plate, *chop, 12-inch diameter, #49*	$ 350–400
Plate, *dinner, 10-inch diameter, #101*	$ 450–525
Plate, *grill, 10^1/2-inch diameter*	$ 1,750–2,000
Platter, *round, 15-inch diameter, #31*	$ 375–425
Shakers, *barrel, salt and pepper, set, #45 and #46*	$ 475–550
Shakers, *hourglass, "S" and "P" holes on top, #117 and #118*	$ 300–325
Shakers, *hourglass, "S" and "P" embossed on sides, #117 and #118*	$ 300–325
Sugar bowl, *lidded, #98*	$ 100–125
Teapot, *32-ounce, #505*	$ 2,400–2,600
Teapot, *6-cup, #112*	$ 1,300–1,750

Kitchenware

Baking dish, *rectangular, lug-handled, 10 inches by 5^1/4 inches, #85*	$ 1,100–1,250
Bean pot, *two handles, three-leaf, #76*	$ 235–260
Bean pot, *two handles, two-leaf, #76*	$ 275–350
Bowl, *deep, 2-pint, #63*	$ 70–85
Bowl, *deep, 4-pint, #64*	$ 70–85
Bowl, *deep, 6-pint, #65*	$ 70–85
Bowl, *mixing, lipped, three-leaf, 5-inch diameter, #5*	$ 70–85
Bowl, *mixing, lipped, two-leaf, 5-inch diameter, #5*	$ 80–100
Bowl, *mixing, lipped, three-leaf, 6-inch diameter, #6*	$ 70–85
Bowl, *mixing, lipped, two-leaf, 6-inch diameter, #6*	$ 80–100
Bowl, *mixing, lipped, three-leaf, 7-inch diameter, #7*	$ 70–85
Bowl, *mixing, lipped, two-leaf, 7-inch diameter, #7*	$ 80–100
Bowl, *mixing, lipped, three-leaf, 8-inch diameter, #8*	$ 70–85

Watt Pottery mixing bowl, "Apple," two-leaf, #7,
$80–$100.
*Item courtesy of Needful Things, Hendersonville, North
Carolina.*

Bowl, *mixing, lipped, two-leaf, 8-inch diameter, #8*	$ 80–100
Bowl, *mixing, lipped, three-leaf, 9-inch diameter, #9*	$ 70–85
Bowl, *mixing, lipped, two-leaf, 9-inch diameter, #9*	$ 80–100
Bowl, *mixing, ribbed, three-leaf, 5-inch diameter, #5*	$ 60–80
Bowl, *mixing, ribbed, three-leaf, 6-inch diameter, #6*	$ 60–80
Bowl, *mixing, ribbed, three-leaf, 7-inch diameter, #7*	$ 60–80
Bowl, *mixing, ribbed, three-leaf, 8-inch diameter, #8*	$ 60–80
Bowl, *ribbed, 4-inch diameter, #04*	$ 55–70
Bowl, *ribbed, 5-inch diameter, #05*	$ 55–70
Bowl, *ribbed, 6-inch diameter, #06*	$ 55–70
Bowl, *ribbed, 7-inch diameter, #07*	$ 55–70
Bowl, *ribbed, $4^3/_4$-inch diameter, #602*	$ 145–165
Bowl, *ribbed, $5^3/_4$-inch diameter, #603*	$ 90–110
Bowl, *ribbed, $6^3/_4$-inch diameter, #604*	$ 90–110
Bowl, *ribbed, $7^3/_4$-inch diameter, #600*	$ 35–50

Bowl, *ribbed, 7³/₄-inch diameter, lidded, #600*	$ 145–165
Bowl, *ribbed, 8³/₄-inch diameter, #601*	$ 35–50
Bowl, *ribbed, 8³/₄-inch diameter, lidded, #601*	$ 145–165
Canister, *"Coffee," 7 inches, #82*	$ 375–425
Canister, *"Flour," 8 inches, #81*	$ 375–425
Canister, *"Sugar," 8 inches, #81*	$ 375–425
Canister, *"Tea," 7 inches, #82*	$ 375–425
Canister, *dome top, 10³/₄ inches, #72*	$ 425–475
Cookie jar, *7¹/₂ inches, #21*	$ 350–400
Cookie jar, *8¹/₄ inches, #503*	$ 425–500
Roaster, *lidded, three-leaf, #20*	$ 1,600–1,750
Warmer base for casserole, *electric, #133*	$ 900–1,100

"Autumn Foliage"

This pattern was introduced in 1959, and consists of a very simple decoration of brown leaves and stems.

Dinnerware

Baker, *open, #94*	$ 35–50
Baker, *open, #95*	$ 35–50
Baker, *open, #96*	$ 35–40
Bowl, *salad, serving, 9¹/₂-inch diameter, #73*	$ 65–85
Bowl, *salad, serving, 11-inch diameter, #106*	$ 85–100
Bowl, *spaghetti, 13-inch diameter, #39*	$ 145–165
Carafe, *ribbon handle, open, 9¹/₂ inches, #115*	$ 165–190
Casserole, *2-quart, 8 inches, #110*	$ 95–110
Creamer, *#62*	$ 190–220
Cruet, *oil and vinegar, china-tipped cork, set, #126*	$ 375–450
Fondue, *stick handle, 9 inches, #506*	$ 275–350
Ice bucket, *flat lid, 7¹/₄ inches, #59*	$ 175–225
Jug, *1-pint, 5¹/₂ inches, #15*	$ 85–100
Jug, *2-pint, 6¹/₂ inches, #16*	$ 110–125

Jug, *5-pint, 8 inches, #17*	$ 145–175
Mug, *barrel-shaped, #501*	$ 145–175
Mug, *coffee, #121*	$ 145–175
Pie baker, *9-inch diameter, #33*	$ 150–180
Platter, *round, 15-inch diameter, #31*	$ 110–135
Shakers, *hourglass, embossed "S" and "P," #117 and #118, set*	$ 80–95
Shakers, *hourglass, "S"- and "P"-shaped holes on top, #117 and #118, set*	$ 80–95
Sugar bowl, *lidded*	$ 250–325
Teapot, *#505*	$ 650–750

Kitchenware

Bean pot, *two handles, 6^1/$_2$ inches, #76*	$ 185–210
Bowl, *deep, 2-pint, 6^1/$_2$-inch diameter, #63*	$ 55–70
Bowl, *deep, 4-pint, 7^1/$_2$-inch diameter, #64*	$ 55–70
Bowl, *deep, 6-pint, 8^1/$_2$-inch diameter, #65*	$ 55–70
Bowl, *mixing, ribbed, 5-inch diameter, #5*	$ 30–45
Bowl, *mixing, ribbed, 6-inch diameter, #6*	$ 30–45
Bowl, *mixing, ribbed, 7-inch diameter, #7*	$ 30–45
Bowl, *mixing, ribbed, 8-inch diameter, #8*	$ 30–45
Bowl, *mixing, ribbed, 9-inch diameter, #9*	$ 30–45
Bowl, *ribbed, 4^3/$_4$-inch diameter, #602*	$ 45–60
Bowl, *ribbed, 5^3/$_4$-inch diameter, #603*	$ 45–60
Bowl, *ribbed, 6^3/$_4$-inch diameter, #604*	$ 45–60
Bowl, *ribbed, 7^3/$_4$-inch diameter, #600*	$ 45–60
Bowl, *ribbed, 8^3/$_4$-inch diameter, #601*	$ 45–60
Drip jar, *5^1/$_2$ inches, #01*	$ 165–185
Refrigerator set, *two bowls and a lid, #02*	$ 700–825

"Cherry"

The "Cherry" line was introduced in the early 1950s. The design consists of a cluster of red cherries (either two or three, depending on the size of the object on which they appear), with green leaves and brown stems, plus a red flower with a yellow center.

Dinnerware

Bowl, *berry, 5^1/$_2$-inch diameter, #4*	$ 30–45
Bowl, *cereal/salad/individual popcorn 6^1/$_2$-inch diameter, #52*	$ 140–165
Bowl, *spaghetti, 13-inch diameter, #39*	$ 165–185
Casserole, *stick handle with grooves, #18*	$ 140–165
Jug, *1-pint, #15*	$ 225–275
Jug, *2-pint, #16*	$ 175–225
Jug, *5-pint, #17*	$ 250–325
Platter, *round, 15 inches, #31*	$ 110–135
Shaker, *barrel, "S" and "P" holes in top, #45 and $46, each*	$ 70–85

Kitchenware

Bowl, *mixing, lipped with shoulder, 5-inch diameter, #5*	$ 45–60
Bowl, *mixing, lipped with shoulder, 6-inch diameter, #6*	$ 45–60
Bowl, *mixing, lipped with shoulder, 7-inch diameter, #7*	$ 45–60
Bowl, *mixing, lipped with shoulder, 8-inch diameter, #8*	$ 45–60
Bowl, *mixing, lipped with shoulder, 9-inch diameter, #9*	$ 45–60
Cookie jar, *7^1/$_2$ inches, #21*	$ 325–400

"Dutch Tulip"

This is a Pennsylvania Dutch (Deutsch) design. First made in 1956, it features a blue tulip blossom with red and green leaves.

Dinnerware

Baker, *1-quart, lidded, 7 inches, #66*	$ 145–165
Baker, *1^1/$_2$-quart, lidded, 8 inches, #67*	$ 145–165
Baker, *5-inch diameter, open, #68*	$ 110–135
Bowl, *spaghetti, 13-inch diameter, #39*	$ 400–475
Casserole, *individual, stick handle with grooves, #18*	$ 165–195
Creamer, #62	$ 225–275

Jug, *1-pint, #15*	$ 190–210
Jug, *2-pint, #16*	$ 190–210
Jug, *5-pint, square, #69*	$ 425–500
Plate, *grill, 10¹/₂-inch diameter*	$ 375–425
Shakers, *barrel-shaped, "S" and "P" holes on top, #45 and #46, each*	$ 375–425

Kitchenware

Bean pot, *two handles, 6¹/₂ inches, #76*	$ 375–425
Bowl, *deep, 2-pint, #63*	$ 85–100
Bowl, *deep, 4-pint, #64*	$ 85–100
Bowl, *deep, 6-pint, #65*	$ 85–100
Bowl, *ribbed, lidded, 5 inches*	$ 210–235
Canister, *"Coffee," 7 inches, #82*	$ 375–425
Canister, *"Flour," 8 inches, #81*	$ 375–425
Canister, *"Sugar," 8 inches, #81*	$ 375–425
Canister, *"Tea," 7 inches, #82*	$ 375–425
Cheese crock, *#80*	$ 450–500

"Eagle"

Unlike other Watt Pottery products, pieces in the "Eagle" line feature a stenciled rather than hand-painted design. The pattern consists of a maroon eagle with outstretched wings, with three stars above.

Dinnerware

Baker, *ribbed, covered, #601*	$ 200–250
Dish, *cereal/salad, 5¹/₂ inches, #74*	$ 125–150
Jug, *ice lip, 5-pint, #17*	$ 550–650

Kitchenware

Bean pot, *two handles, #76*	$ 425–475
Bowl, *mixing, lipped with shoulder, 10-inch diameter, #10*	$ 150–200
Bowl, *mixing, lipped with shoulder, 12-inch diameter, #12*	$ 150–200
Bowl, *mixing, ribbed, 5-inch diameter, #5*	$ 120–145

Bowl, *mixing, ribbed, 6-inch diameter, #6*	$ 120–145
Bowl, *mixing, ribbed, 7-inch diameter, #7*	$ 120–145
Bowl, *mixing, ribbed, 8-inch diameter, #8*	$ 120–145
Bowl, *mixing, ribbed, 9-inch diameter, #9*	$ 120–145
Canister, *7¹/₄ inches, #72*	$ 325–375

"Morning Glory"

Pieces bearing this unusual Watt pattern have embossed depictions of morning glories on a lattice background. There were several different color schemes used for "Morning Glory"; the most common featured red flowers with green leaves against an ivory or yellow background. "Morning Glory" originated in 1958, and the line consisted of just 17 shapes.

Dinnerware

Casserole, *2-quart, 8¹/₂ inches, #94*	$ 135–165
Creamer, *#97*	$ 325–400
Jug, *ice lip, 5-pint, #96*	$ 375–450
Sugar bowl, *open, #98*	$ 225–275

Kitchenware

Bowl, *mixing, 5-inch diameter, #5*	$ 85–110
Bowl, *mixing, 6-inch diameter, #6*	$ 85–110
Bowl, *mixing, 7-inch diameter, #7*	$ 85–110
Bowl, *mixing, 8-inch diameter, #8*	$ 85–110
Bowl mixing, *9-inch diameter, #9*	$ 85–110
Cookie jar, *brown and ivory coloration, #95*	$ 375–450

"Rio Rose"

This pattern is officially called "Rio Rose," but collectors sometimes refer to it as "Pansy." The design features a red flower consisting of almost-round petals surrounding a yellow center with green leaves. There are several variations of this pattern, including "Cut Leaf" (which features veining in the leaves), "Solid Leaf" (which has no veining in the leaves), "Bull's Eye" (in which pieces are painted with bands of red and green), and "Cross-Hatch" (the rarest variation, which features a white cross in the yellow center of the rose). Prices listed below are for pieces other than "Cross-Hatch."

Watt Pottery spaghetti bowl, 13-inch diameter, "Rio Rose," $90–$110.
Item courtesy of Kingston Pike Antique Mall, Knoxville, Tennessee.

Dinnerware

Bowl, *flat soup/individual spaghetti, 8-inch diameter, #44*	$ 30–45
Bowl, *spaghetti, 11-inch diameter, #24*	$ 65–85
Bowl, *spaghetti, 13 inches, #39*	$ 90–110
Casserole, *individual, stick handle, #18*	$ 85–100
Casserole, *7¹/₂ inches, #48*	$ 70–85
Casserole, *9 inches, #19*	$ 85–100
Creamer	$ 120–140
Cup and saucer, *cutout handle, #40 and #41*	$ 85–100
Cup and saucer, *#27 saucer, regular cup*	$ 75–90
Jug, *old-style, 7 inches*	$ 185–220
Jug, *1-pint, #15*	$ 145–195
Jug, *2-pint, #16*	$ 145–195
Jug, *5-pint, #17*	$ 175–225
Plate, *7¹/₂-inch diameter, #28*	$ 25–35

Plate, *6¹/₂-inch diameter, #42*	$ 25–35
Plate, *chop, 12-inch diameter, #49*	$ 65–95
Platter, *15-inch diameter, #31*	$ 65–95
Sugar bowl, *open*	$ 140–165

Kitchenware

Bowl, *mixing, lipped, 5-inch diameter, #5*	$ 60–85
Bowl, *mixing, lipped, 6-inch diameter, #6*	$ 60–85
Bowl, *mixing, lipped, 7-inch diameter, #7*	$ 60–85
Bowl, *mixing, lipped, 8-inch diameter, #8*	$ 60–85
Bowl, *mixing, lipped, 9-inch diameter, #9*	$ 60–85
Cookie jar, *#21*	$ 145–185
Dutch oven, *lidded, # 20*	$ 85–125
Pie baker, *9-inch diameter*	$ 135–175

"Rooster"

This pattern was first made in 1955. As its name suggests, it consists of a black, green, and red rooster standing in green grass. There are many variations in the rooster's form—some roosters are skinny, others are fat.

Dinnerware

Baker, *1-quart, lidded, #66*	$ 150–225
Baker, *1¹/₂-quart, lidded, #67*	$ 150–225
Baker, *5-inch diameter, no lid, #68*	$ 85–100
Bowl, *salad, 9¹/₂-inch diameter, #73*	$ 225–275
Bowl, *spaghetti, 12-inch diameter, #39*	$ 300–350
Casserole, *individual, French handle, #18*	$ 165–195
Creamer, *#62*	$ 200–250
Ice bucket, *flat lid, 7¹/₄ inches, #59*	$ 275–325
Jug, *1-pint, #15*	$ 165–185
Jug, *2-pint, #16*	$ 150–175
Jug, *square, 5-pint, #69*	$ 550–650
Mug, *#61*	$ 1,100–1,250

Shaker, *barrel, "S" and "P" holes in top, #45 and #46, each*	$ 210–240
Shaker, *hourglass, "S" and "P" holes in top, #117 and #118, each*	$ 190–220
Sugar bowl, *lidded, #98*	$ 425–500

Kitchenware

Baking dish, *rectangular, lug-handled, 10 inches by 5¹/₄ inches, #85*	$ 700–800
Bean pot, *two-handled, #76*	$ 375–425
Bowl, *deep, 2-pint, #63*	$ 100–125
Bowl, *deep, 4-pint, #64*	$ 100–125
Bowl, *deep, 6-pint, #65*	$ 100–125
Bowl, *mixing, ribbed, 5-inch diameter, #5*	$ 90–110
Bowl, *mixing, ribbed, 6-inch diameter, #6*	$ 90–110
Bowl, *mixing, ribbed, 7-inch diameter, #7*	$ 90–110
Bowl, *mixing, ribbed, 8-inch diameter, #8*	$ 90–110
Bowl, *mixing, ribbed, 9-inch diameter, #9*	$ 90–110
Bowl, *ribbed, lidded, 5-inch diameter, #05*	$ 175–225
Canister, *"Coffee," 7 inches, #82*	$ 475–525
Canister, *"Flour," 8 inches, #81*	$ 475–525
Canister, *"Sugar," 8 inches, #81*	$ 475–525
Canister, *"Tea," 7 inches, #82*	$ 475–525
Cheese crock, *#80*	$ 700–800

"Starflower"

This pattern started out as a red six-petal flower with a bud, stem, and veined green leaves. In the early 1950s, the pattern was simplified: it became a five-petal shape with no detailing on the leaves. In the late 1950s the design was simplified once again, and it became a four-petal flower with no bud. Another type of "Starflower" pattern—known to collectors as "Special Starflower"—consists of a simple white four-petal flower, with stem and leaves, against a red, blue, or green background. Unless otherwise noted, prices listed below are for regular "Starflower" items.

Dinnerware

Bean cup, *#75*	$ 85–100
Bowl, *salad, 9¹/₂-inch diameter, #73*	$ 45–60

Watt Pottery jug, "Starflower" pattern, five petals, #15,
$80–$100.
*Item courtesy of Kingston Pike Antique Mall, Knoxville,
Tennessee.*

Bowl, *spaghetti, 13-inch diameter, #39*	$ 110–135
Bowl, *spaghetti, 13-inch diameter, "Special Starflower," red, #39*	$ 100–125
Bowl, *spaghetti, 13-inch diameter, "Special Starflower," blue, #39*	$ 175–225
Bowl, *cereal/salad/individual popcorn, 6^1/$_2$-inch diameter, #52*	$ 50–65
Bowl, *7^1/$_2$-inch diameter, #53*	$ 50–65
Bowl, *8^1/$_2$-inch diameter, #54*	$ 50–65
Bowl, *salad, #55*	$ 65–85
Casserole, *individual, tab handles, lidded, 5 inches, #18*	$ 60–75
Casserole, *individual, stick handle, 7^1/$_2$ inches, #18*	$ 60–75
Creamer, *four petals, #62*	$ 225–275
Creamer, *five petals, #62*	$ 185–220
Ice bucket, *flat lid, four petals, #59*	$ 190–250
Ice bucket, *flat lid, five petals, #59*	$ 165–190
Jug, *1-pint, four petals, #15*	$ 90–110

Jug, *1-pint, five petals, #15*	$ 80–100
Jug, *2-pint, four petals, #16*	$ 110–135
Jug, *2-pint, five petals, #16*	$ 85–100
Jug, *5-pint, ice lip, four petals, #17*	$ 190–225
Jug, *5-pint, plain lip, five petals, #17*	$ 165–195
Jug, *square, 5-pint, four petals, #69*	$ 450–550
Jug, *square, 5-pint, five petals, #69*	$ 425–475
Mug, *barrel, #501*	$ 85–100
Mug, *coffee, #61*	$ 150–200
Plate, *chop, #49*	$ 150–200
Platter, *round, 15-inch diameter, #31*	$ 125–150
Shaker, *hourglass, embossed "S" and "P," #117 and #118, pair*	$ 250–300
Shakers, *barrel, #45 and #46, pair*	$ 145–175
Tumbler, #56	$ 200–275

Kitchenware

Baker with lid, *with metal stand, #96*	$ 90–120
Bean pot, *two handles, #76*	$ 175–225
Bowl, *mixing, lipped with shoulder, 5-inch diameter, #5*	$ 65–85
Bowl, *mixing, lipped with shoulder, 6-inch diameter, #6*	$ 65–85
Bowl, *mixing, lipped with shoulder, 7-inch diameter, #6*	$ 65–85
Bowl, *mixing, lipped with shoulder, 8-inch diameter, #7*	$ 65–85
Bowl, *mixing, lipped with shoulder, 9-inch diameter, #8*	$ 65–85
Bowl, *deep, 2-pint, #63*	$ 90–110
Bowl, *deep, 4-pint, #64*	$ 90–110
Bowl, *deep, 6-pint, #65*	$ 90–110
Bowl, *ribbed, 4-inch diameter, #04*	$ 35–50
Bowl, *ribbed, 5-inch diameter, #05*	$ 35–50
Bowl, *ribbed, 6-inch diameter, #06*	$ 35–50
Bowl, *ribbed, 7-inch diameter, #07*	$ 35–50
Bowl, *ribbed, 7-inch diameter, "Special Starflower," blue, #07*	$ 225–275

Cookie jar, #21	$ 150–200
Drip jar, 4^1/$_2$ inches, #47	$ 300–350
Drip jar, 5^1/$_2$ inches, #01	$ 350–450
Pie baker, 9-inch diameter, #33	$ 225–275

"Tulip"

This pattern originated around 1963, and was sold exclusively through F. W. Woolworth stores. The design consists of red and blue tulip blossoms with green leaves. This pattern should not be confused with "Dutch Tulip," which is more stylized and was produced somewhat earlier.

Dinnerware

Bowl, salad, 9^1/$_2$ inches, #73	$ 175–225
Bowl, spaghetti, 13-inch diameter, #39	$ 325–375
Creamer, #62	$ 210–235
Jug, 1-pint, #15	$ 375–450
Jug, 2-pint, #16	$ 140–175
Jug, ice lip, 5-pint, #17	$ 210–240

Kitchenware

Bowl, deep, 2-pint, #63	$ 90–110
Bowl, deep, 4-pint, #64	$ 90–110
Bowl, deep, 5-pint, #65	$ 90–110
Bowl, ribbed, 4^3/$_4$-inch diameter, #602	$ 145–165
Bowl, ribbed, 5^3/$_4$-inch diameter, #603	$ 145–165
Bowl, ribbed, 6^3/$_4$-inch diameter, #604	$ 145–165
Bowl, ribbed, 7^3/$_4$-inch diameter, #600	$ 65–85
Bowl, ribbed, 8^3/$_4$-inch diameter, #601	$ 65–85
Cookie jar, #503	$ 275–325

Miscellaneous

Bean pot, "Campbell Kids," brown	$ 90–110
Bowl, chili, Mexican man, #603	$ 10–12

Cookie Jar, *"Cookie Barrel"*	$ 60–80
Cookie Jar, *Policeman, 11 inches*	$ 1,000–1,200
Dish, *"Dog," 6-inch diameter, #6*	$ 65–85
Dish, *"Dog," 7-inch diameter, #7*	$ 65–85
Dish, *"Purina Mink Chow," 9-inch diameter*	$ 25–35
Dish, *snack set, "Nuts," #4*	$ 125–175
Dish, *snack set, "Corn," #52*	$ 125–150
Dish, *snack set, "Chips," #7*	$ 125–150
Dish, *snack set, "Pretzels," #54*	$ 125–150
"Goodies Jar," ice bucket, #59	$ 275–350
"Goodies Jar," canister, #72	$ 275–350
"Goodies Jar, bean pot, #76	$ 275–350
Jardinière, *quilted pattern, green/white, 6¹/₂ inches*	$ 40–60
Jardinière, *quilted pattern, green/white, 7¹/₂ inches*	$ 40–60
Jardinière, *quilted pattern, green/white, 8¹/₄ inches*	$ 40–60
Jardinière, *quilted pattern, green/white, 10¹/₂ inches*	$ 50–75
Jardinière, *quilted pattern, green/white, 13 inches*	$ 50–75

WELLER POTTERY

Weller Pottery
Since 1872

Mark found on *Weller* pottery.

Weller "half-kiln" mark

Weller "half-kiln" mark.

Samuel A. Weller was an entrepreneur. He opened a pottery in Fultonham, Ohio, in 1873, where he made ordinary flowerpots. To increase business, Weller began decorating his products with house paint and selling them door-to-door in nearby Zanesville, Ohio. Weller prospered, and by the late 1880s he had built additional facilities in Zanesville. Through his connections with William Long and the Lonhuda pottery, Weller began making underglaze slip-decorated pottery with atomized shaded backgrounds as early as 1893. By 1895, however, Weller had learned all he needed to learn from Long, and he severed the relationship while continuing to make pottery under the name "Louwelsa"—a combination of his daughter's name ("Louise"), his family name ("Weller"), and his first two initials ("S. A.").

Weller continued to introduce new art lines in the early 20th century, but the line that is of most interest to collectors is called "Sicard" or "Sicardo." (Serious collectors tend to avoid using the name "Sicardo," and disdain those who do, even though it is the line's original name.) The line takes its name from Jacques Sicard, a former ceramist at the Clement Massier pottery in Golfe-Juan, France. In 1902, Weller hired Sicard to come to Zanesville and develop a lustrous metallic glaze pottery similar to a type of glaze that was being made in France.

Mindful of the way in which Weller had severed his relationship with William Long, Sicard insisted on working in secret with his assistant, Henri Gellie. Weller did everything he could to learn how to make the glaze, with its variegated surface of iridescent green, blue, purple, crimson, and copper. He is even said to have drilled a hole in the wall of Sicard's laboratory to spy on the work, but Sicard always outfoxed him, and Weller never learned the secret. When Sicard left Zanesville in 1907, his secret method went with him, and wares made using this method are the Weller products most eagerly sought after by today's collectors.

In the late 1800s, Doulton Pottery in England (later known as "Royal Doulton") began producing wares based on the novels of Charles Dickens. These products were very successful, and Sam Weller, who was never one to worry about stealing an idea, decided to produce his own version of these wares. Weller reportedly joked that if Charles Dickens could name a character after him—Dickens's *Pickwick Papers* features a character named "Sam Weller"—then the real Sam Weller could name an art line after the great English author.

There are actually three lines of "Dickensware." Pieces in the first line resemble "Louwelsa" pieces, only their backgrounds are generally unshaded, and they were produced in hues of brown, green, or blue. Pieces in the second line of "Dickensware" feature sgraffito decoration, usually on a shaded matte ground, though high-gloss pieces were also made. Decorations include scenes from Dickens's novels, as well as images of Native Americans, monks, fish, birds, golfers, tavern scenes, birds, and historical scenes. Pieces in the third line of "Dickensware" feature underglaze slip-painted scenes from Dickens's fiction on a high-gloss background, usually in brown or blue-gray. There were also figural "Dickensware" tobacco jars shaped like the head of an Admiral, a Chinaman, a Turk, or an Irishman.

Other early Weller art pottery lines of importance include:

- **"Aurelian."** Pieces in this line are similar to "Louwelsa" pieces, except their backgrounds have been sponged, producing a surface that is said to resemble a forest fire.

- **"Auroro."** These pieces feature high-gloss glazes with splotched background colors of gray and pink. Pieces are underglaze slip-decorated with fish, flowers, and other subjects.

- **"Eocean."** Pieces feature high-gloss pastel-colored shaded backgrounds, and are decorated with underglaze slip painting. This line was later renamed "Rochelle."

- **"Hudson."** These pieces feature matte finish with underglaze slip-painted decoration. High-gloss examples are called "Glazed Hudson."

- **"Jap Birdimal."** Pieces feature brown, blue, gray, yellow-green, and terra-cotta backgrounds, and are decorated with incised line designs depicting Japanese women, birds, trees, or animals. The incised lines are filled with color and covered with a high-gloss glaze.

- **"La Sa."** Pieces feature metallic glaze with a gold or reddish-gold tone, and are decorated with landscapes.

- **"Turada."** Pieces feature lacy decoration in hues of white, orange, or blue against a dark background with a high-gloss glaze. The designs on these pieces were first incised, and then filled with colored slip in the same manner as the designs on "Jap Birdimal" pieces. However, the designs on "Turada" pieces are not pictorial, and the raised slip lines are higher than those on "Jap Birdimal" pieces.

The history of Weller Pottery can be divided into three distinct periods. The early period lasted from 1895 until 1918, and at the end of this period the making of art pottery was largely suspended in favor of making molded commercial art wares. The middle period, which lasted from 1918 to 1935, saw the introduction of many lines, and some hand-painted wares such as "Hudson" and "Blue and Decorated" were still being made. The late period lasted from 1935 until the factory's closing in 1948.

Art Lines

"Aurelian"
Introduced in 1898, "Aurelian" pieces have a brown, high-gloss glaze similar to that found on "Louwelsa" pieces, but these pieces are brushed with brighter colors such as red or yellow. It is said that, in many cases, the backgrounds of these pieces resemble a forest fire. Designs generally depict fruit and flowers, and pieces were sometimes marked "Aurelian."

Ewer, *7 inches, floral decoration, artist-signed* $ 300–350

"Dickensware" (Second Line)
First produced in 1897, pieces in this line feature either matte or high-gloss glaze, with incised decorations depicting scenes from Charles Dickens's novels, monks, Native Americans, golfing or drinking scenes, fish, or birds. This line was made until 1905, and pieces are generally marked "Dickens Ware." Some pieces are signed by the artist.

Mug, *5¹/₂ inches, monk drinking from stein* $ 400–450

Tankard pitcher, *12 inches tall, portrait of Native American chief in headdress, artist-signed* $ 1,400–1,600

Weller "Dickensware" (Second Line) vase, 14¼ inches
tall, portrait of a cavalier, $2,000–$2,400.
*Item courtesy of Richard Hatch and Associates,
Hendersonville, North Carolina.*

Vase, 7¹/₂ *inches, scene with a golfer swinging his club,* *artist-signed*	$ 1,100–1,250
Vase, *14 inches, cylindrical, knight on a horse in plumed helmet,* *artist-signed*	$ 2,800–3,000
Vase, *14¹/₄ inches, Cavalier*	$ 2,000–2,400

"Eocean"

This Weller line was made between 1898 and 1915. Pieces are underglaze slip-decorated with flowers, birds, animals, fish, and other subjects against light-colored, high-gloss backgrounds. Pieces can be unmarked, marked "Eocean Weller," or simply marked "Weller."

Vase, *6 inches, floral decoration, some crazing*	$ 200–225
Vase, *11 inches, floral decoration*	$ 550–600

"Etched Matt"

This line is similar to Weller's second line of "Dickensware," and its pieces have incised decorations, often against shaded backgrounds in shades of gray or brown.

Weller "Etna" mug, 6 inches, $150–$185.
Item courtesy of Kingston Pike Antique Mall, Knoxville, Tennessee.

This line originated around 1905, and pieces are often marked "Weller Etched Matt." Pieces are usually decorated with flowers or fruit, though rare pieces also feature portraits.

Vase, 6³/₄ inches, bulbous body tapers to cylindrical neck, floral decoration	$ 450–500
Vase, 10¹/₂ inches tall, waisted cylinder, incised grapes and stems run the length of the vase, some glaze damage	$ 500–550

"Etna"

Pieces in this line generally feature shaded backgrounds of blue to gray, shaded to darker colors at the top, and an embossed line. Floral decoration is most common, but some pieces were also produced with cameolike depictions of people (such as Beethoven), and other pieces can be found with three-dimensional depictions of lizards and snakes. Pieces are often marked "Etna Weller," or impressed with the word "Weller."

Mug, *grapes, leaves, and stems, 6 inches*	$ 150–185
Vase, 5 inches, gray ground, pansy decoration, bulbous-shaped, marked "Etna Weller"	$ 150–185

Vase, 5¹/₄ inches, gray ground with pink floral decoration	$ 150–185
Vase, 6 inches tall, mismarked "Etna," shaded brown "Louwelsa"-style high-gloss glaze, floral decoration	$ 150–185

"Floretta"

This line was introduced in 1904. Pieces feature a brown or pastel (often gray) background, with fruit or flowers either in low relief or incised. Pieces were produced in both high-gloss and matte-glaze versions, and are often marked with "Floretta Weller" in a circle, though some pieces are unmarked.

Vase, 4 inches, fruit (grapes)	$ 200–225
Vase, 4¹/₄ inches, globular form, cherries, marked	$ 175–225
Vase, 12 inches, unmarked, cherries	$ 600–675

"Hudson"

This is a very complicated grouping, and pieces actually fall into several categories. Pieces in the "Hudson" line have shaded backgrounds in blue to pink, buff to blue, or pink to gray or green. The glaze is semimatte, and the underglaze decoration is heavily slip-painted—usually in floral motifs, though a great variety of other designs were also produced, including birds, animals, people, and landscapes. Pieces in the "Hudson-Perfecto" line are decorated with mineral colors under the semimatte glaze in the style of china painting. "Blue and Decorated Hudson" pieces have solid blue backgrounds, while "White and Decorated Hudson" pieces feature solid white backgrounds. "Hudson Rochelle" pieces have shaded brown backgrounds. This line was made in the 1920s and 1930s, and pieces are either unmarked or marked with an impressed "Weller," "Weller Pottery" with the half-kiln mark, or simply "Weller Pottery."

Bowl, 6-inch diameter, shallow, "White and Decorated," floral	$ 175–210
Bowl, 12-inch diameter, shallow, floral decoration, standard-quality art work, signed	$ 125–150
Vase, 4¹/₂ inches, "Hudson Perfecto," fruit decoration around shoulder of globular form	$ 400–450
Vase, "Hudson Light," 5¹/₂ inches, pansies on a light-colored background	$ 375–425
Vase, 7¹/₄ inches, "Hudson Rochelle," flower painted, average-quality	$ 450–550
Vase, 8 inches tall, floral decoration, signed "Timberlake" by the artist, average quality for this artist	$ 500–575

Weller "Hudson" ("Hudson-Light") vase,
5½ inches, $375–$425.
*Item courtesy of Tony McCormack, Sarasota,
Florida.*

Weller "Hudson" vase, 8¾ inches,
$475–$525.
*Item courtesy of Charles Seagrove and Don
Griffin, Old School Antique Mall, Sylva,
North Carolina.*

Weller "Hudson" vase, 17½ inches,
$2,250–$2,500.
*Item courtesy of Richard Hatch and
Associates, Hendersonville, North Carolina.*

Vase, 8½ inches, "White and Decorated," cylinder band of floral decoration around the top, signed	$ 350–400
Vase, 8¾ inches tall, pink to blue shading, floral	$ 475–525
Vase, 9½ inches, large floral decoration, artist-signed, above-average quality	$ 700–775
Vase, 10 inches, large floral decoration, signed by artist Hester Pillsbury, above-average quality	$ 1,000–1,200
Vase, 10½ inches, "Blue and Decorated," band of flowers near flared top, signed	$ 350–400

Vase, 11¹/₂ inches, "White and Decorated," panel sides, band of decoration near top, average work, not signed by artist	$ 275–350
Vase, 12 inches tall, panel sides, average art work, not signed by artist	$ 275–350
Vase, 12 inches, large floral decoration, above-average work, once drilled to be a lamp, repaired	$ 700–825
Vase, 17¹/₂ inches, grape decoration, not artist-signed	$ 2,250–2,500

"Louwelsa"

Pieces in this line feature atomized high-gloss brown backgrounds. The line was first made around 1895, and continued to be produced until about 1918. Pieces are often unmarked, but were sometimes marked with the "Weller Louwelsa" back-stamp, or simply impressed "Weller." Occasionally a piece will turn up that has a shaded blue background and is marked "Weller Louwelsa"; such pieces are generally referred to as "Blue Louwelsa" pieces.

Ewer, 7 inches, artist-signed, leaves and flowers	$ 600–675
Jardinière, typical underglaze slip-painting of tulips and foliage, 8 inches	$ 650–750
Jug, 5³/₄ inches, berry decoration	$ 225–250
Vase, 3¹/₂ inches, pansy decoration	$ 175–225
Vase, pillow, 4¹/₈ inches by 5 inches, silver overlay	$ 2,200–2,400
Vase, 5¹/₂ inches, typical floral decoration	$ 200–250
Vase, 6¹/₂ inches, globular form, typical floral decoration, signed	$ 200–250
Vase, 6¹/₄ inches, "Blue Louwelsa," typical decoration of holly berries with leaves, signed	$ 700–800

"Sicard" (or "Sicardo")

Perhaps Weller's most highly desired line, "Sicardo" was introduced in 1902 and was produced for only about five years. Pieces in this metallic-glazed line are often signed "Sicard" on the side, and are sometimes marked "Weller" or "Weller Sicardo" on the base.

Vase, 5³/₄ inches, average color, signed	$ 1,200–1,400
Vase, 6¹/₂ inches, two handles, melon-ribbed, good color, signed	$ 2,400–2,600
Vase, 14 inches, good color, signed "Sicard" on side	$ 4,800–5,250

LOUWELSA WELLER

Mark sometimes found on Weller "Louwelsa" pieces.

Weller "Louwelsa" jardinière, 8 inches, $650–$750.
Item courtesy of Francis and Suzie Nation, Old School Antique Mall, Sylva, North Carolina.

Weller "Louwelsa" pillow vase, silver overlay, $2,200–$2,400.
Item courtesy of Tony McCormack, Sarasota, Florida.

Commercial Art Wares

"Bonito"

This line was produced between 1927 and 1933. Pieces feature matte glaze in cream with painted flowers. On occasion, a rare high-gloss "Bonito" piece will turn up. Pieces are marked "Weller Pottery" with a half-kiln stamp.

Jardinière, *6¹/₂ inches, flower-and-leaf band around center, green interior, artist-signed* $ 175–225

Vase, *5 inches tall, handles at waist, flared rim, flowers with green leaves, green interior, artist-signed* $ 125–150

SICARDO WELLER.

Mark sometimes found on Weller "Sicardo" (or "Sicard") pieces.

Weller "Sicard" vase, two handles, ribbed, 6½ inches, $2,400–$2,600.
Item courtesy of Tony McCormack, Sarasota, Florida.

Vase, *7 inches, two handles, floral with green leaves, green interior, artist-signed*	$ 140–160
Vase, *8 inches, handles with ring near top, green interior, floral decoration, artist-signed*	$ 200–225

"Coppertone"

Pieces in this middle-period Weller line (from the 1920s) feature a mottled semi-gloss green glaze over brown with yellow accents. Decorations consist of frogs, turtles, and fish on the sides of vases and bowls or as the handles of pitchers. Pieces are often unmarked, but may be marked with the words "Weller Hand Made" or with the "Weller Pottery" logo.

Frog, *5 inches by 4 inches*	$ 200–250
Pitcher, *7³/4 inches, three-dimensional fish handle, embossed aquatic design on body, marked*	$ 1,900–2,000
Vase, *7¹/4 inches, frog on side*	$ 1,200–1,400

Weller "Coppertone" vase with frog on side,
$1,200–$1,400.
*Item courtesy of Kingston Pike Antique Mall, Knoxville,
Tennessee.*

"Lido"

First produced in the 1930s, pieces in the middle-period "Lido" line feature shaded solid-color glaze in a variety of pastel shades including pink, blue, and green. Decoration consists of either leaves or flowing draperies. "Lido" pieces are generally marked "Weller Pottery Since 1872" or "Weller" in molded script.

Candelabra, *two cups, pink, each*	$ 120–145
Cornucopia, *9¹/₂ inches, pink*	$ 100–120

"Roma"

Designed by Rudolph Lorber around 1914, "Roma" pieces are characterized by matte-glazed ivory backgrounds with embossed designs of flowers, garlands, and fruit, and are accented in colors of red and/or green. Pieces are often marked with and impressed "Weller," though some pieces are unmarked. This is one of Weller's most common lines.

Bowl, *6¹/₄ inches, garland of roses*	$ 75–110
Compote, *5¹/₂ inches, band of stylized leaves, marked*	$ 200–225

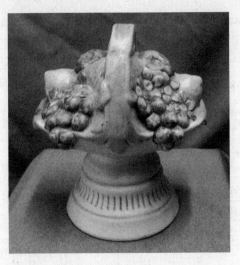

Weller "Roma" doorstop, $375–$425.
*Item courtesy of Pattie and Howard Tower, Old School
Antique Mall, Sylva, North Carolina.*

Doorstop, *basket of fruit*	$ 375–425
Vase, *7 inches, three panels of decoration, horizontally ribbed top that projects over base*	$ 175–225
Vase, *9 inches, rose garland, marked*	$ 175–225
Vase, *10¹/₂ inches, sculpted panel of pinecone with pine needles, unmarked*	$ 250–300

"Scenic"

Pieces in this late-period line (produced circa 1937) have a blue or green matte glaze with embossed landscapes. Color schemes usually feature shaded blues or greens, but some brown pieces were also produced. Pieces are generally marked "Weller Pottery Since 1872," or simply "Weller" in script.

Vase, *6¹/₂ inches, palm tree, ruffled top*	$ 165–200

"Silvertone"

Made during the 1920s, pieces in this line have a matte, multicolored glaze in shades of pink, blue, green, or lavender, with embossed representations of flowers, fruit, and occasionally butterflies. This is an attractive line, and it is popular with Weller collectors. "Silvertone" pieces are generally marked with the name "Weller" around the half-kiln design.

Vase, 8¹/₂ inches, globular with two small handles on shoulder, ruffled top, signed	$ 400–475
Vase, 9¹/₂ inches, floral, two handles from shoulder of bulbous base to lip, signed	$ 425–500
Vase, 10¹/₂ inches, dogwood design, two handles	$ 550–625
Vase, 11 inches tall, bulbous body to tapered neck	$ 575–650
Wall pocket, 10 inches, artist-signed, marked	$ 450–500

"Velva"

Made between 1928 and 1933, "Velva" pieces feature panels of embossed flowers and leaves against brown or beige backgrounds. Pieces are generally marked "Weller" or "Weller Pottery."

Jar, covered ginger, 8 inches, both lid and body have panel of decoration	$ 700–800

"Woodcraft"

This pattern often confuses collectors, because it resembles several other Weller patterns, including "Flemish" and "Voile." Examples are often wood-tone with matte finish, and are often in the shapes of stumps, tree trunks, and entwined branches. Pieces are generally brown with polychrome details, though some pieces are primarily polychrome. Some of the more desirable forms feature three-dimensional owls or foxes. Produced in the 1920s and 1930s, pieces in this line are generally marked with an impressed "Weller."

Bowl, 3 inches tall, raised squirrel among tree branches and leaves	$ 250–300
Vase, fan, 6 inches, embossed tree trunk with leaves, flowers and fruit, unmarked	$ 250–300
Vase, bud, 8³/₄ inches, in the shape of a tree trunk with two cut-off limbs, signed	$ 150–200
Vase, chalice-shaped, with twiglike supports of cup, embossed flowers and leaves, unmarked	$ 300–350
Wall pocket, 10 inches, with owl peering through hole in tree trunk	$ 600–700

Weller "Flemish" basket, 4½ inches tall, $225–$275.
*Item courtesy of Charles Seagrove and Don Griffin, Old
School Antique Mall, Sylva, North Carolina.*

Miscellaneous

Basket, *"Flemish," 4¹/₂ inches tall*	$ 225–275
Bowl, *"Patricia," 7¹/₂ inches, four swan's head handles, embossed leaves, high-gloss cream glaze, circa 1935*	$ 100–135
Bowl, *"Pumila," 7³/₄ inches, matte light-green glaze on exterior, pumpkin-colored interior, relief leaves that form a spikey top*	$ 125–150
Bowl, *"Rosemont," 12 inches, dark background, stylized red rose, white band, middle period*	$ 125–150
Candleholders, *"Ansonia," 3 inches, gray, appearance of being hand-turned, handled, pair*	$ 140–165
Candleholders, *"Malvern," 1³/₄ inches high, relief decoration of swirling leaves and flowers, matte green, mulberry, and yellow, middle period*	$ 150–175
Candlesticks, *"Florala," 11 inches, vertical band of embossed flowers, cream background with pastel tinting, middle period, pair*	$ 250–300

Jardinière, *"Clinton Ivory,"* 6 inches, embossed flowers and stems in panel, ivory with brown accents, unmarked, middle period	$ 85–110
Jardinière, *"Fairfield,"* 6¹/₂ inches, band of cherubs with fluted base, similar to Roseville's *"Donatello,"* middle period	$ 125–150
Jardinière, *"Selma,"* 6 inches, embossed swans in aquatic scene with trees, ivory ground with tan and green accents, middle period	$ 200–225
Pitcher, *"Zona,"* 8¹/₂ inches, embossed woodpecker	$ 550–600
Pitcher, *waisted tankard,* 11¹/₂ inches, Native American-style decorations, black triangles against white, terra cotta-colored top and bottom	$ 350–400
Planter, *"Claywood,"* 3¹/₄ inches, dark brown or charcoal background, band of flowers in style of burnt-wood decoration, middle period	$ 65–85
Planter, *"Elberta,"* 6¹/₂ inches, bands of buff/brown on green matte	$ 100–120
Vase, *"Blo Marblo,"* 5¹/₂ inches, caramel and dark-brown marbling, broad base, flared top, circa 1915	$ 145–170
Vase, *"Blo Marblo,"* 7 inches tall, dark and light marbling, circa 1915	$ 175–200
Vase, *"Bouquet,"* 12 inches tall, blue ground, white flowers	$ 200–250
Vase, *"Chase,"* 7 inches tall, dark-blue ground with white embossed figure of a man in top hat leaping a fence on horseback	$ 350–400
Vase, *"Louella,"* 4¹/₂ inches, ribbed, vertical, draperylike folds with embossed flowers, ruffled top, pink ground, middle period	$ 125–145
Vase, *"Louella,"* 7¹/₂ inches, ribbed, vertical, draperylike folds with embossed flowers, pastel-gray background, middle period	$ 150–175
Vase, *"Nile,"* 8 inches, shades of green with drip decoration, ruffled top, middle period	$ 135–160
Vase, *"Raceme,"* 5¹/₂ inches, stylized modern floral, two-tone with blue top and black bottom, late period, artist-signed	$ 475–525
Vase, *"Roba,"* 11¹/₄ inches, realistically colored embossed flowers against a shaded blue background, late period	$ 200–225

Weller "Zona" pitcher with woodpecker,
8½ inches, $550–$600.
*Item courtesy of B and D Antiques and Art
Pottery.*

Weller "Bouquet" vase, 12 inches, blue
ground with white flowers, $200–$250.
*Item courtesy of Kingston Pike Antique Mall,
Knoxville, Tennessee.*

Weller "Chase" vase, 7 inches, $350–$400.
*Item courtesy of Tony McCormack, Sarasota,
Florida.*

Vase, *"Scandia,"* 7³/₄ inches, vertical slatlike forms in brown with square indentions at top and bottom, against a black background, circa 1915, unmarked	$ 250–300
Vase, *"Tutone,"* 5 inches, embossed flowers and leaves, green on pink, middle period	$ 150–175
Wall pocket, *"Blue Drapery,"* 7³/₄ inches, vertical band of red roses and pastel flowers against a dark-blue background with draperylike folds, circa 1925	$ 200–250

Wall pocket, *"Greora,"* 10 inches, orange-brown modeling with green, middle period	$ 425–475
Wall pocket, *"Marvo,"* 7 inches, embossed ferns and leaves, matte green and tan	$ 250–275
Wall pocket, *"Panella,"* 8 inches, raised pansy and leaf against matte blue background, late period	$ 175–225
Wall pocket, *"Tivoli,"* 8 inches, cream-colored ground with band of raised florals against black, middle period	$ 200–250

WILLETS MANUFACTURING COMPANY

Most common mark of the
*Willets Manufacturing
Company.*

In 1879, brothers Joseph, Daniel, and Edmund Willets took over the old William Young and Sons Pottery facility in Trenton, New Jersey, and founded the Willets Manufacturing Company. The company produced a wide variety of wares from white granite, semiporcelain, and porcelain, and also reportedly produced majolica. Though Willets also made toilet wares, electrical wares, and doorknobs, it is best known to current collectors for its fine Belleek china.

William Bromley Sr., who had been instrumental in bringing Belleek china to Ott and Brewer, came to Willets in 1884, and within a year the company was producing its own Belleek wares. (Walter Lenox also worked at Willets, before starting his own company to manufacture fine Belleek porcelain.) Belleek porcelain continued to be made at Willets until about 1909, and the company closed in 1912.

Basket in the Irish Belleek style, *9-inch diameter, spaghetti strand woven with applied flowers on rim, expected losses to petals, ivory ground, double handles on each side*	$ 2,500–3,000
Bowl, *centerpiece, 13-inch diameter, dragon handles, floral decoration, not signed by the artist, may have been done by an outside china painter*	$ 800–1,000

Willets Manufacturing Company cup and saucer,
$250–$300.
Item courtesy of Richard H. Crane, Knoxville, Tennessee.

Chalice, *11 inches tall, gold ground with stylized flowers in bands around the foot and bowl, artist-signed in body of work*	$ 600–700
Cup and saucer, *interpretation of Irish Belleek "Nautilus" pattern, gray lustre glaze*	$ 250–300
Mug, *tankard, 6 inches, foliage-and-floral design, not artist-signed, may not be factory-decorated*	$ 200–250
Pitcher, *nautilus shell with coral handle, 7¹/₂ inches, ivory ground with pink lip and some gilding*	$ 1,400–1,600
Tea set, *three pieces, teapot, creamer, covered sugar, elaborate silver overlay on burgundy-red ground*	$ 1,250–1,500
Vase, *8¹/₂ inches, two crescent handles on the shoulder, lavish silver overlay on green-to-pink ground*	$ 1,800–2,000
Vase, *9³/₄ inches, conical-shaped narrowing to short neck with flared lip, beautiful decoration of large roses and leaves, not artist-signed but good work*	$ 1,000–1,100
Vase, *10 inches, cylindrical, monochromatic decoration of cranes with Japanese-style pine tree, artist-signed but not factory work*	$ 500–650

Vase, $12^1/_2$ inches tall, monotonal roses with a red-to-gold background, cylindrical with scooped-out lip, not artist-signed, and painting may not have been factory-done	$ 400–450
Vase, $15^1/_2$ inches, cylindrical, painting of Japanese-style cranes, with trees and river, fine work, not artist-signed	$ 800–1,000

GLOSSARY

This glossary provides explanations of words found in this book that pertain to pottery and porcelain, but may not be familiar to nonspecialists.

Art Deco: A high-style art movement that originated in France in the early 20th century as an attempt to replace Art Nouveau and other 19th-century expression with something "modern." Many trace its origins to the bold, vividly colored scenery that was prepared for the first appearance of Sergei Pavlovich Diaghilev's Ballet Russe in Paris in 1909. World War I interrupted the development of Art Deco, and the movement did not reach its full flower until the Paris Exposition Internationale des Arts Decoratifs et Industriels Modernes in 1925. There were two main components of the Art Deco style. The first was a voluptuous look characterized by lush depictions of women attired in skimpy (or no) clothing dancing with the moon or striding along with greyhounds at their sides. This type of Art Deco work also included depictions of geometrically stylized fruit and flowers rendered in bright colors. The second component was based on industry and the machine, and used straight, clean lines, squares, rectangles, chrome, glass, and spare forms. In the minds of today's collectors, Art Deco also encompasses the artistic movements known as "Cubism" and "Futurism." By the mid- to late 1930s, the artistic nature of Art Deco had given way to commercialism, and items made after that time period should not be called "Art Deco."

Art Nouveau: Like Art Deco (discussed above), Art Nouveau has its roots in France. The style began developing in the 1880s, but items from this time frame are generally called "proto-Art Nouveau." True Art Nouveau came into being about 1890, and lasted as a popular fashion until the period from 1905 to 1910. Art Nouveau was a revolt against Victorian eclecticism and mass-produced ornamentation, and was based on natural forms—particularly the curved lines associated with plant tendrils. Art Nouveau abhorred the straight line. This type of art is often associated with depictions of flowers, animals, and women with long, curly hair, often languidly reclining or staring at the moon.

Arts and Crafts: This movement began in 19th-century England as a reaction to everything that was Victorian—particularly a perceived lack of Victorian craftsmanship and the eclecticism of Victorian design elements. Such English tastemakers as author John Ruskin and poet-craftsman William Morris sought a return to medieval standards of workmanship, and wanted to establish work guilds so that groups of craftsmen could share ideas and collaborate. In furniture, the proponents of English Arts and Crafts favored items made from oak. Unlike American Arts and Crafts pieces, these items could be quite elaborate, with long strap hinges, pieced metalwork, and elaborate inlay. For smaller items such as metalwork and pottery, the English craftsmen wanted the pieces to be handmade and based on naturalistic forms. The Arts and Crafts movement came to the United States in the late 19th century, with Elbert Hubbard (of "Message to Garcia" fame) establishing his Roycroft community in East Aurora, New York, in 1895, and Gustav Stickley opening his Craftsman Workshops in Eastwood, New York, in the late 1890s. American Arts and Crafts furniture tended to be much simpler than the English variety, with rectangular forms accented with handmade copper hardware. In pottery, Newcomb College, Grueby, Teco, and Fulper are often associated with this movement.

Backstamp: The mark or logo found on the bottom or reverse side of a ceramic item. It can be printed or stamped in ink, or transfer-printed either under or over the glaze. In addition, it can be impressed into the body of the clay. Backstamps can be very important identification tools, but they should not be relied upon entirely when determining the age and authenticity of a piece of pottery or porcelain.

Baker: An oval dish used for baking food in the oven and also for serving at the table. Bakers generally do not have covers.

Batter Set: A set consisting of a jug for holding waffle batter, a syrup pitcher, and a tray. These originated when electric waffle makers were introduced into the American home as a "must-have" modern convenience. Soon, it became fashionable to make waffles at the dining table rather than at the stove. Making them in the dining or breakfast room required attractive equipment to go along with the shiny new waffle maker, and the batter set was born.

Belleek China: A type of porcelain introduced in 1863 in the village of Belleek, which is located in County Fermanagh, Ireland. Belleek was based on fine statuary porcelain, or "parian" china, which was first produced by Copeland and Garrett of Stoke, Staffordshire, England in 1844. While working in Belleek, craftsmen who had once worked at the Goss factory pioneered a process in which a beautiful iridescent glaze was added to thin parian china. Collectors refer to the product resulting from this process as "Irish Belleek," because a variety of Belleek china was also made in the United States ("American Belleek"). Ott and Brewer, Lenox, and a number of other companies all tried to copy the Irish product, and produced wares marked with the word "Belleek." Some were successful copies, and most were not, but such "Belleek"-inspired wares nonetheless comprise their own category of collectibles.

Bennington: This is the name that Americans give to a type of pottery distinguished by a mottled brown-and-white glaze. The name "Bennington" comes from the town of Bennington, Vermont, where this type of glaze was used by several companies, including the Norton Pottery and the Lyman Fenton Company, which later became the United States Pottery Company. However, the "Bennington" designation is technically incorrect: this type of glaze should rightfully be called "Rockingham," after Earl Fitzwilliam, Marquis of Rockingham of Yorkshire, England, on whose property this type of glaze was reportedly first produced.

Bisque: The first firing given to a piece of porcelain is called the "bisque firing," and an unglazed piece that is only fired once is referred to as "bisque ware," "bisque china," or "bisque porcelain." Because the surface and texture of bisque porcelain reminds some people of human skin, dolls' heads are made from this type of ceramic. On occasion, bisque is painted or colored, but such painting or coloring is considered applied decoration rather than glaze.

Blank: A piece of pottery or porcelain that has yet to be decorated, but is intended for decoration. Blanks were often sold by manufacturers to amateur china painters, who would then apply decorations of their own design.

Body: The part of a ceramic item that is made from solid clay. Glaze and decoration are applied to the body of a piece, and are not an integral part of the body, except insofar as the glaze and decoration, in certain cases, may actually fuse to it.

Bone China: An artificial porcelain produced by mixing clay with bone ash made from calcined cow bones. It was first made in England during the mid-18th century at either the Chelsea or Bow factories, but it was the famous Spode factory that actually developed it.

Bouillon Cup: A two-handled cup, resembling a teacup, that is used to serve clear soups. It is typically accompanied by a saucer, and without the saucer is generally considered part of an incomplete set.

Bread and Butter Plate: A flatware piece in a dinnerware set, generally 6 inches to 6^1/$_2$ inches in diameter, designed to hold bread or rolls and butter. In many cases, these plates can also serve as dessert or cake plates.

Breakfast Set: An abbreviated dinnerware service typically consisting of a small or demitasse coffeepot (sometimes called an "after-dinner" coffeepot), a regular-size cup and saucer, covered muffin dish (sometimes used for serving pancakes), egg cup, cereal dish, and breakfast plate. Breakfast services for two were also made.

Cake Set: A specialized grouping of dinnerware made up of a large cake plate (usually with handles), a cake server, and six to eight smaller plates in the 6- to 7-inch size range.

Casserole: A round or oval baking dish with a cover that can be used at the table as a serving dish.

Casting: A method of forming a ceramic body by pouring liquid clay (slip) into a plaster mold. The plaster mold draws the moisture out of the liquid clay, causing it to harden so the body can be withdrawn from the mold, handled, and finished.

Ceramic: Refers to any item, made from clay or another nonmetallic mineral, that has been shaped and fired at a high temperature. "Ceramics" refers to the art or craft of making objects from clay.

China: A term applied to items made from Chinese-style hard-paste porcelain, though the term may also be applied to artificial porcelains such as bone china.

Chop Plate: A round serving platter resembling a large dinner plate. Chop plates were designed to be used to serve meat such as lamb chops, pork chops, and veal chops, hence their name. In most cases, chop plates are between 12 and 16 inches in diameter, with 12 inches being the most common diameter.

Cold Paint: Oil paint that is hand-applied over the glaze and not fired in the kiln. It is very susceptible to wear.

Compote: A bowl elevated above a base with a stem or shaft. It is designed to hold candy, fruit, or sweetmeats.

Commercial Art Ware: Decorative or useful ceramics that are formed by molding, and then given a little hand-finishing. These wares are mass-produced, and are also referred to as "production line wares."

Console Set: A three-piece set intended for use in the center of a dining table. It consists of a bowl for holding flowers and two candlesticks to be placed on either side of the bowl.

Coupe: A modern shape that does not feature a pronounced rim or shoulder. Pieces with a coupe shape are essentially flat, but they roll up slightly at the edges. This term is generally used to describe soup bowls, plates, and platters.

Cozy Set: A set of two rectangular pitchers on a tray. One pitcher has a short spout and is designed to hold hot water, while the other has a longer spout and is designed to hold tea.

Crackling: Similar to crazing (see definition below), except the network of tiny cracks is intentionally induced during the manufacturing process as a decorative effect, and does not constitute a defect.

Crazing: A network of tiny cracks that occur during the manufacturing process when the glaze and the body do not "fit" and one contracts more than the other, causing the glaze to develop the characteristic system of cracks. This effect can also occur over time or with use, when excessive heat or moisture (often fat particles) get underneath the glaze. Crazing is considered a defect in most cases, and will often cause a collector to reject a piece.

Cream Soup Cup: A two-handled cup used to hold thick, cream-based soup. Like the similar bouillon cup, a cream soup cup has an accompanying saucer, but is broader and flatter than a bouillon cup.

Cruet: A small lidded bottle designed to hold oil or vinegar and to be displayed at the table. In certain applications, a cruet might also hold other condiments.

Decal: A medium for transferring decoration to a piece of ceramic. A design, which may be either multicolored or monochromatic, is printed on a special type of paper that may or may not be coated with plastic. An area on the item to be decorated is then covered with "size," which is a kind of gelatinous substance made from glue, wax, or clay. Next, if the decal has a plastic backing, the plastic is removed and the paper with the design on it is positioned on the area that has been prepared with size, which holds the paper in place. When the piece is fired in a kiln, the paper burns away and the decoration is incorporated into the glaze, thus becoming permanent. The decal is a modern form of transfer-printing.

Demitasse: Taken from the French word for "half cup," this term applies to the small cups used to hold strong after-dinner coffee. It can also refer to the coffee itself.

Dinner Plate: One of the flatware pieces in a typical dinnerware service. A dinner plate is generally 10 inches to $10^1/_2$ inches in diameter, but may be as small as 8 inches or as large as 11 inches in diameter.

Dinnerware: Any items used to set a table, such as plates, cups and saucers, bowls, and platters from which people will eat or that hold the food to be served at the table. Dinnerware usually comes in extended services to accommodate a certain number of diners. Sets designed to serve four people are generally the smallest sets available, and services for even numbers up to twelve are commonplace. Larger services are somewhat more unusual, but do exist. Dinnerware is divided into two types of items: flatware and hollowware.

Dipping: The process of covering a once-fired piece of ceramic with glaze by immersing it into the liquid, either by hand or by machine.

Dish: In modern usage, the term "dish" might refer to a piece of dinnerware. Technically, however, a dish is an item that is shallow, concave, uncovered, and meant to hold or serve food.

Drip Jar: A container in vogue during the early to mid-20th century for holding bacon drippings or other types of fats retained from cooking for later use. These were kept on or near the stove, usually labeled "Drips," and were often part of a range set that consisted of a grouping of other containers used in cooking, such as salt and pepper shakers or a flour container. A more health-conscious diet in the last quarter of the 20th century sparked the general disappearance of the drip jar from the American kitchen—except as a collectible.

Dutch Casserole: A round dish, with straight sides and lug handles opposite each other on or near the rim for easy transport.

Earthenware: A term applied to all pottery, either glazed or unglazed, that is not either stoneware or porcelain. Earthenware is opaque and porous when it is not covered with a glaze. True earthenware is fired at a relatively low temperature.

Embossing: A raised decoration achieved by the molding process and not applied separately to the body.

Encrustation: A decoration of gold or platinum on the body of a piece of pottery or porcelain, applied in liquid form and then fired. This type of decoration is often pictorial or geometric, and is not simply a band on the edge or at the verge of a plate. Encrustation generally feels raised to the touch.

Engobe: A decorative technique in which slip (liquid clay) is put on the body of a piece before the final glaze is applied. The slip may be white or colored.

Engraving: Decoration that has been cut or impressed into the body of a piece of ceramic. This type of recessed, below-the-surface decoration is sometimes called "intaglio."

Epergne: A table or buffet decoration meant to hold flowers, fruit, or sweet-meats in lily-shaped trumpets, in baskets, or in some other container attached to a center support with a container underneath.

Faststand Gravy Boat: A gravy boat with an attached under plate. Sometimes these gravy boats have two spouts.

Finial: In ceramics, a finial is the knob on top of a lid that is grasped in order to remove the lid. In a larger sense, a finial is any decorative knob on top of something, such as a lampshade or bedpost.

Finishing: The process of cleaning up a piece of pottery or porcelain after it has come out of the mold. This process usually involves smoothing away seam lines and rough spots with a tool designed for this purpose or with a damp sponge.

Firing: The process of heating pottery, porcelain, or stoneware in a kiln to harden it, give it strength, affix decoration or gilding, and/or make the shape permanent. An item might go through several firings for different purposes and at different temperatures before it is finished.

Flatware: In dinnerware, the term "flatware" refers to pieces that are flat or nearly so, such as plates and platters. Flatware is usually the largest component of any dinnerware service. This term is also applied to the eating utensils such as knives, forks, and spoons that are used with dinnerware.

French Casserole: A casserole with a single long sticklike handle. This shape of casserole dish comes in a variety of sizes, and the larger ones often have lug handles opposite the stick handles to aid in picking up, handling, and stabilizing the vessels during transport.

Frog or Flower Frog: A device shaped like an oval, round, or square mound with scattered holes across the surface that are designed to keep the stems of flowers used in a flower arrangement in place. Often, flower frogs are found in conjunction with a shallow bowl, and the frog may have a figural element in the center, such as a bird or a human figure.

Gadroon: A decorative edge composed of embossed ovals and lines that is found on pieces of silver and furniture, as well as on pottery and porcelain.

Gilding: The application of a thin layer of precious metal, usually either gold or platinum, to the body of a piece of ceramic as a decorative element. An extremely small amount of precious metal is actually used in this process.

Glaze: The covering of the surface of a piece of ceramic, made from minerals that are either transparent or colored. When the glaze is applied to the surface of an object and the piece is heated in a glost kiln, the glaze melts and forms a glass-like covering. Glaze is applied to ceramic surfaces in order to make an object nonporous, to strengthen the body and make it more permanent, or to beautify the surfaces.

Glost Firing: This is the firing that fixes the glaze; it is cooler than the first (or "bisque") firing.

Glost Kiln: A special kiln used for firing glazes and decorations.

Greenware: Unfired, undecorated ceramic that has been formed (usually molded) and is dry. It is said to be "leather hard," and can be handled to be decorated and cleaned up, though it is extremely fragile.

Grill Plate: A dinner-size plate that is divided into three or more sections.

Ground: The solid color background on a piece of ceramic. Usually, this color does not cover the entire surface of the piece of ceramic, but has areas or "reserves" that are left blank for decoration.

Hollowware: In dinnerware, this term refers to the containers that are meant to hold food for serving, such as bowls, tureens, casseroles, creamers, and sugar bowls. In determining the value of a dinnerware service, the hollowware pieces are generally the most valuable items, and the presence of a significant number of these items can raise the value of a service significantly.

Impressed: Pressed into clay either using a mold or by hand. This term is used to refer to decorative elements.

Institutional Ware: Items designed to be used by institutions such as airlines, hospitals, schools, and the like. Institutional wares are generally fairly heavy and durable. Items made for railroads, restaurants, hotels, and steamships also fall into this category, but are sometimes called "hotel ware," "railroad china," or "restaurant ware." In many instances, institutional ware is decorated with the logo of the applicable organization, or with some other sort of identifying mark or decoration.

Ironstone: Introduced in 1813 by C. J. Mason, ironstone is a heavy, durable earthenware. It is made traditionally by using ground-up stone, and is nonporous. It goes by a number of other names, including "Graniteware," "Stone China," and "Opaque China."

Jardinière: A decorative container for ferns or flowers that is designed to hold a utilitarian flowerpot. Jardinières often come with a separated pedestal on which they are designed to sit.

Jiggering: This process is used for making plates and other flat items of dinnerware. Clay is placed on a form that represents the top of the piece, pressed down, and spun. As it spins, a template that will form the bottom side is placed against the clay, and the excess clay is eliminated or cut away.

Jug: Term used by many manufacturers to refer to a pitcher.

Jumbo Cup and Saucer: Oversized cup and saucer, sometimes quite large.

Kiln: A furnace designed to "fire" ceramics (greenware) to make them hard, or to make glazes and decorations permanent. There are different kinds of kilns, many of which have specific purposes, such as glost kilns.

Kitchenware: Any ceramic item intended to be used in a kitchen, such as a leftover container, refrigerator jug, mixing bowl, drip jar, or bean pot.

Lead Glaze: A glaze containing lead oxide. Lead glazes have a shiny appearance and are now considered dangerous.

Liner or Underliner: A plate or saucer-shaped piece designed to go under such items as gravy boats and cream soup bowls to prevent drips or to rest spoons.

Lining: The contrasting interior color of a cup or piece of hollowware, or a thin line of gold, silver, platinum, or color used to accent rims, verges, knobs, spouts, or handles.

Lug Handle: A tablike handle that usually sits parallel to the tabletop.

Lug Soup Bowl: A soup bowl with lug handles, also called an "onion soup bowl."

Luncheon Plate: A plate that is generally about one inch smaller in diameter than a dinner plate. Most lunch plates have diameters in the 8-inch to 9-inch range, and are used to serve the entrée course at luncheon or breakfast.

Luster: A metallic glaze that gives an iridescent finish to ceramics. In some cases, as when gold, silver, or platinum is used all over the body, the intention is to create a surface that makes the object appear as if it were made from precious metal.

Matte Glaze: Also spelled "Matt" or "Mat," a matte glaze is a nonshiny or nonreflective glaze.

Nappy: Uncovered vegetable or salad dish, usually 8 inches or 9 inches in diameter. This term can also refer to a small round dish with a single handle.

Nove Rose: This decoration consists of a bouquet of flowers with a large rose in the center and tulips extending out from the grouping. The origins of this term are unclear, but the term may refer to a type of design associated with the Nove pottery in Italy.

Ohio Jug: A jug that is wider at the base than at the top. It has a flat base, and is rounded. Some may be paneled, and handle and finial designs vary.

Ovenware: Kitchenware made from ceramic material that will withstand the heat of the oven without damage, and will then be usable as a serving dish on the table.

Overglaze Decoration: After the glost firing, decoration that is applied on top of the glaze and then not fired again. Many colors are destroyed or weakened in the kiln, and overglaze decoration can make use of a wide variety of vibrant colors that would not withstand the heat of the kiln. Cold-painting is an example of overglaze decoration.

Parian: This is a special type of porcelain that originated in England in the 1840s, and formed the basis for Belleek porcelain. Parian was supposed to resemble Parian marble, and it is generally only bisque-fired. Belleek porcelain is parian modeled very thin with an iridescent glaze.

Party or Snack Plate: A plate with a ring near the edge to hold a cup so it will be more secure when the plate is held on the lap or in the hand.

Pate-sur-Pate: Literally "paste-on-paste," this is a decorative technique developed in China during the 18th century, but widely used in Europe. It involves decorating a surface by using semiliquid clay and brushing on a design repeatedly until it is built up and slightly three-dimensional. This technique requires talent, skill, and patience.

Plaque: A decorative, flat piece of ceramic that is intended to hang on the wall. A plaque may be square, rectangular, round, or any other shape.

Platter: An oval serving piece, usually 8 inches to 20 inches in length. In some instances, platters may also be square or oblong.

Porcelain: Any item made from a combination of kaolin (also called "china clay") and petuntse (also called "china stone") is porcelain—and, more specifically, hard-paste porcelain. Hard-paste porcelain, which was invented in China, may be translucent, but does not have to be. It will hold water without being glazed, and is so hard that it cannot be scratched with a steel-bladed knife. It is fired at very high temperatures that usually range between 1,300 and 1,450 degrees centigrade. There is another type of porcelain called "soft-paste porcelain" that, for all intents and purposes, was first made in Europe during the 18th century. This is actually an artificial porcelain that was made by adding "frit" or ground glass, soapstone, or bone ash (thus the term "bone china") to white clay. This was invented because the Europeans did not have the formula for Chinese-style hard-paste porcelain, and soft-paste porcelain represented an attempt at making a serviceable imitation. As one might surmise from the name, soft-paste porcelain is softer than hard-paste porcelain, and can be scratched with the steel blade of a knife. It is generally very translucent, showing a faint green, gray, or orange color when a light is shone through it.

Pottery: This term refers to any item made from clay that has been baked in a fire or kiln, or even hardened in the sun. Technically, this is a term that encompasses a lot of other words such as "china," "earthenware," "porcelain," and "stoneware." However, most ceramics specialists who use the word "pottery" tend to exclude these other terms from the definition, and define "pottery" as being a product made from clay that is opaque, soft enough to be scratched with a steel-bladed knife, and porous to the point that it will not hold water without being covered with a glaze. Pottery is generally fired at a relatively low temperature, and in some instances is just hardened in the sun.

Premium: An item given away by a manufacturer to induce sales. Sometimes the premium item is included in the box with the product, or it may have to be ordered using coupons or some other type of proof of purchase.

Print-and-Paint: Refers to the process in which the outline of a design is printed on a piece of ceramic and then colored in by hand. The piece is then fired and covered with a clear glaze.

Ramekin: A small flat-bottomed dish with vertical sides, used for serving individual portions of food. A ramekin sometimes has an underliner.

Range Set: Vessels designed to sit on or near the range for use during cooking. The most common range sets have salt and pepper shakers and a drip jar, but other items such as flour and spice containers are sometimes included.

Range Shaker: A large shaker for salt, pepper, or, rarely, flour that is usually part of a range set. Range shakers generally have handles.

Reamer: Another name for a citrus juicer.

Redware: Earthenware made from clay that has a high ferrous oxide content. When fired, redware has a red or pinkish tint. In order to hold water, it must be glazed. Typically, shiny lead glazes were used for this purpose.

Rockingham: See "Bennington."

Salt Glaze: The result of a process in which, during the firing of pottery, salt (common NaCl) is introduced into the kiln, where it vaporizes in the head and then condenses on the pottery to form a glaze that is clear. Salt glaze feels like orange peel to the touch, and can be a bit pitted.

Semiporcelain: Fine earthenware that is made from refined clay and fired at a high temperature until it becomes semivitreous. Like common earthenware, it is still porous unless covered with a glaze, but it is a somewhat stronger material and was widely used for dinnerware in the United States.

Service or "Place" Plate: An ornate plate that is slightly larger than a regular dinner plate. It is used to set the table at a formal dinner party. The first course is served on top, and then both the service plate and the first-course plate or bowl are removed.

Sgraffitto: A decorative technique in which a design is carved into a piece of pottery after the piece has been glazed but before it has been fired. Sometimes, the grooves thus created are filled with color.

Shelf Sitter: A figure that is designed to appear to be sitting on the edge of a shelf, or some other flat surface, with its legs hanging over the edge.

Slip: Clay mixed with water and color to make a mixture with creamlike consistency that can be used to decorate pottery. Slip can be applied by brush or by squeeze bag.

Sponge Ware: A type of pottery that has been decorated with color applied with a sponge or a rag to give the color a distinctive texture.

Squeeze-Bag Technique: A method of applying slip in a decorative manner. It is also called "slip trailing." This technique leaves a three-dimensional line, and somewhat resembles cake decorating.

St. Denis Cup and Saucer: A large cup and saucer, with the cup having a ring handle. This form was used by a number of different potteries, including Hall.

Stock Decal: A decal that was sold by jobbers to any number of manufacturers, and was not the exclusive decoration of any one company.

Stoneware: Pottery that is hard (stonelike) and vitrified, but not translucent. It will hold water without being glazed. Impurities in the clay generally give stoneware a dark color, and the body usually has a lead or salt glaze.

Toiletware or Sanitary Ware: One of the mainstays of many 19th- and early 20th-century potteries, these types of products include such items as chamber pots, slop jars, bowl and pitcher sets, soap dishes, and so forth.

Transfer Printing: A process in which an image is etched or engraved onto a copper plate and color or oil is rubbed into the grooves. Next, a piece of tissue paper is pressed on top of the plate, and the image is transferred to the tissue. The tissue is then placed on the piece of ceramic that is to be decorated, and a sponge is used to remove the tissue, leaving the image on the surface of the ceramic. The color is set by firing the piece in a kiln.

Verge: On a piece of flatware, the place where the rim and the center well meet.

Vitrified: Glasslike.

Wall Pocket: A flat-backed wall vase with a hole in the back for hanging.

Well: The center of a plate or bowl, surrounded by the rim.

White Ware: Undecorated porcelain, also called a "blank."

Yellowware: Earthenware made from naturally occurring clays that have a color ranging from buff to mustard.

BIBLIOGRAPHY

Altman, Seymour and Violet. *The Book of Buffalo Pottery.* West Chester, Pa.: Schiffer Publishing, Ltd., 1987

Boshears, James R., and Carol Sumilas. *Gonder Ceramic Arts: A Comprehensive Guide.* Altglen, Pa.: Schiffer Publishing, Ltd., 2001.

Chipman, Jack. *Collector's Encyclopedia of Bauer Pottery, Identification and Value Guide.* Paducah, Ky.: Collector Books, 1998.

Coates, Carole. *Catalina Island Pottery and Tile, 1927–1937, Island Treasures.* Altglen, Pa.: Schiffer Publishing, Ltd., 2001.

Cunningham, Jo. *The Collector's Encyclopedia of American Dinnerware.* Paducah, Ky.: Collector Books, 1982.

Dilley, David D. *Haeger Potteries through the Years.* Gas City, Indiana: L-W Book Sales, 1997.

Dollen, B. L. and R. L. *Red Wing Art Pottery, Identification and Value Guide,* Book II. Paducah, Ky.: Collector Books, 1998.

Dommel, Darleen Hurst. *Collector's Encyclopedia of Rosemeade Pottery: Identification and Values.* Paducah, Ky.: Collector Books, 2000.

Elliot-Bishop, James. *Franciscan, Catalina, and Other Gladding, McBean Wares, Ceramic Table and Art Wares: 1873–1942.* Atglen, Pa.: Schiffer Publishing, Ltd., 2001.

Eng, Loman and Petula. *Collecting American Belleek.* Altglen, Pa.: Schiffer Publishing, Ltd., 2003.

Evans, Paul. *Art Pottery of the United States.* New York, N.Y.: Feingold & Lewis Publishing Corporation, 1987.

Feldman, Anna Mary, and Fara Holtzman. *Uhl Pottery, Identification and Value Guide.* Paducah, Ky.: Collector Books, 2001.

Gibbs, Carl Jr. *Collector's Encyclopedia of Metlox Potteries, Identification and Values.* Paducah, Ky.: Collector Books, 2001.

Gifford, David Edwin. *Collector's Encyclopedia of Camark Pottery, Identification and Values,* Book II. Paducah, Ky.: Collector Books, 1999.

———. *Collector's Encyclopedia of Niloak Reference and Values.* Paducah, Ky.: Collector Books, 2001.

Hahn, Frank, L. *Collector's Guide to Owens Pottery.* Lima, Oh.: Golden Era Publishing, 1996.

Huxford, Sharon and Bob. *The Collector's Encyclopedia of Roseville Pottery.* Paducah, Ky.: Collector Books, 1976.

———. *The Collector's Encyclopedia of McCoy Pottery.* Paducah, Ky.: Collector Books, 1980.

———. *The Collector's Encyclopedia of Roseville Pottery,* Second Series. Paducah, Ky.: Collector Books, 1976

———. *The Collector's Encyclopedia of Weller Pottery.* Paducah, Ky.: Collector Books, 1979.

Johnson, Donald-Brian, Timothy J. Holthaus, and James E. Petzold. *Ceramic Arts Studio, The Legacy of Betty Harrington.* Altglen, Pa.: Schiffer Publishing, Ltd., 2003.

Keller, Joe, and David Ross. *Russel Wright Dinnerware, Pottery, & More: An Identification and Price Guide.* Altglen, Pa.: Schiffer Publishing, Ltd., 2000.

Kerr, Ann. *A Collector's Encyclopedia of Russel Wright.* Paducah, Ky.: Collector Books, 1998.

Kovel, Ralph and Terry. *The Kovels' Collector's Guide to American Art Pottery.* New York, N.Y.: Crown Publishers, Inc., 1974.

Lehner, Lois. *Lehner's Encyclopedia of U. S. Marks on Pottery, Porcelain & Clay.* Paducah, Ky.: Collector Books, 1988.

Magus, Jim and Bev. *Shawnee Pottery, An Identification and Value Guide.* Paducah, Ky.: Collector Books, 1994.

Miller, C. L. *The Jewel Tea Company, Its History and Products.* Altglen, Pa.: Schiffer Publishing, Ltd., 1994.

Moran, Mark L. *Warman's McCoy Pottery.* Iola, Wis.: Krause Publications, 2004.

Nelson, Maxine Feek. *Collectible Vernon Kilns,* Second Edition. Paducah, Ky.: Collector Books, 2004.

Newborn, Betty and Bill. *Best of Blue Ridge Dinnerware, Identification and Value Guide.* Paducah, Ky.: Collector Books, 2003.

————. *Southern Potteries Inc., Blue Ridge Dinnerware, An Illustrated Value Guide.* Paducah, Ky.: Collector Books, 1989.

Paradis, Joe. *Abingdon Pottery Artware, 1934–1950, Stepchild of the Great Depression.* Altglen, Pa.: Schiffer Publishing, Ltd., 1997.

Rans, Jon, and Mark Eckelman. *Collector's Encyclopedia of Muncie Pottery, Identification and Values.* Paducah, Ky.: Collector Books, 1999.

Reed, Alan B. *Collector's Encyclopedia of Pickard China.* Paducah, Ky.: Collector Books, 1995.

Rinker, Harry L. *Dinnerware of the 20th Century: The Top 500 Patterns.* New York, N.Y.: House of Collectibles, 1997.

Roberts, Brenda. *The Collector's Encyclopedia of Hull Pottery.* Paducah, Ky.: Collector Books, 1980.

Rosson, Joe. *Collecting American Dinnerware.* New York, N.Y.: House of Collectibles, 2004.

Runge, Robert C., Jr. *Collector's Encyclopedia of Stangl Artware, Lamps, and Birds.* Paducah, Ky.: Collector Books, 2002.

Saloff, Tim and Jamie. *The Collector's Encyclopedia of Cowan Pottery, Identification and Values.* Paducah, Ky.: Collector Books, 2001.

Schaum, Gary V. *Collector's Guide to Frankoma Pottery, 1933 through 1990.* Gas City, Ind.: L-W Book Sales, 1997.

Schneider, Mike. *California Potteries, The Complete Book.* Altglen, Pa.: Schiffer Publishing, Ltd., 1995.

Smith, Timothy J. *Universal Dinnerware and Its Predecessors.* Altglen, Pa.: Schiffer Publishing, Ltd., 2000.

Supnick, Mark and Ellen. *The Wonderful World of Cookie Jars.* Gas City, Ind.: L-W Book Sales, 1995.

Thompson, Dennis, and Bryce W. Watt. *Watt Pottery: A Collector's Reference with Price Guide,* Second Edition. Altglen, Pa.: Schiffer Publishing, Ltd., 2003.

Whitmyer, Margaret and Ken. *Collector's Encyclopedia of Hall China,* Third Edition. Paducah, Ky.: Collector Books, 2001.